FOURTH EDITION

SOCIAL MARKETING

This book is dedicated to all current and future social marketers working to influence behaviors that improve health, decrease injuries, protect the environment, build communities, and enhance financial well-being.

We hope you'll find that this 10-step strategic planning approach enhances your success.

FOURTH EDITION

SOCIAL MARKETING
Influencing Behaviors for Good

Nancy R. Lee
Social Marketing Services, Inc.

Philip Kotler
Northwestern University

Los Angeles | London | New Delhi
Singapore | Washington DC

Los Angeles | London | New Delhi
Singapore | Washington DC

FOR INFORMATION:

SAGE Publications, Inc.
2455 Teller Road
Thousand Oaks, California 91320
E-mail: order@sagepub.com

SAGE Publications Ltd.
1 Oliver's Yard
55 City Road
London EC1Y 1SP
United Kingdom

SAGE Publications India Pvt. Ltd.
B 1/I 1 Mohan Cooperative Industrial Area
Mathura Road, New Delhi 110 044
India

SAGE Publications Asia-Pacific Pte. Ltd.
33 Pekin Street #02-01
Far East Square
Singapore 048763

Acquisitions Editor: Lisa Cuevas Shaw
Editorial Assistant: Mayan White
Production Editor: Libby Larson
Copy Editor: Rachel Keith
Typesetter: C & M Digitals (P) Ltd.
Proofreader: Sally Jaskold
Indexer: Judy Hunt
Cover Designer: Janet Kiesel
Marketing Manager: Helen Salmon
Permissions Editor: Karen Ehrmann

Copyright © 2011 by SAGE Publications, Inc.

Printed in the United States of America

Library of Congress Cataloging-in-Publication Data

Lee, Nancy, 1932-

Social marketing : influencing behaviors for good/
Nancy R. Lee, Philip

Kotler.—4th ed.

p. cm.
Prev. ed. entered under: Kotler, Philip.

Includes bibliographical references and index.

ISBN 978-1-4129-8149-1 (pbk.:alk. paper)

1. Social marketing. 2. Behavior modification.
I. Kotler, Philip. II. Kotler, Philip. Social marketing.
III. Title.

HF5414.K67 2012
658.8—dc23   2011033241

This book is printed on acid-free paper.

11 12 13 14 15 10 9 8 7 6 5 4 3 2 1

CONTENTS

FOREWORD

As someone who has had experience revising a popular textbook, I can particularly appreciate—and recommend—this fourth edition of *Social Marketing: Influencing Behaviors for Good*. The field of social marketing is on a major growth trajectory. Since the last edition, there have been two worldwide conferences on social marketing, each drawing more than 500 participants from all continents. The keynote addresses and individual reports and papers attested to three things: the growing sophistication of the field, the widening array of applications to social problems, and the increasing interest of a broadened range of commercial and nonprofit enterprises in the field. This new volume captures this momentum and excitement exceedingly well.

Important developments incorporated in this edition include greater attention to what the authors call midstream and upstream behaviors that are needed to give downstream targets both the opportunity and the ability to carry out valuable social behaviors. Much more space is devoted to the use of social media such as Facebook, Twitter, blogs, and electronic mailing lists to both promote desirable behavioral outcomes and to link students and practitioners. (The authors also stress the need for the social marketing field to distinguish itself in the minds of the general public and potential practitioners from the *tool* of social media.)

The fourth edition is also particularly timely in that more universities and online programs are offering courses—even master's degrees—in social marketing. This growth and recognition is facilitated by the emergence of a second social marketing academic journal and the systematic collection of concepts and tools in a greater variety of Web sites. Both this edition and the aforementioned courses and journals also reflect increasing attention to categories of problems beyond traditional health care applications. These include community mobilization, financial behavior, environmental protection, and public policy. This volume also incorporates frameworks and approaches from heretofore peripheral fields such as behavioral economics, environmental psychology, and social norming.

Finally, as in the previous editions, the text is replete with hands-on case examples—all of them entirely new. These show innovative, well-managed interventions that tackle a range of problem social behaviors and serve—again—to make the drier frameworks and checklists elsewhere in the book directly usable and not just interesting ideas.

This edition continues to play a very valuable role in advancing the social marketing field and acquainting and training students and practitioners in the latest and best tested concepts and tools. I hope that this is not the last of such a useful and inspiring series.

Alan R. Andreasen
Georgetown University

PART I

UNDERSTANDING SOCIAL MARKETING

Chapter 1

DEFINING SOCIAL MARKETING

I believe the genius of modern marketing is not the 4Ps, or audience research, or even exchange, but rather the management paradigm that studies, selects, balances, and manipulates the 4Ps to achieve behavior change. We keep shortening "the marketing mix" to the 4Ps. And I would argue that it is the "mix" that matters most. This is exactly what all the message campaigns miss—they never ask about the other 3Ps and that is why so many of them fail.

—Dr. Bill Smith
Executive Vice President
Academy for Educational Development

Social marketing, as a discipline, has made enormous strides since its distinction in the early 1970s, and has had a profound positive impact on social issues in the areas of public health, injury prevention, the environment, community involvement, and more recently, financial well-being. Fundamental principles at the core of this practice have been used to help reduce tobacco use, decrease infant mortality, stop the spread of HIV/AIDS, prevent malaria, help eradicate guinea worm disease, make wearing a bike helmet a social norm, decrease littering, stop bullying, increase recycling, encourage the homeless to participate in job training programs, and persuade pet owners to license their pets and "scoop their poop."

Social marketing as a term, however, is still a mystery to most, misunderstood by many, and increasingly confused with others such as behavioral economics (a framework we consider in this book) and social media (one of many potential promotional tactics to choose from). A few even worry about using the term with their administrators, colleagues, and elected officials, fearing they will associate it with socialism, manipulation, and sales. This chapter is intended to create clear distinctions and to answer common questions. How does social marketing differ from commercial marketing, nonprofit marketing, cause marketing, and public education? Everyone argues it is more than communications, but what's the "more"? Do people who do social marketing actually call themselves social marketers? Where do they work?

We support the voices of many who advocate an expanded role for social marketing and social marketers, challenging professionals to take this technology "upstream" to influence other factors that effect positive social change, including laws, enforcement, public policy, built environments, school curricula, community organizations, business practices, and the media. We also encourage distinguishing and considering "midstream" audiences, those influential others closer to our target audiences (e.g., family, friends, neighbors, healthcare providers).

We begin this and all chapters with an inspiring case story, this one from Africa. We conclude with one of several Marketing Dialogues that feature discourses among practitioners on the social marketing listserv seeking to shape, evolve, and transform this discipline.

MARKETING HIGHLIGHT

Sustainable Malaria Prevention NetMark's Success Story in Africa (1999–2009)

Background

In Africa alone, almost 3,000 people die from malaria every day.[1] That number bears repeating: Almost 3,000 people die from malaria every day in Africa, more than 1 million each year. Additional statistics[2] are just as astonishing:

- Malaria is the number one cause of death for pregnant mothers and children under five years of age
- One out of 20 children in Africa dies of malaria before the age of five
- The primary cause of absenteeism in African schools is malaria
- Families spend approximately 20% of their income on malaria treatments
- Public health institutions spend up to 40% of their budgets on outpatient treatment for malaria

And perhaps the greatest tragedy is that many of these illnesses, deaths, and related expenditures are preventable. The World Health Organization (WHO) recommends insecticide-treated nets (ITNs) as the best way for families to protect themselves from malaria, proven to reduce the risk of infection by up to 45% and the risk of death by 30%. In 1999, the United States Agency for International Development (USAID) funded an effort called NetMark to increase demand for and appropriate use, availability, and affordability of ITNs, through the commercial sector if possible. At the time, ITNs were not even available for sale in most African countries. ITNs were provided by governments and donors. By 2009, more than 60 million nets had been sold by NetMark's partners in its seven countries of operation.[3]

This case highlight describes the program's rigorous application of social marketing principles, including the use of all 4Ps in the traditional marketing mix. Case information was provided by Dr. Willard Shaw at the Academy for Educational Development (AED) in Washington, D.C., the agency implementing the project.

Target Audiences and Desired Behaviors

Although primary audiences (*downstream*) were the most-at-risk populations—pregnant women and children under five—net availability and affordability would depend on strategies that would also reach and influence net and insecticide manufacturers, national product distributors, and retailers (*midstream*) as well as policy makers (*upstream*).

For families, the desired behavior was to purchase, properly hang, and consistently use an ITN. NetMark would also need to persuade multinational manufacturers to invest in the retail market, help them identify national distributors for their brands, assist distributors in introducing ITNs into the marketplace and recruiting retailers, and convince the public sector to allow the commercial sector to build ITN markets and to focus its limited resources on providing ITNs to high-risk populations who could not afford to pay.

Audience Insights

Extensive consumer research was conducted regarding knowledge of and beliefs about mosquitoes and malaria. Barriers to purchasing and using ITNs included lack of awareness of ITNs, the perceived high cost of the nets, little or no availability of commercial ITNs, concern about potential adverse health effects from treated nets, and perceived "hotness" when sleeping. In Nigeria, for example, 92% of respondents said that the nearest place they could buy an untreated net "was an outdoor market, and that the average time to get there would be approximately one hour by bus."[4]

Strategies

Product strategies focused on ensuring an adequate supply chain of at least two to five competing, high-quality ITN brands in each country. Supplies were enhanced by helping

distributors manage stocks, cash flow, and financing, and by providing technical support to expand local manufacturing capacity and quality. A "seal of quality" (see Figure 1.1) was developed to reassure consumers that products carrying the seal met international standards, including the use of WHO-recommended insecticides. Partners incorporated the seal into their packaging designs, which served to link their brand with the generic marketing campaign. And new, unpatented technology for producing long-lasting ITNs was developed and adopted by several manufacturers.

NetMark worked to lower the *price* of the nets through market competition and price reviews with distributors, as well as to make them available for those who could not pay the full retail price. As a stronger and more compelling messenger for policy makers than for-profit businesses could have been, NetMark successfully advocated reducing taxes and tariffs in the interest of the public good in

Figure 1.1 The program's seal assuring product quality.[5]

all its countries. It constantly encouraged public health authorities to promote market segmentation by focusing publicly funded free and highly subsidized ITNs on high-risk and poor populations while allowing the commercial sector to market to the people who could afford to buy an ITN. It also lobbied national regulatory agencies to streamline the process of registration for quality ITN brands. After convincing multinational net and insecticide manufacturers to invest in developing retail ITN markets, NetMark helped them identify country distributors (*place*) willing to invest in promoting retail sales. NetMark worked with both groups on annual brand marketing plans using a joint risk/joint investment process, with NetMark investing in market research, generic promotion of ITNs, and coordination with the public sector and donors, and the commercial firms doing what they do best—manufacturing, distributing, and promoting their own brands. NetMark provided some "matching funds" to distributors for activities aimed at expanding the reach of their retail networks (e.g., sales teams, marketing materials), reimbursing distributors for 50% of specific investments. Manufacturers also provided distributors with brand promotion support and technical assistance. The confidential brand marketing plans identified special audiences to target, with some distributors targeting special groups (nongovernmental organizations, churches, boarding schools, etc.) in addition to the general public. There was ongoing tension between NetMark's public health focus on reaching as many at-risk people as possible and the commercial sector's more conservative approach of managing risk and ensuring return on investment.

NetMark's *promotional* efforts sought to build demand for ITNs by informing the public about the dangers of malaria and the benefits of sleeping under treated nets. Two multinational advertising and product promotion agencies helped develop an advertising and communication campaign with region- and country-specific components. The initial tagline "Mosquitoes KILL. KILL Mosquitoes" (see Figure 1.2) was based on research showing that consumers valued the killing power of any insect control product. Each brand conducted a marketing campaign of its own, which was coordinated with the generic campaign. The generic campaign included mass media (print, television, and radio) as well as special promotions such as wall murals, point-of-purchase materials, street theatrics, and road shows (see Figure 1.3).

Figure 1.2 Initial campaign tagline.[6]

MOSQUITOES
KILL.

KILL
MOSQUITOES.

Use Insecticide

Treated Nets

NetMark™

Figure 1.3 Painted wall murals promoting benefits.[7]

Outcomes

A quick summary of accomplishments included the following:

- *Creating Supply:* In 1999, there were only 2 ITN brands commercially available in Africa; by 2008, there were 22, with 50 commercial partners providing increased access, higher net quality, lower prices, more brands in the marketplace, and creation of jobs for manufacturing, promoting, distributing, and selling ITNs.
- *Creating Demand:* In 2009, awareness of ITNs among women ages 15 to 49 was more than 90% and ownership was as high as 64% in Ghana and 91% in Ethiopia. NetMark partners sold more than 60 million nets by 2009.

- *Ensuring Equity:* NetMark's commercial discount voucher program enabled 2.2 million families with children under five to buy an ITN in a local shop at discounts from 40% to 100% and served as an excellent tool to attract new retailers. In addition, NetMark helped governments and donors distribute 2.3 million ITNs.
- *Ensuring Sustainability:* NetMark partnered with 42 African and 9 multinational commercial partners who invested over $90 million in creating national ITN markets and made organizational changes to support growing retail markets. This will help ensure a sustainable supply of ITNs when donors are no longer willing or able to supply free nets.

WHAT IS SOCIAL MARKETING?

Social marketing is a distinct marketing discipline, one that has been labeled as such since the early 1970s and refers primarily to efforts focused on influencing behaviors that will improve health, prevent injuries, protect the environment, contribute to communities, and, more recently, enhance financial well-being. Several definitions from social marketing "veterans" are listed in Box 1.1, beginning with one we have adopted for use in this text. It seems clear there are several common themes. Social marketing is about (a) influencing behaviors, (b) utilizing a systematic planning process that applies marketing principles and techniques, (c) focusing on priority target audience segments, and (d) delivering a positive benefit for society. Each of these themes is elaborated upon in the next four sections.

Box 1.1
Definitions From a Few Social Marketing Veterans

Social Marketing is a process that uses marketing principles and techniques to influence target audience behaviors that will benefit society as well as the individual. This strategically oriented discipline relies on creating, communicating, delivering, and exchanging offerings that have positive value for individuals, clients, partners, and society at large.

—Nancy R. Lee, Michael L. Rothschild, and Bill Smith, 2011

Social Marketing is the application of commercial marketing concepts and tools to influence the voluntary behavior of target audiences to improve their lives or the society of which they are a part.

—Alan Andreasen, 2011

Social Marketing 2.0, more specifically, is the systematic application of interactive marketing principles and techniques that harness audience participation to deliver value and achieve specific behavioral goals for a social good.

—Jay Bernhardt, 2011

Social Marketing is the application of commercial marketing principles and tools where the primary goal is the public good.

—Rob Donovan, 2011

(Continued)

(Continued)

Social Marketing is a set of evidence- and experience-based concepts and principles that provide a systematic approach to understanding behaviour and modifying it for social good. It is not a science but rather a form of 'technik'; a fusion of science, practical know-how, and reflective practice focusing on continuously improving the performance of programmes aimed at producing net social good.

—Jeff French, 2011

Social Marketing critically examines commercial marketing so as to learn from its successes and curb its excesses.

—Gerard Hastings, 2011

Social Marketing is the application of marketing principles to shape markets that are more effective, efficient, sustainable, and just in advancing people's well-being and social welfare.

—Craig Lefebvre, 2011

Social Marketing is a process that involves (a) carefully selecting which behaviors and segments to target, (b) identifying the barriers and benefits to these behaviors, (c) developing and pilot testing strategies to address these barriers and benefits, and, finally, (d) broad scale implementation of successful programs.

—Doug McKenzie-Mohr, 2011

Social Marketing is a way to reduce the barriers and increase the facilitators to behaviors that improve the quality of life for individuals and society. It uses concepts and planning processes from commercial marketing to make behaviors "fun, easy, and popular." It goes beyond communication, public service announcements, and education to give you a 360-degree view of potential causes and solutions for health and human service problems.

—Mike Newton-Ward, 2011

Social Marketing is the activity and processes for understanding, creating, communicating, and delivering a unique and innovative offering to overcome a societal problem.

—Sharyn Rundle-Thiele, 2011

Social Marketing is the use of marketing principles and techniques to promote the adoption of behaviors that improve the health or well-being of the target audience or of society as a whole.

—Nedra Weinreich, 2011

We Focus on Behaviors

Similar to commercial sector marketers whose objective is to sell goods and services, social marketers' objective is to successfully influence desired behaviors. We typically want to influence target audiences to do one of four things: (a) *accept* a new behavior (e.g., composting food waste); (b) *reject* a potentially undesirable behavior (e.g., starting smoking), which is why we refer more often to behavior influence than behavior change; (c) *modify* a current behavior (e.g., increase physical activity from three to five days of the week or decrease the number of fat grams consumed); or (d) *abandon* an old undesirable behavior (e.g., talking on a cell phone while driving). It may be the encouragement of a one-time behavior (e.g., installing a low-flow showerhead) or the establishment of a habit and the prompting of a repeated behavior (e.g., taking a five-minute shower). More recently, Alan Andreasen suggested a fifth arena, in which we want to influence people to *continue* a desired behavior (e.g., giving blood on an annual basis), and a sixth, in which we want people to *switch* a behavior (e.g., take the stairs instead of the elevator).[8]

Although benchmarks may be established for increasing knowledge and skills through education and efforts may need to be made to alter existing beliefs, attitudes, or feelings, the bottom line for the social marketer is whether the target audience adopts the behavior. For example, a specific behavior that substance abuse coalitions want to influence is women's consumption of alcohol during pregnancy. They recognize the need to inform women that alcohol may cause birth defects and convince them that this could happen to their baby. In the end, however, their measure of success is whether the expectant mother abstains from drinking.

Perhaps the most challenging aspect of social marketing (also its greatest contribution) is that it relies heavily on "rewarding good behaviors" rather than "punishing bad ones" through legal, economic, or coercive forms of influence. And in many cases, social marketers cannot promise a direct benefit or immediate payback in return for adopting the proposed behavior. Consider, for example, the task of influencing gardeners to pull their dandelions instead of using harmful chemicals. It's tough to show the healthier fish their actions helped to support. And it's tough to convince youth who want to look good to use sunscreen so they will (maybe) avoid skin cancer later in life. As you will read in subsequent chapters, this is why a systematic, rigorous, and strategic planning process is required—one that is inspired by the wants, needs, and preferences of target audiences and focuses on real, deliverable, and near-term benefits. It should be noted, however, that many believe this heavy reliance on individual voluntary behavior change is outdated and have moved on to applying social marketing technologies to influence other change factors in the environment (e.g., laws, policies, media). These are elaborated upon later in this chapter.

We Use a Systematic Planning Process That Applies Traditional Marketing Principles and Techniques

The American Marketing Association defines marketing as "the activity, set of institutions, and processes for creating, communicating, delivering, and exchanging offerings that have value for customers, clients, partners, and society at large."[9] The most fundamental principle underlying this approach is application of a *customer orientation* to understand barriers target audiences perceive to adopting the desired behavior and benefits they want and believe they can realize. The process begins with an *environmental scan* to establish a purpose and focus for the plan. A *situation analysis* (SWOT) helps identify organizational strengths the plan can maximize and weaknesses to minimize, as well as environmental opportunities to take advantage of and threats to prepare for. Marketers then select *target audiences* they can best affect and satisfy. We establish clear *behavior objectives* and *goals* the plan will be developed to achieve. *Formative research* is conducted to identify audience barriers, benefits, and the competition. This inspires the *positioning* of the offer, one that will appeal to the desires of the target audience, and the game requires that we do this more effectively than the competition. We then consider the need for each of the major intervention tools in the marketer's toolbox, the "4Ps," to influence target audiences: Product, Price, Place, and Promotion, also referred to as the *marketing mix*. An *evaluation* methodology is established, leading to a *budget* and *implementation* plan. Once a plan is implemented, ideally first with a pilot, results are *monitored* and *evaluated,* and strategies are altered as needed. Table 1.1 summarizes this strategic planning process using the 10-step model this text follows. Examples of marketing techniques are included.

We Select and Influence a Target Audience

Marketers know that the marketplace is a rich collage of diverse populations, each having a distinct set of wants and needs. We know that what appeals to one individual may not appeal to another and therefore divide the market into similar groups (market segments), measure the relative potential of each segment to meet organizational and marketing objectives, and then choose one or more segments (target audiences) on which to concentrate our efforts and resources. For each target, a distinct mix of the 4Ps is developed, one designed to uniquely appeal to that segment's barriers, benefits, and the competition.

Considering, again, a more expanded view of social marketing, Robert Donovan and Nadine Henley (among others) advocate also targeting individuals in communities who have the power to make institutional policy and legislative changes in social structures (e.g., school superintendents). In this case, efforts move from influencing (just) an individual with a problem or potentially problematic behavior to influencing those who can facilitate behavior change in individuals.[10] Techniques, however, remain the same.

The Primary Beneficiary Is Society

Unlike commercial marketing, in which the primary intended beneficiary is the corporate shareholder, the primary beneficiary of the social marketing program is society. The question many pose and banter about is, who determines whether the social change created by the program is beneficial? Although most causes supported by social marketing efforts tend to draw high consensus that the cause is good, this model can also be used by

Table 1.1 Social Marketing Planning Process: Phases, Steps, Techniques, and Feedback Loops

Phase	Scoping		Selecting		Understanding	Designing		Managing		
Step	1. Purpose and focus	2. Situation analysis	3. Target audience	4. Behavior objectives and goals	5. Barriers, benefits, and competition	6. Positioning	7. Marketing mix: The intervention tools	8. Evaluation plan	9. Budget	10. Plan to implement
Technique examples	Literature reviews, epi and scientific data	SWOT analysis, peer interviews	Andreasen's nine criteria (see Chapter 6)	McKenzie-Mohr's three criteria (see Chapter 7)	Knowledge, attitudes, and practice studies	Perceptual maps	The 4Ps	Logic model	Objective and task method	Include a pilot prior to rollout
Feedback loops					Findings at this step may suggest adjustments to the target audience and/or behavior objectives and goals		A pretest of draft strategies may suggest changes in the 4Ps design			A pilot may suggest changes, especially in the marketing mix

Figure 1.4 "Rosie the Riveter," created by the War Ad Council to help recruit women[11]

organizations who have the opposite view of what is good. Abortion is an example of an issue where both sides argue that they are on the "good" side, and both use social marketing techniques to influence public behavior. Who, then, gets to define "good"? Some propose the United Nations' Universal Declaration of Human Rights (http://www.un.org/en/documents/udhr/) as a baseline with respect to the common good, while other perspectives and discussions are elaborated upon in the Marketing Dialogue at the end of Chapter 2.

WHERE DID THE CONCEPT ORIGINATE?

When we think of social marketing as "influencing public behavior," it is clear that this is not a new phenomenon. Consider efforts to free slaves, abolish child labor, influence women's right to vote, and recruit women into the workforce (see Figure 1.4).

Launching the discipline formally more than 40 years ago, the term *social marketing* was first introduced by Philip Kotler and Gerald Zaltman, in a pioneering article in the *Journal of Marketing*, to describe "the use of marketing principles and techniques to advance a social cause, idea or behavior."[12] In intervening decades, growing interest in and use of social marketing concepts, tools, and practices has spread from public health and safety to use by environmentalists, community advocates, and poverty workers, as is evident in the partial list of seminal events, texts, and journal articles in Box 1.2. (See Appendix B for additional resources.)

Box 1.2
Social Marketing: Seminal Events and Publications

1970s

1971: A pioneering article by Philip Kotler and Gerald Zaltman, "Social Marketing: An Approach to Planned Social Change" in the *Journal of Marketing*, coins the term *social marketing*.

More distinguished researchers and practitioners join the voice for the potential of social marketing, including Alan Andreasen (Georgetown University), James Mintz

---

(Federal Department of Health, Canada), Bill Novelli (cofounder of Porter Novelli Associates), and Dr. Bill Smith.

1980s

The World Bank, World Health Organization, and Centers for Disease Control start to use the term and promote interest in social marketing.

1981: An article in the *Journal of Marketing* by Paul Bloom and William Novelli reviews the first 10 years of social marketing and highlights the lack of rigor in the application of marketing principles and techniques in critical areas of the field, including research, segmentation, and distribution channels.

1988: An article in the *Health Education Quarterly*, "Social Marketing and Public Health Intervention" by R. Craig Lefebvre and June Flora, gives social marketing widespread exposure in the field of public health.

1989: A text by Philip Kotler and Eduardo Roberto, *Social Marketing: Strategies for Changing Public Behavior*, lays out the application of marketing principles and techniques for influencing social change management.

1990s

Academic programs are established, including the Center for Social Marketing at the University of Strathclyde in Glasgow and the Department of Community and Family Health at the University of South Florida.

1992: An article in the *American Psychologist* by James Prochaska, Carlo DiClemente, and John Norcross presents an organizing framework for achieving behavior change, considered by many the most useful model developed to date.

1994: A publication, *Social Marketing Quarterly* by Best Start Inc. and the Department of Public Health, University of South Florida, is launched.

1995: A text by Alan Andreasen, *Marketing Social Change: Changing Behavior to Promote Health, Social Development, and the Environment*, makes a significant contribution to both the theory and practice of social marketing.

1999: The Social Marketing Institute is formed in Washington, DC, with Alan Andreasen from Georgetown University as interim executive director.

1999: A text by Doug McKenzie-Mohr and William Smith, *Fostering Sustainable Behavior*, provides an introduction to community-based social marketing.

2000s

2003: A text by Rob Donovan, *Social Marketing: Principles & Practice*, is published in Melbourne, Australia.

(Continued)

(Continued)

2005: The National Social Marketing Centre, headed by Jeff French and Clive Blair-Stevens, is formed in London, England.

2005: The 10th annual conference for Innovations in Social Marketing is held.

2005: The 16th annual Social Marketing in Public Health conference is held.

2006: A text by Alan Andreasen, *Social Marketing in the 21st Century*, describes an expanded role for social marketing.

2007: Gerard Hastings's book *Social Marketing: Why Should the Devil Have All the Best Tunes?* is published.

2008: The first World Social Marketing Conference is held in Brighton, England.

2010s

2010: The 20th annual Social Marketing in Public Health conference is held.

2010–2011: More books are published, including the second edition of *Hands-On Social Marketing* by Nedra Weinreich; *Social Marketing for Public Health: Global Trends and Success Stories* by Hong Cheng, Philip Kotler, and Nancy Lee; *Social Marketing to Protect the Environment: What Works* by Doug McKenzie-Mohr, Nancy Lee, Wesley Schultz, and Philip Kotler; *Social Marketing and Public Health: Theory and Practice* by Jeff French; and the third edition of *Fostering Sustainable Behavior* by Doug McKenzie-Mohr. The *Journal of Social Marketing* is launched in Australia.

2011: The second World Social Marketing Conference is held in Dublin, Ireland, and the International Social Marketing Association is launched.

HOW DOES SOCIAL MARKETING DIFFER FROM COMMERCIAL MARKETING?

There are a few important differences between social marketing and commercial marketing.

In the commercial sector, the primary aim is selling goods and services that will produce a *financial gain* for the corporation. In social marketing, the primary aim is influencing behaviors that will contribute to *societal gain.* Given their focus on financial gain, commercial marketers often favor choosing primary target audience segments that will provide the greatest volume of profitable sales. In social marketing, segments are selected based on a different set of criteria, including prevalence of the social problem, ability to reach the audience, readiness for change, and others that will be explored in depth in Chapter 6 of this text. In both cases, however, marketers seek to gain the greatest returns on their investment of resources.

Although both social and commercial marketers recognize the need to identify and position their offering relative to the competition, their competitors are very different in nature. Because, as stated earlier, the commercial marketer most often focuses on selling goods and services, the *competition is often identified as other organizations offering similar goods and services.* In social marketing, *the competition is most often the current or preferred behavior of our target audience* and the perceived benefits associated with that behavior, including the status quo. This also includes any organizations selling or promoting competing behaviors (e.g., the tobacco industry).

For a variety of reasons, we believe social marketing is more difficult than commercial marketing. Consider the financial resources the competition has to make smoking look cool, yard cleanup using a gas blower easy, and weed-free lawns the norm. And consider the challenges faced when trying to influence people to do any of the following:

- Give up an addictive behavior (e.g., stop smoking)
- Change a comfortable lifestyle (e.g., reduce thermostat settings)
- Resist peer pressure (e.g., be sexually abstinent)
- Go out of their way (e.g., take unused paint to a hazardous waste site)
- Be uncomfortable (e.g., give blood)
- Establish new habits (e.g., exercise five days a week)
- Spend more money (e.g., buy recycled paper)
- Be embarrassed (e.g., let lawns go brown in the summer)
- Hear bad news (e.g., get an HIV test)
- Risk relationships (e.g., take the keys from a drunk driver)
- Give up leisure time (e.g., volunteer)
- Reduce pleasure (e.g., take shorter showers)
- Give up looking good (e.g., wear sunscreen)
- Spend more time (e.g., flatten cardboard boxes before putting them in recycling bins)
- Learn a new skill (e.g., create and follow a budget)
- Remember something (e.g., take reusable bags to the grocery store)
- Risk retaliation (e.g., drive the speed limit)

Despite these differences, we also see many similarities between the social and commercial marketing models:

- *A customer orientation is critical.* The marketer knows that the offer (product, price, place) will need to appeal to the target audience, solving a problem they have or satisfying a want or need.
- *Exchange theory is fundamental.* The target audience must perceive benefits that equal or exceed the perceived costs they associate with performing the behavior.[13] As Dr. Bill Smith often purports, we should think of the social marketing paradigm as "Let's make a deal!"[14]

- *Marketing research is used throughout the process.* Only by researching and under-standing the specific needs, desires, beliefs, and attitudes of target adopters can the marketer build effective strategies.
- *Audiences are segmented.* Strategies must be tailored to the unique wants, needs, resources, and current behavior of differing market segments.
- *All 4Ps are considered.* A winning strategy requires an integrated approach, one utilizing all relevant tools in the toolbox, not just relying on advertising and other persuasive communications.
- *Results are measured and used for improvement.* Feedback is valued and seen as "free advice" on how to do better next time.

HOW DOES SOCIAL MARKETING DIFFER FROM NONPROFIT MARKETING, PUBLIC SECTOR MARKETING, AND CAUSE PROMOTIONS?

As you will read, social marketing efforts are most often initiated and sponsored by those in the public and nonprofit sectors. However, in the nonprofit sector, marketing is more often used to support utilization of the organization's services (e.g., ticket sales), purchases of ancillary products and services (e.g., at museum stores), volunteer recruitment, advocacy efforts, and fundraising. In the public sector, marketing activities are also used to support utilization of governmental agency products and services (e.g., the post office, community clinics) and engender citizen support and compliance. In summary, social marketing efforts are only one of many marketing activities conducted by those involved in nonprofit or public sector marketing.

Cause promotions primarily focus on efforts to raise awareness and concern for a social issue (e.g., global warming, domestic violence) but typically stop short of charging themselves with influencing specific behaviors. This change in knowledge and belief may be a necessary prelude to impacting behaviors, and social marketers may contribute to this awareness building and attitude change—but the ball their eyes will be on is whether the desired behavior was adopted.

WHAT IS SOCIAL MARKETING'S UNIQUE VALUE PROPOSITION?

In March 2011, Nancy Lee, Mike Rothschild, and Bill Smith wrote a document to address two very narrow questions: What does social marketing add to the already considerable understanding of social change developed by many other disciplines? What is social marketing's unique value proposition? See Box 1.3 on pages 16 and 17 for their response.

WHO DOES SOCIAL MARKETING?

In most cases, social marketing principles and techniques are used by those on the front lines responsible for improving public health, preventing injuries, protecting the environment, engendering community involvement, and, more recently, enhancing financial well-being. It is rare that these individuals have a social marketing title. More often, they are program managers or those working in community relations or communication positions. Efforts usually involve multiple change agents who, as Robert Hornik points out, may or may not be acting in a consciously coordinated way.[15] Most often, organizations sponsoring these efforts are *public sector agencies*: international agencies such as WHO; national agencies such as the Centers for Disease Control and Prevention, departments of health, departments of social and human services, the Environmental Protection Agency, the National Highway Traffic Safety Administration, and departments of wildlife and fisheries; and local jurisdictions, including public utilities, fire departments, schools, parks, and community health clinics.

Nonprofit organizations and foundations also get involved, most often supporting behaviors aligned with their agency's mission. For example, the American Heart Association urges women to monitor their blood pressure, the Kaiser Family Foundation uses their Know HIV/AIDS campaign to promote testing, and the Nature Conservancy encourages actions that protect wildlife habitats.

Professionals working in a for-profit organization in positions responsible for corporate philanthropy, corporate social responsibility, marketing, or community relations might support social marketing efforts, often in partnership with nonprofit organizations and public agencies that benefit their communities and customers. Although the primary beneficiary is society, they may find that their efforts contribute to organizational goals as well, such as a desired brand image or even increased sales. Safeco Insurance, for example, provides households with tips on how to protect rural homes from wildfire; Crest supports the development of videos, audiotapes, and interactive lesson plans to promote good oral health behaviors; and thousands of customers at Home Depot's stores have attended weekend workshops focusing on water conservation basics, including drought-resistant gardening (see Figure 1.5).

Finally, there are marketing professionals who provide services to *organizations*

Figure 1.5   Home Depot's Arizona stores offered weekend workshops on water conservation basics, including drought-resistant gardening. More than 3,100 consumers attended.

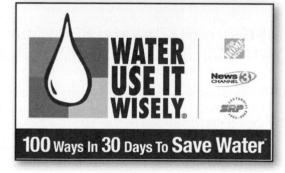

Box 1.3
A Declaration of Social Marketing's Unique Principles and Distinctions

Nancy R. Lee, Michael L. Rothschild, Bill Smith
March 2011

Principles Shared With Other Disciplines

Many of social marketing's key characteristics have been widely adopted by other fields, and in turn social marketing has integrated practices developed elsewhere. Among the important characteristics it shares with others are:

- AUDIENCE ORIENTATION: Social marketers view their audience as decision-makers with choices, rather than students to be educated, or incorrigibles to be regulated. Social Marketing begins with a bottom-up versus a top-down perspective, and therefore rejects the paternalist notion that "experts know what is best and will tell people how to behave for their own good" in favor of an audience-centered approach which seeks to understand what people want and provides them support in acquiring it.
- SEGMENTATION: In order to enhance efficiency and effectiveness, subsets of populations are selected, evaluated, and then prioritized as targets based on useful aggregation variables. The segments selected are those most likely to adopt the intended behavior or most important to the organization's goals, and to provide value in yielding societal benefit. Even among difficult to reach populations, strategies are developed that appeal to those within the chosen population that are the "most ready for action."
- BEHAVIOR FOCUS: Behavior is defined as an individual's observable action or lack of action. Social marketing is interested in behavior that results in societal benefit. Many marketing strategies also have intermediate responses, but Social Marketing success is ultimately measured on whether the desired behavior was adopted. It is not sufficient to merely change awareness, knowledge, attitudes, or behavioral intentions.
- EVALUATION: Efforts are evaluated, focusing on ongoing measurement of outcomes (levels of target audience behavior change), and the intended impact this has had on societal benefits. Social Marketing is a continuous process in which evaluation and monitoring provide data on the audience's preferences and the environmental changes necessary to maintain and expand the impact of programs.
- CONSIDERATION OF UPSTREAM & MIDSTREAM TARGET AUDIENCES: Efforts to influence individuals downstream are often enhanced by also targeting those who are upstream (policy makers, corporations), and/or those who are midstream (e.g. friends, family and influential others).

Unique Principles

While social marketing integrates many characteristics common to other forms of behavior change, four core principles remain truly unique to social marketing.

- VALUE EXCHANGE: Social Marketing is unique with respect to other behavior change tools in that the offer that is made is based on an understanding of the target audience's perceived self-interest that will be rewarded for performing the desired behavior. The concept of value exchange states that consumers will choose a behavior in exchange for receiving benefits they consider valuable and/or reducing barriers that they consider to be important. An exchange may result when the marketer has created a program that is perceived by each side to provide value.
- RECOGNITION OF COMPETITION: In a free-choice society there are always alternative options available. Competition can be described in terms of choice offerings available in the environment that lead to alternative behaviors. Social Marketing strategies lead to a unique exchange offering that is perceived by the audience to have greater value than that of any other available option.
- THE 4Ps OF MARKETING: Product, Place, Price and Promotion represent the fundamental building blocks of Social Marketing interventions. These tools are used to reduce the barriers that make it difficult for people to behave as desired, and to increase the benefits that induce people to be more likely to behave. The tools are used in concert to develop a favorably perceived relationship that is more appealing than all alternate choices. Social marketers assess and then balance the need for, and use of, these four elements to influence optimal change.
- SUSTAINABILITY: Sustainability results from continuous program monitoring and subsequent adjustment to changes occurring in the audience and environmental condition. This is necessary to achieve long run behavior.

Distinctions

It also is important to be clear about how it differs from other important approaches to behavior change. Being different does not make any approach superior to any other, but these distinctions signal opportunities for Social Marketing to make a unique contribution.

- COMMERCIAL MARKETING: Social marketing is built upon many of the traditional processes and principles of commercial marketing, especially Customer Orientation, Exchange Theory, Competition, Segmentation, the 4Ps, Relationships, and a Service Orientation. Social Marketing differs in that the primary responsibility of commercial marketers is to increase the company's wealth by increasing individuals' well-being, whereas the primary responsibility of social marketers is to increase individual and societal well-being.
- COMMUNICATIONS: Communications is a process involved with every human activity and is widely used by many approaches to behavior change. In Social Marketing, communications refers to the activity that describes the benefits of the offering, its price and accessibility to the target audience. Communicating the integrated value of the marketing mix is unique to social marketing, and is not offered by any other communication discipline. Communications alone generally is not sufficient to influence behaviors.
- REGULATION: Regulation also seeks to influence behaviors for the benefit of society, but often does so by increasing the cost of undesired competing behaviors (e.g., penalties for breaking laws), rather than increasing the benefits of desired behaviors. Those regulations that offer a benefit for an appropriate behavior (e.g., various tax incentives) more closely fit within the rubric of social marketing. Social marketers also have a role to play in influencing policy makers to adopt regulations (upstream changes) that complement and accelerate behavior changes among large-scale audiences, and to increase compliance with existing regulations.
- SOCIAL MEDIA: Social media leverage the social networks of target audiences, and are more personal and interactive forms of message delivery than are the traditional mass media. From a conceptual perspective, though, these electronic systems are similar to print, broadcast, and outdoor, in that each are ways of delivering messages and are, therefore, a subset of Communications.
- NONPROFIT MARKETING: The marketing function for nonprofit organizations often focuses on fund-raising, advocacy and program development, as well as supporting utilization of the organization's products and services.
- BEHAVIORAL ECONOMICS: Behavioral economics merges economics, psychology, sociology, and anthropology theory and research that focus on how changes in the external environment prompt and promote voluntary individual level behavior change. Social marketing is a process that should apply these insights along with others to maximize the efficiency and effectiveness of large-scale behavior change.

Unique Value Proposition

Social Marketing's unique position in the marketplace of behavior change ideas is to integrate the shared and unique characteristics described above into a program of behavior change. Social marketing is a process rooted in the belief that more than words and/or regulations are needed in order to succeed at influencing people's behavior. Social marketers understand and build upon the consumer's perception of:

- Self-interest
- Barriers to behavior, and
- Competitive forces that create attractive choices.

These lead to interventions that

- Reduce barriers, and
- Increase benefits that matter to the audience and, in the end, move people to action.

Acknowledgements

We wish to thank the following colleagues whose feedback and insights were invaluable to this document. Alan Andreasen, John Bromley, Carol Bryant, Stephen Dann, Rob Donovan, Jeff French, Phil Harvey, Gerard Hastings, Phil Kotler, Francois Lagarde, Craig Lefebvre, Rowena Merritt, Mike Newton-Ward, Sharyn Rundle Thiele. Ultimately any flaws are ours, not theirs.

engaged in social marketing campaigns, firms such as advertising agencies, public relations firms, marketing research firms, and marketing consulting firms—some that specialize in social marketing.

WHAT SOCIAL ISSUES CAN BENEFIT FROM SOCIAL MARKETING?

Table 1.2 presents 50 major social issues that could benefit from the application of social marketing principles and techniques. This is only a partial list but representative of the aforementioned five major arenas social marketing efforts usually focus on: health promotion, injury prevention, environmental protection, community involvement, and financial well-being. For each of the social issues listed, the status could improve if and when we are successful in increasing the adoption of desired related behaviors.

Table 1.2 50 Major Issues Social Marketing Can Impact

Health-Related Behaviors to Impact	
Tobacco Use	One in five (20.6%) adults 18 and older smokes cigarettes.[a]
Heavy/Binge Drinking	More than a fourth (26%) of 18- to 24-year-olds binge drink (have five or more drinks on one occasion).[b]
Fetal Alcohol Syndrome	3.3% of pregnant women binge drink and 8.3% drink frequently.[c]
Obesity	Almost half (49.4%) of adults do not exercise at recommended levels.[d]
Teen Pregnancy	37% of sexually active 9th through 12th graders did not use a condom during their last sexual intercourse.[e]
HIV/AIDS	About a fourth (24% to 27%) of Americans living with HIV are unaware of their infection.[f]
Fruit and Vegetable Intake	More than three out of four adults (76.5%) do not consume the recommended five or more servings a day.[g]
High Cholesterol	23% of adults have never had their cholesterol checked.[h]
Breastfeeding	57% of mothers do not meet recommendations to breastfeed infants until they reach at least six months.[i]
Breast Cancer	25% of women 40 and older have not had a mammogram within the past two years.[j]
Prostate Cancer	48% of men 40 and older have not had a PSA test within the past two years.[k]
Colon Cancer	In 2010, 35% of adults 50 and older had never had a sigmoidoscopy or colonoscopy.[l]
Birth Defects	60% of women of childbearing age are not taking a multivitamin containing folic acid.[m]

Immunizations	10% of 29- to 35-month-old children are not receiving all recommended vaccinations.[n]
Skin Cancer	Only 9% of youths wear sunscreen most of the time.[o]
Oral Health	30% of adults have not visited a dentist or dental clinic in the past year.[p]
Diabetes	One third of 20.8 million Americans with diabetes are not aware that they have the disease.[q]
Blood Pressure	30% of the estimated 60 million Americans with high blood pressure don't know they have it.[r]
Eating Disorders	57% of college students cite cultural pressures to be thin as a cause of eating disorders.[s]
Injury Prevention–Related Behaviors to Impact	
Drinking and Driving	16% of high school students report having ridden one or more times in the past year in a car driven by someone who had been drinking.[t]
Seatbelts	Observation surveys nationwide indicate that at least 16% of people do not wear a seatbelt.[u]
Head Injuries	More than a third (35%) of children riding bicycles wear helmets improperly.[v]
Proper Safety Restraints for Children in Cars	83% of children ages four to eight ride improperly restrained in adult safety belts.[w]
Suicide	8.4% of 9th through 12th graders attempted suicide one or more times during the past 12 months.[x]
Domestic Violence	Around the world, at least one woman in every three has been beaten, coerced into sex, or otherwise abused in her lifetime. Most often the abuser is a member of her own family.[y]
Gun Storage	An estimated 3.3 million children in the United States live in households with firearms that are always or sometimes kept loaded and unlocked.[z]
School Violence	5% of students in high schools reported carrying a gun onto school property during a given month.[aa]
Fires	Roughly half of home fire deaths result from fires in the small percentage (4%) of homes with no smoke alarms.[bb]
Falls	More than one third of adults 65 and older fall each year. In 2003, more than 13,700 people 65+ died from injuries related to falls.[cc]
Household Poisons	More than 4 million accidental poisonings are reported each year; 65% of those involve children, and the most common poisoning agents among small children are vitamins, aspirins, cleaning products, and beauty supplies.[dd]
Environmental Behaviors to Impact	
Waste Reduction	Only 50% of all paper, 45% of all aluminum beer and soft drink cans, and 34% of all plastic soft drink bottles are recycled.[ee]

(Continued)

Table 1.2 (Continued)

Wildlife Habitat Protection	Roughly 70% of the major marine fish stocks depleted from overfishing are being fished at their biological limit.[ff]
Forest Destruction	About 15 million trees are cut down annually to produce the estimated 10 billion paper bags we go through each year in the United States.[gg]
Toxic Fertilizers and Pesticides	An estimated 76% of households use harmful insecticides, and an estimated 85% have at least one pesticide in storage.[hh]
Water Conservation	A leaky toilet can waste as much as 200 gallons a day.[ii]
Air Pollution From Automobiles	An estimated 76% of commuters in the United States drive alone to work.[jj]
Air Pollution From Other Sources	If every household in the United States replaced their five most frequently used light fixtures with bulbs that have the ENERGY STAR® label, more than 1 trillion pounds of greenhouse gas emissions would be prevented.[kk]
Composting Garbage and Yard Waste	30% to 50% of all trash that ends up in a landfill in the United States could have been composted.[ll]
Unintentional Fires	An average of 106,400 wildfires are estimated to break out each year in the United States; about 9 out of 10 are started by carelessness.[mm]
Litter	Each year, over 4.5 trillion nonbiodegradable cigarette butts are littered worldwide.[nn]
Watershed Protection	At least 40% of Americans don't pick up their dogs' waste.[oo]
Community Involvement Behaviors to Impact	
Organ Donation	As of June 30, 2011, 111,814 patients were on a waiting list for an organ transplant.[pp]
Blood Donation	60% of the U.S. population is eligible to give blood, but only 5% do in a given year.[qq]
Voting	Only 64% of the eligible voting-age population voted in the 2008 U.S. presidential election.[rr]
Literacy	Only 16% of children are read a bedtime story every night compared to 33% of their parents' generation.[ss]
Identity Theft	About 3.6 million U.S. households (3%) were victims of at least one type of identity theft during a six-month period in 2004.[tt]
Animal Adoption	Over 10 million animals in shelters are not adopted and are euthanized each year.[uu]
Financial Behaviors to Impact	
Establishing Bank Accounts	Nearly a quarter of the workforce in the U.S. has no bank account.[vv]
Bankruptcy	Job loss is a big cause of bankruptcy because people who don't have emergency funds often live off credit cards while they are unemployed.[ww]
Fraud	More than a quarter (26%) of U.S. adults have been victimized by fraudulent telemarketing techniques at some point in their lives.[xx]

Note: Statistics are estimated and approximate. Data are for the United States, and dates for these statistics are given in Chapter 1 Table Notes.

WHAT ARE OTHER WAYS TO IMPACT SOCIAL ISSUES?

Social marketing is clearly not the only approach to impacting a social issue, and social marketers are not the only ones who can be influential. Other forces and organizations, which some describe as upstream factors and midstream influential others, can affect individual behaviors downstream. Included upstream are technological innovations, scientific discoveries, economic pressures, laws, improved infrastructures, changes in corporate business practices, new school policies and curricula, public education, and the media. Midstream influences are family members, friends, neighbors, church leaders, healthcare providers, entertainers, Facebook friends, and others our target audiences listen to, observe, or look up to.

Technology: Many new gas pumps inhibit the ability to top off the tank, thus avoiding ozone-threatening spillage. Some cars have automatic seatbelts that wrap around the passenger when the door is closed. In some states, ignition locks require Breathalyzers for serious offenders, and Mothers Against Drunk Driving (MADD) is advocating that automobile manufacturers be required to include high-tech alcohol sensors in all new cars. Imagine the impact on trip reduction if cars were designed to give feedback on how much that trip to the grocery store just cost, given the current price of a gallon of gas.

Science: Medical discoveries may eventually provide inoculations for certain cancers, such as one released in 2009 for 11- to 26-year-olds to help prevent cervical cancer. And in 2006, researchers at the Mayo Clinic announced they felt they were close to discovering a shot that could be given that would help a smoker to quit (if not ensure smoking cessation).[16]

Legal/political/policy making: Sometimes when all else fails, the laws have to get tougher, especially when the vast majority of the market has adopted the behavior and only the most resistant are still holding out (late adopters and laggards, as they are labeled in marketing). As of April 2011, 31 states and the District of Columbia ban text messaging for all drivers.[17] All U.S. states now have a 0.08% blood alcohol level limit for drinking and driving, more strict than the prior 0.10%. Some states have considered laws requiring deposits on cigarettes similar to those requiring deposits on beverage containers (and rewarding their return). And in a policy statement published in December 2006 in the journal *Pediatrics*, the American Academy of Pediatrics asked Congress and the Federal Communications Commission to impose severe limits on children-targeted advertising, including banning junk food ads during shows viewed predominantly by those under age eight.[18]

Improved infrastructures and built environments: If we really want more people to ride bikes to work, we'll need more bike lanes, not just bike paths. If we really want to reduce cigarette butt littering on roadways, perhaps automobile manufacturers could help out by building in smoke-free cigarette butt containers so that disposing a cigarette inside the car is just as convenient as tossing it out the window. If we want to reduce electricity consumption, perhaps more hotels could ensure that lights in rooms can only be turned on when the room key is inserted in a master switch and therefore automatically turned off when guests leave the room with their key. And if we want more people at work to take the stairs instead of the elevators, we may want to have elevators skip the first three floors except in cases of emergency or to accommodate those with a physical disability,

Figure 1.6   Making the calories per container more obvious.

and we certainly want to take a look at the cleanliness and lighting of the stairway. How about a little music? And social marketers can play a huge role in influencing policy makers and corporations to make these changes.

Changes in corporate policies and business practices: In 2010, the American Beverage Association announced their Clear on Calories initiative in support of First Lady Michelle Obama's antiobesity campaign. Instead of printing the number of calories per serving on the back of a can in small print, members will print the number in large print on the front of the can—and the number will represent the total calories per container, versus per serving, since most consumers drink the entire can (see Figure 1.6).

Each of these efforts will positively impact the same social issues that social marketers are trying to address.

Schools: School district policies and offerings can contribute significantly in all social arenas, providing channels of distribution for social marketing efforts: health (e.g., offering healthier options in school cafeterias and regularly scheduled physical activity classes), safety (e.g., requiring students to wear ID badges), environmental protection (e.g., providing recycling containers in each classroom), and community involvement (e.g., offering school gymnasiums for blood donation drives).

Education: The line between social marketing and education is actually a clear one, with education serving a useful tool for the social marketer, but one that does not work alone. Most often, education is used to communicate information and/or build skills but does not give the same attention and rigor to creating and sustaining behavior adoption. It primarily applies only one of the four marketing tools, that of promotion. Many in the field agree that when the information is motivating and "new" (e.g., the finding that secondhand tobacco smoke increases the risk of sudden infant death syndrome), it can move a market from inaction—even resistance—to action very quickly. This, however, is unfortunately not typical. Consider the fact that death threats for tobacco use have been posted right on cigarette packs for decades, and yet WHO estimates that 29% of youths and adults (ages 15 and older) worldwide still smoke cigarettes.[19] Marketing (benefits in exchange for behaviors) has often been missing in action.

Media: News and entertainment media have powerful influences on individual behaviors as they shape values, are relied on for current events/trends, and create social norms. Many argue, for example, that the casual and sensational attitude of movies and television toward sex has been a major contribution to the problems we see among young people today.[20] On the flip side, the media was a powerful factor influencing people to donate time and resources to victims of the earthquake in Haiti and the tsunami in Japan.

WHAT IS THE SOCIAL MARKETER'S ROLE IN INFLUENCING UPSTREAM FACTORS AND MIDSTREAM AUDIENCES?

As noted earlier, many believe that to date we have been placing too much of the burden for improving the status of social issues on individual behavior change and that social marketers should direct some of their efforts to influencing upstream factors and midstream influentials. We agree.

Alan Andreasen, in his book *Social Marketing in the 21st Century,* describes this expanded role for social marketing well:

> Social marketing is about making the world a better place for everyone—not just for investors or foundation executives. And, as I argue throughout this book, the same basic principles that can induce a 12-year-old in Bangkok or Leningrad to get a Big Mac and a caregiver in Indonesia to start using oral dehydration solutions for diarrhea can also be used to influence politicians, media figures, community activists, law officers and judges, foundation officials, and other individuals whose actions are needed to bring about widespread, long-lasting positive social change.[21]

Consider the issue of the spread of HIV/AIDS. Downstream, social marketers focus on decreasing risky behaviors (e.g., unprotected sex) and increasing timely testing (e.g., during pregnancy). If they moved their attention upstream, they would notice groups and organizations and corporations and community leaders and policy makers that could make this change a little easier or a little more likely, ones that could be a target audience for a social marketing effort. The social marketer could, with others, influence pharmaceutical companies to make testing for HIV/AIDS quicker and more accessible. They could work with physician groups to create protocols to ask patients whether they have had unprotected sex and, if so, encourage them to get an HIV/AIDS test. They could encourage offices of public instruction to include curricula on HIV/AIDS in middle schools. They could support needle exchange programs. They could provide the media with trends and personal stories, maybe even pitching a story to producers of soap operas or situation comedies popular with the target audience. They might look for a corporate partner that would be interested in setting up testing at their retail location. They could organize meetings with community leaders such as ministers and directors of nonprofit organizations, even providing grants for them to allocate staff resources to community interventions. If they could, they might visit hair salons and barbershops, engaging owners and staff in spreading the word with their clients. They could testify before a senate committee to advocate increased funding for research, condom availability, or free testing facilities. And midstream, they might appeal to parents to talk with their teens about how HIV/AIDS is spread and to midwives to speak to pregnant women about the importance of testing.

The marketing process and principles are the same as those used for influencing individuals: utilizing a customer orientation, establishing clear objectives and goals, conducting audience research, crafting a position statement, developing a marketing mix, and conducting monitoring and evaluation efforts. Only the target audience has changed.[22]

CHAPTER SUMMARY

Social marketing is a process that uses marketing principles and techniques to promote target-audience behaviors that will benefit society as well as the individual. This strategically oriented discipline relies on creating, communicating, delivering, and exchanging offerings that have positive value for individuals, clients, partners, and society at large.[23]

There are a few important differences between social marketing and commercial marketing. Social marketers focus on influencing behavior for societal gain, whereas commercial marketers focus on selling goods and services at a financial gain for the organization. Commercial marketers position their products against those of other companies, while the social marketer competes with the audience's current behavior and its associated benefits.

Social marketing principles and techniques are most often used to improve public health, prevent injuries, protect the environment, increase involvement in the community, and enhance financial well-being. Those engaged in social marketing activities include professionals in public sector agencies, nonprofit organizations, corporate marketing departments and advertising, public relations, and market research firms. A social marketing title is rare, and social marketing is most likely to fall within the responsibility of a program manager or community relations or communications professional.

Other approaches to changing behavior and impacting social issues include technological innovations, scientific discoveries, economic pressures, laws, improved infrastructures, changes in corporate business practices, new school policies and curricula, public education, and the media. Many agree that influencing these factors and audiences is well within the purview of social marketers—and even their responsibility.

MARKETING DIALOGUE

When Is Social Marketing "Social Marketing"?
When Is It Something Else?

In February 2010, a member of the social marketing listserv of 2,000-plus members sent a message with the subject line "To Stir the Pot." The message included a link to an announcement of a new type of speed bump unveiled in West Vancouver, Canada, one intended to persuade motorists to slow down in the vicinity of an elementary school. A pavement painting appears to rise up as the driver gets closer to it, reaching a full 3D image of a child playing, creating the illusion that the approaching driver will soon hit the child (link: http://beta.news.yahoo.com/blogs/upshot/canada-unveils-speed-bump-optical-illusions-children.html). As anticipated, several members were adamant that this effort was not social marketing: "This is not marketing. Where's the exchange? What does the driver get [benefit] in exchange for slowing down?" Counter-arguments stressed that "by slowing down [the cost], the driver gets a great benefit—a reduced probability of hitting a child!" Some were troubled by unintended secondary effects ("cultivating resentful drivers not liking to be tricked"), and others weren't impressed with the potential efficacy, convinced that "it might work once but then wouldn't be sustainable." A few felt it met the basic criteria for social marketing: "Since social marketing's basic purpose is to change behavior for the good or betterment of society as a whole, I think this initiative seems to fit well into that criteria. However, I question whether or not it will work."

The authors of this text offer the following opinions on common questions and reactions, such as whether an effort is social marketing—or not. As will be apparent, we make a distinction between what defines social marketing and what are its best practices:

- *Does the effort have to use all 4Ps in order to be called social marketing?* No, but this is a best practice. Your efforts will be more successful when you do, because most of the time all four intervention tools are needed to overcome audience barriers, increase benefits, and upstage the competition.

- *Does there have to be a narrowly defined and targeted audience segment?* No, but this is also a best practice, based on there being very few homogeneous populations, and that different segments within these populations have different barriers and benefits and therefore require different interventions.

- *Is a communications-only campaign a social marketing campaign?* It might be. A campaign intended to influence a behavior (e.g., putting infants on their back to sleep) to benefit individuals and society (e.g., prevent sudden infant death syndrome) but that uses only words (e.g., "Back to Sleep" printed on the strip of a newborn diaper) meets the basic criteria for a social marketing effort. However, it is more likely to be successful if other influence tools are used as well (e.g., demonstrations as part of a free class for new moms at a local hospital).

- *What needs to be present for an effort to be called social marketing?* An effort can be considered a social marketing effort when it is intended to influence a target audience behavior to benefit society as well as the target audience. And we should keep in mind that the target audience may be a school district or corporation upstream.

CHAPTER 1 NOTES

1. Retrieved September 7, 2010, from AED NetMark Web site: http://www.netmarkafrica.org/
2. Ibid.
3. Ibid.
4. Netmark. *NetMark Baseline Survey on Insecticide Treated Materials (ITMs) in Nigeria* (p. 10). (2001, May). Retrieved June 29, 2011, from http://www.netmarkafrica.org/research/index.html

5. Academy for Educational Development for Netmark.

6. Ibid.

7. Ibid.

8. Personal communication from Alan Andreasen to Philip Kotler, April 28, 2011.

9. American Marketing Association. (2007, December 17). *AMA definition of marketing.* Retrieved July 31, 2007, from http://www.marketing power.com/mg-dictionary.php?SearchFor= marketing&Searched=1

10. Donovan, R., & Henley, N. (2003). *Social Marketing: Principles and Practices.* Melbourne, Australia: IP Communications.

11. Provided by National Archives and Records Administration, Washington, DC.

12. Kotler, P., & Zaltman, G. (1971, July). Social marketing: An approach to planned social change. *Journal of Marketing, 35,* 3–12.

13. Bagozzi, R. P. (1978, March/April). Marketing as exchange: A theory of transactions in the marketplace. *American Behavioral Science,* pp. 535–556.

14. Smith, W. (2002, Summer). Social marketing and its potential contribution to a modern synthesis of social change. *Social Marketing Quarterly, 8*(2), 46.

15. Hornik, R. (2002, Summer). Some complementary ideas about social change. *Social Marketing Quarterly, 8*(2), 11.

16. Marchione, M. (2006). Doctors test anti-smoking vaccine. Retrieved July 31, 2007, from http://www.foxnews.com/printer_friendly_wires/2006Ju127/0,4675,TobaccoVaccine,00.html

17. Governors Highway Safety Association. (2011, April). *Cell phone and texting laws.* Retrieved April 27, 2011, from http://www.ghsa.org/html/stateinfo/laws/cellphone_laws.html

18. Teinowitz, I. (2006, December 4). Pediatricians demand cuts in children-targeted advertising: Doctors' group asks federal government to impose severe limits. *Advertising Age.* Retrieved June 29, 2011, from http://adage.com/print?article_id=113558

19. World Health Organization, Tobacco Free Initiative. (2003). Statistics for the year 2000, published in the HNP Discussion Paper No. 6, Economics of Tobacco Control Paper No. 6, The World Bank.

20. Andreasen, A. R., & Kotler, P. (2003). *Strategic marketing for non-profit organizations* (6th ed., p. 490). Upper Saddle River, NJ: Prentice Hall.

21. Andreasen, A. R. (2006). *Social marketing in the 21st century* (p. 11). Thousand Oaks, CA: Sage.

22. Kotler, P., & Lee, N. (2006). *Marketing in the public sector: A roadmap for improved performance.* Upper Saddle River, NJ: Wharton School.

23. Lee, N. R., Rothschild, M. L., & Smith, W. (2011, March). *A declaration of social marketing's unique principles and distinctions.* Unpublished manuscript.

CHAPTER 1 TABLE NOTES

a. Centers for Disease Control and Prevention. (n.d.). *Adult cigarette smoking in the United States: Current estimate.* Retrieved April 27, 2011, from http://www.cdc.gov/tobacco/data_ statistics/fact_sheets/adult_data/cig_smoking/index.htm

b. Centers for Disease Control and Prevention. (2010, October 8). Vital signs: Binge drinking among high school students and adults. *Morbidity and Mortality Weekly Report.* Retrieved April 27, 2011, from http://www.cdc.gov/mmwr/preview/mmwrhtml/mm5939a4.htm?s_cid=mm5939a4_w

c. March of Dimes. (n.d.). *Alcohol and drugs.* Retrieved April 27, 2011, from http://www.marchofdimes.com/alcohol_indepth.html

d. Centers for Disease Control and Prevention. (2009). *Behavioral Risk Factor Surveillance System prevalence and trends data.* Retrieved April 27, 2011, from http://www.cdc.gov/brfss/index.htm

e. Centers for Disease Control and Prevention. (2006, June 9). Youth risk behavior surveillance—United States, 2005. *Morbidity and Mortality Weekly Report, 55*(SS-5).

f. Fleming, P., Byers, R. H., Sweeney, P. A., Daniels, D., Karon, J. M., & Janssen, R. S. (2002, February). *HIV prevalence in the United States, 2000* [Abstract #11]. Paper presented at the ninth Conference on Retroviruses and Opportunistic Infections, Seattle, WA.

g. Centers for Disease Control and Prevention. (2009). *Behavioral Risk Factor Surveillance System prevalence and trends data.* Retrieved April 27, 2011, from http://www.cdc.gov/brfss/index.htm

h. Centers for Disease Control and Prevention. (2005). *Behavioral Risk Factor Surveillance System prevalence and trends data.* Retrieved October 20, 2006, from http://www.cdc.gov/brfss/index.htm

i. Centers for Disease Control and Prevention. (n.d.). *Breastfeeding report card, United States: Outcome indicators.* Retrieved July 1, 2011, from http://www.cdc.gov/breastfeeding/data/reportcard2.htm

j. Centers for Disease Control and Prevention. (2004). *Behavioral Risk Factor Surveillance System prevalence and trends data.* Retrieved October 20, 2006, from http://www.cdc.gov/brfss/index.htm

k. Ibid.

l. Centers for Disease Control and Prevention. (2010). *Behavioral Risk Factor Surveillance System prevalence and trends data.* Retrieved July 1, 2011, from http://www.cdc.gov/brfss/index.htm

m. Medical News Today. (2004, September 18). *Folic acid vitamin use by women reaches all-time high, March of Dimes survey finds.* Retrieved October 20, 2006, from http://www.medicalnewstoday.com/medicalnews.php?newsid=13625

n. Centers for Disease Control and Prevention, CDC Online Newsroom. (2010, September 16). *CDC survey finds childhood immunization rates remain high* [Press release]. Retrieved July 2, 2011, from http://www.cdc.gov/media/pressrel/2010/r100916.htm

o. Centers for Disease Control and Prevention. (2006). Youth risk behavior surveillance—United States, 2005.

p. Centers for Disease Control and Prevention. (2004). *Behavioral Risk Factor Surveillance System prevalence and trends data.* Retrieved October 20, 2006, from http://www.cdc.gov/brfss/index.htm

q. American Diabetes Association. (n.d.). *All about diabetes.* Retrieved October 20, 2006, from http://www.diabetes.org/about-diabetes.jsp

r. American Heart Association. (2002). *High blood pressure statistics.* Retrieved October 20, 2006, from http://www.americanheart.org/presenter.jhtml?identifier=2139

s. National Eating Disorders Association. (2006, September 26). *National Eating Disorders Association announces results of eating disorders poll on college campuses across the nation* [Press release]. Retrieved October 20, 2006, from http://www.edap.org/ nedaDir/files/documents/PressRoom/CollegePoll_9–28–06.doc

t. Centers for Disease Control and Prevention. (2005). *Behavioral Risk Factor Surveillance System prevalence and trends data.* Retrieved October 20, 2006, from http://www.cdc.gov/brfss/index.htm

u. National Highway Traffic Safety Administration. (2010, May 24). *U.S. DOT targets 45 million Americans still not buckling up.* Retrieved July 1, 2011, from http://www.nhtsa.gov/PR/ DOT-101-10

v. National Safe Kids Campaign. (2004, May). *Headed for injury: An observational survey of helmet use among children ages 5 to 14 participating in wheeled sports.* Retrieved October 20, 2006, from http://www.usa.safekids.org/content_documents/ACFC7.pdf

w. Safe Kids USA. (n.d.). *Preventing accidental injury. Injury facts: Motor vehicle occupant injury.* Retrieved November 20, 2006, from http://www.usa.safekids.org/tier3_cd .cfm?content_item_id= 1133&folder_id=540

x. Centers for Disease Control and Prevention. (2006). Youth risk behavior surveillance— United States, 2005.

y. Heise, L., Ellsberg, M., & Gottemoeller, M. (1999, December). *Ending violence against women.* (Population Reports, Series L, No. 11). Baltimore, MD: Johns Hopkins University School of Public Health, Population Information Program.

z. Safe Kids. (n.d.). *Facts about unintentional firearm injuries to children.* Retrieved November 20, 2006, from http://www.usa.safekids.org/content_documents/Firearm_facts.pdf

aa. Centers for Disease Control and Prevention. (2006). Youth risk behavior surveillance— United States, 2005.

bb. National Fire Protection Association. (n.d.). *Smoke alarms.* Retrieved November 20, 1996, from http://www.nfpa.org/categoryList.asp?categoryID=278&URL=Research%20&%20 Reports/Fact% 20sheets/Fire%20protection%20equipment/Smoke%20alarms

cc. Centers for Disease Control and Prevention. (n.d.). *Falls among older adults: An overview.* Retrieved June 29, 2011, from http://www.cdc.gov/ncipc/factsheets/adultfalls.htm

dd. Powell, A. (2006, March 20). Happy Birthday Mr. Yuk [Web log post]. Retrieved November 20, 2006, from http://pittsburgh.about.com/b/2006/03/20/happy-birthday-mr-yuk.htm

ee. U.S. Environmental Protection Agency. (n.d.). *Municipal solid waste—recycling.* Retrieved November 20, 2006, from http://www.epa.gov/epaoswer/non-hw/muncpl/states.htm

ff. Bill Moyers reports: Earth on edge. (2001, June). *Discussion guide* (p. 4.). Retrieved October 10, 2001, from http://www.pbs.org/earthonedge/

gg. Gore, A. (2006). *An inconvenient truth* (p. 316). New York, NY: Rodale.

hh. Northwest Coalition for Alternatives to Pesticides. (n.d.). *Pesticide use reporting program.* Retrieved January 31, 2007, from http://www.pesticide.org/PUR.html

ii. U.S. Environmental Protective Agency. (n.d.). *At home.* Retrieved January 29, 2007, from http://epa.gov/climatechange/wycd/home.html

jj. U.S. Census Bureau. (n.d.). *United States—selected economic characteristics: 2007– 2009.* Retrieved July 1, 2011, from http://factfinder.census.gov/servlet/ADPTable?_bm=y&-qr_ name=ACS_2009_3YR_G00_DP3YR3&-geo_id=01000US&-gc_url=null&-ds_ name=ACS_2009_3YR_G00_&-_lang=en&-redoLog=false

kk. U.S. Environmental Protective Agency. (n.d.). *At home.* Retrieved January 29, 2007, from http://epa.gov/climatechange/wycd/home.html

ll. Van Cleef, L. (2001, April 30). *Landfill saver: Put a pile of rotting waste to work in your garden and save the world, too* (InformationWeek BreakAway). Retrieved June 30, 2011, from http://www.informationweek.com/breakaway/835/landfill.htm

mm. Only You Can Prevent Wildfires. (n.d.). Retrieved January 31, 2007, from http://www .smokeybear.com/couldbe.asp nn. CigaretteLitter.org. (2001). *Facts about cigarette butts and litter.* Retrieved September 19, 2001, from http://www.cigarettelitter.org

oo. Watson, T. (2002, June 7). *Dog waste poses threat to water.* Retrieved January 6, 2002, from http://www.usatoday.com/news/science/2002–06–07-dog-usat.htm

pp. United Network for Organ Sharing Web site: http://www.unos.org/

qq. American Red Cross. (n.d.). *50 quick facts.* Retrieved January 31, 2007, from http://www.givelife2.org/sponsor/quickfacts.asp

rr. U.S. Census Bureau. (n.d.). *Voting and registration in the election of November 2008.* Retrieved April 27, 2011, from http://www.census.gov/prod/2010pubs/p20–562.pdf

ss. *Reading research: Parent reading.* (n.d.). Retrieved January 31, 2007, from http://www.m2fbooks.com/research

tt. Bureau of Justice Statistics. (2006, April 2). *Identity theft, 2004* [Press release]. Retrieved June 30, 2011, from http://bjs.ojp.usdoj.gov/index.cfm?ty=pbdetail&iid=454

uu. American Humane™: Protecting Children & Animals Since 1877. (n.d.). *Care & issues: Spay and neuter.* Retrieved January 31, 2007, from http://www.americanhumane.org/site/PageServer? pagename=pa_care_issues_spay_neuter

vv. Get a New Bank Account: Banks That Do Not Use ChexSystems. (n.d.). *The plight of the unbanked population.* Retrieved April 28, 2011, from http://www.getanewbankaccount.com/the-plight-of-the-unbanked-population.html

ww. TFGI.com. (n.d.). *The top five causes for bankruptcy.* Retrieved April 28, 2011, from http://www.tfgi.com/201003/the-top-five-causes-for-bankruptcy/

xx. Retirement Industry Trust Association. (n.d.). *Senior fraud initiative.* Retrieved April 28, 2011, from http://www.ritaus.org/mc/page.do?sitePageId=77992&orgId=rita

10 Steps in the Strategic Marketing Planning Process

I find the social marketing process is a great way to mobilize groups and coalitions around a common goal. It is a logical, step-by-step process that makes sense. It provides a concise map for how the project will be conducted. It ensures that efforts will be measured. And it demands continuous monitoring that allows for midcourse corrections. Sometimes I get asked if it's okay to skip a step. My response: If you do, then it's not social marketing.

—Heidi Keller
Keller Consulting

Although most agree that having a formal, detailed plan for a social marketing effort "would be nice," that practice doesn't appear to be the norm. Those in positions of responsibility who could make this happen frequently voice perceptions and concerns such as these:

- We just don't have the time to get this all down on paper. By the time we get the go-ahead, we just need to spend the money before the funding runs out.
- The train already left the station. I believe the team and my administrators already know what they want to do. The target audience and communication channels were chosen long ago. It seems disingenuous, and quite frankly a waste of resources, to prepare a document to justify these decisions.

We begin this chapter with an inspiring case story that demonstrates the positive potential return on your investment in the planning process. Ten steps to developing a compelling social marketing plan are then outlined—ones we hope will demonstrate that the process can be simple and efficient and that those who have taken the time to develop a formal plan realize numerous benefits. Readers of your plan will see evidence that recommended activities are based on strategic thinking. They will understand why specific target audiences have been recommended. They will see what anticipated costs are intended to produce in specific, quantifiable terms that can be translated into an associated return on investment. They will certainly learn that marketing is more than advertising and will be delighted (even surprised) to see you have a system, method, timing, and budget to evaluate your efforts.

We conclude with comments on why a systematic, sequential planning process is important and where marketing research fits in the process. The Marketing Dialogue at the end of the chapter gives a glimpse at the ongoing, passionate debate over the first step in the planning process—deciding "what is good."

MARKETING HIGHLIGHT

Scooping the Poop in Austin, Texas (2001–2009)

Background

The Humane Society of the United States estimates that 39% of U.S. households own at least one dog.[1] Austinites are no exception, with the current population of canine residents estimated at more than 120,000. Further, many consider Austin an especially dog-friendly city, evidenced by off-leash areas in 11 city parks as well as frequent sightings of dogs with their owners on excursions along neighborhood streets and local trails, lounging on restaurant patios, and attending public events in the parks.

The problem is that pet waste contains dangerous bacteria such as *Salmonella* and *E. coli* as well as harmful parasites such as *Giardia* and roundworms. When not properly disposed of and left in public places and as many as 120,000 backyards in the city, it poses a direct-contact health hazard for people and pets. And when washed into creeks and lakes, pet waste can make the water unsafe for recreation and cause aquatic weeds and algae to flourish, eventually reducing levels of oxygen in the water and killing fish. With each dog producing an average of one half pound of waste daily, that adds up to 60,000 pounds deposited each day in Austin (a citywide total of nearly five dump truck loads)—approximately *22 million pounds per year.*

Beginning in 1992, the City relied on an ordinance, carrying a potential fine of up to $500, requiring that pet owners pick up after their pets. The code is a helpful deterrent, but hard to enforce as it requires a law officer to witness the offense, and it does nothing to engender public concern for the environmental and health impacts of pet waste. To increase this influence, in 2000 the City's Watershed Protection and Parks and Recreation departments launched a new effort called Scoop the Poop. As you will read, the program continues to this day (2011), with new strategic components being added each year. Information for this case was provided by Kathy Shay, Environmental Program Manager, City of Austin, Texas.[2]

Target Audiences and Desired Behaviors

Initially, the primary target audience was dog owners taking their pets to public parks. Eventually, in response to citizens' complaints regarding neighborhood dogs' defecating on private property, the campaign expanded its outreach to include people walking their dogs in community neighborhoods.

Three behaviors for waste disposal were encouraged: (1) Scoop the poop, (2) bag it, and (3) place it in the trash.

Audience Insights

To identify perceived *barriers*, program managers interviewed professionals around the country and reviewed existing surveys, including some from the Center for Watershed Protection. Common barriers to poop scooping and proper disposal included (a) not having convenient access to disposable bags, (b) not having enough trash cans around for quick disposal, (c) finding the task messy and smelly, (d) not believing that "one little pile" is a problem, and (e) considering dog waste a good/natural fertilizer.

In one survey conducted by the City, potential *benefits* were quantified and ranked: 53% expressed that pressure from others would probably make them more likely to pick up after their pet; 46% indicated that more dispensers with plenty of bags would help; 40% said more trash cans were important; 35% wanted more information about why they should pick it up and what to do with it; and 35% "admitted" that enforcement of fines would make a difference.

Strategies

In 2000, 25 Mutt Mitt stations dispensing disposable bags were installed in city parks (see Figure 2.1). Mutt Mitt plastic bags are degradable and designed to "protect the hand like a glove," easing some of the concerns about mess and smell. By 2010, there were more than 150 stations in 90 city parks (*product*).

In 2002, the program expanded to reach citizens walking their dogs in neighborhoods and other public places and began giving away reusable pet trash bag holders with a clasp to clip to a dog leash (see Figure 2.2).

As noted earlier, there is a preexisting $500 fine. To make the law more visible and increase the perception of enforcement, citizens are now encouraged to report violators via the City's nonemergency telephone number (311), which is highlighted on signage and promotional materials (*disincentive*). The City also offers a Green Neighbor program that lists more than 100 actions citizens can do to improve the environment. Any neighborhood that distributes Green Neighbor guides to its residents, marks storm drains, adopts a

Figure 2.1 Mutt Mitt dispenser[3]

Figure 2.2	Bag holder giveaway[4]

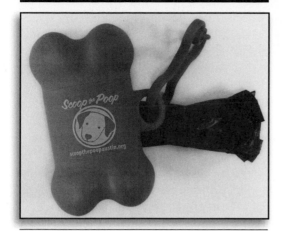

Source: City of Austin

park, or performs other earth-wise actions qualifies as a Green Neighborhood and can receive a free Mutt Mitt dispenser (*incentive*).

To help ensure bags are always available at stations, there is a message on the dispenser with a number to call to let the City know when the dispenser is empty. Yard signs to prompt pet owners to pick up waste on private properties can be ordered online and are then mailed directly to the citizen. Additional trash cans have been added in many of the parks to make disposal more convenient (*place*).

Until 2008, primary strategies consisted of the pet waste dispensers with bags (*product*), signage regarding the City code and how to report violators (*price*), and placement of more trash receptacles along with provision of a phone number for letting the City know if there were no bags in the dispenser (*place*). In 2009, the program was enhanced with more *promotional* elements to spread the word beyond the city parks. These included:

- *Broadcast media:* a 30-second animated television spot funded by the Watershed Protection Department
- *Public events:* creation of a temporary dirt pile sculpture next to a popular downtown lake; the pile represented one day's worth of poop (60,000 pounds) and was unveiled at a press conference hosted by the mayor and showcasing an original "Scoop the Poop" song performed by a local singer/songwriter
- *Outdoor and print media:* promotional advertisements placed in newspapers
- *Signage:* signage based on the Snohomish County, Washington, pet waste campaign, adapted by Austin, and placed in many off-leash areas
- *Brochures and flyers:* two small Austin Guide brochures, one on the Scoop the Poop program and one to describe issues specific to the off-leash pet areas
- *Enhanced Web site* for downloading program materials and ordering yard signs
- *Program mascot:* Scoop the Poop's mascot, Eco—Austin's #1 dog for the environment
- *Social media:* a Facebook page that encourages visitors to interact with Eco, the campaign mascot; the most popular feature asks pet owners to send photos of their dogs, who then become "friends" of Eco
- *Articles* for neighborhood newsletters
- *Face-to-face promotions:* staff talking to dog owners in off-leash areas about pet waste and attending

environment-, pet-, and park-themed city events

- *Direct mail:* educational postcards mailed to pet-related businesses and organizations to distribute to their clientele
- *Additional distribution channels for program materials:* veterinary clinics, animal shelters, libraries, recreation centers

Results

Program outcomes, impact, and cost/benefit are tracked and reported every year. As indicated in Table 2.1, outcomes are measured in terms of number of Mutt Mitts distributed; impact is stated in terms of estimated number of pounds of pet waste collected and disposed of properly; and cost per pound disposed of correctly is calculated based on annual program budgets. Number of Mutt Mitts distributed reflects those taken from the City's dispensers. (It should be noted that this number of bags does not include those carried by dog owners, including the contents of the 2,000 clip-on bag containers distributed by the City.) Impact is based on an assumption of an average of one half pound per bag. In 2001, approximately $10,000 was spent on the program. In 2009, $72,000 was spent on Mutt Mitts and dispensers; an additional $20,000 was spent on signs, brochures, giveaways, T-shirts, advertising, and staff time. Yard sign requests increased from 50 in 2007, to 140 in 2008, to 271 in 2009. Monthly Web hits to the Scoop the Poop Austin homepage, which numbered less than 400 before the campaign, increased to nearly 4,000 after the campaign began.

Table 2.1 Cost Per Pound to Properly Collect and Dispose of Pet Waste

Year	Annual Program Budget	Mutt Mitts Distributed	Pounds Collected and Disposed of Properly (@ 0.5 lb. per bag on average)	Estimated Cost Per Pound Properly Collected and Disposed Of
2001	$10,000	75,000	37,500 lbs.	$.27/lb.
2003	$53,000	535,000	267,500 lbs.	$.20/lb.
2006	$72,500	967,000	483,500 lbs.	$.15/lb.
2008	$87,000*	2,000,000	1,000,000 lbs.	$.09/lb.
2009	$92,000	2,400,000	1,200,000 lbs.	$.08/lb.

*Costs were reduced in 2008 by switching to less expensive bags

MARKETING PLANNING: PROCESS AND INFLUENCES

To set the stage for developing a tactical social marketing plan, we begin with a description of the traditional marketing planning process, the evolution of the marketing concept, and a few of the most recent shifts in marketing management philosophy.

The Marketing Planning Process

In theory, there is a logical process to follow when developing a marketing plan—whether for a commercial enterprise, nonprofit organization, or public sector agency. You begin by clarifying the purpose and focus of your plan; you move on to analyzing the current situation and environment, identifying target audiences, establishing marketing objectives and goals, conducting research to deepen your understanding of your target audiences, determining a desired positioning for the offer, and designing a strategic marketing mix (4Ps); and then you develop evaluation, budget, and implementation plans. Some conceptualize the process more easily with these broader headings: Why are you doing this? Where are you today? Where do you want to go? How are you going to get there? How will you keep on track?

Evolution of the Marketing Concept

The cornerstone of the marketing concept is a customer-centered mindset that sends marketers on a relentless pursuit to sense and satisfy target audiences' wants and needs and to solve their problems—better than the competition does. Marketers haven't always thought this way. Some still don't. This customer-centered focus didn't emerge as a strong marketing management philosophy until the 1980s and is contrasted with alternative philosophies in the following list provided by Kotler and Keller.[5] We have added a few examples relevant to social marketing.

- The Production Concept is perhaps the oldest philosophy and holds that consumers will prefer products that are widely available and inexpensive, and therefore the organization's focus should be to keep costs down and access convenient. Early efforts to encourage condom use to prevent the spread of HIV/AIDS may have had this philosophical orientation, unfortunately falling on deaf ears for those who did not see this behavior as a social norm and feared their partner's rejection.
- The Product Concept holds that consumers will favor products that offer the most quality, performance, or innovative features. The problem with this focus is that program and service managers often become caught up in a love affair with their product, neglecting to design and enhance their efforts based on customers' wants and needs. Otherwise known as the "build it and they will come" or "make it and it will sell" philosophy, this orientation may explain the challenges community transit agencies face as they attempt to increase ridership on buses.

- The Selling Concept holds that consumers and businesses, if left alone, will probably not buy enough of the organization's products to meet its goals, and as a result, the organization must undertake an aggressive selling and promotion effort. Communications encouraging adults to exercise and eat five or more servings of fruits and vegetables a day do not begin to address the barriers perceived by many in the target audience—such as how to make time when holding down a full-time job or raising a family, or simply not liking vegetables.
- The Marketing Concept stands in sharp contrast to the product and selling concepts. Instead of a "make and sell" philosophy, it is a "sense and respond" orientation. Peter Drucker went so far as to proclaim, "The aim of marketing is to make selling superfluous. The aim of marketing is to know and understand the customer so well that the product or service fits him and sells itself."[6] If a city utility's natural yard care workshop is exciting, and better yet those who attend are able to keep their lawn weed free without the use of harmful chemicals, they are bound to share their enthusiasm and this newfound resource with their neighbors—and go back for more!
- The Holistic Marketing Concept is a 21st-century approach, recognizing the need to have a more complete, cohesive philosophy that goes beyond traditional applications of the marketing concept. Three relevant components for social marketers include relationship marketing, integrated marketing, and internal marketing. The Farmers' Marketing Nutrition Program of the U.S. Department of Agriculture encourages clients in the Women, Infants, and Children (WIC) program to shop at farmers' markets for fresh, unprepared, locally grown fruits and vegetables. Keys to success include relationship building (e.g., counselors in WIC offices who work with clients to overcome barriers to shopping at the markets, such as transportation), integrated marketing (e.g., farmers' stands at the markets carry signage and messages regarding the program similar to those clients see in WIC offices), and internal marketing (e.g., counselors in WIC offices are encouraged to visit the markets themselves so they are more able to describe places to park and what clients are likely to find fresh that week).

Shifts in Marketing Management

Kotler and Keller also describe philosophical shifts in marketing management that they believe smart companies have been making in the 21st century.[7] A few that are relevant to social marketers in the planning process include the following:

- From "marketing does the marketing" to "everyone does the marketing." Programs encouraging young partygoers to pick a designated driver are certainly supported (even funded) by more than public information officers within departments of transportation. Schools, parents, police officers, law enforcement, judges, health care providers, advertising agencies, bars, and alcohol beverage companies help spread the word and reinforce the program.
- From organizing by product units to organizing by customer segments. Clearly, an effective drowning-prevention program plan would need to have separate strategies—even separate marketing plans—based on the differing ages of children. Focuses might

be toddlers wearing life vests on beaches, young children taking swimming lessons, and teens knowing where they can buy cool life vests that won't "ruin their tan."

- From building brands through advertising to building brands through performance and integrated communications. The "Makeover Mile," launched in the U.S. in 2011, is well on its way to building a brand that is a catalyst for positive change, one supported by communications that are both consistent and pervasive. Seeking to turn back the tide of obesity-related diseases that threaten nearly two thirds of Americans, on February 23, 2011, Dr. Ian Smith announced the launch of this grassroots initiative that stages a one-mile walk ending at a health fair in communities most adversely affected by weight-related illnesses and lack of access to health care.[8] The walks are constructed with the intention of influencing participants to "seize the moment today in order to steer their lives towards a healthier tomorrow."[9] At the end of the mile walk, participants participate in a sponsored health fair that provides free health screenings for adults, including eye exams, blood pressure checks, cholesterol screening, and bone density tests; healthy cooking and fitness demonstrations; and giveaways and activities for children. As of April 1, 2011, a total of 3,947 people had pledged, "I'm going to the Makeover Mile," in one of seven cities: Houston, Dallas, Los Angeles, Atlanta, Philadelphia, Chicago, and Washington, DC.[10]

- From focusing on profitable transactions to focusing on customers' lifetime value. We would consider the approach many city utilities take to increasing recycling among residential households to be one focused on building customer relationships and loyalty (to a cause). Many begin with offering a container for recycling paper and then eventually offer those same households a separate container for glass and plastic. Some then take the next relationship-building step as they add containers for yard waste and food waste to the mix. A few are now providing pickup of used cooking oils, which can then be used to produce biodiesel fuel, and some cities (San Francisco for one) are considering collecting pet waste and turning it into methane to use for heating homes and generating electricity. At least one state (Minnesota) also suggests to customers that they put unwanted clean clothing and rags in a plastic trash bag and set it out for pickup on regular curbside recycling days.

- From being local to being "glocal"—both global and local. Efforts by the U.S. Environmental Protection Agency (EPA) to encourage households to use energy-saving appliances seems a great example, where communications regarding ENERGY STAR® appliances and fixtures stress the link between home energy use and air pollution and at the same time provide detailed information on how these options can both save taxpayer dollars and lower household utility bills.

10 STEPS TO DEVELOPING A SOCIAL MARKETING PLAN

Our first of several primers in this book is presented in Table 2.2, outlining the 10 distinct and important steps to developing a strategic social marketing plan. They are described briefly in this chapter. Chapters 5 through 17 provide more detailed information on each step, and worksheets are also presented in Appendix A.

Table 2.2 Social Marketing Planning Primer

Executive Summary

Brief summary highlighting the plan's purpose, target audiences, major marketing objectives and goals, desired positioning, marketing mix strategies (4Ps), and evaluation, budget, and implementation plans.

1.0 Background, Purpose, and Focus

What social issue is this plan intended to impact (e.g., water quality)? On what population (e.g., single-family homes) and/or solution (e.g., natural yard care) will we focus? Why? Who is the sponsor?

2.0 Situation Analysis

    2.1 SWOT: organizational Strengths and Weaknesses and environmental Opportunities and Threats

    2.2 Key learnings from a review of similar prior efforts and additional exploratory market research

3.0 Target Audience(s)

    3.1 Descriptions of priority target audience(s), including demographics, geographics, readiness to change, relevant behaviors, values and lifestyle, social networks, and community assets relative to the plan's purpose and focus

    3.2 Market research findings providing a rationale for targeted audiences, including factors such as size, problem incidence, problem severity, defensiveness, reachability, potential responsiveness to marketing mix elements, incremental costs, and organizational match, relative to the plan's purpose and area of focus

4.0 Behavior Objectives and Goals

    4.1 Behaviors that target audience(s) will be influenced to adopt (e.g., planting native plants), ones that are single and simple with lowest current penetration, highest willingness, and most potential impact

    4.2 SMART (Specific, Measurable, Achievable, Relevant, Time-bound) goals quantifying desired behavior outcomes as well as changes in knowledge, beliefs, and behavior intent

5.0 Target Audience Barriers, Benefits, the Competition and Influential Others

    5.1 Perceived barriers and costs associated with adopting the desired behavior

    5.2 Potential unique and meaningful benefits that will help influence and sustain targeted behaviors

    5.3 Competing behaviors/forces/choices

    5.4 Influence of importance to others

6.0 Positioning Statement

How we want the target audience to see the targeted behavior, highlighting unique benefits and the value proposition

7.0 Marketing Mix Strategies (4Ps)

    7.1 Product: *Benefits from performing behaviors and features of goods or services offered to assist adoption*

        Core product: Audience-desired benefits promised in exchange for performing the behavior

        Actual product: Features of any goods or services offered/promoted (e.g., 100 native plants to choose from)

        Augmented product: Additional goods and services to help perform the behavior or increase appeal (e.g., workshops on how to design a native plant garden)

7.2 Price: *Costs that will be associated with adopting the behavior and price-related tactics to reduce costs*

Costs: money, time, physical effort, psychological, lack of pleasure

Price-related tactics:

Monetary incentives (e.g., discounts, rebates)

Nonmonetary incentives (e.g., pledges, recognition, appreciation)

Monetary disincentives (e.g., fines)

Nonmonetary disincentives (e.g., negative public visibility)

7.3 Place: *Convenient access*

Creating convenient opportunities for audience(s) to engage in the targeted behaviors and/or access products and services, including developing partnerships for distribution channels and reinforcing desired behaviors

7.4 Promotion: *Persuasive communications highlighting benefits, features, fair price, and ease of access*

Decisions regarding messages, messengers, creative strategies, and media channels

Consideration of incorporating prompts for sustainability

8.0 Plan for Monitoring and Evaluation

8.1 Purpose and audience for monitoring progress and evaluating final results

8.2 What will be measured: inputs, outputs, outcomes (from Step 4), and (potentially) impact and return on investment (ROI)

8.3 How and when measures will be taken

9.0 Budget

9.1 Costs of implementing the marketing plan, including additional research and monitoring/evaluation plan

9.2 Any anticipated incremental revenues, cost savings, or partner contributions

10.0 Plan for Implementation and Program Management

Who will do what, when—including partners and their roles

Note: This is an iterative, nonlinear process, with numerous feedback loops (e.g., barriers to a behavior may be determined to be so significant that a new behavior is chosen). Marketing research will be needed to develop most steps, especially exploratory research for Steps 1 and 2, formative research for Steps 3 through 6, and pretesting for finalizing Step 7.

Developed by Philip Kotler and Nancy Lee with input from Alan Andreasen, Carol Bryant, Craig Lefebvre, Bob Marshall, Mike Newton-Ward, Michael Rothschild, and Bill Smith in 2008.

Although this outline for the most part mirrors marketing plans developed by product managers in for-profit organizations, three aspects of the model stand out:

1. Target audiences are selected before objectives and goals are established. In social marketing, our objective is to influence the behavior of a target audience, making it important to identify the target (e.g., seniors) before determining the specific behavior the plan will promote (e.g., joining a walking group).

2. The competition isn't identified in the situation analysis. Because we haven't yet decided the specific behavior that will be encouraged, we wait until Step 4, when we conduct audience research related to the desired behavior.

3. Goals are the quantifiable measures of the plan (e.g., number of seniors you want to join a walking group) versus the broader purpose of the plan. In this model, the plan's purpose statement (e.g., increase physical activity among seniors) is included in Step 1. Certainly, labels for any part of the plan can and probably should be changed to fit the organization's culture and existing planning models. The important thing is that each step be taken and developed sequentially.

Steps in the plan are described briefly in the following sections and illustrated using excerpts from a marketing plan to reduce litter in Washington State.

Step 1: Describe the Background, Purpose, and Focus

Begin by noting the social issue the project will be addressing (e.g., carbon emissions) and then summarize factors that have led to the development of the plan. What's the problem? What happened? The problem statement may include epidemiological, scientific, or other research data related to a public health crisis (e.g., increases in obesity), a safety concern (e.g., increases in cell phone use while driving), an environmental threat (e.g., inadequate water supply), or need for community involvement (e.g., need for more blood donations). The problem may have been precipitated by an unusual event such as a tsunami or may simply be fulfilling an organization's mandate or mission (e.g., to promote sustainable seafood).

Next, develop a purpose statement that clarifies the benefit of a successful campaign (e.g., improved water quality). Then, from the vast number of factors that might contribute to this purpose, select one focus (e.g., reducing the use of pesticides).

Litter Plan Excerpt: Every year in Washington State, over 16 million pounds of "stuff" is tossed and blown onto interstate, state, and county roads. Another 6 million pounds is tossed into parks and recreation areas. Programs funded through the Department of Ecology (Ecology) spend over $4 million each year, but staff estimate that only 25% to 35% gets picked up. Litter creates an eyesore, harms wildlife and their habitats, and is a potential hazard for motorists, who may be struck by anything from a lit cigarette to an empty bottle of beer, or even a bottle of "trucker's pee." In 2001, Ecology developed a three-year social marketing plan with the *purpose* of decreasing littering and a *focus* on intentional littering on roadways.

Step 2: Conduct a Situation Analysis

Now, relative to the purpose and focus of the plan, conduct a quick audit of factors and forces in the internal and external environments that are anticipated to have some impact on or relevance in subsequent planning decisions. Often referred to as a SWOT (strengths, weaknesses, opportunities, and threats) analysis, this audit recognizes organizational *strengths* to maximize and *weaknesses* to minimize, including factors such as available resources, expertise, management support, current alliances and partners, delivery system capabilities, the agency's reputation, and priority of issues. Then make a similar list of environmental forces in the marketplace that represent either *opportunities* your plan should take advantage of or *threats* it should prepare for. These forces are typically not within the marketer's control but must be taken into account. Major categories include cultural, technological, natural, demographic, economic, political, and legal forces.[11]

Time taken at this point to contact colleagues, query listservs, and conduct a literature—even Google—search for similar campaigns will be well spent. Lessons learned from others regarding what worked and what didn't should help guide plan development, as should reflection on prior similar campaigns conducted by the organization sponsoring this new effort.

Litter Plan Excerpt: The greatest organizational strengths going into the campaign included the state's significant fines for littering, social marketing expertise on the team, management support, and other state agency support, including critical involvement and buy-in from the state patrol and Department of Licensing. Weaknesses to minimize included limited financial resources, competing priorities faced by law enforcement (traffic safety issues such as drinking and driving and use of seatbelts), and lack of adequate litter containers in public areas.

Environmental opportunities to take advantage of included the fact that litterers were not always aware of the significant fines for littering (as indicated by formative research), the strong environmental ethic of many citizens, and many businesses that were "part of the problem" but also potential campaign sponsors (e.g., fast-food establishments, beverage companies, mini-marts). Threats to prepare for included the argument that litter was not a priority issue and that litterers were not motivated by environmental concerns.

Step 3: Select Target Audiences

In this critical step, select the bull's-eye for your marketing efforts. Provide a rich description of your target audience using characteristics such as stage of change (readiness to buy), demographics, geographics, related behaviors, psychographics, social networks, community assets, and size of the market. A marketing plan ideally focuses on a primary target audience, although additional secondary markets (e.g., strategic partners, target audience opinion leaders) are often identified and strategies included to influence them as well. As you will read further in Chapter 6, arriving at this decision is a three-step process that involves first segmenting the market (population) into similar groups, then evaluating segments based on a set of criteria, and finally choosing one or more as the focal point for positioning and marketing mix strategies.

Litter Plan Excerpt: Surveys indicate that some of us (about 25%) would never consider littering. Some of us (about 25%) litter most of the time. Almost half of us litter occasionally but can be persuaded not to.[12] There were two major audiences for the campaign: litterers and nonlitterers. Target audiences for littering include the five behavior-related segments creating the majority of intentional litter on roadways: (a) motorists or passengers who toss (1) cigarette butts, (2) alcoholic beverage containers, and (3) food wrappers and other beverage containers out the window, and (b) those who drive pickup trucks and are (1) not properly covering or securing their loads and (2) not cleaning out the backs of their pickup trucks before driving on roadways. Campaign strategies were also developed and aimed at nonlitterers traveling on Washington State roadways.

Step 4: Set Behavior Objectives and Goals

Social marketing plans always include a *behavior* objective—something we want to influence the target audience to do. It may be something we want our target audience to accept (e.g., start composting food waste), reject (e.g., purchasing a gas blower), modify (e.g., water deeply and less frequently), or abandon (e.g., using fertilizers with harmful herbicides). Often our research indicates that there may also be something the audience needs to know or believe in order to be motivated to act. *Knowledge objectives* include information or facts we want the market to be aware of (e.g., motor oil poured down the street drain goes directly to the lake)—including information that might make them more willing to perform the desired behavior (e.g., where they can properly dispose of motor oil). *Belief objectives* relate more to feelings and attitudes. Home gardeners may know the pesticide they are using is harmful, and even that it works its way into rivers and streams, but they may believe that using it once or twice a year won't make "that much difference."

This is also the point in the marketing plan where we establish quantifiable measures (goals) relative to our objectives. Ideally, goals are established for behavior objectives, as well as any knowledge and belief objectives—ones that are specific, measurable, attainable, relevant, and time sensitive (SMART). You should recognize that what you determine here will guide your subsequent decisions regarding marketing mix strategies. It will also have significant implications for your budgets and will provide clear direction for evaluation measures later in the planning process.

Litter Plan Excerpt: Campaign strategies were developed to support three separate objectives: (a) a short-term objective to create *awareness* that there were significant fines associated with littering and that there was a (new) toll-free number to report littering, (b) a midterm objective to convince litterers to *believe* that their littering would be noticed and they could be caught, and (c) a long-term objective to influence litterers to *change their behaviors*: to dispose of litter properly, cover and secure pickup truck loads, and clean out the backs of their trucks before driving on roadways. Telephone surveys were conducted to establish a baseline of public awareness and beliefs about the littering, and field research was done to measure current quantities and types of litter.[13]

Step 5: Identify Target Audience Barriers, Benefits, the Competition, and Influential Others

At this point you know who you want to influence and what you want them to do. You (theoretically) even know how many, or what percentage, of your target audience you are hoping to persuade. Before rushing to develop a positioning and marketing mix for this audience, however, take the time, effort, and resources to understand what your target audience is currently doing or prefers to do (the competition) and what real and/ or perceived barriers they have to this desired behavior and what would motivate them to "buy" it. In other words, what do *they* think of your idea? What are some of the reasons they are not currently doing this or don't want to? What do they come up with when asked what it would take for them to do it? Do they think any of your potential strategies would work for them? Their answers should be treated like gold and considered a gift.

Litter Plan Excerpt: Focus groups with motorists who reported littering (yes, they came) indicated several perceived barriers to the desired behaviors of disposing of litter properly, covering pickup loads, and cleaning out backs of trucks: "I don't want to keep the cigarette butt in the car. It stinks." "If I get caught with an open container of beer in my car, I'll get a hefty fine. I'd rather take the chance and toss it." "I didn't even know there was stuff in the back of my truck. Someone in the parking lot keeps using it as a garbage can!" "The cords I have found to secure my load are just not that effective." "What's the problem, anyway? Doesn't this give prisoners a way to do community service?"

And what would motivate them? "You'd have to convince me that anyone notices my littering and that I could get caught." "I had no idea the fine for littering a lit cigarette butt could be close to a thousand dollars!" (Notice their concerns were not about helping keep Washington green!)

Step 6: Develop a Positioning Statement

In brief, a positioning statement describes how you want your target audience to see the behavior you want them to buy, relative to competing behaviors. Branding is one strategy to help secure this desired position. Both the positioning statement and brand identity are inspired by your description of your target audience and its list of competitors, barriers, and motivators to action. The positioning statement will also guide the development of a strategic marketing mix. This theory was first popularized in the 1980s by advertising executives Al Ries and Jack Trout, who contended that positioning starts with a product, but not what you do to a product: "Positioning is what you do to the mind of the prospect. That is, you position the product in the mind of the prospect."[14] We would add, "where you want it to be."[15]

Litter Plan Excerpt: We want motorists to believe that they will be noticed and caught when littering and that fines are steeper than they thought. In the end, we want them to believe disposing of litter properly is a better, especially cheaper, option.

Step 7: Develop a Strategic Marketing Mix (4Ps)

This section of the plan describes your product, price, place, and promotional strategies.

It is the blend of these elements that constitutes your marketing mix, also thought of as the determinants (independent variables) used to influence behaviors (the dependent variable). Be sure to develop the marketing mix in the sequence that follows, beginning with the product and ending with a promotional strategy. After all, the promotional tool is the one you count on to ensure that target audiences know about your product, its price, and how to access it. These decisions obviously need to be made before promotional planning.

Product

Describe core, actual, and augmented product levels. The *core product* consists of benefits the target audience values that they believe they will experience as a result of acting and that you will highlight. Your list of motivators and positioning statement is a great resource for developing this component of the product platform. The *actual product* describes actual features of the desired behavior (e.g., how a pickup load should be secured) and any tangible goods and services that will support the desired behavior. The *augmented product* refers to any additional tangible objects and/or services that you will include in your offer or that will be promoted to the target audience (e.g., guaranteed anonymity when reporting litterers).

Litter Plan Excerpt: It was determined that a new service, a toll-free number, would be launched for motorists witnessing people throwing trash from vehicles or losing materials from unsecured loads. When they called the hotline, they would be asked to report the license number, a description of the vehicle, time of day, type of litter, whether it was thrown from the passenger or driver's side of the car, and approximate location. Within a couple of days, the registered owner of the car would receive a letter from the state patrol, alerting the owner, for example, that "a citizen noticed a lit cigarette butt being tossed out the driver's side of your car at 3 P.M. on Interstate 5, near the University District. This is to inform you that if we had seen you, we would have pulled you over and issued a ticket for $1,025." All "Litter and it will hurt" campaign materials, from road signs (see Figure 2.3) to litterbags, stickers, and posters, would feature the campaign slogan and the litter hotline telephone number.

Price

Mention here any program-related *monetary costs* (fees) the target audience will pay (e.g., cost of a gun lockbox) and, if offered, any *monetary incentives* such as discount coupons or rebates that you will make available. Also note any *monetary disincentives* that will be emphasized (e.g., fines for not buckling up), *nonmonetary incentives* such as public recognition (e.g., plaques for backyard sanctuaries), and *nonmonetary disincentives* such as negative public visibility (e.g., publication of names of elected

Figure 2.3   Road sign for reporting littering.[16]

Litter and it will hurt.

REPORT VIOLATORS
866-LITTER-1

officials owing back taxes). As you will read in Chapter 11 on pricing, arriving at these strategies begins with identifying major costs the target audience associates with adopting the behavior—both monetary (e.g., paying for a commercial car wash versus doing it at home) and nonmonetary (e.g., the time it takes to drive to the car wash).

Litter Plan Excerpt: Fines for littering would be highlighted in a variety of communication channels with an emphasis on targeted behaviors (lit cigarette butts $1,025, food or beverage container $103, unsecured load $194, illegal dumping $1,000 to $5,000 plus jail time), with notes that fines would be subject to change and might vary locally. The image in Figure 2.4 was used on billboards, posters, and litterbags.

Place

In social marketing, place is primarily where and when the target audience will perform the desired behavior and/or acquire any campaign-related tangible goods (e.g., rain barrels offered by a city utility) or receive any services (e.g., tobacco quitline hours and days of the week) associated with the campaign. Place is often referred to as your delivery system or distribution channel, and you will include here any strategies related to managing these channels. Distribution channels are distinct from communication channels, through which promotional messages are delivered (e.g., billboards, outreach workers, Web sites).

Figure 2.4   Washington State's litter campaign focused on a hotline and stiff fines.[17]

Litter Plan Excerpt: The hotline would be available 24 hours a day, seven days a week, as would a Web site where littering could be reported (www.litter.wa.gov/c_hotline.html). Litterbags (printed with fines for littering) were to be distributed at a variety of locations, including fast-food restaurant windows, car rental agencies, and vehicle licensing offices. A litterbag was also enclosed with each letter sent in response to a litter hotline report.

Promotion

In this section, describe persuasive communication strategies, covering decisions related to *key messages* (what you want to communicate), *messengers* (any spokespersons, sponsors, partners, actors, or influential others you use to deliver messages), and *communication channels* (where promotional messages will appear). Include decisions regarding slogans and taglines as well. Information and decisions to this point will guide your development of the promotional plan—one that will ensure your target audiences know about the offer (product, price, place), believe they will experience the benefits you promise, and are inspired to act.

Figure 2.5 Washington State's litter poster at truck weigh stations.[18]

Okay, one last time: This is not a urinal.

Get caught tossing a bottle of urine and you'll pay $1,025.
Fines for littering range from $103 to $5,000. Remember, Washington State Patrol has eyes out for violators. (Not to mention their noses).

Litter and it will hurt. **REPORT VIOLATORS 866-LITTER-1**

Litter Plan Excerpt: Communication channels selected to spread the "Litter and it will hurt" message included roadway signs, television, radio, publicity, videos, special events, Web sites, and messages on state collateral pieces, including litterbags, posters, stickers, and decals. There were even special signs to be placed at truck weigh stations targeting one of the state's "most disgusting" forms of litter—an estimated 25,000 jugs of urine found on the roadsides each year (see Figure 2.5).

Step 8: Develop a Plan for Monitoring and Evaluation

Your evaluation plan outlines what measures will be used to evaluate the success of your effort and how and when these measurements will be taken. It is derived after first clarifying the purpose and audience for the evaluation and referring back to goals that have been established for the campaign—the desired levels of changes in behavior, knowledge, and beliefs established in Step 4. This plan is developed before devising a budget plan, ensuring that funds for this activity are included. Measures typically fall into one of three categories: *output* measures (campaign activities), *outcome* measures (target audience responses and changes in knowledge, beliefs, and behavior), and *impact* measures (contributions to the effort's purpose, e.g., improved water quality).

Litter Plan Excerpt: A baseline survey of Washington State residents was planned to measure and then track (a) awareness of the stiff fines associated with littering and (b) awareness of the toll-free number for reporting littering. Internal records would be used to assess the number of calls to the hotline, and periodic litter composition surveys would be used to measure changes in the targeted categories of roadway litter.

Step 9: Establish Budgets and Find Funding Sources

On the basis of draft product benefits and features, price incentives, distribution channels, proposed promotions, and the evaluation plan, summarize funding requirements and compare them with available and potential funding sources. Outcomes at this step may necessitate revisions of strategies, the audience targeted, and goals, or the need to secure additional funding sources. Only a final budget is presented in this section, delineating secured funding sources and reflecting any contributions from partners.

Litter Plan Excerpt: Major costs would be associated with campaign advertising (television, radio, and billboards). Additional major costs would include signage at governmental facilities and operation of the toll-free litter hotline number. Funding for litterbag printing and distribution and retail signage was anticipated to be provided by media partners and corporate sponsors who would augment advertising media buys.

Step 10: Complete an Implementation Plan

The plan is wrapped up with a document that specifies *who* will do *what*, *when*, and for *how much*. It transforms the marketing strategies into specific actions. Some consider this section "the real marketing plan," as it provides a clear picture of marketing activities (outputs), responsibilities, time frames, and budgets. Some even use this as a stand-alone piece they can then share with important internal groups. Typically, detailed activities are provided for the first year of a campaign along with broader references for subsequent years.

Litter Plan Excerpt: Three phases were identified for this three-year campaign. In summary, first-year efforts concentrated on awareness building. Years two and three would sustain this effort as well as add elements key to belief and behavior change.

A news release from the Department of Ecology in May 2005 regarding the results of Washington State's litter prevention campaign touted the headline "Ounce of Prevention Is Worth 4 Million Pounds of Litter." The results from a litter survey in

2004 found a decline from 8,322 tons to 6,315 tons (24%) compared to a similar survey conducted in 1999. This reduction of more than 2,000 tons represented 4 million pounds less litter on Washington's roadways. And calls to the hotline were averaging 15,000 a year.

WHY IS A SYSTEMATIC, SEQUENTIAL PLANNING PROCESS IMPORTANT?

Only through the systematic process of clarifying your plan's *purpose and focus* and *analyzing the marketplace* are you able to select an appropriate target audience for your efforts. Only through taking the time to *understand your target audience* are you able to establish realistic *objectives and goals*. Only through developing an *integrated strategy* will you create real behavior change—an approach that recognizes that such change usually takes more than communications (promotion) and that you need to establish what product benefits you will be promising, what tangible goods and services are needed to support desired behaviors, what pricing incentives and disincentives it will take, and how to make access easy. Only by taking time up front to establish how you will measure your performance will you ensure that this critical step is budgeted for and implemented.

The temptation, and often the practice, is to go straight to advertising or promotional ideas and strategies. This brings up questions such as these:

- How can you know whether ads on the sides of buses (a communication channel) are a good idea if you don't know how long the message needs to be?
- How can you know your slogan (message) if you don't know what you are selling (product)?
- How can you know how to position your product if you don't know what your audience perceives as the benefits and costs of their current behavior compared with the behavior you are promoting?

Although planning is sequential, it might be more accurately described as spiral rather than linear. Each step should be considered a draft, and the planner needs to be flexible, recognizing that there may be a good reason to go back and adjust a prior step before completing the plan. For example:

- Research with target audiences may reveal that goals are too ambitious, or that one of the target audiences should be dropped because you may not be able to meet its unique needs or overcome its specific barriers to change with the resources you have.
- What looked like ideal communication channels might turn out to be cost prohibitive or not cost effective when more carefully examined while preparing the budget.

WHERE DOES MARKETING RESEARCH FIT IN THE PLANNING PROCESS?

You may have questions at this point regarding where marketing research fits into this process, other than at the step noted for conducting research to determine barriers and motivators. As you will read further in Chapter 4, and as is evident in Figure 2.6, research has a role to play in the development of each step. And properly focused marketing research can make the difference between a brilliant plan and a mediocre one. It is at the core of success at every phase of this planning process, providing critical insights into the target audience, the marketplace, and organizational realities. For those concerned (already) about the resources available for research, we will discuss in Chapter 4 Alan Andreasen's book *Marketing Research That Won't Break the Bank*. [19]

Figure 2.6 Summary of marketing planning steps and research input.

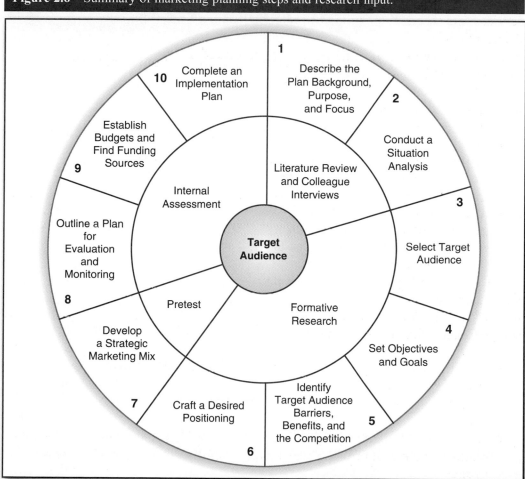

CHAPTER SUMMARY

Marketing planning is a systematic process, and a 10-step model is recommended for developing social marketing plans. You begin by clarifying the purpose and focus of your plan, then move on to analyzing the current situation and environment, identifying target audiences, establishing marketing objectives and goals, understanding your target audience's position, determining a desired positioning for the offer, designing a strategic marketing mix (4Ps), and then developing evaluation, budget, and implementation plans.

Although planning is sequential, the process is more accurately described as spiral rather than linear—a draft the first time around—as you may need to go back and adjust a prior step before completing the plan. Given the customer-centered nature of all great marketing programs, planning efforts will revolve around the target audience, and research—both external and internal—will be essential to your success.

MARKETING DIALOGUE

Social Marketing Contributes to Social Good ("Good" Defined by Whom?)

Most agree that social marketing is a technology used to promote behaviors that then benefit the individual and the society. What causes concern—even fury—is whether we should still call it social marketing if we (or even you) don't agree that the intended behaviors are good for the individual or society. Who gets to define good? Excerpts taken from the social marketing listserv in 2006 present varied perspectives.

Many think like social marketing consultant Craig Lefebvre, who said,

It is in the eye of the beholder. What I consider to be an absolute right and therefore worthy of extensive publicly funded social marketing campaigns, you may consider to be an

absolute wrong. Organ donation is an absolute wrong for those whose religious beliefs preclude the desecration of bodies yet it is considered an important cause worthy of social marketing dollars by those not constrained by the same belief structure.[20]

Alan Andreasen's comments focused on the role of the social marketing consultant versus the client or funder:

We need to be clear that social marketers are "hired guns" (excuse the metaphor). That is, give us a behavior you want influenced and we have some very good ways of making it happen. Each of us is free to work on behavior-influence challenges with which we feel comfortable and "comfort" is both a matter of personal ethics and a matter of expertise. The decision about which behaviors ought to be influenced is not ours to make. Clients, or even societies or governments, make those judgments.[21]

Others, such as Elisabeth Gleckler in Louisiana, expressed discomfort with the "neutral hammer tool of value-free hired guns." She suggested, "A good check and balance would be the inclusion of the 'target adopter' in the planning, implementation, and hopefully evaluation of the social marketing endeavor."[22] Additional ideas mentioned for deciding if the campaign is "for good," and therefore should be considered and labeled social marketing, included using public consensus (e.g., reducing drunk driving) or the United Nations' Universal Declaration of Human Rights as a baseline (http://www.un.org/en/documents/udhr/).

CHAPTER 2 NOTES

1. The Humane Society of the United States. (2009, December 30). *U.S. pet ownership statistics.* Retrieved March 1, 2010, from http://www.humanesociety.org/issues/pet_overpopulation/facts/pet_ownership_statistics.html

2. Information for this case was provided in 2010 by Kathy Shay, Environmental Program Manager, City of Austin, Watershed Protection Department, Kathy.shay@ci.austin.tx.us. For a more in-depth write-up on this case, see McKenzie-Mohr, D., Lee, N. R., Schultz, P.W., & Kotler, P. (2011). *Social marketing to protect the environment: What works.* Thousand Oaks, CA: Sage.

3. City of Austin.

4. Ibid.

5. Kotler, P., & Keller, K. L. (2005). *Marketing management* (12th ed., pp. 15–23). Upper Saddle River, NJ: Prentice Hall.

6. Drucker, P. F. (1973). *Management: tasks, responsibilities, practices* (pp. 64–65). New York, NY: Harper & Row.

7. Kotler & Keller, 2005, *Marketing management* (pp. 27–29).

8. PR Newswire. (2011, February 28). *Dr. Ian Smith, celebrity physician and diet expert, launches The Makeover Mile to raise health and wellness awareness in underserved communities* [Press release]. Retrieved April 4, 2011, from http://thestreet.com/print/story/11025223.html

9. Retrieved April 1, 2011, from Makeover Mile Web site: http://www.makeovemiles.com

10. Ibid.

11. Kotler, P., & Lee, N. (2006). *Marketing in the public sector* (pp. 283–284). Upper Saddle River, NJ: Wharton School.

12. Washington State Department of Ecology. (2006). *Litter campaign.* Retrieved October 10, 2006, from http://www.ecy.wa.gov/programs/swfa/litter/campaign.html

13. Washington State Department of Ecology. (2005, March). *Washington 2004 State litter study: Litter generation and composition report.* Olympia, WA: Author.

14. Ries, A., & Trout, J. (1986). *Positioning: The battle for your mind* (p. 2). New York, NY: Warner Books.

15. Kotler & Lee, 2006, *Marketing in the public sector* (p. 113).

16. Courtesy of Washington State Department of Ecology.

17. Ibid.

18. Ibid.

19. Andreasen, A. (2002). *Marketing research that won't break the bank.* San Francisco, CA: Jossey-Bass.

20. Message posted to the Social Marketing Institute's listserv, March 16, 2006.

21. Ibid.

22. Ibid.

Chapter 3

16 TIPS FOR SUCCESS

You will have a much better chance of influencing people to adopt a behaviour if you: know more about them; understand that not all are likely to be at the same starting point; consider your competition; actually make it attractive and easy for people; partner with influential people; communicate effectively; and are in it for the long run.

—Francois Lagarde[1]
Views From the World Social Marketing Conference 2008, p. 15.

For a variety of reasons, social marketers have a tough job. You are (or will be) tackling huge social issues that have been around for decades, such as HIV/AIDS, teen pregnancy, malaria, senior falls, water quality, air pollution, traffic injuries, and colonies of feral cats. Your goliath competition (e.g., good-tasting trans fat, the tobacco industry, MTV, the status quo) usually has more resources, experience, expertise, distribution channels, and fans than you do. On top of that, you don't always (or even often) have something you can give your customer in return for the exchange, especially in the near term. Your marketplace is diverse, and yet you may be forced to be equitable with your services, making them known and available to everyone, especially the hardest to reach. And to achieve real change, you can't usually do it on your own. You need partners in the legislature, school districts, law enforcement, local government, health care industry, and the corporate world—ones who take additional money, time, and patience to reach and influence.

This chapter presents 16 tips to make this job a little easier and to increase your chances of success. Some are simple, commonsense approaches. Others will take practice. Many are backed by theories that will be elaborated upon in subsequent chapters.

Our introductory case from Australia serves well to remind us of the role social marketing can play to increase compliance with existing regulations—especially when using principles for success.

Reducing "Drink Driving" in Australia[2] (2003–2009)

Background

In 1989, 776 people were killed on the roads in Victoria, Australia. By 2009, 20 years later, that number had been reduced to 290, a 63% decrease.[3] Efforts of the state's Transport Accident Commission (TAC) and its partners had paid off. The TAC is a government-owned organization in Victoria, Australia (a state in the southwest region of the country), whose role is to pay for treatment and benefits for people injured in transport accidents. This is a "no-fault" scheme, meaning medical benefits are paid to an injured person regardless of who caused the accident. Perhaps this explains the motivation for the TAC's strategic vision of "a future where every journey is a safe one."[4]

Drink driving remains one of the biggest killers on Victoria's roads, with one out of four fatal crashes involving a driver or rider with an illegal blood alcohol concentration (BAC). The legal BAC is 0.05, with zero tolerance for probationary drivers, first-year motorcyclists, and drivers of heavy trucks, buses, trains, and trams. Unlike in the United States, the term "drunk driving" is rarely used in Australia. When it is, it is used mainly to refer to someone observably suffering from the effects of alcohol, such as a slurring of words or stumbling.[5]

On the surface, you may see this effort as using only one of the 4P tools: promotion. Read on. A clear understanding of audience beliefs and behaviors, and an integrated approach and partnerships relying on the other three tools, were also key

to success. This highlight will focus on more recent strategies, beginning in 2003.

Target Audience Profile, Insights, and Desired Behavior

Beginning in 2003, the TAC's efforts have been increasingly directed at "low-level" drink drivers, those with BAC levels at or just over the legal limit of 0.05. This behavior was found to be most common among 26- to 39-year-old males.

A study of the attitudes of drivers willing to take the risk and drive near or over the BAC limit was conducted to assist the TAC in campaign development. Several findings were important.[6] Although many drinkers were convinced that drink driving can cause harm, a sizable proportion of them took the risk and drove at low but illegal BACs. They didn't think driving when "only a little bit over" was dangerous. The study revealed that when drinkers drove their car to a venue (often unplanned) where alcohol would be consumed, the chances were very high that they would drive home even with an illegal BAC— hoping not to be over the limit and not breath tested. The most powerful legal sanction was felt to be loss of license, and the greatest fear was a crash causing injury to oneself or others. Social embarrassment and shame were also significant deterrents for these otherwise law-abiding citizens.[7]

The behavior objective was for drivers to keep their alcohol intake moderate (BAC less than 0.05).

Strategies

Strategies were developed to convince drivers that even moderate levels of drinking and then driving could cause harm to themselves and others—that "this could happen to me." The TAC also needed to increase the perception that offenders would be caught and fined, or perhaps even lose their license. The TAC recognized, even at the beginning in 1989, that they would need the support of various state and community-based road safety bodies, including Victoria Police and VicRoads. The "Only a Little Bit Over?" campaign was their answer.

One high-profile component is the TAC's funding and support of a fleet of *booze buses* that "roam" the state, concentrating on the Melbourne metropolitan area as well as major rural cities. Victoria Police use these to perform random breath tests; by 2008, the number of tests by bus had reached around 1.4 million per year. The TAC also funds *enhanced enforcement efforts*, making it possible for Victoria Police to run traffic operations over and above their normal duties. *Online resources* include a downloadable guide that provides locations and schedules for trains, trams, buses, and taxis near licensed (alcohol-serving) establishments. Promotional efforts focus on making sure drinkers know about these booze buses, enhanced enforcement efforts, and online resources (*products*).

The key message of the "Only a Little Bit Over?" campaign is that if you drink and drive over the BAC limit, you are breaking the law and endangering the lives of innocent passengers and other road users (*price*). The campaign was developed by GREY Advertising Melbourne, the agency's promotional partner from the beginning. The "look and feel" of the campaign is attention grabbing and confronting (see Figure 3.1).

Mass media are a driving feature of the campaign, with channels including paid television, outdoor, and radio ads. Promotional products distributed have ranged from T-shirts to bike lights, helping to reinforce the TAC's position as a road safety organization committed to the Victorian community. At regular intervals along all major roads, TAC signs remind drivers of the consequences of drinking and driving. At peak times, media releases are sent to major outlets announcing the locations of BAC testing sites and reminding people not to drink and drive. Events at which people are likely to drink, such as music festivals and university

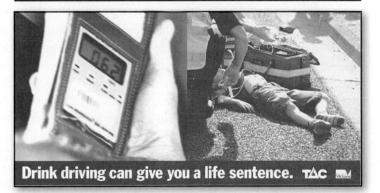

Figure 3.1 The look and feel of the campaign is attention grabbing and confronting.[8]

Drink driving can give you a life sentence. TAC

orientations, are targeted via a converted booze bus where people can self-assess their BAC and get tips about how to get home safely. In addition, anywhere there are motoring events, TAC sponsorship ensures that people are aware of the TAC's many road safety messages regarding issues ranging from drink driving to speeding. TAC sponsorship of major sporting events, such as Australian Rules Football, provides them with a presence via broadcasting of the events and in association with the clubs' communication strategies.

Results

The TAC measures its target audience's reactions to its advertising campaigns, as well as the changing attitudes of the community regarding road safety issues, using weekly telephone interviews conducted by an independent research organization. Respondents are asked, among other things, what they think the risk of a crash is with a BAC of over 0.05 and what they think their chances are of being caught by police if driving over the limit.

Results in 2007 were encouraging: 39% of drivers rated their likelihood of being caught as "high" if they were to drink and drive. Overall, the level of drink driving has decreased steadily, with a much smaller proportion of people caught exceeding the limit, and of those who are caught, fewer whose BAC is in excess of 0.15 (three times the legal limit).

16 TIPS FOR SUCCESS

The sequence in which we present these 16 tips for success is deliberate. It follows the marketing planning model outline, offering one or more principles to keep in mind when developing the related step in the marketing plan. Each tip is illustrated with an inspirational example.

Tip #1: Take Advantage of Prior and Existing Successful Campaigns

Beginning a social marketing campaign planning process with a search for similar efforts around the world is one of the best investments of a planner's time. Benefits can be substantial, including learning from the successes and failures of others, having access to existing research and detailed information on market segmentation and ideal targets, finding innovative and cost-effective strategies, and discovering ideas and materials for creative executions. And because social marketers most often are working with or for public sector agencies or nonprofit organizations, you may even be able to borrow campaigns that others have spent time and money to develop. The following exemplifies this opportunity.

Example: Physical Activity and Healthy Eating for Youth

Let's Go! is a community-based initiative with the goal of increasing physical activity and healthy eating among children and youth. The success of a pilot program launched in Portland, Maine, in 2006 inspired others around the state, and then the country, to implement the program's model and tools. Four clear behaviors form the foundation of the 5–2–1–0 branded program: 5 servings of fruits and vegetables a day; no more than 2 hours of TV or computer a day; 1 hour of exercise or more, and 0 sugar drinks (see Figure 3.2). Importantly, the program includes support for these activities. For example, bracelets are used to keep track of getting five fruits and veggies, and parents are encouraged to refrigerate cut-up fruits and vegetables in small bags for easy snacks on the run. The initiative's core principles are also clearly stated:

- Environmental and policy change is needed to influence behavior change
- Interconnectivity across sectors is essential
- Strategies are to be evidence based and continuously evaluated

The program collaborates with many organizations that serve families and children. By 2010, these included 345 schools, 163 child care sites, 65 healthcare sites, and 24 after-school recreation sites.

Importantly, the program has a comprehensive evaluation plan, and evaluative research efforts showed that between 2007 and 2009, there was a 27% increase in the proportion of children in the 12 Greater Portland communities meeting at least three out of four recommended 5–2–1–0 behaviors.[9]

Figure 3.2 Logo for the Let's Go! initiative.[10]

Tip #2: Start With Target Audiences Most Ready for Action

In a nutshell, the social marketer's job is to influence some number of people to do some desired behavior or abstain from an undesirable one. It would follow, then, that efforts and resources should be directed toward market segments most likely to buy (the low-hanging fruit) rather than those least likely (hardest to reach and move).[11] Campaigns increase their chances of success (actual number of behaviors "sold") when they start with market segments most ready for action—those that have one or more of the following ideal characteristics:

- A want or need the proposed behavior will satisfy or a problem it will solve (e.g., households wanting to reduce their water bill and contribute to sustainable water supplies)

- Knowledge/information regarding the benefits of the behavior and the costs of current alternative behaviors (e.g., hearing on the news about the new $86 fine for not picking up after a pet)
- The belief that they can actually perform the behavior and that they will experience important benefits (e.g., believing that exercising five times a week, 30 minutes at a time, can improve sleep)
- Current engagement in the desired behavior, but not on a regular basis, and the perception of some initial benefit (e.g., trying to quit smoking)

The following example illustrates the increased markcting and operational efficiencies one organization achieves by focusing on a very attractive segment.

Example: Blood Donations

The Puget Sound Blood Center defines marketing as relationship building and places the highest value on the repeat donor segment—for good reason. Their experience shows that it costs 10 times as much to acquire a new donor as it does to keep an established one. They know that if they can persuade just 10% of all donors to give blood just one more time each year, they will reach their annual donation goals, increase operational efficiency, and reduce expenditures. They have identified clear benefits of targeting current donors: They are the most likely future donors, they have a lower reaction risk, they have a higher blood-usability rate, collection is more efficient, and they are the most credible recruiters of new donors.

Marketing tactics to increase repeat donations are aggressive and persuasive. Efforts are focused on making the first experience a pleasant one. Volunteers are the first and last people a donor sees, and their sincerity is clear. After giving blood and sitting with a cup of juice and a cookie, donors are asked by volunteers whether they want to set up the next appointment, usually two months later. A reminder call or e-mail is placed the week prior to the next appointment.

Figure 3.3 Postcard used to thank and remind donors.[12]

The only lifesaving technique that involves eating a cookie.

First-time donors are mailed a donor card along with a message of thanks (see Figure 3.3). After 56 days, they are called by a telerecruiting team, who know from the information on computer screens that their previous donations were their first with the blood center and recognize the donors for that.

In 2005, this center attracted 208,000 people to give blood, and 54% of those were repeat donors. Over time, 50% of first-time donors, on average, have become repeat donors, implying a 50% customer retention rate.[13]

Tip #3: Support and Promote Single, Doable Behaviors With Significant Potential Impact

In this world of information and advertising clutter, you often have only a few moments to speak to your target audience before they switch channels, click the mouse, hang up, leave the room, or turn the page. A simple, clear, action-oriented message is most likely to persuade your target audience to adopt, reject, modify, or abandon a specific behavior. Your message should help the target audience know exactly what to do and whether it has been accomplished. Remember, as well, that if you are targeting those (most) ready for action, you won't have to spend as much time, money, and space convincing them they should do something. They are probably just waiting for clear instructions.[14]

Example: Safe Water Project

In 2006, in Malawi in southeast Africa, 90% of women in a pilot program developed by PATH, an international nonprofit organization, knew about an effective water treatment product called WaterGuard, but only 2% were currently using it. Nine months into the program, 61% were using it, as were 25% of their friends and relatives with young children.[15] How did this happen? The intervention succeeded because it addressed initial barriers and then focused on a single, simple solution.

Initial interviews with mothers identified primary barriers as affordability, availability, and taste and smell. A free trial offer included a sample of WaterGuard, a safe storage container, and up to three refills. This trial period let women experience firsthand how easy the product was to use and how much it could improve their family's health. It also gave them time to get used to the taste, which over time many came to associate with treated or safe water. Careful instruction about how to use WaterGuard also reduced the chances of overdosing, which had contributed to the strong smell and taste of chlorine. Health workers taught pregnant women about the health benefits of safe water, and outreach workers made follow-up home visits to reinforce the message.

Three years later, after the trial program had expired, 26% of participants (compared with 2% prior to the trial) and 18% of their friends and relatives were continuing to buy and use WaterGuard, and many others were treating their water with a free chlorine solution supplied by the government.[16]

Tip #4: Identify and Remove Barriers to Behavior Change

As mentioned in an earlier chapter, a list of concerns and real reasons why your target audience members perceive they can't or don't want to do your desired behavior (their barriers) should be considered a gift. After all, when you have this, you are more likely to know what to say to them, what to do for them, and/or what to give them that will make it more likely they will adopt the desired behavior. Identifying these barriers can actually be as simple as asking your target audience (in groups or individually) a few questions relative to the desired behavior: "What are some of the reasons you haven't done this in the past? What might get in the way of your doing this in the future? What do you prefer to do instead? Why?"[17] As you will read in the following example, be prepared for an earful.

Example: Alternative Transportation

Employers encouraging employees to abandon their single-occupant vehicles (SOVs) and take the bus, ride a bike, join a car pool, or walk to work—even one day a week—are likely to find one or more of the following "complaints." As discouraging as the list might be, consider the inspiration and strategic direction each barrier gives the marketer:

- I need my car to run personal errands during the day. (Offer loaner cars.)
- I have to drop off and pick up my child at day care. (Provide on-site day care.)
- I don't like all the chatter in a car pool. (Give iPods to people committing for a year.)
- I get all sweaty when I ride my bike. (Provide showers and lockers.)
- If I walk to work and it rains, I'll get soaked going home. (Make ponchos and umbrellas available to borrow.)
- I'll have to transfer buses, so it will take longer. (Issue free bus passes and increase on-site parking rates.)
- It's too hard to find a car pool partner. (Develop an intranet match service.)

Tip #5: Bring Real Benefits Into the Present

Benefits are something your target audience wants or needs that the behavior you are promoting can provide. Although this idea is simple in theory, one of your challenges and keys to success is to first ensure that the benefits you select are real for the target audience—ones they truly value and believe your behavior will deliver. A second is to highlight benefits that the target audience is likely to realize sooner rather than later. Michael Rothschild at the University of Wisconsin asserts that this is because the rewards you promise are "worth less in the future" and "costs are less onerous in the future."[18]

Example: Saving the Crabs in Chesapeake Bay[19]

For centuries, Chesapeake Bay blue crabs were considered the best blue crabs in the world, but in 2003, the Chesapeake harvest hit a near historic low. With this knowledge at hand, the campaign theme of "saving the seafood" was born. While people in the DC area might have only limited concern for the bay, many are passionate about their seafood, as is evidenced by the many thriving seafood restaurants throughout DC and its Maryland and Virginia suburbs. *Reframing the problem of a polluted bay as a culinary, not an environmental, problem was the cornerstone of the campaign developed by the nonprofit Academy for Educational Development (AED).*

Branded "Save the Crabs. Then Eat 'em," promotional messages focused on "wait until fall to fertilize," as this was the desired behavior for 84% of the target audience. Three television ads were developed, each encouraging viewers to wait until fall to fertilize their lawns and each using humor to lighten the message. One ad explained that "no crab should die like this . . . ," and as a man bites into a lump of crabmeat, opines that "they should perish in some hot, tasty butter." Print ads ran in the *Washington Post* and in a free tabloid handed out at Metro stops (see Figure 3.4). Drink coasters were printed and distributed without charge for local seafood restaurants to use and hand out to patrons (see Figure 3.5).

Figure 3.4 Out-of-home ad promoting fertilizing in the fall.[20]

Figure 3.5 Drink coasters distributed to local seafood restaurants.[21]

To assess campaign outcomes early on, random-digit-dial telephone surveys were administered to measure behavior intent before and after the campaign was launched. Interviews were completed with 600 area residents who reported they cared for their lawn or hired someone to do it. In 2004, prior to the campaign, 52% of those surveyed reported that they planned to fertilize that spring. In 2005, after the campaign had launched, that number had dropped to 39%.

Tip #6: Highlight Costs of Competing Behaviors

Now switch to the other side of the exchange equation and focus on identifying the competition for the behavior you are promoting and the costs your target audience may (or may not yet) associate with it.

As mentioned earlier, the competition in social marketing is the behavior your target audience prefers, might be tempted to do, or is currently doing—instead of the one you would like them to do. It may also be defined as an organization or group that encourages or sells the competing behavior (e.g., the tobacco industry). As in commercial marketing, one key to attacking the competition is to highlight the downside of this choice in an honest and credible way (e.g., according to the National Cancer Institute, cigarette smoking causes 87% of lung cancer deaths). Some concerned about fear-appeal tactics stress the importance of quickly offering a solution (e.g., don't start smoking). Others suggest simply framing the issue as "choice and consequences," then letting the market decide (e.g., having middle school students touch and feel tumors in the lungs of people who died from lung cancer and compare them with the smooth and soft lungs of someone who hadn't smoked).

In many cases, your competition is the target audience's inclination to "do nothing," as it was in the following example.

Example: Pet Adoption

On Saturday morning, October 14, 2006, an interview on a Seattle, Washington, radio station with a spokesperson for the Humane Society for Tacoma and Pierce County certainly highlighted the costs of doing nothing: "We have over a hundred cats and kittens that are likely to be euthanized tonight if they are not adopted today." Television news programs, newspaper articles, and blogs also helped spread the word to "*skadoodle over to Kittenkaboodle* and help us end the heartache of euthanasia by adopting a homeless cat or kitten." The event promised to be festive and was decked out with balloons and offered free face paintings. An incentive topped off the offer—a $20 discount on the regular adoption fee, which ("today only") included spaying or neutering, a veterinary exam, a cat carrier, and even a cat toy.

On the following Monday, it was announced that a record-breaking 180 shelter pets found homes in just eight hours! Follow-up news stories and Web site postings assured those who missed out, "No problem. The shelter will be open all week, and there is sure to be a new and ample supply of adoptable animals."[22]

Tip #7: Promote Tangible Goods or Services to Help Target Audiences Perform the Behavior

Although tangible goods, such as tablets to test for leaky toilets, and services, such as tobacco quitlines, may be considered an optional component of a social marketing effort, they are sometimes exactly what is needed to help the target audience perform or sustain the behavior, provide encouragement, or remove barriers.[23] They can also enhance opportunities for branding campaign messages and measuring impact. Wiebe concluded from an analysis of more than four social change campaigns that "the more a campaign resembles a commercial product campaign, the more successful it is likely to be."[24] The following example certainly represents that opportunity.

Example: Text4baby

Every year in the U.S., an estimated 28,000 children die before their first birthday,[25] and more than 500,000 babies are born prematurely.[26] To address this public health crisis, in December 2010 the National Healthy Mothers, Healthy Babies Coalition (HMHB) launched text4baby, a free mobile information service providing pregnant women and moms whose babies are less than a year old with information to influence them to perform behaviors that will give their babies the best possible start in life. As of February 2011, about 135,000 women had signed up.[27] Many consider this a success and have asked, "What are they doing right?" A strategic mix of the 4Ps is certainly part of the answer.

First, the service (*product*) was developed with input from potential users. The HMHB tested the content and style of text messages in, for example, community clinics and Healthy Start programs. According to Judy Meehan, the chief executive officer of HMHB, "We worked on tone—so the messages sound like they're coming from a friend. Not 'you should do this' but 'have you thought about this?'"[28] Balanced, informative, 160-character messages are delivered directly to cell phone inboxes.

Second, the service is free (*price*). One program partner, CTIA–The Wireless Association, a nonprofit advocacy group, persuaded wireless carriers to transmit messages free of charge, similar to what had been done to send "Amber alerts"—messages about child abductions.

Third, sign-up is simple (*place*): All you need to do is send a text message to the number 511411 with the message BABY or BEBE (for Spanish messages). You are then prompted for your due date or your child's birth date, and your zip code, and immediately you begin receiving three messages a week offering actionable, evidence-based information relevant to your stage in pregnancy or your child's development.

Finally, information (*promotion*) reaches mothers in all 50 states in a variety of ways, including through libraries, churches, billboard ads, health care providers, employers, health fairs, and networks such as the American Academy of Pediatrics. In some states, women learn about the program when applying for Medicaid, and in others, such as New York City, every birth certificate promotes the program.

Tip #8: Consider Nonmonetary Incentives in the Form of Recognition and Appreciation

Pricing strategies in social marketing can utilize traditional monetary incentives such as discount coupons for compost and rebates for outdated car seats. The good news is that there are also effective ways to encourage changes in behavior that don't involve cash incentives and don't cost a lot of money. These nonmonetary incentives typically provide something else the target audience values—recognition or appreciation. This can be given to individuals by recognizing, for example, a household that commits to practicing natural yard care by putting a branded ladybug sticker on its yard waste container. It can also be a way to recognize organizations for supporting healthy, safe, or environmentally friendly behaviors. As you will read in the following example, this can also be popular in the private sector, as it can provide a way to do well by doing good.

Example: Ecolabels

Ecolabeling entered mainstream environmental policy making in the late 1970s when the German government established the Blue Angel program. According to the United Nations, "Since that time, ecolabels have become one of the more high-profile market-based tools for achieving environmental objectives."[29] There are now a variety of schemes in operation throughout the world, including a number within the European Union.

For one type of environmental labeling, ecolabels are awarded by an impartial third party that determines that certain products or services meet established environmental criteria. Labels are then granted to products judged to be less harmful to the environment than others within the same product category. Ecolabels, then, indicate that a brand is more environmentally friendly than an unlabeled brand of the same type and are seen as a simple way to present complex environmental information to consumers. The rationale behind these systems is that credible environmental information will affect consumer brand choice and increase the market shares of companies with (more) environmentally friendly products.[30]

Many claim this is working for the common good: consumers, businesses, and the environment. The German Blue Eco Angel, for one, now (2011) covers over 10,000 products, in 80 different product categories, that are judged to have positive environmental features.[31]

Tip #9: Make Access Easy

In a society that places a premium on time, convenient access can be a deal breaker. Successful social marketing efforts provide target audiences *easy ways to sign up* (e.g., organ donation registration via the Internet), *convenient locations* to acquire tangible objects (e.g., gun lockboxes available at major retail outlets) and receive services (e.g., flu shots at grocery stores), and *reasonable hours and days of the week* for accessing services (e.g., natural yard and garden hotlines open on Saturdays, when homeowners are most likely doing their gardening).

Efforts to make adoption easy were worth it to the utility featured in the following example.

Example: Water Conservation[32]

Seattle Public Utilities' Home Water Savers Program was designed to make conserving water simple and extremely convenient for homeowners.

During the summer of 1992, 300,000 showerheads were distributed door to door to about 90% of households in the utility's service area. A package was left at each doorstep with a high-quality showerhead and easy-to-follow installation instructions (see Figure 3.6).

Figure 3.6 Promotional materials carried a consistent message.[33]

Prior consumer research had tested several potential strategies to influence residents to do two things: (1) install this water-efficient model and (2) put their old showerhead, in a bag provided in the package, on their doorstep to be picked up within a few days. This was critical in order for program managers to know their installation rates. The messages from potential adopters were loud and clear: Make sure this showerhead is of high quality and make the process simple, easy, and convenient.

The simplicity and ease of participation in the program resulted in the highest rate of installation of water-efficient showerheads in the nation. The rate of installation was 65%, twice the expectation using national standards. And as an added benefit, approximately one third of residents reported in telephone surveys that they now took shorter showers and used less hot water for showering.

Tip #10: Have a Little Fun With Messages

Using humor to influence public behaviors can be tricky, especially if a governmental agency is the messenger. There are times when humor just isn't appropriate for the target audience (e.g., victims of sexual assault). Some agencies have a brand personality where humor doesn't quite fit (e.g., Homeland Security). Some messages are so complex they could be dismissed or lose their impact with a humorous approach (e.g., keeping household poisons away from children). And there are certain behaviors that are more likely to be inspired by an emotion other than humor (e.g., getting people to evacuate their homes in the path of a wildfire).

You are encouraged, however, to look for opportunities where humor might be appropriate and persuasive with your audience, where it wouldn't be inconsistent with your program or agency's brand, and where it might be just "the right emotion to garner the attention, appeal, and memorability you want in your campaign."[34] We think the following example fits the bill.

Figure 3.7 Poster for a breastfeeding campaign in partnership with the Ad Council.[37]

BREASTFEED FOR 6 MONTHS. YOU MAY HELP REDUCE YOUR CHILD'S RISK FOR CHILDHOOD OBESITY.

Recent studies show babies may be less likely to develop childhood obesity when exclusively breastfed for six months. Call 800-994-WOMAN or visit www.4woman.gov to learn more. Or talk to your healthcare provider. **Babies were born to be breastfed.**

U.S. Department of Health and Human Services

Example: Breastfeeding

Recent studies show that babies who are breastfed for six months are less likely to develop ear infections, diarrhea, and respiratory illnesses. And some studies suggest that infants who are not breastfed have higher rates of obesity, diabetes, leukemia, and asthma. Yet, in 2004 in the United States, only about 33% of mothers were breastfeeding at the recommended six months postpartum, one of the lowest breastfeeding rates in the developed world.[35] The Healthy People 2010 goal was to raise this to 50%. The U.S. Department of Health and Human Services, Office of Women's Health, took on this challenge.

Their precampaign research findings provided a direction and focus for the campaign, revealing that there was no clear understanding of the duration goal for breastfeeding and that there were no perceived real disadvantages of not breastfeeding. Campaign messages were designed to address this confusion and to highlight these misperceptions. A media campaign was launched in June 2004 with the support of the Advertising Council, using ads driving home the message "Babies were born to be breastfed" and highlighting real, tangible benefits—with a little humor (see Figure 3.7).[36]

In addition to mass media and the Internet, resources were directed to support community-based demonstration projects (CDPs) throughout the country. These projects involved funding of local coalitions, hospitals, universities, and other organizations to offer breastfeeding services, provide outreach to their communities, train health care providers, implement the media aspects of the campaign, and track breastfeeding rates in their communities.

Research after the first year of the campaign was encouraging. Awareness about breastfeeding had risen from 28% to 38%. More than half of respondents (63%) either correctly identified six months as the recommended length of time to exclusively breastfeed a baby or said the recommended duration was longer than six months. The number agreeing that babies should be exclusively breastfed in the first six months increased from prewave (53%) to postwave (62%). And, most important, more of the women surveyed had breastfed a child (any duration) in the 2005 study (73%) than in the 2004 study (63%).

Tip #11: Use Media Channels at the Point of Decision Making

Many social marketers have found that an ideal moment to speak to the target audience is when they are about to choose between alternative, competing behaviors. They are at a fork in the road, with your desired behavior in one direction and their current behavior, or a potential undesirable one, in the other. Presenting the offer at a target audience's point of decision making can be powerful, giving you one last chance to influence their choice, even the choices of those around them, as demonstrated in the following example.

Example: Ask for Healthier Food in Singapore—And Get a Discount!

When a national nutrition survey in Singapore in 1998 showed that the majority (70%) of Singaporeans ate out at food courts and hawker centers, the Health Promotion Board knew right where to take their National Healthy Lifestyle Program messages.

By September 2002, 5,756 stall holders at hawker centers and 1,600 stall holders at food courts in Singapore were carrying point-of-purchase tent cards for tables, stickers, and posters with branded labels, including "Ask for more vegetables," "Ask for less gravy," "Ask for less oil," "Ask for less sugar," "Ask for less syrup," "Ask for plain rice," and "Ask for skin to be removed" (see Figure 3.8). Stall vendors displaying the labels were then responding to customers' requests for healthier choices (e.g., hawkers displaying the "Ask for more vegetables" label were giving at least two Chinese spoonfuls of vegetables upon request).

By 2003, it looked as if Singaporeans were having even more fun with this, with Scotts Picnic Food Court announcing that it would be participating in its first-ever Great Singapore Sale by offering a 10% discount to customers who requested healthier food, and (from June 15 to June 30) that customers who asked for healthier food (e.g., with less oil, less gravy) would be entitled to a 10% discount on their favorite dishes.[39]

Tip #12: Try for Popular/ Entertainment Media

Successful campaigns use media vehicles and formats that effectively reach target audiences with appealing spokespersons, sponsors, and settings (e.g., situation comedies, rap songs, movies, entertainers, sports figures). For example, Bob Barker, host of

Figure 3.8   A point-of-purchase campaign in Singapore influencing healthier choices.[38]

daytime TV's longest-running daily game show in the United States, was known for his passionate closing words each day: "Help control the pet population. Have your pets spayed or neutered." The following example also illustrates the impact that a small publicity stunt can have when a credible spokesperson is involved.

Example: Energy Conservation[40]

During an energy crisis on the U.S. West Coast in the winter of 2001, a popular, well-respected radio talk show host, Dave Ross of 710 KIRO in Seattle, Washington, was intrigued when he heard of a successful conservation effort in Israel more than 20 years before. He then tried a similar strategy with his listening audience of several hundred thousand.

The campaign in Israel had taken place immediately after a popular television show dramatized Israel's overuse of electricity. The show's host asked the audience to leave the room and go around the house and turn off all extra lights. The viewers then saw the impact of their actions on their television screens, from a camera focused on the Israeli Electric Company's electricity consumption gauges. Within a few seconds, the gauges dropped sharply. The experiment that helped alter the belief that "my lights don't make a difference" saved an estimated 6% in aggregate electricity consumption during the eight months of the campaign.[41]

Taking a similar approach, Dave announced on a preview for his show that he would try an experiment at 11:30 that morning and would be asking listeners to turn off and unplug anything electric that wasn't being used. He emphasized that he didn't want people to make any sacrifices; he just wanted them to turn off what they didn't need. At 11:28, the city's electric utility staff were standing by and read the current level of megawatts in use: "We're at 1,400 megawatts." At 11:30, the talk show host said, "Go!" and for the next five minutes he walked around the studios of the station with a handheld microphone and turned off conference room lights and computer monitors in empty offices. He then called his daughter at home to make sure she was participating, all as an example for the listening audience.

At 11:35, the city utility public information officer came back on the air and reported impressive results. Usage had dropped by 40 megawatts to 1,360. The decrease was enough to power 40,000 homes and represented $300,000 worth of electricity. Excitement over the success generated an hour-long program the next day on ways to conserve electricity (e.g., doing laundry in nonpeak hours and purchasing energy-saving appliances). Dave was presented a conservation award on air (an energy-saving lightbulb) by a member of the city council. For several weeks thereafter, local home and garden supply stores featured energy-saving appliances and lightbulbs.

Tip #13: Get Commitments and Pledges

Obtaining commitments and pledges to perform a behavior has been proven surprisingly effective, increasing the likelihood that your target audience will actually follow through with a good intention. McKenzie-Mohr and Smith report this may work because "when individuals agree to a small request, it often alters the way they perceive themselves."[42] It also makes them even more likely to agree to a subsequent, more demanding activity, and to sustain it. Perhaps that's one of the reasons the following program is so successful.

Example: Teleworking

AT&T promotes teleworking as a way to achieve a good family balance, increase productivity, save money, and protect the environment. Its telework initiative was launched in the United States in 1992, in part as a response to the new Clean Air Act, and provides information and support to all staff and management (part time and full time), corporate-wide, who are interested in teleworking. A simple but comprehensive Web site has been the primary means of promoting and delivering the program and includes steps for setting up a telework location, tips, telework research, and links to employees and management involved in program delivery. The initiative, which was launched using several pilot programs in different locations, includes a commitment (teleworking agreement) from each employee.

In 2000, reports indicated that since initiation of the program, 56% (36,000) of AT&T staff had teleworked from home at least once a month. Consider the estimated environmental impact of the program during that year alone:

- 110 million fewer miles of driving to the office
- 5.1 million fewer gallons of gas
- 50,000 fewer tons of carbon dioxide emissions

And although up-front costs are incurred to set up teleworkers, AT&T estimates that those costs are recouped within a year, through savings in real estate and related costs (e.g., energy) and the 15% to 20% increases in productivity of teleworking employees due to enhanced morale and fewer meetings and interruptions.[43]

Tip #14: Use Prompts for Sustainability

According to McKenzie-Mohr and Smith, prompts are

> visual or auditory aids which remind us to carry out an activity that we might otherwise forget. The purpose of a prompt is not to change attitudes or increase motivation, but simply to remind us to engage in an action that we are already predisposed to do.[44]

In other words, it works to address the most human of traits—simply forgetting. And it can be a simple, life-saving intervention, as illustrated in the following example.

Figure 3.9 A just-in-time reminder on Pampers newborn diapers.[45]

Example: Sudden Infant Death Syndrome (SIDS)

SIDS is a term used to describe the sudden, unexplained death of an infant younger than one year of age. In the United States, it is the leading cause of death in infants between one month and one year old. Some call it "crib death" because many babies who die of SIDS are found in their cribs. Health care providers don't know exactly what causes SIDS, but they do know that placing a baby on his or her back to sleep is one of the easiest ways to reduce the risk of SIDS.[46]

The Back to Sleep campaign included, along with other cosponsors, the National Institute of Child Health and Human Development (NICHD), the Maternal and Child Health Bureau, the American Academy of Pediatrics, the First Candle/SIDS Alliance, and the Association of SIDS and Infant Mortality Programs. And Pampers, a strong and early partner of the program, helped to expand the reach of the campaign message by printing the Back to Sleep logo (a baby sleeping on its back) across the fastening strips of its newborn diapers (see Figure 3.9). This prompt helped ensure that every time caregivers changed a baby's diaper, they would be reminded that back sleeping is best to reduce a baby's risk of dying from SIDS. Most important, the Back to Sleep logo on diapers was printed in three different languages—English, French, and Spanish.[47]

In 2006, it was announced by the NICHD that since the campaign had been launched in 1994, the percentage of infants placed on their backs to sleep had increased dramatically and the rate of SIDS had declined by more than 50%.[48]

Tip #15: Create Plans for Social Diffusion

Social diffusion, or diffusion of innovations,[49] is a model that describes the diffusion or spread of an idea or behavior through a population. Doug McKenzie-Mohr describes this phenomena well: "Think of the last book that you read, restaurant you ate at, or movie that you watched. What do each of these seemingly unrelated events have in common? All three were likely influenced by friends, family members, or colleagues."[50] You are encouraged to take advantage of this natural "force" and create a plan that supports diffusion of the desired behavior you have in mind, as illustrated in the following example.

Example: Walking to the Grocery Store

In 2008, Feet First, a pedestrian activist group, launched a pilot in a small Seattle, Washington, neighborhood, funded by a grant from the Robert Wood Johnson Foundation, to increase physical activity by making personal shopping carts "a norm." The funding was used in part to purchase 90 carts, branded "Go! Cart for Groceries," that would be sold at a minimal cost ($15) to promote user buy-in, or distributed at multi-unit housing establishments for residents to share. Feet First's choice of the Westwood Neighborhood was strategic because of its dense housing, two grocery stores close by, and highly visible sidewalks and crosswalks that would ensure residents would see others rolling their groceries home. Their 4P strategies were inspired by focus groups and personal interviews that revealed barriers (e.g., "I don't walk to the store because my canvas bag gets too heavy to carry all I buy"), highlighted potential benefits (e.g., "Oh, I can take this on the bus and go up to the Farmer's Market"), and inspired product selection. Those living in the single-family area, for example, expressed concerns about "looking like a bag lady" and wanted a cart that would be "hip." For these residents, Feet First found an urban and fashionable cart made from a French company (see Figure 3.10). Elderly and low-income residents did not care about aesthetics and just wanted a cart that was functional, large,

and stable. For this, the group found the four-wheeled "VersaCart" (sec Figure 3.11). In five months, all 90 carts were sold, primarily at local grocery stores at a Feet First–staffed booth to people living within a quarter mile of the store. Others were distributed to multi-unit housing residences, where they were shared.

Figure 3.10   Fancy cart (Perigot).[51]

Tip #16: Track Results and Make Adjustments

Successful campaigns establish ways to monitor progress and make important adjustments so that current or planned strategies support objectives and goals. This effort is obviously most important when there is still time to alter the plan. In the following example, a campaign's target audiences and objectives were altered when research on audience perspectives raised insurmountable barriers to desired behaviors.

Figure 3.11   Functional cart (VersaCart).[52]

Example: Eating Disorder Awareness and Prevention[53]

GO GIRLS! (Giving Our Girls Inspiration and Resources for Lasting Self-Esteem) is an advocacy project launched in 1998 by the national non-profit organization National Eating Disorders Association. The initial purpose of the effort was to encourage and support teens by promoting positive images of youth in advertising, television programs, fashion shows, and retail displays. Research by this organization and others indicated that teenagers' self-esteem is significantly influenced by their images of their bodies as compared with those portrayed by these industries.

An initial project began with a group of marketing students from three high schools who developed a plan to influence modeling agencies, advertising firms, and retail stores to use a diversity of body sizes and shapes in ads, fashion shows, and displays. Initial objectives were ambitious: to (a) persuade modeling agencies to use teen models of various weights and sizes, (b) persuade advertising agencies to request a diversity of models for ads, and (c) persuade retail department stores to use a variety of mannequins in teen displays. Planned efforts included interviews of executives in these industries at the beginning to understand any perceived barriers to using diverse images.

Initial interviews and presentations dampened the student marketers' enthusiasm as they listened to their target audience's problems. Modeling agencies provided models requested by advertisers, advertisers used models who fit into (small-sized) sample outfits from brand manufacturers, and retail executives indicated they had few, if any, options from mannequin manufacturers for teen displays.

The students adjusted their plan. They narrowed their audience to the merchandise managers of the retail stores, a segment with real decision making authority and a problem they thought they could solve. Armed with media support from a local television station and a major newspaper reporter "at their side," they presented retail executives with a new idea, one they thought would help teens and would also work for the retailers. Given that factory-ordered mannequins would take several years to alter, they suggested stuffing existing soft-cloth mannequins so that they had larger-sized torsos.

The teens were jubilant when one of the department stores agreed to display mannequins with larger-sized torsos in its popular teen department. Local television and newspapers covered their successful efforts, spreading goodwill for one retail giant and casting a negative light over the other.

CHAPTER SUMMARY

The most credible and reliable indicator of success for your social marketing effort is the extent to which meaningful and relevant program objectives and goals are met. Sixteen tips that can contribute to achieving targeted results were presented in this chapter, illustrated with programs chosen to provide a balanced overview of the range and nature of successful campaigns:

1. Take advantage of prior and existing successful campaigns

2. Start with target audiences most ready for action

3. Support and promote single, doable behaviors with significant potential impact

4. Identify and remove barriers to behavior change

5. Bring real benefits into the present

6. Highlight costs of competing behaviors

7. Promote tangible goods or services to help target audiences perform the behavior

8. Consider nonmonetary incentives in the form of recognition and appreciation

9. Make access easy

10. Have a little fun with messages

11. Use media channels at the point of decision making

12. Try for popular/entertainment media

13. Get commitments and pledges

14. Use prompts for sustainability

15. Create plans for social diffusion

16. Track results and make adjustments

MARKETING DIALOGUE

The Seatbelt Man

Sussex Safe Roads in the United Kingdom is a partnership funded by a government grant through three local highway authorities. Their role is to support partner authorities to achieve national traffic safety targets through education, engineering, and enforcement.[54] In January 2010, they launched a campaign to increase seatbelt usage with a video posted on YouTube titled "Embrace Life: Always Wear Your Seat Belt" (see http://www.youtube.com/watch?v=h-8PBx7isoM). The emotional public service announcement features a father not wearing a seatbelt who is involved in a fictitious crash and then embraced and protected by his daughter's and wife's arms in the form of a seatbelt. It generated more than 1 million views in its first two weeks online, and by April 2011, more than 13 million views. It was also featured on CNN and became one of YouTube's videos of the year, and one Facebook viewer was even moved to create a group dedicated to getting the campaign on TV.[55]

Members of the social marketing listserv, however, shared challenges they saw regarding the ad's potential effectiveness, many related to the tips for success discussed in this chapter:

- "I'm not sure who the target audience is. Is it family men, who are more likely to wear their seatbelts anyway, is it their wives and children, or is it younger men who are more at risk?"
- "They must be assuming the reason people don't wear their seatbelt is they don't think they'll be in an accident. How did they determine this was the main barrier?"
- "They are only using one of the 4Ps. Isn't this just social advertising?"
- "I thought fear appeals have been proven not to work." To this, one listserv member pointed out that, according to the sponsor, the ad was "deliberately developed to provide a counter-point to the hard-hitting 'shock and awe' advertising so common to road safety."[56]
- "How are they going to evaluate this (well)? So far they point only to the number of people who have seen the spot on YouTube. And if they point eventually to a reduction in people killed or seriously injured through not wearing their seatbelt, how will they know it had anything to do with this campaign?"

CHAPTER 3 NOTES

1. Lagarde, F. (2008). *Views from the World Social Marketing Conference 2008* (p.15). Retrieved July 11, 2011, from www.nsmcentre.org.uk

2. Our thanks to Linda Brennan, School of Media and Communication, RMIT University, Melbourne, Australia, for reviewing this case.

3. Transport Accident Commission. (n.d.). *Road toll annual.* Retrieved November 29, 2010, from http://www.tac.vic.gov.au

4. Transport Accident Commission. (n.d.). *Statement of corporate intent.* Retrieved November 29, 2010, from http://www.tac.vic.gov.au/jsp/content/NavigationController.do?area ID=25&tierID=1&navID=DEB4B70F7F00000101A5D193AADEE0E1&navLink=null&pag eID=787

5. Snitow, S., & Brennan, L. (2009). Reducing drink driving road deaths [Case study]. In H. Cheng, P. Kotler, & N. Lee, *Social marketing for public health: Global trends and success stories.* Sudbury, MA: Jones and Bartlett.

6. Transport Accident Commission. (2009). *Drink driving case study.* Retrieved November 29, 2010, from http://www.tacsafety.com.au/jsp/content/NavigationController.do? areaID=13&tierID=2&navID=47AABBA17F00000100A0BA6C43C70BF9&navLink=null &pageID=442

7. Ibid.

8. Victoria Transportation Accident Commission.

9. Let's Go! (2010, November 23). *FY10 annual report* (p. 8). Retrieved April 15, 2011, from http://www.letsgo.org/About/documents/LGAnnualReportYear4.pdf

10. Courtesy of Let's Go!, www.letsgo.org

11. Kotler, P., & Lee, N. (2006). *Marketing in the public sector* (p. 199). Upper Saddle River, NJ: Wharton School.

12. Reprinted with permission of Puget Sound Blood Center.

13. Puget Sound Blood Center. (n.d.). Retrieved October 23, 2006, from http://www.psbc.org/home/index.htm

14. Kotler & Lee, 2006, *Marketing in the public sector* (p. 200).

15. PATH. (n.d.). *Promoting water treatment in Malawi.* Retrieved April 7, 2011, from http://path.org/projects/safe-water-malawi.php

16. Ibid.

17. Kotler & Lee, 2006, *Marketing in the public sector* (pp. 201–202).

18. Rothschild, M. (2003, June). *Road crew.* Plenary presentation at the 13th annual Social Marketing in Public Health Conference, University of South Florida, Tampa.

19. Adapted from the Marketing Highlight "Save the Crabs. Then Eat 'em (2005–2006)," by Bill Smith, in the 3rd edition of this book (pp. 4–7).

20. Source: Academy of Educational Development for Chesapeake Bay Club.

21. Source: Academy of Educational Development for Chesapeake Bay Club.

22. The Humane Society, Tacoma and Pierce County. (n.d.). *Kittenkaboodle.* Retrieved October 25, 2006, from http://thehumanesociety.org/2006/09/kittenkaboodle/

23. Kotler & Lee, 2006, *Marketing in the public sector* (p. 206).

24. Wiebe, G. D. (1951–1952, Winter). Merchandising commodities and citizenship on television. *Public Opinion Quarterly, 15,* 579–690.

25. Xu, J., Kochanek, K. D., Murphy, S. L., & Tejada-Vera, B. (2010). Deaths: Final data for 2007. *National Vital Statistics Reports, 58*(19), 1–135.

26. Heron, M., Sutton, P., Ventura, S., Strobino, D., & Guyer, B. (2010). Annual summary of vital statistics: 2007. *Pediatrics, 125*(1), 4–15.

27. Bornstein, D. (2011, February 7). Mothers-to-be are getting the message. *The New York Times.* Retrieved April 15, 2011, from http://opinionator.blogs.nytimes.com/2011/02/07/pregnant -mothers-are-getting-the-message/?pagemode=print

28. Ibid.

29. United Nations Environment Program. (2006). *Assessing trade & environmental effects of ecolabels.* Retrieved October 2006 from http://www.unep.org/Documents.Multilingual/Default .asp?DocumentID=457&ArticleID=5061&1=en and http://www.unep.fr/shared/docs/publica tions/Ecolabelpap141005f.pdf

30. Ecolabels. (2006). *Ecolabelling.* Retrieved October 2006 from http://www.envirohelp .co.uk/ireland/bestpractices/ecolabels.html

31. Centre for the Promotion of Imports from Developing Countries. (n.d.). *German environmental label Blue Angel for several products.* Retrieved April 15, 2011, from http://www.cbi.eu/ marketinfo/cbi/docs/german_environmental_label_blue_angel_for_several_products)

32. Case source: Pretti Shridhar, Seattle Public Utilities.

33. Reprinted with permission of Seattle Public Utilities.

34. Kotler & Lee, 2006, *Marketing in the public sector* (p. 209).

35. U.S. Department of Health and Human Services. (2007, June 4). *Public service campaign to promote breastfeeding awareness launched* [Press release]. Retrieved April 6, 2007, from http:// www.hhs.gov/news/press/2004pres/20040604.html

36. U.S. Department of Health and Human Services. (2005). *National breastfeeding awareness campaign: Babies are born to be breastfed.* Retrieved April 2007 from http://www.4woman .gov/breastfeeding/index.cfm?page=campaign

37. The National Women's Health Information Center (womenshealth.gov), a service of the Office on Women's Health in the U.S. Department of Health and Human Services.

38. Health Promotion Board. (n.d.). "Ask for Healthier Food—And Get a Discount"

39. Health Promotion Board. (n.d.). *Ask for healthier food—and get a discount.* Retrieved October 31, 2006, from http://www.hpb.gov.sg/hpb/default.asp?

40. Case source: Nancy Lee, Social Marketing Services, Inc.

41. Kotler, P., & Roberto, E. L. (1989). *Social marketing: Strategies for changing public behavior* (p. 102). New York, NY: Free Press.

42. McKenzie-Mohr, D., & Smith, W. (1999). *Fostering sustainable behavior: An introduction to community-based social marketing* (2nd ed., p. 48). Gabriola Island, British Columbia, Canada: New Society.

43. Environment Canada. (n.d.). *Program: AT&T Telework Program Government of Canada.* Retrieved in 2000 from http://www.fhio-ifppe.gc.ca/default.asp?lang=En&n=A6D35B68–1

44. McKenzie-Mohr & Smith, 1999, *Fostering sustainable behavior* (p. 61).

45. National Institutes of Child Health and Human Development (NICHD), Back to Sleep Campaign. (n.d.). "Safe Sleep for Your Baby: Ten Ways to Reduce the Risk of Sudden Infant Death Syndrome." Retrieved 10/31/06 from http://www.nichd.nih.gov/publications/pubs/safe_ sleep_gen.cfm#backs

46. National Institute of Child Health and Human Development (NICHD), Back to Sleep Campaign. (n.d.). *Safe sleep for your baby: Ten ways to reduce the risk of sudden infant death syndrome.* Retrieved October 31, 2006, from http://www.nichd.nih.gov/publications/pubs/safe_ sleep_gen.cfm#backs

47. NICHD, Back to Sleep Campaign. (n.d.). *Pampers will print the Back to Sleep logo across the diaper fastening strips of newborn diapers.* Retrieved October 31, 2006, from http://www .nichd.nih.gov/sids/pampers.cfm

48. NICHD, n.d., *Safe sleep for your baby.*

49. Rogers, E. M. (2003). *Diffusion of innovations* (5th ed.). New York, NY: Free Press.

50. McKenzie-Mohr, D. (2011). *Fostering sustainable behavior: An introduction to community based social marketing* (3rd ed.). Gabriola Island, British Columbia, Canada: New Society.

51. Feet First.

52. Feet First.

53. Case source: National Eating Disorders Association.

54. Sussex Safer Roads Partnership. (n.d.). *Latest campaigns.* Retrieved April 18, 2011, from http://www.sussexsaferroads.gov.uk/latest-campaigns.html

55. Embrace life video: Seat belt campaign emphasizes family. (n.d.). *Huffpost Living.* Retrieved April 18, 2011, from http://www.huffingtonpost.com/2010/02/22/embrace-life-video -seat-b_n_471799.html

56. Sussex Safer Roads Partnership. (n.d.). *Embrace life* (para. 2). Retrieved July 11, 2011, from http://www.sussexsaferroads.gov.uk/latest-campaigns/embrace-life.html

PART II

ANALYZING THE SOCIAL MARKETING ENVIRONMENT

Chapter 4

DETERMINING RESEARCH NEEDS AND OPTIONS

Social marketing demands a passionate commitment to understanding consumers. Although existing data are used whenever possible, original research is usually needed to fully understand how people view the benefits, costs, and other factors that influence their ability to adopt new behaviors. This research does not always need to be expensive or complex, but it must be done. Without these unique insights, it is impossible to develop an effective, integrated marketing plan.

—Dr. Carol Bryant
University of South Florida

Alan Andreasen, a renowned marketing professor and social marketer at Georgetown University, captures the mood of many regarding research with his list of common myths below—coupled with his counterpoints for each:[1]

Myth 1: "*I'm Already Doing Enough Research.*" Almost always, they aren't, but there are simple decision frameworks that will help you find out.

Myth 2: "*Research Is Only for Big Decisions.*" Research is not only for big decisions, and sometimes big decisions do not even need it.

Myth 3: "*Market Research Is Simply Conducting Surveys and Surveys Are Expensive.*" All research is not surveys, and even surveys can be done inexpensively.

Myth 4: "*Most Research Is a Waste.*" Research can be a waste, but it need not be, especially if you use a systematic approach to developing a plan, beginning with determining key decisions to be made using the research results.

This chapter on research will only begin to debunk these myths and only scratch the surface of this important discipline and its contribution to successful campaigns. Its focus is on ensuring you are familiar with some of the research jargon, common research instruments and techniques, statistical procedures, sampling methodologies, and the nature of focus groups. More-detailed research case stories appear at the end of Chapters 4 through 15 and Chapter 17 and are intended to cover the range of research methodologies as well as applications for social marketing campaigns. We open with an inspiring case, one that benefited from formative, pretest, and evaluative research.

MARKETING HIGHLIGHT

Increasing Family Planning in Pakistan[2] (2007)

Gulbibi (living in Pakistan) was married at the age of 16. By the time she was 26, she had been pregnant five times, suffered one miscarriage and given birth to four children. Gulbibi is illiterate, and so are her husband and all their relatives and ancestors as far back as anyone can recall. They migrated to the city two years ago in search of opportunity and better living conditions, yet could only afford to live in a slum.[3]

According to the United Nations Family Planning Association (UNFPA), there are at least 200 million women like Gulbibi in the world who want to use safe and effective family planning methods but are unable to do so because they lack access to information and services or do not have the support of their husbands and communities (*barriers*).[4] And providing these family planning services is an important poverty reduction solution, for when couples can choose the number, timing, and spacing of their children, they are better able to adequately feed their families, educate their children, reduce healthcare costs, and maintain good jobs.

Although the use of contraceptives by married women worldwide increased from 10% in the 1960s to 63% in 2008,[5] fertility rates are still high, with as many as seven births per woman in some countries.[6] And according to the UN, the current trajectory is likely to take us from 6.6 billion to more than 9 billion by 2050.[7] Almost all of this increase will take place in the less developed countries, whose populations are expected to reach 7.9 billion in 2050, a 41% increase over 2009 estimates of 5.6 billion. By contrast, projections are that the population of the more developed countries will remain around 1.15 billion.[8]

Improved access to modern and natural family planning options is the goal of all Population Services International (PSI) family planning programs. Starting with one condom social marketing project in Kenya in 1973, PSI's family planning programs have expanded to include oral and injectable contraceptives, IUDs, emergency contraceptives, vasectomy, and natural family planning methods such as the Standard Days Method using CycleBeads. In 2007, PSI programs provided 12.2 million couple years of protection against pregnancy, averting an estimated 2.6 million unintended pregnancies and 13,400 maternal deaths.[9]

The following case highlights PSI's successful Greenstar program in Pakistan. As you will read, a clear up-front understanding of client barriers and motivators inspired their strategic marketing mix.[10]

Background

Gulbibi's story, introduced earlier, does have a happy ending. She eventually convinced her husband they could not afford to have any more children for a while, and he agreed she should visit a neighborhood health clinic (*place*), one with a green star on the sign (*brand* and *prompt*), which she had heard meant it offered quality family planning services (see Figure 4.1). She returned home with an effective method for birth spacing (*product*) and told others about it (*promotion*)—an important and credible social influence, as many couples in Pakistan were poorly informed about family planning.

Target Audiences and Strategies

In 1991, PSI established a nonprofit nongovernmental organization, Social Marketing Pakistan, and together they designed and then launched the Greenstar Network with a mission to improve the quality of life among people throughout Pakistan by increasing access to and use of health products, services, and information, particularly in the lower socioeconomic population groups. Contraceptive choices and access to information and services had been limited; 76% of women were illiterate and contraceptive use was low, with only 9% of married couples using a modern method of any type, according to

Figure 4.1   Clinic displaying Greenstar logo.[11]

the 1990–91 Demographic and Health Survey of Pakistan. Overall, contraceptive use was 12% in 1990–1991. The network focused on existing clinics and pharmacies and worked with them to be even more viable for family planning by expanding the number of services they offered and increasing their numbers of clients. From the beginning, the Greenstar social marketing program had five components:

1. *Medical training:* There are two main types of providers in the Greenstar Network: medical doctors and lady health visitors (LHVs, paramedics with 18 months' training in primary health care). Greenstar was started as an IUD training

network in which doctors and LHVs were trained to provide counseling in family planning and IUD insertion. After 2005, Greenstar expanded the training it provided doctors and LHVs to include maternal and child health services.

2. *Reliable supply:* Subsidies from program donors make it possible to provide international-quality contraceptive pills, injectable contraceptives, IUDs, and condoms at prices affordable for low-income clients. Regular supply of IUDs is a powerful predictor of the number of IUD insertions made by providers every month.

3. *Communications:* Creation of demand for Greenstar reproductive health services and products is conducted through mass media promotion of family planning and reproductive health services featuring the Greenstar logo. The logo, promoted as the symbol of high-quality, affordable

family planning products and services, is placed on signboards of certified clinics and pharmacies, and also appears on the packaging of its four contraceptive products (see Figure 4.2). Outreach workers work in communities around clinics and conduct "clinic sahoolats," event days when subsidized family planning services are provided at Greenstar clinics to low-income women. In addition, neighborhood meetings are held in the home of a woman from the neighborhood and obstacles to the adoption of family planning addressed in a more intimate setting. Importantly, a recent assessment showed that clinic sahoolats were associated with a 21-percentage-point increase in contraceptive use among women who participated in the event. About 300,000 women attended 15,000 of these events during 2010, generating about 63,000 new contraceptive users during 2010.

Figure 4.2   Greenstar logo.[12]

4. *Technical support and quality control:* Greenstar quality assurance teams make regular visits to Greenstar clinics to follow up on service quality and product availability. This model permits provision of on-the-job support to private medical providers in Pakistan, a largely unregulated sector. The support provided by Greenstar's quality assurance team increases provider self-efficacy. A medical detailing force also visits Greenstar doctors and pharmacists to ensure that contraceptive stockouts do not occur.

5. *Program evaluation:* The program has conducted a series of evaluations that assess improvements in quality of care, increases in service delivery, and program impact.

Outcomes

The Greenstar Network has achieved concrete results on three very important measures: increased sales of contraceptives, increased numbers of clients, and improved family planning services. An evaluation early in Greenstar's development indicated that among Greenstar female doctors, over 90% of clinics had oral contraceptives, injectables, and IUDs available. Doctors discussed three or more birth spacing methods with more than 85% of PSI researchers posing as patients, and over 75% of doctors discussed how to use the contraceptive method chosen.

In addition to the Greenstar private provider network, traditional contraceptive social marketing has been a mainstay of PSI's work in Pakistan since 1986. Because of the long-term investment in developing the market for condoms, condoms are the most widely used reversible method of contraception in Pakistan. The 2006–07 Demographic and Health Survey of Pakistan showed that 7% of married couples were using the male condom. This is equivalent to about 2 million Pakistani couples relying on the male condom for protection against unwanted pregnancy. A recent evaluation using data from a nationally representative panel survey of married men showed that a mass media condom advertising campaign implemented in 2010 generated 190,000 condom users.[13] Overall, modern contraceptive use rose to 22% by 2006–2007.

MAJOR RESEARCH TERMINOLOGY

The first primer in this chapter presents some of the most commonly used research terms (see Table 4.1). They have been grouped according to whether they refer to the objective of the research, when the research is conducted in the planning process, the source of data and information, the technique used, or approaches to collecting primary data. More-detailed descriptions and an illustrative example are presented in the next several sections.

Research Characterized by Research Objective

Exploratory research has as its objective gathering preliminary information that helps define the problem.[14] It would be most characteristic of research conducted at the beginning of the marketing planning process, when you are seeking to determine the purpose and focus for your plan. A city wanting to persuade restaurants to recycle their cooking oil, for example, might begin by reviewing data on the estimated amount of cooking oil that is currently being dumped down drains or put in garbage cans and the impact it is having on infrastructures and the environment.

Table 4.1   A Marketing Research Primer

Marketing Research is the systematic design, collection, analysis, and reporting of data and findings relevant to a specific marketing situation facing the organization.[a]

Characterized by Research Objective:

Exploratory research helps define problems and suggest hypotheses.
Descriptive research helps understand marketing problems, situations, or markets.
Causal research tests hypotheses about cause-and-effect relationships.

Characterized by Stage in Planning Process:

Formative research is used to help select and understand target markets and develop the draft marketing mix strategy.
Pretest research is used to evaluate draft marketing mix strategies and then make changes prior to finalizing the marketing plan and communication elements.
Monitoring research provides ongoing measurement of program outcomes through periodic surveys.
Evaluation research most often refers to research conducted at the conclusion of a campaign effort.

Characterized by Source of Information:

Secondary data were collected for another purpose and already exist somewhere.
Primary data are freshly gathered for a specific purpose or for a specific research project.

Characterized by Approach to Collecting Primary Data:

Key Informant interviews are conducted with colleagues, decision makers, opinion leaders, technical experts, and others who may provide valuable insight regarding target markets, competitors, and strategies.
Focus Groups usually involve 8-10 people gathered for a couple of hours with a trained moderator who uses a discussion guide to focus the discussion.
Surveys use a variety of contact methods, including mail, telephone, online/Internet, intercept, and self-administered surveys, asking people questions about their knowledge, attitudes, preferences, and behaviors.
Experimental research is used to capture cause-and-effect relationships, gathering primary data by selecting matched groups of subjects, giving them different treatments, controlling related factors, and checking for differences in group responses.[b]
Observation is the gathering of primary data by observing target audiences in action, in relevant situations.
Ethnographic research is considered a holistic research method, founded in the idea that to truly understand target markets, the researcher will need an extensive immersion in their natural environment.
Mystery Shoppers pose as customers and report on strong or weak points experienced in the buying process.

Characterized by Technique:

Qualitative research is exploratory in nature, seeking to identify and clarify issues. Sample sizes are usually small, and findings are not usually appropriate for projections to larger populations.
Quantitative research refers to research that is conducted in order to reliably profile markets, predict cause and effect, and project findings. Sample sizes are usually large, and surveys are conducted in a controlled and organized environment.

Note: See page 105 for Chapter 4 Table Notes.

Descriptive research has as its objective describing factors such as the market potential for a product or the demographics and attitudes of potential target audiences.[15] It would be expected, for example, that the city developing the cooking oil recycling campaign would want to know the numbers, types, and locations of restaurants in the city that were generating the most cooking oil and where and how they were currently disposing of the oil.

Causal research is done to test hypotheses about cause-and-effect relationships.[16] We can now imagine the city managers "running the numbers" to determine how much in oil disposal costs they might be able to defray if they concentrate on Chinese restaurants in Phase 1 of their efforts and how this potential outcome stacks up against the suggested funding at various cooperation (market penetration) levels.

Research Characterized by Stage in Planning Process

Formative research, just as it sounds, refers to research used to help form strategies, especially to select and understand target audiences and draft marketing strategies. It may be qualitative or quantitative. It may be new research that you conduct (primary data), or it may be research conducted by someone else that you are able to review (secondary data). In June 2002 in Washington State, for example, formal observation studies indicated that 82% of drivers wore seatbelts. Although some might think this market share adequate, others, such as the Washington Traffic Safety Commission, were on a mission to save more lives and wanted to increase this rate. And formative research helped select target markets and form strategies. Existing data from the National Highway Traffic Safety Administration helped identify populations with the lowest seatbelt usage rates (e.g., teens and men 18 to 24, among others). Focus groups conducted around the state with citizens who didn't wear seatbelts on a regular basis presented clear findings that current positive coaching messages, such as, "We love you. Buckle up," were not motivating. A primary seatbelt law, tougher fines, and increased enforcement were what they said it would take (although they wouldn't like it).

Pretest research is conducted to evaluate a short list of alternative strategies and tactics, ensure that potential executions have no major deficiencies, and fine-tune possible approaches so that they speak to your target audiences in the most effective way.[17] It is typically qualitative in nature (e.g., focus groups, intercept interviews), as you are seeking to identify and understand potential responses your target audiences may have to various campaign elements. It is most powerful when you can participate in, or at least observe, the interviews. Referring back to the Washington State seatbelt story, potential slogans, highway signs, and television and radio ad concepts were developed based on findings from the formative research and then shared once more with focus groups. Among the concepts tested was a successful campaign from North Carolina called "Click It or Ticket." Although focus group respondents certainly "didn't like it" (i.e., that they would be fined $86 for not wearing a seatbelt and that a part of the effort included increased law enforcement), their strong negative reaction indicated that it would certainly get their

Figure 4.3 New road sign emphasizing night seatbelt usage.[18]

attention and likely motivate a behavior change. Findings indicated that elements of the North Carolina television and radio spots, however, left people with the impression that the enforcement effort was happening somewhere else in the country, and thus they could psychologically dismiss the message. Advertisements were developed locally to counteract this.

Monitoring research provides ongoing measurement of program outputs and outcomes and is often used to establish baselines and subsequent benchmarks relative to goals. Most important, it can provide input that will indicate whether you need to make course corrections (midstream), alter any campaign elements, or increase resources in order to achieve these goals. Once launched, the state's Click It or Ticket campaign was monitored using several techniques, including reviewing data from the state patrol on the number of tickets issued, analyzing news media coverage, and, most important, conducting periodic formal observation studies the first year. Findings indicated that in the first three months after the campaign was launched, seatbelt usage rates increased from 82% to 94%. Even though strategies appeared to be working, decisions were made to increase the fine from $86 to $101, and more grants were provided to support increased enforcement in hopes of reaching a goal of zero traffic deaths and serious injuries by 2030 (Target Zero). In 2007, data from research and monitoring efforts turned the state's attention to nighttime drivers, whose seatbelt usage was lower; motorists driving at night had a death rate about four times higher than that of those driving during the day. Twice-yearly law enforcement and publicity mobilizations stressed the importance of buckling up at night and that special patrols "were watching" (see Figure 4.3).

Evaluation research, distinct from monitoring research, according to Andreasen "typically refers to a single final assessment of a project or program, and may or may not involve comparisons to an earlier baseline study."[19] Important attempts are made in this effort to measure and report in the near term on campaign outcomes and in the longer term on campaign impacts on the social issue being addressed—both relative to campaign outputs. (Both monitoring and evaluation techniques will be discussed in depth in Chapter 15.) Each year a nationwide observational seatbelt survey is conducted. In Washington State, over 90,000 vehicle drivers and passengers are observed. Summarizing the results of the seatbelt campaign in Washington State, a press release in August 2006 from the Washington Traffic Safety Commission reported that results from the latest observational research survey of seatbelt use had shown that the use rate had climbed to 96.3%. It was the highest seatbelt use rate in the nation and the world, and research indicated that buckling up was attributed to seatbelt road signs, aggressive local law enforcement, and educational activities at all levels of government. And by 2010, the numbers were getting even better, reaching 97.6% (see Table 4.2). Most important, in terms of impact on the social issue, vehicle occupant deaths dropped from 503 in 2002 to 337 in 2009, and an estimated 642 serious injuries were avoided in that same period (see Table 4.2).

Table 4.2   Vehicle Occupant Deaths and Serious Injuries in Washington State

Year	Passenger vehicle occupant Deaths			Passenger vehicle occupant Serious injuries		
	All Hours	Daytime	Nighttime	All Hours	Daytime	Nighttime
1994	489	277	208	NA	NA	NA
2002	503	266	233	2349	1549	800
2007	401	212	188	1779	1147	632
2009	337	164	173	1707	1066	641
2010 (As of 9/27/10)	133	74	58	NA	NA	NA

Research Characterized by Source of Information

Secondary research, or secondary data, refers to information that already exists somewhere, having been collected for another purpose at an earlier time.[20] It is always worth a first look. The agency's internal records and databases will be a good starting point. Searching through files for information on prior campaigns and asking around about what has been done before and what the results were is time well spent. It is likely, however, that you will need to tap a wide variety of external information sources, ranging from journal articles to scientific and technical data to prior research studies conducted for other, similar purposes. Some of the best resources are peers and colleagues in similar organizations and agencies around the world, who often have information on prior similar efforts that they are willing to share. Unlike commercial marketers competing fiercely for market shares and profits, social marketers are known to rally around social issues and to treat each other as partners and team players. Typical questions to ask peers responsible for similar issues and efforts include the following:

- What target audiences did you choose? Why? Do you have data and research findings that profile these audiences?
- What behaviors did you promote? Do you have information on what benefits, costs, and barriers your target audience perceived? Did you explore their perceptions regarding competing alternative behaviors?
- What strategies (4Ps) did you use?
- What were the results of your campaign?
- What strategies do you think worked well? What would you do differently?
- Are there elements of your campaign that we could consider using for our program? Are there any restrictions and limitations?

There may also be relevant electronic mailing lists to query (e.g., the social marketing listserv at listproc@listproc.georgetown.edu and Fostering Sustainable Behavior at fsb@ cbsmlist.com), online database services (e.g., LexisNexis for a wide range of business magazines, journals, research reports), and Internet data sources (e.g., CDC's Behavior Risk Factor Survey Surveillance, which will be described further in the research highlight in Chapter 6). (See Appendix B for additional resources.)

Primary research, or primary data, consists of information collected for the specific purpose at hand, for the first time. This journey should be undertaken only after you have exhausted potential secondary resources. A variety of approaches to gathering this data will be described in the following section. A hypothetical example of a water utility interested in a sustainable water supply will be used throughout.

Research Characterized by Approaches to Collecting Primary Data

Key informant interviews are conducted with decision makers, community leaders, technical experts, and others who can provide valuable insights regarding target markets, competitors, and potential strategies. They can be useful in helping to interpret secondary data, explain unique characteristics of the target audience (e.g., in a country other than where you live), shed light on barriers to desired audience behaviors, and provide suggestions for reaching and influencing targeted populations. Though typically informal in nature, a standard survey instrument (questionnaire) is often used to compile and summarize findings. For example, a water utility interested in persuading households to fix leaky toilets to conserve water might interview engineers on staff to understand more about what causes toilets to leak and what options customers have to fix them. They might then want to interview a few retail managers of home supply and hardware stores to learn more about what types of questions customers come to them with regarding leaky toilets and what advice they give them.

Focus groups are a very popular methodology for gaining useful insights into target audiences' thoughts, feelings, and even recommendations on potential strategies and ideas for future efforts. Perceived as a group interview, a focus group usually involves 8 to 10 people "sitting around a table" for a couple of hours participating in a guided discussion—hence the term *focus group*. In terms of numbers of groups to conduct, Craig Lefebvre offers,

> My rule of thumb is to plan to do as many as you can afford ONLY for segments that you will truly develop a specific marketing mix for. The advice I have gotten is to do at least three for any segment, but stop once you start hearing the same thing.[21]

This chapter's second primer highlights focus group terminology and key components (see Table 4.3). For the leaky toilet project, focus groups with homeowners could help identify reasons they did not test their toilets (*barriers*) and what it would take to persuade them (*benefits*). Households in targeted areas of the city might be contacted by a market research firm that would screen potential participants and then invite to the upcoming group those with the following profile: homeowner, person in the home most responsible for household maintenance and repairs, having a toilet older than 1994 that has not been checked for leaks in the past five years.

Surveys use a variety of contact methods and include mail, telephone, online/Internet, intercept, and self-administered surveys, asking people questions about their knowledge, attitudes, preferences, and behaviors. Findings are typically quantitative in nature, as the intent of the process is to project findings from a representative segment of the population to a larger population and to then have large enough sample sizes to enable the researcher to conduct a variety of statistical tests. These samples are designed by determining first *who* is to be surveyed (sampling unit), then *how many* people should be surveyed (sample size), and finally how the people will be *chosen* (sampling procedure).[22] Back to our leaky toilet example. A telephone survey might be conducted following the focus groups to help prioritize and quantify barriers and benefits identified by participants in the groups. Findings might also be used to identify the demographic and attitudinal profile of target audiences (those most likely/ready to test their toilets) and to test potential marketing strategies. How would interest increase (or not) if the utility were to host demonstrations on how to fix leaky toilets (*product*), provide monetary incentives to replace old high-water-use toilets with new water-efficient ones (*price*), and offer to pick up old toilets (*place*)?

Experimental research is the gathering of primary data to capture cause-and-effect relationships by selecting matched groups of respondents (similar on a variety of characteristics), giving them different treatments (exposing them to alternative marketing strategies), controlling related factors, and checking for differences in group responses.[23] Some might even call it a pilot, where you measure and compare the outcomes of one or more potential strategies among similar market segments. For example, let's assume the utility was trying to decide whether they needed to provide homeowners with dye tablets to use to test for a leak or whether it worked just as well to provide instructions on how

Table 4.3	Focus Group Primer

Focus Groups: A research methodology where small groups of people are recruited from a broader population and interviewed for an hour to an hour and a half utilizing a focused discussion led by a trained moderator. Results are usually considered qualitative in nature and therefore not projectable to the broader population.

Planning: The first step in the focus group planning process is to establish the **purpose** of the group. What decisions will this research support? From there, **informational objectives** are delineated, providing guidance for discussion topics.

Participants: The ideal number of participants is between 8 and 12. With fewer than 8 participants, discussions may not be as lively nor input as rich. With more than 12 participants, there is not typically enough time to hear from each person in depth.

Recruitment: Ten to 14 participants are usually recruited in order to be assured 8 to 12 will show up. A marketing research firm is often involved in recruiting participants, using a **screener** developed to find participants with the desired demographic, attitudinal, and/or behavioral profile.

Discussion Guide: This detailed outline of discussion topics and related questions distributes the 60 to 90 minutes to ensure informational objectives are achieved. It usually begins with a welcome, statement of purpose, and ground rules and concludes with opportunities for the moderator and participants to summarize highlights of the discussion. It is likely to include time allowed for numerous probes (e.g., "Please say more about that") to achieve the intended in-depth understanding and insights.

Moderator: The group facilitator is usually (but doesn't have to be) a trained professional. Important characteristics include strong listening and group dynamics skills, knowledge of the topic, genuine curiosity for the findings, and ability to synthesize and report on findings relative to research objectives.

Facility: Many groups are held in designated focus group rooms at market research firms, which include two-way mirrors so that observers (e.g., the client for the research) can witness participants' expressions and body language, as well as slip notes to the moderator regarding additional questions or probes. Groups are often audiotaped and sometimes videotaped in order to prepare reports and share findings with others. Some focus groups are now conducted online, via the telephone, and/or video conferencing.

Incentives: Participants are usually provided monetary incentives for their time (e.g., $50–$60) and provided light refreshments when they arrive. The opportunity to share opinions, even contribute to an important social issue, is a strong motivator as well.

to use ordinary food coloring from the household pantry. If the incidence of testing for leaks is not higher among households who have been mailed a tablet than those who have simply been mailed instructions, the utility will likely decide to roll out the campaign without the added costs of the tablet.

Observational research, not surprisingly, involves gathering primary data by observing relevant people, actions, and situations. In the commercial sector, consumer packaged-goods marketers visit supermarkets and observe shoppers as they browse the store, pick up products, examine the labels (or not), and make purchase decisions.[24] In social marketing, observational research is more often used to provide insight into difficulties people have performing desired behaviors (e.g., recycling properly), to measure actual versus reported behaviors (e.g., seatbelt usage), or to simply understand how consumers navigate their environments in order to develop recommended changes in infrastructures (e.g., removing their computers from their bags as they approach airport security screeners). It would be useful for the managers working on the leaky toilet project to watch people at local home supply stores as they check out repair kits for their toilets.

Ethnographic research is considered a holistic research method, founded in the idea that to truly understand target audiences, the researcher will need an extensive immersion in their natural environment. It often includes observation as well as face-to-face interviews with study participants. For example, the utility might want to actually observe and interview people in their homes as they test their toilets for leaks and (if warranted) make decisions regarding repair or replacement. Findings can then be used to develop instructional materials that will be most helpful to others as they then engage in these behaviors.

Mystery shoppers pose as customers and report on strong or weak points experienced in the buying process. This technique may include interfacing with an agency's personnel with an interest in observing and reporting what the target audience sees, hears, and feels during the exchange and how personnel respond to their questions. For example, utility managers may want to call their own customer service center and ask questions regarding the mailer on testing for leaky toilets "they" received as well as questions regarding options for repairing and replacing the toilets. They may also want to visit the Web site for the project, post a comment or question, and note how quickly their question is acknowledged.

Research Characterized by Technique

Sometimes a research project is characterized as either a qualitative or a quantitative study. The differences between these two techniques are described in the following section and illustrated by a research effort conducted to inform the development of a social marketing campaign to combat the spread of HIV/AIDS in Ethiopia, where the infection rate is one of the world's highest.

Qualitative research generally refers to studies where samples are small and the findings are not reliably projected to the greater population. That isn't their purpose. The focus instead is on identifying and seeking clarity on issues and understanding current knowledge, attitudes, beliefs, and behaviors of target audiences. Focus groups, personal interviews, observations, and ethnographic studies are commonly used, as they are often qualitative in nature.[25]

In October 2005, an article titled "Managing Fear in Public Health Campaigns" by Cho and Witte appeared in *Health Promotion Practice*, a journal of the Society for Public Health Education (SOPHE).[26] It described, in depth, the role that formative research played in the development of strategies to influence HIV/AIDS-preventive behaviors among teens and young adults (ages 15 to 30) living in Ethiopia. This research was grounded in a fear appeal theory called the Extended Parallel Process Model.[27] Thus, the variables studied were not selected at random but were purposely chosen. Once the researchers discovered what people believed regarding these variables, they would have specific guidance from the theory about how to influence their beliefs in the direction providing the most behavior change.

Focus groups were conducted first to better understand urban youths' perceptions about HIV/AIDS prevention issues by exploring, among other factors, their current knowledge, attitudes, beliefs, and behaviors regarding HIV/AIDS and condom use. Four focus groups were conducted in the two most populous towns in each of five regions in Ethiopia. Of specific interest were perceptions of consequences associated with HIV/AIDS. Participants in groups identified a variety: dysentery, weight loss, family breakdown, increase in orphans, social stigma, long-term disability, and death. The groups also revealed negative perceptions of condoms, including embarrassment, reduction of sexual pleasure, breakage during sexual intercourse, reduction of faithfulness between partners, and a perception among some that condoms actually spread HIV/AIDS. Also interesting was who participants considered most at risk for HIV infections: commercial sex workers, drivers, soldiers, youth in and out of school, government employees, and sexually active young adults. Most important, "participants expressed that condom promotion campaigns were either absent or ineffective in most of their localities" and that some totally ignored the HIV/AIDS-prevention messages.[28]

Quantitative research refers to studies conducted to reliably profile markets, predict cause and effect, and project findings. This reliability is created as a result of large sample sizes, rigorous sampling procedures, and surveys conducted in a controlled and organized environment.

For the HIV/AIDS-prevention study in Ethiopia, a quantitative effort followed the qualitative focus group phase. The study plan included a sample of 160 households per region, for a total of 800 households, drawn from a representative sample. A total of 792 household participants ages 15 to 30 years were interviewed from the 10 towns of priority regions. Of interest was the measurement and analysis of levels of agreement on a five-point scale (strongly agree, agree, neutral, disagree, and strongly disagree) with statements related to four beliefs often considered to be predictive of behavior change:

- Perceived susceptibility: "I am at risk of getting infected with HIV/AIDS."
- Perceived severity: "Getting infected with HIV/AIDS would be the worst thing that could happen to me."
- Perceived response efficacy: "Condoms work in preventing HIV/AIDS infection."
- Perceived self-efficacy: "I am able to use condoms to prevent HIV/AIDS infection."

Next, the data were analyzed within the theoretical framework. Based on previous research, the researchers knew they needed high levels of each of the four variables listed above to promote behavior change. If just one of the variables was at a low level, then they knew they had to focus on that variable in a subsequent campaign. The authors of the article embarked on five steps to analyze the data:

1. Examine the frequency distribution of each variable (agreement levels for each of the four variables).

2. Compare the mean score for each variable (average level of agreement) to assess whether average beliefs are all at high levels (i.e., 4 or 5).

3. Categorize the four variables into weak, moderate, and strong belief categories. Perceived severity was strong, and thus there was no need to address it in a campaign. However, perceived susceptibility was weak and response and self-efficacy moderate, thus needing to be strengthened in a subsequent campaign.

4. Strengthen targeted beliefs by examining the psychological, social, cultural, and structural bases of these beliefs to determine what caused low perceived susceptibility and only moderate levels of self-efficacy and response efficacy. For example, the researchers found that simply talking with partners about condom use was one key to increased perceived self-efficacy.

5. Then the research was entered into a chart of key beliefs to introduce, change, and reinforce. This chart guided writers and program planners in the development and production of a 26-week radio soap opera.[29] (See Table 4.4.)

Table 4.4 Chart of Beliefs to Change, Introduce, and Reinforce for HIV/AIDS Prevention

Theoretical Variables	Beliefs to Introduce	Beliefs to Change	Beliefs to Reinforce
Susceptibility	Talk with partner(s) about HIV/AIDS and prevention methods.	HIV/AIDS prevention services are easy to get.	Talk with partner(s) about HIV/AIDS and prevention methods.
Severity	Partner(s) believes HIV/AIDS is serious problem.		Partner(s) believes HIV/AIDS is serious problem
Response Efficacy	Using condoms is good, positive, safe, accepted idea.	Quality of HIV/AIDS prevention services is good.	Using condoms is good, positive, safe, accepted idea.
Self-Efficacy	Talk with partner(s) about HIV/AIDS and prevention methods. Generate positive, nonjudgmental talk in community about HIV/AIDS and prevention methods. Best friends are supportive of HIV/AIDS prevention methods.	Generate positive, nonjudgmental talk in community about HIV/AIDS and prevention methods. Generate approval of condoms as a prevention method. Quality of HIV/AIDS prevention services is good.	Using condoms is good, positive, safe, accepted idea.

Source: Cho, H., & Witte, K. (2005). "Managing Fear in Public Health Campaigns."

STEPS IN DEVELOPING A RESEARCH PLAN

Andreasen recommends that we begin our research journey with the end in mind. He calls this "backward research" and states, "The secret here is to start with the decisions to be made and to make certain that the research helps management reach those decisions."[30]

Nine traditional steps to take when planning a research project are described in the following section, beginning with this critical purpose statement. We'll use a case example to illustrate this process from an article by Simons-Morton, Haynie, Crump, Eitel, and Saylor that appeared in *Health Education & Behavior*.[31] Here the authors present a comprehensive research study they conducted for the National Institutes of Health to assess "Peer and Parent Influences on Smoking and Drinking Among Early Adolescents."

1. *Purpose:* What decisions will this research help inform? What questions do you need this research to help answer?

Existing research indicated to the study team that less than 10% of sixth graders reported smoking or drinking in the past 30 days, and yet 19.1% of eighth graders and 33.5% of 12th graders reported smoking and 24.6% of eighth graders and 51.3% of 12th graders report drinking in the past 30 days.[32] The purpose of the new research effort was to help determine what interventions would be most effective in reducing this prevalence, and with what audiences. Key to this decision were data answering the question, "To what extent do peers and parents influence smoking and drinking among middle school students?"

2. *Audience:* For whom is the research being conducted? To whom will it be presented?

Research findings would be presented to and utilized by health professionals working with youth populations.

3. *Informational objectives:* What specific information do you need to make this decision and/or answer these questions?

Major topics to be explored included those related to dependent variables (e.g., incidence of smoking and drinking among middle school students) and independent variables (e.g., peer- and parent-related factors). Relative to dependent variables, factors to be queried included demographics (gender, race, school attended, mother's education, family structure) and whether any adults living at the student's home smoked cigarettes. Relative to the students' peers, topics of interest included levels of direct peer influence (e.g., peer pressure) and indirect influence (e.g., how many of the respondent's five closest friends smoked and how many drank alcohol). Relative to their parents, insights were needed regarding perceived parent awareness, expectations, monitoring, support, involvement, and conflict—primarily related to drinking and smoking behaviors.

4. *Respondents:* From whom do you need information? Whose opinion matters?

Sixth-, seventh-, and eighth-grade students in all seven middle schools in a Maryland school district located in a suburb of Washington, DC, would be recruited for the study. The county was predominantly white but included a relatively large minority of African-Americans. Student and parent consent would be needed, as would review and approval of the study protocol by the Institutional Review Board of the National Institute of Child Health and Human Development. Authorization would be needed from the school district.

5. *Technique:* What is the most efficient and effective way to gather this information?

An anonymous self-administered questionnaire would be used for data collection. Once the technique is determined, draft the survey instrument.

6. *Sample size, source, and selection:* How many respondents should you survey, given your desired statistical confidence levels? Where will you get names of potential respondents? How do you select (draw) your sample from this population to ensure your data are representative of your target audience?

A total of 4,668 students were selected after 417 special education students with reading difficulties were excluded. (In the end, the parents of 302 students refused to allow their children to participate, and 103 students were absent on both the initial and makeup dates for taking the survey. In total 4,268, or 91.3%, of the students completed the survey, having the following demographic profile: 49.1% boys, 50.9% girls, 67.1% white, 23.5% African-American, and 7.2% another race.)

7. *Pretest and fielding:* With whom will the survey instrument (e.g., questionnaire, focus group discussion guide) be pretested? Who will conduct the research, and when?

Extensive pretesting of the measures and the questionnaire was done with repeated samples of volunteer students in the same schools the year prior to initiation of the study. These assessments included small group sessions where students were asked about the meanings of certain words, phrases, and statements being considered for use in the survey. For the final survey, students were to complete the questionnaire in class or during a makeup session, and two trained proctors were to oversee data collection in each class of 20 to 30 students. Classroom teachers were to remain in the classroom and be responsible for student discipline but were instructed not to circulate around the room or otherwise be involved while students completed surveys.

8. *Analysis:* How and by whom will data be analyzed to meet the planners' needs? A variety of statistical procedures will be considered and applied. This chapter's third primer, on basic statistical terminology, is presented in Table 4.5.

The prevalence of drinking and smoking behaviors within the past 30 days was to serve as the dependent variable for all analyses. Advanced statistical techniques would be used to determine the impact of each of the independent variables on these behaviors.

Table 4.5 A Statistical Primer

Statistics are numbers that help make sense of data. Statistical procedures are tools that are used to organize and analyze the data in order to determine this meaning. The following terms are described very briefly and are only a few among those used in the field.[c]

Terms Describing the Distribution of the Data

Mode: The response or score that occurs with the greatest frequency among findings

Median: The value (score) halfway through the ordered data set, below and above which lies an equal number of values

Mean: The simple average of a group of numbers, often thought of as the one number that best describes the distribution of all other numbers/scores

Range: Determined by subtracting the lowest score from the highest score

Terms Describing Measures of Variability

Margin of Error: A measure indicating how closely you can expect your sample results to represent the entire population (e.g., plus or minus 3.5%).

Confidence Interval: A statistic plus or minus a margin of error (e.g., 40% plus or minus 3.5%)

Confidence Level: The confidence level is the probability associated with a confidence interval. Expressed as a percentage, usually 95%, it represents how often the true percentage of the population lies within the confidence interval.

Standard Deviation: A measure of the spread of dispersion of a set of data. It gives you an indication of whether all the data (scores) are close to the average or whether the data are spread out over a wide range. The smaller the standard deviation, the more "alike" the scores are.

Terms Describing Analytical Techniques

Cross-Tabs: Used to understand and compare subsets of survey respondents, providing two-way tables of data with rows and columns allowing you to see two variables at once (e.g., the percentage of men who exercise five times a week compared to the percentage of women who exercise five times a week)

Factor Analysis: Used to help determine what variables (factors) contribute (the most) to results (scores). This analysis, for example, might be used to help determine the characteristics of people who vote (or don't) in every election.

Cluster Analysis: Used to help identify and describe homogeneous groups within a heterogeneous population, relative to attitudes and behaviors used to identify market segments

Conjoint Analysis: Used to explore how various combinations of options (alternatives features, prices, distribution channels, etc.) affect preferences and behavior intent

Discriminant Analysis: Used to find the variables that help differentiate between two or more groups

Terms Describing Samples

Population: A set that includes all units (people) being studied, usually from which a sample is drawn

Sample: A subset of the population being studied

Probability Sample: Based on some form of random selection. Each population member has a known chance of being included in the sample. This chance measure helps determine the confidence level to be used when interpreting data.

Nonprobability Sample: A sample that was not selected in a random fashion. As a result, results are not representative of the population, and a confidence level cannot then be determined and used when interpreting data.

Note: See page 105 for Chapter 4 Table Notes.

9. *Report:* What information should be included in the report, and what format should be used for reporting?

Final reports and discussions of findings were to include tables displaying results for each of the dependent variables (e.g., friends' problem behavior), cross referenced by each of the independent variables (e.g., smoking in the past 30 days), and the "odds" that these variables would influence the youths' behavior. Discussions would include a description of the prevalence of drinking and smoking relative to national data as well as the degree to which the findings supported (or not) a positive association between direct and indirect peer pressure and smoking and drinking.

RESEARCH "THAT WON'T BREAK THE BANK"

Alan Andreasen's book *Marketing Research That Won't Break the Bank* has more than 250 pages of suggestions for reducing research costs, a few of which are described in the following section.[33]

- Use available data, because they are almost always cheaper to gather than new data and are often "simply lying about as archives waiting to be milked for their marketing and management insights."[34] One place to look is at prior primary research projects conducted for your organization but not analyzed thoroughly or with your new research questions in mind. There may also be existing internal records or documents, such as attendance levels at events, tallies of zip codes and ages of clients, and anecdotal comments captured by telephone customer service staff. Externally, there are commercial enterprises that sell major marketing research data (e.g., *Advertising Age* magazine), and there are also free options, often easily found on the Web (e.g., CDC's Behavior Risk Factor Surveillance System).

- Conduct systematic observations, as they represent "the ultimate in cheap but good research."[35] And just because they're "free" doesn't dismiss the need for using a systematic and objective process to collect and interpret the data. For example, a state drowning coalition may decide they want to measure increases in life vest usage among children as a result of their campaign by observing toddlers on beaches in public parks. A standardized form for volunteers to use and a designated time and day of the week to conduct the research will be important to ensure reliability of the data when comparing pre- and postcampaign measures.

- Try low-cost experimentation, a technique often used in the private sector and referred to as "test marketing." In the social sector, it may be more familiar as a "pilot." In either case, the objective is to try things out before rolling them out. There are several advantages, including the ability to control the intervention so that it closely matches the strategic options under consideration. If your experiment is carefully designed, you can control extraneous variables and findings can be used to confirm (or not) cause and effect. And this approach is also "often speedier and more efficient than many other approaches."[36]

- Use quota sampling instead of the more costly probability sampling method by developing a profile of the population to be studied and then setting quotas for interviewers so that the final sample matches the major profile of the broader population. For example, a researcher who wanted a projectable sample of opinions of mental health care providers regarding various recovery models might control interviews to match the types of health care organizations in the state (e.g., clinical settings versus hospital settings versus school-based programs). Some maintain that these results can still be projectable to the larger similar population "if the quotas are complex enough and interviewers are directed not to interview just easy or convenient cases."[37]

Additional options to consider include *participating in shared cost studies*, sometimes called omnibus surveys. With these studies, you can pay to add a few additional questions to a survey being conducted by a research firm for a variety of other organizations, targeting an audience you are interested in. A county department of natural resources, for example, may want to estimate the percentage of households who might be willing to drop off unused prescription drugs at local pharmacies (market demand). They might then take advantage of a marketing research firm's offer to add that question to their monthly countywide survey that queries households on a variety of questions for similar clients. Another option is to *ask professors and students* at universities and colleges to volunteer their assistance. They may find your research proposal to be of interest and benefit to their current projects and publication goals.

CHAPTER SUMMARY

It may be easiest for you to remember (even understand) familiar research terms by recognizing the criteria used to categorize them:

- By research objective: exploratory, descriptive, causal
- By stage in planning process: formative, pretest, monitoring, evaluation
- By source of information: secondary, primary
- By approaches to collecting primary data: key informant, focus groups, surveys, experimental research, observational research, ethnographic research, mystery shoppers
- By technique: qualitative, quantitative

There are nine steps for you to take when developing a research plan, beginning "with the end in mind":

1. Get clear on the purpose of the research

2. Determine the audience for the research findings

3. Identify informational objectives

4. Determine respondents for the research

5. Find the best technique, given the above

6. Establish sample size and source, and how it will be drawn

7. Draft survey instrument, pretest, and field

8. Create an analytical approach

9. Outline contents and format for reporting, helping to ensure methodologies will provide desired management information

RESEARCH HIGHLIGHT

The "Yes" Initiative for Youth Employment in Maldives (2007)

In the introductory section of an article in the Winter 2007 issue of the *Social Marketing Quarterly*, Gideon Arulmani, director of The Promise Foundation in India, and Agisa Abdulla, a marketing consultant in Singapore, identified a real and persistent research challenge for social marketers.[38] They noted that although there appears to be evidence that interventions using social marketing principles can be effective, it is difficult to isolate what it is about any particular social marketing program that causes behavior change. Was it the result of one or more specific aspects of the intervention, the combined effects of the intervention, or some other environmental/cultural variable or trend? This research highlight presents a summary of Arulmani and Abdulla's research to answer these questions for a social marketing initiative in the Republic of Maldives.

Background

Maldives is a small developing nation located in the Indian Ocean, southwest of India and Sri Lanka. It comprises 1,190 small coral islands and had a population of about 400,000 as of 2010.[39] Young people between the ages of 15 and 24 years represent almost 25% of the population, and their employment was the focus of a social marketing effort launched in 2006.[40]

Although the Maldivian government traditionally was the primary employer in the country, this sector had not been able to meet the demand for employment among young people. The real job opportunities available for these youth entailed skilled jobs in the private sector. The problem was that the youth weren't interested in jobs involving such tasks as masonry, electrical wiring, carpentry, boat building and repair, and waiting tables. They also weren't interested in training programs to prepare them for these jobs. Instead, they preferred "trendy courses" that carried high "social prestige."[41] To compound the problem (or as social marketers might say, to tip the scales in favor of the competing behavior), many youth were cushioned by a family safety net that provided basic necessities and thus shielded them from the harsh realities of unemployment.[42] As a result, these skilled labor job opportunities were taken by an expatriate labor force. It is against this backdrop that the government of Maldives, in partnership with The Promise Foundation and Bluemoss Consultants, developed and launched their social marketing effort.

Campaign Summary and Outcomes

A strong branding effort formed the foundation for the campaign. In response to the identified negative attitudes and behavior of the target audience, the brand "Yes," an acronym for Youth Employment Skills, was tested and unanimously approved. The logo, a fingerprint, and slogan "Because I Can" were designed to communicate that personal identity is at the core of the concept and that career development is related to finding yourself and becoming you (see Figure 4.4). Counseling guidance services did more than help make the brand visible. They integrated it into their counseling approach, providing career exploration activities that gravitated around strong action for personal growth and development. For example, the program began with worksheets that stimulated discussion on what it means to say "Yes" and how saying "Yes" means

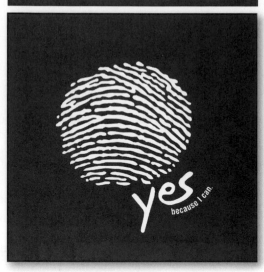

Figure 4.4   The "Yes" program's logo.[43]

dealing with negative career beliefs and barriers to career development. Exercises included students making pictures with their fingerprints and using them to discuss the uniqueness of their identity and the importance of taking responsibility for personal growth. *Promotional* strategies included initial television spots highlighting statistics of the number of school dropouts every year, and the large percentage left doing nothing; free postcards, called Zocards, distributed on the streets and at schools and youth hangouts by young people wearing "Yes" T-shirts; newspaper advertisements carrying the theme "Your future is at your fingertips"; and subsequent television clips showing a teenage schoolgirl with a group of friends writing the word "Yes" on the TV screen. To influence behaviors, TV and radio broadcasts on national networks presented information about counseling and employment opportunities. Importantly, promotional materials elements presented a "call to action" to visit the "Yes" Web site for more information, and/or to call the "Yes" toll-free number to ask any questions. *During the first month of the campaign, there were 49,075 hits to the Web site and 2,251 calls.* And this is in a nation with only about 100,000 youth.

Research Methodology and Findings

As noted earlier, of particular interest in this research was determination of what aspects of a social marketing effort, if any, contribute to intended outcomes. To this end, the researchers studied the impact of the social marketing effort through a series of studies with 10th-grade students. Schools were randomly chosen on every "focus island." In these schools, all 10th-grade students, both boys and girls, participated in the study. These studies focused on measuring changes in career beliefs and used the Career Belief Patterns Scale, a 13-item standardized scale designed to measure levels of negativity toward career development.[44]

As displayed in Table 4.6, there were four study groups. Scores for the control group represent measures taken among 10th-grade students prior to the launch of the "Yes" campaign.

While the findings suggested that "effects" were achieved by both the promotional and counseling interventions, of particular interest is the markedly larger effect size recorded for the combination of the two strategies.

Authors concluded by proposing that promotional campaigns need product "partners" for impact as well as sustainability. Promotional campaigns should consider culminating "with the baton being passed on as it were, to the partner intervention."[45]

Table 4.6 Changes in Career Beliefs: Comparison of Study Groups

Study Group	Size of Study Group	Score (Highest Possible 39) (The higher the score, the more negative the beliefs.)
A. Exposed to "Yes" Promotional Elements Only	105	Mean (SD) at Time 1 = 33.28 (1.77) Mean (SD) at Time 2 = 28.67 (2.45)
B. Exposed to Counseling Elements Only	161	Mean (SD) at Time 1 = 33.04 (1.97) Mean (SD) at Time 2 = 32.91 (1.82)
B. Exposed to Both Counseling and Promotional Elements	109	Mean (SD) at Time 1 = 32.72 (2.37) Mean (SD) at Time 2 = 19.41 (1.93)
C. Control Group: Not exposed to Promotions or Counseling	77	Mean (SD) at Time 1 = 33.15 (1.82) Mean (SD) at Time 2 = 32.44 (1.43)

CHAPTER 4 NOTES

1. Andreasen, A. R. (2002). *Marketing research that won't break the bank* (pp. 6–11). San Francisco, CA: Jossey-Bass.

2. An expanded version of this case appears in Kotler, P., & Lee, N. R. (2009). *Up and out of poverty: The social marketing solution* (pp. 132–138). Upper Saddle River, NJ: Wharton School.

3. PSI. (n.d.). *Pakistan.* Retrieved June 4, 2008, from http://www.psi.org/pakistan

4. United Nations Family Planning Association (UNFPA). (n.d.). *Reproductive health: Ensuring that every pregnancy is wanted.* Retrieved June 4, 2008, from http://www.unfpa.org/rh/planning.htm

5. Population Reference Bureau. (2008, March). *Family planning worldwide 2008 data sheet.* Retrieved July 14, 2011, from http://www.prb.org/Publications/Datasheets/2008/family planningworldwide.aspx

6. Allen, R. H. (2007, November). The role of family planning in poverty reduction. *Obstetrics & Gynecology, 110,* 999.

7. UN News Centre. (2009, March 11). *Revised UN estimates put world population at over 9 billion by 2050.* Retrieved July 15, 2011, from http://www.un.org/apps/news/story.asp?NewsID= 30159&Cr=family+planning&Cr1=S#

8. Ibid.

9. PSI. (n.d.). *Family planning.* Retrieved June 4, 2008, from http://www.psi.org/reproduc tive-health/

10. PSI. (n.d.). *Pakistan.* Retrieved June 4, 2008, from http://www.psi.org/pakistan

11. Used with permission. Population Services International.

12. Ibid.

13. Agha, S., & Meekers, D. (2010). Impact of an advertising campaign on condom use in urban Pakistan. *Studies in Family Planning, 41*(4), 277–290.

14. Kotler, P., & Armstrong, G. (2001). *Principles of Marketing* (9th ed., p. 140). Upper Saddle River, NJ: Prentice Hall.

15. Ibid.

16. Ibid.

17. Andreasen, A. R. (1995). *Marketing social change: Changing behavior to promote health, social development, and the environment* (p. 120). San Francisco, CA: Jossey-Bass.

18. Reprinted with permission from the Washington Transportation Safety Commission.

19. Andreasen, A. R. (1995). *Marketing social change: Changing behavior to promote health, social development, and the environment* (p. 127). San Francisco, CA: Jossey-Bass

20. Kotler & Armstrong, 2001, *Principles of marketing* (p. 141).

21. Lefebvre, C. Message posted to the Social Marketing Institute's listserv, January 21, 2007.

22. Kotler & Armstrong, 2001, *Principles of marketing* (p. 152).

23. Ibid., p. 146.

24. Ibid., p. 144.

25. Kotler, P., & Lee, N. (2007). *Marketing in the public sector: A roadmap for improved performance* (p. 259). Upper Saddle River, NJ: Wharton School.

26. Cho, H., & Witte, K. (2005). Managing fear in public health campaigns: A theory-based formative evaluation process. *Health Promotion Practice, 6*(4), 483–490.

27. Witte, K. (1992). Putting the fear back into fear appeals: The Extended Parallel Process Model. *Communication Monographs, 59,* 329–349.

28. Cho & Witte, 2005, Managing fear in public health campaigns (p. 484).

29. Ibid., pp. 484–489.

30. Andreasen, A. R. (1995). *Marketing social change: Changing behavior to promote health, social development, and the environment* (p. 101).

31. Simons-Morton, B., Haynie, D., Crump, A., Eitel, P., & Saylor, K. (2001). Peer and parent influences on smoking and drinking among early adolescents. *Health Education & Behavior, 23*(1), 95–107.

32. Johnston, L. D., O'Malley, P. M., & Bachman, J. G. (1995). *National survey results on drug use from the Monitoring the Future study, 1975–1994: Vol. 1. Secondary school students* (NIH Pub. No. 95–4206). Rockville, MD: United States Department of Health and Human Services, National Institute on Drug Abuse.

33. Andreasen, 2002, *Marketing research that won't break the bank.*

34. Ibid., p. 75.

35. Ibid., p. 108.

36. Ibid., p. 120.

37. Ibid., p. 167.

38. Arulmani, G., & Abdulla, A. (2007, Winter). Capturing the ripples: Addressing the sustainability of the impact of social marketing. *Social Marketing Quarterly, XIII*(4), 84–105.

39. United States Central Intelligence Agency. (n.d.). *The world factbook.* Retrieved July 14, 2011, from https://www.cia.gov/library/publications/the-world-factbook/geos/mv.html

40. Ministry of Planning and National Development. (2006). *Statistical yearbook of Maldives.* Malé, Republic of Maldives: Author.

41. Castley, R. (2006). *Employment skills training project: Proposal for a localisation policy.* Malé, Republic of Maldives: Ministry of Higher Education, Employment and Social Security.

42. Ibid.

43. Used with permission of The Yes Program.

44. Arulmani, G., & Nag-Arulmani, S. (2004). *Career counseling: A handbook.* New Delhi, India: Tata McGraw-Hill.

45. Arulmani & Abdulla, 2007, Capturing the ripples (p. 105).

CHAPTER 4 TABLE NOTES

a. Kotler, P., & Armstrong, G. (2001). Principles of Marketing (9th ed., p. 140). Upper Saddle River, NJ: Prentice Hall.

b. Ibid., p. 146.

c. *Webster's New World Dictionary.* (1980). Cleveland, OH: William Collins; Senter, R. J. (1969). *Analysis of Data: Introductory Statistics for the Behavioral Sciences.* Glenview, IL: Scott, Foresman; Andreasen, A. R. (2002). *Marketing Research That Won't Break the Bank.* San Francisco: Jossey-Bass; Rumsey, D. (2003). *Statistics for Dummies.* Indianapolis, IN: Wiley; Kotler & Armstrong, *Principles of Marketing* (9th ed.); Ellen Cunningham of Cunningham Environmental Consulting.

Chapter 5

CHOOSING A PURPOSE AND FOCUS FOR YOUR PLAN AND CONDUCTING A SITUATION ANALYSIS

Bring as many people from all disciplines to the table as you can, as early as possible, and find out how they would define success in the initiative.

—Dr. Katherine Lyon Daniel[1]
Deputy Associate Director for Communications, CDC

With this chapter, the strategic marketing planning process begins, following the 10-step model presented in Chapter 2. Whether you are a student developing a plan for a course assignment or a practitioner working on a project for your organization, this practical approach is intended to guide you in creating a final product destined to "do good." (In Appendix A, you will also find worksheets that follow this planning outline and a resource to receive an electronic copy.) For those among you who are reading this "just for fun," the process is illustrated with a variety of examples to make it come to life.

Step 1: Describe the Background, Purpose, and Focus for your plan, and *Step 2: Conduct a Situation Analysis,* are both relatively brief and will be covered together in this chapter. As mentioned earlier, this model begins "with the end in mind," inspiring your decision-making audiences with the problem your plan will address and the possibility it intends to realize. With this background, you then paint a vivid picture of the marketplace where you will be operating and are honest about the challenges you face and what you will need to address and prepare for to be successful.

In our opening case story, a compelling purpose with a single focus inspired a lifesaving marketing strategy.

MARKETING HIGHLIGHT

Reducing Diarrheal Disease in India
The ORS-Zinc Solution
(2008–2010)

Background

Diarrheal disease is a significant but highly preventable contributor to child morbidity and mortality worldwide, second only to pneumonia as the leading cause of death for children under five.[2] It is estimated that 1.9 million children worldwide die every year from diarrhea.[3] In India, the under-five diarrheal mortality rate is 74 per 1,000 children. In the state of Rajasthan, in 2005–2006, that rate was even higher, at 85 per 1,000 children.[4]

Diarrheal disease creates dehydration and the loss of electrolytes in young children and can lead to death if not properly treated. Nearly all of these dehydration-related deaths could be prevented by prompt administration of rehydration solutions. In 2008, in collaboration with UNICEF and the government of Rajasthan, Population Services International (PSI) launched a social marketing effort with a clear *purpose* to reduce the incidence of this disease and a *focus* on increasing the use of highly effective products—zinc and oral rehydration salt (ORS). Research had shown that when zinc tablets were added to ORS, the length of a diarrheal episode was reduced by as much as 40%.

The program strategy and associated social marketing effort had three key strategic intents: (a) Generate demand for the products, (b) increase accessibility of the products, and (c) build local capacity. As you

will read, the success of the effort on all three fronts reflects the program designers' clear understanding of existing target audience barriers and lack of perceived benefits, and the need to address each to be successful.

Case information was provided by Jaidev Balakrishnan, Regional Director, North West Region, PSI, and Sanjeev Dham, Program Director, PSI.

Target Audiences and Desired Behaviors

Downstream, the program targeted parents with at least one child below the age of five, in the lower socioeconomic strata, residing in areas with prevalent poor health indicators. Poor hygiene combined with a lack of safe drinking water leads to a propensity for diarrhea in infants and children, who are then unable to access cost-effective treatment and cure. Both fathers and mothers were targeted, as men were the primary decision makers in the household regarding health and financial issues and women were the primary caregivers of children under five. The program was designed to influence parents to obtain and administer the ORS-zinc solution, and to provide continuous feeding during episodes of diarrhea.

Engaging health care providers (*midstream*) in both the public and private sector was understandably critical to providing an enabling environment. In addition, the effort would need to influence decision makers in key retail distribution channels (*upstream*) to stock and support the sale of these products.

Audience Insights

A major barrier to the use of ORS among targeted households was that although awareness of the product was high, understanding of its benefits was low, resulting in a low usage level. In addition, zinc tablets were considered "pricey."

Strategies

PSI developed and promoted its own brand of low-osmolarity ORS, Neotral. It was (and still is) orange flavored and packaged in two different sizes of sachets that must then be dissolved in water. The *price* of the zinc tablets promoted was less than that of an existing brand. PSI tapped its existing distribution network in Rajasthan to start carrying ORS with zinc in both rural and urban areas (*place*). Sales managers were responsible for hiring a sales force at ground level to ensure product availability by recruiting and restocking retail outlets, as well as working with chemist shops and local grocery stores. The distribution network was also expanded to include rural health care providers. Between April 2008 and June 2009, 690 urban outlets and 298 unique rural outlets were established, with 93% of rural areas having at least one outlet.

A variety of *promotional* strategies were used to surround and engage the target audience, including:

- *Personal outreach to mothers:* A local nongovernmental organization was engaged to conduct the outreach activities by distributing fliers and making door-to-door visits. Messages to mothers focused on the benefits of using ORS-zinc and gave instructions on preparation and administration. During the project period, 55,573 females were contacted through the outreach activity, exceeding the target of 20,000 households.

- *Interactive tools:* To help make the benefits of using ORS-zinc real and concrete, two interactive tools were developed and utilized (see Boxes 5.1 and 5.2).

- *Street theatrics:* Male outreach workers reached fathers through *street plays* conducted at male congregation points such as bus stands, railway stations, and tea stalls. The message in the street plays concentrated on areas most relevant to males, such as the financial benefits of diarrhea management. In total, 1,130 street plays were conducted during the project period, reaching 116,337 people, against a target goal of 560 shows to reach 16,800 people.

- *Prompts:* With little access to billboards and print media, wall paintings were used instead, functioning as more sustainable reminders as well as reinforcing the message within the community. A total of 100 square feet of wall paints were applied across all villages with a population of 200 or more in the intervention area.

- *Signage* was placed at retail outlets in rural areas to signify places in the villages where products were available.

- *Special events:* At local fairs and festivals, outreach workers put up demonstration tents where they conducted product demonstrations. A total of 12 fairs were attended, reaching 2,104 participants.

To reach and influence public and private health care providers (*midstream*), PSI worked in close collaboration with the state government to develop and provide trainings. Training manuals and materials were developed on continued feeding and the use of ORS with zinc. An experienced medical consultant was used to ensure a quality training. A total of 46 trainings were conducted for public health providers, with 2,567 trained. An additional 20 training sessions were conducted with private health care providers, reaching 449 providers.

Box 5.1
Inflated Beach Ball Tool

An inflated beach ball was used to symbolize a child who is healthy, active, playful, and full of life. The ball was then deflated, symbolizing a child who is suffering from diarrhea and has become weak and lifeless. The ball was again inflated (symbolizing rehydration through ORS) and a cap (symbolizing the action of zinc) was placed on the nozzle so that it did not deflate again. The message presented was that using ORS-zinc during diarrhea helps a child regain his health.

Figure 5.1 Inflated beach ball tool.[5]

Box 5.2
Tree Cycle Tool

The target group was shown the image of a withered tree and asked for their reaction. All agreed that if a tree becomes dry and diseased, we give it water, pesticide, and manure so that it can recover and grow again.

Next, they were shown the other side of the sheet depicting the child's cycle and were again asked to respond. It was then explained that just as the insects make the tree dry and lifeless, diarrhea makes the child's body weak and dehydrated. To make him healthy again we have to give him ORS that hydrates the body, and zinc supplements to reduce the duration and severity of diarrheal episodes.

Figure 5.2 Tree cycle tool.[6]

Results

A total of 80,730 ORS sachets and 445,000 zinc tablets were sold during this first 15-month effort (April 2008–June 2009). The project complemented efforts of the Government of Rajasthan in achieving the objective of increasing the use of ORS to 90%.

Based on the project's learnings, a "how-to" manual has been developed that describes, in detail, steps on implementing a similar social marketing intervention to promote zinc with ORS in any district of any state. This document is significant for program managers, as it provides a lucid step-by-step process for selection of the intervention district, selection of the target population, the implementation strategy, and a logical framework for the project. This document has been shared with the state government and is in the process of being disseminated among program managers. The manual also holds significance for donor agencies and organizations wishing to support a social marketing intervention for reduction in mortality from diarrhea in children under five.

STEP 1: DESCRIBE THE BACKGROUND, PURPOSE, AND FOCUS OF YOUR PLAN, AND

STEP 2: CONDUCT A SITUATION ANALYSIS

To illustrate the first two steps in planning, we have chosen, for the most part, scenarios from China that represent social marketing opportunities to address a variety of social issues. Our intention is for you to capture the worldwide applicability of this very portable model.

Step 1: Describe the Background, Purpose, and Focus

Background

Begin the first section of your social marketing plan by briefly identifying the social issue your plan will be addressing—most likely a public health problem, safety concern, environmental threat, or community need. Then move on to present information and facts that led your organization to take on the development of this plan. What's the problem? How bad is it? What happened? What is contributing to the problem? How do you know? This description may include epidemiological, scientific, or other research data from credible sources— data that substantiate and quantify the problem for the reader. The development of the plan may have been precipitated by an unusual event, such as a school shooting, or it may simply be a means of fulfilling one of your organization's mandates. In either case, this section should leave the reader understanding why you have developed the plan and wanting to read on to find out what you are proposing to do to address the social issue.

It wouldn't be surprising, for example, to find the following paragraphs in the background information of a social marketing plan developed to reduce air pollution in Hong Kong.

In June 2006, a front page article in the *South China Morning Post* reported that according to a major study released the day before, air pollution was costing Hong Kong over 1,600 lives and at least $1.5 billion a year in direct health care costs and $504 million in lost productivity. The research had been conducted and analyzed by experts from three Hong Kong universities and a public policy think tank. The study also found that the city could save, each year, up to 64,000 bed days in hospitals and 6.8 million visits to family doctors if it improved its air quality from "average" to "good." Hong Kong's air quality standards were further reported to be below those of Paris, New York, London, and Los Angeles, and the city's concentration of air pollutants exceeded World Health Organization standards by 200%.[7]

Some believe a decade of passive approaches to tackling air pollution is to blame. The good news is that other cities are "recovering," and there are many options and solutions to consider that a social marketing effort could support, including increasing use of public transportation, energy-efficient appliances and fixtures, electric bikes, and replacing old vehicles more quickly.

Purpose

Given this background, you now craft a broad purpose statement for the campaign. It answers the questions, "What is the potential impact of a successful campaign?" and "What difference will it make?" This statement is sometimes confused with objective or goal statements. In this planning model, it is different from each of these. An *objective* in a social marketing campaign is what we want our target audience to do (behavior objective) and what they may need to know (knowledge objective) or believe (belief objective) to be persuaded. Our *goals* establish a desired level of behavior change as a result of program and campaign efforts. They are quantifiable and measurable. The campaign *purpose*, by contrast, is the ultimate impact (benefit) that will be realized if your target audience performs the desired behaviors at the intended levels. Typical *purpose* statements, like the background information, should inspire support for the plan. They don't need to be long or elaborate at this point. The following are a few examples:

- Decrease the spread of HIV/AIDS among African-Americans
- Reduce the amount of time it takes to get through airport security
- Improve water quality in Lake Sammamish
- Increase the percentage of spayed and neutered pets in the county
- Eliminate the stigma surrounding mental illness

A plausible social marketing plan addressing pedestrian injuries in China illustrates this sequential thought process.

The background section of this plan would have likely included statistics describing pedestrian-related injury rates, locations where injuries occurred, and populations most affected—such as the estimate that traffic injuries claim the lives of more than 18,500 children ages 14 and under in China each year. And that further analysis of motor vehicle collisions typically shows two main reasons for child traffic injuries: children (a) suddenly running into driveways and (b) crossing a street behind or just in front of a car. Surveys also indicate that 65% of children ages 8 to 10 walk to school, but only 15% are accompanied by adults. And among the 40% of children surveyed who had problems crossing roads, lack of traffic signs and crosswalks were the major problems.[8]

Several related *purpose* statements might then be considered, including *increasing proper use of crosswalks by students* and *decreasing accidents among children in driveways*. As you can probably tell, each of these purpose statements will lead you in a different strategic direction, with the crosswalk problem more likely solved by products such as pedestrian flags and fluorescent vests and the driveway problem more likely addressed by adults walking with children to school and teaching them about navigating driveways. In the end, one would be chosen for the plan (as a start).

Focus

Now, to narrow the scope of the plan, a *focus* (e.g., adults walking with children to school) is selected from the vast number of potential options contributing to the plan's *purpose* (e.g., decreasing accidents among children in driveways). This decision making process can begin with brainstorming several major potential approaches (*focuses*) that might contribute to the plan's *purpose.* These may be approaches that the agency has discussed or undertaken in the past; they may be new for the organization, recently identified as areas of greatest opportunity or emerging need; or they may be approaches other organizations have used that should be considered for your organization. Table 5.1 lists different social issues and possible focuses of each. The areas of potential focus may be behavior-related, population-based (although a target market segment has not yet been chosen), or product-related strategies, but they are broad at this point. They will be narrowed further in the subsequent planning process.

Several criteria can be used for choosing the most appropriate focus from your initial list of options:

- *Behavior change potential:* Is there a clear behavior within this area of focus that can be promoted to address the issue?
- *Market supply:* Is this area of focus already being addressed adequately in this way by other organizations and campaigns?

Table 5.1 Identifying Potential Focuses for Your Campaign

Social Issue (and Hypothetical Sponsoring Organization)	Campaign Purpose	Options for Campaign Focus
Family planning (nonprofit organization)	Decrease teen pregnancies	• Condoms • Birth control pills • Abstinence • Sexual assault prevention • Talking to your child about sex
Traffic injuries (state traffic safety commission)	Decrease drinking and driving	• Designated drivers • Underage drinking and driving • Advocating tougher new laws with policy makers • Military personnel • Repeat offenders
Air pollution (regional air quality council)	Reduce fuel emissions	• Carpooling • Mass transit • Walking to work • Telecommuting • Not topping off gas tanks • Gas blowers
Senior wellness (city department of neighborhoods)	Increase opportunities for community senior gatherings	• Tai chi classes in parks • Walking groups in pedestrian malls • Disco dancing under overpasses • Neighborhood watch programs

- *Organizational match:* Is this a good match for the sponsoring organization? Is it consistent with its mission and culture? Can the organization's infrastructure support promoting and accommodating the behavior change? Does it have staff expertise to develop and manage the effort?
- *Funding sources and appeal:* Which focus area has the greatest funding potential?
- *Impact:* Which area has the greatest potential to contribute to the social issue?

The best focus for a social marketing campaign would then have high potential for behavior change, fill a significant need and void in the marketplace, match the organization's capabilities, and have high funding potential (see Table 5.2).

Table 5.2 Potential Rationale for Choosing a Campaign Focus

Campaign Purpose	Campaign Focus	Rationale for Focus
Decrease teen pregnancies (nonprofit organization)	Abstinence	• Recent governmental funding for campaigns promoting abstinence in middle schools and high schools • Controversial nature of "safe sex" campaigns in school environments
Decrease drinking and driving (state traffic safety commission)	Designated drivers	• Opportunities to work with restaurants and bars • Familiarity with brand, yet little recent promotion in past several years
Reduce fuel emissions (regional air quality council)	Not topping off gas tanks	• Consumer research in other regions revealing a high level of willingness to stop topping off gas tanks after hearing the (low) costs and potential benefits • Ease of getting the message out in partnership with gas stations
Increase opportunities for community senior gatherings (city department of neighborhoods)	Tai chi classes in parks for seniors	• Availability of space at parks and existing roster of tai chi instructors • Increasing popularity of this form of exercise and camaraderie for seniors

Step 2: Conduct a Situation Analysis

Now that you have a purpose and focus for your plan, your next step is to conduct a quick audit of organizational strengths and weaknesses and environmental opportunities and threats that are anticipated to have some impact on or relevance for subsequent planning decisions. As may be apparent, it is critical that you selected a *purpose* and *focus* for your plan first, as they provide the context for this exercise. Without it, you would be scanning all aspects of the environment versus just the strengths, weaknesses, opportunities, and threats (SWOT) relevant to your specific plan. It would be overwhelming indeed.

Figure 5.3 presents a graphic overview of these factors and forces anticipated to have some impact on your target audience and therefore your efforts. As indicated, picture your target audience at the center of your planning process. (A specific segment of the population you will be targeting will be selected in Step 3, in part based on this analysis.)

Figure 5.3   Factors and forces.

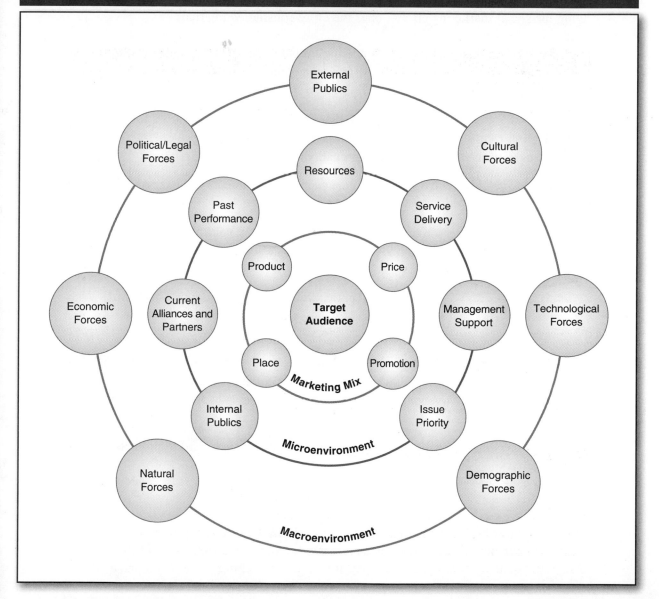

In the first concentric circle are the 4Ps, the variables that you as a marketer have the most control over. Next, a little farther away from the target, are factors associated with the sponsoring organization for the campaign, thought of as the *microenvironment*. The outer concentric circle depicts the *macroenvironment*, forces the marketer has little or no control over but that have influence on your target audience and therefore your effort.

The Microenvironment: Organizational Strengths and Weaknesses

The microenvironment consists of factors related to the organization sponsoring or managing the social marketing effort—ones therefore considered internal:

Resources: How are your levels of funding for the project? Is there adequate staff time available? Do you have access to expertise related to the social issue or target populations that you can easily tap?

Service delivery capabilities: Does the organization have distribution channels available for current products and services or ones you might develop? Are there any concerns with the current or potential quality of this service delivery?

Management support: Does management support this project? Have they been briefed on it?

Issue priority: Within the organization, is the social issue your plan will be addressing a priority for the organization? Are there other issues you will be competing with for resources and support, or is this one high on the list?

Internal publics: Within the organization, who is likely to support this effort? Who might not? Are there groups or individuals whose buy-in will be needed for the campaign to be successful?

Current alliances and partners: What alliances and partners does the sponsoring organization have that could potentially provide additional resources such as funding, expertise, access to target populations, endorsements, message delivery, and/or material dissemination?

Past performance: What is the organization's reputation in regard to projects such as this? What successes and failures are relevant?

Strengths

Make a (bulleted) list of major organizational strengths relative to this plan, based at least in part on an audit of these seven internal factors. These points will be ones your plan will want to *maximize*. You may not have something to note for each of the factors. You should be aware that this list will guide you in many subsequent decisions, such as which target audiences you can best reach and serve, what products (programs and services) you have the resources and support to develop, prices you will (need to) charge, incentives you will be able to afford to offer, and existing alliances you might be able to tap for delivery of products, services, promotional materials, and messages.

For another brief illustration from China, consider a plan with the purpose of reducing energy consumption and a focus on reducing commercial electrical use, a plan spurred by statistics indicating that the energy efficiency rate of China stood (in 2005) at 33%, 10 percentage points lower than the average advanced world level.[9] We can imagine that a national group charged with the responsibility of developing this plan would begin fully aware of one of their major strengths—that as a result of blackouts experienced in dozens of provincial-level power grids, energy saving had topped the government agenda. (In the end, this may have led to changes in infrastructure found today in China—such as self-activated escalators in hotel lobbies and hotel rooms that require room keys to be inserted for lights to go on. And of course lights then go off as guests leave the room with the key they will need when they return.)

Weaknesses

On the flip side, a similar list is made of factors that don't look as positive for your effort—ones you may need a few action items, even strategies, to *minimize.* This bulleted list is constructed by reviewing each of the same seven internal factors, noting ones that stand out as potential concerns in developing and implementing a successful plan. Most frequently for governmental agencies and nonprofit organizations (the likely sponsors of a social marketing effort), concerns involve resource availability and issue priority, as in the following example.

Consider internal factors challenging those charged with developing a plan to reduce teen smoking in China, where there are more than 100 million smokers under the age of 18.[10] According to an article in the *China Daily* in May 2006, a nongovernmental organization, the China Tobacco Control Association, wants to educate the public about the dangers of teen smoking, "but without money, what can we do?"[11] The article cites a lack of government funds (resources*)* for antismoking education and a historical lack of priority for this issue. In Beijing, for example, a regulation was issued 10 years ago banning smoking in public areas, but enforcement is apparently weak (an issue priority for a key partner organization in this case) and "smoking is still rampant in these places."[12]

The Macroenvironment: Environmental Opportunities and Threats

The macroenvironment is the set of forces typically outside the influence of the social marketer that must be taken into account, as they either currently have an impact on your target audience or are likely to in the near future. In each of the following seven categories, you will be noting any major trends or events you may want to take advantage of (*opportunities*) or prepare for (*threats*). Remember, you are interested in those related to the purpose and focus of your plan.

Cultural forces: Trends and happenings related to values, lifestyles, preferences, and behaviors often influenced by factors such as advertising, entertainment, media, consumer goods, corporate policies, fashion, religious movements, health concerns, environmental concerns, and racial issues

Technological forces: Introduction or potential introduction of new technologies and products that may support or hinder your effort

Demographic forces: Trends and changes in population characteristics, including age, ethnicity, household composition, employment status, occupation, income, and education

Natural forces: Forces of "nature," including famine, fires, drought, hurricanes, energy supply, water supply, endangered species, and floods

Economic forces: Trends affecting buying power, spending, and perceptions of economic well-being

Political/legal forces: Potential or new laws and actions of governmental agencies that could affect campaign efforts or your target audience

External publics: Groups outside the organization other than current partners and alliances, including potential new partners, that could have some impact on your efforts (good or bad) and/or your target audience

As discussed in Chapter 1, it is important to note that social marketing experts are now recommending that you also consider the role you can play to influence decision makers who can impact these upstream forces (e.g., focusing on school district administrators to increase formal physical activity programs in elementary schools).

Opportunities

A major purpose for scanning the external environment is to discover opportunities that you can take advantage of and build into your plan. Your activities can be leveraged by benefiting from the visibility and resources that other groups may be bringing to your issue or the increased awareness and concern that you find is already out there in the general public, as it was in the following example.

According to another article in the *China Daily* in May 2006, the number of pet owners in China had been soaring, as were the associated social problems—pet waste left on sidewalks, increases in rabies, and abandonment of pets when owners turned out to be ill prepared for the responsibility. Several organizations were picking up the challenge, including the country's Ministry of Health and the International Fund for Animal Welfare. An environmental scan on their part would likely identify several macroenvironmental forces impacting their target populations, ones they would consider potential opportunities as they prepared their approach to influencing public behaviors. Most cities in China removed the ban on dog rearing in the urban area in the 1980s after food rationing was scrapped (*political/legal*); 2006 was the Year of the Dog on the Chinese calendar (*cultural*); having a pet is now a symbol of prosperity, whereas it was once looked upon as a bourgeois way of life (*economic*); and some have attributed the popularity of pets to a growing sense of loneliness among city dwellers, particularly the elderly living alone and single white-collar workers (*demographic*).[13]

Threats

On the other hand, some of these forces will represent potential threats to your project, and you will want your plan to address or prepare for them. Understanding the influences on your target population can provide insight, as shown in the following example.

Referring again to the problem with tobacco use in China and the interest in reducing teen smoking, numerous external factors threaten success of the campaign along with the internal weaknesses noted earlier. Imagine the following powerful and entrenched cultural, economic, and legal forces operating in the marketplace—also mentioned in the May 2006 *China Daily* article: [14]

- People begin smoking at an early age, especially in tobacco-planting areas.
- Parents and teachers smoke in front of children.
- China is the world's largest tobacco producer and consumer, so smoking is accepted, even supported, given the close relationship between the production and consumption of tobacco and the national economy.
- Cigarette companies are still allowed to advertise their brands.
- There are no national laws or regulations in China to forbid selling cigarettes to youngsters.

Review of Past or Similar Efforts

One of the principles for success mentioned in Chapter 3 is to begin your social marketing planning with a search and review of prior efforts undertaken by your agency and similar campaigns planned and launched by others. When reviewing past efforts, you are looking for lessons learned. What worked well? What didn't? What did evaluators think should have been done differently? What was missing? One of the benefits of working in the public and nonprofit sectors is that your peers and colleagues around the world often can and will help you. They can share research, plans, campaign materials, outcomes, and war stories. Finding these resources (and people) can be as simple as joining social marketing listservs, such as those mentioned in Appendix B of this book, that have thousands

Figure 5.4 Bicycle lanes.

of members around the world. It can also be as simple as watching what others have done, as illustrated in this next example from China.

Nations and communities around the world interested in increasing bicycling (especially as a mode of commuting) could benefit from observing what China has done over the decades to make bicycling a social norm. They provide bike lanes, not just paths, that are protected from cars that might be opening a door (see Figure 5.4). At many intersections, there's a traffic signal—just for cyclists—that gives them their own time and space (see Figure 5.5). In Beijing, there are sports coliseums, adding to the excitement (and status) of bikers. For those concerned about "overexertion," electric bicycles costing about the same as a cell phone and getting the equivalent of 1,362 miles per gallon of gas are common and certainly not a "sign of weakness." For those concerned about costs, the government makes the competition (cars) very unattractive through escalating gas prices and high fees for vehicle licensing, such as the $5,000 licensing fee in Shanghai that doubles the cost of the cheapest cars.[15] And for those concerned about rain, they've thought of everything, including form-fitting heavy-duty ponchos that protect legs, heads, packages—even two riders (see Figure 5.6).

Figure 5.5 Traffic signals.

The Role of Exploratory Research in Steps 1 and 2

As mentioned in Chapter 4, exploratory research is conducted to describe the marketplace relative to the social issue you are addressing, a process that assists in making decisions regarding the *purpose* and *focus* for your plan (Step 1). Consider, for example, a program manager developing a plan to address a country's continued increase in new cases of HIV/AIDS. Exploratory research can help determine a purpose and focus for the plan by answering several important questions: (a) What are the number of new cases each year? (b) What populations represent the greatest increases? (c) What are the major ways this disease was transmitted in the past year? (d) What percentage of those infected are aware of their status? Findings may point, as they did for the Centers for Disease Control and Prevention (CDC) in 2006, to developing a social marketing plan with the purpose of increasing testing and a focus on African-Americans, the population segment representing the greatest number of new cases.[16] (Note: A specific target audience within this heterogeneous population would be selected in Step 3.)

Exploratory research also assists in identifying *organizational strengths and weaknesses* (Step 2) by assessing such factors as

Figure 5.6 Ponchos.

levels of support from management and key internal publics, resources available for the effort, the organization's past performance on similar efforts, and the capacity for incremental service delivery. For example, this research would be insightful for a large metropolitan hotel interested in increasing water conservation (*purpose*) with a *focus* on water utilized for laundering guest towels and sheets. Before selection of target audiences and desired behaviors, a work team would be interested in knowing the levels of behaviors influenced by existing cards in bathrooms that encourage guests to leave towels on the rack if they don't need a clean one and a card on a pillow if sheets don't need to be changed. They would also be curious about any feedback from guests and anecdotal comments from staff regarding the program.

Finally, exploratory research will enrich the identification of environmental forces that represent *opportunities* as well as *threats*. A citizen advocacy group interested in having the state legislature pass a law making texting while driving a primary, versus secondary, offense will find it useful to conduct informal interviews before speaking at a senate subcommittee hearing. What if they heard, for example, that four of the eight members of the committee were planning to recommend against the bill? This potential threat would certainly guide their selection of a target audience (Step 3) and underscore the urgent need to conduct subsequent formative research with these four to identify perceived barriers and potential benefits (Step 5) relative to a "yes" recommendation.

ETHICAL CONSIDERATIONS WHEN CHOOSING A FOCUS FOR YOUR PLAN

Conscientious social marketers will no doubt face ethical dilemmas and challenges throughout the planning and implementation process. Although ethical considerations are varied, several themes are common: social equity, unintended consequences, competing priorities, full disclosure, responsible stewardship, conflicts of interest, and whether the end justifies (any) means.

For each of the planning steps covered in this text, major potential ethical questions and concerns will be highlighted at the completion of most chapters, beginning with this one. We present more questions than answers, with the intention of increasing awareness of "ethical moments" and the chances that your decisions will be based on a social conscience that leads all of us to "higher ground."

When you brainstormed potential focuses and then picked one for your current plan, your first ethical question and challenge probably popped up: "What will happen to the ones we didn't pick?" For decreasing drunk driving, potential focuses include choosing designated drivers, promoting a tougher new law, and focusing on specific populations, such as military personnel or repeat offenders. Since each of these choices would lead to a different marketing strategy, you can only (effectively) deal with one at a time. One potential way to address this challenge is to present a comprehensive organizational plan for the social issue, indicating when important areas of focus will be handled and why they have been prioritized as such.

An additional common question and challenge regarding your focus may also come up, often from a colleague or peer: "If you push your desired behavior, won't you make it tougher for me to accomplish mine?" Some argue, for example, that if you focus on a campaign to increase the number of teens who choose a designated driver, won't you increase the number of teens who drink? Won't it look like "the government" approves of teen drinking? Good questions. And to answer, you will want to be prepared with your background and SWOT data as well as outcomes from prior similar efforts conducted by other agencies in other markets that support your decision-making.

CHAPTER SUMMARY

This chapter has introduced the first two of the 10 steps in the social marketing planning model.

Step 1 is intended to help you (and others) clarify why you are embarking on this project and, in broad and brief terms, what you want to accomplish and where you will focus your efforts. This will include:

- Gathering and presenting background information relative to the social issue your plan will address
- Choosing a campaign purpose
- Brainstorming and then selecting a focus for this plan

Step 2 provides rich descriptions of the marketplace where you will be vying for your customers and entails creating a common understanding of the internal and external challenges you will face by conducting an analysis of:

- *Organizational strengths* to maximize and *weaknesses* to minimize related to organizational resources, service delivery, management support, issue priority, internal publics, current alliances and partners, and past performance

- *Environmental opportunities* to take advantage of and *threats* to prepare for related to cultural, technological, demographic, natural, economic, and political/legal forces, as well as external publics other than current partners and alliances
- *Prior similar campaigns*, with an interest in lessons learned as well as opportunities for using existing research, plans, and materials developed by others

Exploratory research informs the process of identifying a purpose and focus and conducting a situation analysis and also provides a rationale for your decisions.

RESEARCH HIGHLIGHT

Focus Groups to Inform *Nuestro Barrio*
An Edutainment Soap Opera
(2006)

Background

The mission of the Community Reinvestment Association (CRA) of North Carolina is to promote and protect community wealth. A special focus is on changing "the lending practices of financial institutions to promote wealth building of underserved communities and to end predatory lending practices that strip wealth" with a strong commitment to "creative advocacy, using research, education, mobilization, media, litigation, regulatory changes, legislative advocacy and stockholder actions to initiate change."[17] One of their efforts, *Nuestro Barrio*, uses the popular "telenovela," or television soap opera, format to influence Latino immigrants in the U.S. to take two actions: (a) open a bank account and make regular deposits, and (b) save for a down payment or build credit to qualify for a home mortgage. This research highlight presents a summary of exploratory research conducted by Sentient Research in 2006 that identified barriers

and motivators to these two desired behaviors (*research purpose*).[18]

Methodology

Three Latino immigrant focus groups were conducted during two Saturdays in the fall of 2006. Participants were recruited from information fairs that had been held for Latinos in North Carolina. A screener administered at the fairs ensured participants were 18 years of age or older, Spanish dominant, working in the U.S., and television viewers. There were two female groups and one male group. Sessions were conducted in Spanish and videotaped, and participants received $50 as compensation for their time.

After a brief warm-up exercise, discussions focused on the following *informational objectives* for the groups, which would help inform the content of the series:

- What are their current sources of information and advice about money?

- What are they currently doing with their earnings?
- What barriers do they perceive to opening a bank account in the U.S. and to applying for a home mortgage?
- What are the motivators for having an account and owning a home?

Findings

1. *Current sources of financial information and advice:* Respondents agreed that the most valued sources were those with expertise on the subject, citing credit unions, banks, the Internet, and financial segments on television and news as the most reliable. Family members who owned homes and/or businesses were also given priority, but virtually no mention was made of friends as a trusted source.

2. *Current uses for money:* Two themes emerged from all three groups: taking care of living expenses (e.g., food and rent), and sending money to their country of origin (e.g., to help family members build a home or start a business). Some, especially the single women in the groups, expressed difficulty in having anything left to spend after sending money home.

3. *Barriers to opening bank accounts:* The overriding theme in all three groups was the required identification, especially the confusion about it. Although many believed that a social security number was required to open an account, some claimed a tax identification number (ITIN) was sufficient, along with a photo ID such as one from Sam's Club. There was also confusion regarding whether or not banks gave different interest rates based on whether the account was opened with a social security number or an ITIN. Additional barriers, though not as significant, included concern about possible "hidden" bank fees and trust issues regarding use of personal information. Interestingly, language was seen as a "barrier of the past," with many participants indicating that banks had at least one bilingual staff member for Spanish-speaking customers.

4. *Motivators for opening bank accounts:* These Latino immigrants were clear that they saw advantages of having an account, mentioning it would keep their money safer from theft, make it easier to pay for things, and help them establish a credit history. They would be motivated to learn more about how to use the account to better transfer money to their native country and to clear up confusion regarding identification, fees, and interest rates.

5. *Barriers to getting a home mortgage:* Barriers were even greater for owning a home. As with bank accounts, the number one concern was the perception that a lack of a social security number would mean a higher interest rate on their mortgage. Many believed they had to have a 20% down payment, and some worried what would happen to the home if they were deported. Some were actually planning to return to their native country, and the way to establish a good credit history was not understood.

6. *Motivators for home ownership/ mortgages:* Respondents saw the investment advantages of home ownership and indicated they would be most interested if there were reduced closing costs and their ITIN was accepted for the application.

Postscript

Content in the 13-part mini-series, now funded by Freddie Mac, addresses many of the barriers identified and highlights important perceived benefits. One series, for example, involves a married couple with children who live in an apartment complex with noisy neighbors. After being woken up at night once more, the irritated wife asks her husband to find out about buying a home. The husband's erroneous belief of needing a 20% down payment and other concerns are tackled head on.

This is the first Spanish language show distributed on English-speaking networks.

The series has aired in media markets in North and South Carolina, Miami, Austin, Dallas, Houston, and Phoenix (as of 2010) and is used by bank partners to market their banking services and to provide financial literacy to Latino immigrants. A DVD of the first season is also distributed by partner banks. The CRA currently (fall 2010) anticipates distributing *Nuestro Barrio* into the top Latino media markets across the country, eventually reaching an estimated 50% of Latino households in the United States. This would make *Nuestro Barrio* the most widely distributed financial literacy program in the country.

CHAPTER 5 NOTES

1. National Social Marketing Centre. (2008). *Effectively engaging people: Views from the World Social Marketing Conference 2008* (p. 10). Retrieved July 15, 2011, from http://www.tcp-events.co.uk/wsmc/downloads/NSMC_Effectively_engaging_people_conference_version.pdf

2. Black, R. E., Morris, S. S., & Bryce, J. (2003). Where and why are 10 million children dying every year? *Lancet, 361,* 2226–2234.

3. Bryce, J., Boschi-Pinto, C., Shibuya, R., Black, R. E., & WHO Child Health Epidemiology Reference Group. (2005). WHO estimates of the causes of death in children. *Lancet, 365,* 1147–1152. Retrieved July 15, 2011, from http://www.ncbi.nlm.nih.gov/pubmed/15794969

4. Black, R. E., Morris, S. S., & Bryce, J. (2003). Where and why are 10 million children dying every year?

5. PSI (Population Services, Inc.)

6. Ibid.

7. Majithia, R. (2006, June 9). Report finds HK's bad air claims a heavy toll. *South China Morning Post,* p. 1.

8. Qide, C. (2004, April 1). Campaign to teach kids about road safety. *China Daily.* Retrieved November 20, 2006, from http://www.chinadaily.com.cn/english/doc/2004–04/01/content_319588.htm

9. China focus: Energy conservation highlighted at level of national strategy. (2005, June 17). *People's Daily Online.* Retrieved November 27, 2006, from http://english.people.com.cn/200506/17/eng20050617_190751.html

10. Quanlin, Q. (2006, May 30). Campaign aims to smoke out young addicts. *China Daily,* pp. 1, 5.

11. Feng, Z. (2006, May 30). Current anti-smoking efforts failing to make an impact. *China Daily,* p. 1.

12. Ibid.

13. Qi, L. (2006, May 29). Pets bring host of problems. *China Daily,* p. 5.

14. Feng, 2006, Current anti-smoking efforts failing to make an impact (pp. 1, 5).

15. Holder, K. (2006). China road. *UCDAVIS Magazine Online.* Retrieved November 28, 2006, from http://www-ucdmag.ucdavis.edu/current/feature_2.html

16. Kotler, P., & Lee, N. (2007). *Social marketing: Influencing behaviors for good* (3rd ed., pp. 132–134). Thousand Oaks, CA: Sage.

17. Community Reinvestment Association of North Carolina. (n.d.). *Our history.* Retrieved July 12, 2011, from http://www.cra-nc.org/our-history

18. Montoya, J. (2007, December). Appendix: Nuestro Barrio *qualitative evaluation: Focus group report.* In Center for Community Capital at the University of North Carolina at Chapel Hill, *The bold and the bankable.* Chapel Hill, NC: Center for Community Capital.

PART III

SELECTING TARGET AUDIENCES, OBJECTIVES, AND GOALS

Chapter 6

SEGMENTING, EVALUATING, AND SELECTING TARGET AUDIENCES

We need to value segmentation beyond the "casting call" for images and voices and think about it as it can impact behavior offerings, product and service design, benefits offered and distribution strategies.

—Dr. Craig Lefebvre[1]
University of South Florida

Selecting target audiences probably makes sense to you by now and sounds good in theory. It's the practice that creates the greatest angst for many, reflected in these common musings:

- "We're a governmental agency and expected to treat everyone the same. How can we justify allocating a disproportionate share of our resources to a few population segments? Even worse, how can we justify eliminating some segments altogether?"
- "I keep hearing about 'the low-hanging fruit' and that we should go after them first. In my community clinic, I interpret that to mean that we focus our resources on clients who are ready to lose weight, ready to exercise. I don't get it. Don't the ones who aren't ready need us the most to convince them they should?"
- "If a marketing plan is built around and for a particular segment of the population, does that mean we'll need separate and multiple marketing plans for every audience we try to influence? That seems over the top, especially in these tough economic times."
- "Sometimes this just sounds like fancy language for something that never really happens. When we do a billboard for organ donation, everyone in town sees it. How is that target marketing?"

We believe this inspiring opening case describing four unique market segments and tobacco-cessation strategies targeted to each will begin to answer these questions and address these concerns.

Reducing Tobacco Use in the United States: Legacy's Small Innovative Grants Program Recognizes "One Size Never Fits All" (2010)

Background

Legacy is an independent public health foundation created in 1999 out of the landmark Master Settlement Agreement between the tobacco industry, 46 state governments, and five U.S. territories. Located in Washington, DC, it is a 501(c)(3) nonprofit organization with a mission to build a world where young people reject tobacco and anyone can quit.

In 2001, Legacy launched its Small Innovative Grants (SIG) program to explore tobacco control solutions among segments of the population in which traditional tobacco control approaches are not proving effective. Over the life of the initiative, it has supported efforts focused on using existing tobacco control strategies in new communities or tailoring proven strategies to the needs of a specific population. Program administrators recognize the power of community-level behavior influencers, including friends, family, employers, coworkers, and cultural practices. They also are clear that each subpopulation, whether based on ethnicity, income, geography, gender, or education, has special and specific tobacco control issues that need to be addressed and that tailored strategies are required to be successful.

One of the strengths of the SIG program is its ability to scour the landscape for newer, nontraditional players and to bring myriad community-based organizations into the field of tobacco control. This case highlights four of these grantee programs, featured in a January 2010 Legacy publication called *Legacy's Small Innovative Grants: Exploring Programming in Tobacco Control.*[2] As you scan the list, it is probably immediately apparent that one strategy would never work for all:

- Prisoners in New York State
- Coal miners in West Virginia
- Arab American waterpipe users in Pennsylvania
- South Asian communities in California

Target Audiences, Strategies, and Results

Although support for cessation and prevention is an underlying theme in each of the cases, the types of support (*products*), distribution channels, incentives, messages, messengers, and media channels were tailored to unique target audience characteristics and perceived barriers to and benefits of action.

Prisoners in New York State

Founded in 1931, The Osborne Association, a nonprofit organization in New York, focuses on the prison population, which is at a disproportionately higher risk for tobacco use; studies have concluded that up to 70% of inmates are smokers or use other forms of tobacco.[3] Although indoor areas of facilities may be smoke free, according to The Osborne Association inmates are still often free to smoke in exercise areas and other outdoor common areas. A Legacy grant initiative with The Osborne Association piloted a program to reduce the disparities in access to tobacco education and cessation support in the prison system.

Two major services (*product*) were developed and offered. Calls Without Walls gave prisoners interested in quitting smoking or needing support to stay tobacco free an opportunity to pick up the phone and make a collect call (*price*) to Osborne's help line and talk with a counselor, such as Diarra Steward, who describes the experience:

> The first thing I do is to congratulate them on the decision to stop smoking. . . . Then I start to tell them about all the chemicals in tobacco, and when I hear that silence, that's when I know I have their attention. I tell them that tobacco has killed more people than AIDS, illegal drugs, hit-and-runs, or people getting murdered on the street. . . . Then I tell them I was a smoker for 25 years and I stopped smoking in prison.

For those wanting nicotine replacement therapy (NRT), information is relayed to the prison medical provider and then on to the prison pharmacy. To support those waiting for their NRTs (which can take up to five weeks) and for those having a tough time even with the therapy, Osborne supported the development of Lean on Me, an all-volunteer peer counseling program and support group. Building on the success of the Osborne pilot and model, individuals in any prison facility in New York State can now call the state quitline and receive counseling and NRT support.

Coal Miners in West Virginia

In McDowell County in southern West Virginia, coal mines are the largest economic engine in the region, but coal mining also carries a dark legacy of health risks. In addition to the risks associated with coal dust inhalation, the Southern Coalfields Regional Tobacco Prevention Network Office (SCRTPNO) estimated that cigarette use prevalence among coal miners was 60%, chew tobacco 30%, and rates of "polyuse"—miners who smoke above ground and chew while on the job—as high as 25%. A Small Innovative Grant from Legacy allowed SCRTPNO to focus on this underserved population that had not received formal tobacco cessation programs in the past.

SCRTPNO viewed trusted and credible community *partnerships* as essential for entry and buy-in with targeted audiences. One partnership with the Brooks Run Mining Company developed and implemented a program that paid miners (*price*) to come to a cessation workshop (*product*). The company hosted intervention and education sessions, first with SCRTPNO, and then partnered with a physician who traveled to the mine site itself (*place*) to conduct required consultations. Interested miners were provided with prescription cessation medication. Eighteen miners came to the workshops, and 20% of those miners have stayed off tobacco to date. SCRTPNO also worked with Brooks Run to create billboards featuring miners who completed the program (*promotion*; see Figure 6.1). Now when McDowell County residents head out to the bank and the grocery store, they are likely to see one of these large signs providing the number for the West Virginia Quit Line and the message, "We're helping our people quit and you can, too." The financial benefits of Brooks Run's support for on-site tobacco intervention cannot be overlooked. The mining company pays 100% of the healthcare premiums for its miners.

SCRTPNO also views partnerships with faith-based organizations such as Hands of Hope Ministries (HOHM) as a way to tap into one of the strongest and farthest-reaching networks in the county. One of HOHM's most popular initiatives is its "Ladies' Night Out," featuring monthly meetings with a potluck meal and activities specifically designed to appeal

Figure 6.1   Spit tobacco prevention barn in Monroe County, West Virginia.[4]

to women. Because of the low literacy rate of the men in these communities, HOHM and SCRTPNO have found it effective to take a trickle-down approach—"to educate the women and the men will get an earful at home."[5]

Arab American Waterpipe Users in Pennsylvania

Pennsylvania's Lehigh Valley is home to some 16,000 Arab Americans, mostly of Syrian and Lebanese descent.[6] In some communities, almost 40% of Arab Americans are cigarette smokers.[7] According to the Bethlehem Health Bureau, waterpipe usage in this community is prevalent, understudied, and a serious health risk. Common throughout the cultures of the Middle East, the waterpipe is an ancient smoking device whereby the smoke of flavored tobacco passes through a chamber of water. Compared to cigarette smokers, waterpipe smokers may actually inhale higher levels of harmful toxins because of more prolonged smoking and the deeper inhalation involved.[8]

The Bethlehem Health Bureau applied for a Small Innovative Grant from Legacy to collect information on waterpipe use. Findings were insightful:

- First, although the waterpipe is commonly known as a "hookah," to the Arab American community it is an "arghile" and never referred to as a "hookah"
- In Middle Eastern cultures, the arghile signifies hospitality and is present at most family events and used as a marker of maturity

- Although many parents disapproved of their teenagers' smoking cigarettes, they were often more lenient when it came to the arghile
- Originally, the health bureau had intended to create tailored cessation for arghile users only, but consistently heard that that selective approach would not be effective; rather, it was suggested that it would be better to target polyusers, that is, smokers of multiple forms of tobacco
- Group cessation support might be effective

At the heart of the initiative was a goal to increase awareness of the serious dangers of arghile use, believing this realization would be effective in reducing use as well as initiation. A network for dissemination was created that included faith-based and lay community leaders, as well as dedicated peer educators working on an informal level among family and friends and on a formal level within the business and social sectors. Very large summertime family picnics with hundreds of attendees (*place*) were ideal locations for arghile interventions. The initiative also took the intervention and education directly into homes by targeting parents directly. As reported by program partners,

We have generated buzz. Pastors are talking about it in their sermons. We've had our two local papers report main stories about it, and the local TV station as well. Two years ago when we started this, there were just a couple of us having this discussion. Now there are many.

South Asian Communities in California

The city of Artesia, California, 25 miles southeast of downtown Los Angeles, has long been a gateway community for immigrants from South Asia—a blend of Indians, Sri Lankans, Pakistanis, Nepalis, Bangladeshis, and many others from the subcontinent. And although government survey data indicate that South Asians as a group have a lower tobacco use prevalence rate than most other major Asian immigrant groups in the United States, the statistics are misleading. Such surveys generally tally only the use of Western tobacco products, but South Asians consume a high variety of other South Asian smokeless tobacco products (e.g., *zarda, paan masala, paan parag, gutka, gul, mishri,* etc.), with one survey of South Asians in Southern California estimating that 34% of male residents and 21% of female residents used these culturally specific products.[9,10] With the help of a Small Innovative Grant from Legacy, the South Asian Network (SAN) set out to lower usage of these products in this population. Two strategies are especially intriguing.

Looking for shoes in the doorway: The staff at SAN speak many languages and realized early on that no tobacco-outreach or education materials were available in these languages and dialects. Once these resources were created, the teams hit the streets, visiting temples, cultural events, motels, and grocery stores. They knocked on countless doors. They knew where to focus, as they figured that if they saw shoes outside the doorway or clothes hung outside to dry, they were probably South Asian. They also knew that South Asians commonly work at gas stations, liquor stores, and as taxi drivers. As might be expected, there was cultural resistance among many South Asians to seeking help. But—as might not be expected—if people were inclined to seek help, they wanted to speak with someone they saw as an expert, not necessarily a friend or family member. This rapport was necessary to conduct roughly 150 individual customized tobacco interventions.

Point of sale: Getting the business community on board: These culturally specific tobacco products were exceptionally inexpensive, some costing just 25 cents per package. To make the products even more appealing and accessible, they could be found in just about every South Asian storefront, regardless of whether it sold groceries, DVDs, or clothing. SAN discovered further that shopkeepers rarely verified the age of the purchaser, and many had no idea they were selling a tobacco product. Shopkeepers could even list all the products' supposed benefits, including lowering blood pressure, freshening breath, fighting cavities, and preventing hernias. After the team thoroughly educated local business owners about state tobacco laws (*price*) and the harmful effect of the seemingly beneficial products, they began to notice changes in the storefronts of Artesia (see Figure 6.2). Shopkeepers have now posted notices that tobacco sales to minors are illegal, and when SAN staff find businesses that have

Figure 6.2 Educating South Asian business owners on the harmful effects of tobacco use.[11]

changed their ways, they publicly recognize them for being in compliance (*price*).

Concluding Comment

Reflecting on the concerns about market segmentation mentioned earlier, this case uniquely highlights the need to select strategies custom designed to appeal to and influence a specific market segment. Can you imagine one strategy that would have been effective with inmates of New York prisons, coal miners in West Virginia, Arab American waterpipe users in Pennsylvania, and South Asian communities in California?

STEP 3: SELECT TARGET AUDIENCES

At this point in the planning process, you have established the following components of your plan (illustrated using a utility as a hypothetical example):

- *Purpose* (e.g., decrease landfill and hauling costs)
- *Focus* (e.g., backyard composting of foodwaste)
- *Strengths* to maximize (e.g., as a utility, access to the customer base)
- *Weaknesses* to minimize (e.g., the utility's curbside yardwaste collection service just started accepting foodwaste, an internal competitor for the foodwaste)
- *Opportunities* to capture (e.g., continued community interest in natural gardening)
- *Threats* to prepare for (e.g., potential to increase rodent populations)
- Possible discovery of *existing campaigns* that will be useful for your efforts (e.g., one from a list of success stories on a state department of ecology's Web site)

You are now ready to select one or more target audiences for your campaign, defined as *a set of buyers sharing common needs or characteristics that the company decides to serve.*[12] They are subsets of the larger group (population) that may also be exposed to your efforts. In the utility example, residential households are the implied population of focus for the backyard composting campaign. Your marketing strategy will be crafted, however, to be particularly effective with one or more subsets of these diverse residents.

STEPS INVOLVED IN SELECTING TARGET AUDIENCES

Determining these targets for your campaign is a three-step process involving *segmentation*, *evaluation*, and then *selection*. Each of these steps is described briefly in the following section and elaborated upon in remaining sections of the chapter.

1. Segment the market.

First, the most relevant (larger) population for the campaign is divided into smaller groups who will likely require unique but similar strategies in order to be persuaded to change their behavior. The groups you end up with should have something in common (needs, wants, barriers, motivations, values, behavior, lifestyles, etc.)—something that makes them likely to respond similarly to your offer. Based on background information about attitudes toward composting indicating that avid gardeners are the most interested in composting, this city utility might identify four market segments to consider. As you will see, their segmentation is based initially on a combination of values and lifestyle and behavior variables:

- Avid gardeners putting most of their foodwaste in their *yardwaste container*
- Avid gardeners putting most of their foodwaste in the *garbage* or *down the drain*
- Avid gardeners putting most of their foodwaste in a *backyard composter*
- Remaining households who aren't avid gardeners

2. Evaluate segments.

Each segment is then evaluated based on a variety of factors described later in the chapter, ones that will assist you in prioritizing (perhaps even eliminating some) segments. For the foodwaste composting scenario, planners should be very eager to know more about each of these segments, beginning with *size* (number of households in the group), as a way to understand the impact the segment is having on the solid waste stream. They should also consider their *ability to reach* each identified segment and *how receptive* they might be to the idea of composting foodwaste in their backyard. Avid gardeners, for example, are likely to be the most interested in taking on this new practice, as they will likely see the value in the compost for their gardens.

3. Choose one or more segments to target.

Ideally, you are able to select only one or a few segments as target audiences for the campaign and then develop a rich profile of their distinguishing characteristics that will inspire strategies to uniquely and effectively appeal to them. Keep in mind that if you select more than one audience, it is likely you will need a different marketing mix strategy for each. A campaign to influence avid gardeners who are currently putting their foodwaste with their yardwaste to instead put it in a composter would have different incentives and messages, perhaps even communication channels, than one intending to persuade those who aren't avid gardeners to start composting their foodwaste. In fact, it is likely the utility would make the latter segment its last priority, given the challenges they would face in creating and delivering value to this segment in exchange for their effort.

This segmentation and targeting process, though sometimes tedious and complex, provides numerous benefits—ones long familiar to corporate sector marketers who "know that they cannot appeal to all buyers in their markets, or at least not all buyers in the same way":[13]

- *Increased effectiveness:* Outcomes (numbers of behaviors successfully influenced) will be greater, as you have designed strategies that address your target audience's unique wants and preferences and therefore "work." (It's like fishing. If you use the bait that the fish you want like, you're more likely to catch the ones you want . . . and more of them!)
- *Increased efficiency:* Outcomes relative to outputs (resources expended) are also likely to be greater, again as a result of targeting your efforts and resources to market segments with a higher likelihood of responding to your offer. (And back to the fish analogy. You are also likely to catch all these fish in a shorter time and with less bait.)
- *Input for resource allocation:* As a result of evaluating each of the segments, you have objective information that will assist you in distributing your resources and providing this rationale to others.
- *Input for developing strategies:* This process will leave you with detailed profiles of a segment that will then provide critical insights into what will influence an audience to buy your behavior.

Even if, for a variety of purposes, programs are developed for all markets, segmentation at least organizes and provides a framework for developing strategies that are more likely to be successful with each of the markets.

VARIABLES USED TO SEGMENT MARKETS

Potential variables and models for segmenting a market are vast, and still expanding.

Traditional approaches used by commercial marketers for decades are described in this section, as are unique models successfully applied by social marketing theorists and practitioners.

Keep in mind that in this initial segmentation process, before you have actually chosen a target audience, your objective is to create several attractive potential segments for consideration. You will select variables to characterize each group that are the most meaningful predictors of market behavior, ending up with groups that are likely to respond similarly to your offer (*products*, *price*, *place*) and your promotional elements (*messages*, *messengers*, *media channels*).

Traditional Variables

Segmentation variables typically used to categorize and describe consumer markets are outlined in Table 6.1 on page 139. Each is applicable to a social marketing environment (marketplace) as well.[14]

Demographic segmentation divides the market into groups on the basis of variables common to census forms: age, gender, marital status, family size, income, occupation (including the media, legislators, physicians, etc.), education, religion, race, and nationality. Sometimes referred to as sociodemographic or socioeconomic factors, these are the most popular bases for grouping markets, for several reasons. First, they are some of the *best predictors* of needs, wants, barriers, benefits, and behaviors. Second, this type of information about a market is *more readily available* than it is for other variables, such as personality characteristics or attitudes. Finally, these are often the easiest ways to *describe and find a targeted segment* and to share with others working to develop and implement program strategies.

Example: A demographic basis for segmentation could be quite appropriate in planning an immunization campaign, because immunization schedules vary considerably according to age. Planners might understandably create unique strategies for each of the following population segments in their local community:

- Birth to 2 years (3%)
- 3 to 6 years (5%)
- 7 to 17 years (20%)
- Adults, 18 to 64 years (52%)
- Seniors, 65 years and over (20%)

Geographic segmentation divides a market according to geographic areas, such as continents, countries, states, provinces, regions, counties, cities, and neighborhoods, as well as related elements, such as commute patterns, places of work, and proximity to relevant landmarks.

Example: An organization focused on reducing the number of employees driving to work in single-occupant vehicles might find it most useful to develop strategies based on *where employees live* relative to the worksite, current van pools, current car pools, and each other. The planner might then decide that the first four groups represent the greatest opportunity for "hooking up" employees with attractive alternative and/or existing forms of transportation:

- Employees living on current van pool routes (10%)
- Employees living within 5 miles of current car pools (5%)
- Employees living within 5 miles of each other (15%)

- Employees living within walking or biking distance of the workplace (2%)
- All other employees (68%)

Psychographic segmentation divides the market into different groups on the basis of social class, lifestyle, values, or personality characteristics. You may find that your market varies more by a personal value, such as concern for the environment, than by some demographic characteristic, such as age.

Example: A campaign to reduce domestic violence might find it most important to develop campaign programs based on levels of self-esteem among potential victims:

- High self-esteem (20%)
- Moderate self-esteem (50%)
- Low self-esteem (30%)

Behavior segmentation divides the market on the basis of knowledge, attitudes, and behaviors relative to the product being sold. Several variables can be considered within this approach: segmenting according to *occasion* (when the product is used or decided on), *benefit sought* (what the segment wants from using the product), *usage levels* (frequency of use), *readiness stage* (relative to buying), and *attitude* (toward the product/ offering).

Example: A blood donation center may increase efficiency by prioritizing resource allocation according to donation history, allocating the most resources to loyal donors (those who have given in the past):

- Gave more than 10 times in the past five years (10%)
- Gave 2 to 10 times in the past five years (10%)
- Gave only once, less than five years ago (5%)
- Gave only once, more than five years ago (5%)
- Never gave at this blood center (70%)

In reality, marketers rarely limit their segmentation to the use of only one variable as we did to illustrate each of these variables. More often, they use a combination of variables that provide a rich profile of a segment or help to create smaller, better defined target groups.[15] Even if, for example, the blood center decided to target the 20% of the market who had given more than once in the past five years, they might further refine the segment by blood type if a particular type was in short supply and high demand.

Stages of Change

The *stages of change model*, also referred to as the *transtheoretical model*, was originally developed by Prochaska and DiClemente in the early 1980s[16] and has been tested and

Table 6.1 Major Segmentation Variables for Consumer Markets

Variable	Sample Classifications
Geographic	
World, region, or country	North America, Western Europe, Middle East, Pacific Rim, China, India, Canada, Mexico
Country or region	Pacific, Mountain, West North Central, West South Central, East North Central, East South Central, South Atlantic, Middle Atlantic, New England
City or metro size	Under 5,000; 5,000–20,000; 20,000–50,000; 50,000–100,000; 100,000–250,000; 250,000–500,000; 500,000–1,000,000; 1,000,000–4,000,000; 4,000,000 or over
Density	Urban, suburban, rural
Climate	Northern, southern
Demographic	
Age	Under 6, 6–11, 12–19, 20–34, 35–49, 50–64, 65+
Gender	Male, female
Family size	1–2, 3–4, 5+
Income	Under $10,000; $10,000–$20,000; $20,000–$30,000; $30,000–$50,000; $50,000–$100,000; $100,000 and over
Occupation	Professional and technical; managers, officials, proprietors; clerical, sales; craftspeople; supervisors; operatives; farmers; retired; students; homemakers; unemployed
Education	Grade school or less, some high school, high school graduate, some college, college graduate
Religion	Catholic, Protestant, Jewish, Muslim, Hindu, other
Race	Asian, Hispanic, black, white
Generation	Baby boomer, Generation X, echo boomer
Nationality	North American, South American, British, French, German, Italian, Japanese
Psychographic	
Social class	Lower lower, upper lower, working class, middle class, upper middle, lower upper, upper upper
Lifestyle	Achievers, strivers, strugglers
Personality	Compulsive, gregarious, authoritarian, ambitious
Behavioral	
Occasions	Regular occasion, special occasion
Benefits	Quality, service, economy, convenience, speed
User status	Nonuser, ex-user, potential user, first-time user, regular user
Usage rate	Light user, medium user, heavy user
Loyalty status	None, medium, strong, absolute
Readiness stage	Unaware, aware, informed, interested, desirous, intending to buy
Attitude toward product	Enthusiastic, positive, indifferent, negative, hostile toward product

Source: From *Principles of Marketing,* 9th ed. (p. 252), by P. Kotler and G. Armstrong. Copyright © 2001. Reprinted by permission of Pearson Education, Inc., Upper Saddle River, NJ.

refined over the past two decades. In a 1994 publication, *Changing for Good*, Prochaska, Norcross, and Di Clemente describe six stages that people go through to change their behavior.[17] As you read about each one, imagine the implications for a specific population you are working with or, if you are a student, one you have chosen for the focus of a class project.

Precontemplation: "People at this stage usually have no intention of changing their behavior, and typically deny having a problem."[18] Relative to the behavior you are "selling," you could think of this market as "sound asleep." They may have woken up and thought about it at some point in the past, but they have gone back to sleep. In the case of an effort to convince people to quit smoking, this segment is not thinking about quitting, doesn't consider their tobacco use a problem, or tried once in the past but decided not to try again.

Contemplation: "People acknowledge that they have a problem and begin to think seriously about solving it."[19] Or they may have a want or desire and have been thinking about fulfilling it. They are "awake but haven't moved." This segment of smokers is considering quitting for any number of reasons but hasn't definitely decided and hasn't taken any steps.

Preparation: "Most people in the Preparation Stage are (now) planning to take action . . . and are making the final adjustments before they begin to change their behavior."[20] Back to our analogy, they are sitting up—maybe they even have their feet on the floor. In this segment, smokers have decided to quit and may have told others about their intentions. They probably have decided how they will quit and by when.

Action: "The Action Stage is one in which people most overtly modify their behavior and their surroundings. They stop smoking cigarettes, remove all desserts from the house, pour the last beer down the drain, or confront their fears. In short, they make the move for which they have been preparing."[21] They have "left the bed." This segment has recently stopped smoking cigarettes. However, it may not be a new habit yet.

Maintenance: "During Maintenance (individuals) work to consolidate the gains attained during the action and other stages and struggle to prevent lapses and relapse."[22] Individuals in this segment have not had a cigarette for perhaps six months or a year and remain committed to not smoking. But at times they have to work to remind themselves of the benefits they are experiencing and distract themselves when they are tempted to relapse.

Termination: "The termination stage is the ultimate goal for all changers. Here, a former addiction or problem will no longer present any temptation or threat."[23] This segment is not tempted to return to smoking. They are now "nonsmokers" for life.

One of the attractive features of this model is that the authors have identified a relatively simple way to assess a market's stage. They suggest four questions to ask, and, on the basis of responses, respondents are categorized in one of the four stages.[24] Table 6.2 summarizes the groupings by stage of change, on the basis of the four responses.

Table 6.2 Determining Stage of Change					

	Decision/Response Taken By:				
Decision/Response Taken	**Precontemplation Segment**	**Contemplation Segment**	**Preparation Segment**	**Action Segment**	**Maintenance Segment**
I solved this problem more than 6 months ago	No	No	No	No	Yes
I have taken action within the past 6 months	No	No	No	Yes	Yes
I intend to take action in the next month	No	No	Yes	Yes	Yes
I intend to take action in the next 6 months	No	Yes	Yes	Yes	Yes

In the model shown in Box 6.1, the "name of the marketer's game" is to move segments to the next stage. The authors (Prochaska, Norcross, and DiClemente) offer cautions:

Linear progression is a possible but relatively rare phenomenon. In fact, people who initiate change begin by proceeding from contemplation to preparation to action to maintenance. Most, however, slip up at some point, returning to the contemplation, or sometimes even the precontemplation stage, before renewing their efforts.[25]

Box 6.1
Stages of Change Progression

Precontemplation ⇒ Contemplation ⇒ Preparation ⇒

Action ⇒ Maintenance ⇒ Termination

Figure 6.3 is these authors' graphic representation of the more likely patterns of change, a spiral one.

Diffusion of Innovation

Some consider this model one of the more important ones for attempting to segment the market and influence the behavior of large groups of people. Kotler and Roberto describe this concept of diffusion (or spread) of the adoption of new behaviors through a population and its applicability to social marketing by referencing original work by Rogers and Shoemaker:

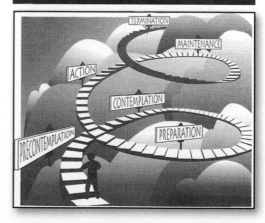

Figure 6.3 The spiral of change.[26]

The ability of social marketers to plan and manage the diffusion or spread of adoptions to the largest possible target-adopter population requires an understanding of both individual behavior and the mechanisms by which new ideas and practices spread to the larger group or population of target adopters. . . .

Innovation diffusion research suggests that different types of adopters accept an innovation at different points in time. Table 6.3 summarizes the size, timing of adoption, and motivations for adoption of each target-adopter segment. The diffusion process begins with a small (2.5 percent) segment of innovative-minded adopters. These adopters are drawn to novelty and have a need to be different. They are followed by an early segment of target adopters (13.5 percent), who are drawn by the social product's intrinsic value. A third early majority segment (34 percent) perceive the spread of a product and decide to go along with it, out of their need to match and imitate. The late majority (34 percent) jump on the bandwagon, and the remaining segment, the laggards (16 percent), follow suit at the product attains popularity and broad acceptance.[27]

For example, this segmentation model might be applicable to a campaign influencing citizens to consider renewable energy resources such as solar power, wind power, and biodiesel fuel. Early efforts would be designed to appeal to the innovators and early

---

Table 6.3 Elements of the Diffusion Innovation Model That Are Useful for Diffusion Planning

Target-Adopter Segments	Hypothetical Size (%)	Timing Sequence of Adoption	Motivation for Adoption
Innovator segment	2.5	First	Need for novelty and need to be different
Early adopter segment	13.5	Second	Recognition of adoption object's intrinsic/convenience value from contact with innovators
Early majority segment	34.0	Third	Need to imitate/match and deliberateness trait
Late majority segment	34.0	Fourth	Need to join the bandwagon triggered by the majority opinion legitimating the adoption object
Laggard segment	16.0	Last	Need to respect tradition

Source: Adapted with permission of The Free Press, a division of Simon & Schuster, Inc., from *Communications of Innovations: A Cross-Cultural Approach* (2nd ed.), by Everett M. Rogers, with F. Floyd Shoemaker. Copyright @ 1962, 1971 by The Free Press

adopters, which would be different from efforts that would appeal to the late majority and especially the laggards.

Healthstyles Segmentation

Another segmentation model used for health-related program planning appears in Table 6.4. This system incorporates several segmentation variables including demographics, psychographics, and knowledge, attitudes, and current behaviors related to personal health. Resulting segments provide planners with a rich and memorable picture of each potential target audience, aiding in the development of winning strategies for that market. For example, a physical activity campaign wanting to influence "Decent Dolittles," who may not have confidence in their ability to exercise, might emphasize the benefits of moderate physical activity, how it can fit into everyday life and activities, and the opportunities to "hang out with friends" while doing it. By contrast, a strategy to influence the "Tense but Trying" segment would switch the emphasis to the health benefits of exercise, especially for stress-related illnesses.

Environmental Segmentation

With a goal of improving climate-change public engagement initiatives, Maibach, Leiserowitz, and Roser-Renouf conducted a national study to identify distinct and motivationally coherent groups within the American public.[28] In the fall of 2008, they conducted a nationally representative Web-based survey to measure Americans' climate change beliefs, issue involvement, policy preferences, and behaviors. Using market segmentation techniques, they identified six distinct groups and described them as follows (see also Figure 6.4 on page 145):

- The *Alarmed* (18%) are the segment most engaged in the issue of global warming. They are completely convinced it is happening, caused by humans, and a serious and urgent threat. The Alarmed are already making changes in their own lives and support an aggressive national response.
- The *Concerned* (33%) are moderately convinced that global warming is a serious problem, but while they support a vigorous national response, they are distinctly less involved in the issue and less likely than the Alarmed to take personal action.
- The *Cautious* (19%) also believe that global warming is a problem, although they are less certain that it is happening than the Alarmed or the Concerned. They don't view it as a personal threat and don't feel a sense of urgency to deal with it through personal or societal actions.
- The *Disengaged* (12%) haven't thought much about the issue. They are the segment most likely to say that they could easily change their minds about global warming, and they are the most likely to select the "don't know" option in response to every survey question about global warming where "don't know" is presented as an option.

Table 6.4	Healthstyles Segmentation System, American Healthstyles Audience Segmentation Project

Decent Dolittles (24%)

They are one of the less health-oriented groups. Although less likely to smoke or drink, they also are less likely to exercise, eat nutritiously, and work to stay at their ideal weights. Decent Dolittles know that they should be performing these behaviors to improve their health, but they do not feel that they have the ability. Their friends and family tend to avoid these behaviors as well. They describe themselves as "religious," "conservative," and "clean."

Active Attractives (13%)

They place a high emphasis on looking good and partying. Active Attractives are relatively youthful and moderately health oriented. They tend not to smoke and limit their fat intake more than do other groups. They are highly motivated, intending to exercise and keep their weight down, but they do not always succeed at this. Alcohol consumption is an important part of their lifestyle, and Active Attractives often are sensation seekers, constantly looking for adventure. They describe themselves as "romantic," "dynamic," "youthful," and "vain."

Hard-Living Hedonists (6%)

They are not very interested in health and tend to smoke and drink alcohol more heavily and frequently than do other groups. They also enjoy eating high-fat foods and do not care about limiting their fat intake. Despite this, they tend not to be overweight and are moderately physically active. Although they are the group least satisfied with their lives, they have no desire to make any health-related changes. Hard-Living Hedonists also are more likely to use stimulants and illicit drugs than are other segments. They describe themselves as "daring," "moody," "rugged," "independent," and "exciting."

Tense but Trying (10%)

They are similar to the more health-oriented segments except that they tend to smoke cigarettes. They are average in the amount of exercise they get and in their efforts to control their fat intake and weight. They have a moderate desire to exercise more, eat better, and control their weight more effectively as well. The Tense but Trying tend to be more anxious than other groups, with the highest rate of ulcers and use of sedatives and a higher number of visits to mental health counselors. They describe themselves as "tense," "high-strung," "sensitive," and "serious."

Noninterested Nihilists (7%)

They are the least health oriented and do not feel that people should take steps to improve their health. Accordingly, they smoke heavily, actively dislike exercise, eat high-fat diets, and make no efforts to control their weight. Despite this, they tend to drink alcohol only moderately. Of all the groups, Noninterested Nihilists have the highest level of physical impairment, the most sick days in bed, and the most medical care visits related to an illness. They describe themselves as being "depressed," "moody," and "homebodies."

Physical Fantastics (24%)

They are the most health-oriented group, leading a consistently health-promoting lifestyle. They are above average in not smoking or drinking, exercising routinely, eating nutritiously, and making efforts to control their weight. They tend to be in their middle or latter adult years and have a relatively large number of chronic health conditions. Physical Fantastics follow their physicians' advice to modify their diets and routinely discuss health-related topics with others.

Passive Healthy (15%)

They are in excellent health, although they are somewhat indifferent to living healthfully. They do not smoke or drink heavily and are one of the most active segments. Although they eat a high amount of dietary fat, they are the trimmest of all the groups. The Passive Healthy do not place much value on good health and physical fitness and are not motivated to make any changes in their behaviors.

Source: Reprinted by permission of Sage Publications Ltd. from Maibach, E. A., Ladin, E. A. K., and Slater, M., "Translating Health Psychology Into Effective Health Communication: The American Healthstyles Audience Segmentation Project," in *Journal of Health Psychology, I,* pp. 261–277. As appeared in Weinreich, N., *Hands-on social marketing: A step-by-step guide* (p. 55).

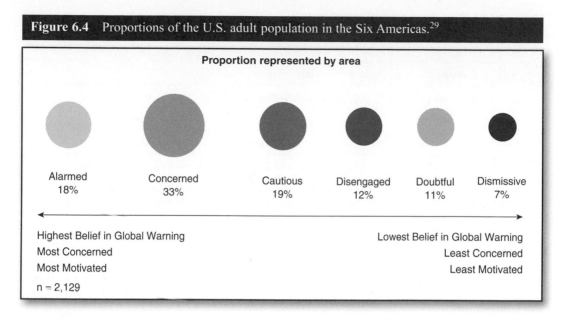

Figure 6.4 Proportions of the U.S. adult population in the Six Americas.[29]

- The *Doubtful* (11%) are evenly split among those who think global warming is happening, those who think it isn't, and those who don't know. Many within this group believe that if global warming is happening, it is caused by natural changes in the environment, that it won't harm people for many decades into the future, if at all, and that America is already doing enough to respond to the threat.
- The *Dismissive* (7%), like the Alarmed, are actively engaged in the issue, but on the opposite end of the spectrum. The large majority of the people in this segment believe that global warming is not happening, is either not a threat to people or is not caused by humans, and is not a problem that warrants a personal or societal response.

Subsequently, Maibach and colleagues developed a brief (15-item) survey instrument—and accompanying SPSS and SAS macros—so that other researchers and campaign planners can identify the prevalence of the Six Americas within their target population.

Generational Segmentation

Some researchers and theorists point to the power of market segmentation on the basis of generation. Every generation is profoundly influenced by the times in which it grows up—the music, movies, politics, technological advances, economics, and defining events of the period (e.g., the Great Depression, 9/11, world wars). Demographers refer to generational groups as *cohorts*, members of which share similar major cultural, political, and economic experiences.[30] The five groups in Table 6.5 are a blend of several popular generational segmentation typologies:[31]

| **Table 6.5** | Generational Segments | | |

Born	Name	Age (2010)	Major characteristics
1927–1945	Traditionalists	65–83 yrs.	Loyal, hardworking, disciplined, patriotic, civic minded
1946–1964	Baby Boomers	45–64 yrs.	Optimistic, driven, competitive, career centered
1965–1977	Generation X	23–45 yrs.	Cynical, self-starters, independent, resourceful, media savvy
1978–1994	Generation Y	16–22 yrs.	Edgy, focused on urban style, more idealistic than Gen-X
1995–2002	Millennials	8–15 yrs.	Tech savvy, multicultural, grew up in affluent society

Of significance to social marketers is that these cohort segments and characteristics may provide unique insight into current beliefs, attitudes, and other behavioral influences. Kotler and Keller suggest, however, that we consider the impact that additional variables have on these cohorts. For example, two individuals from the same cohort (Baby Boomers) may differ in their *life stages* (e.g., one recently divorced and the other never married); *physiographics*, that is, conditions related to a person's age (e.g., one coping with hair loss and the other diabetic); and/or *socioeconomics* (e.g., one recently losing a job and the other receiving an inheritance).[32] This more multivariate analysis will lead to greater insights and therefore more efficient and effective targeting.

Cluster Systems: PRIZM & VALS

Two well-known commercial models used to group consumer markets into homogeneous segments, often referred to as clusters, are the PRIZM NE and VALS products.

PRIZM NE is a geodemographic classification system offered by the Claritas Corporation that describes every U.S. neighborhood in terms of 66 distinct social group types, called "segments."[33] Each zip code is assigned one or several of these 66 clusters, based on the shared socioeconomic characteristics of the area. It is based on the fundamental premise that "birds of a feather flock together" and that when choosing a place to live, people tend to seek out neighborhoods compatible with their lifestyles, where they find others in similar circumstances with similar consumer behavior patterns. Segments are given snappy, memorable names like "God's Country," "Red, White & Blues," "Kids & Cul-de-Sacs" and "Blue Blood Estates." Each segment is then described for the user, providing demographic as well as lifestyle-related behaviors. For example, a state department of ecology interested in reducing litter might be interested in having Claritas analyze the addresses and zip codes of citizens receiving tickets for littering, providing information that will help the department with messages and communication strategies, such as what bus routes in the city would be best for ads promoting the $1,025 fine for littering lit cigarette butts. (See Appendix B for more information on this resource.)

The well-known VALS segmentation system categorizes U.S. adult consumers into one of eight segments, indicative of personality traits considered to be determinants (drivers) of buying behaviors. The eight primary VALS consumer types are shown graphically in the VALS framework (see Figure 6.5.) The horizontal dimension in the figure represents the primary motivations and the vertical dimension represents resources. Using the primary motivation and resources dimensions, VALS defines eight primary types of adult consumers who have different attitudes and exhibit distinctive behavior and decision making patterns. How would you use this? If you are a nonprofit organization with a mission to increase voter turnout, this system might be very helpful in first identifying segments representing the greatest opportunities for increased voting, creating an offer this group would find particularly motivating, and then, by using the GeoVALS system, targeting a direct-mail campaign or get-out-to-vote effort in zip codes with high concentrations of these types. (See Appendix B for more information on this resource, including a Web site where you can complete the questionnaire and determine your VALS type.)

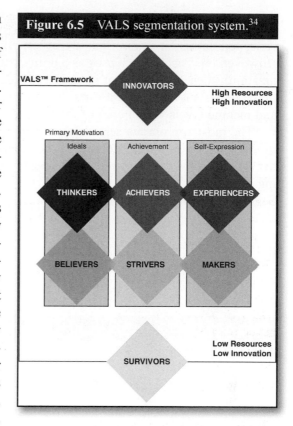

Figure 6.5   VALS segmentation system.[34]

Segmenting Target Audiences Upstream

To this point, we have been focusing on consumer market segmentation variables. As you read in Chapter 1, however, real social change strategies often need to focus on influencing markets upstream from the individual—politicians, media figures, community activists, corporations, schools, foundations, and others with influence over your target audience and their environments. The segmentation process is the same for these populations, but the variables are likely to differ. Politicians, for example, might be segmented by what committees they serve on or by political party. The corporate market will more likely be segmented by industry type, schools by administrative level, foundations by areas of focus, and media figures by type of media. Once the market is segmented, you will still proceed to the next two steps of evaluation and selection.

Combination of Variables

As noted earlier, it is rare that a market will be segmented using only one variable. However, one base is often used as a primary way to group a market (e.g., age for immunization); then each segment is further profiled, and perhaps narrowed, by using additional important and relevant variables that predict response to strategies (e.g., education and income levels within each of the age segments for immunization).

"The most appropriate segmentation variables are those that best capture differences in the behavior of target adopters."[35] For social marketing planning, we encourage you to consider using behavior-related segmentation variables as the primary base for profiling the market, similar to the ones in the stages of change model described earlier. Segments are then profiled using other meaningful variables. Table 6.6 illustrates a hypothetical profile of market segments that a planner might compile at this stage in the planning process. It uses Andreasen's version of the stages of change model, which collapses the six stages to four, a model more manageable for some programs. The issue is litter on roadways. The market is people who smoke in cars.[36]

Table 6.6   Hypothetical Segmentation Using Stages of Change as Primary Bases

Stage of Change	Precontemplation	Contemplation	Preparation for or in Action	Maintenance
Behavior and intent	Throw cigarette butts out the window and aren't concerned about it.	Throw cigarette butts out the window, feel bad about it, and have been thinking about not doing it.	Sometimes throw cigarette butts out the window and sometimes use ashtray. Trying to increase use of ashtray.	Never throw cigarette butts out the window; use ashtray instead.
Size	20%	30%	30%	20%
Geographics (residence)	Rural (10%) Suburban (40%) Urban (50%)	Rural (8%) Suburban (55%) Urban (37%)	Rural (6%) Suburban (65%) Urban (29%)	Rural (5%) Suburban (70%) Urban (25%)
Demographics (age)	16–20 (60%) 21–34 (25%) 35–50 (10%) 50+ (5%)	16–20 (53%) 21–34 (22%) 35–50 (15%) 50+ (10%)	16–20 (45%) 21–34 (20%) 35–50 (20%) 50+ (15%)	16–20 (30%) 21–34 (18%) 35–50 (27%) 50+ (25%)
Psychographics (environmental ethic)	Environmentally: Concerned (10%) Neutral (30%) Not concerned (60%)	Environmentally; Concerned (15%) Neutral (45%) Not concerned (40%)	Environmentally; Concerned (30%) Neutral (40%) Not concerned (30%)	Environmentally: Concerned (60%) Neutral (30%) Not concerned (10%)

CRITERIA FOR EVALUATING SEGMENTS

Once the marketplace has been grouped into meaningful population segments, the next task is to evaluate each segment in preparation for decisions regarding selection of target audiences.

For social marketers, Andreasen cites nine factors for evaluating segments relative to each other.[37] A list of these factors follows, with typical questions that might be asked to establish each measure. To further illustrate each factor, a situation is described in which a state health agency is deciding whether middle school students would be the most attractive segment for promoting safe sex. This segment would then be compared to a similar evaluation of high school students.

1. *Segment size:* How many people are in this segment? What percentage of the population do they represent? (How many middle school youth are sexually active?)

2. *Problem incidence:* How many people in this segment are either engaged in the "problem-related behavior" or not engaged in the "desired behavior"? (What percentage of middle school youth are having unprotected sex?)

3. *Problem severity:* What are the levels of consequences of the problem behavior in this segment? (What is the incidence of sexually transmitted diseases and pregnancy among middle school youth?)

4. *Defenselessness:* To what extent can this segment "take care of themselves" versus needing help from others? (What percentage of middle school youth have easy access to condoms?)

5. *Reachability:* Is this an audience that can be easily identified and reached? (Are there media channels and other venues that we can use for safe sex messages specifically targeting middle school youth?)

6. *General responsiveness:* How "ready, willing, and able" to respond are those in this segment? (How concerned are middle school youths with sexually transmitted diseases and pregnancy? How do they compare with high school students or college students in this regard? Which group has been most responsive to similar campaign messages in the past?)

7. *Incremental costs:* How do estimated costs to reach and influence this segment compare with those for other segments? (Are there free or inexpensive distribution channels for condoms for middle school youth? How does this compare with those for high school and college students? Are there campaigns from other states that have been proven to work well with middle school youth, or will we need to "start from scratch"?)

8. *Responsiveness to marketing mix:* How responsive is this market likely to be to social marketing strategies (product, price, place, and promotion)? (What are the greatest influences on middle school youths' decisions relative to their sexual activity? Will the parents of middle school youth, more so than those of high school or college students, be concerned with potential programs and messages?)

9. *Organizational capabilities:* How extensive is our staff expertise or availability to outside resources to assist in the development and implementation of activities for this market? (Is our experience and expertise with middle school youth as strong as it is with high school and college students?)

One potential evaluation methodology would use these nine factors to quantitatively score each segment, creating a rational way to then rank them. Two major steps are involved, the first calculating a *potential for effectiveness* score and the second a *potential for efficiency* score.

1. *Effectiveness scores* are determined from statistics and incidence data on four of the factors: segment size, problem incidence, problem severity, and defenselessness. The segment's population size is multiplied by percentages for incidence, severity, and defenselessness (i.e., size x incidence x severity x defenselessness). The resulting number becomes the segment's "true" market size relative to potential effectiveness.

2. *Efficiency scores* are determined from assessments of segments on the next five factors: reachability, responsiveness, incremental costs, responsiveness to marketing mix elements, and organizational capabilities. This process requires assigning some quantitative value or score to each segment relative to each factor.

HOW TARGET AUDIENCES ARE SELECTED

Market segmentation has identified and described relevant market segments. *Evaluation activities* provide information on each segment that will help you take the next step, deciding which and how many segments will be *target audiences* for the campaign or program being planned.

Three approaches are typical for commercial sector marketers and are useful concepts for the social marketer to consider:[38]

Undifferentiated marketing: The organization decides to use the same strategy for all segments, focusing on what is "common in the needs of consumers rather than on what is different."[39] This approach is sometimes referred to as *mass-marketing* and involves trying to reach and influence the most people at one time. Undifferentiated campaigns include those promoting issues of concern to a large cross section of the population (e.g., drinking eight glasses of water a day, wearing seatbelts, not drinking and driving, flossing teeth, sun protection, water conservation, learning CPR, voting, organ donation).

Differentiated marketing: The organization develops different strategies for different audiences. This approach often includes allocating more resources to priority segments. Campaigns that would benefit from a differentiated strategy are those in which segments have clear and distinguishable wants and needs as well as recommended behaviors. This approach might be used for campaigns promoting water safety, physical activity, breast cancer screening, and commute reduction.

Concentrated marketing: In this approach, some segments are eliminated altogether, and resources and efforts often concentrate on developing the ideal strategy for one or only a few key segments. Campaigns with narrow and concentrated focuses might include those promoting folic acid to women of childbearing age, encouraging horse farmers to cover manure piles to avoid contamination of streams, offering AIDS prevention outreach programs to drug abusers, or recruiting young single men as volunteers for mentoring youth at risk.

As introduced in the prior section, segments can be prioritized and ranked at this point using effectiveness and efficiency scores. This would be especially useful for campaigns using a differentiated or concentrated approach in which the most efficient and effective segments will be targeted.

WHAT APPROACH SHOULD BE CHOSEN?

Most organizations involved in social marketing (public sector agencies and nonprofit organizations) are faced with limited budgets. Segments will need to be prioritized, with a disproportionate amount of resources allocated to the most effective and efficient segments. Some segments will need to be eliminated from the plan.

Target audiences (markets of greatest opportunity) emerge as those with the greatest need and are the most ready for action, easiest to reach, and best match for the organization. Measures used to assess each of these are as follows:

- *Greatest need:* size, incidence, severity, and defenselessness
- *Most ready for action:* ready, willing, and able to respond
- *Easiest to reach:* identifiable, venues for distribution channels and communication
- *Best match:* organizational mission, expertise, and resources

Targeting audiences of *greatest market opportunity* may run counter to a social marketer's natural desire and inclination (or mandate) to either (a) ensure that all constituent groups are reached and served (markets are treated equally) or to (b) focus resources on segments in which the incidence and severity of the problem is the gravest (markets of greatest need). Concerns can be addressed by emphasizing that this is the most effective and efficient use of scarce resources, reassuring others that segmentation allows plans to be developed that are likely to succeed with individual segments, and explaining that additional segments can be addressed overtime. You are simply prioritizing resources and efforts in an objective, systematic, and cost-effective way.

ETHICAL CONSIDERATIONS WHEN SELECTING TARGET AUDIENCES

The musings at the beginning of the chapter expressing concern regarding resource allocation represent well the ethical dilemma at this phase in the planning process. In campaigns in which a majority of resources have been allocated to one or a few market segments, how do you address concerns about social inequity? Or what about reverse situations in which resources are allocated equally, when in fact only one or a few market segments have the greatest need? For example, a state water conservation effort may send messages to all residents in the state to voluntarily reduce water usage by a goal of 10% over the next six months. Take shorter showers. Flush one less time. But what if water levels and resources are actually adequate in half the state? Should residents on one side of the mountain (where it rains "all the time") be asked to make these sacrifices as well? What is fair?

Our recommendation, as it was when selecting a focus for your campaign, is that you present (or at least mention) a long-range plan that will eventually address groups you are not addressing in this phase. Additionally, as you will read in the Research Highlight at the end of this chapter, be prepared to present the rational criteria and evaluation that led to your decision to focus resources on the target audience you have selected.

CHAPTER SUMMARY

Selecting target audiences is a three-step process: (1) Segment the market, (2) evaluate segments, and (3) choose one or more segments for targeting. Traditional variables used to describe consumer markets include demographics, geographics, psychographics, and behavior variables. Five additional models frequently used by social marketing practitioners include stages of change, diffusion of innovation, Healthstyles segmentation, environmental segmentation, and generational segmentation.

Target audiences are evaluated based on efficiency and effectiveness measures, using nine variables outlined by Andreasen and presented in this text: segment size, problem incidence, problem severity, defenselessness, reachability, general responsiveness, incremental costs, responsiveness to marketing mix, and organizational capabilities.

Three common targeting approaches include undifferentiated marketing (same strategy for all segments), differentiated marketing (different strategies for different audiences), and concentrated marketing (only a few key segments are targeted and with unique strategies).

It is recommended that the markets of "greatest opportunity" be recognized as those that have the greatest need, are most ready for action, are easiest to reach, and are the best match for the organization.

RESEARCH HIGHLIGHT

"You Know Different": Barriers and Benefits Research Informing a Youth HIV Testing Campaign (2005)

Background

In the United States, youth and young adults are at persistent risk for HIV infection. This risk is especially notable for youth of minority races and ethnicities, with African-Americans accounting for 55% of all HIV infections reported among persons ages 13 to 24.[40] These high rates are due in large part to the fact that these youth are not regularly testing for HIV infection. In 2004, the National Youth Advocacy Coalition (NYAC), through a grant from the Centers for Disease Control and Prevention (CDC), designed and piloted a national model intended to enhance the organizational capacity of agencies to reach young African-American men having sex with men and gain their participation in HIV testing and retrieval of test results (*product*). A promotional effort to support increased utilization of these services was also launched, including a community-based grassroots campaign developed by the Metropolitan Group, a social marketing firm in Portland, Oregon.[41]

At the end of the first pilot, participating organizations experienced an average 153% increase in HIV testing among the target population, with African-Americans representing 58% of the young people tested. The campaign subsequently expanded geographically and into the transgender community with similar results. This research highlight focuses on the qualitative research that inspired this success.

Methodology

During the first project year, NYAC conducted 10 youth focus groups between September 2004 and January 2005. Six of the youth discussions were focused on *barriers to service utilization* and four were designed to *inform promotional efforts*. Community-based organizations assisted with youth recruitment, and groups were held in five cities in the mid-eastern, northern, and southern regions of the United States. Groups consisted of 10 to 12 youth who were provided with incentives, which included gift cards from shopping venues and transportation passes. For extremely marginalized populations (e.g., transgender and homeless youth), as well as rural youth, a cash stipend was offered. Participants were 13 to 24; 56% were lesbian, gay, or bisexual; 23% identified as transgender; 73% were African-American or Latino/a; and 12% were homeless.

Findings

When the youths were asked, "What keeps people like you from accessing HIV testing services?" four themes emerged: denial, fear, stigma, and misinformation.

- Many youths were quick to deny their risk and thought they were safe, and subsequent comments suggested these perceptions were reinforced by misinformation and myths. For example, although the participants self-identified as educated and informed about HIV/AIDS, many could not cite modes of transmission and many believed myths such as, "Tops don't get infected" and "Persons who are HIV positive knowingly spread the disease."

- Multiple expressions of *fear* kept youths from accessing HIV testing services. These included the fear of knowing you have HIV, fear of death, fear of the unknown, and fear of rejection. One reason for youths' not finding out their status was their ability to truthfully say they don't know their status. And for at least one group of young gay men, not knowing was evidently better than knowing.

- When the youths were asked what *scares* them most about knowing their HIV status, responses included "rejection by everyone," "rejection by the whole society," and the "loss of sex." Knowing your status was described as "stressful." Most of the youths continued to link HIV infection to death. Many of them believed that even if they tested negative for HIV, the fear that they would test positive later would remain.

- The *stigma* surrounding HIV, specifically testing, was a barrier expressed in multiple groups. Youths expressed being afraid of what being HIV positive meant, being afraid of being rejected, being afraid that loved ones would leave, and being afraid of being seen getting an HIV test. One female participant even stated, "I would kill myself if I found out I was HIV positive." During the rural focus group, it was expressed that a person with HIV/AIDS would be discriminated against in that town. "That person could be beat up and nobody would talk to them."

When the youths were asked to list the benefits of testing, two themes emerged: if positive, early treatment and notification of partners; if negative, "a warning to protect yourself." In terms of testing methods, youths clearly preferred the rapid test over the two-week wait period for standard testing methods.

Focus groups to inform promotional efforts explored recommended messages, the look and feel of the campaign, and media channels:

- Youths recommended that messages should be direct. They should "come hard," "give useful information," and "tell us why we should get tested."
- When asked what would be good venues or places to run prevention messages, instead of mass media, participants recommended more targeted channels including hip-hop magazines, T-shirts and posters, and direct peer outreach. The best places for posters would be at social gathering places such as clubs, movie theaters, and other community venues. A few youths suggested attending a poetry slam addressing issues such as HIV among youth, and some expressed a strong desire to perform live drama as a social marketing tool in their community.
- In terms of "look and feel," common themes included highlighting "real people" and "being direct." Also mentioned was the need for age-specific images and the inclusion of transgender images. "We want someone to represent us."

Implications

Campaign planners took these findings and recommendations seriously. Through subsequent focus groups, "You Know Different" emerged as the theme, playing on strong values of self-determination and self-respect (*positioning*)—values that were perceived to be missing from other outreach efforts. A rapid test (*product*) was chosen, and community organizations were provided training to help ensure testing would be culturally appropriate and more welcoming to youth of color (*service quality*). NYAC partnered with community-based organizations in high-impact locations to ensure that the testing was available and convenient (*place*). Community partners received posters to customize with information about their testing locations and display throughout the community. A set of palm cards carrying the campaign imagery and key messages were passed out at clubs and other youth gatherings. Peer educators and volunteers from the community organizations then blanketed their stomping grounds (e.g., clubs, balls, Chelsea Piers in New York) with these cards (see Figures 6.6 and 6.7).

As the campaign expanded further to reach new audiences and geographic areas, audience-driven research and campaigning remained at the forefront. As of this writing, the campaign was about to expand into Latino communities with a slightly modified theme, "We Know Different," reflecting the audience's assertion that they would never tell a friend to get tested, but rather would go with him.

Figure 6.6 Campaign poster.[42]

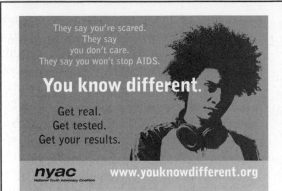

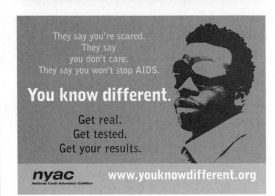
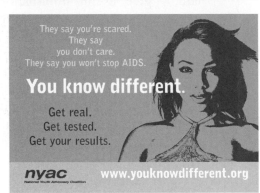

Figure 6.7 Campaign palm cards.[43]

CHAPTER 6 NOTES

1. Lefebvre, R. C. (2011). An integrative model for social marketing. *Journal of Social Marketing, 1*(1), 62.

2. Legacy. (2010, January). *Legacy's small innovative grant: Exploring promising programming in tobacco control.* Retrieved July 25, 2011, from http://www.legacyforhealth.org/PDF/SIG_Dissemination_Booklet.pdf

3. National Network on Tobacco Prevention and Poverty. (2004). *Tobacco policy, cessation, and education in correctional facilities.* West Sacramento, CA: Author.

4. Used with permission of Legacy.

5. Legacy, 2010, *Legacy's small innovative grant* (p. 18).

6. Arab American Institute. (n.d.). *Pennsylvania.* Retrieved October 6, 2009, from www.aaiusa.org/page/file/6651d8562611b437c3_y89mvyhcj.pdf/PAdemographics.pdf

7. Shara, H., Carter, E., Abu-Bader, A., Deshields, A., Fokar, A., & Howard, B. (2010). Cardiovascular disease risk factors in Arab Americans living in metropolitan Washington, DC. *Current Cardiovascular Risk Reports, 2010*(4), 181–185; Rice, V, & Kulwicki, A. (1992). Cigarette use among Arab Americans in the Detroit metropolitan area. *Public Health Reports, 107*(5), 589–594.

8. American Lung Association. (2007). *An emerging deadly trend: Waterpipe tobacco use.* Washington, DC: Author. Retrieved October 14, 2009, from http://slati.lungusa.org/reports/Trend%20Alert_Waterpipe.pdf

9. Surani, Z., et al. (2005). *South Asian needs assessment survey 2003–2005* (p. 8). Los Angeles, CA: UCLA Center for Community Partnerships, UCLA School of Public Health, and South Asian Network.

10. Glenn, B., Surani, Z., Chawla, N., Patel, M., Parikh, P., & Bastani, R. (2007, April 19). *Tobacco use and cancer screening among South Asians: Results of a community-university collaborative study.* Presentation at the Bridging the Health Care Divide Conference, American Cancer Society, New Orleans, LA. Retrieved October 9, 2009, from http://cancer.confex.com/cancer/disparities/techprogram/P1413.HTM

11. Used with permission of Legacy.

12. Kotler, P., & Armstrong, G. (2001). *Principles of marketing* (p. 265). Upper Saddle River, NJ: Prentice Hall.

13. Ibid., p. 244.

14. Ibid., pp. 253–259.

15. Ibid., p. 259.

16. Prochaska, J., & DiClemente, C. (1983). Stages and processes of self-change of smoking: Toward an integrative model of change. *Journal of Consulting and Clinical Psychology, 51,* 390–395.

17. Prochaska, J., Norcross, J., & DiClemente, C. (1994). *Changing for good* (pp. 40–56). New York, NY: Avon Books.

18. Ibid., pp. 40–41.

19. Ibid., pp. 40–41.

20. Ibid., pp. 41–43.

21. Ibid., p. 43.

22. Ibid., p. 44.

23. Ibid., p. 45.

24. Ibid., p. 46.

25. Ibid., p. 47.

26. "The Spiral of Change" From *Changing for Good* by James O. Prochaska and John C. Norcross and Carlo C. Diclemente. Copyright © 1994 by James O. Prochaska. Used by permission of the author.

27. Kotler, P., & Roberto, E. L. (1989). *Social marketing: Strategies for changing public behavior* (pp. 119, 126–127). New York, NY: Free Press.

28. Leiserowitz, A., & Maibach, E. (2010). *Global warming's "six Americas": An audience segmentation.* George Mason University, Center for Climate Change Communication, Fairfax, VA.

29. Global Warming's "Six Americans." An Audience Segmentation.

30. Kotler, P., & Keller, K. (2006). *Marketing management* (pp. 251–252). Upper Saddle River, NJ: Prentice Hall.

31. Tsui, B. (2001, January 1). Generation next. *Advertising Age, 72*(3), 14–16; Anna Liotta, Resultance Incorporated, www.resultance.com

32. Kotler & Keller, 2006, *Marketing management* (pp. 251–252).

33. PRIZM® NE. (n.d.). *The new evolution in segmentation.* Retrieved January 2, 2007, from http://www.claritas.com/claritas/Default.jsp?ci=3&si=4&pn=prizmne

34. SRI Consulting Business Intelligence (SRIC-B1).

35. Kotler & Roberto, 1989, *Social marketing* (p. 149).

36. Andreasen, A. R. (1995). *Marketing social change: Changing behavior to promote health, social development, and the environment* (p. 148). San Francisco, CA: Jossey-Bass.

37. Ibid., pp. 177–179.

38. Kotler, P., & Armstrong, G. (2001). *Principles of marketing* (pp. 265–268). Upper Saddle River, NJ: Prentice Hall.

39. Ibid., p. 266.

40. Centers for Disease Control and Prevention. (n.d.). *HIV/AIDS among youth.* Retrieved November 24, 2010, from http://www.cdc.gov/hiv/resources/factsheets/print/youth.htm

41. For more-in-depth information on this case, the National Youth Advocacy Coalition at www.nyacyouth.org has two reports: "Executive Summary of National Youth HIV Testing Data 2006" and "National Youth HIV Testing Initiative: You Know Different, Evaluation Summary of 2006 Social Marketing Pilot."

42. Used with permission of Metropolitan Group.

43. Ibid.

Chapter 7

SETTING BEHAVIOR OBJECTIVES AND GOALS

Focus. Tackle one "non-reducible" behavior at a time. As the name suggests, and Doug McKenzie-Mohr describes, a non-reducible behavior is one that cannot be divided further into more specific behaviors. This is critical, as barriers and benefits differ dramatically for different behaviors.

—Dr. Ed Maibach[1]
Director, Center for Climate Change Communication,
George Mason University

We recognize the challenges, even resistance, some of you may have when it comes to this section in the planning process—that of setting campaign objectives (desired behaviors) and target goals (levels of behavior change). Do any of the following sound familiar?

- "I always have trouble choosing among the numerous optional good behaviors we want to promote. Why do we need to (once more) narrow our focus, as we did with target audiences? It seems to me the more we can get them to do, the better."
- "When I look at this model and the use of the terms *objective* and *goal*, I get confused, even discouraged. We were taught in public health programs that goals were what we were trying to accomplish, like decrease obesity. This model says that goals are the quantifiable measure of your objective. Does it matter?"
- "This goal setting is nice in theory but near to impossible, in my experience. If we haven't done this particular behavior change campaign before, how could we possibly know what kind of a target goal or milestone to set?"

We chose this opening case to highlight the power of not only establishing clear desired behavior objectives, but also then prioritizing them based on audience research. As you will read, what the Monterey Bay Aquarium discovered after doing barriers research with their initial upstream priority audience, the fisheries, was that they would have to go downstream first, to consumers.

MARKETING HIGHLIGHT

Seafood Watch: Influencing Sustainable Seafood Choices (2010)

Background

The Monterey Bay Aquarium in California envisions a world where our oceans are healthy and people are committed to protecting the integrity of Earth's natural systems. When it opened its doors in 1984, the global catch of wild fish had nearly peaked. That catch is now in decline, and as of 2010 it is anticipated that farmed species will for the first time overtake wild-caught fish as the leading source of seafood in the human diet.[2]

To help make its vision of healthy oceans a reality, in 1999 the aquarium created the Seafood Watch program to influence sustainable seafood choices, where sustainable seafood is defined as coming from sources, whether fished or farmed, that maintain or increase production without jeopardizing affected ecosystems.[3] With an estimated two thirds of all U.S. seafood (by dollar value) reaching consumers through restaurants and an additional 24% sold through retail outlets, consumers have an unprecedented opportunity to assist ocean conservation efforts through sustainable seafood choices.[4] As you will read, the aquarium's strategy is to use innovative tools that address audience barriers and create incentives that increase marketplace demand for sustainable seafood. Its outcomes, both short term and long term, are inspiring.[5]

Target Audiences and Desired Behaviors

The following planned chain of events reflects the program's strategic intent to influence audiences *downstream* (consumers) to request and make purchases that then influence audiences *midstream* (e.g., restaurants, food service companies, grocery stores, and fish markets) to persuade those *upstream* (wholesalers and the fishing/aquaculture industry) to change their practices. They began with the end in mind:

1. Consumers decide to buy more (or only) sustainable seafood

2. Consumers start asking questions and making requests at restaurants, grocery stores, and fish markets, creating salience for the sustainable seafood issue

3. These purveyors work with their suppliers to increase availability of sustainable seafood

4. Suppliers shift purchasing

5. In response to customer demand from major buyers, the fishing/aquaculture industry changes its harvesting practices or shifts to a different operation

The priority initial consumer audience was identified as "green consumers," those a 2004 survey of 3,690 Americans revealed are likely to be opinion leaders, information seekers, interested in new products, careful in their shopping habits, and, perhaps most important, actively engaged in sharing product information related to the environment with others.[6] This audience was also a "natural" for the aquarium, as they represent a significant portion of its visitors, as well as those of sister zoos and aquariums.

This case example will focus primarily on strategies used to influence consumers, and how their actions ultimately influenced audiences further upstream.

Audience Insights

Perceived barriers to purchasing sustainable seafood at the time were significant, even for the "green" consumer:

- Lack of information on sustainable choices at point of purchase, whether in stores or restaurants
- A feeling of being overwhelmed with information to take into consideration when buying
- A concern that sustainable seafood would be more expensive
- Lack of trust in recommendations—concerns about "What is their agenda?" and "How do they know this fish is sustainable and this one isn't?"
- Interest in knowing how, if at all, sustainable seafood choices relate to better personal health

The primary benefit for this environmentally oriented target audience was to contribute to a sustainable supply of seafood.

Strategies

The *products* Seafood Watch has created over the past decade tackle many of these barriers head on.

The initiative began with the Seafood Watch Pocket Guides, one for each of six regions in the United States (see Figure 7.1). More than a promotion, this card is designed for point-of-purchase decision making. The most popular seafood options in each region are listed as either green (best choices), yellow (good alternatives), or red (avoid). To address health concerns, an asterisk (*) following any of the items listed warns that consumption should be limited because of concerns about mercury or other contaminants. And to address potential concerns with the credibility of the recommendations, information on the Seafood Watch Web site explains that categorizations are determined based on reports generated by the aquarium's scientists, who review government studies, journal articles, and white papers. From these reports, recommendations are developed and updated every six months. In 2009, a new iPhone application was offered, loading the right guide for the current location using the phone's GPS. The application offers the ability to sort seafood by rank or to search for a rank for a specific fish (see Figure 7.2).

Pocket guides are free, including shipping, as is the iPhone application (*price*). A link to download the iPhone application is provided on the Seafood Watch Web site. Outreach partners are key to distribution of pocket guides, with aquariums, zoos, and restaurants in major metropolitan areas around the country extending the reach of the guide (*place*).

Figure 7.1 Seafood Watch pocket guide.[7]

Figure 7.2 Seafood Watch iPhone application.[8]

Seafood Watch raises consumer awareness primarily through its pocket guides, Web site, mobile applications, a presence on Facebook and Twitter, and special events (*promotion*). As the program has gained credibility, it has been featured in a broad array of popular media—from Oprah Winfrey's *O* magazine to Martha Stewart's television program, and from the *New York Times* and *TIME* magazine to Web sites including TreeHugger.com and Grist.org.

Results

Evaluations were conducted for audiences downstream, midstream, and upstream: consumers, partners, retailers, suppliers, and fisheries.

Consumer Outputs and Outcomes

- *Pocket guides:* By 2010, more than 34 million guides reached the pockets of consumers across the United States. Most were distributed by partners in epicenters, including more than 900,000 to visitors at the Monterey Bay Aquarium alone. Each year, several hundred thousand guides are inserted or reprinted in publications. In 2007, a unique partnership with Warner Brothers Studios inserted 9 million pocket guides in the DVDs of the award-winning film *Happy Feet.*

- *Web site.* In 2009 alone, there were 535,559 visitor sessions to seafood-watch.org, a 43% increase over 2008. There were more than 1 million page views and more than 200,000 visits the week the *State of Seafood Report* was released.
- *Special events:* Annual Cooking for Solutions events are attended by close to 6,000 people, and additional presentations at various conferences, trade shows, and special events reach an audience of more than 10,000 each year.
- *Advocates:* To date (2010), more than 1,200 people have agreed to be program advocates and to have their activities tracked via regular e-mail surveys. Surveys completed by a subset of advocates indicated that a majority distributed at least one of the items, 18% distributed everything in the action kit, and nearly two thirds (63%) approached at least one restaurant with the materials.

Partnership Outcomes

By 2010, 161 partnerships had been formed with nonprofit organizations, quasi-government agencies, and businesses. These include 67 *full partners*, organizations that have formally agreed to distribute at least 10,000 pocket guides per year, develop displays, exhibits, or educational curricula to interpret the pocket guide, and conduct outreach activities in their area; 45 *associate partners* who commit to distributing 5,000 pocket guides per year; and 49 *business partners*, primarily restaurants that pledge to remove all items listed in the red "avoid" column from their menu.

Retail Outcomes

Several leading supermarket retailers in the U.S. now have sustainable seafood sourcing policies in place. In January 2010, for example, Target committed to eliminate all farmed salmon and Safeway agreed to stop selling grouper, red snapper (*Lutjanus campechanus*), and monkfish— species it said have been overfished.

Supplier Outcomes

Two of the largest food service companies in the U.S., Compass Group North America and Aramark, have made sustainable seafood commitments through agreements with the Monterey Bay Aquarium.

STEP 4: SET OBJECTIVES AND TARGET GOALS

Once target audiences for a campaign have been selected, your next step is to establish *campaign objectives*, with the primary objective always being the very specific *behaviors* you want to influence your audience to accept, modify, abandon, or reject. As you will read, the key to success is to select single, doable objectives—and then explain them in simple, clear terms.

This chapter presents examples of the three types of objectives associated with a social marketing campaign:

1. *Behavior objectives* (what you want your audience to do)

2. *Knowledge objectives* (what you want your audience to know)

3. *Belief objectives* (what you want your audience to believe or feel)

A social marketing campaign always has a behavior objective. When and if you determine there is something your audience needs to know or believe in order to "act," that objective is identified and incorporated as well. As will become clear, campaign objectives (e.g., buy "green" fish) are different from the campaign purpose (e.g., increase supply of sustainable fish), defined earlier in this model as the ultimate impact of a successful campaign on the social issue being addressed.

After determining campaign objectives, campaign *target goals* are established that are specific, measurable, attainable, relevant, and time sensitive (SMART).[9] Ideally, they specify targeted rates of change in behaviors, such as the increase in numbers of those in the target audience who will be performing the desired behavior at some future date. They may also establish desired changes in knowledge and belief, especially in cases where behavior change may be a long-term effort. We recognize that in some models, such as those used in public health, goals are the nonquantifiable components of a campaign. These, however, are usually referred to as "overarching goals." Target goals at this step in the planning process refer to campaign goals. This social marketing model is based on commercial marketing models, where goals are expressed as "sales goals." We recommend, however, that you feel free to reverse these labels to match your organization's language and culture.

Remember the comment in the second chapter that this planning model should be considered spiral in nature? Objectives and goals established at this point should be considered *draft objectives* and *target goals*. You may learn in Step 5, for example, when you "talk" with your target audience about these desired behaviors, that your objectives and target goals are not realistic, clear, and/or appropriate for them and should be revised. Your audience may express a misconception that will require an additional knowledge objective, or an attitude that a new belief objective will need to address. Or you might find when developing preliminary budgets that you will need to reduce your goals because of funding realities.

As a final overview of this step, keep in mind that objectives and goals will affect your campaign evaluation strategy. Given that campaign goals represent the foundation for campaign evaluation, it is crucial that goals are relevant to campaign efforts and are able to be measured.

Table 7.1 illustrates key concepts that will be presented in this chapter, using an example of an effort that might be undertaken by a state department of transportation to reduce traffic injuries and deaths caused by drivers distracted while using cell phones.

Table 7.1 Example of a Campaign's Purpose, Focus, Objectives, and Goal

Campaign Purpose	Reduce traffic injuries and deaths
Focus	Cell phone usage while driving
Campaign Objectives	
Behavior Objective	To wait until you arrive at your destination to use your cell phone
Knowledge Objective	To know the percentage of traffic accidents involving someone talking on a cell phone
Belief Objective	To believe that talking on a cell phone, even a hands-free model, can be a distraction
Target Goal	Increase the number of people who wait to use their cell phones by 25% in one year

BEHAVIOR OBJECTIVES

All social marketing campaigns should be designed and planned with a specific behavior objective in mind. Even if the planner discovers that the campaign needs to include additional knowledge and belief objectives, a behavior objective will need to be identified that these additional elements will support. As you develop and consider potential behavior objectives for your efforts, the following five criteria should help you choose one(s) with the greatest potential for meaningful change, or at least assist you in prioritizing them:

1. *Impact:* If your audience adopts the behavior, will it make a difference relative to the purpose of your campaign (e.g., decreasing teen pregnancies)? How does this compare with other behaviors being considered?

2. *Willingness:* Has your target audience heard of doing this behavior before? How willing or interested are they in doing this behavior? Do they perceive it will solve some problem or concern they have, or will it satisfy some unfulfilled need?

3. *Measurability:* Can the behavior be measured, either through observation, record keeping, or self-reporting? You should be able to "picture" your target audience performing the behavior (e.g., removing the plastic insert from the cereal box before sorting for recycling). And your target audience should be able to determine that they have performed the behavior (e.g., placing infants in cribs on their backs to reduce the risk of infant death).

4. *Market opportunity:* How many in the target audience are not currently doing the behavior? What, in other terminology, is the current penetration of this behavior? A behavior that few have adopted would garner a high score in terms of market opportunity.

5. *Market supply:* Does the behavior need more support? If some other organization is already "doing all that can be done" to influence this behavior, perhaps a different behavior would be more beneficial to the social issue.

At the end of Al Gore's book *An Inconvenient Truth*, 30 specific desired behaviors to reduce carbon emissions are listed. Ten were then selected for a handout titled *tenthingstodo* and make an interesting prioritization exercise that could be approached using a grid like the one in Table 7.2.[10] Assume that once launched, efforts would then focus on highlighting two behaviors each year based on scores for each of the five criteria just mentioned. To keep it simple, each behavior could be rated on each criterion as high (3), medium (2), or low (1), as illustrated in the first row. Ideally, these would be determined using objective information (e.g., citizen surveys, scientific data). In reality, it might be more subjective in nature—which is still better than prioritizing them based on less rigorous ways, such as informal conversations or hunches.

Table 7.2 Process for Prioritizing Behavior Objectives: High (3), Medium (2), Low (1)

Behaviors	Impact	Willingness	Measurability	Market Opportunity	Supply	Average
Change a light	2	3	3	3	1	2.4
Drive less						
Recycle more						
Check your tires						
Use less hot water						
Avoid products with a lot of packaging						
Adjust your thermostat						
Plant a tree						
Turn off electronic devices						
Spread the word						

To increase the rigor (and value) of the exercise, you could also weight the criteria. For example, you could understandably decide that "Impact" was more important than other criteria and decide to double the score ($2 \times 2 = 4$). That way, something that was low impact (1) but had the highest scores on other criteria would not automatically surface as the number one priority.

A behavior objective should be distinguished from several other planning components. It is not the same as a campaign slogan or campaign message, although it is used to develop both (e.g., "Eat five or more fruits and vegetables a day" became "5 a Day the Color Way^{TM}"). It is not quantifiable as we are defining it. The target goal is the quantifiable, measurable component that has implications for strategies and budget decisions and provides a benchmark for monitoring and measuring program success (e.g., did the average consumption of the number of fruits and vegetables increase from 2.5 to 4 per day by 2010?).

If you are familiar with logic models, you may be curious where social marketing objectives fit in the model. They should be noted as "Outcomes" in the traditional model, reflecting behaviors changed as the result of program "Outputs."

For those not familiar with logic models, these are visual schematics that show links between program processes (inputs, activities, and outputs) and program outcomes and impact. This tool will be discussed in more depth in Chapter 15, which covers evaluation.

Although a campaign may promote more than one behavior, it should be recognized that different tactics or strategies might be necessary to promote each one (e.g., getting people to use a litterbag will take different strategies than getting people to cover their loads in pickup trucks). Table 7.3 presents examples of potential behavior objectives in our familiar arenas of health, injury prevention, the environment, and community and financial well-being.

KNOWLEDGE AND BELIEF OBJECTIVES

When gathering background data and conducting the strengths, weaknesses, opportunities, and threats (SWOT) analysis, you probably learned from existing secondary research or from prior similar campaigns that typical audiences need a little help before they are willing, sometimes even able, to act. They may need to have some *knowledge* (information or facts) and/or *belief* (values, opinions, or attitudes) before they are convinced that the action is doable and/or worth the effort. Those in the precontemplation stage, for example, typically don't believe they have a problem. Those in the contemplation stage may not have made up their mind that the effort (cost) is worth the gain (benefit). Even those in the action stage may not be aware of their accomplishments and therefore be vulnerable to relapses.

Knowledge objectives are those relating to statistics, facts, and other information and skills your target audience would find motivating or important. Typically, the information has simply been unavailable to the audience or unnoticed. Here are examples:

- Statistics on risks associated with current behavior (e.g., percentage of obese women who have heart attacks versus those not medically obese)

Table 7.3 Examples of Potential Behavior Objectives for Specific Audiences

Improving Health	
Tobacco use	Don't start smoking.
Heavy/binge drinking	Drink less than five drinks at one sitting.
Alcohol and drug use during pregnancy	Don't drink alcoholic beverages if you are pregnant.
Physical inactivity	Exercise moderately 30 minutes a day, 5 days a week, at least 10 minutes at a time.
Teen pregnancy	Choose abstinence.
Sexually transmitted diseases	Use a condom.
Fat gram intake	Make sure total fat grams consumed are below 30% of total daily calories.
Water intake	Drink eight glasses of water a day.
Fruit and vegetable intake	Eat five servings of fruits and vegetables a day.
Obesity	Have your body mass index measured by a health care professional.
Breast cancer	Learn the proper procedure for examining your breasts.
Prostate cancer	Talk with your health care provider about an annual prostate exam if you are 50 years of age or older.
Oral health	Use a cup to give an infant juice instead of a bottle.
Osteoporosis	Get 1,000 to 1,200 milligrams a day of calcium.
Avian flu	Limit sources of food for wild and free-flying birds.
Preventing Injuries	
Drinking and driving	Keep your blood alcohol level below 0.08% if you are drinking and driving.
Seatbelts	Buckle your seatbelt before you put your vehicle in gear.
Domestic violence	Have a plan that includes a packed bag and a safe place to go.
Gun storage	Store handguns in a lockbox or safe or use a reliable trigger lock.
Fires	Check smoke alarm batteries every month.
Falls	Include some form of strength building in your exercise routine.
Household poisons	Place recognizable stickers on all poisonous products in the kitchen, bathroom, bedroom, basement, and garage.

(Continued)

Table 7.3 (Continued)

Protecting the Environment	
Waste reduction	Buy bulk and unpackaged goods rather than packaged items.
Wildlife habitat protection	Stay on established paths when walking through forests.
Forest destruction	Use materials made from recycled tires and glass for garden steps and paths.
Toxic fertilizers and pesticides	Follow instructions on labels and measure precisely.
Water conservation	Replace old toilets with new low-flow models.
Air pollution from automobiles	Don't top off the gas tank when refueling your car.
Air pollution from other sources	Use an electric or push mower instead of a gas-powered model.
Forest fires	Chip wood debris that can be used for composting instead of burning it.
Conserving electricity	Turn off computer monitors when leaving work at the end of the day.
Litter	Clean out litter that might blow out of the open back of your pickup truck.
Involving the Community	
Volunteering	Give five hours a week to a volunteer effort.
Mentoring	Encourage and support caring relationships between your child and a nonparent adult.
Enhancing Financial Well-Being	
Bank accounts	Open a checking account.
Savings	Build a savings account equivalent to six months of income.
Using credit	Establish a monthly budget and follow it.

- Statistics on benefits of proposed behavior (e.g., the amount of money you will have saved in a year by making small monthly deposits)
- Facts on attractive alternatives (e.g., lists of flowering native plants that are drought and disease resistant)
- Facts that correct misconceptions (e.g., cigarette butts are not biodegradable and can take more than 10 years to disintegrate completely)
- Facts that might be motivating (e.g., moderate physical activity has been proven to have some of the same important medical benefits as vigorous physical activity)

- Information on how to perform the behavior (e.g., how to prepare a home for an earthquake)
- Resources available for assistance (e.g., phone numbers where battered women can call to find temporary shelter)
- Locations for purchase of goods or services (e.g., locations where handgun lock-boxes can be purchased)
- Current laws and fines that may not be known or understood (e.g., a fine of $1,025 can be imposed for tossing a lit cigarette)

Belief objectives are those relating to attitudes, opinions, feelings, or values held by the target audience. The target audience may have current beliefs that the marketer may need to alter in order for them to act, or you may find that an important belief is missing, such as one of the following:

- That they will personally experience the benefits from adopting the desired behavior (e.g., increased physical activity will help them sleep better).
- That they are at risk (e.g., they currently believe they are capable of driving safely with a blood alcohol level of over 0.08).
- That they will be able to successfully perform the desired behavior (e.g., talk to their teenager about thoughts of suicide).
- That their individual behavior can make a difference (e.g., taking mass transit to work).
- That they will not be viewed negatively by others if they adopt the behavior (e.g., not accepting another drink).
- That the costs of the behavior will be worth it (e.g., establishing a bank account versus cashing paychecks at check cashing services and pawn shops).
- That there will be minimal negative consequences (e.g., worrying that organ donation information might be shared with third parties).

These knowledge and belief objectives provide direction for developing subsequent strategies (positioning and the marketing mix). They have important implications *especially for developing a brand identity and key messages* that provide the information and arguments that will be most motivating. Advertising copywriters, for example, will reference these objectives when developing communication slogans, script, and copy. There are also opportunities for other elements of the marketing mix to support these additional objectives: for instance, an immunization product strategy that incorporates a wallet-sized card to ensure that parents know the recommended schedule; an incentive offered by a utility for trading in gas mowers for mulch mowers as a way to convince homeowners of their harm to the environment; or a special Web site dedicated to purchasing booster seats, sponsored by a children's hospital, as a testimonial to the safety concern.

Table 7.4 Purpose, Audience, and Objectives

Campaign Purpose	Target Audience	Behavior Objective	Knowledge Objective	Belief Objective
Reduced senior falls	Seniors 75 and older	Exercise five times a week, including strength and balance.	One in three adults age 65 and older falls each year.	Risk of falling can be reduced by strengthening muscles and improving balance.
Reduced child injuries from automobile accidents	Parents with children ages 4 to 8	Put children who are ages 4 to 8 and weigh less than 80 pounds in booster seats.	Traffic accidents are the leading cause of death for children ages 4 to 8.	Children ages 4 to 8 weighing less than 80 pounds are not adequately protected by adult seatbelts.
Improved water quality	Small horse farmers within 5 miles of streams, lakes, or rivers	Cover and protect manure piles from rain.	Storm water runoff from piles can pollute water resources.	Even though your manure pile is small, it does contribute to the problem.
Increased number of registered organ donors	People renewing driver's licenses	Register to be an organ donor when you renew your driver's license.	Your family may still be asked to sign a consent form for your donation to occur.	Information will be kept private and can only be accessed by authorized officials.
Decreased number of unbanked in San Francisco	Residents relying on check cashers, pawn shops, and other fringe financial services charging high fees and interest rates	Open a Bank on San Francisco account, one established by a public-private partnership	These accounts offer a low- or no-cost product with no minimum balance; consular identification cards are accepted as primary identification.	Participating banks will be easy to find; you will feel welcomed.

Table 7.4 provides examples of each of the objectives described. It should be noted that even though each campaign illustrated has a knowledge and belief objective, this is neither typical nor required. As stated earlier, the behavior objective is the primary focus.

TARGET GOALS

Ideally, target goals establish a desired level of behavior *change* as a result of program efforts (e.g., from 10% of homeowners who check for leaky toilets on an annual basis to 20% in one year). To establish this target for the amount or percentage of change, you will, of course, need to know current levels of behavior among your target audience. In this regard you are similar to commercial marketers, who establish sales goals for their products when developing annual marketing plans and then develop strategies and resource allocations consistent with these goals. Consider how the specificity and time-bound nature of the following goals would inspire and guide your planning and eventually help justify your resource expenditures:

- Increase by 25% in a 24-month period the percentage of women over the age of 50 in the country who get annual mammograms
- Increase the percentage of people in the state wearing seatbelts at checkpoints from 85% in 2011 to 90% by 2014
- Decrease the amount of glass, paper, aluminum, and plastic litter on interstate road-ways by 4 million pounds in two years
- Increase the average number of caring adults in the lives of middle school youth in the school district from 1.5 to 3.0 over a period of three years

Target goals may also be set for knowledge and belief objectives, as illustrated in Table 7.5. Although the goals are hypothetical for the purposes of this illustration, the effort to increase the intake of folic acid as a way to prevent birth defects is real. The U.S. Public Service and the March of Dimes recommend that all women of childbearing age consume 400 micrograms of folic acid per day in a multivitamin in addition to eating a healthy diet (see Figure 7.3).

In reality, this process is difficult or impractical for many social marketing programs. Baseline data on current levels of behavior for a target audience may not be

Table 7.5 Hypothetical Objectives and Target Goals

Purpose	Behavior	Knowledge	Belief
Reduce birth defects	What we want them to do	What they may need to know before they will act	What they may need to believe before they will act
Objective	Get 400 micrograms of folic acid every day	For it to help, you need to take it before you become pregnant, during the early weeks of pregnancy (see Figure 7.3).	Without enough folic acid, the baby is at risk for serious birth defects.
Target Goal	Increase the percentage of women ages 18 to 45 who take a daily vitamin containing folic acid from 39% in 2008 to 50% by 2012.	Increase the percentage of women ages 18 to 45 who know folic acid should be taken before pregnancy from 11% in 2008 to 15% by 2001.	Increase the percentage of women ages 18 to 45 who believe folic acid prevents birth defects from 20% in 2008 to 30% by 2012.

Figure 7.3 Promoting daily use of a vitamin before pregnancy.[11]

known or may not be available in a timely or economically feasible way. Projecting future desired levels (goal setting) often depends on data and experience from years of tracking and analyzing the impact of prior efforts. Many social marketing efforts are conducted for the first time, and historical data may not have been recorded or retained.

There are several excellent resources in the public health arena you can explore, however, that may provide data that guide efforts to establish baselines as well as goals.

- The Behavioral Risk Factor Surveillance System (BRFSS) was developed by the Centers for Disease Control and Prevention (CDC), headquartered in Atlanta, Georgia. It is used throughout the United States to measure and track the prevalence of major risk-related behaviors among Americans, including tobacco use, sexual behavior, injury prevention, physical activity, nutrition, and prevention behaviors, such as breast, cervical, and colorectal cancer screening. Details on this system are highlighted in Box 7.1.
- *Healthy People 2020* is managed by the Office of Disease Prevention and Health Promotion within the U.S. Department of Health and Human Services. It is a set of objectives with 10-year target goals designed to guide national health promotion and disease prevention efforts to improve the health of all people in the United States (see Box 7.2). It is used as a strategic management tool by the federal government, states, communities, and other public and private sector partners. Its set of objectives and targets is used to measure progress for health issues in specific populations and serves as a foundation for prevention and wellness activities across various sectors and within the federal government, as well as a model for measurement at the state and local levels.[12] Of interest to social marketers is the inclusion, for the first time, of three objectives related to social marketing (see Box 7.3).

- Explore availability of data from peers in other agencies who may have conducted similar campaigns.
- Often nonprofit organizations and foundations with a related mission (e.g., the American Cancer Society) may have excellent data helpful to establishing meaningful campaign goals.

Box 7.1
CDC's Unique State-Based Surveillance

In the early 1980s, CDC worked with the states to develop the Behavioral Risk Factor Surveillance System (BRFSS). This state-based system, the first of its kind, made available information on the prevalence of risk-related behaviors among Americans and their perceptions of a variety of health issues. (See Figure 7.4.)

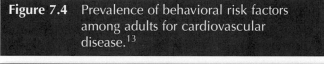

Figure 7.4 Prevalence of behavioral risk factors among adults for cardiovascular disease.[13]

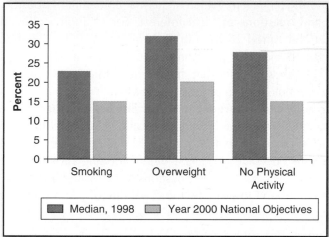

Now active in all 50 states, the BRFSS continues to be the primary source of information on major health risk behaviors among Americans. State and local health departments rely heavily on BRFSS data to:

- Determine priority health issues and identify populations at highest risk
- Develop strategic plans and target prevention programs
- Monitor the effectiveness of intervention strategies and progress toward achieving prevention goals

(Continued)

(Continued)

- Educate the public, the health community, and policy makers about disease prevention
- Support community policies that promote health and prevent disease

In addition, BRFSS data enable public health professionals to monitor progress toward achieving the nation's health objectives outlined in *Healthy People 2020: National Health Promotion and Disease Prevention Objectives*. BRFSS information is also used by researchers, volunteer and professional organizations, and managed care organizations to target prevention efforts.

The benefits of the BRFSS for states include the following:

- **Data can be analyzed in a variety of ways.** BRFSS data can be analyzed by a variety of demographic variables, including age, education, income, and racial and ethnic background. The ability to determine populations at highest risk is essential in effectively targeting scarce prevention resources.
- **The BRFSS is designed to identify trends over time.** For example, state-based data from the BRFSS have revealed a national epidemic of obesity.
- **States can add questions of local interest.** For example, following the bomb explosion at the Alfred P. Murrah Federal Building in Oklahoma City, the Oklahoma BRFSS included questions on such issues as stress, nightmares, and feelings of hopelessness so that health department personnel could better address the psychological impact of the disaster.
- **States can readily address urgent and emerging health issues.** Questions may be added for a wide range of important health issues, including diabetes, oral health, arthritis, tobacco use, folic acid consumption, use of preventive services, and health care coverage. In 1993, when flooding ravaged states along the Mississippi River, Missouri added questions to assess the impact of the flooding on people's health and to evaluate the capability of communities to respond to the disaster.

Although the BRFSS is flexible and allows for timely additions, standard core questions enable health professionals to make comparisons between states and derive national-level conclusions. BRFSS data have highlighted wide disparities between states on key health issues. In 2010, for example, the prevalence of current smoking among U.S. adults ranged from a low of 9% in Utah to a high of 27% in West Virginia. These data have also been useful for assessing tobacco control efforts. For instance, BRFSS data revealed that the annual prevalence of cigarette smoking among adults in Massachusetts declined after an excise tax increase and antismoking campaign were implemented.

Box 7.2
Healthy People 2020: Topic Areas

These topic areas of *Healthy People 2020* identify and highlight specific issues and populations. Each topic area is assigned to one or more lead agencies within the federal government that is responsible for developing, tracking, monitoring, and periodically reporting on objectives.

1. Access to Health Services	21. Heart Disease and Stroke
2. Adolescent Health	22. HIV
3. Arthritis, Osteoporosis, and Chronic Back Conditions	23. Immunization and Infectious Diseases
	24. Injury and Violence Prevention
4. Blood disorders and Blood Safety	25. Lesbian, Gay, Bisexual, and Transgender Health
5. Cancer	26. Maternal, Infant, and Child Health
6. Chronic Kidney Disease	27. Medical Product Safety
7. Dementias, Including Alzheimer's Disease	28. Mental Health and Mental Disorders
8. Diabetes	29. Nutrition and Weight Status
9. Disability and Health	30. Occupational Safety and Health
10. Early and Middle Childhood	31. Older Adults
11. Educational and Community-Based Programs	32. Oral Health
12. Environmental Health	33. Physical Activity
13. Family Planning	34. Preparedness
14. Food Safety	35. Public Health Infrastructure
15. Genomics	36. Respiratory Diseases
16. Global Health	37. Sexually Transmitted Diseases
17. Healthcare-Associated Infections	38. Sleep Health
18. Health Communication and Health Information Technology	39. Social Determinants of Health
	40. Substance Abuse
19. Health-Related Quality of Life and Well-Being	41. Tobacco Use
20. Hearing and Other Sensory or Communication Disorders	42. Vision

Source: U.S. Department of Health and Human Services, Office of Disease Prevention and Health Promotion, ODPHP Publication No. Bp132, November 2010, www.healthypeople.gov

Box 7.3
Healthy People 2020: Health Communications and Health Information Technology Objectives Related to Social Marketing

#13 To increase social marketing in health promotion and disease prevention:

    13.1 Increase the proportion of State health departments that report using social marketing in health promotion and disease prevention programs

(Continued)

(Continued)

13.2 Increase the proportion of schools of public health and accredited master of public health (MPH) programs that offer one or more courses in social marketing

13.3 Increase the proportion of schools of public health and accredited MPH programs that offer workforce development activities in social marketing for public health practitioners

Source: HealthyPeople.gov Health Topics & Objectives http://www.healthypeople.gov/2020/topicsobjectives2020/overview.aspx?topicid=18

Alternatives for Goal Setting

If baseline data are not available and setting target goals relative to behavior change is not practical or feasible at the time, the following alternatives might be considered for goal setting:

- Establish target goals for campaign awareness and recall. For example, a statewide tobacco prevention program establishes a goal for the first three months of an advertising campaign that 75% of the target audience (adults who smoke) will correctly recall the campaign slogan and two of the four television ads on an unaided basis. Results will then be presented to the state legislature to support continued funding of the campaign.
- Establish target goals for levels of knowledge. For example, a program for improved nutrition among low-income families sets a goal that 50% of women participating in a pilot project will correctly identify and describe the recommended daily servings of fruits and vegetables.
- Establish goals for acceptance of a belief. For example, a chain of gas stations is conducting a pilot project to influence customers not to top off their gas tanks and establishes a goal that 80% of customers, versus 25% prior to launch of the campaign, will report they believe topping off a gas tank can be harmful to the environment.
- Establish target goals for a response to a campaign component. For example, a water utility will consider a campaign a success if 25% of residential customers call a well-publicized toll-free number or visit a Web site for a listing of drought-resistant plants.
- Establish target goals for intent to change behavior. For example, a state coalition promoting moderate physical activity is eager to know if a brief six-week pilot program increased interest in physical activity. They establish a goal that states their

"reported intention to increase physical activity in the next six months from 20% to 30%, a 50% increase in behavior intent."

- Establish target goals for the campaign process. For example, a school-based program promoting sexual abstinence has a goal that 40 abstinence campaigns will be developed and implemented by youth in middle schools and high schools around the state during the upcoming school year.

In situations such as these, in which campaign goals are not specifically related to behavior change, it should be emphasized that campaign objectives should still include a behavior objective. Alternative goals relate to some activity that supports and promotes the desired behavior.

OBJECTIVES AND TARGET GOALS ARE ONLY A DRAFT AT THIS STEP

In Step 5 of this planning process, you will deepen your understanding of your target audience. You will learn more about their knowledge, beliefs, and current behavior relative to objectives and goals established at this point. It is often necessary to then revise and finalize objectives and goals that are more realistic, clear, and appropriate.

OBJECTIVES AND TARGET GOALS WILL BE USED FOR CAMPAIGN EVALUATION

One of the last steps (Step 8) in developing a social marketing plan will be to develop an evaluation plan, a process covered in Chapter 15. It is important to emphasize at this point, however, that the planner will need to return to Step 4 of the plan, setting campaign objectives and goals, and select methodologies and develop plans to measure these stated goals. For the examples presented in this chapter, the following items would need to be measured:

- Number of mammograms among women in the pilot community
- Number of people stopped at checkpoints wearing seatbelts
- Pounds of specific types of litter on roadways
- Number of caring adult relationships that middle school youth have
- Number of women in childbearing years taking folic acid
- Number of bank accounts opened by the unbanked in San Francisco

The message is simple. Establish a goal that is meaningful to campaign efforts and that will be feasible to measure.

ETHICAL CONSIDERATIONS WHEN SETTING OBJECTIVES AND TARGET GOALS

What if trends indicate that a behavior objective you are planning to support (e.g., putting foodwaste in curbside pickup containers) is in conflict with the desired behaviors for other agency programs (e.g., backyard composting)? Or what if your research reveals that the goals that your funders or sponsors would like to support are not realistic or attainable for your target audience? For example, a community clinic may know they are to encourage pregnant women to quit smoking—completely. But what if research has shown that cutting down to nine cigarettes a day would have significant benefits for those not able to quit? Can the clinic consider their efforts a success if they persuade pregnant women to decrease from 24 cigarettes a day to nine? Do they suggest a more attainable behavior (maybe using the foot-in-the-door technique) for this segment instead of just sending a "quit" message?

CHAPTER SUMMARY

The primary objective of a social marketing campaign is behavior change. All social marketing campaigns should be designed and planned with a specific behavior objective in mind, something we want our target audience to do. Behavior objectives should be clear, simple, doable acts—ones that can be measured and that the target audience will know they have completed.

Occasionally, the social marketer will also need to establish one or two additional objectives. *Knowledge objectives* (something you want your target audience to know) are those relating to statistics, facts, and other information your target audience would find motivating or important. *Belief objectives* (something you want your target audience to believe) are those relating to attitudes, opinions, or values held by the target audience. The target audience may have current beliefs that the marketer will need to alter in order for them to act, or an important belief may be found missing.

Target goals are quantifiable, measurable, and relate to the specific campaign focus, target audience, and time frame. Ideally, they establish a desired level of behavior change as a result of program and campaign efforts. When establishing and measuring behavior change is not practical or economically feasible, alternatives can be considered, including measuring campaign awareness, response, process, and/or increase in knowledge, beliefs, and intention.

Given that campaign target goals represent the foundation for campaign evaluation, it is critical that goals are relevant to program efforts and measurable.

RESEARCH HIGHLIGHT

Reducing Tractor Rollover Injuries and Deaths:
A Social Marketing Approach That Makes It Look Easy
(2006)

Sometimes, even often, the social marketer's job is to influence a target audience to purchase and properly use existing consumer products (e.g., vegetables, emergency preparedness kits, booster seats, organic fertilizers). Critical to success is understanding why target audiences are not currently buying, what would make the difference, and then working with interested private sector partners to make efforts easy and affordable. That's just what a team at the Northeast Center for Agricultural and Occupational Health (NEC) in New York did, including Julie Sorensen, who works at NEC and provided information for this case.[14]

Of particular interest in this highlight is the use of research at every step: *exploratory research* to understand the problem and identify target audiences; *formative research* to gain insights into audience barriers, motivators, the competition, and influential others; *pretest research* to choose among several potential messages, messengers, creative strategies, and communication channels; and an *evaluation* that inspired other states to replicate the campaign and the *Wall Street Journal* and *USA Today* to write about it.

Exploratory Research

Farming has the highest fatality rate of any industry in the U.S., and tractor overturns are the most frequent cause.[15] Of interest to NCE was research showing that these injuries and deaths are easily prevented by retrofitting unprotected tractors with rollover protective structures (ROPS) that are 99% effective in the event of tractor overturn.[16] And yet, only 59% of U.S. tractors were equipped with these lifesaving structures.[17] NCE's exploratory research also revealed that previous interventions had been largely education focused, seemingly content with simply making farmers aware of the dangers of overturns. Concern with this communications-only approach, however, was confirmed by research in New York State in 2006 indicating that these efforts had indeed increased farmers' awareness of overturn risk but had done little to motivate them to retrofit their tractors.[18] Knowledge wasn't the barrier. Secondary research also indicated that small crop and livestock farmers represented roughly 85% of New York farms that were either completely lacking any ROPS-equipped tractors or had only one tractor that was equipped. NCE had found its target audience.

Formative Research and Strategic Response

Although team interviews with farmers identified numerous barriers to the adoption of ROPS, two stood out—the $1,000 cost per tractor and logistical barriers farmers encountered when retrofitting. There were also strong, long-held beliefs that "this won't happen to me." Motivating factors were clear as well and centered on the risk of death or injury to younger family members using the equipment, and the real possibility of permanently disabling injuries.

In response, in 2006 the team launched the New York State Rebates for Rollbars Program (ROPS), which reimburses farmers for the cost of the safety equipment— eventually up to $703, 70% of the cost. A variety of *product* options were available (i.e., rigid rollbars, folding rollbars, awnings, or cabs). The program also developed and offered a toll-free help line (1–877–ROPS R4U) and a Web site (www .ropsr4u.com) to assist in decision making (*augmented product*), ordering the gear, and applying for the rebate (*place*). Money to run the program came from grants from the CDC, and rebates were initially funded by the state legislature. (A search for additional private sector funding is now under way.)

Pretest Research and Strategic Response

To develop promotional materials and communication channels, the research team worked with marketing consultants from the Academy of Educational Development (AED) to conduct a series of triads—focused discussions with groups of three people. Of interest was identifying the most engaging among several draft concepts and providing direction for further refinements. The team got clear advice from respondents:

- It needs to prominently feature financial assistance: "We know what's right. We just can't afford it."
- It needs to be brief: "Farmers don't have a lot of time on their hands to read. You better get to the point."
- It needs to be convincing: "The only time they're concerned about a rollover is when someone else is out there operating the tractor."
- It needs to be eye-catching: "Our farmers don't really have time to read, so they will sit down with their coffee at breakfast or something, and leaf through. They are not really reading; they just want to see something visual first and then if it catches their eye, then they will stop and read it."

See Figure 7.5 for one of the finalized promotional materials based on the insights and recommendations from the triads.

Evaluation

In the six months following the intervention, tractor dealers in the five targeted counties sold approximately 10 times more rollbars than in the six months prior to the intervention. Over the four years of the program, 800 farmers have accepted the offer.[19] Dealers have reported selling roughly eight times as many retrofits as those in comparison counties, and this is a conservative estimate, since 40% of the farmers who received rebates bought their rollbars directly from the manufacurer. Importantly, 58 program participants reported that they had subsequently overturned a tractor or had a close

Figure 7.5 Announcing the rebate and increasing perception of risk, especially for family members.[20]

call and had not experienced injuries or fatalities.[21]

Similar expansion programs are under way in other northeastern states, including Vermont, Pennsylvania, and New Hampshire. Rebate money in these states has been provided by insurance companies, equipment dealers, and other agricultural service providers, with the only qualifying condition being that the applicant must be a resident of the state where he or she is applying.

CHAPTER 7 NOTES

1. National Social Marketing Centre. (2008). *Effectively engaging people: Views from the World Social Marketing Conference 2008* (p. 8). Retrieved July 15, 2011, from http://www.tcp-events.co.uk/wsmc/downloads/NSMC_Effectively_engaging_people_conference_version.pdf

2. Monterey Bay Aquarium. (2009, October 20). *Turning the tide: The state of seafood* (p. 11). Retrieved July 15, 2011, from http://www.montereybayaquarium.org/cr/cr_seafoodwatch/content/media/MBA_SeafoodWatch_StateofSeafoodReport.pdf

3. For a more in-depth write-up of this case, see McKenzie-Mohr, D., Lee, N. R., Schultz, P. W., & Kotler, P. (2011). *Social marketing to protect the environment: What works.* Thousand Oaks, CA: Sage.

4. Compass Group. (2006). *Seafood choices evaluation prepared for the David & Lucile Packard Foundation.* Bridgespan Group.

5. Information for this case was provided in 2010 by Ken Peterson, Communications Director, Monterey Bay Aquarium.

6. Wolfe, L., & Lilley, L. (2004). *Seafood Watch literature review.* Quadra Planning Consultants Ltd. and Galiano Institute for Environmental and Social Research.

7. Monterey Bay Aquarium.

8. Ibid.

9. Project Smart. (n.d.). *Smart goals.* Retrieved August 11, 2007, from http://www .projectsmart.co.uk/smart-goals.html

10. Climate Crisis. (n.d.). *Ten things to do.* Retrieved in 2006 from http://www.climatecrisis .net/pdf/10things.pdf

11. © March of Dimes Birth Defects Foundation, 1999. Reprinted with permission.

12. Healthy People 2020. Source: U.S. Department of Health and Human Services, Office of Disease Prevention and Health Promotion, ODPHP Publication No. B0132, November 2010, www.healthypeople.gov

13. Northeast Center for Agricultural and Occupational Health.

14. Some of the information in this highlight appears in a lengthier case write-up: Sorensen, J., May, J., O'Hara, P., Ostby, R., Lehman, T., Viebrock, S., & Emmelin, M. (2008, Winter). Evaluating tractor safety messages: A concept development project. *Social Marketing Quarterly, XIV*(4), 22–44.

15. Donham, K. D., Osterburg, D., Myers, M., & Lehtola, C. (1997). *Tractor risk abatement and control: The policy conference final report.* Iowa City: University of Iowa.

16. New York State ROPS Rebate Program. (n.d.). *Rollover facts.* Retrieved December 10, 2010, from http://ropsr4u.com/ny/rollover-facts/

17. NASS. (2008). *2006 farm and ranch safety survey.* Washington, DC: United States Department of Agriculture, National Agricultural Statistics Service.

18. Sorensen, J. A., May, J., Jenkins, P., Jones, A., & Earle-Richardson, G. (2006). Risk perceptions, barriers, and motivators to tractor ROPS retrofitting in New York state farmers. *Journal of Agricultural Safety and Health, 12*(3), 215–226.

19. Barbara Bayes, NY Rebate Program Hotline Facilitator, personal communication, December 13, 2010.

20. Northeast Center for Agricultural and Occupational Health.

21. New York State ROPS Rebate Program. (n.d.). *Rollover facts.* Retrieved December 10, 2010, from http://ropsr4u.com/ny/rollover-facts/

Chapter 8

Identifying Barriers, Benefits, the Competition, and Influential Others

Stand in the shoes of your target audience. What may seem illogical and irrational attitudes and/or behavior to you, might look different from their viewpoint.

—Dr. Sue Peattie
Lecturer in Marketing, Cardiff Business School

By the time you reach this stage in the planning process, you may (understandably) just want to "get going." You will probably be eager to design the product, brainstorm incentives, search for convenient locations, dream up clever slogans, and envision beautiful billboards. After all, you have analyzed the environment, selected a target audience, and know what you want that audience to do. And you may think you know what they need to know or believe in order to act. The problem is, unless you are the target audience, you probably don't know how they really feel about what you have in mind for them, or what they may be thinking when approached to "behave" in ways such as these:

- Put all your liquids in a quart-sized resealable plastic bag before reaching security checkpoints.
- Reduce your lawn by half.
- Eat five or more fruits and vegetables a day, the color way.
- Take one of these flags and wave it at cars when you cross the crosswalk.

You may not know what's really in the way of their taking you up on your offer, what they want in exchange for your proposed behavior, and who or what you are competing with. This is the time to find out, and by conducting this investigation well, the rest of your planning process will be grounded in reality and guided by the customer's hand, as it was in this opening case.

Be Active
An Award-Winning Program in Birmingham, England
(2008–2010)

This case highlights the evolution of a program from a small pilot in one neighborhood to a citywide program. It also highlights the power of understanding and responding to even just one barrier to behavior change, especially when it is a big one.

The Inspiration

The City of Birmingham is in the West Midlands region of England. Ladywood, an inner-city location within Birmingham, has one of the most economically deprived populations in Britain, with 17% of adults on Jobseeker's Allowance, compared to 8% for Birmingham as a whole, and as many as 44% classified as economically inactive. Almost half (48%) of households have an annual income of less than

£15,000, and the average income is £19,600, compared to the Birmingham city average of £25,600.[1] It is a multicultural population, with minority communities accounting for 62%. Poor health and childhood obesity statistics exceed the city's and national averages.

In February 2008, there were only 90 people in Ladywood using public gyms on a regular basis. Seven months later, there were 6,555 people! That's more than a 7,000% increase. What happened? They called it the "Gym for Free" scheme, and it was named the overall winner of the *Guardian*'s 2009 Public Services Award.

On Valentine's Day, February 2008, residents of Ladywood "were made an offer that proved hard to refuse."[2] A letter was mailed to every household offering residents over the age of 16 free use (*price*) of civic facilities across the city that included swimming pools, gyms, and exercise classes (*product*). The scheme was conceived as a way to remove cost as the *barrier* to participation in exercise. A commitment to attend four times a month to maintain free membership was motivating (*price: incentive*). Residents could register at a local sports center (*place*). The effort was a joint initiative of the Birmingham City Council and the Heart of Birmingham Primary Care Trust (PCT), and funds were made available by the

PCT's public health budget. Take-up of the scheme turned out to be high among groups that are typically underrepresented in sporting activities, including women from ethnic minority communities. Reports indicated that users were inspired to reassess other aspects of their health as well, evidenced by a significant increase in demand for weight management and smoking cessation programs.[3] And the attention of the Birmingham City Council was captured.

The Rollout

On September 1, 2009, the initiative was rebranded Be Active and went live to all 1.1 million people in the city, entitling them to use the city's 25 leisure centers for free. All 50,000 (by then) members of the Gym for Free scheme were transferred to the new program. The offer was similar, including free swimming, fitness classes, and gym sessions for all residents, although the offer was limited to an "off peak" time. And, as with the previous program, there was no upper limit to the number of times they could attend exercise sessions. But the *Be Active* program took it to yet another level.

First they offered a membership Leisure Card, with the look and feel of a debit or credit card (see Figure 8.1). Citizens are encouraged to "simply pop into" their local leisure or fitness center and fill out an application (*place*). Alternatively, they can apply for the card online. Customers simply show the Leisure Card every time they visit the center for free access to the facilities. This also provides a tracking mechanism, ensuring customers keep their commitment to exercise at least once a week or

Figure 8.1 Member card for the *Be Active* program.[4]

four times a month to remain on the scheme. And new programs were added, including tai chi, activities for mothers with their babies, and sessions for family sports.

In the spring of 2010, the initiative launched a promotional campaign to get even more people active over the summer. In addition to encouraging people to join the Be Active program, they also encouraged residents to join other activities, such as going for walks with friends, playing sports in the park, or simply spending some time doing gardening. Leaflets with maps and directions for walks in parks and around the city were made available at park visitor centers and libraries, or could be downloaded and printed. Promotional elements included posters and radio adverts featuring Be Active customers benefiting from the program.

Outcomes

By June 2010, over 300,000 people had joined Be Active, and the program "scooped" the 2010 Local Government Association's LGcomms Reputation Campaign Award for improving health with additional impressive outcomes:

- 74.3% of users had not previously been a member of a leisure center, gym, or swimming pool before joining

- 40% of users confirmed cost had been the major barrier to regular exercise
- 83% cited health and fitness benefits; 75% wanted to lose weight
- 73% said that Be Active had made them feel more positive about Birmingham as a city

STEP 5: IDENTIFY TARGET AUDIENCE BARRIERS, BENEFITS, THE COMPETITION, AND INFLUENTIAL OTHERS

In the marketing game, the winners almost always have one "maneuver" in common—a customer-centered focus. The best have a genuine curiosity, even hunger, to know what the potential customer thinks and feels about their offer. This fifth step in the planning process is designed to do just that—deepen your understanding of your target audience.

This chapter will first identify and discuss what current and specific knowledge, beliefs, attitudes, and practices will be helpful for you to know and understand. You then will read about how to gather this information; behavior change theories, models, and frameworks to consider; and finally, how you will use these insights in developing your strategies. First, a word about the exchange theory, another marketing cornerstone—one that will help you envision this "deal making" process.

The Exchange Theory

The traditional economic exchange theory postulates that, for an exchange to take place, target audiences must perceive benefits equal to or greater than perceived costs.[5] In other words, they must believe they will get as much or more than they give. In 1972, Philip Kotler published his article in the *Journal of Marketing* asserting that exchange was the core concept of marketing and that free exchange takes place when the target audience believes they will get as much or more than they give.[6] And earlier, in 1969, Kotler argued that exchange theory applies to more than the purchase of tangible goods and services, that it can in fact involve intangible or symbolic products (e.g., recycling), and that payments are not limited to financial ones (e.g., time and effort may be the only major perceived costs).[7] In 1974 and 1978, Richard Bagozzi broadened this framework by adding several ideas, including that more than two parties may be involved in the transaction and that the primary beneficiary of an exchange may in fact be a third party (e.g., the environment).[8] This is certainly consistent with the definition of social marketing used throughout this text, as it acknowledges that the intent is always to better society as well as the target audience.

Given this, four target audience perspectives are crucial and will be elaborated upon in the remainder of the first section of this chapter:

1. *Barriers:* What do they think they will have to give (up) in order to perform the behavior? What concerns do they have regarding the behavior? Do they think they can do it? Why haven't they done it in the past, or on a regular basis? Why, perhaps, did they quit doing it? These could also be thought of as the "costs" the target audience perceives.

2. *Benefits:* What do they think they will get if they perform the behavior (as suggested)? How likely do they think it is that they will get this? What do they really want to get? These are also sometimes referred to as potential "motivators" for the target audience.

3. *Competition:* What behaviors are they doing instead? Why? What benefits do they perceive in this competing offer? What does it cost and how does that compare with your offer?

4. *Influential others:* Relative to your desired behavior, who does your target audience listen to (most)? Are these influential others engaged in the desired behavior? What are they saying, or likely to say, to your target audience about this behavior?

WHAT MORE DO YOU NEED TO KNOW ABOUT THE TARGET AUDIENCE?

Barriers

Doug McKenzie-Mohr, an environmental psychologist known and respected for his community-based social marketing approach, notes that barriers may be *internal* to the individual, such as lack of knowledge or skill needed to carry out an activity, or *external*, as in structural changes that need to be made in order for the behavior to be more convenient. He also stresses that these barriers will differ by target audience and by behavior. In our planning process, that is why target audiences and the desired behavior (activity) are identified up front.[9]

Barriers may be related to a variety of factors, including knowledge, beliefs, skills, abilities, infrastructures, technology, economic status, or cultural influences. They may be *real* (e.g., taking the bus will take longer than driving alone to work) or *perceived* (e.g., people who take the bus can't really afford any other mode of transportation). In either case, they are always from the target audience's perspective and often something you can address.

To illustrate both barriers and benefits, we'll use an example of blood donation. Founded in 1962, America's Blood Centers (ABC) is the national network of nonprofit, independent community blood centers, and in 2006, ABC members served more than 180 million people at 600-plus collection sites and more than 4,200 hospitals and health care facilities across North America.[10]

In May 2001, ABC conducted a survey to determine nationwide attitudes toward blood donation. The objective of the survey was to determine effective public messages and program changes that would increase blood donations. Telephone interviews were conducted with 600 adults from May 7 through May 9, 2001. The 95% confidence interval that is associated with a sample of this type produces a margin of error of plus or minus 4.1%.

When nondonors cite their reasons for not giving blood, there is an interesting split. About half the respondents (44%) cite health issues as their reason for not giving blood. However, as seen in Table 8.1, more than half of nondonors (52%) cite other reasons for not donating. As you review the list, begin imagining what you would do to address that barrier. This is what you will do when you develop a positioning statement and marketing strategy in Steps 6 and 7.

Table 8.1 Major Barrier (Reason) for Not Donating Blood Among Nondonors	
Health issues/not qualified	44%
Never thought about it	17%
Too busy	15%
Scared of process	10%
Afraid of infection	4%
Don't know where/how	4%
Don't know anyone in need	2%

Benefits

Benefits are something your target audience wants or needs and therefore values that the behavior you are promoting has the potential to provide.[11] They are what will motivate your target audience to act. Again, these will be benefits in the eyes of the customer—not necessarily the same as yours. Dr. Bill Smith asserts that these benefits may not always be so obvious. For example,

> The whole world uses health as a benefit. [And yet] health, as we think of it in public health, isn't as important to consumers—even high-end consumers—as they claim that it is. What people care about is looking good (tight abdominals and buns). Health is often a synonym for sexy, young, and hot. That's why gym advertising increases before bathing suit time. There is not more disease when the weather heats up, just more personal exposure.[12]

Returning to our blood donation example, as seen in Table 8.2, current and prior blood donors cite humanitarian reasons as their primary reason for giving blood (perceived benefits). Five of the top six responses are altruistic motives, such as helping the community or responding to a blood shortage.

Table 8.2 Major Benefit Perceived in Donating Blood Among Donors	
Wanting to help others	34%
Responding to a blood drive	25%
Helping the community	13%
Hearing about a shortage	7%
Because I might need it someday	4%
Helping a local child	2%

In this same survey, potential messages were tested in terms of their ability to increase intent to give blood in the next 12 months. Before exposure to potential messages, findings indicated that 34% of respondents planned to give blood in the next 12 months. After hearing the potential message series, this increased to 41%, and, not surprisingly, humanitarian reasons tested well both in terms of intensity and in the multiple regression analysis. The most effective messages included, "A family member, friend, or child is in need," which 86% said was an "extremely compelling" reason, and "4 million Americans would die every year without lifesaving blood transfusions," which 56% rated "extremely compelling."[13] One appeal even focused on saving the lives of emergency response professionals (see Figure 8.2).

The Competition

Identifying the Competition

The third area you'll want to explore with your target audience is the competition. Social marketers have tough competitors, for we define *the competition* as follows:

- Behaviors our target audience would prefer over the ones we

Figure 8.2   Highlighting the beneficiary of the lifesaving gift of blood.[14]

are promoting (e.g., condoms may be preferred over abstinence as a way to prevent unwanted pregnancies)

- Behaviors they have been doing "forever," such as a habit that they would have to give up (e.g., driving alone to work or having a cigarette with a morning cup of coffee)
- Organizations and individuals who send messages that counter or oppose the desired behavior (e.g., the Marlboro Man)

Table 8.3 illustrates the challenges you (will) face. Consider the pleasures and benefits we are asking our target audience to give up. Consider the economic power of organizations and sponsors that are sending messages countering those you are sending. Consider the persuasiveness and influence of typical key messengers. And consider that the competition may even be your own organization! We call this "friendly" competition, where one program within the organization (e.g., a needle exchange program) may in fact potentially erode the success of another (e.g., a drug use reduction program).

Table 8.3   What and Who You May Be Competing With

Behavior Objective	Competing Behaviors	Competing Messages and Messengers
Drink less than five drinks at one sitting	Getting really "buzzed"	Budweiser
Wear a life vest	Tanning	Fashion ads showing tan shoulders, midriffs, and arms
Give five hours a week to a volunteer effort	Spending time with family	Your kids
Compost organic foodwaste	A habit of pushing scraps down the drain when cleaning dishes	Neighbors who say the backyard composter will attract rats

Another potential framework (and way to identify the competition) is offered by Sue Peattie and Ken Peattie of Cardiff University in Wales.[15] They suggest that in social marketing, the competition is better thought of as a "battle of ideas" and that these competing ideas can come from four sources that can be considered potential competitors: (a) *commercial counter-marketing* (e.g., cigarette companies), (b) *social discouragement* of your desired behavior (e.g., anti-gun-control activists), (c) *apathy* (e.g., when considering whether to vote), and (d) *involuntary disinclination* (e.g., physical addictions).

Identifying Barriers and Benefits of the Competition

Once competitors are identified, there is more you want to know while you're at it. McKenzie-Mohr and Smith provide a useful framework to capture your research findings—one that will prepare you for developing your product's positioning and 4Ps marketing mix strategy in Steps 6 and 7. The name of this marketing game is to change the ratio of benefits to barriers so that the target behavior becomes more attractive. McKenzie-Mohr and Smith propose four ways (tactics), which are not mutually exclusive, to accomplish this:

1. Increase the benefits of the target behavior

2. Decrease the barriers (and/or costs) of the target behavior

3. Decrease the benefits of the competing behavior(s)

4. Increase the barriers (and/or costs) of the competing behaviors[16]

Table 8.4 is a simple illustration of what in reality (ideally) would include a more exhaustive list of benefits and barriers/costs created from audience research. Keep in mind there is likely to be more than one preferred or alternative behavior identified as the competition.

Table 8.4 Identifying Perceived Barriers and Benefits of the Competition

Audience Perceptions	Desired Behavior: Use a Litterbag in the Car	Competing Behavior: Tossing Fast-Food Bags Out the Window
Perceived benefits/ motivators	It's good role modeling for my kids. I am doing my part for the environment. I help save tax dollars. I don't feel as guilty.	It's easier. I avoid the smell of old food in my car. I avoid the trash all over my car. It gives prisoners a job to do.
Perceived barriers/costs	Having to find one and remember to put it in the car. Having liquid spill out of it. Looking like a nerd with a white plastic bag in my black leather interior car.	I might have to do community service and pick up litter. I could get caught and fined. I'm contributing to the litter on the roadways that looks bad and will have to be picked up.

An important component of this research process will include attempting to prioritize these benefits and barriers/costs within each of the quadrants. You are most interested in the "higher values"—the key benefits to be gained or costs that will be avoided by adopting the desired behavior. In the example in Table 8.4, your research won't be complete until you determine how your target audience ranks benefits and barriers in each quadrant (e.g., what is the number one benefit for using a litterbag?).

Influential Others

The fourth area to consider at this point is those your target audience listens to, watches, and/or looks up to, especially related to the desired behavior you have in mind. We think of them as midstream audiences, and they include social groups your target audience belongs to (e.g., a moms' support group or Facebook friends) as well as coworkers, classmates, neighbors, family members, physicians, counselors, and pharmacists. In some cases, it may be individuals the target audience finds trustworthy, credible, and likable (e.g., a highly regarded scientist or entertainer). Knowing what these groups and individuals are saying and doing (or might say and do) regarding the desired behavior will have significant implications especially for promotional strategies, perhaps warranting an additional target audience for your plan.

For example, beginning in 2007, efforts to increase timely immunizations among children from birth to 24 months in the United States were significantly negatively impacted by one well-known entertainer—Jenny McCarthy. Convinced her son's autism was triggered by MMR shots (immunization for measles, mumps, and rubella), she became a vocal anti-immunization activist, appearing on popular shows such as *The Oprah Winfrey Show* and *Larry King Live*. Despite the lack of medical evidence for her claims, her books, columns, blogs, and public demonstrations raised doubts and fears regarding immunization safety.

HOW DO YOU LEARN MORE FROM AND ABOUT THE TARGET?

Formative research, as the name implies, will help you gain insights into audience barriers, benefits, the competition, and influential others. It will assist you in developing draft strategies to then pretest. Existing behavior change theories and models will then help deepen your understanding of your customer—even develop empathy and compassion.

Formative Research

As usual, you should begin with a review of existing literature and research and discussions with peers and colleagues. If, after this review, informational gaps still exist, it may be important to conduct original research using qualitative methods, such as focus groups and personal interviews, to identify the barriers, benefits, the competition, and important influential others. Quantitative instruments, such as telephone and Web-based surveys, would be very helpful in prioritizing the benefits and barriers to, say, using a litterbag, such as those listed in Table 8.4.

One popular survey model to know about is the knowledge, attitudes, practices, and beliefs (KAPB) survey. As described by Andreasen,

> these are comprehensive surveys of a representative sample of the target population designed to secure information about the social behavior in question and on the

current status of the target audience's Knowledge, Attitudes, Practices, Beliefs. KAPB studies are relatively common in social marketing environments, especially in the area of health. They are very often carried out routinely by local governments, the World Bank, or the United Nations. For this reason, they are sometimes available to social marketers as part of a secondary database.[17]

For example, a KAPB-type study has been conducted annually by the Gallup Organization for the March of Dimes, beginning in 1995, and is supported by the Centers for Disease Control and Prevention.[18] Telephone surveys conducted nationwide among women ages 18 to 45 are designed to track knowledge and behavior related to the importance of taking folic acid before becoming pregnant to decrease the chances of birth defects. Consider how these summary findings in the year 2008 would shape campaign strategies and priorities:

- 9 out of 10 women (89%) did not know that folic acid should be taken prior to pregnancy
- 8 out of 10 women (80%) did not know that folic acid could help prevent birth defects
- Only about one in three women (39%) not pregnant at the time of the survey reported consuming a multivitamin containing folic acid daily

Behavior Change Models, Theories, and Frameworks

Information on target audience barriers, benefits, and the competition will help deepen your understanding, but it may not be enough. Sometimes it helps to understand underlying behavior change theories. One of these theories, the stages of change theory, was mentioned in our Chapter 6 on segmentation. Additional theories, frameworks, and models of interest include the social norms theory, diffusion of innovation model, health belief model, ecological framework, theory of planned behavior, social cognitive theory, behavioral economics framework, science of habit framework, and nudge factor. At the end of this section, you will read about themes that reflect all models.

Social Norms Theory

Linkenbach describes the social norms approach to prevention, which has clear potential implications for strategy development:

The social norms approach to prevention emerged from college health settings in the mid-1980s in response to the seemingly intractable issue of high-risk drinking by college students. Wesley Perkins and Alan Berkowitz, social scientists at Hobart, Williams, and Smith Colleges, discovered that a significant disparity existed between actual alcohol use by college students and their perceptions of other students' drinking. Simply put, most college students reported that they believed drinking norms were higher and riskier than they really were.

The major implication of these findings is that if a student believes that heavy alcohol use is the norm and expected by most students, then regardless of the accuracy of the perception, he or she is more likely to become involved in alcohol abuse—despite his or her own personal feelings. Perkins came to call this pattern of misperception the "reign of error" and suggested that it could have detrimental effects on actual student drinking. According to Berkowitz, if students think "everyone is doing it," then heavy drinking rates rise due to influence from "imaginary peers."[19]

This norming theory highlights the potential benefit of understanding perceived versus actual behaviors among target audiences. Results may signal an opportunity to correct the perception. The research highlight at the conclusion of this chapter presents a more in-depth case on this social norms marketing approach.

The Diffusion of Innovations Model

In the fifth edition of his book *Diffusion of Innovations* (2003), Everett Rogers defines diffusion as a process by which (1) an innovation (2) is communicated through certain channels (3) over time (4) among the members of a social system. Innovation diffusion research suggests that different types of adopters accept an innovation at different points in time. Five groups have been identified:

1. *Innovators* are motivated by a need for novelty and a need to be different

2. *Early adopters* are drawn by the product's intrinsic value

3. *Early majority* perceive the spread of a product and decide to go along with it out of their need to match and imitate

4. *Late majority* jump on the bandwagon after realizing that "most" are doing it

5. *Laggards* finally follow suit as the product attains popularity and broad acceptance

The implication for social marketers is that, for a relatively new behavior, you would start by targeting innovators and early adopters, and once that adoption was successful, you would move to the early majority, then the late majority. After these groups are on board, the assignment gets easier, as the laggards will be "outnumbered." Beginning in January 2010 in Washington DC, for example, a 5-cent tax was charged for grocery bags. Later, in October of that year, the *Wall Street Journal* reported on outcomes. Retail outlets went from handing out 68 million bags per quarter to only 11 million. The article, how-ever, attributed this success to something more than the 5-cent tax. "No one got bags automatically anymore. Instead, shoppers had to ask for them—right in front of their fellow customers."[20] The article concluded that the magic ingredient was not the financial incentive. It was "peer pressure."

The Health Belief Model

Kelli McCormack Brown describes clearly the model originally developed by social psychologists Hochbaum, Kegels, and Rosenstock, who were greatly influenced by the theories of Kurt Lewin:

> The Health Belief Model states that the perception of a personal health behavior threat is itself influenced by at least three factors: general health values, which include interest and concern about health; specific health beliefs about vulnerability to a particular health threat; and beliefs about the consequences of the health problem. Once an individual perceives a threat to his/her health and is simultaneously cued to action, and his/her perceived benefits outweigh his/her perceived costs, then that individual is most likely to undertake the recommended preventive health action. Key descriptors include:
>
> - Perceived Susceptibility: Perception of the likelihood of experiencing a condition that would adversely affect one's health
> - Perceived Seriousness: Beliefs a person holds concerning the effects a given disease or condition would have on one's state of affairs: physical, emotional, financial, and psychological
> - Perceived Benefits of Taking Action: The extent to which a person believes there will be benefits to recommended actions
> - Perceived Barriers to Taking Action: The extent to which the treatment or preventive measure may be perceived as inconvenient, expensive, unpleasant, painful, or upsetting
> - Cues to Action: Types of internal and external strategies/events that might be needed for the desired behavior to occur[21]

This model suggests you would benefit from reviewing or conducting research to determine each of these forces (susceptibility, seriousness, benefits, barriers, and perceptions of effective "cues to action") *before* developing campaign strategies. The National High Blood Pressure Education Program (NHBPEP) understands this well, as illustrated in the following highlight of their social marketing efforts and successes.

More than 65 million American adults, one in three, had high blood pressure in 2006, and less than 30% were controlling their condition.[22] Key to influencing desired behaviors (increasing monitoring and lifestyle and medication plans) is an understanding of perceived susceptibility, seriousness, and barriers such as the following:

- It is hard for me to change my diet and to find the time to exercise.
- My blood pressure is difficult to control.
- My blood pressure varies so much, it's probably not accurate.
- Medications can have undesirable side effects.
- It's too expensive to go to the doctor just to get my blood pressure checked.
- It may be the result of living a full and active life. Not everybody dies from it.

As you read on, you can see how messages in NHBPEP materials and related strategies reflect an understanding of these perceptions:

- "You don't have to make all of the changes immediately. The key is to focus on one or two at a time. Once they become part of your normal routine, you can go on to the next change. Sometimes, one change leads naturally to another. For example, increasing physical activity will help you lose weight."[23]
- "You can keep track of your blood pressure outside of your doctor's office by taking it at home."[24]
- "You don't have to run marathons to benefit from physical activity. Any activity, if done at least 30 minutes a day over the course of most days, can help."[25]

The year the program began in 1972, less than one fourth of the American population knew of the relationship between hypertension, stroke, and heart disease. In 2001, more than three fourths of the population was aware of this connection. As a result, virtually all Americans have had their blood pressure measured at least once, and three fourths of the population have it measured every six months.

The Ecological Model

One criticism of many theories and models of behavior change is that they emphasize the individual behavior change process but pay little attention to sociocultural and physical environmental influences on behavior—the ecological perspective.[26] The ecological approach places significant importance on the role of supportive environments, and four are typically cited: individual factors (demographics, personality, genetics, skills, religious beliefs), relationship factors (friends, families, colleagues), community factors (schools, work sites, healthcare organizations, media), and societal factors (cultural norms, laws, governance). This model argues that the most powerful behavior change interventions are those that simultaneously influence these multiple levels and that this will lead to greater and longer-lasting behavioral changes. The key to success is to assess each of these levels of influence and determine what is needed that will provide the greatest influence on the desired behavior.[27]

The Theory of Reasoned Action and the Theory of Planned Behavior

The theory of reasoned action (TRA), developed by Ajzen and Fishbein in 1975 and restated in 1980, suggests that the best predictor of a person's behavior is his or her intention to act. This intention is determined by two major factors: our beliefs about the outcomes associated with the behavior and our perceptions of how people we care about will view the behavior in question. Using language from other theories presented throughout this text, our likelihood of adopting the behavior will be greatly influenced by perceived benefits, costs, and social norms. In 1988, Ajzen extended the TRA to include the influence of beliefs and perceptions regarding control—beliefs about our ability to actually perform the behavior (e.g., self-efficacy). This successor is called the theory of planned behavior (TPB).[28]

Stated simply, a target audience is most likely to adopt a behavior when they have a positive attitude toward it, perceive that "important others" would approve, and believe they will be successful in performing it.

Social Cognitive Theory/Social Learning

Fishbein summarized Bandura's description of the social cognitive theory, also referred to as the social learning theory:

> The Social Cognitive Theory states that two major factors influence the likelihood that one will take preventive action. First, like the Health Belief Model, a person believes that the benefits of performing the behavior outweigh the costs (i.e., a person should have more positive than negative outcome expectancies). [This should remind you of the exchange theory mentioned frequently throughout this text.] Second, and perhaps most important, the person must have a sense of personal agency or self-efficacy with respect to performing the preventive behavior, . . . must believe that he or she has the skills and abilities necessary for performing the behavior under a variety of circumstances.[29]

Andreasen adds that this self-efficacy comes about at least in part from learning specific skills and from observing social norms; hence the name "social learning." This learning of specific new behaviors, he explains, has three major components: sequential approximation, repetition, and reinforcement. Sequential approximation acknowledges that individuals do not often instantly leap from not doing a behavior to doing it. They may prefer to work their way up to it. For example, one way of teaching smokers how to adopt a nonsmoking lifestyle is to reduce their consumption step by step, perhaps one cigarette at a time, starting with the easiest behavior to give up and working up to the most difficult. Encouraging repetition (practice) and providing reinforcement strategies will then make it more likely the behavior will become a "part of a permanent behavioral repertoire."[30]

The Behavioral Economics Framework and the Nudge Factor

Behavioral economics is a growing body of science that looks at how environmental and other factors prompt personal decisions. The core idea that humans don't behave like rational economic agents was introduced several decades ago by Daniel Kahneman, Amos Tversky, and others. The central thesis is that people move between states of emotional hot and cold. As it sounds, when in a hot state, we are emotionally aroused (irrational), and in a cold state we are calm or neutral (rational). And as might be expected, arousal more often than not overrides reason. A young woman watching her budget may think before going to the mall to shop that she will only buy the shoes she heard were

50% off. When she gets there and sees the newest fashions, however, she is likely to succumb to her desires and pay full price.

In their book *Nudge*, Professors Richard Thaler and Cuss Sunstein go beyond the more psychology-oriented behavioral economics theory to suggest concrete ways this can inspire and improve public policy. They call them "nudges." Consider, for example, organ donation in Europe. In Germany, they note, only an estimated 12% of citizens consent to organ donation when getting or renewing their driver's license. By contrast, in Austria, nearly everyone (99%) does.[31] Why the difference? In Germany, citizens must "opt in"—check a box indicating they agree to be an organ donor. By contrast, in Austria citizens need to "opt out"—check a box indicating they don't agree. The same "choice architecture," as the authors call it, could be used to bolster retirement-savings plans (companies automatically enroll employees unless told otherwise) or to increase the chances that students in school cafeterias will choose healthier foods (healthy options are at the beginning of the line).

Dr. Bill Smith argues in an article in the Summer 2010 *Social Marketing Quarterly* that "we have a new ally in Behavioral Economics"—one he is particularly excited about, as it has the potential to encourage the government "to arrange the conditions of life . . . and build policy contingencies so that it is fun, easy, and popular for people to make the right decision."[32]

The Science of Habit Framework

Charles Duhigg's 2008 article in the *New York Times*, "Warning: Habits May Be Good for You," encourages those interested in influencing "good behaviors" to take a lesson from the playbooks of the Proctor & Gambles and Unilevers of the world:

> If you look hard enough, you'll find that many of the products we use every day—chewing gums, skin moisturizers, disinfecting wipes, air fresheners, water purifiers, antiperspirants, colognes, teeth whiteners, fabric softeners, vitamins—are results of manufactured habits. A century ago, few people regularly brushed their teeth multiple times a day. Today . . . many Americans habitually give their pearly whites a cavity-preventing scrub twice a day.[33]

How is this useful to social marketers? Consider opportunities to "manufacture" new habits (e.g., walking a new puppy 30 minutes a day), or try embedding a new behavior into an existing habit (e.g., flossing your teeth while watching your favorite late night show.)

Themes From All Models

Fishbein's summary of behavior change interventions melds themes from most of the models presented in this section and provide a quick reference for gauging whether your target audience is "ready for action" and, if not, what might be needed to help them out.

Generally speaking it appears that in order for a person to perform a given behavior one or more of the following must be true:

1. The person must have formed a strong positive intention (or made a commitment) to perform the behavior;

2. There are no environmental constraints that make it impossible to perform the behavior [even better, there are "nudges" in the environmental infrastructure that make it more likely the audience will choose the desired behavior];

3. The person has the skills necessary to perform the behavior;

4. The person believes that the advantages (benefits, anticipated positive outcomes) of performing the behavior outweigh the disadvantages (costs, anticipated negative outcomes);

5. The person perceives more social (normative) pressure to perform the behavior than to not perform the behavior;

6. The person perceives that performance of the behavior is more consistent than inconsistent with his or her self-image, or that its performance does not violate personal standards that activate negative self-actions;

7. The person's emotional reaction to performing the behavior is more positive than negative; and

8. The person perceives that he or she has the capabilities to perform the behavior under a number of different circumstances.[34]

Based on the science of habit framework, we would add a ninth point: The person is encouraged to form a *new habit* by connecting the new behavior with an existing one or new environmental cue.

HOW WILL THIS HELP DEVELOP YOUR STRATEGY?

If you understand (better yet, empathize with) your target audience's real and perceived barriers, benefits, competitors, and influential others relative to your desired behavior, it will be akin to having a guiding hand as you craft your positioning statement and 4Ps strategies. We'll illustrate this application and process with a brief case.[35]

In 2006, the Washington State Department of Health developed a social marketing plan with the purpose of decreasing falls among seniors and a focus on developing fitness classes that could be offered by a variety of community organizations. The target audiences for the pilot (first year) were seniors ages 70 to 79 living in one county of the state.

Formative research with key informants and seniors in the target audience identified the following major perceived benefits, barriers, competition, and important others influencing seniors regarding joining and attending classes:

- Benefits: "It could improve my strength, balance, and fitness, and then perhaps I can live independent longer. I also want it to be fun and a chance to make new friends."
- Barriers to joining: "It depends on how much it will cost, where the class is located, the time of day it is offered, and who will be leading the class. I don't want some young instructor I can't relate to!"
- Barriers to attending regularly: "I'd probably drop out if it's too strenuous, I hurt myself, or I couldn't keep up. And I'd need to see improvements in my fitness for it to seem worthwhile."
- Competition: "I can probably just do my own thing at home for free, at my own pace, by watching an exercise video or going out for a walk. I guess the advantage of the class, though, is that it's a way to make sure I do it!"
- Influential others: "My neighbor says that the gym instructor is younger than her grandkids and just as energetic. I wouldn't be able to keep up."

A *positioning* statement, as you will read in the next chapter, describes how you want your target audience to see your desired behavior, especially relative to the competition. Planners wanted the fitness classes to be seen by their target audience of 70- to 79-year-olds as

a fitness class for seniors that *works*, as it will improve strength and balance; is *safe*, as it has experienced skilled instructors offering tested exercises; and is *fun*, as it offers an opportunity to meet others and get out of the house. It is an important and worthwhile activity for seniors wanting to stay *independent*, *be active*, and *prevent falls*.

The *product* platform includes a description of the core, actual, and augmented product, all inspired by your benefits, barriers, and competitive research. For the fitness classes, the *core* product (benefits of the classes) was subsequently refined to be "staying active, independent, and preventing falls." The *actual* product (features of the classes) would be one-hour fitness classes, with up to 20 participants, meeting three times a week. The classes would include strength exercises with wrist and ankle weights, balance exercises, and moderate aerobics. The exercises could be done standing or sitting, and the instructor would be a certified fitness instructor with special training for strength and balance exercises for seniors. The *augmented* product (extras to add value) would include a booklet giving information on fall prevention and describing a way to conduct a self-assessment for fall risk and determine readiness to exercise (see Figure 8.3). External safety effectiveness assessments would be available as well.

Pricing strategies include *costs* for products, *fees* for services, and any *monetary* and *nonmonetary* incentives and *disincentives*. Based on target audience comments, it was determined that the recommended fee per class should be $2.00 to $2.50, enough to help cover the cost of the instructors, add to perceived value, and build commitment. It was also recommended that a coupon be offered for a free first class as well as a punch card giving 12 classes for the price of 11, and it was suggested that organizers build in a reward of a free class to participants who attended at least 10 classes in a month.

Place strategies refer to where and when behaviors are performed and tangible objects and services are accessed. For the exercise classes, nine sites were selected, eight of them at senior centers and one at a senior retirement facility. Suggested ideal start times were 9 or 10 A.M. or 1, 2, or 3 P.M. There was to be free, adjacent parking at each site.

Figure 8.3   Brochure cover for a fall-prevention class for seniors.[36]

Stay Active & Independent for Life

An Information Guide for Adults 65+

Washington State Department of Health

Injury & Violence Prevention Program
DOH Pub 341-013

Promotional elements include messages, messengers, and media channels. The recommended name of the program was S.A.I.L. (Stay Active and Independent for Life), with a tagline of "A strength and balance fitness class for seniors." Consistent with the desired positioning, key messages to incorporate in promotional materials included the following:

- It works. You'll be stronger, have better balance, feel better, and this will help you stay independent, active, and prevent falls.
- It's safe. Instructors are experienced and skilled, and exercises have been tested with seniors.
- It's fun. You'll meet other seniors, make new friends, and this will get you out of the house three days a week.

Types of media channels to promote the class would include flyers, posters, articles in newsletters and local newspapers, packets for physicians, Web site information, sandwich board signs at senior centers, and a Q&A fact sheet for senior center staff.

POTENTIAL REVISION OF TARGET AUDIENCES, OBJECTIVES, AND GOALS

This new in-depth understanding of target audiences may signal a need to revise target audiences (Step 3) and/or objectives (Step 4), because it may reveal one or more of the following situations:

- One of the target audiences has beliefs that you would have a difficult time changing or may not want to: "Moderate physical activity like this is wimpy, and I'd rather increase vigorous activity from two to three days a week if I do anything more."
- The desired behavior has too many insurmountable barriers for one or more target audiences: "I can't get to the farmers' market to use my coupons because they close before I get off work."
- The audience tells us the behavior objective isn't clear: "I don't understand what reducing my BMI means."
- Perceived costs are too high: "Quitting smoking while I'm pregnant looks impossible, but I might be able to cut down to a half a pack a day."
- The behavior objective has already been met: "My child already has five caring adult relationships outside the home, so for you to suggest I go find one caring adult for my child says you're not talking to people like me."
- We learn that a major knowledge objective isn't needed but a belief objective is: "I already know that tobacco kills one out of three users. I just don't believe I'll get addicted."
- The original behavior objective isn't the solution to the problem: "I always cover the load in the back of my pickup truck with a tarp. The problem is, it still doesn't keep stuff from flying out. What we need is a net or cable that holds the tarp down."
- The goal is too high: "This latest survey says that 75% of high school seniors are sexually active, so a goal of 50% choosing abstinence looks impossible with this group!"

ETHICAL CONSIDERATIONS WHEN RESEARCHING YOUR TARGET AUDIENCE

Perhaps the greatest ethical concern when conducting activities to learn more about your target audience is the research process itself. Concerns range from whether questions will make respondents uncomfortable or embarrassed to deceiving respondents regarding the purposes of the research to assurance of anonymity and confidentiality.

Institutional review boards (IRBs) have been formed to help avoid these ethical problems. An IRB is a group formally designated to review and monitor behavioral and biomedical research involving human subjects. The purpose of IRB review is to ensure that appropriate steps are taken to protect the rights and welfare of humans participating as subjects in a research study. In the United States, IRBs are mandated by the Research Act of 1974, which defines IRBs and requires them for all research that receives funding, directly or indirectly, from the Department of Health and Human Services (HHS). These IRBs are themselves regulated by the Office for Human Research Protections within HHS and may be based at academic institutions or medical facilities or conducted by for-profit organizations.[37]

CHAPTER SUMMARY

In this important step in the marketing planning process, you take time out to deepen your understanding of your target audience. What you are most interested in knowing are perceived *barriers*, *benefits*, *competitors*, and *influential others*. What you are most interested in feeling are compassion and a desire to develop marketing strategies that decrease these barriers, increase benefits, upstage your competition, and engage influential others.

These insights may be gathered through a literature review or other secondary research resources. They are more likely to involve at least some qualitative surveys, such as focus groups or personal interviews. Quantitative surveys, such as a KAPB (knowledge, attitudes, practices, and beliefs) survey, will help prioritize your findings and provide sharp focus for your positioning and marketing mix strategies.

Several behavior change theories and models may also help explain why your audience thinks and feels the way they do regarding your desired behavior: exchange theory, social norms theory, diffusion of innovations model, health belief model, ecological model, theory of reason, theory of planned behavior, social cognitive theory/social learning theory, behavior economics framework, and science of habit framework. Fishbein's summary pulling all theories and models together is worth rereading, even keeping close at hand.

RESEARCH HIGHLIGHT

Reducing Drinking and Driving in Montana:
Evaluating a Social Norms Approach
(2003)

Background

When a social marketing effort uses the social norms theory to inspire a campaign strategy, it is often referred to as *social norms marketing*. In 2001, The *New York Times Magazine* listed social norms marketing as one of the most significant ideas of the year, describing it as "the science of persuading people to go along with the crowd. The technique works because people are allelominimetic—that is, like cows and other herd animals, our behavior is influenced by the behavior of those around us."[38]

The theory was first introduced in a study by H. Wesley Perkins, a professor of sociology, who found that students consistently overestimated how much alcohol their fellow students drank. And then in an attempt to be more "normal," they drank more themselves. The theory states that

> overestimations of problem behavior will increase these problem behaviors, while underestimations of healthy behaviors will discourage individuals from engaging in them. Thus, correcting misperceptions of group norms is likely to result in decreased problem behavior or increased prevalence of healthy behaviors.[39]

One of the first social norms campaigns took place at Northern Illinois University in 1990, where the message that "most students have fewer than five drinks when they party" was distributed using newspaper ads, posters, and handouts. By 1999, incidents of heavy drinking (five or more drinks at one sitting) was down 44%.[40]

While patterns of misperceptions were evident in college populations, they had never been identified in statewide populations of young adults.[41] If such misperceptions did exist, then a statewide campaign might have positive impacts.

The following case highlights a more recent effort and presents impressive evaluative results confirming the behavior change potential of this approach. Case information was provided by Dr. Jeffrey Linkenbach, director of the Center for Health and Safety Culture and a senior research scientist at

Montana State University in Bozeman, Montana, where he directs the nationally acclaimed MOST of Us® Campaign (www.mostofus.org).

Campaign Overview

In 2002, Montana ranked first in the nation for alcohol-related fatalities per vehicle miles traveled, up from fourth in 1999.[42] Alcohol and drug-related vehicle crashes accounted for approximately 10% of all crashes in Montana.[43] And young adults represented a disproportionate share of these crashes, with 21- to 30-year-olds accounting for nearly half of all alcohol- and drug-related crashes in Montana. In 2001, a statewide social norms media campaign was developed and then implemented from January 2002 to March 2003 (15 months) to test the potential for this model to reduce drinking and driving among youth ages 21 to 34. Campaign elements included television, radio, newspapers, theater slides, billboards, promotional items (e.g., T-shirts, key chains, pens, and windshield scrapers), and indoor advertisements in restaurants (see Figure 8.4). One TV ad depicted a ski lodge window with snow falling. A male voice read the following script: "In Montana there are two things you need to know about snow: how to drive in it and how to ski on it. After a day on the slopes and some time in the lodge, my friends and I all take turns being designated drivers." The view widens to reveal the message written on the window, "Most of us (4 out if 5) don't drink and drive." The commercial closes with the voice asking, "How are you

Figure 8.4 Posters used in a 15-month campaign in western counties of Montana.[44]

getting home?" Additional campaign messages pointed out that the majority of Montana young adults practice protective behaviors, such as taking cabs or using designated drivers.

Research Methodology

Researchers Perkins, Linkenbach, Lewis, and Neighbors used this opportunity to conduct a research study, for several reasons.[45] First, to date there had not been a peer-reviewed publication evaluating a social norms marketing campaign implemented on a statewide level. Second,

rigorous evaluative results were needed, given the surge of social norms marketing campaigns being implemented widely in the U.S., especially on college campuses. Third, the vast majority of interventions incorporating the social norms approach had been limited to school settings, so this would be one of the first studies to measure whether the approach worked in a broader marketplace. The research objectives were to evaluate whether the social norms media marketing campaign reached the target audience, whether it was effective in correcting misperceptions, and whether it resulted in adoption of key desired behaviors, including using a designated driver and not driving within an hour of having two or more drinks.

A quasi-experimental design was used, with regions of Montana assigned to one of three groups. Fifteen counties in the western Montana region were assigned to receive a "high dosage" of the campaign. These counties were an optimal choice, as a majority of Montanans ages 21 to 34 lived in those counties. Because radio and television messages could not be completely contained in intervention counties, counties in the buffer region (central Montana) were used to adjust for diffusion of social norms media messages outside the intervention counties. Counties in the control region were those on the eastern half of Montana and thus not in close geographical proximity to the counties in the campaign regions.

The target population was selected and surveyed a total of four times: once prior to the campaign (n = 1,000), once during the media interventions (n = 1,000), once immediately following the intervention (n = 1,005), and once three months after the conclusion (n = 517), with the final sample being reduced on account of cost considerations. Ten- to twelve-minute telephone interviews were conducted. Sampling frames were purchased that provided targeted lists of Montana households with residing adults ages 21 to 34, and numbers were then selected at random.

Table 8.5 Differences Between Intervention and Control Counties for Perceived and Reported Behavior in November 2001 (Prior to Campaign) and June 2003 (Three Months After Completion of Campaign)

	Western Intervention Counties			Eastern Control Counties			Difference of Change
	Nov.	June	Change	Nov.	June	Change	
Percentage recalling social norms media as main message (unprompted recall)	53.8	70.5	16.7	50.7	42.6	−8.1	24.8
Percentage thinking average Montanan drove within one hour of consuming two drinks in past month	91.8	86.7	−5.1	91.9	94.3	2.4	−7.5
Percentage perceiving majority of peers almost always have a designated driver when using a car after drinking	29.9	39.2	9.3	24.9	23.2	−1.7	11.0
Percentage driving within one hour of consuming two drinks in past month	22.9	20.9	−2.0	16.9	28.6	11.7	−13.7
Percentage reporting they always make sure they have a designated driver when using a car after drinking	41.7	46.4	4.7	42.3	32.0	−10.3	15.0

Results

As presented in Table 8.5, findings were encouraging. Overall, results revealed that the target audience noticed and recalled one or more of the campaign messages (70.5% in intervention counties versus 42.6% in control counties). (It should be noted that there had been MOST of Us campaigns in several locations around the state in previous years. Thus, some recognition or recall at baseline was not unexpected. Therefore, analysis of the findings focused on difference of change.) Misperceptions of peer norms were reduced, with those in the intervention counties less likely to believe the average Montanan their age had, in the past month, driven within one hour of consuming one or more drinks (86.7% versus 94.3%) and more likely to believe the majority of peers almost always had a designated driver when using a car after drinking (39.2% versus 23.2%). Behaviors changed as well. The percentage of those in the intervention counties having driven, in the past month, within an hour after having two or more drinks decreased by 10%, and the percentage reporting they used a designated driver increased by 11%. And, most important, in 2003, alcohol-related crashes declined by 5% over 2001 in the intervention counties, while in the control counties, the rate actually increased by 2%.[46]

Details related to implementing this approach can be found in Linkenbach's toolkit titled *How to Use Social Norms Marketing to Prevent Driving After Drinking: A MOST of Us® Toolkit* (a publication of the MOST of Us® Institute, Montana State University–Bozeman, 2006, available at www.mostofus.org).

CHAPTER 8 NOTES

1. Ramrayka, L. (2009, November 25). Winner: Birmingham city council in partnership with Heart of Birmingham PCT. *The Guardian.* Retrieved July 16, 2011, from http://www.guardian .co.uk/publicservicesawards/fit-for-free

2. Ibid.

3. Birmingham Health and Wellbeing Partnership. (n.d.). The Guardian: *Fit for service.* Retrieved December 2, 2010, from http://www.bhwp.nhs.uk/Apps/Content/News/-ViewArticle .aspx?id=264

4. Birmingham Health and Wellbeing Partnership.

5. Bagozzi, R. P. (1978, March/April). Marketing as exchange: A theory of transactions in the marketplace. *American Behavioral Scientist, 21,* 535–556.

6. Kotler, P. (1972, April). A generic concept of marketing. *Journal of Marketing, 36,* 46–54.

7. Kotler, P., & Levy, S. J. (1969, January). Broadening the concept of marketing. *Journal of Marketing, 33,* 10–15.

8. Bagozzi, R. P. (1974). Marketing as an organized behavioral system of exchange. *Journal of Marketing, 38,* 77–81; Bagozzi, R. P. (1978). Marketing as exchange: A theory of transactions in the marketplace.

9. McKenzie-Mohr, D. (n.d.). *Community based social marketing: Quick reference.* Retrieved January 30, 2007, from http://www.cbsm.com/Reports/CBSM.pdf

10. America's Blood Centers. (2006). *About ABC.* Retrieved December 28, 2006, from http://www.americasblood.org/go.cfm?do=Page.View&pid=29#research

11. Kotler, P., & Lee, N. (2006). *Marketing in the public sector: A roadmap for improved performance* (p. 199). Upper Saddle River, NJ: Wharton School.

12. Smith, B. (2003). Beyond "health" as a benefit. *Social Marketing Quarterly, 9*(4), 22–28.

13. Key findings from America's Blood Centers' nationwide survey on blood donation, 2001. Summary information provided by Brightline Media of Arlington, Virginia: Mike Broder, President, and Eric Wilk, Research Manager.

14. Reprinted with permission of Puget Sound Blood Center. Photo by Craig Harrold.

15. Peattie, S., & Peattie, K. (2003). Ready to fly solo? Reducing social marketing's dependence on commercial marketing theory. *Marketing Theory Articles, 3*(3), 365–385.

16. McKenzie-Mohr, D., & Smith, W. (1999). *Fostering sustainable behavior: An introduction to community-based social marketing* (p. 5). Gabriola Island, British Columbia, Canada: New Society.

17. Andreasen, A. R. (1995). *Marketing social change: Changing behavior to promote health, social development, and the environment* (pp. 108–109). San Francisco, CA: Jossey-Bass.

18. March of Dimes. (2001). *United States: Quick facts: Folic acid overview.* Retrieved December 23, 2010, from http://www.marchofdimes.com/peristats/tlanding.aspx?reg=99&top=13&lev=0&slev=1%20

19. Personal communication, 2001.

20. Simon, S. (2010, October 18). The secret to turning consumers green. *The Wall Street Journal.* Retrieved July 16, 2011, from http://online.wsj.com/article/SB10001424052748704575304575296243891721972.html

21. Brown, K. R. M. (1999). *Health belief model.* Retrieved April 2, 2001, from http://www.hsc.usf.edu/-kmbrown/Health_Belief_Model_Overview.htm

22. United States Department of Health and Human Services, National Institutes of Health, National Heart Lung and Blood Institute. (n.d.). *National High Blood Pressure Education Program (NHBPEP).* Retrieved September 18, 2001, from http://hin.nhlbi.nih.gov/nhbpep_kit_about_m.htm

23. United States Department of Health and Human Services, National Institutes of Health, National Heart Lung and Blood Institute. (n.d.). *Taking action to control high blood pressure.* Retrieved January 19, 2001, from http://www.nih.gov/health/hbp tifl/3.htm

24. Ibid.

25. Ibid.

26. Grizzell, J. (n.d.). *Behavior change theories and models.* Retrieved June 9, 2008, from http://www.csupomona.edu/~jvgrizzell/best_practices/betheory.html#Ecological%20Approaches

27. Kotler, P., & Lee, N. (2009). *Up and out of poverty: The social marketing approach* (p. 151). Upper Saddle River, NJ: Wharton School.

28. Ajzen, I. (1991). The theory of planned behavior. *Organizational Behavior and Human Decision Processes, 50,* 179–211.

29. Fishbein, M., summarizing Bandura (1986, 1989, 1999) in *Developing effective behavior change interventions* (p. 3), as quoted in The Communication Initiative, *Summary of change theories and models* (Slide 5). Retrieved April 2, 2001, from http://www.comminit.com/power_point/change_theories/sld005.htm

30. Andreasen, A. R. (1995). *Marketing social change: Changing behavior to promote health, social development, and the environment* (pp. 266–268). San Francisco, CA: Jossey-Bass.

31. Thaler, R., & Sunstein, C. (2009). *Nudge: Improving decisions about health, wealth, and happiness* (pp. 180–181). New York, NY: Penguin Group.

32. Smith, B. (2010, Summer). Behavioral economics and social marketing: New allies in the war on absent behavior. *Social Marketing Quarterly, XVI*(2), 137–141.

33. Duhigg, C. (2008, July 13).Warning: Habits may be good for you. *The New York Times.* Retrieved July 16, 2011, from http://www.nytimes.com/2008/07/13/business/13habit.html

34. Fishbein, M., in *Developing effective behavior change interventions* (pp. 5–6), as quoted in The Communication Initiative, *Summary of change theories and models* (Slide 6). Retrieved April 2, 2001, from http://www.comminit.com/power_point/change_theories/sld005.htm

35. This case was taken from a draft of a social marketing plan for the Washington Department of Health, 2006. Ilene Silver, lead project manager.

36. Washington State Department for Health.

37. Wikipedia. (n.d.). *Institutional review board.* Retrieved January 16, 2007, from http://en.wikipedia.org/wiki/Institutional_Review_Board

38. Frauenfelder, M. (2001, December 9). The year in ideas: A to Z.; social-norms marketing. *The New York Times.* Retrieved July 16, 2011, from http://www.nytimes.com/2001/12/09/magazine/the-year-in-ideas-a-to-z-social-norms-marketing.html

39. Berkowitz, A. (2004, August). *The social norms approach: Theory, research, and annotated bibliography.* Retrieved July 16, 2011, from http://www.alanberkowitz.com/articles/social_norms.pdf

40. Frauenfelder, 2001, The year in ideas.

41. Linkenbach, J., & Perkins, H. W. (2003). Misperceptions of peer alcohol norms in a statewide survey of young adults. In H. W. Perkins (Ed.), *The social norms approach to preventing school and college age substance abuse: A handbook for educators, counselors, and clinicians.* San Francisco, CA: Jossey-Bass.

42. National Highway Traffic Safety Administration. (2003). *State alcohol-related fatality rates 2002.* Washington, DC: United States Department of Transportation.

43. Montana Department of Transportation. (2003). *Traffic safety problem identification (FY 2004)* (State and Local Traffic Safety Program section). Helena, MT: Author.

44. Linkenbach, J. W., and Perkins, H. S. (2005). *Most of us prevent drinking and driving: A successful social norms campaign to reduce driving among young adults in Western Montana.* A publication by the National Highway Traffic Safety Administration - U.S. Department of Transportation. DOT HS 809 869

45. Perkins, H. W., Linkenbach, J. W., Lewis, M. A., & Neighbors, C. (2010). Effectiveness of social norms media marketing in reducing drinking and driving: A state wide campaign. *Addictive Behaviors, 35,* 866–874. doi:10.1016/j.addbeh.2010.05.004

46. Linkenbach, J. W., & Perkins, H. W. (2005). *Most of us prevent drinking and driving: A successful social norms campaign to reduce driving after drinking among young adults in western Montana* (DOT HS 809 869). Washington, DC: United States Department of Transportation, National Highway Traffic Safety Administration.

PART IV

DEVELOPING SOCIAL MARKETING STRATEGIES

Chapter 9

CRAFTING A DESIRED POSITIONING

It's about more than education! If communication and information based on rational process were enough, no one in the entire world would ever smoke a cigarette! Human behavior often occurs in an emotional context; the tobacco and fast-food industries depend on it! That's why changing behavior means addressing all the 4Ps: Product, Price, Place, and Promotion.

—Bob Marshall
Rhode Island Department of Health

Back in the early 1970s, a couple of advertising executives, Al Ries and Jack Trout, started a small revolution—a marketing revolution, that is. They introduced the concept and art of positioning. It was more than a new approach. It was, as they described it, a creative exercise.

Positioning starts with a product—a piece of merchandise, a service, a company, an institution, or even a person. But positioning is not what you do to a product. Positioning is what you do to the mind of the prospect. That is, you position the product in the mind of the prospect.[1]

Ries and Trout's premise was that our mind, as a defense against the volume of today's communications, screens and rejects much of the information offered it and accepts only that which matches prior knowledge or experience. They advocated the oversimplified message as the best approach to take in our overcommunicated society:

The average mind is already a dripping sponge that can only soak up more information at the expense of what's already there. Yet we continue to pour more information into that supersaturated sponge and are disappointed when our messages fail to get through. . . . In communication, as in architecture, less is more. You have to sharpen your message to cut into the mind. You have to jettison the ambiguities, simplify the message, and then simplify it some more if you want to make a long-lasting impression.[2]

And as you no doubt have discovered, or at least have read so far in this text, different markets have different needs, and your challenge is to position your offer "perfectly" in the mind of your desired prospect. The positioning exercise you will explore in this chapter will help provide that clarity. And in the following opening case story and the closing Research Highlight, you'll experience the power this can have.

MARKETING HIGHLIGHT

Get Some: "Get Yours. Grab a Handful and Go!" New York City's Bold Campaign to Increase Condom Use (2007–2010)

On Valentine's Day 2007, the New York City Department of Health and Mental Hygiene (DOHMH) unveiled the NYC Condom, the first municipally branded condom in the nation. The NYC Condom is a premium lubricated Lifestyles condom with a specialty wrapper and the slogan *Get Some*. This case highlights several fairly bold moves for a governmental agency, ones we hope will inspire others to position their products "to sell."

Background

New York City continues to be the epicenter of HIV/AIDS in the U.S., with a case rate almost three times the U.S. average and HIV as the leading cause of death for residents ages 35 to 54.[3] And each year, nearly 1,000 people in NYC don't find out they are HIV positive until they are already sick with AIDS.[4]

Despite these odds and challenges, Mayor Michael Bloomberg and Dr. Thomas Frieden, NYC DOHMH commissioner of health at that time, wanted to make NYC a national and global model for HIV/AIDS prevention, treatment, and care. And making condoms *more accessible* and *more the norm* was a cornerstone strategy.

The City's condom initiative dates back to 1971, when the health department started making them available for free through their STD clinics. In the 1980s, the program expanded to include community-based organizations and needle exchange venues, and then in 2005, distribution increased more than sevenfold when the department launched an Internet-based bulk ordering system. But even with such enhanced access, they were only distributing about 18 million free condoms per year by 2007.[5] With a population of over 6 million adults 18 and older, they knew the potential demand was much higher and wanted to fill it.

Target Audience

Several key segments were identified as most at risk in a 2005 *Report of the New York City Commission on HIV/AIDS*.[6]

Since the mid 1980s, the city's epidemic had increasingly affected *blacks* (44% of AIDS cases), *Latinos* (32%), *women* (31%), and the *poor.* By 2005, blacks and Hispanics accounted for 80% of new AIDS diagnoses and deaths. In addition, evidence suggested a resurgence of risky behavior among men having sex with men (MSM), both nationwide and in New York City. Young people were also increasingly affected, with some estimates indicating that as many as half of new HIV infections were occurring in people under age 25. At the same time, there was an aging of the epidemic in NYC where, between 1993 and 2003, the number of people with AIDS over age 50 increased sixfold.[7]

Desired Behavior

The NYC Commission on HIV/AIDS' report made nine prevention-related recommendations, with a focus on reducing risky unprotected sexual intercourse. Their first was to "make condoms much more widely available." Their suggestions included making both male and female condoms easily available in a wide variety of locations beyond the health clinics and community organizations. The mayor and commissioner took their recommendations seriously.

Positioning

Although New York City's health department didn't articulate it in their formal positioning statement, we think their strategies fit Dr. Bill Smith's recommendation to make desired behaviors "fun, easy, and popular." Their brand name and slogans are lighthearted, and their "everywhere"

Figure 9.1   Campaign poster highlighting condom dispensers around town.[8]

locations have increased convenient access as well as perception of the condom as a social norm (see Figure 9.1).

Strategy

On Valentine's Day 2007, during the morning rush hour, community volunteers and others handed out more than 150,000 NYC Condoms (*product*) across the five boroughs (*promotion*).[9] More than 100 night spots and retail outlets—including Kenneth Cole and M-A-C Cosmetics—gave condoms to interested customers throughout the day. At a press conference, the CEO of Gay Men's Health Crisis stressed that "safer sex is better sex, whatever one's orientation."[10] And fashion designer and cochair of the condom campaign, Kenneth Cole, made this statement: "Any successful product has a strong brand, and condoms are no different." Cole also unveiled a new line of T-shirts and boxer shorts, each sporting a condom-sized pocket and discreet woven label that read, "Safety Instructions: This garment and its contents should be worn whenever conceivable."[11]

As cochair of the condom campaign, Cole also led a coalition of businesses in an effort to keep free NYC Condoms in wide circulation. Consider how easy the City made it for more and more potential distribution sites to come on board. Any New York City establishment—be it a health club, coffee house, bar, hair salon, nail salon, African hair braiding parlor, wine and liquor store, Laundromat, mini-mart, bathhouse, spa, tattoo parlor, theater, bar, tavern, saloon, ethnic cafe—even a church—can become a partner in the campaign by calling 311 or visiting www .nyccondom.org (*place*). The health department then delivers free NYC Condoms in bulk and replenishes them as needed (*price*). (See Figure 9.2.)

The launch was also supported by bilingual (English/Spanish) subway ads, radio spots, club launch parties, and street teams distributing the NYC Condom at high-pedestrian traffic spots throughout the city (*promotion*). The hope was that these expanded efforts would increase the number from 2.5 million per year to some 18 million per year.[12] In fact, the month following the launch, 5 million NYC Condoms were distributed to city organizations and businesses. Subsequently,

Figure 9.2 Poster encouraging businesses to call for free condoms.[13]

average monthly distribution stabilized at about 3 million; in 2010, over 36 million condoms were distributed through 3,000 condom distribution community partners.

In 2008, new ads, set to hip-hop, jazz, and Latin beats, featured images of New Yorkers against bold cityscapes. Display ads also appeared in more than 1,000 subway cars citywide, as well as on phone kiosks and in check cashing outlets (*media channels*).

To sustain interest and enthusiasm for the brand, in December 2009 the DOHMH featured a wrapper design contest that asked residents of NYC (age 17 and older) to design a special, limited edition wrapper for the NYC Condom. Over 600 entries were obtained from as far away as St. Petersburg, Russia, and Paris, France. The top five finalists' designs were put on the NYC Condom Web page, and the people of New York were asked to vote for their favorite. Over 15,000 people voted, and the winner was the power button

Figure 9.3 NYC's 2010 limited edition wrapper.[14]

design. To celebrate the condom wrapper's arrival, the health department launched the NYC Condom with the new power button wrapper at the Village Halloween Parade and at five live condom distribution events at major transportation hubs across the city; over 40,000 condoms were distributed that one evening. The winning "power on" logo was a creation of Luis Acosta, a designer from Queens, who said, "I wanted to associate it with something we see in our daily lives so it wasn't taboo for people"[15] (see Figure 9.3). It sounds as if he understands social norming theories!

Results

The following brief summary of an evaluative research effort is a great example of the value and necessity of carrying out research to monitor your campaign once it is launched, keeping your eyes and ears open for possible, even critical, campaign enhancements.

In 2007, a team of health professionals and researchers with the DOHMH assessed awareness of and experience with the NYC Condom via street intercept surveys at seven public events targeting priority condom distribution populations.[16] One of the motivations for the survey was to address anecdotal reports from organizations that the public wanted larger condoms for free as well. Findings suggested high levels of NYC Condom awareness, and that awareness translated into use. The study also confirmed that demand existed for alternatives to the current NYC Condoms, as most respondents:

- were aware of NYC Condoms (76%)
- used them (69% of those who obtained them)
- wanted alternative condoms offered for free (80%)
  - 22% wanted ultra thin
  - 18% wanted extra strength
  - 14% wanted a larger size

On the basis of these results, the DOHMH began distributing alternative condoms in November 2008, including this study's most frequently named types—ultra thin/extra sensitive, extra strength, and larger size.

POSITIONING DEFINED

Positioning is the act of designing the organization's actual and perceived offering in such a way that it lands on and occupies a distinctive place in the mind of the target audience—where you want it to be.[17] Keep in mind that your offering, which you will design in the next three chapters, includes your product, its price, and how it is accessed—place. The desired positioning for this offer is then supported by promotional elements including messages, messengers, and media channels.

Think of your target audience as having a perceptual map that they will use to locate your offer. Consider further that they have a different map for each product category (one each for cars, airlines, fast food, beverages, etc., and, more relevant for social marketers perhaps, one each for exercise, workplace safety, recycling, organ donation, etc.). Figure 9.4 illustrates a simplified version of a perceptual map, showing which brands are perceived as being similar and which are competing against each other. Most perceptual maps for products and services use data from consumer surveys evaluating those products and services on specific attributes.

There is a good reason we present and recommend you take this step *after* you have selected and researched your target audience and *before* you develop your marketing mix strategy. Since offers are positioned differently for different markets (e.g., exercise for tweens versus seniors), choosing an audience comes first. And since your product, price, place, and promotion will determine (to a great extent) where you land, it makes sense to know your desired destination. This will help guide your marketing strategy by clarifying the brand's

Figure 9.4 A perceptual map.

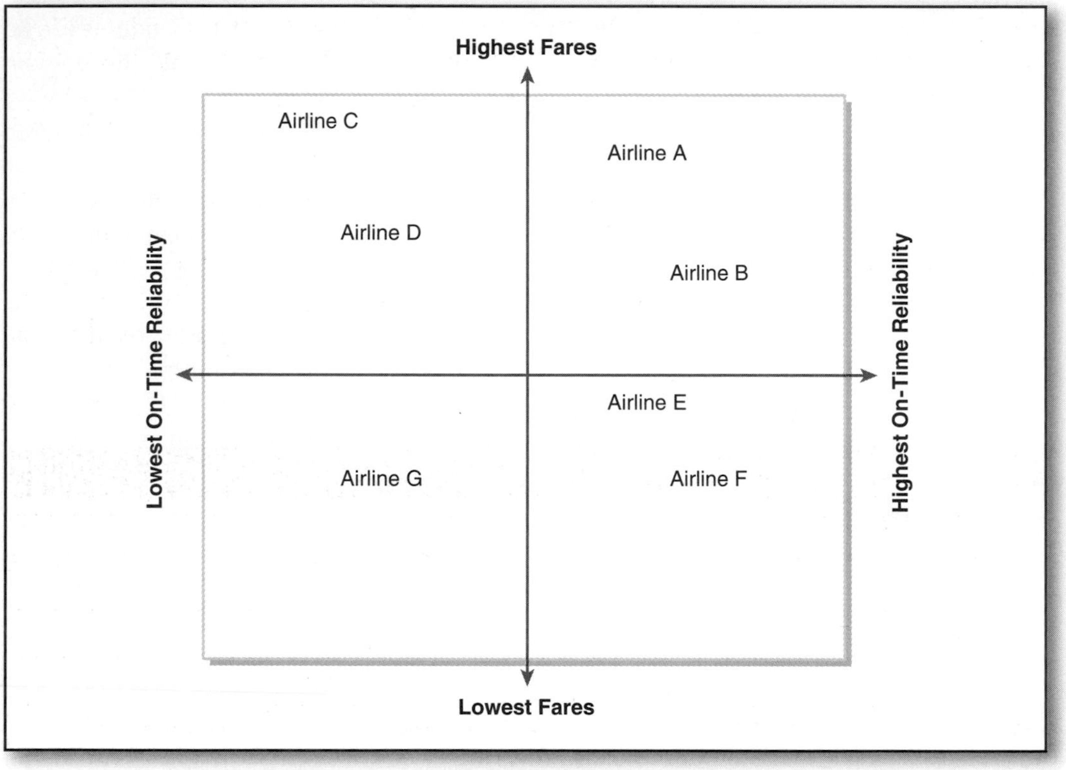

essence, what goals it helps the consumer achieve, and how it does so in a unique way.

As you may recall, we have defined social marketing as a process that applies marketing principles and techniques to create, communicate, and deliver value in order to influence target audience behaviors. The result of positioning is the successful creation of a customer-focused value proposition; that is, a cogent reason why the target audience should buy the product—from you![18]

Positioning in the Commercial Sector

Perhaps because the commercial sector has embraced this positioning concept for decades, great examples of clear positioning and the value proposition are easy to find, as suggested in Table 9.1. In the Focus column, we have linked these value propositions to social marketing theories and models we have discussed in prior chapters: benefits, barriers, and competition. One new option, now that we have introduced the positioning concept, would be a focus on repositioning—where a brand manager is interested in moving a product from its current location in the mind of target audiences to a new, more desirable one (see Figure 9.5).

Commercial marketers also often consider and establish *points of difference* and *points of parity*, which are described by Kotler and Keller.[20] Points of difference are attributes or benefits consumers strongly associate with a brand and believe they could not find with a competitive brand. Examples include FedEx (guaranteed overnight delivery), Costco (lower costs for similar products), and Lexus (quality). Points of parity, by

Figure 9.5 Repositioning milk as "cool."[19]

Table 9.1 Commercial Sector Brand Positioning Examples

Category	Brand	Focus	Value Proposition
Car	Volvo	Benefits	Safety
Fast food	Subway	Barriers	Fresh, healthy options
Airlines	Southwest	Competition	No frills; lower costs
Beverages	Milk	Repositioning	From boring to cool

contrast, are associations that are not necessarily unique to the brand but may be considered essential to a legitimate offering within a certain product or service category (e.g., a bank needs to at least offer access to ATM machines, online banking services, and checking accounts in order to be considered a bank). Competitive points-of-difference positioning might instead or also work to negate the competitors' points of difference. One good example Kotler and Keller highlight is a Miller Lite advertising strategy that ends with the tagline, "Everything you've always wanted in a beer . . . and less."[21]

STEP 6: DEVELOP A POSITIONING STATEMENT

Positioning principles and processes for social marketing are similar to those of commercial marketing. With the profile of your target audience in mind, including any unique demographic, geographic, psychographic, and behavior-related characteristics and the findings from your research on perceived barriers, benefits, competitors, and influential others, you will now "simply" craft a positioning statement.

One way to develop a positioning statement is to fill in the blanks to this phrase, or one similar to it:

> We want [TARGET AUDIENCE] to see [DESIRED BEHAVIOR] as [SET OF BENEFITS] and as more important and beneficial than [COMPETITION].

Keep in mind this positioning statement is "for internal use only." It is not your ultimate message to your target audiences. It will, however, be shared with others working with you on your effort to develop your marketing mix strategy, helping to unify and strengthen decision making. Consider how agreement on the following statements would guide these teams:

- "We want pregnant women to see breastfeeding exclusively for the first six months as a way to bond with their child and contribute to their health and as more important than concerns about nursing in public."
- "We want media reporters to see using nonstigmatizing mental health labels (e.g., 'this person has schizophrenia' versus 'this person is schizophrenic') as a way to help those with mental illnesses and as a way to be a respected and leading role model in the profession."
- "We want homeowners who love gardening to see composting foodwaste as an easy way to contribute to the environment and create great compost for their garden at the same time, and to see that this is better for the environment than putting it in the garbage, which then goes to the landfill, or down the kitchen disposal and into water that has to be treated."
- "We want people shopping for a puppy to visit the Humane Society's Web site first to see if the pet they have in mind is just waiting for someone to adopt it, and that this is likely to be a less expensive and more convenient option than going to the classified ads."

Inspiration for your descriptive phrase will come from the lists of barriers and benefits identified in your research. As you may recall, the ideal research will have included a prioritization of barriers and benefits, giving you a sense of what factors would be most important to highlight. You are searching for the "higher value," the key benefits to be gained or costs that will be avoided by adopting the desired behavior.

To leverage prior steps in the planning model, you may find it advantageous to consider a focus for your positioning statements, choosing from among those that drive home specific *behaviors*, highlight *benefits*, overcome *barriers*, upstage the *competition*, or *reposition* an "old brand." More detail on each of these options is presented in the next five sections, with a couple of brief examples and one longer illustration.

BEHAVIOR-FOCUSED POSITIONING

For some social marketing programs, especially those with a new and/or very specific desired behavior in mind, you may benefit from a behavior-focused positioning. In these cases, a description of your behavior will be highlighted, as shown in these examples:

- 3 Days 3 Ways, a campaign sponsored by King County (Washington) Emergency Management, encourages citizens to be prepared for emergencies and disasters in three ways: (1) Make a plan, (2) build a kit, and (3) get involved[22]
- 311, Transportation Security Administration's travel tip effort, was developed in 2006 to support travelers in knowing what liquids and gels they could carry on and how many (see Figure 9.6)

In these cases, making sure target audiences know the specifics of the desired behavior is key to successful outcomes, as illustrated in the following example.

Example: 5 a Day

In 1991, the National Cancer Institute (NCI), in cooperation with the Produce for Better Health Foundation, created "5 a Day for Better Health," a national program that approaches

Figure 9.6 A behavior-focused positioning from the TSA on a wallet card for travelers[23]

Figure 9.7 The Produce for Better Health Foundation's behavior-focused positioning.[24]

Americans with a simple, positive message: "Eat five or more servings of vegetables and fruit daily for better health" (see Figure 9.7).

This key message has been repeated using a well-integrated strategy and a multitude of venues over the years: plastic produce bags, grocery bags, in-store signage and displays, produce packaging labels, supermarket tours, recipe cards, brochures, grocery store flyer ads, magazine articles, newspaper ads, news stories, the Internet, radio news inserts, television news inserts (cooking/recipe spots), radio public service announcements (PSAs), television PSAs, billboards, CD-ROMs in elementary schools, nutrition newsletters, patient nutrition education materials, pay stubs, school curricula, preschool programs, food assistance program materials, church bulletins and newsletters, posters, restaurant menus, Girl/Boy Scout badges, 4-H materials, food bank program materials, health fairs, county fairs, cookbooks, children's coloring books, and videotapes. In 2006, a new slogan, "The Color Way," was added to promote more variety in the 5 a Day mix we choose.

A press release from the Produce for Better Health Foundation in November 2005 reported good outcome news. According to the ACNielsen study of nearly 2,600 households, the number of Americans claiming to eat five or more daily servings was 18% in 2004, up 50% from 2003. The study also found a clear link between awareness and consumption, with a jump in consumption of five or more daily servings reported by those claiming awareness of the foundation's Color Way messages. More than 30% of those who were most aware of the Color Way message reported consuming five or more servings of fruits and vegetables a day, compared to less than 10% of those who were not aware of the campaign. This is further backed up by purchasing data, which show that those most aware of the Color Way message spent $111 more annually on fruits and vegetables than those not aware of the campaign.[25]

BARRIERS-FOCUSED POSITIONING

With this type of focus, you want your offer's positioning to help overcome or at least minimize perceived barriers, such as concern about self-efficacy, fear, or perceived high costs associated with performing the behavior:

- For tobacco users who want to quit, quitlines are often positioned as hopeful and encouraging, as in the following poem (perhaps more like a rap) that appeared on the Washington State Department of Health's Web site in 2007:

In the New Year, make smoking a thing of the past
Put yourself first and your habit last
Start the year right; start out on top
And make '07 the year that you stop

Tobacco products will harm your health
They'll deplete your energy as well as your wealth
Although smoking is a hard habit to break
With determination and support it's a change you can make

Call the Washington State Tobacco Quit Line to learn how
A quit coach will assist you at 1–800–QUIT–NOW
A customized plan and one-on-one counseling you'll get
To help make '07 smoke-free, and your best year yet

The call is confidential, the service is free
And can double your chance of quitting successfully
More than 80,000 Washingtonians have made the call
For free counseling and quit kits available for all

Don't hesitate; call the quit line today
And in the New Year, you'll be well on your way![26]

- Some women avoid or postpone having mammograms when they are afraid to get bad news. This explains why many organizations have positioned mammograms as "early detection," a way to get treatment before it spreads.

In the following illustration, the positioning reflects audience concerns about time, effort, cost, and "know-how."

Example: Recycling Your Cell Phone Is as Easy as 1, 2, 3

According to some estimates, there are over 800 million retired cell phones discarded in drawers and desks in the United States, and over 140 million more enter the waste stream each year.[27] Perceived barriers to recycling them range from not knowing how and where to considerations about the time involved in going to a special recycling station to understanding why it even matters. Inform, a nonprofit organization in the U.S., has a goal to "empower citizens, businesses and government to adopt practices and policies that will sustain our planet for future generations."[28] One of their initiatives is to support cell phone recycling, and their offer and its positioning appear to address consumer barriers head on. They say, "It's as easy as 1–2–3!" Just follow these steps posted on their Web site:

1. Print out the pre-paid mailing label and cut it out along the dotted line.

2. Place your cell phone, charger and accessories in the envelope and affix the mailing label.

3. Drop it off at the post office or in a mailbox. Postage is already paid, so shipping is free![29]

Additional messages on the Web site stress the problem with disposing of unwanted cell phones in the garbage, describing their toxic substances and how, when dumped in landfills, they pollute the environment and potentially harm human health.

BENEFITS-FOCUSED POSITIONING

When the best hook seems to be related to the WIFM ("what's in it for me") factor, perceived benefits become the focus of the positioning:

- Natural yard care practices, such as pulling weeds versus spraying them, are positioned as ways to ensure the health of your children and pets
- Moderate physical activity, such as raking leaves and taking the stairs instead of the elevator, is positioned as something you can fit into your daily routine
- Reading to your child 20 minutes each night is positioned as a way to help ensure he or she will do well in school

In the following illustration of benefit-focused positioning, the focus is once more on benefits your target audience wants and believes they can get.

Example: Road Crew

Michael Rothschild, Professor Emeritus at the University of Wisconsin, believes that good positioning begins with a clear understanding of the target and their competitive choices. He also believes that when developing this positioning, a marketer needs to learn about the target, current usage patterns, and why existing competitive brands are succeeding. This is exactly what a team he led in Wisconsin in the spring of 2000 did for the Wisconsin Department of Transportation.

The "assignment" was to reduce alcohol-related crashes in rural Wisconsin. There was ample prior evidence that the group of people most likely to drink, drive, and crash were 21- to 34-year-old single men. The team conducted 17 focus groups, 11 with the target audience and 6 more with those who observed the target (e.g., bar owners, law enforcement ambulance drivers, judges). Meetings with the target were held in the back of local taverns so that respondents would feel comfortable discussing the issues. By asking the target why they drove after drinking, the team learned about reasons for driving drunk: to get home; to avoid the hassle of coming back in the morning to get the vehicle; everybody does it; at 1:00 A.M. the target is fearless; and there is a low risk of getting caught. When asked to help design a ride program that they would use, they asked for:

- Vehicles that were at least as nice as their own
- A ride from home to the bar, between bars, and then home again, as they wouldn't want to leave their cars behind and wanted to go between bars
- The right to smoke and drink in the vehicles

This is exactly what they were then offered. The resulting service uses limousines and other luxury vehicles to pick people up at their home, business, or hotel; take them to the bar of their choice; take them between bars; and then take them home at the end of the evening. As allowed by local ordinances, passengers may smoke and drink in the vehicles. The cost to the passenger is $15 to $20 for the evening.

Figure 9.8 shows the initial poster that was used to raise awareness. It doesn't tell people not to drive drunk; it focuses on Road Crew's position. That is, it tells people that they can have more fun if they use Road Crew than if they drive themselves. Research had shown that the target wanted to have fun and that drinking was a part of having fun. The target didn't feel that driving drunk was fun, but that it was necessary in order to have fun earlier in the evening.

By 2008, the program was operating in 32 small communities in rural Wisconsin and had provided over 97,000 rides and prevented an estimated 140 alcohol-related crashes and six alcohol-related fatalities. The costs incurred from an alcohol-related crash are approximately $231,000, but the cost to avoid a crash through the use of Road Crew is approximately $6,400. This means that it is about 37 times more expensive to incur a crash than it is to avoid one. Total net savings through the use of Road Crew has been more than $31 million. Of special note is that research shows that while driving behavior has changed dramatically, people are not drinking more as a result of getting rides. After receiving seed money to begin the program, communities are able to self-sustain from ride fares and tavern contributions.[31]

Figure 9.8 Repositioning Road Crew as a cool way to get around and have fun.[30]

Road Crew has succeeded because it is well positioned relative to its competition. Rather than telling people that drunk driving is bad, they are told that using Road Crew is more fun than the competitive choice. Road Crew offers more benefits than driving. In the past, driving was often the only choice available; anyone who admitted to not being able to drive home was seen as a "wimp." But now, choosing the Road Crew is a sign of being cool. (For more insights on Road Crew, go to www.roadcrewonline.org.)

COMPETITION-FOCUSED POSITIONING

A fourth option for focus is the competition, one quite appropriate when your target audience finds "their offer" quite appealing and your offer "a pain":

- Youth abstinence advocates have tough competitors, including the media, entertainment, peer pressure, and raging hormones. Positioning abstinence as postponing sex, versus "no sex," has become an easier sell for many.
- In 2003, New York City announced a convenient and cost-saving alternative to dialing 911—dialing 311 instead. With a vast majority of the more than 8 million annual calls to 911 representing nonemergency situations, the service was anticipated to delight citizens and decrease operating costs. All calls are answered by a live operator, 24 hours a day, seven days a week, and can be translated into 170 languages.[32]
- Consequences of tobacco use are often positioned as gross, realistic, and shocking (see Figure 9.9).

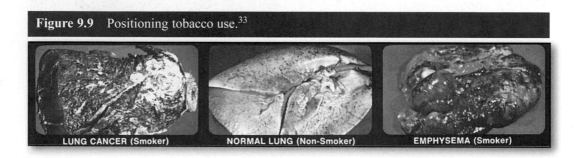

Figure 9.9   Positioning tobacco use.[33]

LUNG CANCER (Smoker)   NORMAL LUNG (Non-Smoker)   EMPHYSEMA (Smoker)

Because consumers typically choose products and services that give them the greatest value, marketers work to position their brands on the key benefits that they offer relative to competing brands. Kotler and Armstrong illustrate this with six possible value propositions as shown in Table 9.2.[34]

An additional model for developing competitive advantage focuses on creating *competitive superiority*, a more rigorous objective. The same four tactics mentioned in Chapter 8 are used in tandem, as illustrated in Table 9.3. A *benefit-to-benefit superiority* tactic appeals to values higher than those perceived for the competition (e.g., a child who wants and needs a parent is compared to the short-term pleasures of smoking). A *cost-to-benefit superiority* tactic focuses on decreasing costs of or barriers to adopting the desired

Table 9.2   Illustrating Value Propositions Based on Price and Product Quality

More for More	Starbucks
More for the Same	Lexus vs. Mercedes Benz
Same for Less	Amazon
Less for Much Less	Motel 6
More for Less	Costco
Less for Much Less	Southwest Airlines

behavior and, at the same time, decreasing perceived benefits of the competition (e.g., success stories from cessation classes include a testimonial from a spouse about how nice it is to have clean air in the house). A *benefit-to-cost superiority* tactic emphasizes the benefits of the desired behavior and the costs of the competing behavior(s) (e.g., abilities of teen athletes who don't smoke as compared with those who do). A *cost-to-cost superiority* tactic relies on a favorable comparison of costs of the desired behavior relative to those of the competition (e.g., short-term nicotine withdrawal symptoms are compared with living with emphysema).

Table 9.3   Creating Competitive Superiority

Competing Behavior	Desired Behavior	
	Increase Benefits	Decrease Costs/Barriers
Decrease Benefits	Tactic A: Benefit-to-benefit superiority tactic	Tactic B: Cost-to-benefit superiority tactic
Increase Costs/Barriers:	Tactic C: Benefit-to-cost superiority tactic	Tactic D: Cost-to-cost superiority tactic

Example: The truth® Campaign

truth®, launched in February 2000, is the largest national youth smoking prevention campaign in the United States. The campaign targeting youth aged 12–17 was created by Legacy®, a national public health foundation with the mission to keep young people from smoking and help all smokers quit. truth® exposes the tactics of the tobacco industry, the truth about addiction, and the health effects and social consequences of smoking. In 1999, one year prior to the campaign's launch, an estimated 35% of youth in 9th, 10th, 11th, and 12th grades had used tobacco one or more times in the past 30 days.[35]

At the core of the truth® campaign's promotional strategies are messages about the marketing tactics of the tobacco industry, as well as the health effects, social costs, addictiveness, and ingredients/additives of tobacco. To ensure that truth® is relevant to teens, teens are involved in testing advertising concepts and are encouraged to provide suggestions and feedback through the truth® Web site at http://www.thetruth.com/. The style and tone of truth® ads are "in-your-face" and hard-hitting, responding to teens' desire for powerful messages that display courage and honesty in a forceful way:

- Sodium hydroxide is a caustic compound found in hair removal products. It's also found in cigarettes.
- Tobacco companies' products kill 36,000 people every month. That's more lives thrown away than there are public garbage cans in New York City.
- Human sweat contains urea and ammonia. So do cigarettes.
- Benzene, arsenic, and cyanide are all poisons. They're all in cigarette smoke, too.
- There are more than 5 million deaths worldwide from smoking each year.[36]

A growing body of research has found that the truth® campaign accelerated the decline in youth smoking rates between 2000 and 2004. According to research published online in February 2009 by the *American Journal of Preventive Medicine* (*AJPM*), truth® was directly responsible for keeping 450,000 teens from starting to smoke during its first four years. A second study released through *AJPM* in February 2009 found that the campaign had not only paid for itself in its first two years, but also saved between $1.9 and $5.4 billion in medical care costs to society.

REPOSITIONING

What happens when your program has a current positioning that you feel is in the way of your achieving your behavior change goals? Several factors may have contributed to this wake-up call and sense that you need to "relocate":

- You might need to attract *new audiences* to sustain your growth, and these new markets may not find your current position appealing. For example, adults over 50 not engaged in regular physical activity may have tuned out messages regarding exercise long ago, as they could hear only the "vigorous aerobic" recommendation. Planners turned to moderate physical activity.
- You may be suffering from an image problem. When bike helmets were first promoted to youth, they balked. Making the behavior "fun, easy, and popular" for the audience is Dr. Bill Smith's recommendation and could well describe the strategy in Figure 9.10. These three words focus program managers on how to change behavior by giving people what they want along with what we feel they need.

○ *Fun* in this context means to provide your audience with perceived benefits they care about

○ *Easy* means to remove all possible barriers to action and make the behavior as simple and accessible as possible

○ *Popular* means to help the audience feel that this is something others are doing, particularly others the audience believes are important to them[37]

Or you may have just received (as do lots of others) the results of an *evaluation* research project indicating disappointing outcomes as a result of your current positioning strategy, as was the case in the following example.

Example: The New D.A.R.E. Program

The Drug Abuse Resistance Education (D.A.R.E.) program was considered a pioneer prevention effort when it was founded in Los Angeles in 1983. But the old-style approach where an officer stands behind a podium and lectures students in straight rows is gone. The New D.A.R.E., revitalized as a result of a national research effort funded by a $13.7 million grant from the Robert Wood Johnson Foundation in 2001, has gone high tech, incorporates interactive exercises, and is using a decision-based model. Now D.A.R.E. officers are trained and positioned as "coaches," supporting kids who are using research-based refusal strategies in high-stakes peer-pressured environments. As described on the program's Web site, "students are getting to see for themselves—via stunning brain imagery—tangible proof of how substances diminish mental activity, emotions, coordination, and movement. Mock courtroom exercises are bringing home the social and legal consequences of drug use and violence."[39] (See Figure 9.11.)

Figure 9.10 Positioning of wearing protective gear as fun, easy, and popular.[38]

Safety Tips

1: Wear protective gear, including a helmet, pads or guards on the arms, wrists and knees, and be sure to wear proper shoes, not flip-flops or bare feet

2: Never ride a scooter at night. Unlike bikes, scooters don't have reflectors.

3: Children under 8 should always be supervised by an adult when riding a scooter. Older kids should be supervised if crossing streets on a scooter.

Figure 9.11 Repositioning D.A.R.E.

According to Charlie Parsons, president and chief executive director of D.A.R.E. America,

> New D.A.R.E. is setting the gold standard for the future. Prevention inside the 21st century school house will need to be effective, diverse, accountable, and mean more things to more people, particularly with the safety issues that have emerged since Columbine and terrorist alerts.[40]

HOW POSITIONING RELATES TO BRANDING

Although the concept of the brand and the branding process will be covered in the next chapter focusing on product, you may have immediate questions regarding positioning and how it relates to branding that we will address briefly at this point. It helps to distinguish the two by referring to a few basic definitions:

- Brand is a name, term, sign, symbol, and/or design that identifies the maker or seller of a product (e.g., ENERGY STAR® identifies products that are energy efficient, according to the Environmental Protection Agency [EPA])[41]
- Brand identity is how you (the maker) want your target audience to think, feel, and act with respect to your brand (e.g., EPA wants citizens to see products with the ENERGY STAR label as a way to help the environment and save on electrical power bills)
- Brand image is how your target audience actually ends up thinking, feeling, and acting relative to your brand (e.g., what citizens know about the ENERGY STAR label and whether they associate it with energy and cost savings)
- Branding is the process of developing an intended brand identity (e.g., activities that EPA has undertaken to determine and ensure this desired brand identity)

Your positioning statement is something you and others can count on to provide parameters and inspiration for developing your desired brand identity—how you want the desired behavior to be seen by the target audience. It will provide strong and steady guidance for your decision making regarding your marketing mix, as it is the 4Ps that will determine where your offer lands in the minds of your target audience. And when your brand image doesn't align with your desired positioning (brand identity), you'll look to your 4Ps for "help" in repositioning the brand.

ETHICAL CONSIDERATIONS WHEN DEVELOPING A POSITIONING STATEMENT

When developing your positioning statement, several ethical questions may (actually should) come to your mind. You will notice many of these relate to the familiar "truth in advertising" code.

If your positioning statement is *behavior focused*, ensure your recommendations are accurate. For 5 a Day the Color Way, detailed information on the Web site clarified why these specific behaviors are important. "Blue/purple fruits and vegetables contain varying amounts of health-promoting phytochemicals such as anthocyanins and phenolics, currently being studied for their antioxidant and anti-aging benefits."[42]

If your positioning statement focuses on *benefits* for the target audience, you will want to be certain that you can really deliver these benefits. A campaign promoting moderate physical activity should make it clear to potential "buyers" what levels and types of physical activity are needed to achieve any health gains promised, and at what levels.

If your positioning statement focuses on how the target audience will be able to overcome their *barriers*, you will want to be certain you paint a realistic picture. Communications promoting quitlines as a way to quit smoking should be certain to include rates of success and the fact that not all those who call will be able to quit. If you reread the poem from the Washington State Department of Health's Web site, note that the quitline delivers on its positioning as "hopeful and encouraging" but doesn't mention any guarantees.

If your positioning statement focuses on the *competition*, be certain what you say about them is really true and not exaggerated. As you read, New York City promises better and "seamless" service when you call 311 rather than 911 for a missing car. It wouldn't take many citizens not getting quick help to spread the word that 911 will get you better service faster.

And if your positioning statement focuses on *repositioning* the brand, be sure your offer is really "new and improved." The New D.A.R.E program will need to be obviously distinct from the prior program.

CHAPTER SUMMARY

Positioning is the act of designing the organization's offering in such a way that it lands on and occupies a distinctive place in the mind of the target audience—where you want it to be. Step 6 in the marketing planning process recommends that you develop a positioning statement at this point. The research on your target audience's barriers, benefits, competitors, and influential others in Step 5 will provide the inspiration you need. It will also help build consensus among your colleagues and partners, ensuring fewer surprises and disappointments as you move forward to developing your strategies.

Positioning statements may be focused on behaviors, barriers, benefits, the competition, and/or on repositioning. Your decisions will reflect your value proposition, a reason why the target audience should buy the product—from you!

Take time and care to develop this statement, as you will refer to it frequently when developing each of the 4Ps. This will help ensure the "proper landing" you have in mind.

Stopping Aquatic Hitchhikers:
A Branding Strategy
(2010)

Background

Invasive species represent one of the greatest threats to global biodiversity (a term used to describe the variety of living things—the different plants, animals, and microorganisms; the genes they contain; and the ecosystems of which they are a part).[43] Aquatic invasive species are particularly problematic. Because they are underwater, and thus out of sight and out of mind, they can be transported to another lake or stream where, if conditions are right, they become established and create drastic results. Unfortunately, most people don't understand the scope and meaning of this concept or the various threats it poses. A branding strategy with a multitiered engagement platform developed by Joe Starinchak and fellow team members at the U.S. Fish and Wildlife Service provided a solution.[44] Secondary research that included an *extensive literature search and review of prior and existing campaigns* shed light on "what not to do." Informal *focus groups* and *personal interviews* provided direction that guided the brand development and selection process. And a pilot that included *qualitative evaluative research* with target audiences provided the inspiration for national campaign adoption and rollout.

Target Audiences and Desired Behaviors

Efforts to decrease transporting aquatic invasive species target audiences downstream (aquatic recreational users), midstream (governmental agencies and nonprofit organizations), and upstream (policy makers). Specific behaviors to influence are highlighted in Table 9.4. This case will focus on the recreational users downstream.

Table 9.4   Desired Behaviors for Audiences Downstream, Midstream, and Upstream

	Aquatic Recreational Users	Federal and State Resource Local Government Agencies	Policy Makers
Target Audience	Boaters, anglers, personal watercraft operators, rafters, kayakers, sailors, float plane operators, recreational bait harvesters, waterfowl hunters	Resource management agencies, parks and recreation, water	Elected officials and senior administrators of agencies responsible for managing fish and wildlife resources
Desired Behavior	Inspect, clean, and dry your aquatic recreational equipment every time you leave the water to prevent the continued spread of aquatic invasive species	Promote a simple prevention message to the aquatic recreational community, build community prevention infrastructure, and embed aquatic resource conservation into the community's social fabric	Support increased funding to address the invasive species issue

Audience Insights

Research activities to understand barriers and benefits began with an extensive *literature review* and *inventory of prior and existing outreach materials and efforts.* The team then conducted *informal focus groups* and *personal interviews* with recreational users. In the end, this six-month effort convinced the team that a focus on developing and distributing species-specific materials in the past had not addressed key audience barriers to action or major perceived benefits:

- Barriers
  - Lack of understanding and awareness of the problem
  - Misperceptions about the impacts of individual action
  - Alienation from technical jargon used to describe the issue
  - Lack of infrastructure to assist with and reinforce behaviors
  - Multiple and conflicting messages
  - Fallacies and myths that undermined successes in outreach
- Perceived benefits
  - Protection of home waters
  - Maintenance of traditional recreational uses
  - Reduced equipment maintenance costs

Branding Strategy

Joe and his team were clear about their desired brand identity—how they wanted the target audience to think, feel, and act with respect to the brand. They wanted aquatic recreational users to perceive the brand as collaborative, responsive, and innovative. They wanted those performing the desired actions to be clear about the desired behavior and feel environmentally responsible as a result. Based on this direction, they worked with a branding agency that developed 75 concepts that were eventually narrowed down to the five most viable options. Using a "feet-on-the-street" research strategy, they tested the conceptual brands with shoppers at tackle and fly shops, West Marine retail outlets, public boat ramps, bait shops, water access points, and marinas. In the end, the "stop sign" theme resonated most positively with these audiences and provided the most support for the desired brand identity.

Results From Pilots in Three States

In 2006–2007, the brand and alternative communication channels were pilot tested in three states. Joe's team then created two surveys to help select the most efficient and effective channels for campaign rollout. One survey was conducted using face-to-face interviews; the other used a self-administered questionnaire. Both were pretested and then fielded at water access sites, taking only about five minutes to complete. Table 9.5 shows how the respondents rated the variety of media channels in the three pilot states: Minnesota, Iowa, and Wisconsin. Table 9.6 addresses the extent to which respondents believed Stop Aquatic Hitchhikers messaging would influence their future actions.

As findings suggest, three channels rose to the top for all three states: (1) signs at water accesses, (2) watercraft inspectors who would help boaters look for "hitchhikers" (*product*), and (3) billboards adjacent to boat launches (see Figures 9.12, 9.13, and 9.14).

Table 9.5 Perceived Effective Media Channels

"What are the three best ways to reach you regarding boating and fishing information?"		
Minnesota (*n* = 219)	**Iowa** (*n* = 48)	**Wisconsin** (*n* = 47)
Signs at water accesses (79%)	Signs at water accesses (65%)	Signs at water accesses (81%)
Watercraft inspectors (58%)	Billboards (19%)	Watercraft inspectors (43%)
Regulation booklets (47%)	Aquatic invasive species ID cards (13%)	Billboards (32%)
Television ads (47%)	Watercraft inspectors (13%)	Television ads (26%)
Billboards (35%)	Radio ads (13%)	Regulation booklets (21%)
Radio ads (25%)	Stickers (10%)	Newspaper ads (17%)
Stickers (23%)	Television ads (10%)	Radio ads (15%)
Newspaper ads (18%)	Windshield flyers (6%)	Other (13%)
Signs along roadways (9%)	Newspaper ads (6%)	Stickers (6%)
Gas pump ads (8%)	Highway radio ads (6%)	Kiosk at Cabela's (6%)
Displays at rest areas (1%)		Signs along roadways (6%)
Invasive species ID cards (1%)		
Windshield flyers (1%)		

Table 9.6   Whether Strategies Will Influence Future Behaviors

| "To what extent will these messages influence you to remove aquatic hitchhikers in the future?" | | | | |
Level of Influence	Minnesota ($n = 219$)	Iowa ($n = 48$)	Wisconsin ($n = 47$)	Overall ($n = 314$)
Large	90%	38%	55%	77%
Moderate	9%	46%	43%	20%
Subtotal	99%	84%	98%	97%
Small	1%	15%	2%	3%
None	0%	2%	0%	1%

Figure 9.12   Watercraft inspectors.[45]

Figure 9.13   Billboard. [47]

Figure 9.14   Signs at water access points.[46]

These findings provided clarity and confidence when selecting communication channels and were promising relative to behavior intent. They were used to engage and persuade state and federal resource management agencies and their partners to adopt the brand and key messages. To date (2011), 1,030 organizations have joined the campaign, including national environmental organizations (The Nature Conservancy, Sierra Club), national conservation organizations, businesses, other federal agencies, and state fish and wildlife agencies in all 50 states. Additional communication channels have included promotional items (e.g., hats, T-shirts, and boat key chains), social media (e.g., Facebook, and blogs), broadcast media (e.g., ESPN Outdoors), and national print media to provide additional exposure.

Pledges have also been used in some communities, with watercraft inspectors and other agency personnel engaging individuals at sports events, boating shows, and boat ramps to take prevention pledges (see Box 9.1). Individuals making the pledge are given a wallet card as a reminder, and participating retailers honor the Stop Aquatic Hitchhikers pledge by providing a nominal discount on merchandise. Additionally, the campaign has catalyzed state partners and local nonprofit organizations to develop prevention infrastructures, such as installing high-powered pressure washers at water access sites and scrubbing and cleaning stations to support individuals in adopting the prevention behaviors.

Box 9.1
A Pledge Used in Some Communities

Stop Aquatic Hitchhikers Pledge

I want to do my part to protect the waters where I recreate and any waters that I might visit. I pledge to abide by the following each time I visit a body of water.

- Remove any visible mud, plants, fish or animals before transporting equipment
- Drain water from equipment before transporting
- Clean and dry anything that came in contact with water (boats, trailers, equipment, clothing, dogs, etc.)

Postscript

The Combined Power and Stickiness of Social Marketing and Social Media

Unfortunately, zebra mussels, a highly invasive mussel species, were recently found (November 2010) in a lake in southeast Nebraska. These mussels were originally introduced into the Great Lakes through the ballast water of large oceangoing ships in the late 1980s. Since then, these mussels have spread westward to many different states. The likely vector for spreading these mussels is recreational boats trailed overland from the Great Lakes to other bodies of water.

A 13-year-old Boy Scout named Addison Krebs found the invader. Since then, the Nebraska Game and Parks Commission has confirmed the presence of zebra mussels and is taking steps to contain this harmful species. However, the finding has piqued Krebs's curiosity, and he has learned more about the invasive species issue. Because of the finding, Krebs has done some research and has joined the Stop Aquatic Hitchhikers Facebook page. Also, he has adopted the campaign brand as his Facebook avatar and switches among the two different brand signatures and a picture of the zebra mussel. This example shows the power of combining theory-based social marketing with social media and social networking sites such as Facebook as complementary ways to maximize different channels and promote behavior change.

CHAPTER 9 NOTES

1. Ries, A., & Trout, J. (1982). *Positioning: The battle for your mind* (p. 3). New York, NY: Warner Books.

2. Ibid., pp. 7–8.

3. New York City Department of Health and Mental Hygiene (DOHMH). (n.d.). *HIV/AIDS information.* Retrieved July 29, 2011, from http://www.nyc.gov/html/doh/html/ah/ah.shtml

4. *Report of the New York City Commission on HIV/AIDS.* (2005, October 31). Retrieved July 19, 2011, from http://www.nyc.gov/html/doh/downloads/pdf/ah/ah-nychivreport.pdf

5. DOHMH. (2007, February 14). *Health Department launches the nation's first official city condom* [Press release]. Retrieved July 19, 2011, from http://www.nyc.gov/html/doh/html/pr2007/pr008-07.shtml

6. *Report of the New York City Commission on HIV/AIDS*, 2005.

7. Ibid.

8. NYC Dept. of Health and Mental Hygiene.

9. DOHMH, 2007, *Health Department launches.*

10. Ibid.

11. Ibid.

12. Ibid.

13. NYC Dept. of Health and Mental Hygiene.

14. Ibid.

15. Smith, R. (2010, March 9). *Official condom design: New York's new sex symbol.* Retrieved July 19, 2011, from http://www.npr.org/templates/story/story.php?storyId=124503824

16. Burke, R., Wilson, J., Bernstein, K., Grosskopf, N., Murrill, C., Cutler, B., . . . Begier, E. (2009, October 15). The NYC Condom: Use and acceptability of New York City's branded condom. *American Journal of Public Health, 99*(12). Retrieved July 29, 2011, from http://ajph.aphapublications.org/cgi/content/short/99/12/2178

17. Adapted from Kotler, P., & Keller, K. L. (2005). *Marketing management* (12th ed., p. 320). Upper Saddle River, NJ: Prentice Hall.

18. Ibid.

19. Photo courtesy of the National Dairy Council.

20. Kotler & Keller, 2005, *Marketing management.*

21. Ibid., pp. 312–313.

22. King County Emergency Management. (2006). *3 days, 3 ways, are you ready?* Retrieved January 19, 2007, from http://www.govlink.org/3days3ways/

23. Transportation Security Administration. (n.d.). *311 for carry-ons.* Retrieved January 19, 2007, from http://www.tsa.gov/assets/pdf/311-credit-card.pdf

24. Photo courtesy of the Produce for Better Health Foundation.

25. Produce for Better Health Foundation. (2005, November 30). *Fruit and vegetable consumption on the rise for first time in nearly 15 years.* Retrieved January 19, 2007, from http://www.5aday.com/html/press/pressrelease.php?recordid=159

26. Washington State Department of Health. (2007). *Tobacco quit line.* Retrieved January 22, 2007, from http://www.quitline.com/

27. Phones 4 Charity Web site: http://www.phones4charity.org/

28. Inform, Inc., Web site: http://www.informinc.org/gs-recycle.php

29. Ibid.

30. Road Crew, University of Wisconsin

31. Rothschild, M. (2007, June). *The impact of Road Crew on crashes, fatalities, and costs.* Available upon request from roadcrew@mascomm.net; Show Case. (n.d.). *Road Crew.* Retrieved July 29, 2011, from http://www.thensmc.com/resources/showcase/road-crew?view=all

32. Sun Microsystems. (2007). *Dial 311.* Retrieved January 22, 2007, from http://www.sun.com/about-sun/media/features/311.html

33. Reprinted with permission of Pilgrim Plastics, Brockton, MA.

34. Kotler, P., & Armstrong, G. (2001). *Principles of marketing* (9th ed, pp. 273–275). Upper Saddle River, NJ: Prentice Hall.

35. Centers for Disease Control and Prevention. (2009). *Fact sheet: Youth and tobacco use: Current estimates.* Retrieved July 28, 2009, from http://www.cdc.gov/tobacco/data_statistics/fact_sheets/youth_data/tobacco_use/index.htm

36. A lengthier version of this case appears in Cheng, H., Kotler, P., & Lee, N. (2011). *Social marketing for public health: Global trends and success stories* (pp. 34–44). Sudbury, MA: Jones & Bartlett.

37. Smith, B. (1999, June). Social marketing: Marketing with no budget. *Social Marketing Quarterly, 5*(2), 7–8.

38. From *Newsweek*, 10/2/00 © 2000 Newsweek, Inc. All rights reserved. Reprinted by permission. Photograph © Nicole Rosenthal.

39. D.A.R.E. America. (n.d.). The new D.A.R.E. program. Substance abuse and violence prevention. Retrieved January 22, 2007, from http://www.dare.com/home/newdareprogram.asp

40. Ibid.

41. Kotler & Armstrong, 2001, *Principles of marketing.*

42. Produce for Better Health Foundation. (n.d.). *5 a Day the Color Way.* Retrieved January 29, 2007, from http://www.5aday.com/html/colorway/colorway_home.php

43. Barnes, D. K. A. (2002, April 25). Invasions by marine life on plastic debris. *Nature, 416,* 808–809.

44. Joe Starinchak is the outreach coordinator for the U.S. Fish and Wildlife Service in Washington, DC. He led the development of the Stop Aquatic Hitchhikers! campaign along with team members Sharon Rushton, SR Enterprises; Gary Isbell, Fisheries Chief, Ohio Division of Wildlife; Jay Rendall, Minnesota DNR; Jim Wentz, Silvertip Productions; Jeff Ivarson, Ivarson, Inc.; Rob Southwick, Southwick and Associates; Phil Seng, DJ Case & Associates; Bob Pitman, U.S. Fish and Wildlife Service; Doug Jensen, Minnesota Sea; Doug Grann, Wildlife Forever; and individuals from the National Oceanic and Atmospheric Administration.

45. U.S. Fish and Wildlife Service.

46. Ibid.

47. Ibid.

Chapter 10

PRODUCT

Creating a Product Platform

Product, not promotion, is the most important component of the marketing mix. Offer them benefits, not fear. Offer them a tangible good or service to help them perform a behavior, not just a brochure. Adopt these principles and you shall win.

—Dr. Sameer Deshpande
University of Lethbridge

You are (finally) ready to develop your marketing strategy.

- You have identified a target audience and developed rich descriptions using relevant demographic, geographic, psychographic, and behavioral variables
- You know what you want your audience to do and what they may need to know and/or believe in order to act, and you've come to some agreement on levels of desired behavior change you will develop a plan to achieve
- You know what benefits and barriers your audience perceives relative to the desired behavior you have in mind
- You know how this stacks up against the competition—most often your target audience's current or preferred behavior or the programs and organizations sponsoring it
- You are aware of others your target audience considers influential
- You have a positioning statement that will align and guide your team's decision making

It is time to decide how you will influence your target audience to accept the desired behavior. You have four tools (product, price, place, and promotion) to help make this happen. And you'll probably need all of them to reduce barriers and create and deliver the value your target audience expects in exchange for this new behavior.

This chapter will focus on developing your product strategy, with an emphasis on exploring opportunities for goods and services that will support desired behaviors. We begin with a case story where the product strategy was key to saving lives.

Reducing Tuberculosis in Peru
With a Product Strategy Key to Success
(1990s)

The tuberculosis challenge is a natural for social marketing. There are specific behaviors of audiences downstream, midstream, and upstream to be influenced. SMART goals have been set for countries by organizations such as the United Nations, which has established targets for tuberculosis control as one of its Millennium Development Goals. There are opportunities for application of all 4Ps in the marketing mix, ones actually needed to reach these ambitious goals. And there are mechanisms in place to monitor and evaluate progress. This case highlight presents key elements of a successful marketing effort to reduce the incidence and prevalence of tuberculosis in Peru.[1]

Background

In 1991, when Peru accounted for about 15% of TB cases in the Americas even though it had only 3% of the population, there were approximately 190 cases of TB per 100,000 adults within the country. The abandonment rate of drug therapy was at 12.1%.[2] Only 50% of people diagnosed with TB were able to get treatment, and of those, only half were cured.[3] Drugs were in short supply, record systems nonexistent, and health workers overworked. Public outcry, including spontaneous street demonstrations by TB patients calling for access to effective drugs, led to high-level commitment and action. The country's incoming government declared TB a significant and widespread public health problem and allocated additional resources to their National Tuberculosis Control Program (NTCP), increasing the annual budget from US$600,000 to US$5 million.[4] The country clearly recognized the impact the disease was having not only on its citizens, but also on the country's economy. With TB affecting primarily the most economically productive age group and a 1999 study showing the economic cost of TB to be between $67 and $108 million, most considered this significant increase a "good investment."[5]

The *purpose* of this bolstered effort was of course to decrease the incidence of TB, with two areas of *focus*. One was on directly observed treatment, short course (DOTS), an internationally recommended approach for TB control programs where a trained healthcare worker monitors the patient as he or she takes each dose of anti-tuberculosis medication. The treatment comprises initial daily doses followed by twice-weekly doses, directly observed to ensure compliance. Without this focus and service, many patients were not completing their regimen or taking medications in a timely manner, leading to prolonged illnesses and increased infections in communities. The second important area of focus was identification of patients currently infected so that treatment could begin.

Target Audiences and Desired Behaviors

Efforts for diagnosis were to focus on reaching high-risk groups, especially the urban poor in crowded areas known as "TB pockets" or "hot spots." The capital city of Lima was one such target, with 60% of all cases in the country but only 29% of the population.[6] As noted earlier, TB mainly affects the most economically productive age group, those between 15 and 54 years of age.[7] "Closed populations," because of their high TB prevalence, were also a priority for outreach and included prisoners, patients in mental institutions, retirement home dwellers, and homeless people sleeping in shelters. As patients were identified, they then became the target for drug therapy along with those currently taking the medications to ensure timely completion.

There were four clear behavior strategies to accomplish with target audiences:

- Influence those with symptoms to get diagnosed
- Influence those already diagnosed to accept treatment
- Influence those receiving treatment to complete the regimen
- Influence those successfully treated to become advocates

Marketing outcome goals for the effort were clear and bold. In 1991, when the NTCP adopted the global targets of the World Health Organization (WHO), the road ahead looked long and steep, and Peru was one of a handful of high-burden TB countries to take it on. The country committed to diagnose 70% of pulmonary TB cases, and for those diagnosed, they accepted the challenge to cure at least 85% of cases; at the time, they were curing only 50%, so this would represent a 70% increase. And they wanted to decrease treatment abandonment; at the time, 12.1% of those being treated were abandoning their treatment.[8]

Audience Insights

Formative research was conducted by the NTCP to assess the public's, as well as healthcare workers', current knowledge and attitudes regarding TB. Findings confirmed suspicions of widespread stigma, misconceptions, and lack of facts about the disease. They also highlighted concerns about access to diagnosis, drugs, and coordinated care.

Many of those infected were unaware that their persistent cough was a signal they should get tested. Others, who suspected they were infected and knew they should be tested, did not know where they should go or imagined they would not be able to afford it. Those being treated were not always convinced they needed to be taking their drugs as prescribed, believing that since they felt better they were cured, or seeing the burden of traveling on foot to a clinic several times a week as too exhausting. These barriers of stigma and access were magnified several times over for those who were homeless, in prisons, or in mental institutions. And then those with multi-drug-resistant (MDR) TB were having difficulty accessing or paying for the type of drugs needed.

Strategies

Given these barriers to getting tested and competing country priorities, planners

Table 10.1 Summary of Marketing Mix Strategies

The 4Ps	Strategies Targeting TB Patients
Product *Core:* Benefits of the behavior *Actual:* Goods and services offered/promoted and any special features *Augmented:* Additional product elements to assist in performing the behavior	*Core:* From testing: Peace of mind From taking drugs: Getting well *Actual:* Tests DOTS therapy *Augmented:* Counseling Patient and family support groups
Price *Monetary and Nonmonetary Incentives*	Free testing Free drugs for those in need Microcredit loans Reimbursement for travel Free lodging Food packages for low-income families
Place *Access to Goods and Services*	Extended clinic hours Home visits for DOTS Transportation for those in need
Promotion *Key Messages* *Key Messengers* *Key Media Channels*	*Key Messages:* "All TB services are free." "If you cough for more than 15 days, you should go to the health center." "Treatment for one is prevention for all." *Key Messengers:* Healthcare workers Family members Community organization volunteers *Key Media Channels:* Mass media: television, radio, billboards, print media Print materials: posters, letters, fact sheets Special events: World TB Day, street theatrics Videos: At healthcare facility waiting areas Personal communications: Health workers Community mobilization: Surveillance groups Advocacy: Local groups targeting families and political leaders

wanted "everyone" to have a sense of urgency about the impact tuberculosis was having on citizens as well as their country. At the same time, they wanted everyone to be hopeful: for patients to know that there were cures and that free help was available; for family members, friends, and healthcare workers to realize their help was needed; for the media to see TB as a major issue of public interest and concern; and for policy makers to see their efforts as a good investment.

All 4Ps in the marketing mix were needed to "get the job done" and are outlined in Table 10.1.

Results

In 2000, WHO reported promising results in Peru, touting its TB program as "one of the world's most successful DOTS programs in the world . . . one of only a handful of high-burden countries to have met the WHO targets for TB control of 70%

case detection rates and 85% cure rates." By 1998, in fact, an estimated 94% of TB cases were being detected and 90% of patients were being cured, preventing close to 70,000 cases and deaths.[9]

Postscript

While Peru succeeded in the late 1990s in meeting the targets set by WHO, the country now faces new challenges: MDR TB and coinfection with HIV/AIDS. Many believe that new commitments have been made to address this and efforts have been redoubled. For example, a grant from the Global Fund will help finance the treatment of MDR TB for 2,000 patients and their families. The grant will also aid Peru in its goal to increase its tuberculosis detection rate to 100%. The program will focus on high-risk populations, including prisoners and residents of the urban areas of Lima and Callao.

PRODUCT: THE FIRST "P"

A product is anything that can be offered to a market to satisfy a want or need.[10] It isn't, as many typically think, just a tangible offering like soap, tires, or hamburgers. It can be one of several types: physical goods, a service, an experience, an event, a person, a place, a property, an organization, information, or an idea.[11]

In social marketing, major product elements include: (a) the benefit the target audience wants in exchange for performing the behavior, (b) any goods and services you will be promoting to your target audience, and (c) any additional product elements you will include to assist your target audience in performing the behavior. As highlighted in the opening case addressing tuberculosis in Peru, the product benefit to patients for completing their drug regimen was *getting well*; the goods were the *drugs* and the services were *direct observations of the patients as they took the drugs*; and an additional product element to assist patients was *a support group*. As you will read, all three elements are key to success. Certainly, what's in it for the audience in exchange for their performing the behavior needs to be highlighted. You will often find social marketing efforts that encourage audiences to increase consumption or utilization of existing products (e.g., childhood immunizations) or products that your program develops and makes available (e.g., a statewide immunization database for healthcare providers). We also encourage you to consider the critical role that additional product elements (augmented products) can play in reducing barriers to behaviors (e.g., providing a wallet-sized immunization card for the parent to use to keep track).

At this point, it is beneficial to distinguish between what we consider goods and what we consider services. We also distinguish between existing products and new products, as depicted in Table 10.2. While goods are usually "consumed" or "utilized" and are purchased/obtained for personal use (e.g., organic fertilizers), services are a product form that is essentially intangible and does not result in the ownership of anything (e.g., a workshop).[12] These distinctions are important primarily so that you are inspired to consider all four categories when developing a product strategy. Additional relevant terms often associated with product strategy in the commercial sector are presented in Table 10.3.

STEP 7: DEVELOP THE SOCIAL MARKETING PRODUCT PLATFORM

Traditional marketing theory propounds that from the customer's perspective, a product is more than its features, quality, name, and style and identifies three product levels you should consider when developing your product: *core product*, *actual product*, and *augmented product*.[13] This platform is illustrated in Figure 10.1, and each of these levels

Table 10.2 Examples of Existing and New Social Marketing Goods and Services

Potential Actual Products	Goods	Services
Existing Products	Condoms	Mammography
	Breast pumps	Gym membership
	Home blood pressure monitors	Taxis
	Immunizations	Blood donation
	Lockboxes for handguns at home	Pet neutering
	Low-flow showerheads	Home energy audits
	Organic fertilizers	Septic tank inspections
New Products Developed To Support Behaviors	Breathalyzers at bars	Road Crew for "bar hopping"
	Hot water temperature gauge cards	Tobacco quitline
	Drug test kits for parents of teens	Home visits for early learning
	Collapsible grocery carts suitable for walking to and from the store	Workshops on natural gardening
	Foodwaste containers for under the sink	Veggie Mobiles for inner-city residents
	Tablets to test for leaky toilets	Walking school bus programs
		Amber Alert for missing children

Table 10.3 A Product Primer

Product Type refers to whether the product is physical goods, services, experiences, an event, a person, a place, a property, an organization, information, or an idea

Product Line refers to a group of closely related products offered by an organization that perform similar functions but are different in terms of features, style, or some other variable[a]

Product Mix refers to the product items that an organization offers, often reflecting a variety of product types

Product Features describe product components (e.g., number of days or hours it takes to obtain results from an HIV/AIDS test)

Product Platform includes decisions regarding the core product (benefit), actual product (goods and services), and augmented product (additional product elements included to support the desired behavior)

Product Quality refers to the performance of the product and includes such valued attributes as durability, reliability, precision, and ease of operation[b]

Product Development is the systematic approach that guides the development and launch of a new product and is managed by a product manager, sometimes called a brand manager

Note: See page 262 for Chapter 10 Table Notes.

Figure 10.1 Three levels of the social marketing product.

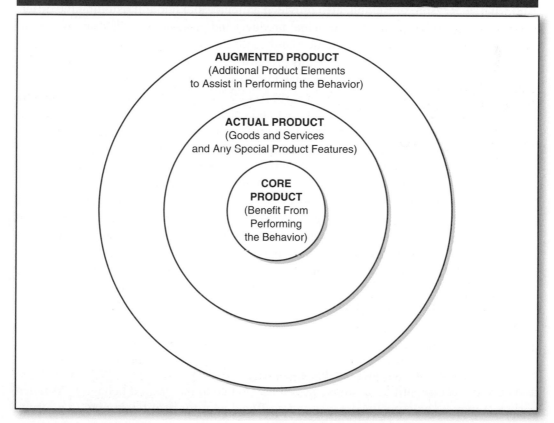

AUGMENTED PRODUCT
(Additional Product Elements
to Assist in Performing the Behavior)

ACTUAL PRODUCT
(Goods and Services
and Any Special Product Features)

**CORE
PRODUCT**
(Benefit From
Performing
the Behavior)

will be described in detail in the next three sections of this chapter. This will be helpful to you in conceptualizing and designing your product strategy.

Briefly, your *core product* is the benefit the target audience wants and expects in exchange for performing the behavior. The *actual product* is any goods or services you will be influencing your target audience to "buy." And the *augmented product* includes any additional product elements that you may develop, distribute, sell, or just promote. Examples are presented in Table 10.4.

Core Product

The core product, the center of the product platform, answers the following questions: What's in it for the customer to adopt the behavior? What benefits will customers receive? What needs will the desired behavior satisfy? What problems will it solve? The core product is not the behaviors or accompanying goods and services you will be developing, providing, and/or promoting. It is the benefits your audience wants and expects to experience when they perform the behavior—benefits *they say* are the most valuable to them (e.g., moderate physical activity will make me feel better, look better, and live longer). The great Harvard marketing professor Theodore Levitt was known to have told his students, "People don't want to buy a quarter-inch drill. They want a quarter-inch hole!" And Charles Revson, of Revlon, also provided a memorable quote illustrating the difference between product features (our actual product) and product benefits (our core product): "In the factory we make cosmetics; in the store, we sell hope."[14]

Decisions about the core product focus primarily on what potential benefits should be stressed. This process will include reviewing (from Step 5) audience perceptions of (a) benefits from the desired behavior and (b) perceived costs of the competing behaviors that the desired behavior can help the target audience avoid. You may have even identified this core product when constructing your positioning statement (in Step 6). Decisions are then made regarding which of these should be emphasized in a campaign. And keep in mind, the key benefit you should highlight is the benefit the target audience perceives for performing the behavior—not the benefit to your organization or agency.

Example: Interviews with teens often reveal several perceived benefits youth associate with not smoking: doing better in school, doing better in sports, being seen as smart, and looking and feeling good. They may also reveal the following perceived costs: You could get addicted and not be able to quit, you might die, you'll stink, and you won't be as good in sports. Further discussions may indicate that one of these (e.g., fear of addiction) is most concerning and should be highlighted in the campaign (see Figure 10.2 on page 248). In this case, the core product for the campaign becomes "By not smoking, you don't risk addiction."

Actual Product

Surrounding the core product are the *specific goods or services* you want your target audience to acquire, utilize, or consume—those related to the desired behavior. As noted earlier, it may be existing goods or services offered by a for-profit company (e.g., fruits

Table 10.4 Examples of Three Product Levels

BEHAVIOR OBJECTIVE	CORE PRODUCT (Benefit from performing the behavior)	ACTUAL PRODUCT (Goods and services and any special product features)	AUGMENTED PRODUCT (Additional product elements to assist in performing the behavior)
For Improved Health			
Get tested for HIV/AIDS within six months of having unprotected six	Early detection, treatment, and prevention of spreading the disease	Rapid HIV/AIDS test with results available in 30 minutes (versus two weeks as before)	Counseling for you and your partner
Conduct monthly breast self-exams and annual mammograms after age 50	Early detection and treatment	Mammogram	Laminated card for a shower to prompt and record exams
For Injury Prevention			
Do not text while driving	Preventing injuries and death	Thumb socks that make it difficult to text, given to teens when they get their driver's licenses	Special attachment for keeping the thumb socks on rearview mirror when not driving
Put a life vest on toddlers at the beach	Preventing drowning	Toddler life vests	Life vests for loan at beaches
To Protect the Environment			
Plant native plants	Protecting wildlife habitats	100 native plants to choose from	Workshops on designing a native plant garden
Reduce home energy consumption	Save money and reduce carbon emissions	Home energy audits	Findings from the audit of recommended actions and anticipated savings
For Community Involvement			
Sign up to become an organ donor	Saving someone's life	Organ donor registry	Form that makes it clear that in the event of death, any family members will be asked to give final approval
To Enhance Financial Well-Being of the Poor			
Make regular deposits to a savings account	Children's education	Lockbox to keep at home for depositing money	Bank personnel make home visits to collect the money and deposit in a savings account

Figure 10.2 A testimonial used to persuade youth that tobacco is addictive.[15]

and vegetables), a nonprofit organization (e.g., rapid HIV/AIDS test), or a governmental agency (e.g., community swimming pool). Or it may be goods or services your organization develops or advocates for development (e.g., Road Crew). In 1952, G. D. Wiebe raised the question, "Why can't you sell brotherhood like you sell soap?" and then embarked on a research journey to find the answer.[16] Dr. Wiebe, at the time a research psychologist for the CBS Radio Network and lecturer in psychology at the City College of New York, concluded after examining four social campaigns that "the more the conditions of a social campaign resemble those of a product campaign, the more successful the campaign will be."[17] One specific factor he felt was critical is a "mechanism" that enables the target audience to translate their motivation (wants, needs, awakened desires) into action. These physical goods and services may well provide this critical mechanism. The following illustrates this principle well.

Example: According to Safe Kids USA, pedestrian injury remains the second leading cause of unintentional injury-related death among children ages 5 to 14.[18] In 2009, the Washington State Department of Transportation saw an opportunity to help reduce this incidence and to use a resource that was going to waste—the extra reflective material they didn't use on their signs. They used it to make reflective feet for kids to put on their backpacks, lunch boxes, and bikes so that drivers would be more likely to see them when walking or riding their bikes. These stickers were distributed by Washington State Patrol officers.

Additional components at the actual-product level may include any *brand names* developed for the behavior (e.g., 5 a Day), the *campaign's sponsoring organization* (e.g., Produce for Better Health Foundation), and any *endorsements and sponsors* (e.g., National Cancer Institute and Centers for Disease Control and Prevention). The following example highlights a product branding strategy, a topic covered in more detail at the end of this chapter.

Example: The City of Seattle and Seattle Public Utilities engage in numerous programs to influence residential gardeners to contribute toward salmon survival. They have named (branded) their program Salmon Friendly Gardening and promote the adoption of six key behaviors: (1) Build healthy soil with compost, (2) choose the right plant for the right place, (3) use water wisely, (4) use natural fertilizers and pest controls, (5) direct rainwater appropriately, and (6) protect shoreline habitats. Campaign materials emphasize the real threat of salmon extinction, how gardening affects salmon, and how Salmon

Friendly Gardens can be beautiful, healthy, and easy to maintain. Residents are assured that Salmon Friendly Gardens (*actual product*) work with natural processes to grow healthy plants with minimal irrigation, fertilizer, and pesticides. In addition to keeping the water clean and protecting habitats, Salmon Friendly Gardens can save time and money (see Figure 10.3).

Sponsor and endorsement decisions are important as well, as they can significantly affect the credibility as well as the appeal of a campaign. Research indicates that credibility is a function of expertise, trustworthiness, and likability, so perceptions of target audiences may need to be explored.[20]

Figure 10.3 Salmon Friendly Gardening logo.[19]

Example: Telephone surveys could ask litterers to rank the impact on their littering of a variety of potential endorsements of an antilitter campaign: department of ecology, state patrol, department of transportation, department of licensing, department of fish and wildlife, department of natural resources, and the state traffic safety commission. It might not be surprising to find that responses indicate that the best (visible) sponsoring organizations for the campaign would be the department of licensing and/or the state patrol, because these organizations are perceived as having the most impact on potential penalties and driving privileges, important personal benefits to these drivers.

Augmented Product

This level of the product platform includes any *additional product elements* you will be providing and/or promoting along with the actual product. Although they may be considered optional, they are sometimes exactly what is needed to provide encouragement (e.g., a walking buddy), remove barriers (e.g., a detailed resource guide and map of local walking trails and organized walking programs), or sustain behavior (e.g., a journal for tracking exercise levels). They may also provide opportunities to brand and to "tangibilize" the campaign, creating more attention, appeal, and memorability for target audiences.[21]

Example: WalkBoston is a nonprofit organization with a mission to create and preserve safe walking environments that build vital communities. One behavior they promote is walking 30 minutes a day. One audience benefit they appeal to is the opportunity to see and experience things that would be missed using other modes of travel. One product they created certainly fits the augmented product profile—maps. One map features lines that indicate five-minute walking increments, helping to plan routes to work, a meeting, or lunch, and lets users estimate how long the walk will be. Other maps feature over 50 places that are wonderful to walk, easy to navigate, and convenient to get around. Created by those who know the area best—either local people or experts in the walk's particular theme—each self-guided walk has a detailed route as well as distances and descriptions of sights and scenes.[22]

You will face several decisions in regard to developing or enhancing physical goods that your campaign will encourage audiences to acquire, utilize, or consume. *Is there a need for new physical goods that would greatly support the behavior change?* For example, many adults with diabetes conduct finger-prick blood tests to monitor their blood sugar levels. A painless, needle-free mechanism that would provide reliable readings would be a welcome innovation and might result in more regular monitoring of blood sugar levels. Not all new products will require retooling or significant research and development costs, as illustrated in the following example:

Example: Research conducted early in 1971 by the Pittsburgh Poison Center of Children's Hospital of Pittsburgh indicated that the old skull and crossbones used in the past to identify poisons had little meaning for the children of the 1970s. In fact, not only had the symbol been exploited in movies, cartoons, commercial products, and amusement parks to denote happy, exciting things such as pirates and adventure, but also their baseball team, the Pittsburgh Pirates, used the symbol as its logo. Six symbols were tested with children in daycare centers, with each affixed to identical bottles of mouthwash. Symbols included a red stop sign, the skull and crossbones, and four others. Children were asked which bottles they wanted to play with—and which they wouldn't. The symbol that proved to be the least appealing was Mr. Yuk (see Figure 10.4). One little boy actually refused to pick up the bottle marked with this green, scowling-faced symbol. He said, "He looks yucky." And so children not only selected Mr. Yuk as the most unappealing poison warning symbol, but they named him as well! Interestingly, the most appealing symbol to the children was, in fact, the skull and crossbones that had been used to date. Mr. Yuk is used in many states and also in Europe, Asia, and Iceland. In 2010, several million stickers were distributed nationwide.[23]

Figure 10.4   Mr. Yuk sticker.[24]

Do current goods need to be improved or enhanced? For example, typical compost bins require the gardener to use a pitchfork to regularly turn the yardwaste to enhance compost development. New and improved models that a social marketing campaign might make known to target audiences are suspended on a bracket that requires only a regular "tumble."

Consider that until recent years, most users (and especially nonusers) have perceived life vests as bulky and uncomfortable. Teens have raised concerns about tan lines and the "ugly" orange color. New options are vastly improved, with a look similar to that of suspenders and a feature for automatic inflation using a pull tab. Consider also the clear need for an improved product in the next example, one mentioned in an article in the *Stanford Social Innovation Review* focusing on "designing thinking for social innovation," coauthored by Tim Brown and Jocelyn Wyatt of IDEO, a global innovation and design firm.[25]

Example: In an area outside Hyderabad, India, a young woman the authors refer to as Shanti was used to fetching water daily from a borehole about 300 feet from her home. She used a 3-gallon plastic container that she carried easily on her head. The water was free and Shanti and her husband depended on it for their drinking and washing. The problem was the water wasn't treated and periodically made her and her family sick. She knew this, but had no plans to stop using it, even though a community treatment center was also within walking distance of her home. The problem was that the jug (*product*) required for use of the facility was a 5-gallon one, and when filled with water was simply too heavy for her. To compound the problem with the product's design, the plastic container was rectangular and couldn't be held on the hip or the head, where she liked to carry heavy objects. Since Shanti's husband worked in the city and didn't return until after the treatment center closed, he couldn't help. The authors make the valid point that,

> time and again, initiatives falter because they are not based on the client's or customer's needs and have never been prototyped to solicit feedback. Even when people do go into the field, they may enter with preconceived notions of what the needs and solutions are. This flawed approach remains the norm in both business and social sectors.
>
> As Shanti's situation shows, social challenges require systemic solutions that are grounded in the client's or customer's needs.[26]

Is there a need or opportunity for a substitute product?[27] A substitute product is one that offers the target audience a "healthier and safer" way to satisfy a want, fulfill a need, or solve a problem. The key is to understand the real benefit (core product) of the *competing* behavior and to then develop and/or promote products offering the same or at least some of the same benefits. These include, for example, food and beverages such as nonalcoholic beers, garden burgers, fat-free dairy products, nicotine-free cigarettes, and decaffeinated coffee; natural fertilizers, natural pesticides, and ground covers to replace lawns; an older sibling (versus a parent) taking a younger teen to a community clinic for STD screening; and a package containing a can of chicken soup, tissues, and aspirin "prescribed" to patients suffering from colds, in an effort to reduce the overuse of antibiotics.

Chakravorty defines a substitute product as "a product offered to a market that is thought of and used by those in the market as a replacement for some other product."[28]She further surmises:

An acceptable and accessible substitute product may promote desirable behaviors by enhancing the user's perceived self-efficacy. Self-efficacy is expected to be strengthened to the extent that many of the behaviors required in using a substitute are similar to behaviors associated with reference product use. . . .[29]

For example, a heavy coffee drinker may come to believe that eliminating coffee will lead to improved cardiac health. The prospective former coffee drinker may decide that she is very likely to quit coffee if she replaces it with decaffeinated coffee. A variety of factors may have contributed to this perception. First, she may feel that as a result of her coffee drinking behavior, she "knows how" to execute the behaviors required in drinking decaf. The beverage will be consumed in the same container, at the same temperature, and she will not have to make great adjustments to the flavor of the substitute. If she is able to consume decaf in all the same situations where she usually drinks coffee (i.e., at home, work, favorite restaurant), her efficacy for "decaf drinking" behavior may rise as she estimates that she will be able to perform the new behavior across a wide variety of settings.[30]

Services are often distinguished as offerings that are intangible and do not result in the ownership of anything.[31] In the social marketing environment, examples of services that support the desired behavior change might include *education-related services* (e.g., parenting workshops on how to talk to your kids about sex), *personal services* (e.g., escorts for students back to their dorms at night), *counseling services* (e.g., a crisis line for people considering suicide), *clinical services* (e.g., community clinics for free immunizations), and *community services* (e.g., hazardous waste mobiles for disposal of toxic waste products). It should be noted that services that are more sales oriented in nature (e.g., demonstrations on the efficiency of low-flow toilets) fall into the promotional category and will be discussed in Chapter 14. You will also face several decisions regarding any services you offer.

Should a new service be developed and offered? For example, given the apparent success and popularity of toll-free tobacco quitlines to support smoking cessation in other states, a community without one might want to develop and launch a line to accompany mass media campaigns encouraging adults to quit smoking. In the past few years, "apps" have become a new popular service for social marketers to explore, such as those highlighted in the following example.

Example: As a part of First Lady Michelle Obama's Let's Move! campaign to reduce childhood obesity, in March, 2010, a competition was announced. Apps for Healthy Kids challenged software developers, game designers, students, and other innovators to develop fun and engaging software tools and games that would influence (even excite) children, especially "tweens" (ages 9 to 12), to eat better and be more physically active. Entries were required to use USDA nutrition guidelines.[32] The tool winning first place, announced in September 2010, was Pick Chow!, an online tool allowing children to create meals by dragging and dropping foods onto their virtual plate (see Figure 10.5). The

Add It Up! meter then shows the nutritional value of the meal, rating it with one to five stars, helping children learn quickly how their choices make a difference in creating a well-balanced meal. And perhaps the most sustainable feature is the one that allows the children to then "send their 'chow' to their parents, who then receive an email with what their child has chosen to be a healthy choice for breakfast, lunch or dinner, along with the menu, recipe, shopping list and coupons."[33]

Does an existing service need to be improved or enhanced? For example, what if customer surveys indicate that an estimated 50% of callers to the state's 800 number for questions about recycling hang up because they typically have to wait more than five minutes on hold? Relative to enhanced services, what if customer feedback also indicates that residents would be interested in (and would pay for) recycling of yardwaste in addition to glass, paper, and aluminum?

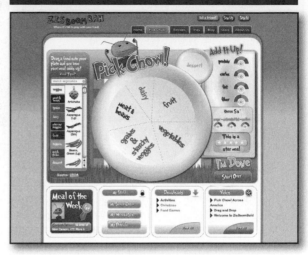

Figure 10.5 Pick Chow! An app developed by Karen Laszio, Mike Carcaise, and Lisa Lanzano.[34]

Example: Doug McKenzie-Mohr is an environmental psychologist specializing in designing programs that support sustainable behaviors. One of the tools he encourages social marketers to use is making norms visible.

> Norms guide how we should behave. If we observe others acting unsustainably . . . we are more likely to act similarly. In contrast, if we observe members of our community acting sustainably, we are more likely to do the same.[35]

Opower, an energy efficiency and smart grid software company, has developed a program whereby residents receive information about their own level of household energy consumption compared with the norm for their local community. They say their company was "founded on a simple premise: It's time to engage the 300 million Americans who are in the dark about their energy use."[36] One of their products is a Home Energy Report that not only provides the utility's customers information and trends on their energy usage, but also includes comparisons to their neighbors, including the use of symbolic "smiley faces" (see Figure 10.6 on next page). According to Opower, leading utilities across the country provide Home Energy Reports to nearly 1 million households nationwide, and these utility customers have cut their annual gas or electricity usage by 1.5% to 3.5% annually after receiving these reports.[37]

Figure 10.6 Home Energy Report comparing "you" to your neighbors.

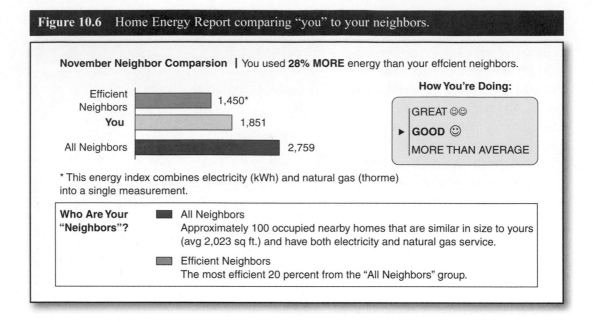

November Neighbor Comparsion | You used **28% MORE** energy than your effcient neighbors.

Efficient Neighbors: 1,450*
You: 1,851
All Neighbors: 2,759

How You're Doing:

GREAT ☺☺
▶ **GOOD** ☺
MORE THAN AVERAGE

* This energy index combines electricity (kWh) and natural gas (thorme) into a single measurement.

Who Are Your "Neighbors"?

All Neighbors
Approximately 100 occupied nearby homes that are similar in size to yours (avg 2,023 sq ft.) and have both electricity and natural gas service.

Efficient Neighbors
The most efficient 20 percent from the "All Neighbors" group.

BRANDING

Branding in the commercial sector is pervasive and fairly easy to understand and recognize. A brand, as mentioned earlier, is a name, term, sign, symbol, or design (or a combination of these) that identifies the maker or seller of a product (see Table 10.5).[38] You have contact with brands when you start your day with a Starbucks, drive your Volvo, listen to music on your iPod, use Microsoft Word, run in your Nikes, and TiVo the CBS News.

Branding in social marketing is not as common, although we would like to encourage more of it, as it helps create visibility and ensure memorability. The following list includes a few of the stronger brands. In these cases, brand names that have been used to identify programs and products are used consistently in an integrated way. Most are accompanied by additional brand elements, including graphics and taglines:

- Wildfire prevention: **Smokey Bear**
- Poison prevention: **Mr. Yuk**
- Nutrition: **5 a Day**
- Traffic safety: **Click It Or Ticket**
- Physical activity: **VERB**
- Crime protection: **McGruff the Crime Dog**
- Safe produce: **USDA Organic**
- Sustainable seafood: **Seafood Watch**
- Waste reduction: **Reduce. Reuse. Recycle.**
- Drinking and driving: **Road Crew**
- Tobacco prevention: **truth**®
- Litter prevention: **Don't Mess With Texas**

Table 10.5 A Branding Primer

Brand is a name, term, sign, symbol, or design (or a combination of these) that identifies the maker or seller of a product or service.

Brand Identity is how you (the maker) want consumers to think, feel, and act with respect to your brand.

Brand Image is how your target audience actually does think, feel, or act with respect to your brand.

Branding is the process of developing an intended brand identity.

Brand Awareness is the extent to which consumers recognize a brand.

Brand Promise is the marketer's vision of what the brand must be and do for consumers.

Brand Loyalty refers to the degree to which a consumer consistently purchases the same brand within a product class.

Brand Equity is the value of a brand, based on the extent to which it has high brand loyalty, name awareness, perceived quality, strong brand associations, and other assets such as patents, trademarks, and channel relationships. It is an important, although intangible, asset that has psychological and financial value to a firm.

Brand Elements are those trademarkable devices that serve to identify and differentiate the brand.

Brand Mix or **Portfolio** is the set of all brands and brand lines a particular firm offers for sale to a buyer in a particular category.

Brand Contact can be defined as any information-bearing experience a customer of prospect has with the brand.

Brand Performance relates to how well the product or service meets customers' functional needs.

Brand Extension is using a successful brand name to launch a new or modified product in a new category.

Cobranding is the practice of using the established brand names of more than one company on the same product or marketing them together in the same fashion.

Source: From Kotler, P., & Lee, N. (2006). *Marketing in the Public Sector: A Roadmap to Improved Performance.* Upper Saddle River, NJ: Wharton School. Reprinted with permission.

- Pet waste: **Scoop the Poop**
- Youth drug prevention: **Parents. The Anti-Drug.**
- Voting: **Rock the Vote**
- SIDS: **Back to Sleep**
- Water conservation: **Water—Use It Wisely**
- Water quality: **Chesapeake Club**
- Energy conservation: **ENERGY STAR**
- Schoolchildren's safety: **Walking School Bus**
- Senior fall prevention: **S.A.I.L. (Stay Active and Independent for Life)**
- Protected sex: **Number One condoms**

In 1994, PSI Cambodia (PSI/C) launched the Number One condom brand and aggressively grew it over time through well-funded promotion and distribution efforts. By 2006, however, PSI/C was becoming a victim of its own success. The Number One

Figure 10.7 Previous packaging and new packaging.[39]

brand had a disproportionately large share of the condom market (88%), which led donors to question how much longer they would have to support the costs. To this end, PSI/C decided to reposition this flagship condom as a more upscale brand, one that would be designed to appeal to those engaged in unprotected "sweetheart sex" (e.g., between two people who share an affectionate bond) and priced to recover costs. They also wanted to leverage the tremendous brand equity of Number One that had built up over 15 years. Changes to the product's packaging appear in Figure 10.7. It kept the visual elements that were so closely associated with the brand (such as the color blue and the boxy logo) while updating them to better express the new positioning (impressing one's partner) and brand personality (being successful and classy).[40]

ETHICAL CONSIDERATIONS RELATED TO CREATING A PRODUCT PLATFORM

One way to highlight ethical considerations relative to product decisions is to revisit each component of the product platform.

The *core product* promises the target audience a benefit they will receive (or cost they will avoid) if they perform the behavior. Can you be sure? How much should you disclose about the probability of success? Tobacco prevention specialists emphasize the health costs of smoking cigarettes, and yet how many times have you seen or read the research that claims that much of the physiological damage done by smoking during the first 10 to 20 years will be repaired by the body if and when you quit? Should this information be prominently displayed?

For the *actual product*, decisions are made relative to a specific behavior you will be promoting and any name and sponsors that will be associated with the behavior. Perhaps one major ethical consideration here is whether you make the actual sponsor/funder of the project very visible or not. For example, should the funder of the campaign be visible on a teen pregnancy prevention campaign poster? And consider this product introduced in January, 2011, in Placer, California. Law enforcement and schools there began offering parents a home alcohol and drug screening kit at a deeply discounted price. The kit included a 10-panel drug screening for $10, which would sell for about $40 in stores; alcohol test strips sell for $2. A deputy who launched the program said authorities were not asking parents to turn in kids who tested positive for illicit drugs and that it was meant to help keep kids safe. Are you as concerned as one representative of the New York–based Drug Policy Alliance, who noted that "asking kids to urinate in a cup could further erode a rocky relationship with parents"?[41] This may be where the rule of thumb "Do more good than harm" can help you decide.

For the *augmented product*, decisions regarding tangible goods and services are similar to those in the private sector, although in this case you are often dealing with taxpayer-funded programs, a different constituent group with agendas different from those of shareholders. Does your product "perform as promised"? If you distribute condoms in high school, do those concerned with sending a "sex is okay" message have a good point? In terms of services, can you deliver and provide good service if you are successful in generating demand?

CHAPTER SUMMARY

The *product* platform has three levels: the core product (the benefit of the behavior), the actual product (any goods and/or services your effort will be developing or promoting), and the augmented product (any additional product elements needed to support behavior change).

Decisions are faced at each level. At the core product level, decisions will need to be made regarding what potential benefits should be stressed. At the actual product level, you will consider whether existing goods (e.g., bike helmets) or services (e.g., home energy audits) should be promoted or whether new or improved products are needed to support behavior adoption (e.g., a tobacco quitline). We encourage you to also consider whether there are additional product elements (augmented products) that would provide support for the target audience, ones not "required" but that might make the difference in whether the audience is moved to action (e.g., life vests available for loan at beaches).

RESEARCH HIGHLIGHT

Ethnographic Research to Study the Use of Water Treatment Devices in Andhra Pradesh, India: PATH's Safe Water Project (2006–2011)

Background and Purpose of Research

To increase access to clean water among low-income households, PATH, an international nonprofit organization focusing on sustainable, culturally relevant public health solutions, launched the Safe Water Project in 2006. The five-year project is funded by the Bill and Melinda Gates Foundation.[42]

One of the primary challenges in developing a household water treatment and safe storage (HWTS) product for low-income households earning between

$1 and $5 a day is a lack of understanding of how, when, why, and by whom such products might be used—or not. To address this challenge, PATH contracted with Quicksand Design to codesign and conduct a *longitudinal ethnographic study* on user experiences with existing HWTS products in India. The study revealed much about what works and does not work and helped identify key product attributes that might influence the adoption and sustained, correct use of future iterations of HWTS products.

Audience for the Research

The sample for the study focused on families living on less than US$5 a day per capita. Twenty households were selected from four districts in Andhra Pradesh, based on a purposive sample that included both rural and urban residents as well as upper and lower ends of the income spectrum. The study team also sought diversity in family size, education, water access and quality, and relationships with other community members. The sample included 10 rural, six semiurban, and four urban households.

Methodology

Five different durable HWTS products were placed in study households, all in commercial production and chosen to represent as much diversity as possible in product features. These included a ceramic water pot, a stainless steel filter, two multistage filters, and one portable hollow-fiber filter.

After obtaining the informed consent of study participants, research teams made six visits to each household over a six-month period. Each visit lasted four to six hours. During the first visit, baseline information on participants' attitudes, perceptions, behaviors, and motivations related to water, HWTS, and health was gathered. A water treatment device was randomly assigned and introduced to each household at the second visit. Some households received an unopened package without any detailed instructions. In other cases, members of the research team posed as shopkeepers who provided cursory instructions about how to set up and use the product, or as traveling salespeople who set up the product for the family and demonstrated cleaning and maintenance procedures. And another group of households were sent to an actual retail store and given money to purchase the product.

Research activities conducted during the home visits ranged from observational to interactive and participatory exercises, including:

- Video ethnography and shadowing
- Structured individual interviews
- Unstructured contextual discussions
- User journals
- Photography by participants
- Card sorting exercises (see Figure 10.8)

Toward the end of the study, the team conducted focus groups with members of the study households, mining deeper insights about the products.

Highlights and Implications of Findings

Findings and implications from the study appeared in PATH's *Extended User Testing of Water Treatment Devices in*

Andhra Pradesh project brief in August 2010, and will help inform guidelines for the development of new products:

• *Product design and development:* Design and development efforts need to focus on product features and attributes that improve the user's experience. For example, devices should be designed to let users know how much water is left by using transparent containers or water level indicators. Clear signals of a product's operational status and prompts for maintenance can reduce frustration and enable users to correct problems. Designers can make HWTS products more desirable by responding to consumers' preferences for certain materials and forms and also by appealing to their desire for modernity. Steel is respected for its durability and traditional place in the kitchen. And although plastic has a more modern appeal, consumers are extremely sensitive

to the grade and quality of plastic. Cylindrical shapes that resemble existing vessels in homes may be considered old fashioned when compared with asymmetrical or angular shapes.

• *Pricing:* Low-income consumers clearly viewed the HWTS products as aspirational goods, which—like mobile phones, bicycles, televisions, and refrigerators—are purchased in the hope of improving one's lifestyle. Therefore, their price point should fall midway between those of solely utilitarian and purely aspirational durable products, somewhere between US$11 and US$21.

• *Accessibility:* Both formal and informal retail channels have a place in distributing HWTS products and replacement parts. Formal channels, such as shops, may be unfamiliar and slightly intimidating environments for low-income consumers in general, but some consumers consider them more credible and trustworthy for durable purchases. Formal channels can also reinforce the aspirational value of water filters and purifiers. For others, informal retail channels, such as mobile vendors, are familiar, accessible, and provide an effective outlet for lower-cost HWTS products. Consumers feel that they offer an acceptable tradeoff between price and quality for everyday, low-risk, low-value purchases. The ready accessibility of informal retail outlets can overcome some of the barriers to sustained use of a water treatment device by making it easy to purchase replacements parts. They also can help maintain awareness of and promote continued consumer engagement with the products.

• *Engaging and informing users:* Low-income consumers feel most comfortable buying goods with which they are already familiar. Since water treatment devices are novel products among low-income households, mass media play a role in building product awareness, but social relationships influence consumers' ultimate decision to purchase. Most study households own televisions and acknowledged that television advertising helps them learn of products. However, they reported that television advertising does not usually drive actual purchases. Seeing a filter in the house of a friend or relative can be an important, perhaps even primary, way to increase acceptability.

In summary, this ethnographic study enabled PATH to document key elements of the daily lives, needs, and preferences of typical low-income consumers in Andhra Pradesh relative to household water treatment and storage. The findings provide valuable insights and direction for future work to improve water treatment and storage for this underserved market segment in India.

CHAPTER 10 NOTES

1. A lengthier version of this case appears in Cheng, H., Kotler, P., & Lee, N. (2011). *Social marketing for public health: Global trends and success stories* (pp. 107–123). Sudbury, MA: Jones & Bartlett.

2. Llanos-Zavalaga, F., Poppe, P., Tawfik, Y., & Church-Balin, C. (2004). *The role of communication in Peru's fight against tuberculosis.* Baltimore, MD: Johns Hopkins Bloomberg School of Public Health, Center for Communication Programs.

3. World Health Organization (WHO). (2008). *Worldwide efforts to confront tuberculosis are making progress but too slowly.* Retrieved January 20, 2009, from http://www.who.int/tb/fea tures_archive/global_tb_control_report08/en/index.html

4. Llanos-Zavalaga, et al., 2004, *The role of communication.*

5. Ibid.

6. Ibid.

7. Ibid.

8. Ibid.

9. WHO, 2008, *Worldwide efforts to confront tuberculosis.*

10. Kotler, P., & Keller, K. L. (2005). *Marketing management* (12th ed., p. 372). Upper Saddle River, NJ: Prentice Hall.

11. Ibid.

12. Kotler, P., & Armstrong, G. (2001). *Principles of marketing* (9th ed., p. 291). Upper Saddle River, NJ: Prentice Hall.

13. Ibid., p. 294.

14. Ibid.

15. Reprinted with permission of the Centers for Disease Control and Prevention's Media Campaign Resource Center.

16. Wiebe, G. D. (1951–1952). Merchandising commodities and citizenship on television (p. 679). *Public Opinion Quarterly, 15,* 679–691.

17. Kotler, P., & Zaltman, G. (1971). Social marketing: An approach to planned social change. *Journal of Marketing, 35,* 3–12.

18. Safe Kids USA. *Preventing injuries: At home, at play, and on the way.* Retrieved January 24, 2011, from http://www.safekids.org/safety-basics/big-kids/on-the-way/pedestrian-safety .html?gclid=CI_Z47GT1KYCFRxqgwodrhHnHg

19. Salmon Friendly Gardening program materials were developed by Seattle Public Utilities. Reprinted with permission.

20. Kotler, P., & Roberto, E. L. (1989). *Social marketing: Strategies for changing public behavior* (p. 155). New York, NY: Free Press; Assael, H. (1981). *Consumer behavior and marketing action.* Boston, MA: Kent.

21. Kotler & Roberto, 1989, *Social marketing*, p. 156.

22. WalkBoston. (n.d.). *Maps.* Retrieved January 24, 2011, from http://www.walkboston.org/ resources/maps.htm

23. Washington Poison Center. (n.d.). *Mr. Yuk.* Retrieved January 25, 2011, from http://www .wapc.org/resources/mryuk.htm

24. Permission to use "Mr. Yuk" provided by the Pittsburgh Poison Center, Pittsburgh University Medical Center.

25. Brown, T., & Wyatt, J. (2010, Winter). Design thinking for social innovation. *Stanford Social Innovation Review.* Retrieved January 25, 2011, from http://www.ssireview.org/articles/ entry/design_thinking_for_social_innovation/

26. Ibid.

27. Chakravorty, B. As quoted in Chakravorty, B. (1996). Product substitution for social marketing of behaviour change: A conceptualization (p. 5). *Social Marketing Quarterly.* Retrieved July 19, 2011, from http://degraysystems.com/aedmichael/Vol%203/3-2/Full%20Text/ III.2.Chakravorty.pdf

28. Ibid., p. 5.

29. Ibid., p. 10.

30. Ibid., pp. 9–10.

31. Kotler & Roberto, 1989, *Social marketing,* pp. 155–157.

32. Apps for Healthy Kids. (n.d.). *Application gallery.* Retrieved January 26, 2011, from http:// www.appsforhealthykids.com/application-gallery

33. ZisBoomBah. (n.d.). *Where it's OK to play with your food!* Retrieved January 26, 2011, from http://www.zisboombah.com/

34. An Application developed by Karen Laszlo, Mike Carcaise, and Lisa Lanzano.

35. McKenzie-Mohr, D., & Smith, W. (1999). *Fostering sustainable behavior: An introduction to community-based social marketing* (2nd ed., p. 156). Gabriola Island, British Columbia, Canada: New Society.

36. Opower. (n.d.). *About us.* Retrieved January 26, 2011, from http://www.opower.com/ Company/AboutUs.aspx

37. Opower. (n.d.). *Special delivery: Energy savings.* Retrieved January 26, 2011, from http:// www.opower.com/Products/HomeEnergyReport.aspx

38. Kotler & Armstrong, 2001, *Principles of marketing* (p. 301).

39. Population Services Inc.

40. Population Services International, Global Social Marketing Department. (2010, March). *A total marketing approach to better marketing in Cambodia.*

41. Drug test kits a bargain for parents. (2011, January 22.). *Chicago Sun-Times.* Retrieved January 26, 2011, from http://www.suntimes.com/lifestyles/3412644–423/parents-drug-kids -schools-test.html

42 Information for this case was taken from PATH's project brief, "Extended User Testing of Water Treatment Devices in Andhra Pradesh," published August 2010.

43. PATH/Quicksand Design

CHAPTER 10 TABLE NOTES

a. Kotler, P., & Armstrong, G. (2001). *Principles of Marketing* (9th ed., p. 300). Upper Saddle River, NJ: Prentice Hall.

b. Kotler & Armstrong, 2001, *Principles of Marketing*, p. 299.

Chapter 11

PRICE

Determining Monetary and Nonmonetary Incentives and Disincentives

Social marketers need to use the whole of the marketing mix to win their target audience's business—there's no use tying one hand behind your back and only using promotion when the competition has price, distribution, and, more often than not, a better product.

—Dr. Stephen Dann
Australian National University

On March 19, 2007, a Canadian news network announced that the new federal budget would include several environmental protection-related strategies, ones that appear to be using, as Michael Rothschild would describe them, carrots as well as sticks: "Gas guzzlers will be dinged with a new tax of up to $4,000, fuel-efficient cars will get a rebate worth up to $2,000 and old wrecks will be offered a short-cut to the junkyard."[1]

This chapter introduces this second tool in your marketing toolbox, one you may find especially helpful in overcoming financial barriers associated with adopting your behavior. You will find it useful in "sweetening the pot" and not necessarily with just monetary incentives that could add significant costs to your program budget. You may also find it effective in reducing the appeal of the competition's offer. You'll read how others have used creative monetary and nonmonetary incentives to add value, sometimes just enough to tip the exchange in their favor:

- How households in Hollywood, Florida, earn points based on how much they recycle, points that can be redeemed at local and national retail stores, restaurants, and grocery stores.
- How coupons helped increase the use of bike helmets from 1% to 57% in one community
- How rewarding youth hockey teams for reducing foul plays decreased (actually eliminated) head injuries for teams in Minnesota

- How a social marketing approach succeeded in persuading legislators to toughen the laws and fines for texting while driving
- How a group of teens convinced their peers to postpone having sex by sharing the pain of pubic lice (crabs)

MARKETING HIGHLIGHT

Increasing Water Availability in Jordan Using Financial Incentives (2010)

Background

Jordan is considered to be one of the world's poorest countries in terms of water resources. This scarcity is exacerbated by rapid population increase (2.8% growth rate), inefficient water management, lack of adequate wastewater treatment capacity, and inappropriate pricing policies. Consequently, the available renewable water resources are dropping drastically, threatening an upcoming national catastrophe. In the 1980s and 1990s, the government initiated a wide range of infrastructure projects to develop fresh water supplies. Options for increasing water supply, however, are limited and expensive. While desalination, for example, is regarded as a possible solution, it has limitations, including the fact that Jordan has an extremely short coastline that is more than 300 kilometers away from the major inhabited areas. The chronic shortage of water available for use and consumption will remain the most serious environmental constraint to development in Jordan.

Most Jordanians experience problems of water supply firsthand, with municipal water supplied through the water network only once a week in the summer months and many rural areas receiving water only once every two weeks or not at all. All households are equipped with water storage tanks. However, given that the average household size is 5.4^2 members, many households end up buying expensive tanker water to help them get through the week until the next municipal water pumping day—especially during the hot summer months when temperatures surge to more than 40°C.

In the coming years, the forecast is for an ever-increasing gap between water supply and demand. This deficit will remain even after an ambitious impressive construction program is carried out. Consequently, more efficient management of existing water resources at all levels is critical.

This case highlights a U.S. Agency for International Development (USAID) success story with a focus on increasing the amount of water available from sources other than the municipal networks and decreasing the amount of water lost in the delivery and access process. Information for this case was provided by Setta Tutundjian, Office of Water Resources and Environment, USAID.[3]

Target Audience

Although all households of Jordan could improve water management techniques, the target for USAID's Community-Based Initiative Project was rural households and communities. Water supply to these communities is not as frequent as in urban areas; incomes are much lower and costs for buying water from tanker trucks is much higher. Generally, poverty rates are higher in rural areas than in urban areas, with 19% of the rural population being poor. Moreover, a large part of the remaining population is just above the poverty line.[4] Employment opportunities are scarce and agricultural expansion as a means for rural development is limited for lack of water.

Desired Behaviors and Audience Insights

Jordan's per capita water usage is already one of the lowest in the world. On average, domestic water is low and barely meets basic household needs for sanitation, cooking, and cleaning. Most consumers are conserving water by turning off taps when brushing their teeth or shaving, not taking baths, and taking shorter showers. In some areas they even bathe their children with a bucket. Further conservation behaviors would not achieve desired impacts, even if successfully influenced. The focus of this effort, instead, was on improvements (*behaviors*) that increased efficiency as well as tapped new water resources:

1. Constructing rainwater harvesting cisterns and reservoirs

2. Installing greywater systems

3. Renovating leaking internal water networks

4. Installing drip irrigation systems

5. Maintaining communal agricultural channels and springs (this entails either lining dirt canals to reduce water seepage into the ground or installing plastic pipes to reduce seepage and evaporation)

The problem (*barrier*) is that these measures are costly, and the target audiences are the poorest segment of Jordanian society. They lack the financial resources to implement the measures needed and have limited access to the banking sector for financing them. To compound matters, the majority of the targeted communities are conservative Muslim with strong religious positions against paying interest, which excluded the option of trying to work with the banking sector to facilitate access to credit.

Strategies

Given these major financial barriers, a strategy was developed that would enable the target audience to access credit to implement these improvements from a source that was religiously acceptable, one with a soft payback plan in which the monthly installment didn't exceed US$50.

To begin, revolving loan funds (*product*) were offered in 135 communities to support households so they could implement water saving and efficiency measures. The seed money for the loan fund was provided as a grant by USAID to a community-based local volunteer or cooperative society through a competitive and transparent process. *Augmented products* included a revolving loan management handbook, extensive formal management and technical trainings, and ongoing technical assistance and mentoring for the recipient society.

Each recipient community managing a loan fund was given the freedom to design a *price* scheme acceptable to those it served. The only condition was that the seed money provided by USAID could be used only for the loans and not for covering administrative costs, even those related to the credit fund. This ensures that the initial USAID grant fund remains constant and the credit fund viable in the future. While some communities chose to have interest rates and others chose a fixed management fee, the majority gave an interest-free loan and opted to cover the administrative expenses of the credit fund from their own resources. This allowed spreading the price of the intervention over a two- to three-year period, with affordable monthly installments ranging from US$20 to US$50.

The revolving funds were established in the communities being served and are managed by community members. This has made taking a loan accessible, convenient, and trustworthy. Each community-based organization establishing a credit fund proposed its own selection criteria that adhere to the general criteria set by USAID to ensure inclusiveness, openness, and transparency. Each organization established its own loan selection committee that includes at least three community members. Community members are then solicited to fill out a unified application form that elicits data on current water usage and estimated water savings, plus information on income, number of household members,

and education levels. As sufficient funds are collected from the payback of given loans, new loans are awarded. The key aspect to the success of the system is ensuring a transparent, fair, and inclusive process of lending and relending funds.

Promotional strategies targeted those midstream as well as downstream. To promote the establishment of the revolving loans within the communities, the local governor held a one-day workshop for voluntary and cooperative community societies. During the workshop, project staff introduced the concept of the revolving loans, discussed the water challenges in their communities and possible responses, described the grant proposal process, and asked them to go back to their communities and discuss what water saving measures their community members would find most appealing as well as feasible. Downstream (at the community level), meetings were held with community members to identify what water conservation measures were needed and for which members were willing to take loans. After the credit fund was established, flyers for public meetings were prepared by the community organizations and distributed at local mosques and schools to promote the program and to solicit the first loan beneficiaries. Subsequently, awareness was increased through visible evidence of increased water efficiencies (*social diffusion*) and word of mouth. As one woman from Ajloun put it,

> When my neighbors see that I have hung washed clothes to dry, while they don't have water to wash themselves, they come and inquire! I show them the rainwater harvesting

cistern. Now, the local society has a long list of beneficiaries waiting for their turn to take a loan.

Results

As of June 2010, 3,396 loans had been dispersed, benefiting more than 19,696 individuals; 161,939 cubic meters of rainwater had been harvested and 39,945 cubic meters of treated municipal water saved because of the residential network maintenance projects. Overall repayment rates are high at 92%. Moreover, 135 communities across the country are now avid advocates of water efficiencies. Because of high demand, USAID decided to increase the size of the credit funds in the original 135 communities where the program was ongoing (see Box 11.1), establish new funds in other rural areas, and pilot this program in urban communities.

Box 11.1

Basma's house is remarkably spotless for a mother of seven children, the majority of whom are under the age of 10. With so many children, she says, she scarcely has the time to keep them all washed and fed, let alone worry about where she might get the water to do so. With six girls and one boy, water for drinking, washing and cooking is an extremely precious commodity. Fortunately, after building a water cistern with a loan funded by USAID and Mercy Corps, taking care of her large family has become much more achievable.

Figure 11.1 Basma with her family.[5]

Source: United States Agency of International Development in Jordan. (n.d.). *Features—Success stories: Water management.* Retrieved July 29, 2011, from http://jordan.usaid.gov/features_disp .cfm?id=144&type=success

(Continued)

(Continued)

Before this year, Basma depended on pressurized water from the municipality, which her family would pay to fill a tank in their home. However the service was irregular, and water was often shut off to the area without warning. Last year, water service was interrupted for 18 consecutive days. In the hot summer heat of her village 'Ein Jenna, the result was crippling. Basma had to send her children daily to the nearest spring to carry water back in heavy jugs, but she constantly feared for their safety. Not only were there many reckless drivers on the road that might not see a small child with a heavy burden, but she was afraid to let her young daughters walk the long distance on isolated roads by themselves.

Four months ago, that all changed when she received a loan to build a cistern that captures precious rainwater, as part of the USAID and Mercy Corps funded Community Based Initiatives for Water Demand Management (CBIWDM) project. Over the course of five years, Mercy Corps has partnered with local Community Based Organizations in each region of Jordan to provide loans to households for water savings and efficiency activities. In Ajlun, Basma received her loan from Fatmah Al-Zahra Cooperative, a women's organization that promotes employment and development. She had worked with the organization before, had demonstrated need, and was interested in improving her family's water situation. After some financial planning with her husband, the family took a US$ 1,400 loan repaid over 30 months to construct a 30 m^3 cistern for harvesting rainwater. Although they still use municipal water when it's available, they save US$14 per month with the cistern, making their loan repayment easy.

It will be three months before the lending organization, Fatima al-Zahra, can grant another loan for a rainwater cistern, but there are already three families on the waiting list. Basma says many of her neighbors and relatives are interested in the project. As she serves mint tea made from rainwater and plump green grapes that are now able to grow in her garden, her daughters giggle shyly from the door. "You don't know the importance of water until you miss it," she said.[6]

PRICE: THE SECOND "P"

Price is the cost that the target audience associates with adopting the desired behavior. Traditional marketing theory has a similar definition: "The amount of money charged for a product or service, or the sum of the values that consumers exchange for the benefits of having or using the product or service."[7]

Adoption costs may be *monetary* or *nonmonetary* in nature. Monetary costs in a social marketing environment are most often related to *goods and services* associated with adopting the behavior (e.g., buying a life vest or paying for a swim class for toddlers). Nonmonetary costs are more intangible but are just as real for your audience and often even more significant for social marketing products. They include costs associated with *time, effort, and energy* required to perform the behavior, *psychological risks and losses* that might be perceived or experienced, and any *physical discomforts* that may be related to the behavior. Most of these nonmonetary costs were probably discovered when you conducted barriers research, identifying concerns your target audience had with adopting the desired behavior. There may be more to add to the list, however, as you may have decided you want to include goods and services such as those listed in Table 11.1. This is the time to do that.

Table 11.1 Potential Costs for Performing the Desired Behavior

Type of Cost	Examples
Monetary: Goods	• Nicotine patches • Blood pressure monitoring equipment • Condoms • Bike helmets, life vests, and booster seats • Breathalyzers • Earthquake preparedness kits • Smoke alarm batteries • Foodwaste compost tumblers • Natural fertilizers (versus regular fertilizers) • Recycled paper (versus regular paper) • Energy-saving lightbulbs • Electric mulch mowers
Monetary: Services	• Fees for family planning classes • Smoking cessation classes • Athletic club fees • Suicide prevention workshops • Taxi rides home from a bar
Nonmonetary: Time, Effort	• Cooking a balanced meal • Pulling over to use the cell phone • Driving to a car wash versus washing at home • Taking the foodwaste outside to a composter
Nonmonetary: Psychological	• Finding out whether a lump is cancerous • Wondering about whether to believe the warning about eating too much fish when pregnant • Having a cup of coffee without a cigarette • Feeling "dorky" carrying a flag across a crosswalk • Listening to the chatter of others in a car pool • Asking your son whether he is considering suicide • Telling your husband you think he drinks too much • Using sunscreen and coming back from Hawaii "pale" • Letting your lawn go brown in the summer
Nonmonetary: Physical Discomfort	• Exercising • Pricking a finger to monitor blood glucose • Having a mammogram • Lowering the thermostat • Taking shorter showers

If your organization is actually the maker or provider of these tangible goods (e.g., rain barrels) or services (e.g., home energy audits), you will want to be involved in establishing the price your customer will be asked to pay. This is the time to do that as well, before developing the incentives that are the emphasis of this chapter. A section at the end of this chapter presents a few tips on price setting.

STEP 7: DETERMINE MONETARY AND NONMONETARY INCENTIVES AND DISINCENTIVES

Your objective and opportunity with this second marketing tool is to develop and provide *incentives* that will increase benefits or decrease costs. (It should be noted that *product* and *place* tools will also be used to increase benefits and decrease costs. The *price* tool is unique in its use of monetary incentives, as well as nonmonetary ones including recognition, appreciation, and reward.) The first four of the six price-related tactics focus on the desired behavior and the last two on the competing one(s).

1. Increase monetary benefits for *the desired behavior*

2. Increase nonmonetary benefits for *the desired behavior*

3. Decrease monetary costs for *the desired behavior*

4. Decrease nonmonetary costs for *the desired behavior*

5. Increase monetary costs for *the competing behavior*

6. Increase nonmonetary costs for *the competing behavior*

The next six sections of this chapter explain each of these in more detail and provide an illustration for each.

1. Increase Monetary Benefits for the Desired Behavior

Monetary rewards and incentives can take many forms familiar to you as a consumer and include *rebates*, *allowances*, *cash incentives*, and *price adjustments* that reward customers for adopting the proposed behavior. Some have been rather "tame" in nature (e.g., 3.5-cent credit for reusing grocery bags), others a little more aggressive (e.g., quit and win contests that offer a chance to win a $1,000 prize for successfully stopping smoking for at least one month;[8] a $20 annual license fee for a neutered dog versus $60 for an unaltered one), and a few quite bold (e.g., offering drug-addicted women a $200 incentive for voluntary sterilization; offering voters a chance at a $1 million lottery just for showing up at the polls). Where would you place the following example on that continuum?

Example: Rewarding Recyclers Like "Frequent Fliers"

In a growing number of communities around the United States, pay-as-you-throw (PAYT) programs are gaining in popularity. What these programs have discovered is that when the cost of managing trash is hidden in taxes, or charged at a flat rate, residents who recycle and prevent waste are not rewarded. In fact, they often pay the same, even more in some cases, than those generating more waste and recycling less. Although PAYT programs vary by community, programs include options such as paying less for a smaller garbage waste container and paying more for garbage waste than recycling waste. Communities typically report reductions in waste amounts of 25% to 35% and an increase in recycling rates.[9] The City of Hollywood, Florida, adds even more to "sweeten the pot." They call in RecycleBank. In 2010, the mayor announced a new incentive. Recycle carts would now have a personalized identification tag. Trucks will read the tag, weigh the recycle bin, and transmit that information to RecycleBank. RecycleBank will then credit the account with RecycleBank points, which can be redeemed at local and national grocery stores, restaurants, and retail stores such as Target and Home Depot.

2. Increase Nonmonetary Benefits for the Desired Behavior

There are also ways to encourage changes in behavior that don't involve cash or free goods and services with significant monetary value. Instead, they provide a different type of value. In the social marketing environment, they often deliver some form of *pledge*, *recognition*, and/or *appreciation* acknowledging the adoption of a desired behavior. In most cases, the benefit is psychological and personal in nature. It can be as simple as an e-mail from a supervisor thanking an employee for signing up for a car pool, or as formal and public as an annual awards program recognizing the dry cleaner who has adopted the most significant green behaviors in the past year. These nonmonetary benefits are distinct from goods and services (e.g., safe bike storage) that are offered to actually help the target audience adopt the behavior. They are also distinct from sales promotion tactics that are more similar to gifts or prizes (e.g., T-shirts and coffee mugs).

Example: Rewarding Fair Play

In 2000, a parent in a Boston suburb was killed by another parent at a grade school hockey game. The incident touched off a national discussion about excess in youth sports, and in 2004 Minnesota Hockey officials decided to do something to change their game's increasingly violent atmosphere. One youth coach described their games then as out of control with "three, four, five fights a game, easy. Any time there was any body contact, they dropped the gloves."[10]

One revolutionary feature they implemented was called the "fair-play point," where a team would get an extra point for each game in which they took fewer than a designated number of penalty minutes. For championship awards, a team earns two points for winning a game and, if it takes fewer than 12 minutes of penalties, a third point for fair play.

The losing team for a game also earns a fair-play point if it is under the penalty threshold. Within a year of instituting the fair-play point, the number of penalties dropped sharply, particularly for fouls from hits to the head, high-sticking, and fighting. The Mayo Clinic, a research partner, reported that penalties for hits to the head dropped from 12.4 per 100 youth games in 2004–2005 season to 2 per 100 games the next season. By 2008–2009, no calls were made for hits to the head.[11]

3. Decrease Monetary Costs for the Desired Behavior

Methods to decrease monetary costs are also familiar to most consumers: discount coupons, cash discounts, quantity discounts, seasonal discounts, promotional pricing (e.g., a temporary price reduction), and segment pricing (e.g., price based on geographic locations). Many of these tactics are also available to you as a social marketer to increase sales. You yourself may have used a discount coupon from a utility for compost, taken advantage of a weekend sales event for water-efficient toilets, or received a discount on parking at work because you are part of a car pool. The social marketing organization may be involved in subsidizing the incentive, distributing coupons, and/or getting the word out, as illustrated in the following example.

Example: Bike Helmet Coupons

Harborview Injury Prevention and Research Center's (HIPRC) Web site reported in February 2000 that "more bicyclists in Seattle wear helmets than bicyclists in any other major city in the country where laws do not require it." The Washington Children's Helmet Bicycle Campaign had been launched in 1986 by physicians at Harborview Medical Center in Seattle, who were alarmed at the nearly 200 children they were treating each year with bicycle-related head injuries.[12]

"Although bicycle helmets were available in 1985, just one child in 100 wears one." HIPRC physicians conducted a study to understand why parents didn't buy bike helmets for their children and what factors influenced whether children actually wore them.

> The results, from a survey of more than 2,500 fourth graders and their parents, shaped the eventual campaign. More than two thirds of the parents said that they had never thought of providing a helmet and *another third cited cost as a factor* [italics added].

> A campaign was designed around "four key objectives: increasing public awareness of the importance of helmets, educating parents about helmet use, overcoming peer pressure among children against wearing helmets, and lowering helmet prices."

The HIPRC formed a coalition of health, bicycling, helmet industry, and community organizations to design and manage a variety of promotions. As a result, parents and children heard about helmets on television, on the radio, in the newspapers, in their doctors' offices, at school, and at youth groups. The advertised discount coupons cut helmet prices by half, to $20. Nearly 5,000 helmets were distributed at no or low cost to needy families.

By September 1993 (seven years later), helmet use had jumped from 1% to 57% among children in the greater Seattle area and adult use had increased to 70%. Five years into the campaign, an HIPRC evaluation revealed its ultimate impact: Admissions at five Seattle-area hospitals for bicycle-related head injuries had dropped by approximately two thirds for children 5 to 14 years old.

4. Decrease Nonmonetary Costs for the Desired Behavior

Tactics are also available for decreasing *time*, *effort*, *physical*, or *psychological* costs. Fox suggests reducing usage time by "embedding" a new behavior into present activities.[13] Thus, people might be encouraged to floss their teeth while they watch television. People can also be encouraged to "anchor" a new behavior to an established habit.[14] To encourage physical activity, for example, you can recommend that people climb the stairs to their third-floor office instead of taking the elevator.

Gemunden proposed several potential tactics for reducing other nonmonetary costs in this model:

1. Against a perceived psychological risk, provide social products in ways that deliver *psychological rewards*.

2. Against a perceived social risk, gather *endorsements from credible sources* that reduce the potential stigma or embarrassment of adopting a product.

3. Against a perceived usage risk, provide target adopters with *reassuring information* on the product or with a free trial of the product so they can experience how the product does what it promises to do.

4. Against perceived physical risk, solicit *seals of approval* from authoritative institutions, such as the American Dental Association, the American Medical Association, or other highly respected organizations.[15]

Example: Redeeming Farmers' Market Checks

Women, Infants, and Children (WIC) program offices often distribute checks to qualified families to purchase fresh fruits and vegetables at local farmers' markets. Yet clients often face significant nonmonetary costs that lead to lower redemption rates than many WIC offices would like to see. Many experience increased *effort* in finding the market and parking, *embarrassment* around other shoppers when using coupons, *difficulty* in identifying qualified produce when signs are inconsistently displayed or hard to see, *concern* about not getting change back from checks, *frustration* with misplacing checks that are often stored in drawers or forgotten in strollers, and *fear* of what the WIC counselor will think if they decline the checks, even though their chances of using them are minimal, given work schedules that conflict with market hours.

These costs could be overcome with a variety of tactics related to the price tool as well as to the other Ps:

- Detailed maps showing the way to the market and parking areas printed on the backs of checks
- Electronic debit cards in place of the checks
- Signs on poles above the stands that display some recognizable logo that doesn't "brand" the client, such as the 5 a Day logo
- Printing checks in lower amounts, such as $1 denominations
- Packaging checks in sturdy check folders
- Offering hesitant clients fewer checks, and more if they use them all

5. Increase Monetary Costs for the Competing Behavior

In the social marketing environment, this tactic is likely to involve influencing policy makers, as the most effective monetary strategies against the competition often require *increasing taxes* (e.g., on gas-guzzling cars), *imposing fines* (e.g., for not recycling), and/or *decreasing funding* (e.g., if a school doesn't offer an hour of physical education classes). Referring back to the bike helmet example, the Harborview Injury Prevention and Research Center is now taking a more legislative and regulatory emphasis, since recent evaluations show that helmet use rates have stabilized—a possible sign, they say, that those not wearing helmets may only respond to laws and fines. As Alan Andreasen lays out in his book *Social Marketing in the 21st Century*, these policy changes may be critical to significant social change, and the social marketer can play a role in making this happen. "Our models and frameworks are flexible enough to guide efforts aimed at this kind of upstream behavior, especially for the many smaller organizations, especially at the local level, that cannot afford lobbyists."[16]

Andreasen proposes that you use familiar components of the social marketing model. You can segment the potential audience using the stages of change model, and in the legislative environment this may be translated into those who are opponents, undecideds, or supporters. You will then benefit from identifying and understanding your target audience's BCOS factors: benefits, costs, others in the target audience's environment and their influence, and self-assurance (perceptions of opportunity and ability).[17] These should sound familiar as well.

In the following example, a social marketing approach upstream helped pass a law to influence behaviors downstream, one expected to save lives.

Example: Persuading Legislators to Pass a Primary Cell Phone and Texting Law

As of January 2010, only 15 states and the District of Columbia had made it a primary offense to text and drive, and only five states and the District of Columbia had made it a primary offense to talk on handheld cell phones while driving. Washington State was one of the states where this was only a secondary offense, meaning a driver must have done something else wrong (e.g., weaving across lane markers) to be ticketed.[18] Two state legislators and a volunteer citizen task force stepped up efforts to persuade the legislature and the governor to pass a new law (*desired behavior*), one that would allow the police to pull over drivers talking on their cell phones or texting while driving. They used a social marketing approach, and their first step was to understand concerns legislators had about voting "yes." Several major barriers were identified. A few are presented in Table 11.2, along with responses presented at testimonies to legislative committees.

Table 11.2   Addressing Barriers to Passing a Primary Cell Phone and Texting Law

Major Concerns Expressed by Legislators	Responses from Advocates
"My constituents will argue that talking on a cell phone is no more dangerous than putting on makeup or eating food. They'll claim laws against this will be next."	Human factors experts tell us that there are three kinds of driving distractions. The first is visual—eyes off the road. The second is mechanical—hands off the wheel. The third is cognitive—when our mind is not fully engaged on the task of driving. Talking on a handheld cell phone or texting involves all three.
	As a result, one study shows that drivers talking on cell phones are as impaired as drunk drivers who have a 0.08% blood alcohol level and those texting while driving are equivalent to those having a 0.24% blood alcohol level.
"I don't understand how talking on a phone is any different than talking with a passenger in the vehicle."	There is one very important difference. A passenger in a vehicle is aware of the driving situation and can even serve as an additional lookout for hazards. He or she also understands when there is a needed pause in a conversation.
"A law like this would not be enforceable."	Although we won't see all offenders, it gives us the important ability, though after the fact, to assess additional penalties on those who have chosen to act recklessly or irresponsibly.

Washington's new law was passed and went into effect on June 10, 2010. Tickets are $124 for talking on handheld cell phones while driving or texting while driving. Teens with intermediate driver's licenses or learner permits may not use a wireless device at all while driving, including a hands-free device, unless they're reporting an emergency.

6. Increase Nonmonetary Costs for the Competing Behavior

Nonmonetary tactics can also be used to increase actual or perceived nonmonetary costs associated with choosing the competing behavior. In this case, you may be creating or emphasizing negative public recognition. In Middlesborough, England, for example, a cyclist was riding through a pedestrian area when he heard on a loudspeaker: "Would the young man on the bike please get off and walk. You are riding in a pedestrian area."[19] The surprised youth stopped, looked about, and although all he saw was a video camera, dismounted and then wheeled his bike through the crowded street, reportedly horrified that the voice was obviously referring to him. Britain's first "talking" security camera had been introduced by the town's mayor, who believed talking cameras would dramatically cut not just antisocial behavior, but violent crime as well. And in Tacoma, Washington, a Web site features properties not in full compliance with municipal codes. They call it "The Filthy 15," and although property owners' names do not appear on the Web site, it does include photos of each building, specific reasons the property is on the list, and what is next in the cleanup process, including something a neighbor or other concerned citizen could track.[20]

In a different scenario, you might be highlighting the downsides of the competition, as illustrated in the following example, in which research was key to understanding what costs should be highlighted.

Example: Encouraging Teen Abstinence

The Teen Aware Project is part of a statewide effort to reduce teen pregnancy and is sponsored by the Washington State Office of Superintendent of Public Instruction. Funds are allocated through a competitive grant process to public middle/junior and senior high schools for the development of media campaigns to promote sexual abstinence and the importance of delaying sexual activity, pregnancy, and childbearing. These campaigns are substantially designed and produced by students. Student media products include video and radio productions, posters, theater productions, print advertising, multimedia, T-shirts, buttons, and Web sites. Campaign messages are distributed in local project schools and communities.

This particular research effort was conducted by teens at Mercer Island High School, a grant recipient. A team of nine students from marketing, health, and communication classes volunteered to develop the campaign, from start to finish. Several teachers and outside consultants served as coaches on the project.[20] At the time this research effort was undertaken, the team had chosen their campaign focus (abstinence), purpose (reducing teen pregnancies), target audience (eighth graders), and campaign objective (to persuade students to "pause and think in a heated moment"). Information from existing student surveys indicated that about 75% of eighth graders—but only 25% of seniors—were abstinent. It was decided that the campaign bull's-eye would be eighth graders, who were seen as being the most vulnerable for making choices regarding sexual activity.

The team of juniors and seniors wanted to refresh their memories about middle school years. As one student expressed, "It's been a long time since I was an eighth grader, and I don't have a clue what they know and think about sex these days." The primary purposes of their research were to (a) help with decision making regarding which benefits of abstinence and costs related to sexual activity should be highlighted in the campaign and

(b) provide input for selecting a slogan for the campaign. More specifically, the study was designed to determine major perceived benefits of abstinence, costs associated with being sexually active, and messages (and tone) that would be most effective in influencing an eighth grader to consider abstinence.

Each of the nine students agreed to conduct casual interviews with at least five eighth graders over a one-week period. They used an informal script that explained the project and assured respondents that their comments would be anonymous. They recorded and summarized responses to the following three open-ended questions:

1. What's the most important reason you can think of for delaying having intercourse until you are older?

2. What are the worst things you can think of that can happen to you if you have intercourse before you are ready?

3. What would you say to your best friend if she or he told you that they thought they were going to have sex for the first time tonight?

Interviews were conducted, with district permission, before and after classes at the middle schools as well as at informal settings such as sports events, after-school programs, and friends' homes. Students returned to class the following week, shared summaries of their findings, and were guided to identify the following themes for each of the informational areas:

- Major reasons for delaying sex:
  o You won't get sexually transmitted diseases (STDs)
  o You can save it for someone special
  o You won't get pregnant
- The worst things that can happen:
  o They could drop you later for someone else
  o You could get pregnant, and childbirth really hurts
  o You can get really bad STDs, like crabs
- Words for a friend:
  o "You should wait until you are older."
  o "Are you sure he really loves you?"
  o "Do you have protection?"
  o "Are you ready for all the things that could happen?"

The team used this input to develop a campaign centered around emphasis on three "gross" consequences of having sex before you're ready. They developed the campaign slogan "Are you ready?" and followed the question with each of the three consequences. Graphic, in-your-face images were reflected on the posters and depicted in radio scripts (see Figures 11.2, 11.3, and 11.4).

Figure 11.2 Abstinence campaign poster.[22]

Radio spots that were played on the high school radio station followed the three gross consequence themes. In one, a male voice says,

> I remember the day I learned what an STD really was. I had seen little things crawling around in my . . . hair. I woke up in the middle of the night, my . . . you know . . . was burning from an itch. My entire crotch was swarming with miniature crabs. Finally, I had to get help. If you think you're going to have sex, ask yourself, "Are you ready for that?" (See Figure 11.2.)

In another approach, a girl graphically recounts the pain of giving birth (see Figure 11.3). And in the third spot, a girl sadly yet frankly relates how the guy she slept with immediately told everyone at school and found a new girlfriend. It took her years to trust a guy again (see Figure 11.4).

SETTING PRICES FOR TANGIBLE OBJECTS AND SERVICES

Prices for tangible goods and services involved in social marketing campaigns are typically set by manufacturers, retailers, and service providers. Social marketers are more often involved in helping to decide what tangible objects and services would be beneficial in facilitating behavior change, recommending discount coupons and related incentives, and then promoting their use.

When a social marketer gets involved in the price setting, however, several principles can guide decision making. The first task is to reach agreement on your pricing objectives. Kotler and Roberto[24] outline several potential objectives:

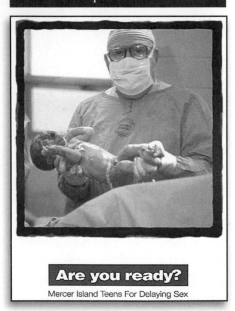

Figure 11.3 Abstinence campaign poster.[23]

- *Maximizing retained earnings* where the primary consideration is money making (e.g., charging advertisers for space on billboards above the Play Pumps in Africa, ones that decrease the time it takes for families to pump water from wells)

- *Recovering costs* where revenue is expected to offset a portion of costs (e.g., charging customers $32 for a rain barrel that cost the utility $45)

- *Maximizing the number of target adopters* where the primary purpose is to influence as many people as possible to use the service and/or buy the product (e.g., providing free condoms to farm workers)

- *Social equity* where reaching underprivileged or high-risk segments is a priority and different prices might be charged according to ability to pay (e.g., a sliding scale fee for bike helmets)

- *Demarketing* where pricing strategies are used to discourage people from adopting a particular social product (e.g., taxes on cigarettes)

Figure 11.4 Abstinence campaign poster.[25]

Once the pricing objective is agreed upon, setting specific prices gets easier. Three options to consider include the following:

1. *Cost-based pricing*, where prices are based on a desired or established profit margin or rate of return on investment (e.g., condoms are sold at community clinics at prices to cover purchase costs)

2. *Competitive-based pricing*, where prices are more driven by the prices for competing (similar) products and services (e.g., a life vest manufacturer partnering on a drowning prevention campaign offers discount coupons to make pricing similar to less expensive vests that are not Coast Guard approved)

3. *Value-based pricing*, where prices are based on an analysis of the target adopters' "price sensitivity," evaluating demand at varying price points (e.g., foodwaste composters that require simple spinning are priced higher than those requiring manual tossing)

ETHICAL CONSIDERATIONS RELATED TO PRICING STRATEGIES

Ethical considerations related to pricing strategies include issues of *social equity* (e.g., fixed versus sliding scale fees), *potential exploitation* (e.g., offering monetary incentives to drug-addicted women for voluntary sterilization or, like a program in North Carolina to reduce teen pregnancy, giving a dollar for each day not pregnant to teens who have never been pregnant, want to attend college, and have a sister who gave birth as a teen), impact and fairness of *public shame* tactics (e.g., what if owners of one of The Filthy 15 buildings had lost their job, and this explains why they haven't repaired their dilapidated building), and *full disclosure* of costs (e.g., requirements to toss food composters daily in order to receive stated benefits). In the case of promoting farmers' markets to WIC clients, each of these issues might apply. Should clients receive additional coupons if they use all of their first set, making it necessary to give some clients only half a pack? What do we do about the fact that many items at the market are less than the $2 coupon denomination, and yet change cannot be given? Are we consistent about telling our clients that they will probably need to pay $3 for parking while at the markets?

CHAPTER SUMMARY

The price of a social marketing product is *the cost that the target audience associates with adopting the new behavior.* Costs may be monetary or nonmonetary in nature. Your task is to use this second tool to help ensure that what you offer the audience (*benefits*) is equal to or greater than what they will have to give up (*costs*). As noted, the *product* and *place* tools are also used to increase benefits and decrease costs (e.g., providing more convenient locations to recycle is a *place* strategy). Your objective (and opportunity) with the *price* tool is to develop and provide *incentives* that can be used to provide one or more of the following six impacts. The first four tactics focus on the desired behavior and the last two on the competing one(s).

1. Increase monetary benefits for *the desired behavior*

2. Increase nonmonetary benefits for *the desired behavior*

3. Decrease monetary costs for *the desired behavior*

4. Decrease nonmonetary costs for *the desired behavior*

5. Increase monetary costs for *the competing behavior*

6. Increase nonmonetary costs for *the competing behavior*

Although most prices for tangible goods and services are established by manufacturers, retailers, and service providers, several principles can guide a social marketer faced with price setting decisions, beginning with establishing pricing objectives. What do you want the price to accomplish for you? Once defined, you will then likely decide to establish your price based on cost, the competition, or the perceived value that your target audience holds for the product.

Formative Research:
Decreasing Use of Plastic Bags and Increasing Use of Reusable Bags in Ireland
(2002–2004)

Background and Purpose of Research

In 1999, it was estimated that around 1.26 billion plastic shopping bags were being handed out free in Ireland each year, with most of the product ending up in the landfill as part of the domestic waste stream.[26] Although an unknown smaller proportion of the bags eventually appeared as litter, even the Irish called it their national flag. Some retailers had tried to encourage the reuse of the bags or the use of cloth and canvas bags, but had not been successful to date. Most blamed consumer apathy, and although there was robust legislation in place to tackle littering, the ability to enforce compliance was understandably difficult.

The Irish government first considered imposing upstream taxes on producers and importers of plastic bags, but decided instead to focus on a downstream strategy that would change consumer behavior. In 2002, they introduced a 15-Eurocent tax on plastic shopping bags, an amount considered sufficiently high to give consumers pause for thought and to stimulate them to bring their own reusable shopping bags more often.[27] As you will read, the effect has been dramatic, with a reduction in the consumption of plastic shopping bags in excess of 90%, and an increase in reusable bags from 36% in 1999 to 90% in

2003.[28] Of interest in this case is the variety of audiences (upstream, midstream, and downstream) included in the *formative research* efforts and the variety of measures used to evaluate the program.[29]

Audience for Research, Methodology, and Findings

The Irish government wanted consumers to bring a reusable bag for their purchases at retail stores, thereby reducing the amount of plastic bag consumption and, ultimately, production and littering. Central to their ultimate success were extensive surveys and consultations with *all* stakeholders that would be affected by the levy, revealing the following barriers:[30]

- *Consumer* "protests" were feared, as many consumers believed increased taxes would benefit the retail stores and/or were primarily a way for the government to increase revenues. Consumers were also concerned they would forget to bring their own bags, having experienced forgetting them frequently in the past. The 15-Eurocent tax was aggressive, but given the reluctance among consumers to pay anything for a bag, policy makers were confident it would give pause. A 2000 survey of 1,003 Irish adults ages 18 and over commissioned by the Department of the Environment, Heritage and Local Government suggested that the proposed tax was more than six times higher than the average amount consumers were willing to pay (around 2.4 Eurocents), and that only 8% of the consumers surveyed felt it was worth paying for a plastic bag at all.[31]

- *Retail industry* leaders were concerned that consumers would blame the retailers for "profiteering," and that the levy would encourage shoplifting, making it easier for customers to put items unseen into their shopping bags. Butchers were strongly opposed to any levy that would apply to all plastic bags, warning that various purchases, including meat, need to be wrapped separately for hygiene reasons.

- *Revenue commissioners and local authorities* were concerned with the amount of additional time, effort, and cost this would require for enforcement, tracking revenue, and allocating funds appropriately.

Program Results

Program evaluations reported the following:

- *Decrease in bags distributed:* In the first year after the launch of the levy, there was a 90% reduction in plastic checkout bags distributed, equating to a reduction of 1 billion plastic bags. The number of plastic bags issued per capita fell from 328 to 21. Of interest to some is whether there was a significant increase in the purchase and use of kitchen "bin liners." Retail data confirmed that there was indeed a 77% increase in the purchase of plastic kitchen bags, but that this only equated to 70 million bags. The net effect is still positive, with an overall reduction in plastic bag use of 930 million bags.[32]

- *Decrease in litter:* Litter surveys found that before levy launch in the spring of 2002, plastic bags were estimated to compose 5% of the litter in Ireland. By August 2003, they were estimated to compose 0.25% of litter, and by August 2004, 0.22%.

- *Consumers' attitudes:* A year after the levy's launch, 100 telephone interviews were completed with a randomly selected sample of householders in Dublin. As indicated in Table 11.3, highlights of findings

Table 11.3   Attitudes Toward Bag Tax One Year Later

	Expense	Environmental Impact
Positive	14%	90%
Neutral	60%	10%
Negative	26%	0%

Note: A 43% response rate from the sample was achieved, and there is a 9.8% margin of error for respondent answers.

indicate that the a majority of the respondents were either neutral or positive about the expense of the bags, and that virtually all felt positive about the environmental impact.[33]

- *Retailers' attitudes:* Surveys of retailers were conducted a year after the levy's introduction. Researchers conducted face-to-face interviews with seven leaders in the retail sector following their completion of a self-administered questionnaire. The cumulative market share of those retailers accounted for 50% of Irish retail sales. Findings indicated that retailers found the effects of the tax neutral or positive, as savings resulting from not having to purchase plastic bags outweighed additional costs of implementation. Findings also indicated that although shoplifting rose initially, it then fell.[34]

CHAPTER 11 NOTES

1. Bueckert, D. (2007). Federal budget hammers gas-guzzlers, leaves Kyoto in the air. *CNEWS.* Retrieved March 20, 2007, from http://cnews.canoe.ca/CNEWS/Canada/2007/03/19/3783431-cp.html

2. Jordan Department of Statistics for the year 2008.

3. Case information was provided by Setta Tutundjian, Project Management Specialist: Policy Reform and Institutional Strengthening Office of Water Resources and Environment, USAID.

4. World Bank Report No. 47951-JO, Hashemite Kingdom of Jordan Poverty Update, November 2009.

5. USAID

6. Quoted from USAID in Jordan. (n.d.). *Water conservation in rural Jordan.* Retrieved July 21, 2011, from http://jordan.usaid.gov/features_disp.cfm?id=144&type=success

7. Kotler, P., & Armstrong, G. (2001). *Principles of marketing* (p. 371). Upper Saddle River, NJ: Prentice Hall.

8. O'Connor, R., Fix, B., Celestino, P., Carlin-Menter, S., Hyland, A., & Cummings, K. M. (2006). Financial incentives to promote smoking cessation: Evidence from 11 quit and win contests. *Journal of Public Health Management and Practice, 12*(1), 44–51. Retrieved March 10, 2007, from http://www.ncbi.nlm.nih.gov/entrez/query.fcgi?cmd=Retrieve&db=pubmed&dopt=Abstract&list_uids=16340515&query_hl=6&itool=pubmed_docsum

9. Environmental Protection Agency, Pay as You Throw. (2010). *Pay-as-you throw success stories.* Retrieved July 28, 2011, from http://www.epa.gov/osw/conserve/tools/payt/tools/success.htm

10. Klein, J. Z. (2010, December 21). Fair play shows up in the standings. *The New York Times.* Retrieved January 28, 2011, from http://www.nytimes.com/2010/12/22/sports/hockey/22youth.html

11. Klein, 2010, Fair play shows up.

12. Information in this example is from Harborview Injury Prevention and Research Center, University of Washington, Seattle. Retrieved October 1, 2001, from http://www.hiprc.org

13. Fox, K. F. (1980). Time as a component of price in social marketing. In R. P. Bagozzi, et al. (Eds.), *Marketing in the '80s* (pp. 464–467). Chicago, IL: American Marketing Association;

as cited in Kotler, P., & Roberto, E. L. (1989). *Social marketing: Strategies for changing public behavior.* New York: Free Press.

14. Ibid.

15. Gemunden, H. G. (1985). Perceived risk and information search: A Systematic meta-analysis of the empirical evidence. *International Journal of Research in Marketing, 2,* 79–100; as cited in Kotler & Roberto, 1989, *Social marketing* (pp. 182–183).

16. Andreasen, A. R. (2006). *Social marketing in the 21st century* (p. 153). Thousand Oaks, CA: Sage.

17. Ibid., p. 102.

18. Driven to Distraction Task Force. (n.d.). *Frequently asked questions. Cell phone legislation proposed by Senator Tracey Eide and Representative Reuven Carlyle.* Retrieved January 28, 2011, from http://www.nodistractions.org/The_Evidence.html

19. Daily Mail. (2006, September 16). *Big Brother is shouting at you.* Retrieved October 10, 2006, from http://dailymail.co.uk/pages/text/print.html?in_article_id=405477&in_page_id=1770

20. City of Tacoma. (2007). *The Filthy 15.* Retrieved March 21, 2007, from http://www.cityoftacoma.org/Page.aspx?nid=167

21. Students received creative and production assistance from Cynthia Hartwig (creative director), Shelley Baker (art director at Cf2Gs Advertising), Marlene Liranzo (Mercer Island High School teacher), Gary Gorland (Teen Aware program manager), and Nancy Lee (consultant).

22. Copyright © 2001 by Washington State Office of Superintendent of Public Instruction.

23. Copyright © 2001 by Washington State Office of Superintendent of Public Instruction.

24. Kotler & Roberto, 1989, *Social marketing,* pp. 176–177.

25. Copyright © 2001 by Washington State Office of Superintendent of Public Instruction.

26. AEA Technology PLC. (2009, August). *Welsh Assembly Government, single use bag study* (Issue Number 8). Report to Welsh Assembly Government. Retrieved July 28, 2011, from http://wales.gov.uk/topics/environmentcountryside/epq/waste_recycling/substance/carrierbags/singleusestudy/?/lang=en

27. Convery, F., McDonnell, S., & Ferreira, S. (2006). The most popular tax in Europe? Lessons from the Irish plastic bag levy. *Environmental and Resource Economics, 38,* 1–11.

28. Irish plastic bag tax set to rise. (2007). *BBC News.* Retrieved July 21, 2011, from http://news.bbc.co.uk/2/hi/uk_news/northern_ireland/6383557.stm

29. An expanded version of this case appears in McKenzie-Mohr, D., Lee, N., Schultz, W., & Kotler, P. (2011). *Social marketing to protect the environment: What works.* Thousand Oaks, CA: Sage.

30. Convery et al., 2006, The most popular tax.

31. Ibid.

32. Evidence to Scottish Parliament, Environment and Rural Development committee hearings, 2005.

33. Convery et al., 2006, The most popular tax.

34. Ibid.

Chapter 12

PLACE

Making Access Convenient and Pleasant

Avoid victim blaming and acknowledge that deficiencies in the structural environment can fuel social inequities and block change.

—Dr. Christine Domegan
National University of Ireland

Store-based retailers say that the three most important things in the success of their businesses are "location, location, location!" You may find this true for many social marketing efforts as well. Consider how much lower the following scores would be without the convenient-access component of these programs, as well as those in the opening case story:

- Recycling: In 2009, Americans recycled 62% of paper, 62% of yard trimmings, 26% of glass, and 20% of aluminum.[1] Although this is certainly not as much as we would like to see, imagine how grim the statistics would be without curbside recycling and recycle containers in office buildings and most public places.
- Pet waste pickup: Although an estimated 40% of dog owners in the United States do not pick up their dog's waste, at least 60% do, and without Mutt Mitts available in parks and public places around the country, we can imagine that number would be smaller.[2]
- Tobacco quitlines: The prevalence of smoking among adults in the United States has declined from about 25% in 1990 to 20.6% in 2009.[3] Most tobacco users across the states have access to quitlines, providing convenient access to telephone counseling to help them quit, and in some cases these lines provide limited access to medication. Quitlines overcome many of the barriers to traditional smoking cessation classes, as they require no transportation and are available at the smoker's convenience.
- Organ donations: Many initiatives around the world aim to increase the number of organs obtained from deceased donors. Convenience of registering as an organ donor is one important strategy, with many countries now offering registration through driver's license bureaus or departments of motor vehicles, where individuals can designate their wish to be an organ donor on their license.[4]

Recycling Made Easy in Cape Town, South Africa (2008)

Background

Surrounded by sea and mountains, Cape Town, South Africa, has limited land available for human habitation and even less for landfills. In fact, out of its six landfill sites, four have been closed over the last decade and the remaining two are nearing their limits. The traditional approach to waste management required technical and engineering solutions focusing on collection and removal as well as landfill design and practices. In 2008, local authorities turned to a voluntary domestic recycling solution. Planners understood that simply creating awareness and educating citizens would not influence action, and that it would take free, accessible, easy-to-use products and services as well.

Information for this case highlight was provided by Hugh Tyrrell, director of GreenEdge, a communications and consulting firm for this project.[5]

Target Audience and Desired Behavior

Targeted households were those that wanted to recycle but for various reasons did not actually do so (*contemplators*). The service was first offered to the more affluent upper-middle and upper income housing areas. With a greater propensity to recycle and with more disposable income, these residents would provide sufficient volumes to make the recycling operation more viable for the contractor. The programs would support recycling of paper, cardboard, cans, plastic bottles, and glass bottles and jars. Households would not recycle wet or food-contaminated paper and cardboard, foodwaste, scraps and peelings, cooking oil, garden refuse, clothing, or empty motor oil, acid solvent, paint, or chemical containers.

Audience Insights

Qualitative interviews with potential recyclers identified only a few barriers to address. There were concerns that the "trolley brigade" (e.g., homeless people/informal collectors) would rip open recyclables bags to gather recyclable items to sell themselves and would leave litter around. Perceived benefits were greater, with most in the target audience eager for an opportunity to receive a convenient way to recycle.

Strategies

Before the programs commenced, open meetings were held where elected representatives of the city *publicly committed* to and endorsed the recycling programs. Their endorsement, as well as those of the ratepayers associations, helped motivate participation in the service. To increase visibility, community newspapers were invited to be present and report on the meetings so that news of local leadership commitment could be disseminated widely in the area. In some instances, support and commitments from local conservation and environmental organizations were also forthcoming and could be communicated to their membership as well.

The recycling offer developed is consistent with a *positioning* intending to deliver a simple and convenient way to recycle.

Householders are given free (*price*) clear bags (*product*) in which to collect their dry mixed-material recyclables (plastic bottles and bags; paper and cardboard; tin/aluminum food and drink cans; and glass bottles and jars). Two weeks before the collections began, starter packs containing four free clear bags—a month's supply—and an explanatory leaflet were dropped in the mailboxes of all residents. This leaflet illustrated what could and couldn't be recycled (*augmented product*) and was intended to be put up as a permanent reminder.

Messages emphasized that getting into the recycling routine would be convenient (*place*) and as "easy as one, two, three":

1. Separate all dry recyclables into the clear plastic bag that will be provided weekly.

2. On your regular weekly refuse removal day, place your clear bag of recyclables on top of your nonrecyclables inside the wheelie bin.

3. The contractor will remove your recyclables bag and leave a new clear bag for collecting the next week's recyclables.

Additional messages helped make clear the environmental benefits of recycling, including reduction in the processing of new materials and the impact on sea life (see Figure 12.1).

A variety of media channels were used, including advertisements in local newspapers announcing the new service (see Figure 12.2); a Web site with details and answers to frequently asked questions about how to

Figure 12.1   Advertisement making the benefit to the environment real.[6]

Figure 12.2 Advertisement announcing the launch of the program.[7]

Get sorted for free door-to-door recycling collection.

From **2 March 2009**, free municipal Think Twice recycling service begins in your area. Each week on the same day as refuse removal, your recyclable materials will be collected.

But first you'll need to sort your waste, gather it in the clear bag you'll be given for recyclables, and get it into your wheelie bin.

What can and can't be recycled

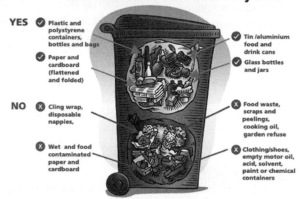

YES
- Plastic and polystyrene containers, bottles and bags
- Paper and cardboard (flattened and folded)
- Tin /aluminium food and drink cans
- Glass bottles and jars

NO
- Cling wrap, disposable nappies,
- Wet and food contaminated paper and cardboard
- Food waste, scraps and peelings, cooking oil, garden refuse
- Clothing/shoes, empty motor oil, acid, solvent, paint or chemical containers

Cut out and put up in your kitchen.

Your starter pack is on its way

It includes clear plastic bags - use one or more for your recyclables each week. Replacement bags will be given to you in exchange for bags of recyclables collected.

Also enclosed is an information leaflet with details on what to recycle and how to get in the recycling routine.

Your contribution is important – every bit of recycling makes a difference!

For more information, contact:
Waste Control: 021 590 3900
City of Cape Town Area Head: 021 704 1005
Email your queries to: info@wastecontrol.co.za
Or visit: www.wastecontrol.co.za

GreenEdge Communications

participate and what could and shouldn't be put into the recycling bags (www.wastecon trol.co.za); signage on sides of refuse-removal trucks in selected suburbs (see Figure 12.3); and special tours for members of the media to observe the process, benefits, and outcomes. Of particular interest was a strategy to motivate householders by providing ongoing feedback on household participation (see Figure 12.5).

And one final note of interest regarding the barriers research that revealed concern about the "poaching" of recycling bags by informal collectors: A program was instituted to buy directly from members of this group who wanted to be formalized. They would be given an ID card and color-coded "bibs" to wear to identify themselves to residents as part of the program. They would then be paid per weight of recyclables brought to the central collection point.

Figure 12.3 Special collection vehicles creating visibility and interest.[8]

Results

Participation rates averaging over 60% of households are being achieved and in some areas are over 80% (see Figures 12.4 and 12.5). Rates are determined using strict

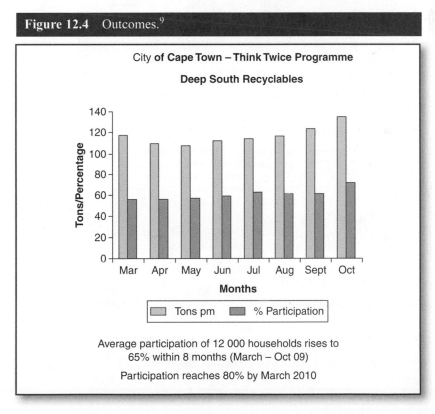

Figure 12.4 Outcomes.[9]

City **of Cape Town – Think Twice Programme**

Deep South Recyclables

Legend: Tons pm / % Participation

Y-axis: Tons/Percentage

X-axis: Months — Mar, Apr, May, Jun, Jul, Aug, Sept, Oct

Average participation of 12 000 households rises to 65% within 8 months (March – Oct 09)

Participation reaches 80% by March 2010

Figure 12.5 Advertisement providing feedback to communities.[10]

Think Twice

Deep South Suburbs Recycling Update - May 2009

Your recycling is saving resources and creating jobs!

Deep South residents recycling through the Think Twice municipal service are saving growing amounts of resources and creating more employment for local people. One out of every two households in the Deep South area are now using the service so it's an increasingly successful programme.

Bags of recyclables are picked up outside homes and taken to the False Bay Recycling company in Lekkerwater Road, Kommetjie. Here the contents are weighed and separated into glass, paper, plastic and metal ready for collection by companies like Consol Glass, SAPPI and SA Metal who reprocess the waste material into new products again.

Evan Saayman with his daughter Yolanda and son Kevin who run False Bay Recycling as a family business, which employs 25 local workers.

False Bay Recycling is run by the Saayman family and the business works every day including public holidays. Since the service began in March, staff numbers from the local community have increased from six to 25 people.

Yes to polystyrene, no to chip packets or tetrapaks

False Bay Recycling accepts polystyrene foam packaging, fruit and meat trays and styrene coffee cups. However no chips or sweet packets, or tetrapak boxes (the tall rectangular fruit juice or milk boxes) can be accepted. Buy in glass or plastic bottles instead.

Recycling bags

Bring a rates statement with you to the Sub-Council Offices in Fish Hoek – a limited supply of bags for keeping your weekly recyclables is available.

For more queries and information:
Waste Control: **021 590 3900**
City of Cape Town Area Manager: **021 704 1005**
Email: **info@wastecontrol.co.za**

THIS CITY WORKS FOR YOU

metrics on collections, comparing the number of households with bags to the number of total households served.

As participation rates rise higher and recycling becomes the normative behavior, advertising campaigns continue to create interest and participation, especially for new people and visitors coming into the area. Regular statistics of the amount of recyclables collected and percentage of participation rates are a constant feature of monthly feedback advertising.

PLACE: THE THIRD "P"

Place is where and when the target audience will perform the desired behavior, acquire any related goods, and receive any associated services.

We live in a convenience-oriented world in which many of us place an extremely high value on our time, trying to save some of it for our families, friends, and favorite leisure activities. As a social marketer, you'll want to be keenly aware that your target audience will evaluate the convenience of your offer relative to other exchanges in their lives. And the convenience bar has been raised over the past decades for all marketers by companies such as Starbucks, McDonald's, Federal Express, Amazon.com, 1–800–Flowers, Netflix for online movie rentals, and of course, the Internet.

In commercial sector marketing, place is often referred to as the distribution channel, and options and potential examples for social marketing are pervasive:

- **Physical locations:** Walking trails
- **Phone:** Domestic violence help line
- **Mail:** Postage-paid plastic bags for recycling mobile phones
- **Fax:** An agreement to quit signed by both patient and physician and faxed to a quitline
- **Internet:** Rideshare matching
- **Mobile unit:** For hazardous waste
- **Where people shop:** Mammograms in a department store
- **Where people hang out:** HIV/AIDS tests at gay bars
- **Drive-throughs:** For flu shots at medical centers
- **Home delivery/house calls:** Home energy audits
- **Kiosks:** For determining your body mass index (BMI)
- **Vending machines:** Condoms

It is important to clarify and stress that place is *not the same as communication channel*, which is where your communications will appear (e.g., brochures, radio ads, news stories, and personal presentations). Chapter 14 presents a detailed discussion of communication channels.

STEP 7: DEVELOP THE PLACE STRATEGY

Your objective with the place marketing tool is to develop strategies that will make it as convenient and pleasant as possible for your target audience to perform the behavior, acquire any goods, and receive any services. It is especially helpful in reducing access-related barriers (e.g., lack of transportation) and time-related barriers (e.g., being at work all day). It can also break down psychological barriers (e.g., providing needle exchange programs on street corners versus at a community health clinic). You will also want to do anything possible and within reason to make the competing behavior (seem) less convenient. The next sections of this chapter will elaborate on 10 successful strategies for you to consider.

1. Make the Location Closer

Example: A Dental Office on Wheels

Many children don't get the regular dental care they need. They may be struggling with language barriers, poverty, rural isolation, or homelessness. A mobile clinic called the SmileMobile travels to communities all across Washington State. This modern dental office on wheels brings dental services directly to children age 13 and younger who don't otherwise have access to care. Children enrolled in Medicaid have no out-of-pocket expenses, and other children are charged on a sliding fee schedule. Families may even enroll in Medicaid at the SmileMobile.

The brightly painted clinic features three state-of-the-art dental operatories and includes x-ray facilities. A full-time dentist and teams of local volunteer dentists and their staffs provide a range of dental services, including diagnostic services (e.g., exams and x-rays), prevention services (e.g., cleaning and sealants), acute and emergent relief of pain (e.g., extractions and minor surgical procedures), and routine restorative services (e.g., fillings and crowns).

The SmileMobile was developed by Washington Dental Service, the Washington State Dental Association, and the Washington Dental Service Foundation (see Figure 12.6). Staff work closely with local health departments and community, charitable, and business organizations to coordinate visits to cities and towns throughout the state. Every effort is made to reach the neediest children and provide translators for non-English-speaking patients and their families. The mobile clinic first hit the road in 1995 and by 2009 had treated more than 25,000 children throughout the state. It currently reaches an average of 60 children per week.[11]

Additional examples illustrating ways to save your target audience a little time and travel include the following:

- Exercise facilities at work sites
- Flu shots at grocery stores
- Breastfeeding consultation provided during home visits
- Print cartridges recycled at office supply stores

Figure 12.6 Making dental care for children more accessible.[7]

- Litter receptacles that make it easy to drive by and deposit litterbags
- Dental floss kept in the TV room or, better yet, attached to the remote control
- Xmas tree recycling drop-off at the local high school
- Bins for unwanted clothing placed in residential buildings
- Mobile libraries reaching rural areas

2. Extend Hours

Example: Vote by Mail

A survey of 15,167 citizens who had not voted in the 2008 presidential election in the U.S. indicated that the number one reason given was that they were "too busy, or had a conflicting schedule."[8] Oregon, however, had one of the highest voter turnouts in the nation—with 86% of registered voters voting in the 2008 presidential election.[11] Perhaps this is because it is so convenient, with Oregonians *voting only by mail*. There are no polling places, and election day is just a deadline to turn in your ballot and has been that way since 1998, when nearly 70% of Oregonians approved the Vote by Mail initiative. Some believe it is the most "effective, efficient and fraud-free way to conduct an election."[12]

Oregon's Vote by Mail system is simple, straightforward, and most of all, convenient. Ballots are mailed to registered voters 14 to 18 days before an election. Voters can complete the ballot "in the comfort of their own home" and on their own schedule. They have two weeks to return the ballot through the mail, or they can drop it off at one of many official conveniently located sites, including ones in a downtown park (see Figure 12.7). And there are additional advantages as well, including reduced election costs (since there are no polling places) and the fact that some feel voters give more thought to how they mark their ballots, having access to campaign materials at their fingertips.

As one editorial opinion expressed it,

> While the idea of the polling place at your local elementary school is something that provokes nostalgia in many of us, the realities of modern life as well as the demands on election officials outstrip any nostalgia we may feel for voting at a polling place. . . . Isn't the true definition of "democracy in action" one where the mechanism for casting ballots advantages the voter, not the system set up to count the ballots?[16]

Additional examples of strategies that offer target audiences more options in terms of time and day of the week include the following:

- Licensed child care searches online (versus calling a telephone center during normal business hours)
- 24-hour help lines for counseling and information
- Recycling centers open on Sundays
- Natural yard care workshops offered weekday evenings

Figure 12.7 One of Oregon's conveniently located ballot boxes in a park in downtown Portland.

3. Be There at the Point of Decision Making

Example: Ecstasy Pill Testing at Nightclubs

DanceSafe is a nonprofit organization promoting health and safety within the rave and nightclub community, with local chapters throughout the U.S. and Canada. They report that they neither condone nor condemn the use of any drug. Rather, they engage in efforts to reduce drug-related harm by providing health and safety information and on-site pill testing to those who do use drugs.[17] Among other programs and services, volunteers in communities with chapters offer *on-site pill testing* to ecstasy users at raves, nightclubs, and other public events where ecstasy is being used socially. Users who are unsure of the authenticity of a pill they possess can bring it to a booth or table where trained harm reduction volunteers will test it for use. DanceSafe reports on their Web site that volunteers staff booths at raves, nightclubs, and other dance events, where they also provide information on drugs, safe sex, and other health and safety issues concerning the dance community (such as driving home safely and protecting one's hearing). [18]

They cite two fundamental operating principles: *harm reduction* and *popular education.* They believe that "combining these two philosophies enables them to create successful, peer-based educational programs to reduce drug abuse and empower young people to make healthy, informed lifestyle choices."[19] They believe that

> while abstinence is the only way to avoid all the harms associated with drug use, harm reduction programs provide non-abstentionist health and safety information under the recognition that many people are going to choose to experiment with drugs despite all the risks involved. Harm reduction information and services help people use as safely as possible as long as they continue to use.[20]

Other creative solutions to influence "just in time" decision making include the following:

- Place a glass bowl of fruits and vegetables at eye level in the refrigerator versus in closed drawers on the bottom shelf.
- Negotiate with retailers to place natural fertilizers in a prominent display at the end of the aisle.
- Place a small, inexpensive plastic magnifier on fertilizer jugs so that gardeners can read the small print, including instructions for safe usage.

4. Make the Location More Appealing

Example: Bicycle Paths and Lanes in Los Angeles

One of the major barriers a potential bicyclist will give for not commuting by bike to work is the lack of safe, pleasant, and interconnected bike paths and lanes. In 1994, the City of Los Angeles, led by its Department of City Planning, developed its first-ever comprehensive Bicycle Plan. It was adopted by the city council in 1996 and then provided the Department of Transportation a template for bicycle paths, lanes, and myriad bicycle amenities and policies to be implemented throughout the city.

Figure 12.8 Making bicycling more appealing and safer in Los Angeles, with the orange line bike path built in conjunction with a metro bus rapid transit project.[21]

And the plan has a goal, that of increasing bicycle travel in the city to *5% of all utilitarian trips taken* by 2025, the year the plan is expected to be fully implemented. Public input for the plan was provided primarily through the city's Bicycle Advisory Committee (no bicycle advocacy group existed in Los Angeles at the time). The public learned about potential bike routes by visiting the committee's "war room," which posted the city's arterial roadway system maps and provided an opportunity for citizen reactions and recommendations.

By 2011 the city had installed 52 miles of bicycle paths, 165 miles of bicycle lanes, 100 miles of bicycle routes, and 8 miles of streets with shared lane markings, or sharrows (see Figure 12.8). In addition, the Los Angeles Department of Transportation has installed over 2,500 inverted-U bicycle racks, has developed and distributed over 250,000 comprehensive city bicycle maps, and is working on numerous funded bicycle path, lane, and parking projects to be put on the ground in the next five years.[22]

Additional examples of enhanced locations include the following:

- Conveniently located teen clinics that have reading materials and decor to which the market can relate
- Stairways in office buildings that employees would want to take, ones that are well lit, carpeted, and have art exhibits on the walls that get changed out once a month
- Organized walking groups for seniors in shopping malls

5. Overcome Psychological Barriers Associated With Place

Example: Pets on the Net

It is estimated that close to 10 million dogs end up in shelters across America every year and only about 25% get adopted.[23] Potential pet owners have several considerations (*barriers*) associated with visiting animal shelters to see what pets are available. In addition to the time it takes to travel to a center, some describe the psychological risk—a concern that they might take home a pet that isn't what they were really looking for. They worry they won't be able to say no. Viewing pets available for adoption on the Internet can help reduce both of these costs.

Many humane societies across the country have created Web sites where all or some of the pets currently available for adoption are featured, 24 hours a day, seven days a week. As illustrated in the photo on Sacramento's Pets on the Net Web site, detailed information on the pet includes a personality profile based on information provided by the previous owner (see Figure 12.9). Web site visitors are told that adoptions are on a first-come, first-served basis, and directions to

Figure 12.9 Pets on the Net reduces concern about not being able to say no.[25]

Name: **Jake**

Sex: Neutered Male

Age: 3 yrs

Breed: German Shepherd/Boxer

Color: Brown/Black, Bicolor

Personality Profile:
Hey there! I'm Jake. I'm a friendly and playful young dog in need of a good home, and a little love and guidance from someone special like you! I walk well on a leash and I like to ride in the car, so maybe we could run errands together! Please come and adopt me and give me the chance I deserve.

CASE: 47862A

the facility are provided.[24] Some Web sites include features such as daily updates, an opportunity to put a temporary hold on an animal, information on how to choose the right shelter pet, and reasons the pet was given up for adoption. A few national sites offer the ability to search nationwide for a pet by providing criteria such as desired breed, gender, age, size, and geographic locale.

Additional examples of strategies that reduce psychological barriers regarding "the place" include the following:

- Needle exchange services provided by a health clinic on a street corner or from a mobile van versus at the facility of a community clinic
- Offering a Web site to help youth quit smoking, with an option to e-mail a counselor instead of calling—an option some research with youth indicates just "isn't going to happen"

And finally, consider this example where well-intentioned program managers wanted to increase convenience of access. The question is whether they will end up creating place-associated psychological costs that will outweigh the attractive product and price components of the offer:

In October 2010, at a Department of Motor Vehicles branch in southwest Washington, DC, a new program was launched, one that would provide residents an opportunity for a confidential HIV test as they waited for their driver's license. The DMV provided the space to a nonprofit organization, Family and Medical Counseling Service, that administered the tests. A spokesperson for the organization commented, "Many people have to wait for some of the DMV services and the rapid HIV test takes only 20 minutes. It fits perfectly with the waiting times."[26] The oral test is free. In fact, test takers are given $15 to go toward the cost of their DMV services that day.

6. Be More Accessible Than the Competition

Example: School Lunch Line Redesign

Brian Wansink, a professor at Cornell University, argues that "the ideal lunchroom isn't one that eliminates cookies. The ideal lunchroom is the one that gets children to choose an apple instead of a cookie, but to think it's their own choice."[27] Wansink's Center for Behavioral Economics and Childhood Nutrition at Cornell aims to provide schools with research-based solutions that encourage healthier eating in the lunchroom. In an October 2010 article in the *New York Times*, Wansink and his colleague, David Just, shared a dozen strategies that they found nudge students toward making better choices on their own by changing the way their options are presented. Several are place-related strategies:

1. Place nutritious foods at the beginning of the lunch line

2. Use more appealing words to label healthy foods (e.g., "creamy corn" rather than "corn")

3. Give choices (e.g., carrots or celery versus just carrots)

4. Keep items like ice cream out of sight in the freezer with an opaque top

5. Pull the salad bar away from the wall

6. Have cafeteria workers ask children, "Do you want a salad?"

7. Provide food trays, as they appear to increase the likelihood of taking a salad

8. Decrease the size of cereal bowls

9. Place the chocolate milk behind the white milk

10. Place fruit in glass bowls, rather than stainless steel pans

11. Lunch tickets should cover fruit as a dessert, but not cookies

12. Provide a "healthy express" checkout line for those not buying chips or desserts

Other examples in which the desired behavior is made more accessible relative to the competition include the following:

- Family-friendly lanes in grocery stores where candy, gum, and adult magazines have been removed from the checkout stand
- High-occupant vehicle lanes that reward high-occupant vehicles with less traffic congestion (most of the time)

7. Make Access to the Competition More Difficult or Unpleasant

Example: Tobacco's "25-Foot Rule"

On December 8, 2005, Washington became the fifth state to implement a comprehensive statewide law prohibiting smoking in all indoor public places and workplaces, including restaurants, bars, taverns, bowling alleys, skating rinks, and nontribal casinos. But this law went further than any state had up to that time. Unlike Washington's measure, most statewide bans exempt some businesses, such as bars, private clubs, card rooms, and cigar lounges. And no state has a deeper no-smoking buffer than Washington's 25-foot rule that prohibits smoking within 25 feet of entrances, exits, windows that open, and ventilation intakes that serve indoor public places or places of employment.

This (upstream) measure, supported by the American Cancer Society and the American Lung Association, created a heated and emotional debate for months before the election on local talk shows and editorial pages. Opponents argued that bars would be put out of business, people would lose their jobs, all the patrons (and revenues) would just move to tribal casinos that would be exempt from the law, and outside dining would decline. And since people can simply choose to work at or frequent a nonsmoking restaurant or bar, why remove their choice? More than a year after the measure went into effect, some are still angry and lobbying with legislators to amend at least the "draconian" 25-foot rule: "It's overly harsh. It's turning my servers into cops. They are working for tips and to take care of customers—not to be authority figures."[28]

But research shows that state tobacco prevention programs must be broad based and comprehensive to be effective and that requiring smokers to "step out in the rain" would be a significant deterrent. With one of the lowest smoking rates in the country (17.6% of adults in 2005), Washington's Tobacco Prevention and Control Program also provides services to help people, restricts the ability of kids to get tobacco, conducts public awareness and media campaigns, supports programs in communities and schools, and evaluates the effectiveness of its activities. [29]

Other examples of limiting access to competitive behaviors include the following:

- Campaigns offering coupons for lockboxes for safe gun storage and distributing brochures listing convenient retail locations for purchase
- Distributing padlocks for home liquor cabinets to reduce alcohol access for minors—better yet, advocating with home builders to make these standard in new homes
- Pruning bushes in city parks so that youth are not able to gather in private and share their cigarettes and beer

8. Be Where Your Target Audience Shops

Example: Mammograms in the Mall

The following excerpt from an article in the *Detroit Free Press* provides an example of reducing barriers through improving access and location appeal.[30]

Many women already pick up birthday gifts, grab dinner, and get their hair cut at the malls, so why not schedule their annual mammograms there, as well? With a concept that screams "no more excuses," the Barbara Ann Karmanos Cancer Institute will open a cancer prevention center at the Somerset Collection South in Troy in September. A first for Michigan and the Detroit Institute, the mall-located screening center will provide a comfortable, spalike atmosphere for patients in a less intimidating setting than a traditional doctor's office or hospital.

Targeting shoppers, mall workers—including about 3,000 women—and the 100,000 employees near the mall, Karmanos is renovating a 2,000-square-foot space in the lower level of the mall. The center initially will focus on breast cancer prevention, with clinical breast exams and mammography available. However, services could expand to prostate, lung, and gastrointestinal cancer screenings and bone density testing, said Yvette Monet, a Karmanos spokeswoman. Taking its cues from the spas, the Karmanos Prevention Center will pamper patients with privacy, peace and quiet, and warm terry cloth robes.

The center is expected to encourage regular mammograms and breast exams. Nearly 44,000 women in the United States died last year from breast cancer—including 1,500 in Michigan—even though American Cancer Society studies show early diagnosis can mean a 97% survival rate. The Karmanos Center is expected to reach women who think they are too busy to get mammograms or are afraid to do so. "This is intended to be a nonclinical-type setting that will feature soothing shades of blue and comfy couches," Monet said.

Other examples of similar opportunities to provide services and tangible objects where your target audience is already shopping include the following:

- Distributing sustainable seafood guides at the fish counter of fish markets
- Providing litterbags at gas pumps, similar to pet waste bags in parks
- Giving demonstrations on how to select a proper life vest at sporting goods stores
- Offering beauty salon clients laminated cards to hang on a shower nozzle with instructions and reminders to conduct a monthly breast self-exam

9. Be Where Your Target Audience Hangs Out

Example: HIV/AIDS Tests in Gay Bathhouses

A headline in the *Chicago Tribune* on January 2, 2004, exemplifies this ninth place strategy: "Rapid HIV Tests Offered Where Those at Risk Gather: Seattle Health Officials Get Aggressive in AIDS Battle by Heading Into Gay Clubs, Taking a Drop Of Blood and Providing Answers in 20 Minutes." The article described a new and aggressive effort for Public Health–Seattle & King County, one that included administering rapid result HIV tests in bathhouses and gay sex clubs.[31]

To this point in time it had been common for health counselors to visit bathhouses to administer standard HIV testing. Although this certainly made taking the test more convenient, it didn't address the place barrier associated with getting the results. They would still need to then make an appointment at a medical clinic and then wait at least a week to hear the results, a critical step in the prevention and early treatment process that was not always taken. With this new effort, counselors would be with clients to present their results within about 20 minutes of taking the test. To address concerns about whether people carousing in a nightclub could handle the sudden news if it turned out they were HIV positive, counselors would refuse to test people who were high, drunk, or appeared emotionally unstable.

Apparently, the bathhouse and sex club owners initially expressed concern with health officials about whether this effort might offend customers, even drive them away. Perhaps the fact that one of the clubs a year and a half later touted the availability of free and anonymous rapid HIV tests every Friday night from 10 P.M. to 2 A.M. on its Web site is an indication of how things actually turned out.[32] Between July 2003 and February 2007, 1,559 rapid HIV tests were administered to gay male patrons of these bathhouses, identifying 33 new cases, a rate of 2.1%. In general, new-case-finding rates of greater than or equal to 1% are considered cost effective, and screening in the baths has substantially exceeded that threshold.[33]

By contrast, consider these dismal results when the place wasn't right. In Denmark, in 2009, a government-sponsored pilot program was launched in Copenhagen to supply addicts with free heroin. You would think this offer would be welcomed. It included a doctor's prescription which guaranteed users a pure dose, and since addicts wouldn't have to steal money to buy their drugs, the crime rate was expected to go down. But the addicts weren't "biting." Out of Denmark's estimated 30,000 heroin addicts, only 80 took the government's offer. The problem was the "place." Users had to show up daily at a medical clinic to get their fix, which was then administered and supervised by a doctor. Evidently, this place took all the "fun and freedom" out of it.[34]

To further explore this strategy, imagine places where these target audiences hang out that you might consider a distribution channel for your services or tangible objects associated with your campaign:

- Where could you find groups of seniors so you can give them small, portable pedestrian flags to wave when entering crosswalks?
- What would be a good place to distribute condoms to Hispanic farm workers who are having unprotected sex with prostitutes while away from home?
- In an effort to increase voting among college students, where could you distribute voter registration packets?
- Where could you efficiently provide dog owners a mail-in pet licensing form?

10. Work With Existing Distribution Channels

Example: Influencing the Return of Unwanted Drugs to Pharmacies

In the fall of 1999, in response to a request from British Columbia's minister of the environment, pharmaceutical industry associations voluntarily created an organization to administer a medications return program in British Columbia, Canada. The program provides the public with a convenient way to return (at no charge) unused or expired medications, including prescription drugs, nonprescription and herbal products, and vitamin and mineral supplements. Easy-to-find links for participating pharmacies are on the association's Web site, and information promoting the program is provided on annual recycling calendars, brochures, flyers, bookmarks, and posters. By 2009, 97.5% of pharmacies were participating, with accessibility and convenient access at over 1,080 locations. Many of the pharmacies are open extended hours, and most offer easy access to those with special needs. All containers returned from a pharmacy are tracked by pickup date, weight, and location and stored in a secure location until ready for safe destruction at a licensed destruction facility. The association's annual report indicated that collection across British Columbia increased from 35,704 kilograms at the beginning of 2009 to 51,297 kilograms at year's end, a 44% increase in medications collected. [35]

MANAGING DISTRIBUTION CHANNELS

In situations in which tangible objects and services are included in your campaign or program, a network of intermediaries may be needed to reach target audiences through the distribution channel.

Kotler and Roberto describe four types of distribution levels to be considered, illustrated in Figure 12.10.[36] In a *zero-level channel*, there is direct distribution from the social marketer to the target audience. Tangible objects and services are distributed by mail, over the Internet, door to door, or through outlets managed by the social marketing organization (e.g., a health department providing immunizations at community clinics). In a *one-level channel*, there is one distribution intermediary, most commonly a retailer (e.g., grocery stores where health care officials set up tables for flu shots). In a *two-level channel*, you would be dealing with the local distributor as well as the retailer (e.g., working with distributors of life vests to include safety tips attached to the product). In a *three-level channel*, a national distributor finds local distributors.

Choices regarding distribution channels and levels are made on the basis of variables such as the number of potential target adopters, storage facilities, retail outlet opportunities, and transportation costs, with a focus on choosing the most efficient and cost-effective option for achieving program goals and reaching target audiences. This process can be guided by several principles offered by Coughlan and Stern:[37]

- The purpose of channel marketing is to satisfy end users, which makes it critical that all channel members have their attention on this focus and that channels are selected on the basis of the unique characteristic of each market segment.
- Marketing channels "play a role of strategic importance in the overall presence and success a company enjoys in the marketplace."[38] They contribute to the product's positioning and the organization's image, along with the product's features, pricing, and promotional strategies.

Figure 12.10 Distribution channels of various levels.

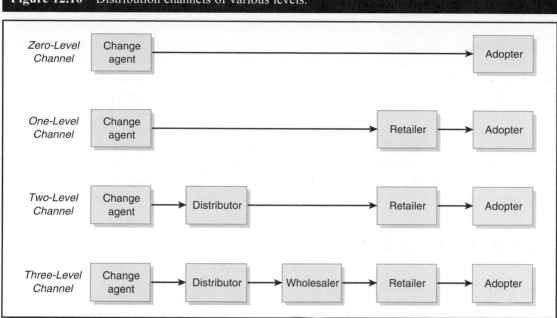

- Marketing channels are more than just a way to deliver the product to the customer. They can also be an effective means to add value to the core product, evidenced, for example, by the fact that employees are often willing to pay a slightly higher price for the convenience of bottled water at a vending machine at a work site than they would in a retail location.
- Issues currently challenging channel managers include increasingly demanding consumers, management of multiple channels, and the globalization of markets.

In the following example from Malcom Gladwell's book *The Tipping Point*, program planners found they had the "perfect" distribution channel and the "perfect" distributors:[39]

In Baltimore, as in many communities with a lot of drug addicts, the city sends out a van stocked with thousands of clean syringes to certain street corners in its inner-city neighborhoods at certain times in the week. The idea is that for every dirty, used needle that addicts hand over, they can get a free clean needle in return. In principle, needle exchange sounds like a good way to fight AIDS, since the reuse of old HIV-infected needles is responsible for so much of the virus's spread. But, at least on first examination, it seems to have some obvious limitations. Addicts, for one, aren't the most organized and reliable of people. So what guarantee is there that they are going to be able to regularly meet up with the needle van? Second, most heroin addicts go through about one needle a day, shooting up at least five or six times—if not more—until the tip of the syringe becomes so blunt that it is useless.

That's a lot of needles. How can a van, coming by once a week, serve the needs of addicts who are shooting up around the clock? What if the van comes by on Tuesday, and by Saturday night an addict has run out?

To analyze how well the needle program was working, researchers at Johns Hopkins University began, in the mid-1990s, to ride along with the vans in order to talk to the people handing in needles. What they found surprised them. They had assumed that addicts brought in their own dirty needles for exchange, that IV drug users got new needles the way that you or I buy milk: going to the store when it is open and picking up enough for the week. But what they found was that a handful of addicts were coming by each week with knapsacks bulging with 300 or 400 dirty needles at a time, which is obviously far more than they were using themselves. These men were then going back to the street and selling the clean needles for $1 each. The van, in other words, was a kind of syringe wholesaler. The real retailers were these handfuls of men—these *superexchangers*—who were prowling around the streets and shooting galleries, picking up dirty needles, and then making a modest living on the clean needles they received in exchange.

At first some of the program's coordinators had second thoughts. Did they really want taxpayer-funded needles financing the habits of addicts? But then they realized that they had stumbled inadvertently into a solution to the limitations of needle exchange programs. "It's a much, much better system," says Tom Valente, who teaches in the Johns Hopkins School of Public Health. "A lot of people shoot on Friday and Saturday night, and they don't necessarily think in a rational way that they need to have clean tools before they go out. The needle exchange program isn't going to be available at that time—and certainly not in the shooting galleries. But these (superexchangers) can be there at times when people are doing drugs and when they need clean syringes. They provide twenty-four seven service, and it doesn't cost us anything."

One of the researchers who rode with the needle vans was an epidemiologist by the name of Tom Junge. He would flag down the superexchangers and interview them. His conclusion is that they represent a very distinct and special group. "They are all very well connected people," Junge says. "They know Baltimore inside and out. They know where to go to get any kind of drug and any kind of needles. They have street savvy. I would say that they are unusually socially connected. They have a lot of contacts. . . . I would have to say the underlying motive is financial or economic. But there is definitely an interest in helping people out." Does that sound familiar? The superexchangers are the Connectors of Baltimore's drug world. What people at Johns Hopkins would like to do is use the superexchangers to start a counter-drug epidemic. What if they took those same savvy, socially connected, altruistic people and gave them condoms to hand out, or educated them in the kinds of health information that drug addicts desperately need to know? Those superexchangers sound as though they have the skills to bridge the chasm between the medical community and the majority of drug users, who are hopelessly isolated from the information and institutions that could save their lives. They sound as if they have the ability to translate the language and ideas of health promotion into a form that other addicts could understand."

ETHICAL CONSIDERATIONS WHEN SELECTING DISTRIBUTION CHANNELS

Issues of equity and unintended consequences are common when planning access strategies. How do working mothers get their children to the free immunization clinic if it is only open on weekday mornings? How do drug addicts get clean needles if they don't have transportation to the exchange site? In these cases, "more" of this place tool may be just the answer, with mobile units, for example, traveling to villages and neighborhoods to reach more of the target population.

Do critics of the ecstasy-testing volunteers at dance clubs have legitimate and higher-priority concerns that this will increase use of the drug? What about those who argue that restricting access (e.g., alcohol to teens in their homes) leads to more serious consequences (e.g., driving home drunk)? And does a safe gun storage campaign that distributes coupons for lockboxes send a message that having guns is a norm and thereby increase ownership? One strategy to consider when addressing the potential for unintended consequences is to conduct a pilot and measure actual behavior changes, both intended and unintended. These data can then be used to conduct a cost-benefit analysis and help guide decision making for future efforts and potentially a quantifiable rationale for a sustainable effort and expanded markets.

CHAPTER SUMMARY

Place, the third "P," is where and when the target audience will perform the desired behavior, acquire any related tangible objects, and receive any associated services.

Distribution channels, as they are often referred to in the commercial sector, include more than physical locations, with other alternatives that may be more convenient for your target audience, including phone, mail, fax, Internet, mobile units, drive-throughs, home delivery, kiosks, and vending machines.

Your objective with the *place marketing tool* is to develop strategies that will make it as convenient and pleasant as possible for your target audience to perform the behavior, acquire any goods, and receive any services. You are encouraged to consider the following winning strategies:

1. Make the location closer.

2. Extend hours.

3. Be there at the point of decision making.

4. Make the location more appealing.

5. Overcome psychological barriers related to "the place."

6. Be more accessible than the competition.

7. Make accessing the competition more difficult.

8. Be where your target audience shops or dines.

9. Be where your target audience hangs out.

10. Work with existing distribution channels.

And, finally, since this tool is often misunderstood, it is worth repeating that place is *not the same as the communication channel*, which is where your communications will appear (e.g., brochures, radio ads, news stories, personal presentations).

RESEARCH HIGHLIGHT

Bicycling in the Netherlands: What Went Right? (2010)

At a minimum, this research highlight represents the application and value of *key informant interviews*. What makes it a rich example is that it also includes *observational*, *experiential*, and *ethnographic* research activities. It is the story of a trip to the Netherlands that a delegation of key decision makers from the San Francisco Bay Area took in search of the "twenty-seven percent" solution. They wanted to understand what the Netherlands had done to influence an impressive 27% of adults to ride a bike to work or to do errands. The trip was sponsored by the Bikes Belong Foundation, a nonprofit organization based in Boulder, Colorado, with a mission "to put more people on bicycles more often."[40] The organization regularly takes public officials on tours of cities where biking is popular.

Their story appeared on September 13, 2010, in an online article written by Jay Walljasper titled "A Week of Biking Joyously: An American Delegation Learns From the Dutch."[41]

Background and Research Purpose

Bikes have so shaped the image of the Netherlands that, for many people throughout the world, the country is almost synonymous with cycling. And evidently it is not, as some might believe, a function of their DNA. Rather, the Dutch made a conscious decision in the early 1970s to make biking safe, convenient, and appealing.[42] Importantly, their efforts have created cycling that appeals to women as well as men, to all age groups, and to all income classes, for a variety of trip purposes.[43]

The September 2010 delegation included elected officials, public sector managers, and other decision makers and influencers from the San Francisco Bay Area. Their research objective seemed simple: "What can we do back home, that they have done here, to increase cycling among adults as well as kids?"

Methodology

The delegation's "investigations" began in Utrecht, where their focus was on the

Table 12.1 Target Audience Barriers and Strategies to Overcome Them

Target Audience	Kids	Adults
Barriers	• Concern with personal safety • Lack of navigation skills	• Concern about personal safety • Concern about/experiences with theft • Lack of parking for bikes
Product	• A municipal program sends teachers into the schools to conduct bike safety classes • Students go to *Trafficgarden*, a miniature city complete with roads, sidewalks, and busy intersections, where they "learn safety by doing"	• Advance green lights for cyclists at most intersections • Well-maintained, fully integrated paths, lanes, and bicycle-dedicated streets • Increased numbers of bike racks and special bike shelters • Bright red asphalt clearly marking bike lanes for motorists to see • "Call a bike" programs where bikes can be rented by cell phone at transit stops • Intersection modifications and priority traffic signals • Traffic-calming mechanisms via speed limits and physical infrastructure deterrents • Regular surveys of cyclists to assess their satisfaction with cycling facilities and programs and to gather specific suggestions for improvement (*product quality research*)
Price	• At age 11, most kids in town are tested on their cycling skills and win a certificate of accomplishment that ends up framed on many bedroom walls	• In Gronigen, a guarded parking facility built in 1982 has a nominal fee, but the city now has 30 of these facilities, and 59% of urban trips made in this city are on bikes • Motorists are assumed by law to be responsible for almost all crashes with cyclists
Place		• Bike-only parking facilities available in the basements of new office developments and at strategic outdoor locations • Conversion of auto parking spaces to 10 bike spaces • Coordination with public transportation on routes and schedules • Bikes available for rent at train stations
Promotion		• Public awareness campaigns focusing on health benefits • Cycling ambassador programs • Annual cycling festivals and car-free days

staggering data indicating that 95% of older students (10 to 12 years) in the town bike to school at least some of the time. (This compares to 15% who either walk or bike to school in the United States, down from 50% in 1970 according to The National Center for Safe Routes to School Program.) Their next stop was The Hague, where bikes account for 27% (the national average) of all trips in the city, which has a population of 500,000. On the third day they visited Rotterdam, where bike traffic share had been increasing by 3% annually for the last several years. And the fourth and final stop was Amsterdam, where their imaginations were further fueled by a bold new vision of urban life embodied in Java Island, where bikes and pedestrians (and boats) take priority over cars.

In each city, delegates attended presentations, interviewed local officials and decision makers, and experienced first-hand the support for cycling.

Findings

Strategies delegates discovered for making cycling safer, more convenient, and more appealing are summarized in Table 12.1 on page 307, grouped by familiar components of the social marketing model, including the *place* "P" highlighted in this chapter. We have also included a few strategies not mentioned in the online article but listed in a separate article by John Pucher and Raphy Buehler at Rutgers University, "At the Frontiers of Cycling: Policy Innovations in the Netherlands, Denmark, and Germany."[44]

Delegates were evidently encouraged when they learned that it took the Dutch more than 25 years to construct their current complex bicycle system. And going home, delegates' comments reflected their research findings were sure to make a difference in the San Francisco Bay area:

The Dutch are not somehow exceptional people when it comes to biking. Everything we see here is the result of a deliberate decision to improve biking here. Even little things, like paint on the street, add up.

They don't just think about bikes. Every presentation we heard tied things together—public transit, parking, cars, streets. The Dutch sense people are going to do what's easiest.

There is actually a road map of doable public policies we can adopt to get us where the Dutch are today.

CHAPTER 12 NOTES

1. United States Environmental Protection Agency. (2010, December). *Municipal solid waste generation, recycling, and disposal in the United States: Facts and figures for 2009* (EPA Report No. 530-F-010-012). Retrieved July 23, 2011, from http://www.epa.gov/osw/nonhaz/municipal/pubs/msw2009-fs.pdf

2. Watson, T. (2002, June 6). Dog waste poses threat to water. *USA Today.* Retrieved February 11, 2007, from http://www.usatoday.com/news/science/2002–06–07-dog-usat.htm

3. United States Department of Health and Human Services, National Institutes of Health, National Cancer Institute. (n.d.). *Smoking.* Retrieved July 23, 2011, from http://www.cancer.gov/cancertopics/tobacco/smoking

4. Nathan, H. M., Conrad, S. L., Held, P. J., McCullough, K. P., Pietroski, R. E., Siminoff, L. A., & Ojo, A. O. (2003). Organ donation in the United States. *American Journal of Transplantation, 3*(4), 29–40. Retrieved February 11, 2007, from http://www.blackwell-synergy.com/links/doi/10.1034/j.16006143.3.s4.4.x/full/?cookieSet=1

5. H. R. Tyrrell, GreenEdge, Cape Town, South Africa, info@greenedge.co.za

6. GREENEDGE

7. Ibid.

8. Ibid.

9. Ibid.

10. Ibid.

11. Delta Dental: Washington Dental Service. (n.d.). *SmileMobile.* Retrieved February 1, 2011, at http://www.deltadentalwa.com/Guest/Public/AboutUs/WDS%20Foundation/SmileMobile.aspx

12. Reprinted with permission from Washington Dental Service Foundation, Making Dental Care for Children More Accessible. SmileMobile was developed by Washington State Dental Services (WDS), the Washington State Dental Association (WSDA) and Washington Dental Service Foundation (WDSF).

13. United States Census Bureau. (n.d.).*Voting and registration in the election of November 2008.* Retrieved February 1, 2011, from http://www.census.gov/prod/2010pubs/p20–562.pdf

14. Oregon voter turnout 85.76% in November. (2008, December 4). *The Oregonian.* Retrieved February 1, 2011, from http://www.oregonlive.com/news/index.ssf/2008/12/oregon_voter_turnout_8567_in_n.html /

15. Wright, J. (2004, November 23). Mail-in ballots give Oregon voters control. *Seattle Post-Intelligencer.* Retrieved from http://seattlepi.nwsource.com/opinion/200682_ore gonvote23.html

16. Ibid.

17. Information retrieved February 14, 2007, from DanceSafe Web site: http://www.dancesafe.org/

18. Ibid.

19. Ibid.

20. Ibid.

21. LA City

22. Healthy Transportation Network. (n.d.). *Safer streets, sidewalks and trails.* Retrieved from http://www.healthytransportation.net/view_resource.php?res_id=7&cat_type=improve; Michelle Mowery, Senior Bicycle Coordinator, City of Los Angeles, Department of Transportation.

23. Rubenstein, E., & Kalina, S. (n.d.). *The adoption option: Choosing and raising the right shelter dog for you.* Retrieved February 17, 2007, from http://www.phsspca.org/store/choosinga dog.htm

24. Sacramento Society's Prevention of Cruelty to Animals. (n.d.). *Pets on the Net.* Retrieved October 31, 2001, from http://www.sspca.org/adopt.html

25. http://www.sspca.org/ContactUs.html

26. Karimi, F. (2010, October 6). Residents can get tested for HIV as they wait for driver's license. *CNN Health.* Retrieved February 1, 2011, from http://www.cnn.com/2010/HEALTH/10/06/washington.hiv.testing/index.html

27. Smith, A. (2010, November 16). *How smart is your school cafeteria? 12 small lunchroom changes that make a big nutritional difference.* Retrieved July 23, 2011, from http://blog.syracuse.com/cny/2010/11/how_smart_is_your_school_cafeteria_12_small_lunchroom_changes_that_make_a_dig_nutritional_difference.html

28. Dawdy, P. (2006, September 27). Broke as a smoke: Powerful state legislators explore ditching the 25-foot rule as barkeeps struggle to weather a butt-free recession. *Seattle Weekly.* Retrieved February 19, 2007, from http://www.seattleweekly.com/2006–09–27/news/broke-as-a -smoke.php

29. Washington's Tobacco Prevention and Control Program. (2006, March). *Secondhand smoke.* Retrieved February 19, 2007, from http://www.doh.wa.gov/tobacco/fact_sheets/second handfacts.htm

30. Bott, J. (1999, April 28). Karmanos site to offer mammograms at mall. *Detroit Free Press.* Retrieved from http://www.freep.com/news/health/qkamra28.htm (Reprinted with permission).

31. Kowal, J. (2004, January 2). Rapid HIV tests offered where those at risk gather: Seattle health officials get aggressive in AIDS battle by heading to gay clubs, taking a drop of blood and providing answers in 20 minutes. *Chicago Tribune.* Retrieved July 23, 2011, from http://www .aegis.com/news/ct/2004/CT040101.html

32. Kotler, P., & Lee, N. (2006). *Marketing in the public sector* (p. 97). Upper Saddle River, NJ: Wharton School.

33. Personal communication, March 2007. Data from the HIV/AIDS Program, Public Health–Seattle & King County.

34. Rytter, N. (2011, January 28). Few takers for free heroin. *The Week,* p. 19.

35. Medications Return Program. (2010, June 30). *Pharmaceutical annual report, January to December 2009.* Retrieved July 23, 2011, from http://www.medicationsreturn.ca/ar2009.pdf

36. Kotler, P., & Roberto, E. L. (1989). *Social marketing: Strategies for changing public behavior* (p. 162). New York, NY: Free Press.

37. Coughlan, A. T., & Stern, L. W. (2001). Market channel design and management. In D. Iacobucci, et al. (Eds.), *Kellogg on marketing* (pp. 247–267). New York, NY: John Wiley.

38. Ibid., p. 250.

39. Gladwell, M. (2000). *From the tipping point: How little things can make a big difference* (pp. 203–206), copyright by Malcolm Gladwell. Boston: Little, Brown. (By permission of Little, Brown and Company, Inc.)

40. The Bikes Belong Foundation is a nonprofit arm of the Bikes Belong Coalition. Information retrieved October 29, 2010, from http://www.bikesbelong.org/what-we-do/

41. Walljasper, J. (2010, September 13). *A week of biking joyously: An American delegation learns from the Dutch.* Retrieved October 19, 2010, from http://www.worldchanging.com/ archives/011581.html

42. Ibid.

43. Pucher, J., & Buehler, R. (2007, December). At the frontiers of cycling: Policy innovations in the Netherlands, Denmark, and Germany. *World Transport Policy and Practice.* Retrieved July 29, 2011, from http://policy.rutgers.edu/faculty/pucher/Frontiers.pdf

44. Ibid.

Chapter 13

PROMOTION

Deciding on Messages, Messengers, and Creative Strategies

Think for a moment about how our everyday lives are dominated by commercial enterprise. We wake in the morning to radio and television programmes interspersed with advertising messages, perform our ablutions courtesy of Procter & Gamble and the Body Shop, breakfast with Kellogg's and Quaker, then dress ourselves with the help of Nike, Topshop and Gap. Before we have even left the house, the commercial sector has not only succeeded in getting us to listen to their messages and use their products—they have turned us into walking adverts. . . . Over a century ago, General William Booth asked, "Why should the devil have all the best tunes?" I am not sure about his demonic metaphor, but the idea of learning from success is clearly a good one.

—Professor Gerard Hastings[1]

Consider for a moment the fact that this chapter on promotion is the 13th of 17 chapters in this book. Twelve chapters precede it. It is placed more than two thirds of the way into the journey to complete a social marketing plan. Those who started this book thinking, as many do, that marketing *is* promotion are probably the most surprised. However, we imagine and hope that, after reading the first 12 chapters, you understand that you wouldn't have been ready before now to explore or use this final tool in the marketing mix.

Many of you who are following the planning process are probably eager for the more creative, often fun-filled exercises associated with brainstorming slogans, sketching out logos, picking out colors, even screening potential actors. Others find this the most intimidating, even dreaded, process of all, having experienced in the past that it can be fraught with internal battles over words, colors, and shapes, and in the end, experienced disappointment and frustration with their final materials or radio and television spots.

This time will be different. You have help. You know your target audience and a lot about them. You have clear behavior objectives in mind and understand what your potential customers really want out of performing the behavior and the barriers that could stop them in their tracks. You know now this understanding is your inspiration, a gift—one that has already helped you craft a powerful positioning statement, build a product platform, find incentives, and select distribution channels.

We predict your promotional efforts will go a lot better this time. And we think you'll be inspired by this opening story.

MARKETING HIGHLIGHT

◆ *PUGET SOUND ENERGY presents*

ROCK ᴛʜᴇ BULB

Puget Sound Energy's Campaign for Increased Energy Efficiency (2010)

Background

Puget Sound Energy (PSE) is Washington State's oldest local energy utility, serving more than 1 million electric customers and nearly 750,000 natural gas customers. In 2009, PSE engaged Colehour+Cohen, a social marketing and public relations firm, to help develop and execute an innovative social marketing campaign focusing on influencing customers to be more energy efficient at home, starting with energy-efficient lighting in the form of compact fluorescent light (CFL) bulbs.[2]

PSE conducted a study between August 2006 and June 2007 to assess the overall current saturation of CFL bulbs in customer homes and to better understand how to increase saturation. Findings indicated that opportunities to install CFL bulbs existed in every area of the home and in each type of lighting fixture and specifically recommended increasing the saturation of specialty bulbs. Another pertinent recommendation was for PSE to continue to expand its CFL rebate and coupon programs in the retail market to increase customer purchasing of the varieties of CFL bulbs available.

Target Audiences and Desired Behaviors

The team developed strategies with two primary targeted audiences in mind: *Green Idealists* (an estimated 14% of PSE customers), who believe that it is socially responsible to limit energy use and are very educated about environmental issues; and *Practical Idealists* (an estimated 23% of PSE customers), who also believe it is important to limit energy use but are more motivated by the practical reasons to do so (e.g., saving money). PSE's campaign goals were ambitious:

1. Distribute 400,000 CFL bulbs through exchange events and community outreach

2. Engage 12,500 customers through attendance at exchange events

3. Recruit 5,000 customers to commit to increased energy efficiency

4. Inspire 500 volunteers to deliver CFL bulbs door to door in their communities

Audience Insights

The August 2006–June 2007 study and other PSE market research identified several customer barriers this campaign would need to address:

1. *Negative stigma* of CFL lighting, primarily among early adopters because of initial poor product quality and high cost when they first came out into the market

2. *Lack of awareness of CFL options* other than the traditional 60-watt replacement bare-spiral CFL bulbs (e.g., specialty bulbs such as reflectors, globes, and a variety of wattages and colors)

3. *Concern about mercury and how to recycle the bulbs* as well as exposure to sometimes confusing messages

4. *Concern about cost* in a down economy

5. *Competition* for time and effort from other "green" initiatives

In summary, strategies would need to "rebrand" CFL bulbs, educating consumers regarding "new and improved options" and economic benefits and providing a product that would be an easy switch, a lead-in to more of PSE's energy-saving programs, and something the whole family could get involved in—a program that would be fun, easy, and vital for families, friends, coworkers, and neighbors to participate in.

Strategies

PSE has a community and educational objective of encouraging more grassroots information exchanges about energy efficiency face to face with customers via PSE energy experts and community members. With consideration of this objective and based on study findings and recommendations, PSE first designed and *piloted* two grassroots public outreach models in the fall of 2008. In the first model, the program team worked with local retailers in four cities to host free lamp and bulb exchanges, during which PSE residential electric customers could trade in incandescent lamps and bulbs for brand new ENERGY STAR® CFL bulbs and portable lamps for free, courtesy of PSE. The exchanges were set up in the parking lots of the retailers and designed so customers would engage with PSE's energy experts as they presented a variety of other energy-efficient programs and rebates and then would be drawn into the store to purchase more items at the end of the line where they picked up their new efficient lighting. A total of 1,600 customers exchanged 2,400 lamps and 5,900 bulbs and received 650 low-flow showerheads, for a total energy savings of 420,000 kilowatt hours. In addition, the events increased sales of PSE-rebated ENERGY STAR lighting products in these stores. One store had weekly sales steadily between 320 and 360 CFL bulbs before the exchange event. The week after the first event, the store had sales of 673 CFL bulbs (an 87%

increase), and the second week after, the store had sales of 605 CFL bulbs (a 68% increase). At event registration, a survey was conducted with participants to summarize how customers heard about the program; 51% heard through print/radio and 29% heard through friends/family.

In the second model, PSE worked with two small cities and a neighborhood association with strong sustainability/energy efficiency initiatives to implement porch light campaigns during which a local community organization or leader recruited volunteers. The volunteers then attended a PSE training and delivered free CFL bulbs and educational materials door to door. The homes visited were directed to switch to more CFL lighting by purchasing PSE-discounted CFL lighting products at local retail stores in their community.

The success of these pilots motivated PSE to combine the models and expand region-wide, targeting 16 cities with the "Rock the Bulb" tour. Several central tactics drove participation and engaged customers:

Tactic #1: The Rock the Bulb Brand

A rock-and-roll theme was chosen for the associations it would undoubtedly produce within a mainstream audience. References and imagery of rock stars and audiences would bring about connections to excellence and community, which would then be applied to the energy efficiency messages.

Tactic #2: PSE's Rock the Bulb Tour

The Rock the Bulb Tour's 16 two-day retail events took place over the summer and fall, from mid-July to the first week of November. With the theme being a mix of green festival, rock concert, and carnival, PSE customers young and old learned about energy efficiency in the home and earned points toward the Be an Energy Rock Star Contest, while engaging in educational activities with community members, event sponsors, and PSE's energy experts. Two tents were set up in the parking lots of Lowe's and Ace Hardware stores for each event, where eligible customers could come to turn in up to 10 incandescent bulbs for ENERGY STAR CFL bulbs (see Figure 13.1). While waiting in line to be verified as a PSE residential electric customer, attendees were greeted by the "singing intern," who sang songs with a lighting or energy theme and told customers about the bulbs available, how the event worked, and details about the contest. If customers were eligible for the contest, the event staff would take down their e-mail address to enter them in the Be an Energy Rock Star contest. Once their profile was created, the number of bulbs they were turning in was recorded in the database and their incandescent bulbs were passed along to Total Reclaim for recycling. While it was required that customers bring incandescent bulbs to exchange for the free CFL bulbs, those who also brought spent CFL bulbs could recycle them at the events. After the customers delivered their bulbs, event staff would then hand them a "backstage pass" to guide them through the remaining event stations.

In addition to exchanging their bulbs, customers participated in a number of activities to boost their energy efficiency knowledge and participate in the contest. They would receive points for visiting stations, which included Battle of the Bulbs, Name that Bulb, Which Bulb Is An Energy (Rock) Star?, and Ask A PSE Energy Expert (see Figure 13.2).

Figure 13.1 Tents at hardware stores to turn in incandescent bulbs.[3]

Figure 13.2 Games at events worth points.[4]

Tactic #3: Project Porchlight

To enhance the grassroots approach to the campaign, PSE contracted with Project Porchlight to build community support for energy efficiency and increase community participation in PSE Rock the Bulb campaign and exchange events. Project Porchlight recruited volunteers, community organizations, and local government officials to get the energy efficiency word out and to drive participation in the events. Project Porchlight staff and volunteers delivered bulbs one to three weeks ahead of each Rock the Bulb event. Each bulb delivered included a brochure promoting the upcoming local event.

Tactic #4: Be an Energy Rock Star Contest

Contest terms were designed to be straightforward and easy to understand, with a variety of prizes to maximize customer interest and attention. PSE secured a total of $45,000 in prizes (courtesy of campaign partner, Feit Electric):

- *One grand prize:* $7,500 gift card to Lowe's or Ace Hardware and a free PSE HomePrint home energy audit
- *Two second prizes:* $2,500 gift card to Lowe's or Ace Hardware and a free PSE HomePrint home energy audit
- *65 third prizes:* $500 gift card to Lowe's or Ace Hardware

Points were earned by participating at a Rock the Bulb Tour event (up to 100 points), volunteering with Project Porchlight (30 points), taking the ENERGY STAR Pledge (5 points), recruiting others into the contest (5 points per recruit up to 100 points total), and saving energy during the month of October compared to usage from the year before (up to 100 points).

Tactic #5: Public Relations

The team executed a launch media event, inviting local media to the first Tour Stop in Bellevue with the city's mayor and PSE officials, to see and film kids from the local YMCA participating in event activities. All four local TV affiliates covered the launch event. News releases and advisories were issued at launch, before every weekend event, and at key milestones. These were followed by outreach to local reporters. The team pitched stories to community papers about each weekend's events. They also sent photos to local papers of notable volunteers (mayors, sports stars, etc.) distributing CFL bulbs door to door. To further midcampaign buzz, PSE hired a magician to perform energy-themed magic tricks at local transit stations and on buses. Spectators and invited media received a free CFL bulb and information on upcoming Rock the Bulb events. The team also conducted extensive media outreach around the ENERGY STAR Exhibit House visit.

Tactic #6: Social Media

Social media were used to help keep the campaign fresh and engaging. Tactics included a blog, Facebook page, and Twitter account. The blog and Facebook page were updated several times a week. To engage customers with the social media portions of the campaign, PSE created a Golden Bulb promotion where 20 yellow CFL bulbs were hidden throughout PSE's service area. Customers who found Golden Bulbs were given a $250 retail partner gift card (provided by Feit Electric). Clues were sent several times a day via Twitter, Facebook, and on the blog.

Tactic #7: Additional Media Strategies

Campaign Web site: PSE's Rock the Bulb Web site was developed to provide an engaging and informative user experience that was easy to navigate and explore and at the same time reflected the event tour energy of this campaign. Visitors were given clear calls to action in each phase of the campaign, and all areas of the site were infused with imagery and attitude fitting the "Rock the Bulb" theme. The home page also included a real-time calculation ticker of campaign effectiveness, as measured in terms of bulbs turned in and the corresponding energy and dollar savings, keeping participants up to date on campaign progress.

E-mail campaign: The C+C team sent out weekly e-mails to contest participants and those who signed up to receive campaign updates. Each e-mail contained a campaign bulb exchange update, encouragement for contest participants to earn more points, and an "Energy-Saving Tip of the Week" to further educate customers about home energy efficiency.

PSE customer-employee communications: The team held a campaign kickoff meeting for employees and promoted the campaign heavily via PSE's internal media vehicles, including bill inserts to residential electric customers, the *Energy at Home* customer e-mail newsletter, the *EnergyWise* customer newsletter, and

prominent placement on PSE.com. Employee communications included the weekly *Friday Focus* employee newsletter and weekly campaign updates on the company's intranet, PSEWeb.

Advertising:

- Web: The team placed banner ads promoting the contest and events, customized for each week's upcoming event, and obtained 30,621,876 total impressions, a click-through rate of 0.18 (national average is .05), and over 70,000 total clicks.
- Radio: The team partnered with three radio stations to drive participation with radio spots promoting the events, contest, social media promotion, and volunteering elements; live remotes at select PSE Rock the Bulb events; and other efforts such as blog postings, listener e-mails, and in-studio interviews; 1,525 spots on 10 stations had 51% reach, 9.6x frequency, and 8,712,000 impressions.
- TV: The team partnered with Comcast to run a "zoned" 60-second spot, customized for each region, to run the week preceding each event, and PSE also partnered with the local Univision affiliate to reach out to Spanish-speaking populations; 2,982 spots had 86.3% reach, 15.9x frequency, and 27,542,000 impressions.
- Print: Print ads were placed in major regional publications as well as smaller community papers in each community hosting an event—including Spanish language paper *La Raza del Noroeste*; 17 newspaper ads had a total circulation of 553,141.

Tactic #8: Partnerships

Partnerships were a key element to successfully implementing the Rock the Bulb campaign. Major partners included Feit Electric, which provided the giveaway CFL bulbs and $50,000 in prize money; Lowe's Home Improvement Warehouse, which provided the majority of retail locations for the Rock the Bulb tour event, served as a warehouse for the weekly shipment of CFL bulbs, and one week prior to the event handed out bag stuffers and placed posters up at each entry and exit; Ace Hardware, which for two out of 16 Rock the Bulb tour events provided partnership assistance similar to that of Lowe's; and ENERGY STAR, which, through its ongoing Change the World campaign, educates the community about the benefits of choosing ENERGY STAR with examples of the many ways to save energy and money and help protect the environment. The ENERGY STAR Campaign Tour Exhibit House visited the Rock the Bulb tour for one of the weekends.

Results

The success of Rock the Bulb is based on the following original scorecard:

Energy and environmental savings (lifetime):		
Total CFL bulbs distributed	511,543	28% above goal
Total kWh savings	118,379,646	
Money saved on energy bills	$22,036,038	
Greenhouse gas emissions avoided (lbs)	130,217,610	
Equivalent cars off the road	10,818	
Drive participation in Rock the Bulb exchange events:		
Customers participated	24,476	91% above goal
CFL bulbs exchanged	224,922	80% above goal
Increase sales of ENERGY STAR CFL lighting at participating Lowe's and Ace Hardware event stores:		
Lowe's store sales week before and after Rock the Bulb events, average combined store increase	218%	
Ace Hardware sales week before and after Rock the Bulb events, average combined store increase	180%	
Number of PSE's retail lighting trainings	330	
Number of employees participating in PSE's retail lighting trainings	767	

Increase participation in PSE's energy efficiency programs and services:		
Heating and cooling contractors that co-boothed at Rock the Bulb events with PSE HomePrint station, # customer leads	568	
PSE's HomePrint, energy audit program, co-boothed at Rock the Bulb events, # customer leads	408	Participated in 1/2 the Rock the Bulb events
PSE's Green Power, renewable energy credit program, co-boothed at Rock the Bulb events, # sign-ups	553	Participated in 3/4 the Rock the Bulb events
Number of ENERGY STAR pledges	More than 4,000	
Distribute 275,000 CFLs via Project Porchlight:		
Volunteers participated	1,179	235% above goal
Community organizations participated	61	122% above goal
CFL bulbs distributed door to door and at community events	286,621	35% above goal
Drive participation in Be an Energy Rock Star Contest and decrease energy use in PSE's electric territory:		
Number of contest participants	7,697	54% above goal
Minimum energy use reduction by each of the top three contestant winners, Oct. 2009 compared to Oct. 2008	82%	
Reduction in energy use by top 1,000 participants	31%	
Number of contestants with year over year reductions of 100 kWh	1,889	
Advertising and public relations:		
Total paid media impressions	67,429,017	
Total earned media value	$344,100	$94,100 added value above budget
Total earned media impressions	3.9 million	
Total earned media value	$180,000	

PROMOTION: THE FOURTH "P"

Promotions are persuasive communications designed and delivered to inspire your target audience to action.

You will be highlighting your product's benefits, features, and any associated tangible goods and services. You will be touting any monetary and nonmonetary incentives. And you will be letting target adopters know where and when they can access any tangible goods and services included in your program's effort and/or where you are encouraging them to perform the desired behavior (e.g., recycle motor oil). In this step, you create the voice of your brand and decide how you will establish a dialogue and build relationships with your customer.[5]

Developing this communication strategy is the last component of Step 7: Develop a strategic marketing mix. Your planning process includes four major decisions:

1. *Messages:* What you want to communicate, inspired by what you want your target audience to do, know, and believe

2. *Messengers:* Who will deliver your messages or be perceived to be sponsoring or supporting your offer

3. *Creative strategy:* What you will actually say and show and how you want to say it

4. *Communication channels:* Where and when your messages will appear (distinct, of course, from distribution channels)

This chapter discusses strategies for developing messages and choosing messengers and presents nine tips for developing creative strategies (how to say it). Chapter 14 covers communication channels.

A WORD ABOUT THE CREATIVE BRIEF

One of the most effective ways to establish clear messages, choose credible messengers, inspire winning creative strategies, and select effective communication channels is to develop a document called a creative brief, usually one to two pages in length.[6] It helps ensure that communications will be meaningful (pointing out benefits that make the product desirable), believable (the product will deliver on the promised benefits), and distinctive (how it is a better choice than competing behaviors).[7] Its greatest contribution is that it helps ensure that all team members, especially those in advertising and public relations firms working on the campaign, are in agreement with communication objectives and strategies prior to more costly development and production of communication materials. Typical elements of a creative brief are illustrated in the following section, with a sample creative brief featured in Table 13.1 on page 322.

Purpose of communications: This is a brief statement that summarizes the purpose and focus of the social marketing effort, taken from Step 1 in your plan.

Target audience: This section presents a brief description of the target audience in terms of key variables determined in Step 3. Most commonly, it will include a demographic and geographic profile of the target audience. It is helpful to include what you know about your audience's current knowledge, beliefs, perceived barriers, and behaviors relative to the desired behavior as well as to competing ones. Ideally, it describes the target's current stage of change and anything else that you think is special about them.

Communication objectives: This section specifies what you want your target audience to *know* (think), *believe* (feel), and/or *do,* based on exposure to your communications. This can be taken directly from decisions made in Step 4. (Individual campaigns may or may not have all three types of objectives.)

Positioning statement: The product positioning established earlier in Step 6 is presented here. This provides guidance to those selecting images and graphics and developing script and copy points.

Benefits to promise: Key benefits the audience hopes they will receive from adopting the behavior were identified as the *core product* when developing the product platform in Step 7. The primary benefit may be expressed in terms of a cost that the audience can avoid by adopting the desired behavior (e.g., stiff penalties for drinking and driving).

Support for the promise: This section refers to a brief list of additional benefits and highlights from product, price, and place strategies established earlier in Step 7. The ones to be highlighted are those that would most help convince the target audience that they can perform the desired behavior, that the benefits are likely, and that they exceed perceived costs. It also includes any available testimonials.

Style and tone: Come to some agreement on any recommended guidelines about the style and tone for creative executions. Also note whether there are any existing graphic standards or related efforts that should be taken into consideration (e.g., the logo and taglines used for any current similar or competing efforts).

Openings: This final important section will be helpful to those selecting and planning communication channels. Siegel and Doner describe openings as "the times, places, and situations when the audience will be most attentive to, and able to act on, the message."[8] Input for this section will come from profiles and audience behaviors explored in Step 5 (barriers and benefits). Additional input may come from secondary and expert resources on the target audience's lifestyle and media habits.

Table 13.1 Creative Brief for a Youth Tobacco Prevention Campaign

Purpose and Focus:
Reduce tobacco use among youth with a focus on addictive components.
Target Audience Description and Insights:
Middle school and high school youth who don't currently smoke or chew tobacco, although they may have experimented with it in the past. They are vulnerable, however, to using tobacco because they have family members and friends who smoke or chew. They know many of the facts about the consequences of using tobacco. They've been exposed to them in health classes and may even have experienced the reality with family members who have smoking-related illnesses or who have died from smoking. The problem is, they don't believe it will happen to them. They don't really believe they will get addicted. There is much peer pressure to fit in by smoking. They also have heard that smoking is a great stress relief and is appealing to pass the time. Some think kids who smoke look older and cool.
Communication Objectives:
To Know: Addiction is real and probable.
To Believe: Smoking-related illnesses are shocking, "gross," and painful.
To Do: Refuse to try cigarettes or chew.
Benefits to Promise:
You will have a longer, healthier, and happier life, free of tobacco addiction.
Supports to Promise:
Real stories from real people who started smoking at a young age
Stories of personal loss about having a family member die or about living with or dying from a smoking-related illness
Graphic visuals depicting real, shocking, and "gross" consequences to the body
Real facts from the American Cancer Society and surgeon general
Style or Tone:
Credible, realistic, and serious
Openings:
Listening to the radio
Watching television
Surfing the Internet
Talking with friends
Positioning:
People who smoke are risking their health and hurting their future families and friends. It's not worth it.

MESSAGE STRATEGY

At this point, you are focused on the content of your communications, not the ultimate slogans, scripts, or headlines. That comes later. What those developing your creative strategies need to know first is what responses you want from your target audience. In our social marketing model, you've already done the hard work here and can simply fill in the blanks to the following by refining and elaborating on campaign objectives established earlier in Step 4 and referencing barriers, benefits, and your competition from Step 5. Bullet points are usually adequate.

What do you want your target audience to do? What specific desired behavior is your campaign focused on (e.g., get an HIV/AIDS test three to six months after having had unprotected sex)? It will include any immediate calls to action (e.g., call this toll-free number for locations in your area for free, rapid HIV/AIDS tests). If your behavior objective was stated in fairly broad terms (e.g., practice natural yard care techniques), this is the time to break these down into more single, simple doable messages (e.g., leave grass clippings on the lawn).

What do you want them to know? Select key facts and information regarding your offer that should be included in campaign messages. If you are offering tangible goods or services related to your campaign (e.g., free quart-sized resealable plastic bags at security checkpoints), you will want messages that inform target audiences *where and when they can be accessed.* There may be key points you want to make on *how to perform* the behavior (e.g., the limit for carry-on liquids is 3 ounces, and they must fit in a quart-sized resealable plastic bag). To highlight benefits of your offer, you may decide that a key point you want your audience to know relates to *statistics on risks* associated with competing behaviors (e.g., makeup and other liquids not in these bags will be taken and discarded) and *benefits you promise* (e.g., having this ahead of time can save you and fellow passengers up to 20 minutes in lines).

What do you want them to believe? This question is different from what you want your target audience to know. This is about what you want your target audience to believe and/ or feel as a result of your key messages. Your best inspiration for these points will be your barriers and benefits research. What did they say when asked why they weren't planning to vote (e.g., "My vote won't make a difference")? Why do they think they are safe to drive home after drinking (e.g., "I've done it before and was perfectly fine")? Why are they hesitant to talk with their teen about suicide (e.g., "I might make him more likely to do it")? These are points you will want your communications to counter. And what was their response when you asked what would motivate them to exercise five days a week (e.g., "believing I would sleep better"), fix a leaky toilet (e.g., saving 200 gallons of water a day), or take the bus to work (e.g., having Wi-Fi available for the duration)? These are points you'll want to put front and center.

Example: Reducing Binge Drinking on College Campuses

To further illustrate these communication objectives, we will use a campaign developed by students at Syracuse University, one that won first prize in the 2009 National Student Advertising Competition sponsored by The Century Council in which over 140 schools competed. The assignment was to develop and present a campaign to curb the dangerous overconsumption of alcohol on college campuses. (A full description of their entry materials can be found at http://www.centurycouncil.org/binge-drinking.)[9]

The student team's formative research included 1,556 in-depth surveys reaching all 50 states, 75 expert interviews, and 15 journals documenting sober and drunk weekends. The first revelation was "difference of opinions," with 92% of college students rejecting the definition of "binge drinking" as having five or more drinks (male) or four or more drinks (female) in about two hours. Students were quick to mention, however, that they were well aware of the negative consequences of drinking too much, and that there was definitely a line between "drinking" and "drinking too much." As one student put it, "There's always that one drink—that one shot that I wish I didn't have. It always makes things go downhill. Always." The problem, as students defined it, was knowing when they "crossed the line." That's when things went wrong.

The team found out what didn't work—statistics and authoritarian messages. And they learned that students got smarter about how they consumed alcohol by the time they were juniors and seniors. The team saw their job as getting students to progress more quickly to that ability to moderate. Their message strategy was developed to do just that.

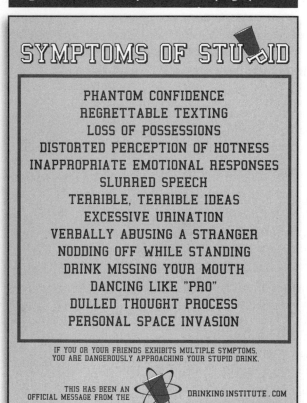

Figure 13.3   The Stupid Drink campaign poster.[10]

What did they want students to do? The Syracuse students wanted their campaign to influence students to refuse that "next drink," the one that would take them "over the line."

What did they need them to know? They wanted them to recognize that the point between drinking and drinking too much is actually . . . a drink.

What did they need them to believe? They wanted them to believe that by refusing that drink that would take them over the line, they would avoid negative consequences, ones their research indicated were "all too familiar" to their target audience and made them feel stupid: "sending drunk texts"; "blacking out"; "getting a DUI"; "ending up in an unwanted hookup"; "throwing up"; "arguing with my girlfriend"; "falling down stairs"; "acting like an idiot."

With this as their inspiration, they developed a creative strategy, one that would identify and stigmatize the one drink that would separate enjoyable drinking from the negative consequences of "drinking too much." They called it The Stupid Drink (see Figure 13.3).

One-Sided Versus Two-Sided Messages

A one-sided message usually just praises the product, while a two-sided one also points out its shortcomings. In this spirit, Heinz ran the message, "Heinz Ketchup is slow good," and Listerine ran the message, "Listerine tastes bad twice a day." [11]

Intuitively, you might think that the one-sided presentations would be more effective (e.g., "Three out of four students drink fewer than four drinks at one sitting"). But research suggests that one-sided messages tend to work better with audiences who are initially favorably predisposed to your product. If your audience is currently "opposed" to your idea or has suspicions or negative associations, a two-sided argument might work better (e.g., "Although 25% of students drink more than four drinks at one sitting, most of us don't"). Furthermore, an organization launching a new brand whose other products are well accepted might think of favorably mentioning the existing products and then going on to praise the new one (e.g., "Click It or Ticket has saved lives, and now Drive Hammered, Get Nailed will too"). Research also indicates that two-sided messages tend to be more effective with better-educated audiences and/or those who are likely to be exposed to counterpropaganda. By mentioning a minor shortcoming in the product, they can take the edge off this communication from the competitor, much as a small discomforting inoculation now prevents a greater sickness later. But you must take care to inject only enough negative vaccine to make the buyer resistant to counterpropaganda, not to your own product. [12]

Example: Booster Seats as a Better Alternative

While great strides have been made to protect infants and toddlers in a motor vehicle crash, preschoolers and young children remain at high risk of injury. Most of the nation's 20 million children ages four to eight ride in motor vehicles either unprotected or use adult seatbelts that do not fit them properly. Seatbelts alone can cause serious internal injuries and even death (see Figure 13.4). Booster seats raise the child so that the lap and shoulder belts fit correctly. A booster seat provides a safe transition from child seats that have their own harness systems to adult lap and shoulder belts.

Figure 13.4 Wanting parents to see booster seats as less costly than the competition. [13]

Messages Relative to Stages of Change

Messages will also be guided by your target audience's current stage of change. As mentioned in Chapter 6 on target audiences, the marketer's role is to move target adopters to the next stage, influencing precontemplators to become contemplators, contemplators to take action, and those in action to make it a habit (maintenance). Most important, there are different recommended message strategies for each stage.[14]

For *precontemplators*, your major emphasis is on making sure your target audience is aware of the costs of competing behaviors and benefits of the new one. These are often stated using statistics and facts, especially those that your target audience was not aware of—ones that serve as a wake-up call. When these facts are big news, they can often move some target audience members very quickly through subsequent stages—all the way to maintenance in some cases (e.g., when it was discovered that aspirin given to children for flu is related to a potentially fatal disease called Reye's syndrome).

For *contemplators* (now that they are "awake"), your message options include encouraging them to at least try the new behavior and/or restructure their environment to make adoption easier (e.g., put a recycle container under the kitchen sink). You'll want to dispel any myths (e.g., air bags are as good as seatbelts) and potentially address any barriers, such as a concern they have about their ability to successfully perform and maintain the behavior.

For those *in action*, you'll want them to start to see the benefits of having "gotten out of bed." Perhaps you will be acknowledging that they reached targeted milestones (e.g., 30 days without a cigarette) or persuading them to use prompts to ensure sustainability (e.g., put the laminated card to track monthly breast self-exams in the shower) or sign pledges or commitments to "keep up the good work." Your messages will target a tendency to return to old habits and at the same time prepare them to create a new one.

For those in *maintenance*, you still have a role to play, for as you learned earlier, behavior change is spiral in nature, and we can easily regress back to any of the stages—even go "back to sleep." This is the group whose behavior you want to recognize, congratulate, feature, and reward. You want to be sure they are realizing the promised benefits, and you may want to occasionally remind them of the long-term gains they are bound to receive or contribute to (e.g., a statement message on a utility bill that selectively thanks residents for helping to reduce peak hour electrical consumption by 6%).

MESSENGER STRATEGY

Who your target audience perceives to be delivering your message and what they think of this particular messenger can make or break the deal. And this is the right time to be choosing the messenger, as this decision will have important implications when you develop the creative strategy as well as select media channels. You have six major messenger options (sole sponsor, partners, spokespersons, endorsements, midstream audiences, mascot), described next, followed by considerations for choosing.

The sponsoring organization can be the *sole sponsor*, with campaign communications highlighting the organization's name (somewhere). A quick audit of social marketing campaigns is likely to indicate a public sector agency sponsor (e.g., EPA promoting energy-efficient appliances) or a nonprofit organization (e.g., the American Cancer Society urging colon cancer screenings). Although it is not as common, the sole sponsor might be a for-profit organization (e.g., Safeco Insurance promoting "10 Tips to Wildfire Defense").

For many efforts, there will be *partners* involved from the beginning in developing, implementing, and perhaps funding the campaign. In this scenario, target audiences may not be certain of the main or actual sponsors. These partners may form a coalition or just a project, one where the target audience may or may not be aware (or clear) what organizations are sponsoring the effort (e.g., a water quality consortium that includes utilities, departments of health, and an environmental advocacy group). In 2006, for example, a public, private, and nonprofit partnership was formed to influence 10,000 of the estimated 50,000 unbanked households in San Francisco to open a bank account. Estimates were that the average unbanked household was spending 5% of its income per year on check cashing alone, relying on check cashers, pawnshops, payday lenders, and other fringe financial services charging high fees and interest rates. City officials were able to persuade 75% of the banks and credit unions in the city to offer what were branded Bank on San Francisco accounts. Even those with a poor banking history were encouraged to open these "second-chance" accounts offering a low- or no-cost product with no minimum balance requirement, accepting consular identification, and waiving one set of overdraft fees per client. Two years after the program launched, more than 31,000 Bank on San Francisco accounts had been opened.[15]

Some organizations and campaigns make effective use of *spokespersons* to deliver the messages, often achieving higher attention and recall as well as increased credibility. In 2006, for example, Barack Obama traveled to Kenya and received a public HIV test. He then spoke about his trip on World AIDS Day:

> So we need to show people that just as there is no shame in going to the doctor for a blood test or a CAT scan or a mammogram, there is no shame in going for an HIV test. Because while there was once a time when a positive result gave little hope, today the earlier you know, the faster you can get help. My wife Michelle and I were able to take the test on our trip to Africa after the Centers for Disease Control informed us that by getting a simple 15-minute test, we may have encouraged as many as half-a-million Kenyans to get tested as well.[16]

Some have used entertainers to draw attention to their effort (e.g., Willie Nelson for the Don't Mess With Texas litter prevention campaign). The best choice would be someone highly recognized and appropriate for the effort. This strategy is not without risk, however, as there are chances they might lose popularity or, even worse, get caught in a scandal or embarrassing situation.[17] You may want to include *endorsements* from outside organizations, which are often then seen as one of the messengers. These can range from simply including an organization's name or logo in your communications to displaying more formal testimonials in support of your campaign's facts and recommendations (e.g., the American Medical Association's verifying that a public health department's statistics on the dangers of secondhand tobacco smoke are scientifically based). In January 2009, Oprah Winfrey gave a big on-air boost for Starbucks' campaign to encourage volunteerism, called

"I'm In," which encourages customers to pledge five hours of volunteer work to an organization of their choosing. Their goal, which seemed ambitious at the time, was to raise pledges for 1 million hours of service. By February 4, 2011, they had received pledges for more than 1.3 million hours.[18]

It may be very advantageous to engage *midstream audiences*, who typically have a closer relationship with your target, to be your messengers. Soul Sense of Beauty, for example, is an outreach program that trains hairstylists, considered confidants by many, to talk to their clients about health issues such as the threat and prevention of breast cancer. Hair salons evidently hold special meaning for African-American women, the target audience for this effort. To many, the salons represent a place where women can go to be pampered and cared for consistently. Although the salon setting is important to the delivery of health messages, including videos and printed material, it is the relationship between the client and her stylist that creates the magic. After all, this confidant is likely to be someone she has had a personal history with for years, and since she "generally stands 6–8 inches from a woman's ear, who better to whisper some potentially lifesaving pearls of wisdom?"[19]

Finally, there is always the option of creating a *mascot* to represent the brand, like Smokey Bear or McGruff the Crime Dog. Others have used current popular characters such as Sesame Street's Elmo, who is featured in a *Ready, Set, Brush Pop-Up Book* intended to feature the fun side of good oral health habits (e.g., a wheel shows how much toothpaste you should use, and there is a pop-up whose teeth can be brushed with an attached toothbrush).[20]

How do you choose? In the end, you want your target audience to see the messenger, or messengers, as a *credible source* for the message. Three major factors have been identified as key to source credibility: expertise, trustworthiness, and likability.[21]

Expertise is the perceived knowledge the messenger has to back the claim. For a campaign encouraging 12-year-olds to receive the new human papillomavirus (HPV) vaccine to help prevent cervical cancer, the American Academy of Pediatrics was an important messenger, in addition to local health care providers. *Trustworthiness* is related to how objective and honest the source is perceived to be. Friends, for example, are more trusted than strangers, and people who are not paid to endorse a product are viewed as more trustworthy than people who are paid.[22] This is why for-profit organizations often need the partnership or at least the endorsement of a public agency or nonprofit organization, with target audiences innately skeptical about the commercial sector's motive (e.g., a pharmaceutical company encouraging childhood immunizations). *Likability* describes the source's attractiveness, with qualities such as candor, humor, and naturalness making a source more likable.

The most credible source, of course, would be the option scoring highest on all three dimensions. Perhaps that's what inspired the strategy in the following example.

Example: The Meth Project in Montana

The United Nations has identified methamphetamine abuse as a growing global pandemic. Law enforcement departments across the United States rank meth as the #1 crime problem in

America. In response to this growing public health crisis, Montana rancher Thomas M. Siebel established the Meth Project to significantly reduce meth use through public service messaging, community action, and public policy initiatives.[23]

Figure 13.5 The primary messengers for this successful effort are youth meth users.[24]

SCABS, HALLUCINATIONS, AND BODY SORES. THEN THINGS REALLY GO DOWNHILL.

The state of Montana, where the Meth Project was first initiated, ranks among the top 10 states nationally in treatment admissions per capita for methamphetamine. The social costs reported on the project's Web site are staggering and the human costs incalculable: 52% of children in foster care are there because of meth, costing the state $12 million a year; 50% of adults in prison are there because of meth-related crime, costing the state $43 million a year; and 20% of adults in treatment are there for meth addiction, costing the state $10 million a year.

The Meth Project, launched in 2005, focuses on informing potential meth consumers about the product's attributes and risks. The integrated program consists of an ongoing, research-based marketing campaign—supported by community outreach and public policy initiatives—that realistically and graphically communicates the risks of methamphetamine use.

At the core of the Meth Project's effort is research-validated, high-impact advertising with the tagline "Not Even Once" and bold images that communicate the risks of meth use. Television, print, radio, and a documentary feature testimonials from youth meth users (see Figure 13.5). Approaching meth use as a consumer product marketing problem, the project aims to unsell meth. It organizes a broad range of community outreach programs to mobilize the people of Montana to assist in meth awareness and prevention activities. Through its Paint the State art contest, thousands of teens and their families were prompted to create highly visible public art with a strong anti-meth message. The Meth Project is now being adopted by other states, including Arizona, Illinois, and Idaho.

CREATIVE STRATEGY

Your creative strategy will translate the content of your desired messages to specific communications. This will include everything from logos, typeface, taglines, headlines, copy, visuals, and colors in printed materials to script, actors, scenes, and sounds in broadcast media. You will be faced with choosing between informational appeals that elaborate on behaviors and their benefits and emotional appeals using fear, guilt, shame, love, or surprise. Your goal is to develop (or approve) communications that will capture

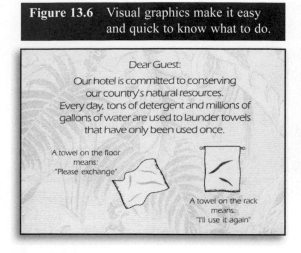

Figure 13.6 Visual graphics make it easy and quick to know what to do.

Dear Guest:

Our hotel is committed to conserving our country's natural resources. Every day, tons of detergent and millions of gallons of water are used to launder towels that have only been used once.

A towel on the floor means: "Please exchange"

A towel on the rack means: "I'll use it again"

the attention of your target audience and persuade them to adopt the desired behavior. We present ten tips in these next sections for you to consider and to help you and others decide.

Creative Tip #1: Keep It Simple and Clear

Given a social marketing campaign's inherent focus on behaviors, try to make your instructions simple and clear.[25] Assume, for a moment, that your target audience is interested, even eager, to adopt the behavior. Perhaps it was something you said or something they were already inclined to do and they are just waiting for clear instructions. Messages like this are probably familiar to you. "Eat five or more fruits and vegetables a day." "Wash your hands long enough to sing the Happy Birthday song twice." "Move right for sirens and lights." "Check your fire alarm batteries when you reset your clocks in the fall and spring." Consider how easy these messages make it for you to know whether you have performed the desired behavior and can therefore count on receiving the promised benefits. Often visual instructions can help make the behavior seem simple and clear. You have, no doubt, seen many versions of messages in hotel rooms asking us to let staff know if we are happy to sleep on our sheets another night and to reuse our towels. Notice how quickly you know what to do in a hotel with a sign such as the one in Figure 13.6.

Creative Tip #2: Focus on Audience Benefits

Since, as Roman and Maas suggest, people don't buy products but instead buy expectations of benefits,[26] creative strategies should highlight benefits your target audience wants (most) and expects in return for costs associated with performing the behavior. This will be especially effective when the perceived benefits already outweigh perceived costs. The target audience just needs to be prompted and reminded of this, as they were in the following example.

Example: "Be Under Your Own Influence"

In an article in the Summer 2006 volume of the *Social Marketing Quarterly*, Kelly, Comello, and Slater described the development of a school and community-based media campaign that was shown to reduce uptake of substances (including marijuana) by 40%.[27] The campaign was tested in a randomized community trial funded by the National Institute on Drug Abuse. Sixteen communities (eight treatment and eight control) from across the United States participated in the study. The campaign, with the tagline "Be Under Your Own Influence," emphasized personal autonomy and future aspirations.

Based on findings from the literature and focus groups, it was decided that messages should not focus on long-term health risks, preach to kids, or put down any particular group. Instead, messages highlighted youth norms and were seen as unique with their emphasis on the inconsistency of drug use with personal aspirations and valued social relationships. Creative executions encouraged youth to aspire to a bright future and to consider the inconsistency of substance use with attaining that future (see Figure 13.7).[28]

Figure 13.7 Posters with a focus on benefits versus costs.[29]

Creative Tip #3: When Using Fear, Follow Up With Solutions and Use Credible Sources

Social marketers frequently debate whether or not to use "fear appeals." Some researchers suggest that part of the reason is the lack of distinction between a fear appeal and what might better be called a "threat appeal."[30] They argue that threats simply illustrate undesirable consequences of certain behaviors (e.g., cancer from smoking) and that the emotion triggered may in fact not be fear, which some worry can immobilize the audience.

Others focus on scenarios and strategies where fear appeals work best. Kotler and Roberto point to research by Sternthal and Craig suggesting that decisions to execute fear-based messages should take several factors into account:[31]

- A strong fear-based appeal works best when it is accompanied by solutions that are both effective and easy to perform. Otherwise, you may be better off with a moderate appeal to fear (see Figure 13.8.).

Figure 13.8 A fear appeal followed by a solution.[32]

Figure 13.9 A fear appeal from a credible source: "The surgeon general warns that smoking is a frequent cause of wasted potential and fatal regret"[33]

- A strong fear-based appeal may be most persuasive to those who have previously been unconcerned about a particular problem. Those who already have some concern may perceive a message of fear as going too far, which will inhibit their change of attitudes or behaviors.

- An appeal to fear may work better when it is directed toward someone who is close to a potential target adopter rather than to the target adopter. This may explain some research indicating that fear appeals are more effective when they are directed toward family members of the target audience.[34]

- The more credible the source, the more persuasive the fear-based appeal. A more credible source reduces the chances that the audience will discount or underestimate the fear-based appeal (see Figure 13.9).

Creative Tip #4: Try for Messages That Are Vivid, Concrete, and Personal

McKenzie-Mohr and Smith believe one of the most effective ways to ensure attention and memorability is to present information that is vivid, personal, and concrete.[35] They point to a variety of ways to make this happen.

Vivid information, they explain, increases the likelihood that a message will stand out against all the other information competing for our attention. Furthermore, because it is vivid, we are more likely to remember it at a later time. For example, one assessor conducting home energy audits was trained to present vivid analogies:

> You know, if you were to add up all the cracks around and under these doors here, you'd have the equivalent of a hole the size of a football in your living room wall. Think for a moment about all the heat that would escape from a hole that size.[36]

Information that is *personalized* uniquely addresses your target audience's preferences, wants, and needs, fully informed by their perceived barriers to and benefits of doing the behavior. For example, McKenzie-Mohr and Smith have a suggestion for utilities on how they might promote energy conservation: Show the percentage of home energy by use item. Rather than using bars for the graph, replace them with a picture of the item itself (furnace, water heater, major appliances, lighting, etc.) and the corresponding energy use in the home.[37]

McKenzie-Mohr and Smith also illustrate information that is *concrete* with an example of a more powerful way to depict waste. Instead of stating that Californians each produce 1,300 pounds of waste annually, Shawn Burn at California Polytechnic State University depicts Californians' annual waste as "enough to fill a two-lane highway, ten feet deep, from Oregon to the Mexican border."[38]

We think the postcard shown in Figure 13.10, used for a youth tobacco prevention campaign in Washington State, demonstrates that a creative strategy can be vivid, personal, and concrete.

Creative Tip #5: Make Messages Easy to Remember

The magic of persuasive communications is to bring your messages to life in the minds of the target audience. And as Kotler and Keller reveal, every

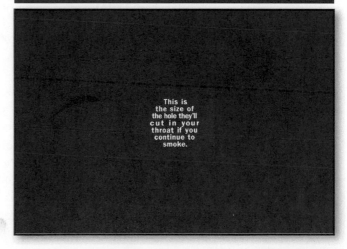

Figure 13.10   A vivid, personal, and concrete creative strategy.[39]

This is the size of the hole they'll cut in your throat if you continue to smoke.

detail matters. Consider, they suggest, how the legendary private sector ad taglines listed in Table 13.2 were able to bring to life the brand themes listed on the left. Consider, as well, how familiar many or most of them (still) are to you.

Table 13.2 Sample Ad Taglines

Brand Theme	Ad Tagline
Our hamburgers are bigger.	Where's the Beef? (Wendy's restaurants)
Our tissue is softer.	Please, Don't Squeeze the Charmin (Charmin bathroom tissue)
No hard sell, just a good car.	Drivers Wanted (Volkswagen automobiles)
We don't rent as many cars, so we have to do more for our customers.	We Try Harder (Avis auto rental)
We provide long-distance phone service.	Reach Out and Touch Someone (AT&T telecommunications)

Source: Kotler, P., & Keller, K. (2005). *Marketing management* (12th ed., p. 545). Upper Saddle River, NJ: Prentice Hall.

In their book *Made to Stick: Why Some Ideas Survive and Others Die*, the Heath brothers suggest six basic traits of sticky ideas—ones that are understood and remembered.[40] Note that they even make the six traits sticky by having them almost, but not quite, spell the word *success*:

1. **S**implicity: The Golden Rule

2. **U**nexpectedness: Southwest: the low-cost airline

3. **C**oncreteness: John Kennedy's "A man on the moon by the end of the decade"

4. **C**redibility: Ronald Reagan's "Before you vote, ask yourself if you are better off today than you were four years ago."[41]

5. **E**motions: "Don't Mess With Texas"

6. **S**tories: David and Goliath

A quick audit of familiar, perhaps even "famous," social marketing messages provides a few additional clues as to what seems to help target audiences remember what to do, especially when your communications aren't close at hand:

- Try rhyming techniques such as "Click It or Ticket" and "If it's yellow, let it mellow; if it's brown, flush it down."

- Those that surprise you may be more likely to stick with you, such as "Save the Crabs. Then Eat 'em."
- Create a simple and memorable mental picture such as "Drop. Cover. Hold" in case of an earthquake.
- Connect the timing to some other familiar event, such as a birthday, as in "Get a colonoscopy when you turn 60."
- Leverage the familiarity of another brand or slogan, as "Just Say No" did with Nike's "Just Do It."

Creative Tip #6: Have a Little Fun Sometimes

Having fun with social marketing messages is often as controversial as using fear-based appeals. We suggest the key here is to know when it is an appropriate and potentially effective solution—and when it isn't. A host of variables will impact your success, including your target audience (e.g., demographics, psychographics, geographics), whether the social issue is one that your target audience can "laugh about," and how a humorous approach contrasts with what has been used in the past to impact this issue.

In general, humorous messages are most effective when they represent a *unique approach* to the social issue. For example, consider how surprised and perhaps delighted you would be to read a sign in a subway in New York like the one in Figure 13.11. There are probably opportunities for humor whenever your target audience would get a kick out of *laughing at themselves or with others*. The Ad Council's Small Steps campaign, launched in 2004 for the U.S. Department of Health and Human Services, is a great example. Campaign elements use humor to inspire overweight adults to incorporate some of the 100 suggested small steps into their hectic lives (see Figure 13.12).[42]

Figure 13.11 A welcome approach in a subway in New York City.[43]

On the other hand, humorous messages are not as effective for *complex messages*. There would be no benefit, and perhaps even a detriment, to a campaign to influence parents to childproof their home, an effort involving multiple, specific instructions. Nor is it appropriate for issues with *strong cultural, moral, or ethical concerns* (e.g., child abuse or domestic violence).

Creative Tip #7: Try for a "Big Idea"

A "big idea" brings the message strategy to life in a distinct and memorable way. [44] In the advertising business, the big idea is thought of by some as the Holy Grail, a creative solution that in just a few words or one image sums up the compelling reason

Figure 13.12 A graphic print ad with copy reading "Starts doing sit-ups during commercials. Gets 30 minutes a day of physical activity. No longer dependent on vertically striped shirts" and "Take a small step to get healthy. Get started at www .smallstep.gov."[45]

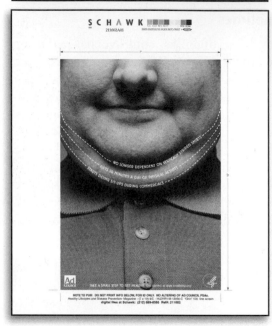

to buy.[46] It takes message strategy statements that tend to be plain, straightforward outlines of benefits and desired positioning and transforms them into a compelling campaign concept.[47] It might be inspired by asking yourself if you had only "one thing" you could say about your product, how would you say it and how would you show it? Others suggest that getting this is not a linear process, but rather a concept that might emerge while in the shower or in a dream. At Porter Novelli, a global public relations firm, the big idea is described as one that has a head, heart, hands, and legs.

> Not only can The Big Idea straddle across a period of time through several campaigns, but at the same time it can stand astride any channel we choose. The Big Idea brings campaigns and channels together, rather than working as disconnected executional elements.[48]

Examples in the commercial sector to model include the well-known "Got milk?" campaign that has been adopted for a variety of celebrities and nondairy products (e.g., "Got junk?"). For a social marketing example, in Chapter 3 you read about the U.S. Department of Health and Human Services' Office on Women's Health's national breastfeeding campaign, with an example of one of the print ads (page 68). The big idea for this campaign will seem more obvious when you see two additional ads intended to increase knowledge about the benefits of breastfeeding exclusively for the first six months (see Figure 13.13).

Creative Tip #8: Consider a Question Instead of a Nag

Are you going to drink eight glasses of water today? Are you going to vote tomorrow? Some believe the very act of asking these questions can be a force for positive change, a technique referred to as the "self-prophecy effect," or the behavioral influence of a person making a self-prediction. Research conducted by Eric Spangenberg, professor of marketing, and Dave Sprott, assistant professor of marketing, both at Washington State University, has led them to believe

Figure 13.13   Part of a big campaign idea.[49]

BREASTFEED FOR SIX MONTHS. HELP REDUCE YOUR CHILD'S RISK FOR EAR INFECTIONS.
Recent studies show you can lower your child's risk of ear infections by breastfeeding exclusively for six months. Call 800-994-WOMAN or visit www.4woman.gov to learn more. Or talk to your healthcare provider.
Babies were born to be breastfed.

U.S. Department of Health and Human Services

BREASTFEED FOR SIX MONTHS. HELP REDUCE YOUR CHILD'S RISK FOR RESPIRATORY ILLNESSES.
Recent studies show you can lower your child's risk for respiratory illnesses and even hospitalizations for illnesses like pneumonia by breastfeeding exclusively for six months. Call 800-994-WOMAN or visit www.4woman.gov to learn more. Or talk to your healthcare provider.
Babies were born to be breastfed.

U.S. Department of Health and Human Services

that having people predict whether they will perform a socially normative behavior increases their probability of performing that target action. They have even demonstrated successful application of self-prophecy through mass-communicated prediction requests.[50] They have also found theoretical support for a dissonance-based explanation for self-prophecy.

Spangenberg and Sprott's studies show that when people predict they will do something, they are more likely to do it. Their analysis of the technique showed an average effectiveness rate of 20% immediately following the asking of the question, and sometimes behavior change would last up to six months after people predicted their behavior.[51] Specific studies have shown that self-prophecy has increased voter turnout in elections, improved attendance at health clubs, increased commitment to recycling aluminum cans, and increased the chances a family will eat dinner together. They believe this result can be explained by the phenomenon of cognitive dissonance, that uncomfortable feeling we humans sometimes get when we say we'll do something and then we don't. (Some of us would probably call it guilt.) This uncomfortable feeling then drives us to act consistently with our predictions. In other words, the prediction becomes a self-fulfilling prophecy.

Spangenberg stresses that for this to be successful, the target audience must see the behavior as a social norm and be predisposed to the behavior, or at least not have strong commitments to the other, undesirable one. For example, asking a group of drug users, "Are you going to stop using today?" is probably not going to work.[52]

Figure 13.14 Social norms marketing corrects misperceptions of the norm.[53]

Creative Tip #9: Make Norms (More) Visible

Social norms marketing, as mentioned in earlier chapters, is based on the central concept of social norms theory—that much of people's behavior is influenced by their perceptions of what is "normal" or "typical." It was listed by the *New York Times Magazine* as one of the most significant ideas of 2001. Jeff Linkenbach, director of the national MOST of Us Institute at Montana State University, points out that what we are doing is turning the problem—that we often severely misperceive the typical behaviors or attitudes of our peers—into an opportunity.

> For example, if people believe that the majority of their peers smoke, then they are more likely to smoke. Using social norms marketing to inform people that the majority of their peers do not smoke can potentially lead them to avoid smoking. There are many areas in which people's behaviors, attitudes or opinions have been shifted by using strategic marketing to realign their perceptions with reality. Informing people that the majority of their peers are acting in a positive or healthy way can create an environment in which people actively strive to emulate what they believe is typical of their peers.[54]

Highlighting the norms in your messages and creative executions can help correct these misperceptions (see Figure 13.14).

Creative Tip #10: Tell Real Stories About Real People

Perhaps one of the reasons that real stories told by real people is such a great creative strategy is that they embody many of the message and messenger best practices mentioned in this chapter. The messenger, because he or she is a real person telling his or her own story, is viewed as *credible* and usually *likable*. And the messages, when they are true stories, have more possibility for providing *concrete* examples and creating *emotion*, two of the "sticky" principles. The following two examples illustrate these well.

Example: Heather Crowe's Story About Secondhand Tobacco Smoke

My name is Heather Crowe. I'm 58 years old, and I'm dying from lung cancer caused by second-hand smoke in the work-place.

I was a waitress for over 40 years.

I worked in the hospitality industry because it let me earn a decent living for myself and my daughter. I worked long hours, sometimes more than 60 hours every week. The air was blue with smoke where I worked, but until recently nobody did or said anything about the smoke in our workplaces. Until last year, I had no idea that second hand smoke was dangerous. People would say, "do you mind if I smoke?" and I said, "I really don't care." I didn't have any idea that the smoke in the restaurants could do me harm. I just wasn't protected. I just wasn't told.

My cancer was diagnosed last year. My health had usually been good, but last spring I noticed some lumps on my neck that didn't go away. Even though I wasn't feeling sick, my daughter encouraged me to visit the doctor. My doctor measured the lumps and sent me for some x-rays and tests. When she told me that results showed a cancerous tumour on my lung that was as big as my hand, I had trouble believing it. "Are you sure it's not tuberculosis?" I asked. "I've never smoked a day in my life."

When she was a university student, my doctor had worked in the same restaurant as me. She remembered how much smoke there was in that restaurant, and told me that she thought my lung cancer might be from second hand smoke. It took many more weeks before they finished the tests and the specialists told me that my cancer was inoperable, and that they identified it as caused by second-hand cigarette smoke. When I learned this, I became exceptionally angry. I thought I had to put my anger and my stress into something positive. I looked for a way to prevent anyone else from getting sick this way. Because I didn't know I was at risk, I figured there were a lot of other people in the hospitality industry that were working in the smoke on a daily basis that also did not know that they might get sick as I had done.

I realized I wanted to increase awareness and I wanted workers in the industry to have some protection if they do happen to get sick. Waiters and waitresses do not have second-class lungs and there is no reason why we should continue to have second-class protection for our health. It's time legislation took over.

The first thing I did was to hire a lawyer to help me make a claim with the Workers Compensation Board. I figured by going forward with Workers Compensation claim it would help give other workers financial support as well as helping change the way workers in the hospitality sector are treated. Then I began to ask for letters to support my claim. I got some letters from my doctor, from the politicians, like the mayor and former mayor, and the medical officer of health for Ottawa, and from some Members of Parliament and councillors. To my surprise, the Board accepted my claim within 8 weeks. I learned that mine was the first claim accepted for illness caused by second hand smoke in restaurants.

On the day after I had a biopsy of my lung, one of my regular clients asked me why I was favouring my left arm. I told him I had lung cancer from second-hand smoke. He worked at Health Canada and asked me if they could use me in an advertisement about second hand smoke. This would help people learn about the need to protect workers, and I said yes. By coincidence, the advertisement started the same day that I learned that my claim for compensation had been accepted. My phone began ringing off the hook, there were so many newspapers and television stations interested in the claim.

Since then I have been across Canada talking to politicians, to schools and to communities about the need to protect workers from smoke. I think I help because I put a face to cancer. There are lots of statistics out there, but I am a person, and I think that helps people understand that this is a real problem. I just want people to become a little more aware of what second hand smoke can do.

I am hoping that the politicians will work at a solution and that we should get smoke-free workplaces right across Canada. I don't expect it all to be done in a very short time, I'm just hoping that they consider this is a very dangerous chemical, and that all workers should be equally protected. Some people say "well, if you don't like the smoke you don't have to work there," to which my reply is "if other people have protection in the workplace then why not us?" All I'm asking for is equal rights. We should not be disposable workers.

I'm not asking the smokers to give up smoking, I'm asking them to step outside when they smoke, to protect all workers.

There are four stages of cancer and that I am at the third stage. That means that there is no way I will be able to get well. I have had five big and five small rounds of chemo-therapy and thirty radiation treatments. The radiation was supposed to kill the actual cancer cells and the chemo-therapy was supposed to shrink the tumour. That may give me two or three years if I go into remission, but eventually the cancer will come back and it will be terminal.

It helps me to do this work. At least I'm out there trying to do something, trying to make a difference. It's too late for me, but it doesn't mean that I have to curl up in a ball and let it go, you know? It's not too late for future generations. My goal is to be the last person to die from second hand smoke. [55]

Heather died at 8:00 P.M. on May 22, 2006.

When Heather started her campaign, very few workers were protected from second-hand smoke at work. Now, all provinces and territories and the federal government have banned smoking in public places and workplaces.

Example: Philipa Davies's Story: Breastfeeding Is Not for Me!

When I was pregnant I was just waiting for my midwife to bring up breast feeding. I knew what she would be like. All, what's that expression—"holier than thou"—full of it being best for baby and free and really easy to do and great for losing weight. Well I had it all planned, I'd just nod at her and keep my gob shut. I mean there is no point in arguing but no one is going to tell me what to do and I'm not having some snotty health professional making me feel guilty and like an uncaring mother. If I didn't care I wouldn't have stopped drinking and smoking when I found out I was pregnant.

No, I didn't feel guilty and I had made up my mind when this baby arrives I wanted some help and I'm sorry but I don't think that is evil. Babies sleep every three hours—I'm not getting my boobs out in public and I don't want to be stuck in the house. We go out on a Friday night—why should I always be the one that has to stay in? Get the baby on the bottle then he can have a turn plus he can do it at night.

And—have you seen how small a new born baby is—it's frightening—surely you want to know that something that small is having enough to eat and how do you know if you breast feed—imagine all that responsibility on you—scary!! So is that enough reasons not to breast feed or shall I add in how much it hurts or how exhausting it is meant to be?

No, my mind was well and truly made up.

My baby is three months now and the most beautiful thing you have ever seen!! Touch wood she is really healthy—so formula is far from evil—if that is what you decide is best for you but after all that I choose to breast feed and I'm so pleased with myself.

I won't lie at first it wasn't easy and it isn't always easy now. I had heard it might hurt well it did—a lot—and it does feel like a massive responsibility but it is not just hippies who enjoy the bond you feel.

So why did I decide to do it?

Well my midwife was great—she did ask me about breast feeding—but she asked me what I thought about it. I tell you, that took the wind out of my sails—I was ready for a lecture but none came. She listened to what I said, told me it was my choice and suggested I might want to go to a class where other women like me were encouraged to talk about their feelings about breast feeding and there were people on hand to answer questions if needed. I went home that night and felt a bit lost—not being lectured had knocked me for six! What did I want to do?

Anyway to cut a long story short—I went to the session and it was quite good. We talked about all sorts of stuff like the pain and the responsibility but also practical stuff like about expressing milk so you are not so tied down—but still no pressure was put on me.

Even up to the day I gave birth I hadn't really decided what to do but then after she was born I thought well what have I got to lose. Now, things were far from perfect—could have done with more help in hospital and when I got home but I guess I am stubborn and didn't want to give in and I haven't. I still have good days and bad days but, not to get all hippy, but the good outweigh the bad. I do take every day at a time. It is my mates birthday next month so who knows I might stop then.

But I might not cos actually I'm enjoying it . . . and there isn't even a hand knit jumper in sight.[56]

PRETESTING

Appropriate Reasons for Testing

The primary purpose for pretesting potential messages and creative executions is to *assess their ability to deliver on the strategies and objectives developed in Step 4 and highlighted in your creative brief.* When faced with several potential executions, the process can also help *choose the most effective options* or eliminate the least effective. It provides an opportunity to *refine materials* prior to production and distribution.

In addition, it helps identify any red flags—something about the potential ad that might interfere with communications or send the wrong message. This often happens when planners and campaign developers are too close to their work or don't have the same profile and characteristics as the target audience. For example, a potential tobacco prevention ad targeting teens with the fact that "all it takes is 100 cigarettes to become addicted" raised a couple of red flags when several youth commented, "Well, then I'll just have 99," and others expressed the idea that 100 cigarettes (to a nonsmoker) "sounds like a lot!"

Potential Pretesting Techniques

Techniques used for pretesting are typically qualitative in nature and most often include *focus groups* or *personal interviews* and *professional review* of materials for technical accuracy and readability (i.e., literacy levels). When a more quantitative, controlled approach is required, methodologies may include *theater* or *natural exposure testing* (e.g., ads are embedded between other spots or in the middle of programming) and/or a *larger number of focus groups*, *intercept interviews*, and *self-administered surveys*. This more extensive testing is often warranted when (a) interested parties are divided on their initial assessments of creative executions, (b) there will be significant economic and political implications to choices, and (c) the campaign needs to have a longer-term shelf life (e.g., years versus months).

Often these techniques vary according to stages in the pretest process. At early stages, when concepts and draft executions are being tested, qualitative instruments are usually most appropriate. After concepts have been refined, quantitative techniques may be important to help you choose from several potential executions.

Typical topics explored with respondents to assess the ability of potential executions to deliver on the strategy are listed as follows. Responses are then compared with intentions developed in the creative brief.

1. What is the main message you get from this ad?

2. What else are they trying to say?

3. What do you think they want you to know?

4. What do you think they want you to believe or think?

5. What action do you think they want you to do?

6. If the respondent doesn't mention the desired behavior, say, "Actually, the main purpose of this ad is to persuade you and people like you to . . ."

7. How likely do you think it is that this ad will influence you to take this action?

8. What about this ad works well for that purpose?

9. What doesn't work well for that purpose?

10. How does the message/ad make you feel about (doing this behavior)?

11. Where is the best place to reach you with this message/ad? Where would you most likely notice it and pay attention to it? Where are you when you make decisions about (this behavior)?

Words of Caution About Pretesting

The idea of pretesting potential messages, concepts, and executions is often dreaded among creative professionals. Many of their concerns are legitimate, grounded in experiences with respondents who typically don't like advertising, don't really want to adopt the desired behavior you're promoting, want to be art directors, want to meet expectations to be an ad critic, can't imagine what the finished ad will really be like, or seize the opportunity to vent about the campaign's sponsor.

Principles and practices that can help to assuage these concerns and produce more effective results from testing efforts include the following:

1. *Inform respondents up front that this testing has nothing to do with whether they like or dislike the ads.* We are trying to find out whether they think the ad will work relative to stated objectives and why or why not. Respondents should be told (at some point) what the intended purpose of the ads are and then be asked to comment relative to that intention. One successful technique is to put the objective on a flip chart or whiteboard and continue to refer to the statement throughout discussions.

2. *Consider testing concept statements* that describe the theme and ad, instead of using storyboards or illustrations, especially when dealing with executions that involve fantasy, humor, or other styles that are difficult to convey with two-dimensional descriptions.

3. *Test potential conceptual spots prior to showing finished ads* when evaluating several potential executions at the same time relative to each other.

4. *Ask respondents to write down their comments before discussing their reactions to ads.* They should be instructed that they can ask for clarification if needed, but to hold their comments until they have had a chance to capture them in writing.

5. *Thoroughly brief clients and colleagues not familiar with the creative testing process* on the limitations of this type of research and the potential pitfalls. Emphasize the importance of listening for what the ads are communicating and what components work and don't work relative to the intended objectives. Warn them not to be surprised or discouraged if participants don't like an ad and not to celebrate just because they do.

ETHICAL CONSIDERATIONS WHEN DECIDING ON MESSAGES, MESSENGERS, AND CREATIVE STRATEGIES

Many of the ethical issues regarding communications seem straightforward. Information should be accurate and not misleading. Language and graphics should be clear and appropriate for audiences exposed to the communications. Gray areas are hard to avoid, however, and what and whose criteria should be used to decide whether something is appropriate? Is this tagline in a teen sexual assault prevention campaign too risky—"If you force her to have sex, you're screwed"—even though it tested well with the target audience? Should someone blow the whistle on a local television station promoting the TV sitcom *Friends* on an outdoor billboard featuring photos of the three slender stars and the headline "Cute Anorexic Chicks"? In most cases, the funders of the effort will likely be the ones to make the final call.

CHAPTER SUMMARY

Promotion is persuasive communication and is the tool we count on to ensure that the target audience knows about the offer, believes they will experience the stated benefits, and is inspired to act. There are four major components of a communications strategy:

- *Messages:* What you want to communicate, inspired by what you want your target audience to do, know, and believe
- *Messengers:* Who will deliver your messages or be perceived to be sponsoring or supporting your offer
- *Creative strategy:* What you will actually say and show and how you want to say it
- *Communication channels:* Where and when your messages will appear (distinct, of course, from distribution channels)

Several tips are suggested to assist you in evaluating and choosing a creative strategy:

1. Keep it simple and clear

2. Focus on audience benefits

3. When using fear, follow up with solutions and use credible sources

4. Try for messages that are vivid, personal, and concrete

5. Make messages easy to remember

6. Have a little fun sometimes

7. Try for a "big idea"

8. Consider a question instead of a nag

9. Make norms (more) visible

10. Tell real stories about real people

Before producing campaign materials, you are encouraged to pretest messages and creative concepts, even if informally. You will be testing their ability to deliver on the objectives for your campaign, especially those outlined in your creative brief. Potential pitfalls in testing are real and can be minimized by carefully constructing questioning and briefing respondents as well as colleagues and clients.

RESEARCH HIGHLIGHT

"No Junk Mail" in Bayside City, Australia: Personal Interviews and Observation Research (2009)

Background

In 2007, two local residents living in Bayside City, a residential suburb to the southeast of Melbourne, formed the Bayside Climate Change Action Group (BCCAG) to advocate firm government action and to persuade other citizens to adopt environment-friendly behaviors. Reducing junk mail was one of their first missions, and five volunteer members designed and implemented an impressive, community-based effort to make it happen. This research highlight begins by describing interviews they conducted to deepen their understanding of the target audience and concludes with an evaluation after 12 months indicating that a third of households (more than 10,000) adopted the desired behavior—placing a

"No Junk Mail" sticker on their mailbox.[57]

Campaign Summary and Outcomes

The campaign focused its research and strategies on household heads whom they described as being well-intended, but not active, environmentalists. Those in the active environmentalists' segment were tapped for advocacy and volunteer efforts. The targeted behavior of putting the sticker on the mailbox was a single, simple, and doable one. It was anticipated that this highly visible act would have the intended normative effect.

The project team conducted 20 face-to-face interviews with residents in targeted neighborhoods to deepen their understanding of their audience. They identified the following attitudes and beliefs:

- Some people liked receiving junk mail, using it to identify discounts and offers or for food/recipe or product research
- There was a concern that the No Junk Mail request would also stop delivery of the two free weekly community newspapers
- Junk mail delivery was a source of income for local teenagers and retirees
- Some local small businesses regarded the junk mail medium as a key channel to drive customers and might ignore or push back efforts
- Not all direct mailers respected the request of a No Junk Mail sticker
- The sticker itself would need to look professional, with an inoffensive design, and be made of durable and waterproof materials

The team heard from this "well-intended" target audience that benefits included a chance to save trees as well as declutter the mailbox.

Description of Program

The *product* was the No Junk Mail sticker itself, a small (3-inch x 1-inch) sticker that could be attached to the mailbox (see Figure 13.15). More than 200 distribution boxes were developed and filled with the 10,000 stickers and placed by the volunteer team in outlets around Bayside City, including coffee shops, bakeries, pharmacies, health clinics, sports clubs, schools, playgroups, youth group halls, local libraries,

Figure 13.15 A sticker signals postal staff that the household declines junk mail.[58]

and council offices (*place*). Messages highlighted potential tree savings, emphasized that the sticker was free, and included instructions to place it on the household mailbox (*promotion*). The cover of the box also listed online sites for catalogs and support, a contact number for refills and questions, and a link to the Bayside Climate Change Action Group. Children were also tapped for distribution of stickers, which were provided at schools for them to take home and given to Boy Scout troops to distribute (*place*).

To accommodate the barrier expressed by several individuals who wanted to read some of the junk mail (e.g., flyers with discount coupons), the BCCAG Web site carried links to mailings that might have been of interest. In addition, several locations, including libraries and coffee shops, agreed to make copies of these publications available for customers to read and use.

Although the stickers were free (*price*), messages on distribution boxes suggested that donations would be appreciated and would be used to help fund the printing of additional stickers. In the end, a total of 350 Australian dollars in donations were collected, fully funding the first as well as the second run of 10,000 stickers each. It was also the intention, and belief, of the group that citizens would feel a sense of pride for their environmentally responsible action.

Further communications were carried out through school speaker programs and promoted in conjunction with similar BCCAG initiatives. At events related to a solar challenge effort, for example, members were provided stickers and were encouraged to disseminate them to friends and neighbors. At local Al Gore *Inconvenient Truth* events, stickers were handed out as a symbol of a clear and immediate action that an individual could take. Additionally, a press release to local media generated visibility for the effort, and the BCCAG's Web site

(http://www.baysideclimatechange.com/) provided additional information on the impact of junk mail and where and how to get a sticker.

Research Methodology and Findings

A *pilot* with 25 houses on two randomly chosen streets in Bayside City provided encouraging results:

- 24 houses were approached and offered a sticker
- 15 accepted stickers
- 7 refused the stickers
- 2 were undecided

The campaign ran initially for 12 months, from October 2007 through September 2008. Campaign effectiveness was evaluated by volunteers auditing eight randomly selected streets within the Bayside City area. Overall, it was estimated that a third of households (10,000) posted one of the 20,000 stickers that had been made available. An audit to estimate impact reported that the average household received over 5,000 pages of junk mail each year (e.g., catalogs, advertising supplements in newspapers). Assuming postal delivery staff observed the No Junk Mail request, as many as 50 million pieces of junk mail were not delivered.

CHAPTER 13 NOTES

1. Hastings, G. (2007). *Social marketing: Why should the devil have all the best tunes?* Burlington, MA: Butterworth-Heinemann.

2. Information for this case was provided by Julie Colehour and Carey Evenson at Colehour+Cohen, a social marketing and public relations firm in Seattle, Washington, and the

Retail and Consumer Channel within PSE's Residential Energy Efficiency Services. Rock the Bulb logo: Permission granted by Colehour & Cohen.

3. Permission granted by Colehour & Cohen.

4. Ibid.

5. Kotler, P., & Keller, K. L. (2005). *Marketing management* (12th ed., p. 536). Upper Saddle River, NJ: Prentice Hall.

6. Reeves, R. (1960). *Reality in advertising.* New York, NY: Knopf.

7. Siegel, M., & Doner, L. (1998). *Marketing public health: Strategies to promote social change* (pp. 332–333). Gaithersburg, MD: Aspen.

8. Ibid., p. 321.

9. Syracuse University, The Newhouse School of Public Communications. (2009, July 29). The stupid drink [Video file]. Retrieved February 5, 2011, from http://www.slideshare.net/prceran/syracuse-universitys-the-stupid-drink-campaign-book?from=ss_embed

10. Courtesy of the Century Council.

11. Crowley, A. E., & Hoyer, W. D. (1994, March). An integrative framework for understanding two-sided persuasion. *Journal of Consumer Research,* 561–574.

12. Kotler, P. (1976). *Marketing management* (3rd ed., pp. 334–335). Upper Saddle River, NJ: Prentice Hall.

13. Reprinted with permission of Harborview Injury Prevention and Research Center.

14. Siegel & Doner, 1998, *Marketing public health* (pp. 314–315).

15. Pioneering S.F. program puts bank accounts in reach of poor. (n.d.). *Irvine Quarterly.* Retrieved July 24, 2011, from http://www.irvine.org/publications/irvine-quarterly/current-issue/947 Irvine Quarterly; City and County of San Francisco, Office of the Treasurer & Tax Collector. (2008, November 20). *Mayor Gavin Newsom and Treasurer José Cisneros announce over 24,000 accounts opened for Bank on San Francisco clients* [Press release]. Retrieved July 24, 2011, from http://www.sftreasurer.org/ftp/uploadedfiles/tax/news/PR%20Bank%20on%20SF.pdf

16. Obama, B. (2006, December 1). *Race against time—World AIDS Day speech.* Retrieved April 11, 2007, from http://obama.senate.gov/speech/061201-race_against_time_world_aids_day_speech/index.html

17. Kotler & Keller, 2005, *Marketing management* (p. 547).

18. Retrieved February 4, 2011, from Starbucks Pledge 5 Web site: http://pledge5.starbucks.com/

19. Browne, R. C. (2006, October). Most Black women have a regular source of hair care—but not medical care. *Journal of the National Medical Association, 98*(10), 1652–1653.

20. Sesame Street Store, Healthy Habits. (n.d.). *Ready, set, brush pop-up book* [Product description]. Retrieved February 4, 2011, from http://store.sesamestreet.org/Product.aspx?cp=21415_21477_21532&pc=6EAM0196

21. Kelman, H. C., & Hovland, C. I. (1953). Reinstatement of the communication in delayed measurement of opinion change. *Journal of Abnormal and Social Psychology, 48,* 327–335; as cited in Kotler & Keller, 2005, *Marketing management* (p. 546).

22. Moore, D. J., Mowen, J. C., & Reardon, R. (1994, Summer). Multiple sources in advertising appeals: When product endorsers are paid by the advertising sponsor. *Journal of the Academy of Marketing Science,* 234–243; as cited in Kotler & Keller, 2005, *Marketing management* (p. 546).

23. Retrieved March 26, 2007, from Montana Meth Project Web site: http://www.montan ameth.org/About_Us/index.php

24. Montana Meth Project. (n.d.) Retrieved 3/26/07 from http://www.montanameth.org/ about_us/index.php

25. McKenzie-Mohr, D., & Smith, W. (1999). *Fostering sustainable behavior: An introduction to community-based social marketing* (2nd ed., p. 101). Gabriola Island, British Columbia, Canada: New Society.

26. Roman, K., & Maas, J. M. (1992). *How to advertise* (2nd ed.). New York, NY: St. Martin's.

27. Kelly, K., Comello, M., & Slater, M. (2006). Development of an aspirational campaign to prevent youth substance use: Be under your own influence. *Social Marketing Quarterly, 7*(2), 14–25.

28. Campaign tagline and materials may not be used without permission from Nori Comello: ncomello@lamar.colostate.edu

29. Reprinted with permission of Maria Leonora Comello.

30. Siegel & Doner, 1998, *Marketing public health* (pp. 335–336).

31. Sternthal, B., & Craig, C. S. (1974). Fear appeals: Revisited and revised. *Journal of Consumer Research, 3,* 23–34; as summarized in Kotler, P., & Roberto, E. L. (1989). *Social marketing: Strategies for changing public behavior* (p. 198). New York, NY: Free Press.

32. Reprinted with permission of Children's Hospital and Regional Medical Center, Seattle, Washington.

33. Image courtesy of www.adbusters.org.

34. Hale, J. L., & Dillard, J. P. (1995). Fear appeals in health promotion campaigns: Too much, too little, or just right? In E. Maibach & R. Parrott (Eds.), *Designing health messages: Approaches from communication theory and public health practice* (pp. 65–80). Thousand Oaks, CA: Sage.

35. McKenzie-Mohr & Smith, 1999, *Fostering sustainable behavior* (p. 101).

36. Ibid., p. 85.

37. Ibid., p. 86.

38. Burn, S. M. (1991). Social psychology and the stimulation of recycling behaviors: The block leader approach. *Journal of Applied Social Psychology, 21,* 611–629.

39. Source: Washington Department of Health.

40. Heath, C., & Heath, D. (2007). *Made to stick: Why some ideas survive and others die.* New York, NY: Random House.

41. Ibid, p. 17.

42. Ad Council. (n.d.). *Obesity prevention.* Retrieved 2006 from http://www.adcouncil.org/ default.aspx?id=54

43. Author photo.

44. Kotler, P., & Armstrong, G. (2001). *Principles of marketing* (9th ed., p. 548). Upper Saddle River, NJ: Prentice Hall.

45. Carducci, V. (n.d.). *The big idea.* Retrieved March 28, 2007, from http://www.popmatters .com/books/reviews/h/how-brands-become-icons.shtml

46. Kotler & Armstrong, 2001, *Principles of marketing* (p. 548).

47. Porter Novelli. (2006). *"The Big Idea": Death by execution.* Retrieved March 28, 2007, from http://www.porternovelli.com/site/pressrelease.aspx?pressrelease_id=140&pgName=news

48. Ad Council.

49. Ibid.

50. Spangenberg, E. R., Sprott, D. E., Grohmann, B., & Smith, R. J. (2003, July). Mass-communicated prediction requests: Practical application and a cognitive dissonance explanation for self-prophecy. *Journal of Marketing, 67,* 47–62. Retrieved from http://www.atyponlink.com/AMA/doi/abs/10.1509/jmkg.67.3.47.18659

51. Guido, M. (2004, Spring). A more effective nag. *Washington State Magazine.* Retrieved July 28, 2011, from http://researchnews.wsu.edu/society/33.html

52. Ibid.

53. MOST of Us. (n.d.) "What Is Social Norms Marketing?" Retrieved 3/29/07 from http://www.mostofus.org/

54. Ibid.

55. Story provided by Physicians for a Smoke-Free Canada,1226A Wellington Street Ottawa, Ontario, Canada, 613–233–4878, http://www.smoke-free.ca/heathercrowe/

56. Story provided by Ray Lowry, http://www.drlowrysocialmarketing.co.uk/

57. Information for this case was provided by Lucy Allinson, Bayside Climate Change Action Group. A more extensive description of this case, along with other successful environmental efforts, can be found in McKenzie-Mohr, D., Lee, N. R., Schultz, P. W., & Kotler, P. (2011). *Social marketing to protect the environment: What works.* Thousand Oaks, CA: Sage.

58. Photo provided by Bayside Climate Change Action Group.

Chapter 14

PROMOTION

SELECTING COMMUNICATION CHANNELS

Social media platforms offer tremendous opportunities to engage our audiences deeply and widely. However, we can't approach social media with the "same old, same old" mindset and treat these channels like cyber brochures that we push to people. Social media is about meeting our audiences where they are both in cyberspace and in their daily lives, engaging them as part of the solution and listening. That being said, social media stills needs to be grounded in good strategic planning, as part of the marketing mix.

—Mike Newton Ward
Social Marketing Consultant,
North Carolina Division of Public Health

In the third edition of this text (2008), there were only two pages describing the social media communication channel. In this edition, there are more than nine, a reflection of the explosion of this channel in just the past three years. Smart marketers have moved from a reliance on traditional channels (e.g., television, radio, outdoor, print advertising, brochures), to an integrated media mix, one that now includes social media options (e.g., mobile phones, interactive Web sites, Facebook pages, YouTube, blogs, Twitter, podcasts, online forums, wikis). Perhaps this shift has occurred in part because many marketers identify with a famous quote from John Wanamaker: "I know that half the money I spend on advertising is wasted; but I can never find out which half." In addition to providing lower costs per impression, social media options provide a more efficient method of collecting real-time data on whether target audiences noticed and responded to the marketers' efforts (e.g., number of times a YouTube video was viewed and shared).

This chapter will guide you through the final step of developing your promotional strategy: deciding on the most efficient and effective mix of media channels to reach and inspire your target audiences to action. It will familiarize you with the options you have and eight factors that can guide your decisions. We begin with a case to illustrate the power of mobile technology to influence healthy behaviors and conclude by describing special events in Africa that are enhancing financial well-being.

MARKETING HIGHLIGHT

Using Text Messaging to Improve Health: A Successful Pilot for Reducing Obesity (2008–2009)

Texting 4 Health Overview

B. J. Fogg, director of the Persuasive Technology Lab at Stanford University, predicts that by 2020, the mobile phone will be the primary platform for influencing people's behaviors—more powerful than TV, radio, or the Web.[1] And this is not only because more than half of the planet's population has a mobile phone (3 billion and growing). It is also because the phone acts as "a heart, a wristwatch, and a magic wand":

- A *heart,* because, "like the love of your life, the mobile phone completes you"
- A *wristwatch*, because "it travels with you almost everywhere"
- A *magic wand* because of its powers that require "no special training"

Fogg's coeditor of *Texting 4 Health*,[2] Richard Adler, believes further that mobile phones have several characteristics that make them an attractive platform for delivering health-related services:

- They are personal, making it possible to target applications to specific individuals

- They are portable, accompanying their users almost everywhere
- They are connected, providing direct access to a wide range of external resources
- They are intelligent, increasingly resembling small personal computers

Fogg and Adler are particularly enamored with the power of text messages on mobile phones. As of 2009, approximately 95% of all mobile phones in the U.S. were capable of sending and receiving text (SMS, or short message service).[3] Although most people are using texting to stay in touch with friends, Fogg and Adler hope that health professionals can see how texting can help influence health-related behaviors. Fogg and graduate student Enrique Allen describe 10 potential specific uses:

Sending Information:

1. Educating people (e.g., symptoms of the H1N1 flu virus)

2. Notifying people (e.g., a warning about air quality)

3. Reminding people (e.g., time to schedule an annual mammogram)

Gathering Information:

4. Collecting data from people for monitoring public health (e.g., "Have you had your flu shot this season? Reply 'yes' or 'no'") and/or for tracking and monitoring personal health status (e.g., reporting blood glucose levels at varying times of day)

5. Journaling by individuals (e.g., recording calories consumed, or steps walked each day)

Getting Answers to Questions:

6. Getting answers from a database (e.g., regarding mercury levels for fish on a menu)

7. Getting answers from a person (e.g., finding out whether a child's fever is related to a recent immunization)

Connecting People to People:

8. Connecting individuals (e.g., a tobacco user with a quit counselor)

9. Connecting groups (e.g., where the new moms' breastfeeding support group is meeting this week)

Performing Transactions:

10. Getting things done (e.g., register for a senior strength and balance exercise class)

The authors are forthcoming about barriers and challenges they see for health professionals as they pursue this technology for citizens, clients, and patients. Screens on mobile phones are small and keyboards are limited. The typical 160 characters available may not form questions that a computer system can understand, and the 160-character response may not provide enough information—even the right information. Posing or responding to open-ended questions can be frustrating with the character limitations. Although journaling may be appealing, users will probably need to access their entries at their computer online, as entry retrieval and reading is cumbersome on most phones today. The authors urge us to "start today to harness the powers of mobile persuasion to change human behavior." And Fogg sees hope for all in doing this.

> In a research lab, like mine at Stanford, we can continue to use text messaging to learn what motivates and persuades people. As we share insights from the field and from the lab, we all get smarter about how to use texting to promote health.[4]

Their first "Texting 4 Health" conference at Stanford University in 2008 brought together 240 experts in health and in text messaging. The following case on "mDIET: A Personalized Approach to Weight Management Using Text Messaging" is one of 15 featured at the first conference and in Fogg and Adler's book.[5]

Background

Strategies to reduce obesity by improving diet and increasing physical activity are often episodic in nature, not intervening in the critical moment-to-moment choices that individuals make as they move through space and time. (Or as we noted in Chapter 8, Michael Rothschild might say we are reaching our target audience in their "cool state" but missing them in their "hot state.") This suggests that we (also) need interventions that provide the right prompt, information, and feedback at the right time. The authors of this case felt that texting fit the bill and undertook the following study in San Diego, California, to find out.

Target Audience

The mDiet system consists of four components: (1) a Web-based application used to enroll participants and set user preferences, (2) a database that stores participants' records, rules, and messages sent and received, (3) an application that determines the appropriate timing and message to send, and to process replies received, and (4) an SMS message-delivery/reception platform.

Their first step in designing specific features of mDIET was to conduct two focus groups with current SMS users ages 25 to 55 who were overweight or obese, one with men and one with women. Of interest was learning more about dietary behaviors, current mobile phone and text messaging habits, the types of text and picture messages that would be helpful for weight loss, and topics that should be included in a weight loss program. Subsequent to the groups, participants tested mDIET by receiving and responding to sample text and picture messages.

Desired Behaviors and Audience Insights

Several themes and design considerations emerged from the focus groups, indicating that their texting service concept to support healthy eating and physical activity was on the right track:

- Participants viewed SMS as fast, immediate, and an easy way to get health information
- They preferred a focus on lifestyle modifications, long-term weight loss, and management versus quick weight loss
- They believed they would benefit from recognition and encouragement as they developed new healthy habits
- They liked support from family members, friends, and coworkers
- They wanted to be able to choose the number of messages they would receive
- They felt they would be more likely to respond to prompted messages and questions versus having to send unprompted ones

Strategies

These preferences inspired the subsequent development of mDIET. Product features were designed to be *personally tailored*, allowing users to choose the number and timing of the receipt of messages each day. To provide *interactivity*, participants were engaged in a "dialogue," with approximately half of the messages requesting a reply. To *minimize the "nag" factor*, if a user chose not to respond to a message, mDIET would reduce the number of messages requesting replies until the user responded. In addition, the user was free to change the time and frequency of the messages after gaining experience with its use. *Topics* included behavioral and dietary strategies known to positively influence weight control, including goal setting, monitoring calories, portion control, and physical activity. To *keep messages fresh and non-repetitive*, type and content of messages were varied throughout the week, with some multimedia messages including illustrations, reference photos, or progress graphs (see Figure 14.1).

Results

A 16-week pilot study was the first evaluation of mDIET. Study participants were males and females, had a body mass index (BMI) of 25 to 39.9, and were between the ages of 25 and 55 years. They were recruited from the community through e-mail and Web sites, flyers, personal referrals, and newspaper advertisements. A total of 65 participants enrolled in the study and were randomly assigned to one of two groups, intervention and control. The intervention group received the mDIET program for 16 weeks. They also received a binder of printed materials on nutrition,

Figure 14.1 Multimedia Messaging Service (MMS) used for images and graphs.[6]

MMS used for Images and Graphs

Add a variety of colorful vegetable to your shopping list this week. Choose green, red, orange and yellow veggies.

A one-cup serving size is about the size of a tennis or baseball.

Nice progress. You're on your way to reaching your goal. It will take time, but you have the motivation to succeed.

physical activity tips and behavioral skills matched to the weekly educational themes, and a brief (5- to 15-minute) monthly phone call from a case manager who assessed their weight loss progress, addressed problems and barriers, and provided encouragement. Control participants received the printed materials but did not participate in the mDIET program or receive personal counseling.

Study measurements were conducted at baseline, at two months, and at the conclusion of the 16-week pilot. Sixty-five participants completed the baseline assessment, 56 completed the two-month evaluation, and 54 completed the final assessment at the end of the pilot. On average, the intervention group lost 4.4 more pounds than the control group. In addition, there were changes in several behaviors important for weight control. While the intervention group included a modest amount of monthly health coaching and a binder of written materials, the impression of research staff was that these were only moderately important in terms of influencing outcomes. The automated daily push and pull of text messages seemed to have had the greater influence.

Satisfaction among mDIET participants was very high, with almost all (96%) indicating they would recommend it to their family, friends, or coworkers. They commented that the SMS messages served as daily reminders ("a steady reminder—keeping health on my mind" and "felt commitment every day—could not let myself forget my goals") and motivators ("kept me on track and motivated!"). They reported it held them accountable ("I enjoyed having to be accountable for my actions and reporting my weight once a week") and provided much-needed support ("I enjoyed receiving the daily messages; they made me feel like someone was working along with me"). A few participants even contacted project staff after the project was over to share that they missed their daily messages.

The authors concluded by acknowledging study limitations (e.g., the pilot's having relatively few participants), but they were encouraged enough to move forward with formative work among Hispanics, a growing population in the U.S. who experience a disproportionate share of a variety of obesity-related problems. Their use of mobile phones suggests a promising and fruitful platform for the mDIET program.

PROMOTION: SELECTING COMMUNICATION CHANNELS

When selecting communication channels, you will be faced with making decisions regarding (a) types of communication channels, (b) specific media vehicles within these broader types, and (c) timing for communications. A brief explanation of each follows (see Box 14.1).

Box 14.1
Major Social Marketing Communication Channels

A. ADVERTISING (PAID MEDIA AND UNPAID PUBLIC SERVICE ANNOUNCEMENTS)

Broadcast:
 Television
 Radio
 Internet: Banner ads
Print:
 Newspaper
 Magazine
Direct Mail:
Separate mailings
 Paycheck and other stuffers
 Internet/Web sites
 Backs of tickets and receipts
 Ads on Internet/Web
 Ads in Theaters

Outdoor/Out of Home:
 Billboards
 Busboards
 Bus shelter displays
 Subways
 Taxis
 Vinyl wrap on cars and buses
 Sports events
 Banners
 Postcard racks
 Kiosks
 Restroom stalls
 Truckside advertising
 Airport billboards and signage

B. PUBLIC RELATIONS AND SPECIAL EVENTS

Stories on television and radio
Articles in newspapers and magazines
Op-eds
Public affairs/community relations
Lobbying
Videos
Media advocacy

Special Events:
 Meetings
 Speakers' bureaus
 Conferences
 Exhibits
 Health screenings
 Demonstrations

C. PRINTED MATERIALS

Brochures
Newsletters
Flyers
Posters
Catalogs

Calendars
Envelope messages
Booklets
Bumper stickers
Static stickers

D. SPECIAL PROMOTIONAL ITEMS

Clothing:
 T-shirts
 Baseball hats
 Diapers
 Bibs
Temporary Items:
 Coffee sleeves
 Bar coasters
 Lapel buttons
 Temporary tattoos
 Balloons
 Stickers
 Sports cards

Functional Items:
 Key chains
 Flashlights
 Refrigerator magnets
 Water bottles
 Litterbags
 Pens and pencils
 Bookmarks
 Book covers
 Notepads
 Tote bags
 Mascots
 Door hangers
 e-Games
 e-Cards
 Podcasts

(Continued)

(Continued)

E. SIGNAGE AND DISPLAYS

Road signs
Signs and posters on government property
Retail displays and signage

F. PERSONAL SELLING

Face-to-face meetings, presentations, speakers' bureaus
Telephone
Workshops, seminars, and training sessions

G. SOCIAL MEDIA CHANNELS AND TYPES

Social networking sites such as Facebook	Buttons and Badges
Mobile technologies such as phones for text messaging	Image sharing
E-mail blasts and alerts	Virtual worlds
YouTube videos	Widgets
Blogs and microblogs such as Twitter	
RSS feeds (really simple syndications) on Web sites	

H. WEB SITES

Banner ads
Links

I. POPULAR AND ENTERTAINMENT MEDIA

Songs	Public art
Movie scripts, television, radio programs	Flash mobs
Comic books and comic strips	Product integration
Video games	

Communication Types

Communication channels, also referred to as media channels, can be categorized by whether they are *mass*, *selective*, or *personal*. Each approach may be appropriate, depending on communication objectives. Many campaigns and programs may warrant all three, as they are mutually reinforcing.

Mass media channels are called for when large groups of people need to be quickly informed and persuaded regarding an issue or desired behavior. There is a need, and perhaps a sense of urgency, for audiences to "know, believe, and/or do something." Typical mass media types for social marketers include *advertising*, *publicity*, *popular and entertainment media*, and *governmental signage*.

Selective media channels are used in cases where target audiences can be reached more cost effectively through targeted media channels and/or when they need to know more than is available in mass media formats. Typical selective media types include *direct mail*, *flyers*, *brochures*, *posters*, *special events*, *telemarketing*, and the *Internet*.

Personal media channels are sometimes important to achieve behavior change objectives and include *social network sites such as Facebook, blogs, and microblogs such as Twitter, face-to-face meetings and presentations, telephone conversations, workshops, seminars, and training sessions.* This approach is most warranted when some form of personal intervention and interaction is required in order to deliver detailed information, address barriers and concerns, build trust, and gain commitment. It is also an effective and efficient way to create social norms and make them more visible.

Communication Vehicles

Within each of the major communication channels (media types) there are specific vehicles to select. Which TV stations, radio programs, magazines, Web sites, mobile technologies, and bus routes should you choose? At what events should you sign up for a booth? When are road signs warranted? Where should you put your fact sheets?

Communication Timing

Timing elements include decisions regarding months, weeks, days, and hours when campaign elements will be launched, distributed, implemented, and/or aired in the media. Your decisions will be guided by when your audience is most likely to be reached or when you have your greatest windows of opportunity for being heard (e.g., a drinking and driving campaign aimed at teens might be most effective immediately prior to and during prom and graduation nights).

TRADITIONAL MEDIA CHANNELS

Advertising and Public Service Announcements

Defined formally, advertising is "any paid form of nonpersonal presentation of ideas, goods, or services by an identified sponsor."[7] More commonly, you probably think of one or more of the popular, traditional mass media communication channels such as *television, radio, newspapers, magazines, direct mail, the Internet,* and a variety of *outdoor* (out-of-home) channels such as billboards, transit signage, and kiosks. In the commercial sector, these advertisements are most often placed (bought) by the organization's advertising or media buying agency.

As a social marketer working for a public sector or nonprofit organization, you will also have opportunities for *unpaid advertising*, something you know of as public service announcements (PSAs). An obvious advantage of PSAs, of course, is the cost (often free, or at least deeply discounted); the disadvantage is that you do not have the same level of control over where the ad will actually appear in the newspaper or magazine or during what program or time of day it will air on television or radio. This perhaps is why some refer to a PSA as "people sound asleep."

There are several tactics you can use to increase your odds of obtaining public service placement of your advertisements and the likelihood they will appear when and where you would like. First, build a relationship with the public affairs or community relations personnel at your local television and radio networks. Know that what they will be most interested in (it's their job) are issues that their listeners and viewing audience care about and ones that their organization has chosen as a community priority. Ensure high quality of your productions, whether for television or radio, as they will consider them a reflection of their organization as well. Be prepared to negotiate. If they can't offer you free placement at times you are targeting, they may have interested corporate sponsors; and if they can't do it free of charge, they may be able to offer a discounted price (e.g., two for the price of one).

Example: Denver Water's Conservation Advertising Campaign

From 2002 to 2006, Denver Water's 1.2 million customers reduced their water usage by about 20% each year. The Denver mayor, however, wanted to continue this trend and announced a partnership in July 2006 to reduce use by 22% a year over the next decade, including a $500,000 advertising campaign intended to help make this happen. The campaign, with the tagline "Use Only What You Need," appeared in community newspapers, magazines, billboards, transit, and other out-of-home media (see Figure 14.2). The ads also appeared in places you might not expect, such as on 20,000 drink coasters that went to local restaurants and bars, offering water conservation tips such as "Be a real man and dry shave, tough guy."[8]

Public Relations and Special Events

Public relations is distinguishable by its most favorable outcome—free visibility for your campaign.[9] Successful activities generate free, positive *mentions of your programs in the media*, most commonly as news and special programming on radio and television and as

Figure 14.2   A creative campaign and use of outdoor advertising for Denver Water.

stories, articles, and editorial comments in newspapers and magazines. Many refer to these accomplishments as *earned media*, contrasting it to paid media. Additional typical efforts in this channel include planning for *crisis communications* (e.g., responding to adverse or conflicting news), *lobbying* (e.g., for funding allocations), *media advocacy* (e.g., working with the media to take on and advance your social issue), and managing *public affairs* (e.g., issue management). Although some organizations hire public relations firms to handle major campaigns, it is more common that internal staff handle day-to-day media relations.

Some believe this is one of the more underutilized channels, and yet a well thought out program coordinated with other communications-mix elements can be extremely effective. It provides more-in-depth coverage of your issue than is often possible with a brief commercial and is often seen as more objective than paid advertising. Tools used to generate news coverage include press releases, press kits, news conferences, editorial boards, letters to the editor, and strong personal relationships with key reporters and editors. Siegel and Doner recommend several keys to success:

> *Build relationships with the media* by first "finding out who covers what and then working to position yourself and your initiative as an important, reliable source of information so that the reporters will call you when they are running a story on your topic." [10]

> *Frame the issues* with the goals of the media in mind, "to appeal to the broadest number of audience members possible, and . . . tell a compelling story that is relevant to their audience and in the public's interest." [11]

> *Create news* by convening a press conference, special event, or demonstration. Consider a technique mastered by the Center for Science in the Public Interest (CSPI) in which their studies create "news that applies pressure to decision makers. For example, after [CSPI's] analysis of the nutrient content of movie popcorn was reported in the media, many major movie chains began using oils lower in saturated fat or offering air-popped options." [12]

Special events can also generate visibility for your effort, offering the advantage of interaction with your target audience and allowing them to ask questions and express attitudes about your desired behaviors that you probably need to hear. The event may be a part of a larger public gathering such as a county fair, or it may be something you have organized just for your campaign. It might include a demonstration (e.g., car seat safety checks), or it might be a presentation at a location where your target audience shops, dines, or commutes, such as the one in the following example.

Example: An Unusual Tour for Colon Cancer Prevention

Times Square in New York City is a cultural hub featuring upscale hotels, Broadway theaters, music, nightlife, quality shops, and gargantuan promotional icons. In 2009 it

Figure 14.3 Inside the Prevent Cancer Super Colon™[13]

added one more feature: a giant colon. Since 2003, the Prevent Cancer Foundation had been sponsoring the Prevent Cancer Super Colon™ exhibit, featuring a tour of an inflatable tube, 20 feet long and 8 feet tall—one that most could easily walk through. On February 27, it arrived in New York City to honor March as Colon Cancer Awareness Month, with the purpose of increasing timely colon cancer screening. As visitors take the tour, they get an up-close look at healthy colon tissue, tissue with nonmalignant colorectal disease, colorectal polyps, and various stages of colorectal cancer (see Figure 14.3). The Prevent Cancer Super Colon™ attracted over 1,500 visitors that week in Times Square, and then throughout 2009 traveled across the nation reaching out to people in small towns as well as big cities, stopping at health fairs, hospitals, and cancer centers.[14] As the Prevent Cancer Foundation is in its 25th year, the Prevent Cancer Super Colon™ is estimated to have reached over 2 million people.

Printed Materials

This is probably the most familiar and utilized communication channel for social marketing campaigns. *Brochures, newsletters, booklets, flyers, calendars, bumper stickers, door hangers, and catalogs* provide opportunities to present more detailed information regarding the desired behavior and the social marketing program. Sometimes, but not as often as you might like, target audiences hold on to these materials, and ideally even share them with others. In some cases, special materials are developed and distributed to other key internal and external groups, such as program partners and the media. Included in this channel category are any collateral pieces associated with the program, such as *letterheads, envelopes, and business cards.*

Example: A Calendar to Increase Workplace Safety

"Keep Washington safe and working," the mission statement of the Washington State Department of Labor & Industries (L&I), also serves as the title of the annual calendar produced by L&I's Division of Occupational Safety and Health. First published in 2007, the calendar explains job hazards and provides safety tips. In 2009, the calendar began featuring real Washington State businesses and employees in a variety of industries. This educational tool brings important safety messages to employers and workers 365 days a year. L&I produces and distributes 12,000 copies a year (see Figure 14.4).

Special Promotional Items

You can reinforce and sometimes sustain campaign messages through the use of special promotional items, referred to by some in the industry as "trinkets and trash." Among the most familiar are messages on *clothing* (e.g., T-shirts, baseball hats, diapers, bibs), *functional items* (e.g., key chains, water bottles, litterbags, pens and pencils, notepads, bookmarks, book covers, refrigerator magnets), and more *temporary mechanisms* (e.g., bar coasters, stickers, temporary tattoos, coffee sleeves, sports cards, lapel buttons). Some campaigns, such as the one in the following example, create a treasure chest of these items.

Figure 14.4 A weekly calendar intended to increase safety practices on construction job sites.[15]

Example: Temporary Tattoos and More for Pooper Scoopers

In Snohomish County, Washington, Dave Ward of the Snohomish County Public Works Department understands the difference between an awareness campaign and a social marketing campaign. He also understands how important it is to research target audiences' current attitudes and practices regarding picking up pet waste and to focus on creative strategies to promote very specific behaviors by solving the customer's problem.

His research among pet owners revealed that 42% picked up their dog's waste regularly and disposed of it properly in the trash; 42% were picking it up regularly but not disposing of it properly (e.g., they were burying it on their property); and 16% were picking it up only sometimes or not at all. To promote "proper behaviors," the county created concrete and vivid communications: "More than 126,000 dogs live in Snohomish County, producing waste equivalent to a city of 40,000 people. More than 20 tons of dog waste are dropped in Snohomish County backyards every day." Observation research then helped define the problem even further. Although citizens appeared to be fairly reliable in picking up pet waste on public property such as sidewalks and parks (where they could be seen), they were less judicious in their own backyards.

Ask dog owners why they don't pick up their dog's waste in their yard, and you might hear what Dave did: "When I come home from work at night and let the dog out to go,

Figure 14.5 A promotional item, a flashlight, that also helps overcome barriers to "scooping the poop" in the dark.[16]

Figure 14.6 A temporary tattoo signaling "Good job, Aja!"

it's too dark to see where they go." To address this barrier, a free functional promotional item was developed, a small flashlight that could be left by the door, serving not only as a way to follow the pet around the yard but also as a prompt for the desired behavior on a regular basis (see Figure 14.5). And to spread the word and recognize these pooper scoopers, another promotional item, a temporary tattoo for the hand with the words "I'm a pooper scooper," was especially popular among youth (see Figure 14.6).[17]

Signage and Displays

Many social marketing campaigns rely on signage and displays to launch and, especially, sustain campaign messages. Examples of those more permanent include *road signs* warning against drinking and driving, reminding people to use a litterbag, and asking motorists to "Move right for sirens and lights." *Signs on government property and establishments regulated by the government* can be used to target messages, such as signs in forests asking people to stay on the path, plaques in bars with messages warning about the dangers of alcohol when pregnant, and signs at airports urging us to remove computers from our bags before reaching the checkpoint. Displays and signage can also be used at point of purchase in *retail environments* (e.g., for life vests, tarps for covering pickup loads, energy-saving lightbulbs, natural pesticides). In this case, signage and special displays will include selling the idea to distribution channel decision makers and coordinating distribution of any special signage and accompanying materials.

Personal Selling

Perhaps the oldest promotional channel is that of face-to-face selling. Kotler and Keller see this tool as the most effective at later stages of the buying process, one that helps build buyer preference, conviction, and action. They cite three distinctive qualities this tool provides: (a) personal interaction—involving an immediate and interactive relationship;

(b) cultivation—permitting relationships to grow; and (c) response—making the buyer feel under some obligation for having listened to the "sales talk."[18] And, as illustrated in the following example, the experience doesn't have to be unpleasant.

Example: Thailand's "Condom King"

Mechai Viravaidya is an ex-senator and founder of the Population and Community Development Association, a leading public health nongovernmental organization in Bangkok, Thailand. He is also known as the "Condom King," credited with increasing the use of condoms in the country and thereby slashing the AIDS infection rate from 140,000 cases per year in 1991 to about 20,000 by 2003.[19] Viravaidya knew that increasing condom usage would take more than traditional messages delivered through traditional channels. To increase usage, his imagination knew no bounds as he sought to make condoms fun, accessible, and the norm. And he wasn't shy, with claims such as, "The condom is a great friend. You can do many things with it. . . . You can use different colors on different days—yellow for Monday, pink for Tuesday, and black when you are mourning."[20] He made special appearances at such events as condom blowing contests at high schools, making sure the media would be there to take photos that he hoped would end up on the front page. He influenced McDonald's to hand condoms out (a program he referred to as "Take this with your Big Mac") and helped make them available at tollbooths, in banks, and in hotels. He even had monks bless them so that Thais would know there would be no ill effects from using them. He promoted a "Cops and Rubbers" program with policemen handing out condoms to youth; and at his popular urban Condoms and Cabbage Restaurants, there are no mints served at the end of the meal.[21]

NONTRADITIONAL AND NEW MEDIA CHANNELS

Social Media

In December 2009, Queen Rania of Jordan delivered a keynote speech at Europe's number one technology event, attended by over 2,000 entrepreneurs, bloggers, and developers. She posed a challenging question, asking how to leverage the power of social media to alleviate social challenges in the real world—especially the state of global education. She sees social media as "a platform to collaborate and a mouthpiece to mobilize," and urged online activists to act on behalf of 75 million children in the world still being denied an education.[22] "You are the ones who can help link online activism to reality, to finally make life-streaming life-changing."[23] The Queen clearly recognizes what many social marketers are discovering—the power of social media. The Social Media Toolkit provided in 2009 by the Centers for Disease Control and Prevention (CDC) articulates these strengths well, seeing the potential of these technologies to:[24]

- Increase the timeliness of communications
- Leverage the networks of target audiences

- Expand your reach
- Personalize and reinforce messages
- Facilitate interaction
- Influence desired behaviors

Example: Letting YouTube Bury the Argument for Brochures

As a sponsor of landmark menu labeling legislation, the California Center for Public Advocacy in 2008 contracted with Brown-Miller Communications to increase support for the nation's first statewide menu labeling law, one that would require chain food facilities to disclose calories for each standard menu item directly on the menu next to the actual item. The fast food industry was backing an alternative bill opting instead for nutrition brochures. Based on the old saying that a picture is worth a thousand words, the agency spent an afternoon filming people standing in line with fast food outlets' complex brochures, trying, unsuccessfully, to quickly find simple information for the item they wanted. They then created a light-hearted man-on-the-street video showcasing their difficulties and posted it on YouTube (http://www.youtube.com/watch?v=zD4m6WN3Tlg) and sent it directly to fast food industry representatives, legislators and their staff, advocates, and the media. The secretary of health and human services and the governor were shown the video in one-on-one meetings. The YouTube video garnered over 5,000 views the first week, and over 80% of the comments directly attacked the fast food industry's bill. Featured on the *New York Times* editorial blog, the video reached beyond the confines of YouTube. The resulting public backlash prompted the fast food industry to withdraw its legislation. State legislators who had been previously skittish about the bill and supportive of the fast food industry's bill passed the first statewide menu labeling law. The governor signed it into legislation, and California became the first state to pass statewide menu labeling legislation.[25]

The CDC's toolkit also provides detailed definitions, descriptions, and tips for social media tools, which are summarized in Box 14.2. In the past several years, the CDC has developed a number of integrated social media campaigns, including the one described in the next example.

Example: 2009–2010 H1N1 and Seasonal Flu Outbreak Campaign

During the 2009–2010 H1N1 and seasonal flu outbreak, the CDC and the U.S. Department of Health and Human Services (HHS) created a media strategy that used a variety of social media tools: *buttons* to inform visitors of steps to take to stop the spread of the disease and direct them to additional information; *badges* that users could post to their individual social networking profiles or personal blogs; *widgets* for sharing guidance and health tips; *online videos*, the most popular being "Symptoms of H1N1 (Swine Flu)," viewed more than 2 million times; *podcasts*, including a special for children about flu prevention; *e-cards* allowing users to send flu-related health messages to friends, family, and coworkers (flu-related e-cards were sent more than 22,000 times and viewed a collective 103,000 times); *text messaging* providing three health messages a week to more than 16,000 subscribers; the *virtual world* Whyville for tweens featuring two different virtual flu viruses, the "Why Flu" and the "WhyMe Flu"; the CDC's *Twitter* accounts (which grew to a collective following of 1.28 million users); and the CDC's *Facebook* account, sharing flu updates and providing additional tools such as badges and widgets and a link to subject matter experts.

Box 14.2
A Social Media Primer

Badges are small graphic elements that include an image, a call to action, and a link for more information, often posted on personal profiles (e.g., "I got my flu shot.").

Image sharing involves posting images such as photos and artwork to Web sites (e.g., a photo of what bacteria on hands looks like before washing).

RSS feeds (really simple syndications) provide ability to aggregate and update information and provide links from many sites in one place (e.g., for emergency preparedness and response recommendations).

Podcasts are a convenient way to listen to or view digital media files by downloading on a portable media device or computer when and where convenient (e.g., preventing Type 2 diabetes).

Online video sharing is the posting of videos on online sites such as YouTube, MSN, and Yahoo (e.g., a YouTube video featuring simple things to do at home to conserve water).

Widgets provide interactive information and fresh content on a subject and can be accessed on an organization's Web site or downloaded to personal Web sites (e.g., a body mass index calculator).

E-cards are electronic greeting cards sent to personal e-mail accounts, often with a colorful greeting and some message that promotes or reinforces a desired behavior (e.g., congratulations for being tobacco free for six months).

E-games are interactive electronic games played through applications such as the Internet, video game console, or mobile phone (e.g., actions youth can take to reduce, reuse, and recycle).

Mobile applications, such as texting, are the most portable and quickly becoming a vital tool for timely and personalized communications (e.g., applications to help choose sustainable seafood while ordering a meal or shopping at a grocery store).

Blogs are regularly updated online journals with one or a team of regular authors (e.g., a physician at a children's hospital participating in a "mommy's" blog regarding childhood immunizations).

(Continued)

(Continued)

Microblogs, such as Twitter, are brief text updates 140 or fewer characters long (e.g., a specific Twitter encouraging sports injury prevention).

Social networking sites are online communities where people can interact with friends, family, coworkers, and others with common interests. They provide social marketers with timely and personal ways to deliver products and promotional communications (e.g., UV alerts through a "Be Smart in the Sun" Facebook page).

Virtual worlds are online environments providing users an opportunity to create a virtual persona, or avatar, and then interact with other avatars in an online virtual environment (e.g., a virtual world on Second Life for preventing bullying).

Source: Adapted from the Centers for Disease Control and Prevention's "The Health Communicator's Social Media Toolkit," August 2010, http://www.cdc.gov/healthcommunication/ToolsTemplates/SocialMediaToolkit_BM.pdf

Twelve lessons learned that the CDC hopes will benefit others when developing, implementing, and evaluating social media efforts include the following:[26]

1. "Make strategic choices" based on the audience's profile and your communication objectives.

2. "Go where the people are" by reviewing user statistics and demographics.

3. "Adopt low-risk tools first," such as podcasts and videos.

4. "Make sure messages are science based," ensuring accuracy and consistency.

5. "Create portable content," such as widgets and online videos that can easily be shared.

6. "Facilitate viral information sharing" through sites such as Facebook and YouTube.

7. "Encourage participation," especially through two-way conversations.

8. "Leverage networks" such as Facebook, where many in your target audience may have more than 100 "friends."

9. "Provide multiple formats" to increase accessibility, reinforce messages, and provide preferred ways to interact.

10. "Consider mobile phones," since 90% of adults in America subscribe to mobile services.

11. "Set realistic goals," as social media alone are unlikely to achieve aggressive communication or behavior change goals.

12. "Learn from metrics and evaluate efforts," an advantage afforded by digital communications.

Craig Lefebvre, a renowned social marketing expert experienced in social media applications, provides additional perspectives for success:[27]

The position a social marketer takes when using social media involves not just a new perspective, but another set of skills that focus on the network, not the individual. *To use these media successfully, we must become collaborators, conveners, facilitators, brokers and weavers.* By collaborators, we mean working inside what others have created—existing blogs, social network sites; creating platforms for group participation from the beginning—not just as static dissemination websites. As conveners we must think about using social media in new ways to bring people of common purpose together to get things done—not simply substitute computer-mediated meetings for in-person ones (aka the burgeoning scheduling of "webinars") to "talk." One of the major barriers to becoming a convener is that few people and organizations understand the effort that must go into changing the behaviors of their collaborators (for a recent discussion see Preece & Shneiderman, 2009). Being a broker means becoming a dynamic resource center—not a place where people go to check out job posts, and download toolkits and case studies, but where people can, among other things, exchange advice and information, solicit creative work, comment on works in progress, allow agencies to see who outside their usual networks might have the ways and means to reach priority groups. For example, why do so few health programs reach poor, underserved and rural populations through agricultural extension services or United Way agencies? And finally, agencies and organizations need to think about themselves as network weavers—pulling together what are usually (when you look for them) a number of diverse and isolated groups working on the same problem but do not have the connectors, or bridges, to bring them into contact with one another.

The creative use of social media and mobile technologies that moves past what they are as technologies, and focuses on how they fit into the lives of people we serve, will allow social marketing to become more effective and efficient at realizing behavior and social change at scale.[28]

Web Sites

To increase visibility for your Web site, *search engine marketing* has evolved immensely in the past several years, and many of us are not fully exhausting recommended strategies to increase the visibility of our Web site when someone conducts a Google-type search (e.g., "natural gardening"). There are paid options to ensure a ranking, often with a "pay per click" fee structure, a strategy that probably makes more business sense in the for-profit sector. There are also numerous unpaid options to improve the chances that your site will make the first results page, if not the top of that page (i.e., your site's ranking). Ranking can be improved by enhancing a Web site's structure, content, and keyword submissions.

Web sites are a critical "touch point" for your customer, one that not only impacts awareness and attitudes toward your organization but also makes a difference in whether your audience is inspired and supported to act (e.g., pledge to keep a lawn pesticide free). Some even believe your Web site could be "the third place," a term referring to social surroundings different from the two usual social environments of home and the workplace. Customers of Starbucks, for example, might classify their coffee spot as one of their third places.

To maximize the influence of your Web site, experts advise that you pay attention to (a) your site's ease of navigation, (b) ability to tailor itself to different users, (c) potential for two-way communications, and (d) availability of related links. And be certain to ensure that the "look and feel" of the site is consistent with your desired brand identity. [29] The following is a good example.

Example: A Web Site and Partnership to Protect Watersheds

In April 2006, CBS 11 in Dallas/Fort Worth, in partnership with the Environmental Protection Agency, the Texas State Soil and Water Conservation Board, and the North Central Texas Council of Governments, introduced a Web site to influence citizen behaviors to protect the Upper Trinity River Watershed in North Texas. The station's new "e-Life" encourages citizens to share story ideas for on-air coverage; photos of people, places, and wildlife in the watershed; Web links with related information that they will then post; events that can be put on a community calendar; and even brochures that they would like posted to e-Life. The site also includes features on a variety of other weather and climate-specific topics, including drought, flooding, and wildfires (see Figure 14.7).[30]

Popular Entertainment Media

A less well-known and underused media category employs popular forms of entertainment to carry behavior change messages, referred to as popular entertainment media by some and edutainment by others. These include movies, television series, radio programs, comic books, comic strips, songs, theater, video games, and traveling entertainers such as puppeteers, mimes, and poets. Social marketing messages integrated into programming, scripts, and performances have included topics such as drinking and driving, use of condoms, eating disorders, recycling, youth suicide, organ donation, HIV testing, avoiding loan fraud, and sudden infant death syndrome.

Alan Andreasen sees this approach as a very effective one in overcoming the problems of selective exposure and selective attention on the part of indifferent target audiences. "This has come to be called the Entertainment Education Approach.[31] It began in the 1960s with a soap opera in Peru called *Simplemente Maria*, which discussed family planning, among other topics."[32] And John Davies, an international social marketing consultant who refers to these initiatives as "edutainment," believes that although they can require substantial budgets, costs might be lowered by selling advertising time to multinational companies that market beneficial, affordable health products such as soap for hand washing, oral rehydration salts for babies, and vitamin/mineral tablets for women.[33]

Figure 14.7 Web site encouraging citizen stories and actions.[34]

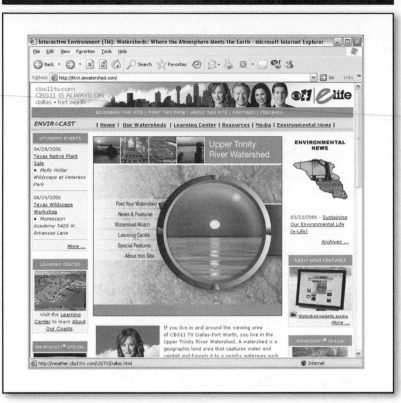

On a local level, you might try persuading local celebrities popular with the target audience to develop special promotional products (e.g., songs on their CDs) to perform at special events or to be featured in advertisements. In a national award-winning television spot for Mississippi's antilitter campaign, for example, former first lady Pat Fordice magically appears in the cab of a pickup truck between two "Bubbas," one of whom has gleefully tossed trash out the window. Pinching the ears of the driver and his offending pal, Fordice admonishes the pair for littering Mississippi highways. The former first lady continued as a spokesperson and representative of the campaign with the tagline "I'm Not Your Mama! Pick It Up, Mississippi!" [35]

Efforts to make this happen on a large scale, however, are likely to be substantial and may include lobbying and partnership efforts with the entertainment industry. The CDC, for example, often partners with Hollywood executives and academic, public health, and advocacy organizations to share information with writers and producers about the nation's pressing health issues. Knowing that an estimated 88% of people in America learn about health issues from television, they believe prime time and daytime television programs are great outlets for health messages. To facilitate this, they provide tip sheets for TV writers and producers, conduct expert briefings for writers, and respond to inquiries for health information. They arrange expert briefings for the entire writing staff of a TV show, set up one-on-one conversations between a producer and a health expert to explore story line possibilities, and help find real people who deal with health issues firsthand. They also present awards and acknowledgments for exemplary portrayal of health issues, as they did in 2003 when they awarded the Sentinel for Health Award to *The Young and the Restless* for "Neil's Alcoholism."[36]

Another impressive trend is also seen as an opportunity for popular media. By 2007, video games surpassed movie rental, music, and box office films in terms of time and dollars spent. In fact, in 2005, a Games for Change Conference was held in New York City to inspire organizations to use video games to further social change, and there is now a Web site (www.socialimpactgames.com) that provides a listing and description of over 200 "serious games," including one described in the following example.

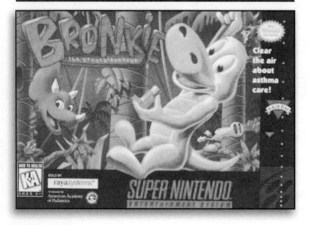

Figure 14.8 A video game helping to reduce asthma attacks.[37]

Example: Video Games for Asthma

Bronkie the Bronchiasaurus, created by Click Health in 1995, is a Super Nintendo video game designed to improve players' asthma self-management. Players take the role of either Bronkie or Trakie, two dinosaurs who have asthma (see Figure 14.8). To win the game, players must keep their dinosaur's asthma under control while also saving their planet from deadly dust clouds. To make sure Bronkie and Trakie stay in top form, the dinosaurs must be guided to measure and monitor their peak flow (breath strength), take medications as needed, follow a sick day plan, use an inhaler correctly, and avoid asthma triggers such as pollen, dust, smoke, and cold viruses shot through the air by Sneezers. The game has been used successfully in homes, hospitals, clinic waiting rooms, and asthma summer camps. Studies found that young people with asthma who had the Bronkie video game available to play at home reduced their asthma-related emergency and urgent care visits by 40% on average.[38]

Public Art

You have, no doubt, experienced public art intended to advocate a cause (e.g., white crosses in a park in protest to a war), attract tourists (e.g., Cows on Parade in Chicago), or raise money for a nonprofit organization (e.g., quilts for AIDS victims). But what about public art intended to actually influence behaviors—behaviors to improve health, safety, the environment, or financial well-being? We think it is another emerging and untapped channel, with unique potentials to sustain behaviors, create media attention, and be seen as a credible messenger. Channel types include *sculptures, exhibits, murals, paintings,* and more recently, "flash mobs," described in the next example.

Example: A Flash Mob to Protect Pedestrians in Crosswalks

Flash mobs are spontaneous public performances by a group (mob) designed to surprise shoppers, diners, commuters, and passers-by in a public place. The mob silently gathers in a public place, indistinguishable from normal passers-by. At a designated time, they break into action, sometimes a synchronized dance, sometimes just a song, maybe even a giant pillow fight. Sometimes participants are organized informally via social networks and consider it an opportunity for artistic expression. Others are more formal, sponsored by an organization with an agenda, as was the case in Seattle in November 2010.

In December 2009, the Seattle Department of Transportation chose the holiday shopping months to organize a flash mob to help reduce pedestrian injuries in the city, where on average there is more than one pedestrian/motor vehicle collision a day. The location was an indoor downtown shopping center near four intersections with the greatest number of collisions, ones that were already well lit, well marked, well signalized, and well engineered. They had run out of upstream engineering solutions and turned to influencing citizen behaviors. Deciding that a group of elected officials speaking at a busy mall might not draw a crowd, they chose a flash mob strategy instead, one that involved 60 people suddenly springing up on the ground floor of the center delivering their messages while doing "The Safety Dance." Then again in December 2010, another city-sponsored mob appeared downtown, this one at the popular Pioneer Square featuring dancers dancing to the tune "Singin' in the Rain" with umbrellas printed with the slogan "See You in the Crosswalk," a message to influence pedestrians to make sure they are seen before crossing the street. Comments on the YouTube blog posted the next day included, "Pretty cool. Fun to learn. Fun to do. Fun to watch. Good work all" (http://www.youtube.com/watch?v=S4CqTV9eEkI).

Product Integration

In the commercial sector, product placement is a specialty of its own, with marketers finding inventive ways to advertise during actual television programs and movies especially. You probably recognize this when you see a familiar logo on a cup of coffee in an actor's hand or the Swoosh on a star's baseball cap. In the James Bond film *Die Another Day*, for example, 7UP, Aston Martin, Finlandia, Visa, and Omega all spent an estimated $100 million for product placement rights, with some critics nicknaming the film *Buy Another Day*. [39]

More relevant for social marketing is the integration of your desired behaviors into commercial products or their packaging. Sometimes corporations decide "all on their own" to take on an initiative. In the fall of 2006, for example, the toymaker Mattel unveiled Tanner, Barbie's new pet dog. Tanner comes with little brown plastic "biscuits" that he can be fed simply by lifting his tail. When he "releases them," Barbie can then scoop them up using her new, magnetic pooper-scooper and place them in the little garbage can included in the package.

More often, the social marketing organization approaches the corporation for support, as Seafood Watch did with Warner Home Video, who then agreed to include the 2007 Seafood Watch pocket guide in every copy of the Academy Award–winning animated film *Happy Feet* when millions of DVD copies became available in March 2007.

FACTORS GUIDING COMMUNICATION CHANNEL DECISIONS

Clearly, you have numerous channel options available for getting your messages to target audiences. Choices and decisions can be guided by a few important factors, eight of which are described in the following sections, in no particular order, since each is an important consideration. Some are even deal breakers.

Factor #1: Your Campaign Objectives and Goals

In Step 4 of your planning process, you ideally set a quantifiable goal for changes in behavior, behavior intent, awareness, and/or attitudes. Those measures/targets are now your guide for selecting communication channels.

For example, it makes sense that if you want 50 homes in a neighborhood of 500 homes on a river to be stream stewards, you will have a very different outreach (communication) strategy than if you want 5 million residents of a state to be aware of an E. coli outbreak. Confirming these numbers ahead of time with funders and team members will help you make the case for the strategies that you then propose.

Factor #2: Desired Reach and Frequency

Kotler and Armstrong describe *reach* as "a measure of the percentage of people in the target audience who are exposed to the ad campaign during a given period of time" and *frequency* as "a measure of how many times the average person in the target audience is exposed to the message."[40] This will be an important decision. For example, a state health department may want radio and television spots to reach 75% of youth ages 12 to 18 living in major metropolitan areas at least nine times during a two-month campaign. Media representatives will then use computer programs to produce media schedules and associated costs to achieve these objectives. The media planner often looks at the cost of the plan and calculates the cost per contact or exposure (often expressed as the *cost per thousand*—the cost of reaching 1,000 people using the medium).

Factor #3: Your Target Audience

Perhaps the most important consideration when planning media strategies will be the *target audience's profile* (demographics, psychographics, geographics, and behaviors) and their *media habits.* This will be especially important when using paid advertising and selecting specific media vehicles, such as radio stations, television programs, sections of the newspaper, magazines, and direct mail lists. Ideally, these were identified as "openings" when developing the creative brief. Again, media representatives will be able to provide audience profiles and recommendations. The goal will be to choose general media types, specific vehicles, and the timing most likely to reach, appeal to, and influence target audiences. *Compatibility* of the social marketing program and associated messages will also be key and will contribute to the ultimate impact of the given medium. For example, a message regarding safe gun storage is more strategically aligned with a parenting magazine than one on home decorating, even though both may have readerships with similar demographic profiles. And the timing of this ad would be best linked to special issues on youth violence or campus shootings.

Factor #4: Being There Just in Time

Many social marketers have found that an ideal moment to speak to the target audience is when they are about to choose between alternative, competing behaviors. They arc at a fork in the road, and the social marketer wants a last chance to influence this decision. Tactics demonstrating this principle include the following:

- The use of the ♥ symbol on menus signifying a smart choice for those interested in options that are low in fat, cholesterol, and/or calories
- Calories posted on menu boards
- The familiar forest fire prevention signs that give updates on the current level of threat for forest fires in the park
- A message on the backs of diapers reminding parents to turn their infants over, onto their backs, to sleep

Figure 14.9   A sign at a beach shows the benefit of a life vest.

- The idea of encouraging smokers (in the contemplation stage) to insert their child's photo under the wrappers of cigarette packs
- A sign at a beach that makes the benefit of a life vest clear (see Figure 14.9)
- A key chain for teens with the message "You Don't Have to Be Buzzed to Be Busted"
- A handmade tent card next to a napkin holder suggesting that customers take only what they need

Factor #5: Being There "In the Event Of"

Communicators also want to prepare for events that are likely to motivate target audiences to listen, learn more, and alter their behaviors. Examples would include an earthquake, a teen suicide in a small community, the listing of an endangered species, threats of drought and power blackouts, a famous female entertainer diagnosed with AIDS, a governor injured in an automobile accident while not wearing a seatbelt, a college student sexually assaulted after a rave party, or a politician diagnosed with prostate cancer. Events such as these often affect levels of awareness and belief relative to costs and benefits associated with behavior change. The amount of time it will take to learn about and prepare a home for a potential earthquake will seem minor compared with suffering the costs and losses in a real earthquake. Though such events are often tragic, the silver lining is that target audiences in the precontemplation stage are often moved to contemplation, even action, and the social marketer can take advantage of the momentum created by heightened publicity and the need for practical information. Just as public relations professionals prepare for crisis communications, the social marketer also wants to prepare for these *opportunity communications*.

Example: A Timely Message on Earthquake Preparedness

On Sunday, March 13, 2011, three days after the 8.9 earthquake off the coast of Japan, a front page headline in the *Seattle Times* read "GETTING READY FOR DISASTER. See Page A13 for a clip-and-save guide to make sure your family are ready if disaster strikes." Editors had likely been ready long before the quake with the full-page checklist, including tips on storing copies of important documents such as birth certificates, making a family emergency plan, having a list of important phone numbers, and knowing how and when to turn off the gas, as well as a list of supplies for the home as well as the car. Publishing this when readers "were awake" to the reality of disasters certainly ensured more would look at the list—even clip it out and start checking off completed items.

Factor #6: Integrated Marketing Communications

Commercial marketers routinely invest millions of dollars in marketing communications, and this experience has led many companies to adopt the concept of *integrated marketing communications* (IMC), "where a company carefully integrates and coordinates its many communication channels to deliver a clear, consistent, and compelling message about the organization and its products."[41]

With integrated marketing communications, you achieve consistency in the use of slogans, images, colors, font types, key messages, and sponsor mentions in all media vehicles and customer touch points. It means that statistics and facts used in press releases are the same as those in printed materials. It means that television commercials have the same tone and style as radio spots and that print ads have the same look and feel as the program's Web site.[42]

In addition, IMC points to the need for a graphic identity and perhaps even a statement or manual describing graphic standards. The integrated approach also addresses the need for coordination and cooperation among those developing and disseminating program materials and, finally, calls for regular audits of all customer touch points.

Benefits of an integrated approach are significant, with (a) increased efficiency in developing materials (e.g., eliminating the need for frequent debates over colors and typefaces and incremental costs for developing new executions) and (b) increased effectiveness of communications, given their consistent presentation in the marketplace.

Example: Friends Don't Let Friends Drive Drunk

In the early 1990s, the Ad Council and the U.S. Department of Transportation's National Highway Traffic Safety Administration introduced a new campaign encouraging friends to intervene in order to prevent a drunk person from getting behind the wheel. It was originally designed to reach 16- to 24-year-olds, who accounted for 42% of all fatal alcohol-related car crashes.[43] Eighty-four percent of Americans now recall having seen or heard a PSA with the now famous "Friends Don't Let Friends Drive Drunk" tagline. More impressive, nearly 80% report they have taken action to prevent a friend or loved one from driving drunk, and 25% report they have stopped drinking and driving as a result of the campaign.[44] This hard-hitting campaign was instrumental, it is reported, in achieving a 10% decrease in alcohol-related fatalities between 1990 and 1991—the single largest one-year drop in alcohol-related fatalities ever recorded.[45] Communication channels have been consistent in their use of the tagline, emotional themes, and memorable stories of "innocent victims" and have included PSAs produced for TV, radio, print, out-of-home, and online media outlets (see Figure 14.10).

Figure 14.10 Magazine insert from a memorable campaign.[46]

Factor #7: Knowing Advantages and Disadvantages of Media Type

Media decisions should also be based on advantages and limitations of each unique media type and should take into consideration the nature and format of key messages established in the creative brief. For example, a brief message such as "Choose a designated driver" can fit on a key chain or bar coaster, whereas a complex one such as "How to talk with your teen about suicide" would be more appropriate in a brochure or on a special radio program. Table 14.1 presents a summary of advantages and limitations for each of the major advertising categories.

Factor #8: Your Budget

Even when all other factors are considered, resources and funding may very well have the final say in determining communication channels. In the ideal scenario, as we have discussed, media strategies and associated budgets are based on desired and agreed-upon campaign goals (e.g., reach 75% of youth at least nine times). In reality, plans are more often influenced by budgets and available funding sources. For example, first estimates of a draft media plan to achieve the above goal may indicate that costs for the desired reach and frequency exceed actual and fixed budgets. In this (all too common) scenario, you will need to prioritize and allocate funding to media types and vehicles judged to be most efficient and effective. In some cases, it may then be necessary and appropriate to reduce campaign goals (e.g., reach 50% of youth at least nine times) and/or create a phased approach to campaign implementation (e.g., achieve the reach and frequency goals in half the state).

ETHICAL CONSIDERATIONS WHEN SELECTING COMMUNICATION CHANNELS

Options for communication channels are numerous, and several factors for consideration have been identified in this chapter, including audience profile and campaign resources. Ethical considerations will also be a factor. Does the end justify the means in a case in which antiabortionists block the entrance to clinics and threaten the lives of doctors? Or what about a case in which activists threaten (but do not physically harm) a woman wearing a fur coat? Considerable mention was made of channels involving access to computers, e-mails, and the Internet. What about the fact that many target audiences don't have this access, or even the skills, to fully utilize and benefit from these new media campaigns?

Organizations, understandably, have ethical and legal concerns with the use of social media, especially regarding security, staff productivity, and negative postings from readers. To address this, many organizations develop and distribute formal policy and best practice statements.

And here's one to ponder. Is it wrong to advertise for a kidney donor? In 2010, in the United States, 19 people on average die each day waiting for an organ transplant, 10 of

Table 14.1 Profiles of Major Media Types

Medium	Advantages	Disadvantages
Newspapers	Flexibility, timeliness, good local market coverage, broad acceptability, high believability	Short life, poor reproduction quality, small pass-along audience
Television	Good mass market coverage; low cost per exposure; combines sight, sound, and motion; appealing to the senses	High absolute costs, high clutter, fleeting exposure, less audience selectivity
Direct Mail	High audience selectivity, flexibility, allows personalization	Relative high cost per exposure, "junk mail" image
Radio	Good local acceptance, high geographic and demographic selectivity, low cost	Audio only, fleeting exposure, low attention ("the half-hear" medium); fragmented audiences
Magazines	High geographic and demographic selectivity, credibility, and prestige; high-quality reproduction; long life; good pass-along readership	Long ad purchase lead time, high cost, no guarantee of position
Outdoor	Flexibility, high repeat exposure, low cost, low message competition, good positional selectivity	Little audience selectivity, creative limitations
Social Media	Timely, leverages target audience networks, provides for interactions and feedback, ability to personalize, ability to prompt and reinforce behaviors	Resource intensive, primarily audience controlled
Web sites	High selectivity, low cost, immediacy, interactive capabilities	Small, demographically skewed audience; relatively low impact
Sales Promotions	Attention getting, stronger and quicker buyer response, incentives add value	Short life, potential image of "trinkets and trash"
Public Relations	High credibility, ability to catch prospects off guard, reaching prospects preferring to avoid salespeople and advertisements	Less audience reach and frequency
Events & Experiences	Relevance, high involvement and active engagement, "softer sell"	Less audience reach, high cost per exposure
Personal Selling	Effective for understanding consumer objections and for building buyer preference, conviction, action, and relationships	Audience resistance, high cost

Source: Adapted from Kotler, P., & Armstrong, G. (2001). *Principles of marketing* (p. 553). Upper Saddle River, NJ: Prentice Hall. Reprinted with permission.

them waiting for a kidney.[47] MatchingDonors.com is a nonprofit organization trying to improve the odds of finding an organ donor for patients needing transplants. Reportedly, they have the world's largest database of available altruistic donors, ones who are not allowed to receive any financial benefit from organ donation. Some physicians wage campaigns against such Web sites, believing the practice is unethical and should be illegal, as it "bypasses" the national organ donor list. Proponents of the Web site argue that those on the organ donor list only get organs harvested from cadavers and that there are currently 70,000 people waiting for a kidney and that half of those on this list will die while waiting.[48]

CHAPTER SUMMARY

Communication channels, also referred to as media channels, can be categorized as one of three types: mass, selective, or personal. *Mass media* channels are called for when large groups of people need to be quickly informed and persuaded regarding an issue or desired behavior; *selective* channels are used when target audiences can be reached more cost effectively through targeted channels such as direct mail and social media; *personal channels* are more costly but sometimes warranted to achieve behavior change objectives.

Traditional communication channels, as the label implies, are those you are probably most familiar with and exposed to:

- Advertising and PSAs
- Public relations and special events
- Printed materials
- Special promotional items
- Signage and displays
- Personal selling

You are encouraged to consider new media and other nontraditional options that may be more successful in "catching your audience by surprise." They may also allow your audience more time to consider your messages:

- Social media: Facebook, YouTube, blogs, online forums, texting, Twitter, mobile phones
- Web sites
- Popular entertainment media
- Public art
- Product integration

Eight factors are presented to guide your selection of communication types, vehicles, and timing:

Factor #1: Your campaign objectives and goals

Factor #2: Desired reach and frequency

Factor #3: Your target audience

Factor #4: Being there just in time

Factor #5: Being there "in the event of"

Factor #6: Integrated marketing communications

Factor #7: Knowing advantages and disadvantages of media type

Factor #8: Your budget

RESEARCH HIGHLIGHT

Financial Literacy Road Shows in Ghana:
A Qualitative Impact Assessment to Inform Future Efforts
(2007–2008)

Background

Access to financial services is key to economic development and poverty reduction. Financial services can help people start businesses, save for the future, and minimize financial risks. In Ghana, however, less than 20% of households benefit from access to formal financial services such as savings, loans, insurance, and investments. The Government of Ghana is convinced, though, that increasing these levels of participation can only be achieved if consumers have increased capabilities of making well-informed financial decisions and financial service providers follow responsible financial principles. In 2007, surveys of urban Ghanaian adults had revealed that consumers' levels of knowledge regarding financial institutions, services, and products was low, and that even when consumers were knowledgeable, this often did not translate into desired behavior changes. At that time, the government of Ghana, in close cooperation with its development partners,

including The Support Programme for Enterprise Empowerment and Development (SPEED), launched an extensive Financial Literacy Program. The aim was not only to create awareness of financial topics, but also to build a relationship of trust between consumers and financial service providers—a prerequisite for increased responsible and sustainable utilization of financial services.[49]

In November 2007, the Consumer Education and Protection Campaign was launched. Major activities carried out the first two years included a Financial Literacy Week, road shows in rural areas, and the development of educational material on loans, saving, (micro)insurance, and investments. This research highlight will focus on the road show component, featuring an evaluation of three road shows held in 15 towns in the Central, Ashanti, and Eastern Regions of Ghana between December 2007 and May 2008.[50] SPEED Ghana commissioned the study.

Road Show Objectives and Strategies

The objectives of the road shows were to address major consumer *barriers* to utilizing financial services, including lack of knowledge (e.g., how do they determine the interest rate for a loan?), lack of trust (e.g., with no established banking relationships, the unbanked poor had been pushed in the past toward expensive alternatives), and lack of convenient access (e.g., in remote rural areas). Most of the road shows (*communication channel*) were held on weekdays at markets in these communities. Most participants were petty traders, market women and artisans. Activities generally started at 9 A.M. and ended by noon. They included parades with engaging giant puppets and a stage with performers discussing difficult financial scenarios, dancing and even singing songs with messages such as "You too can save for the education of your children" and "When you take a loan, make sure you understand the terms and conditions" (see Figure 14.11). Shows focused on savings and loans (*products*), and *promotional materials* included posters, pocket brochures, and flyers. Prior to the performance, staff from the road shows met with personnel at banks, microfinance institutions (MFIs), and nongovernmental organizations in the community to share information on consumer concerns and needs. After performances, representatives from these institutions were on hand to engage further with road show attendees, answering questions, explaining product features—even opening accounts and taking loan applications.

Figure 14.11 Road show performances in Ghana use giant puppets to help deliver positive financial behavior messages.[51]

Assessment Methodology

To measure the effect of the road shows and recommend strategies for subsequent programs, SPEED Ghana contracted a consultant to conduct a qualitative impact assessment of the pilot programs. Both road show participants and MFIs were interviewed between July and August 2008. Questionnaires and guided discussions explored how respondents found out about the shows, what benefits they realized from them, what behavior changes the shows had influenced, and what recommendations participants would make for improving future shows.

Several months after completion of the road shows, 15 towns in the three regions were visited by field interviewers who conducted face-to-face interviews, recording findings on printed survey instruments. Interviews were completed with 41 individuals who had participated in the road shows, and 21 interviews were completed with staff at MFIs. The interview process took 15 to 30 minutes with road show participants, and between an hour and a half and three hours with MFIs.

Results

Interviews with participants at road shows answered several questions important for future planning of road show promotional and content strategies:

- **How did they find out about the road shows?** They either heard and then followed the brass band music, were told about them by bank officials, or heard sounds emanating from program grounds.
- **What did they learn?** They expressed having more knowledge about the importance of savings, especially in order to get loans. They improved their cash management and budgeting skills, and understood the importance of making loan payments on time.
- **What did they like?** The giant puppets and brass band music together with masquerade dances were enjoyed the most.
- **What are they more likely to do in the future and why?** Respondents reported they were more likely to establish a banking relationship, as they could see how their money would be safer. They understood that by increasing their savings they would have better chances of securing loans. They also indicated they

felt more confident to go to the bank and perceived the banks as more client oriented than they had before.

- **What could be done more or better in future road shows?** Respondents suggested getting the word out through adverts on radio and television and having teachers at schools tell children to inform their parents about the event; recording the event so that it could be played again for those not able to attend; providing more mechanisms/souvenirs at the event, such as pens and pencils that would serve as reminders of what they learned; repeating the show several times a year; and including a drama on customer relationship management and presentations on business financial management.

Findings from interviews with MFIs will inform strategies to more effectively engage financial institutions in future shows, especially knowing the numerous potential benefits in their participation:

- **How did the road shows benefit their institution**? Respondents indicated that the events had increased their client base, increased their savings balances, helped them deal with clients usually scared to walk into the bank, taught them how to speak in public, pointed out how much need there was for further consumer education on savings and loans, educated employees, and enhanced the bank's reputation.
- **What are they more likely to do in the future and why?** Road shows

served as an eye opener for many participating financial institutions. For example, some reported that, based on what they had learned at the road shows, they would be changing their operating hours to correspond more to clients' needs. They also made changes to their products and scheduled more time to visit with their clients.

- **What could be done more or better in future road shows?** Suggestions included providing more publicity/ advertising on radio and television prior to the event to increase attendance; informing the financial institutions two weeks before the scheduled event; training staff more thoroughly on their roles at the road show so that they could be better prepared; involving all financial service organizations in the town; and conducting the event at least annually to reach more people and sustain behaviors.

CHAPTER 14 NOTES

1. Fogg, B. J., & Adler, R. (Eds.). (2009). *Texting 4 health: A simple, powerful way to improve lives.* Stanford, CA: Captology Media.

2. Ibid., p.4.

3. Ibid., p.12.

4. Ibid., pp.7–8.

5. Case information on mDIET: A Personalized Approach to Weight Management Using Text Messaging was provided by Kevin Patrick, University of California, San Diego; Fred Raab, University of California, San Diego; Marc Adams, San Diego State University; and Lindsay Dillon, University of California, San Diego.

6. BJ Fogg & Richard Adler.

7. Kotler, P., & Keller, K. (2005). *Marketing management* (12th ed., p. 546). Upper Saddle River, NJ: Prentice Hall.

8. Dunn, J. (2006, July 13). Denver Water's ads already working conservation angle. *Denver Post.* Retrieved April 22, 2007, from http://www.denverpost.com/portlet/article/html/fragments/ print_article.jsp?articleId=4043. Ads developed by Sukle Advertising and Design.

9. Kotler, P., & Lee, N. (2006). *Marketing in the public sector* (p. 152). Upper Saddle River, NJ: Wharton School.

10. Siegel, M., & Doner, L. A. (1998). *Marketing public health: Strategies to promote social change* (p. 393). Gaithersburg, MD: Aspen.

11. Ibid., p. 394.

12. Ibid., p. 396.

13. Prevent Cancer Foundation. (n.d.). *Prevent Cancer Super Colon exhibit.* Retrieved March 7, 2011, from http://www.preventcancer.org/education2c.aspx?id=156&ekmensel=15074 e5e_34_38_btnlink

14. Source: Janet Hudson, Manager, Exhibit Services, Prevent Cancer Foundation,www .PreventCancer.org.

15. Washington State Department of Labor and Industries.

16. Ibid.

17. For more information, go to http://www.petwaste.surfacewater.info

18. Kotler & Keller, 2005, *Marketing management* (p. 556).

19. Melnick, G. A. (2007, September 25). Interview: From family planning to HIV/AIDS prevention to poverty alleviation: A conversation with Mechai Viravaidya. *Health Affairs, 26*(6), w670–w677. doi: 10.1377/hlthaff.26.6.w670

20. Ibid.

21. Kotler, P., & Lee, N. (2009). *Up and out of poverty: The social marketing solution* (pp. 77–81, 156–158). Upper Saddle River, NJ: Wharton School.

22. Queen Rania Al Abdullah: The Hashemite Kingdom of Jordan. (2009, December 11). *Social media for social good: Queen Rania calls on online world to unite on behalf of 75 million out of school children.* Retrieved March 10, 2011, from http://www.queenrania.jo/media/news/ social-media-social-good-queen-rania-calls-online-world-unite-behalf-75-million-out-schoo

23. Ibid.

24. Centers for Disease Control and Prevention. (2010, August). *The health communicator's social media toolkit.* Retrieved March 10, 2011, from http://www.cdc.gov/healthcommunication/ ToolsTemplates/SocialMediaToolkit_BM.pdf

25. Information for this case was provided by Michael Miller of Brown-Miller Communications, March 8, 2011.

26. Source: Adapted from Centers for Disease Control and Prevention's "The Health Communicator's Social Media Toolkit." August 2010. Retrieved March 10, 2011, from http:// www.cdc.gov/healthcommunication/ToolsTemplates/SocialMediaToolkit_BM.pdf

27. For more on social media from a social marketing perspective, see Lefebvre, R. C. (2009). Integrating cellphones and mobile technologies into public health practice: A social marketing perspective. *Health Promotion Practice, 10,* 490–494; Lefebvre, R. C. (2007). The new technology: The consumer as participant rather than target audience. *Social Marketing Quarterly, 13,* 31–42; Lefebvre, R. C., Preece, J., & Shneiderman, B. (2009). The reader-to-leader framework: Motivating technology-mediated social participation in AIS. *Transactions on Human-Computer Interaction, 1,* 13–32; and On Social Marketing and Social Change Web site: http://socialmarket ing.blogs.com

28. Personal communication from Craig Lefebvre, March 8, 2011.

29. Kotler & Keller, 2005, *Marketing management* (12th ed., p. 613).

30. CBS 11. (n.d.). *CBS 11 launches "e-life" website.* Retrieved April 20, 2007, from http:// cbs11tv.com/ press/local_story_114170135.html

31. Rogers, E. M., et al. (1989). *Proceedings from the conference on entertainment education for social change.* Los Angeles, LA: Annenberg School of Communications.

32. Andreasen, A. R. (1995). *Marketing social change: Changing behavior to promote health, social development, and the environment* (p. 215). San Francisco, CA: Jossey-Bass.

33. Davies, J. (n.d.). *Preventing HIV/AIDS with condoms: Nine tips you can use.* Retrieved April 12, 2007, from http://www.johndavies.com/johndavies/new2html/9tips_print.htm

34. Encouraging Citizen Stories and Actions (StormCenter Communications, Inc.)

35. Keep America Beautiful. (n.d.). *I'm not your mama: Mississippi's war against highway litter.* Retrieved April 13, 2007, from http://www.kab.org/aboutus2.asp?id=642

36. Centers for Disease Control and Prevention. (n.d.). *Entertainment education: Overview.* Retrieved October 10, 2006, from http://www.cdc.gov/communication/entertainment_education .htm

37. Social Impact Games.

38. Social Impact Games. (n.d.). *Entertaining games with non-entertainment goals.* Retrieved April 12, 2007, from http://www.socialimpactgames.com/modules.php?op=modload&name=News&file=article&sid=116&mode=thread&order=1&thold=0

39. Weaver, J. (2002, November 17). A license to shill. *MSNBC News.* Retrieved July 25, 2011, from http://www.msnbc.msn.com/id/3073513/

40. Kotler, P., & Armstrong, G. (2001). *Principles of marketing* (p. 552). Upper Saddle River, NJ: Prentice Hall.

41. Kotler & Armstrong, 2001, *Principles of marketing* (pp. 513–517).

42. Ibid.

43. Ad Council. (n.d.). *Drunk driving prevention (1983–present).* Retrieved April 18, 2007, from http://www.adcouncil.org/default.aspx?id=137

44. Ibid., *Campaign description.*

45. Ibid.

46. Courtesy of the U.S. Department of Transportation and the Ad Council.

47. Retrieved March 7, 2011, from Matching Donors Web site: http://www.matchingdonors.com/life/index.cfm?page=main&cfid=12265246&cftoken=12950547

48. Satel, S. (2007, April 13). "Is it wrong to advertise for organs?" *National Review Online,* p. 16.

49. Fact Sheet: Financial Literacy in Ghana, Ministry of Finance and Economic Planning, 2009.

50. Speed Ghana. (2008, August). *Impact assessment on road shows organized in Central, Ashanti, and Eastern regions of Ghana between December 2007 and May 2008.* Prepared by Kwabena Owusu and Belinda Roj Sinemillioglu.

51. GIZ International.

Part V

Managing Social Marketing Programs

Chapter 15

DEVELOPING A PLAN FOR MONITORING AND EVALUATION

Marketing is a learning game. You make a decision. You watch the results. You learn from the results. Then you make better decisions.

—Dr. Philip Kotler[1]
Northwestern University

Now you've reached a step you may not be eager for—developing a plan for monitoring and evaluation. If this is true for you, your experiences and conversations may sound similar to the following common laments:

- "My administrators and additional funders think it's nice I can report on how many PSAs we ran and how many hits we got to our Web site, but I can see it in their eyes. It's not enough. They want to know how many more people got an HIV/AIDS test as a result of our efforts. And actually, that's not even enough. What they really want to know is how many positives did we find and how much did it cost us to find each one."
- "You think that's hard. In my line of work, they want to know if the fish are any healthier."
- "Most of the evaluation strategies I've looked at could cost as much as the small budget I have for this campaign. I honestly can't justify it. And yet, everyone seems to want it."
- "Quite frankly, my concern is with the results. What if it's bad news—that we didn't reach our goal? They like the plan, are going to fully fund it, and trust that we know what we're doing. Bad news could dampen any further work like this."

In this chapter's opening highlight, you'll read how a rigorous evaluative study in the Philippines ended up being able to report even on the program's return on investment—an attractive metric to include in tough economic times. Later in the chapter we'll discuss how to calculate this additional measure.

MARKETING HIGHLIGHT

Evaluating a Commitment Contract for Smoking Cessation in the Philippines
(2006)

Background

In 2006, in the Agusan del Norte province of the Philippines, an innovative smoking cessation alternative was launched and rigorously tested by a unique partnership. One of the partners was Innovations for Poverty Action (IPA), a nonprofit organization based in New Haven, Connecticut, that creates and evaluates solutions to social and economic development problems. Their mission statement commits them to working to scale up successful ideas through dissemination to policy makers, practitioners, investors, and donors.[2] The other partner was the Rural Green Bank of Caraga, key to a program targeting smokers who wanted to quit by encouraging them to open a savings account and deposit the money they would otherwise have spent on cigarettes. Now, perhaps, the program's slogan, "Put your money where your butt is," begins to make a little sense.

Smokers who attempt to quit suffer from side effects including irritability, headache, chest tightness, and coughing. Nicotine replacement therapy is one way to help smokers gradually lessen their dependence on nicotine, but the cost of these therapies, and the ability to access related services, is prohibitive for the low-income smokers in this rural province. IPA thought a savings commitment program would be a less expensive and even potentially more motivating alternative. The program's formal name was Committed Action to Reduce and End Smoking (CARES), and the *target audience* was low-income smokers who wanted to quit, earned an average of 3,500 pesos (about US$70) a month, and spent 92 pesos (almost US$2) a month on cigarettes.[3]

The basic features of this commitment savings program (*product*) require a smoker to sign a commitment contract to make an initial deposit and maintain a minimum balance of 50 pesos (about US$1; *price*). Green Bank gives clients a lockbox at the bank where their money will be kept that they otherwise would have spent on tobacco. Every week, a Green Bank field staff member visits them to collect their deposit (*place*), encouraging them to deposit an amount they would normally have spent on cigarettes (*promotion*). The staff member then makes the deposit in one of the bank's microfinance branches. (Of note is the fact that the account does not pay interest. This is to discourage non-smokers from opening the account merely to receive the convenience of deposit collection services.) The client is not able to withdraw any money during the deposit period. At the end of the sixth month, the client submits to a nicotine test. Clients who pass the test can withdraw their entire savings. Clients who fail (or do not take) the test forfeit their balance, which is then donated to a charity (a local orphanage).

Researchers Xavier Giné at the World Bank and Dean Karlan and Jonathan Zinman with Innovations for Poverty Action (professors at Yale University and Dartmouth College, respectively) led the design and testing of this product. As you will read, they used a randomized controlled trial to isolate and evaluate outcomes of the CARES intervention. Their first objective was to determine whether there was demand for CARES, and their second was to determine whether the CARES strategy—utilizing a commitment contract, monetary incentives, and convenience of access—actually increased smoking cessation. A summary of their evaluation appears in the next sections of this case highlight. For a more in-depth report, see "Put Your Money Where Your Butt Is: A Commitment Contract for Smoking Cessation."[4]

Study Design

The study sample consisted of 2,000 smokers age 18 and older who lived on the island of Mindanao in the southern Philippines. To identify candidates for the study, Green Bank representatives approached people smoking "on the street" and first asked if they smoked regularly. If they did, they were then asked to participate in a short survey. Once this was completed, they were given an informational pamphlet on the dangers of smoking and a tip sheet on how to quit. Each completed survey was then randomly assigned to one of three groups:

Group 1: CARES with deposit collection

Group 2: Cues Only

Group 3: Control

Those in the Cues Only group were offered their choice of one of four cards to keep handy and/or post in locations where they tended to smoke. The cue cards were pocket sized, with graphic and verbal depictions of the negative health consequences of smoking. Each individual was offered to choose one of four pictures: (a) a premature baby with the text "Smoking harms unborn babies," (b) bad teeth with the text "Smoking causes mouth and throat cancer," (c) a black lung with the text "Smoking causes lung cancer," or (d) a child hooked up to a respirator with the text "Don't let children breathe your smoke."

Six months and 12 months after initial launch, the bank attempted to administer the urine test to all study subjects. CARES clients had to take the six-month test or automatically forfeit their deposit balance. Nonclients (including those assigned to the cues and control groups) were paid 30 pesos (US$0.60) for taking the six-month test, and everyone in the sample frame (both treatment and control group participants) was paid 30 pesos for taking the 12-month test.

Results

CARES Study Group

Among the original sample group of 781 individuals who smoked and were offered the CARES program, 83 (11%) were interested and signed a commitment contract. Baseline surveys indicated that those accepting were more likely to want to quit (at some point in life, or now), to be optimistic about quitting (as indicated by responding yes to "Will you quit smoking in the next year?"), and to have a preexisting strategic behavior to manage cravings (as indicated by responding yes to "Do you try to avoid areas or situations that make you want to smoke?").

Results suggest that *CARES helps smokers quit.* At six months, 35% passed the test, and at 12 months, 17% passed. Smokers randomly offered CARES were an estimated 3.3 to 5.8 percentage points more likely to pass the six-month urine test than the control group. To confirm that six-month test results were reliable, researchers also worked with the bank to conduct surprise 12-month tests that would provide sharper evidence on true quit rates. The 12-month results were similar, with the CARES group 3.5 to 5.7 percentage points more likely to pass the test than the control group. Results also suggest that *CARES helps people save.* Ninety percent of clients opened with the minimum balance amount of 50 pesos. Eighty percent of clients then made additional contributions.[5] On average, CARES clients made a deposit every two weeks, and by six months their average balance grew to 553 pesos (about US$10).[6] Based on self-reported smoking rates and a per-cigarette cost of 1 peso, the average CARES client deposited roughly six months' worth of cigarette spending into the account.

Cue Cards Study Group

Although 99% of subjects offered the cue cards accepted them, there was little evidence that this intervention increased quit rates. This was in spite of findings (in a brief follow-up survey conducted along with the "surprise" nicotine test) indicating that one year after receiving the cue cards, 40% reported remembering the cue cards and knowing where theirs was and 6% reported using them actively to help them avoid smoking.

Concluding Thoughts

The research team concluded that the results suggest that the CARES product may be an effective treatment for smoking cessation, comparing favorably to those found for nicotine replacement therapy in randomized controlled trials in other settings.[7] The CARES acceptance rate (11%) also suggests that commitment contracts could help enhance similar public health efforts. Rough calculations relative to a social cost-benefit test were promising. Researchers estimate that the cost per quit was $700 in purchasing-power-parity-adjusted GDP for the U.S. versus the Philippines.[8] In the U.S., the Centers for Disease Control and Prevention reports that employers alone benefit $3,500 per quit-year from increased productivity and reduced health care costs. And of course there were benefits to Green Bank as well: gaining new clients, increasing deposits, and garnering positive public relations.

Nevertheless, the researchers stress, the majority of CARES clients in the study failed to quit, suggesting that there is still much to be done to improve the effectiveness of smoking cessation treatments. They conclude their report with four suggestions for further trials and research:

1. Investigate even longer-term treatment effects—beyond the 12 months in this study.

2. Test whether commitment contracts work best as a complement to other smoking cessation treatments, or as a substitute for them.

3. Study the optimal design of an anti-smoking commitment contract. For example, in this study, CARES was bundled with deposit collection services, making it difficult to know how much of the treatment effect was due to the financial incentive to stick with the program and how much was due to frequent contact with the deposit collector. And if the latter proved to be a persuasive variable, how frequent should the visits be?

4. Determine what drives the decision to accept the CARES offer. Is it the product features, the promotional process, or a combination of the two?

STEP 8: DEVELOP A PLAN FOR MONITORING AND EVALUATION

We recommend that you take time to develop a plan for monitoring and evaluating your social marketing effort before creating your budget in Step 9 and implementation plan in Step 10. You will want your final budget to include funding for this critical activity and your implementation plan to include action items to ensure that it happens.

This chapter will guide you in determining these funding needs and identifying related activities. It is intended to help by outlining components of a monitoring and evaluation plan, posed in the form of questions you'll want to answer sequentially—starting with the toughest one, of course:

- Why are you conducting this measurement and who is the audience for the results?
- What will you measure?
- How will you conduct these measurements?
- When will these measurements be taken?
- How much will it cost?

One distinction is important to clarify up front: the difference between the term *monitoring* and the term *evaluation.*

Monitoring refers to measurements conducted sometime after you launch your social marketing effort but before it is completed. Its purpose is to help you determine whether you need to make midcourse corrections that will ensure that you reach your ultimate marketing goals. Remember the Scoop the Poop campaign in Austin, Texas, discussed in Chapter 2, encouraging citizens to pick up after their pets? A postscript to the program was that in 2008, high levels of bacteria were identified in one of the 12 Austin park facilities designated as off-leash area for dogs, with the highest levels on weekends when park visitors increased. This monitoring effort led to a focus on highlighting health hazards at that beach. It also led to a clean-up event, installation of additional Scoop the Poop boxes, and increased park police and staff presence.

Evaluation, on the other hand, is a measurement and final report on what happened, answering the bottom-line question: Did you reach your goals for changes in behaviors, knowledge, and attitudes? Additional questions are also likely to be addressed in the evaluation. Were activities implemented on time and on budget? Were there any unintended consequences that will need to be addressed now or in future similar projects? Which program elements worked well to support outcomes? Which ones didn't? Was there anything missing? What will you do differently next time, if there is a next time?[9]

WHY ARE YOU CONDUCTING THIS MEASUREMENT?

Your purpose for this measurement often shapes what you measure, how you measure, and when. Consider the differing implications for your plan for each of the following potential reasons for your effort. Notice that audiences for the measurement results will also vary, depending on your purpose.

- To fulfill a grant requirement
- To do better the next time we conduct this same campaign
- To (hopefully) get continued, even increased funding
- To help us decide how to prioritize and allocate our resources going forward
- To alert us to midcourse corrections we need to make to achieve our goals

To fulfill a grant requirement: Sometimes the nature of the monitoring and/or evaluation will be predetermined by specifications in a grant. Consider a case where a city receives a grant from a state department of transportation (DOT) to increase the use of pedestrian flags in the city's eight crosswalks in a downtown corridor. Assume the DOT is hoping that this city's campaign strategies are successful and that these strategies can then be shared by the DOT with other cities in the state. The campaign's evaluation plan will certainly include measuring levels of flag usage before and after the campaign. And the funder (primary audience for the measurement) will need to be assured that the data were collected using a systematic, reliable, and verifiable methodology that can be replicated in other cities.

To do better next time: What if, instead, you are sincerely interested in measuring what happened so that you can improve results in your next similar effort? Perhaps it is a pilot and you want to evaluate the campaign elements to decide what worked well and should be repeated, what could be improved, and what elements should be "dropped" next time around. Imagine a countywide effort to reduce smoking around children in cars. A pilot is carried out the first year to help determine what elements of the campaign should be used when it is rolled out countywide in year two. The pilot includes a packet of materials sent home with children from the elementary schools and contains a secondhand tobacco smoke information card, a plug to replace the cigarette lighter, a smoke-free pledge card, and an air freshener with the campaign's slogan, "Please Smoke Outside." Follow-up surveys with parents will then measure changes in parents' levels of smoking around their child in the car as well as their ratings on which of the materials in the packet they noticed, used, and said were influential. Imagine further that the results indicated that some of the parents thought the air freshener would reduce the harmful effects of the smoke, so they didn't change their habits. This finding, of course, would then lead the county (primary audience for this measurement) to eliminate the $1.50 item when the campaign was rolled out countywide.

To get support for continued funding: Often the purpose of an evaluation is to persuade funders to reinvest in the project to sustain it into the future. As you can imagine, key to the success of this endeavor will be identifying criteria the funders will use to make their decisions and then creating an evaluation plan that includes measures to provide this information. Consider the Road Crew case in Wisconsin, mentioned in Chapter 9, in which a service using limousines and other luxury vehicles picks up people at their home, business, or hotel; takes them to the bars of their choice; and returns them home at the end of the evening—all for about $15 to $20 an evening. A key statistic that funders of the program (the primary audience for this measurement) were interested in was a cost-benefit analysis, and the program's evaluation methodology provided just that. You may recall that it showed an estimated cost of $6,400 to avoid a crash through Road Crew, compared with $231,000, the estimated costs incurred from an alcohol-related crash.

To help determine resource allocation: Management may also, or instead, want to use an evaluation effort to help decide how resources should be allocated in the future. In King County, Washington, for example, the Department of Natural Resources and Parks wanted an evaluation survey to help decide which of some 30 community outreach efforts should receive more funding and which, perhaps, should be pulled back. This objective led to a plan to measure household behaviors that each of these 30 programs sought to influence (e.g., leave grass clippings on the lawn). The programs with the greatest potential market opportunity for growth were then considered first for increased support, with market opportunity being determined by the percentage of households doing the behavior sometimes but not on a regular basis (the action stage of change) or not doing the behavior at all but considering doing it (the contemplation stage of change).

To decide if course corrections are needed: This purpose will lead to a monitoring effort, measuring sometime after an effort launches but before completion, to determine whether goals are likely to be met based on how the market is responding.

Example: Pedestrian Flags

In 2007, the City of Kirkland in Washington State was interested in knowing the difference their 12-year PedFlag program was making. In 1995, in an effort to increase the visibility of pedestrians in crosswalks, they had installed pole holders with orange flags for pedestrians to carry when crossing streets in 37 locations around the city (see Figure 15.1). City officials estimated that about 5% of pedestrians used the flags, but no formal measure had confirmed this. They were interested in knowing what they could do to increase usage to a desired level of 40% by 2011. Observation research of more than 3,000 pedestrians over a 20-day period estimated usage at 11%, and barriers research with those not using the flags provided inspirational feedback. Many did not know what the orange flag was for, thinking it either was intended to alert drivers to a pedestrian crosswalk or signaled a construction zone—*a product problem.* Others noted that often there were no flags on their side of the street—*a place problem.* And the vast majority indicated they felt safe and were sure drivers could see them—*a promotion problem.* Enhancements to the program included redesigning the flags so that they had an immediate connection with pedestrian crosswalks and making them easy to grab by placing them in buckets instead of pole holders (see Figure 15.2). The number of flags at each crosswalk was increased from six to 18, and local businesses were engaged in notifying the city when they saw supplies running low. New promotional

Figure 15.1 Original PedFlags were orange and had to be inserted carefully in the pole holder.

strategies included a slogan, "Take It to Make It," and messages intended to increase perception of risk (see Figure 15.3). Five months after the enhanced strategies had been implemented, the monitoring research methodology was replicated and indicated that usage had increased by 64% (from 11% to 18%).

WHAT WILL YOU MEASURE?

What you will measure to achieve your evaluation purpose is likely to fall into one or more of five categories: *inputs, outputs, outcomes, impacts,* and *return on investment* (ROI). As you will read, required efforts and rigor vary significantly by category.

Overview of a Modified Logic Model

A logic model is a visual schematic that organizes program evaluative measures into categories that can be measured and reported using a "logical" flow, beginning with program inputs and outputs, moving on to program effects in terms of outcomes and

Figure 15.2 Enhanced PedFlags were yellow and were easy to grab and then replace in a bucket.

Figure 15.3 Campaign messages were intended to increase risk perception as well as the benefits of taking a flag.

impact, and ending with (ideally) reporting on returns on investment (see Table 15.1). The difficulty of reporting increases the further one moves to the right on the model.

Input Measures

The easiest and most straightforward measures are those itemizing resources used to develop, implement and evaluate the campaign. The most common elements include money spent and staff time allocated. In many cases there will also be additional contributions to the effort to report on, including any volunteer hours, existing materials, distribution channels utilized, and/or partner contributions. (Developing new partnerships for the effort would be noted in program outcomes.) The quantification of these resources will be especially important when determining return on investment, as they represent the amount invested.

Table 15.1 A Modified Logic Model for Reporting on Social Marketing Efforts

Inputs	Outputs	Outcomes	Impact	Return on investment
Resources allocated to the campaign or program effort	**Program activities conducted to influence audiences to perform a desired behavior**	**Audience response to outputs**	**Indicators that show levels of impact on the social issue that was the focus for the effort**	**Value of changes in behavior and the calculated rate of return on the spending associated with the effort**
• Money • Staff time • Volunteer hours • Existing materials used • Distribution channels utilized • Existing partner contributions	• Number of materials disseminated, calls made, events held, Web sites created, social media tactics employed • Reach and frequency of communications • Free media coverage • Paid media impressions and cost per impression • Implementation of program elements (e.g., whether on time, on budget)	• Changes in behavior • Numbers of related products or services "sold" • Changes in behavior intent • Changes in knowledge • Changes in beliefs • Responses to campaign elements (e.g, YouTube videos shared) • Campaign awareness • Customer satisfaction levels • New partnerships and contributions created • Policy changes	• Improvements in health • Lives saved • Injuries prevented • Water quality improved • Water supply increased • Air quality improved • Landfill reduced • Wildlife habitats protected • Animal cruelty reduced • Crimes prevented • Financial well being improved	• Cost to change one behavior • For every dollar spent, dollars saved or generated • After subtracting expenses, what is the rate of return on investment

Output/Process Measures

The next-easiest measures are those describing your campaign's outputs, sometimes referred to as process measures, which focus on quantifying your marketing activities as much as possible. They represent how you utilized program inputs and are distinct from outcome measures, those focusing on your target audience's response to these activities. Many are available in your records and databases.[10]

- *Number of materials distributed and media channels utilized:* This measure refers to the numbers of mailings, brochures, flyers, key chains, bookmarks, booklets, posters, or coupons put forth. This category also includes numbers and types of additional outreach activities, such as calls made, events held, Web sites created, and social media tactics employed. Note that this does not indicate whether posters were noticed, brochures were read, events were attended, YouTube videos were viewed—only the numbers "put out there."
- *Reach and frequency:* Reach refers to the number of different people or households exposed to a particular image or message during a specified period. Frequency is the number of times within this time frame, on average, that the target audience is exposed to the communication. It is a predictor of audience response but not an indicator of such.
- *Media coverage:* Measures of media and public relations efforts, also referred to as earned media, may include reporting on numbers of column inches in newspapers and magazines, minutes on television and radio news and special programs, and people in the audience attending a planned speaker's events. Efforts are often made to determine and report what this coverage would have cost if it had been paid for.
- *Total impressions/cost per impression:* This measurement combines information from several categories, such as reach and frequency, media exposure, and material dissemination. Typically these numbers are combined to create an estimate of the total number of people in the target audience who were exposed to campaign elements. Taking this to the next level of rigor to achieve a cost per impression, total campaign costs associated with this exposure can be divided by the estimated number of people exposed to the campaign. For example, consider a statewide campaign targeting mothers to increase children's fruit and vegetable consumption; the campaign may have collected exposure information from media buys (e.g., parenting magazines) and any additional efforts (e.g., messages on grocery bags). Let's assume they were able to estimate that 100,000 mothers were exposed to these campaign efforts and that the associated costs were $10,000. Their cost per impression would be $0.10. These statistics can then be used over time to compare the cost efficiency of varying strategies. Suppose, for example, that in a subsequent campaign, efforts reached 200,000 mothers after funds were redirected to sending messages from child care centers and preschools, thus reducing the cost per impression to $0.05.

- *Implementation of program elements:* An audit of major activities planned and implemented (or not) may shed light on campaign outputs and outcomes. Did you do everything you planned to do? Did you complete activities on time and on budget? This audit can help address the tendency many of us have to expect campaign goals to be achieved, even though we did not implement all planned activities or spend originally allocated funds in planned time frames.

Outcome Measures

Measuring outcomes is a little more rigorous, as you are now assessing customer response to your outputs, most likely involving some type of primary research surveys. Ideally, these measures were determined by the goals you established in Step 4, the specific measurable results you want your program to achieve—one or more of the following types:

- *Changes in behavior:* These may be measured and stated in terms of a change in percentage (e.g., adult binge drinking decreased from 17% to 6%), a percentage increase or decrease (e.g., seatbelt usage increased by 20%), and/or a change in numbers (e.g., 40,000 new households signed up for food waste recycling bins, increasing the total number of households participating from 60,000 to 100,000). In 2011, for example, results of a research study conducted by Michael Slater at Ohio State University regarding behavior outcomes for the U.S. federal antidrug campaign "Above the Influence" were encouraging:

  > A study of more than 3,000 students in 20 communities nationwide found that by the end of 8th grade, 12 percent of those who had not reported having seen the campaign took up marijuana use compared to only 8 percent among students who had reported familiarity with the campaign.[11]

  Slater believed the successful outcomes were due in part to the fact that the campaign appears to "tap into the desire by teenagers to be independent and self-sufficient." He cited, for example, one television ad in the campaign ending with the line "Getting messed up is just another way of leaving yourself behind."[12]
- *Changes in behavior intent:* This measure might be appropriate for campaigns with minimal exposure or when campaigns have been running for only short periods of time. It may be the most appropriate measure for campaigns targeting those in the precontemplation stage, when the social marketer's goal is to move them to contemplation and then (eventually) to the action stage.
- *Changes in knowledge:* This may include changes in awareness of important facts (e.g., five drinks at one sitting is considered binge drinking), information (e.g., an estimated 75,000 people are on waiting lists for organ transplants), or recommendations (e.g., eat five or more servings of vegetables and fruit daily for better health).

- *Changes in belief:* Typical indicators include attitudes (e.g., my vote doesn't count), opinions (e.g., native plants are not attractive), and values (e.g., tanning is worth the risk).

- *Responses to campaign elements:* Here you may be counting hits to your Web site, numbers of times a video was shared, numbers of comments on a blog, calls to an 800 number (e.g., for a booklet on natural gardening), coupon redemptions (e.g., for a bike helmet), mail or Internet orders or requests for more information (e.g., for a free consultation on home earthquake preparedness), purchases of tangible objects that have been promoted (e.g., numbers of new low-flow toilets or energy-saving lightbulbs sold compared with the numbers the previous year), or services provided (e.g., number of blood pressure checks given at a mall event).

- *Campaign awareness:* Though not necessarily an indicator of impact or success, measures of awareness of campaign elements provide some feedback on the extent to which the campaign was noticed and recalled. Measurements might include levels of unaided awareness (e.g., what you have seen or heard lately in the news about legal limits for blood alcohol levels while driving); aided awareness (e.g., what have you seen or heard lately in the news about our state's new 0.08% legal limit); or proven awareness (e.g., where you read or hear about this change in the law).

- *Customer satisfaction levels:* Customer satisfaction levels associated with service components of the campaign provide important feedback for analyzing results and for planning future efforts (e.g., ratings on levels of satisfaction with counseling at Women, Infants, and Children [WIC] program clinics).

- *Partnerships and contributions created:* Levels of participation and contributions from outside sources are significant and represent positive responses to your campaign, even though they may not be a reflection of the impact on target audience behaviors. These may include numbers of hours spent by volunteers, partners, and coalition members participating in the campaign, as well as amounts of cash and in-kind contributions received from foundations, media, and businesses.

- *Policy changes:* A legitimate campaign goal may focus on causing an important change in policies or infrastructures that will encourage and/or support behavior change. In the interest of oral health for children, for example, efforts to persuade grocery stores to remove candy and gum from checkout lanes have paid off in some communities.

Impact Measures

This measure is the most rigorous, costly, and controversial of all measurement types. In this category, you are attempting to measure the impact that the changes in behavior you achieved (e.g., more homeowners using natural fertilizers) have had on the social issue your plan is addressing (e.g., water quality). It would indeed be great to be able to report on the following types of impact measures in addition to outputs and outcomes:

- *Lives saved* (e.g., from reducing drinking and driving)
- *Diseases prevented* (e.g., from increased physical activity)

- *Injuries avoided* (e.g., from safer workplace practices)
- *Water quality improved* (e.g., from taking prescription drugs back to pharmacies)
- *Water supply increased* (e.g., from increased purchases of low-flow toilets)
- *Air quality improved* (e.g., from use of fewer leaf blowers in a community)
- *Landfill reduced* (e.g., from composting foodwaste)
- *Wildlife and habitats protected* (e.g., from decreases in littering)
- *Animal cruelty reduced* (e.g., from increases in spaying and neutering)
- *Crimes prevented* (e.g., from increases in the use of motion sensors for outdoor lighting)
- *Financial well-being improved* (e.g., from microcredit loans for farm animals)

The reality is that not only are these measures rigorous and costly to determine, but it may in fact be inappropriate and inaccurate to try to connect your campaign activities with these impacts, even though they were designed with them in mind.

Several key points can assuage you and others: First, you need to trust, or assume, that the behavior that was chosen for your campaign is one that can have an impact on the issue (e.g., that folic acid can help prevent some birth defects). Second, you may need to wait longer to measure, as there may be a lag between adopting the behavior and seeing the impact (e.g., increased physical activity to lower blood pressure levels). Finally, your methodology for measurement may need to be quite rigorous, controlling for variables that may also be contributing to the social issue (e.g., there may not be an improvement in water quality in a lake if during your campaign a new manufacturer in the area started polluting the same waters). You will need to be diligent and forthright about whether you believe you can even determine and claim this victory.

Return on Investment

Determining and reporting on return on investment (ROI) has several benefits. It can provide a solid rationale for *continued funding* for successful programs, funding that might be cut if it is perceived that the program is too costly or is a large-budget item. This will help agency directors address tough budget questions from policy makers, peers, even the media. Second, findings can help administrators *allocate resources*, providing a "disproportionate" share to programs with the highest ROI based on a rational, "apples to apples" comparison. And finally, if more and more programs calculate this, we can build and share a *database of ROIs* that will assist in evaluating programs' efficacy as well as replicating the most cost effective ones.

Most ROIs can be determined with five simple (but not necessarily easy) steps:[13]

1. *Money spent:* Determine total costs of the campaign/program, including value of staff time spent as well as direct expenses associated with research, development, implementation, and evaluation of the program. In other words, calculate total inputs.

2. *Behaviors influenced:* Estimate how many people were influenced to adopt the targeted behavior as a result of the campaign/intervention. Hopefully this was determined when conducting outcome research.

3. *Cost per behavior influenced:* This is the simpler step, completed by dividing the dollars spent by the numbers of behaviors influenced (Step 1 divided by Step 2).

4. *Benefit per behavior:* This step answers the question, "What is the economic value of this changed behavior?" This is the most challenging step for many, as it is most often stated in terms of costs avoided as a result of the behavior adoption (e.g., healthcare costs, response to injuries, landfills developed, environmental cleanup efforts). It some cases, it may be revenue generated by behavior adoption (e.g., from home energy audits conducted by a utility). The problem is that reliable data on the economic benefit of one changed behavior are not often readily available, and many are reluctant to use even reasonable estimates. This concern might be assuaged by being up front with audiences and present information as a "best estimate," explaining the rigor that was taken to create the estimates.

5. *ROI:* This takes three calculations:

    1. Number of behaviors influenced (from Step 2) *times* economic benefit per behavior (from Step 4) *equals* the gross economic benefit (#2 × #4 = gross economic benefit)

    2. The gross economic benefit *minus* the amount spent (Step 1) *equals* the net benefit

    3. The net benefit divided by the investment costs (step 1) times 100 *equals* rate of return on the investment.

Example: A Positive ROI for Smoking Cessation Programs[14]

In December 2010, the American Lung Association reported that a new study conducted by researchers at Penn State University found that "helping smokers quit not only saves lives but also offers favorable economic benefits to state." Researchers with special expertise in health economics and administration compared the costs of providing smoking cessation treatments (including the price of medications and counseling and lost tax revenue) to the savings possible if smokers quit (including savings in health care expenditures, premature death costs, and productivity losses). Their conclusion was that for every $1 spent on helping smokers quit, states would see $1.26 returned, a 26% return on investment. Some states, they noted, would see an even higher rate, with the District of Columbia receiving the highest rate at $1.94 for every dollar spent. Some of the highest rates of smoking are found among people enrolled in Medicaid, and the American Lung Association urged every state to provide all

Medicaid recipients, as well as state employees, with comprehensive, easily accessible tobacco cessation assistance.

HOW WILL YOU MEASURE?

Our third step in developing an evaluation and monitoring plan is to identify methodologies and techniques that will be used to actually measure indicators established in our first step. Chapter 5 outlined typical research methodologies available to you, a few of which are most typical for evaluation and monitoring measures. In general, audience surveys will be the primary technique used in measuring outcomes, given your focus on the actual influence you have had on your target audience in terms of behavior, knowledge, and beliefs. Records will provide information for determining inputs; outputs will rely on records as well but will also tap information on contact reports, anecdotal comments, and project progress reports. Outcome measures usually require quantitative surveys, whereas impact measures may require more scientific or technical surveys.

Quantitative surveys are needed when reliable data are key to evaluation (e.g., percentage increase in levels of physical activity) and are most commonly conducted using telephone surveys, online surveys, self-administered questionnaires, and/or in-person interviews. These may be proprietary or shared-cost studies in which several organizations have questions for similar populations. They may even rely on established surveys such as the Behavioral Risk Factor Surveillance System (BRFSS), presented in Chapter 7.

Qualitative surveys should be considered when evaluation requirements are less stringent or more subjective in nature and include methodologies such as focus groups, informal interviews, and capturing anecdotal comments. Focus groups might be appropriate for exploring with child care providers which components of the immunization tracking kits were most and least useful and why. This information might then refocus efforts for the next kit reprint. Informal interviews might be used to understand why potential consumers walked away from the low-flow toilet display, even after reading accompanying materials and hearing testimonials from volunteers. Anecdotal comments regarding a television campaign might be captured on phone calls to a sexual assault resource line.

Observation research is often more reliable than self-reported data and, when possible, the most appropriate technique. It can be used for evaluating behaviors such as wearing a life vest, washing hands before returning to work, or topping off gas tanks. It may also provide more insight for assessing skill levels and barriers than self-reported data (e.g., sorting garbage and placing it in proper containers or observing a WIC client finding her way around a farmers' market for the first time).

Scientific or technical surveys may be the only sure methodology to assess the impact of your efforts. If you are charged with reporting back on the difference your efforts made in reducing diseases, saving lives, improving water quality, and the like, you will need help designing and conducting reliable scientific surveys that not only are able to measure changes in these indicators but can also link these changes to your social marketing campaign.[15]

Control groups used in combination with quantitative and scientific or technical surveys will further ensure that results can be closely tied to your campaign and program efforts. A drug and alcohol prevention campaign might be implemented in high schools in one community but not in another similar community. Extra precautions can even be taken to ensure the similarity of the control groups by conducting surveys prior to the selection of the groups and then factoring in any important differences. Results on reported drug use in the control group of high schools are then compared with those in the other (similar) communities.

Records and databases will be very useful for several indicators, particularly those measuring responses to campaign elements and dissemination of campaign materials. This may involve keeping accurate track of number of visits to a Web site and length of time spent, numbers of calls (e.g., to a tobacco quitline), comments on Facebook (e.g., regarding tips to avoid the flu), views of a YouTube video (e.g., of a PSA persuading viewers to wear seatbelts), numbers of requests (e.g., for child care references), numbers of visits (e.g., to a teen clinic), numbers of people served (e.g., at car seat inspections), or numbers of items collected (e.g., at a needle exchange). This effort may also involve working with suppliers and partners to provide similar information from their records and databases, such as numbers of coupons redeemed (e.g., for trigger locks), tangible objects sold (e.g., compost tumblers featured in the campaign), or requests received (e.g., organ donation applications processed).

Comparative effectiveness research is a relatively new approach and is utilized primarily to inform healthcare decision making by providing evidence on the effectiveness, benefits, and potential harms of various treatment options. According to the U.S. Department of Health and Human Services, there are two ways this evidence is found. Researchers can look at all available evidence on the benefits and harms of each choice for different groups of people from existing clinical trials, clinical studies, and other research. They might also, or instead, conduct studies that generate new evidence of effectiveness or comparative effectiveness of a test, treatment, procedure, or healthcare service.[16] For social marketers, implications are similar to those of controlled experiments, where one or more interventions are evaluated based on a comparison of results.

WHEN WILL YOU MEASURE?

Earlier, we distinguished between evaluation and monitoring, referring to final assessments of efforts as *evaluation* and ongoing measurements as *monitoring*. Timing for measurement efforts is likely to happen as follows:

1. *Prior* to campaign launch, sometimes referred to as precampaign or baseline measures

2. *During* campaign implementation, thought of as tracking and monitoring surveys, and maybe one time only or over a period of years (i.e., longitudinal surveys)

3. *Postcampaign* activities, referring to measurements taken when all campaign elements are completed, providing data on short-term outcomes and long-term impact

Baseline measures are critical when campaigns have specific goals for change and future campaign efforts and funders will rely on these measures for campaign assessment. These are then compared with postcampaign results, providing a pre- and postevaluation measure. Monitoring efforts during campaigns are often conducted to provide input for changes midstream and to track changes over time. Postcampaign (final) assessments are the most typical evaluations, especially when resources and tight time frames prohibit additional efforts. A few programs will use all points in time for evaluation, most common when significant key constituent groups or funders require solid evidence of campaign outcomes.

HOW MUCH WILL IT COST?

Costs for recommended monitoring and evaluation activities will vary from *minimal* costs for those that simply involve checking records and databases or gathering anecdotal comments, to *moderate* costs for those involving citizen surveys or observation research, to potentially *significant* costs for those needing scientific or technical surveys. Ideally, decisions to fund these activities will be based on the value they will contribute to your program. If such an activity will assist you in getting support and continued funding for your program, it may be a wise investment. If it helps you refine and improve your effort going forward, payback is likely in terms of return on your investment. Once a methodology is determined based on your research purpose, you can assess these potential costs versus potential benefits.

ETHICAL CONSIDERATIONS IN EVALUATION PLANNING

Ethical considerations for monitoring and evaluation are similar to those discussed regarding research and focus mostly on the respondents surveyed for the evaluation.

One additional issue worthy of mention is the extent to which you should (or can) measure and report on unintended outcomes (consequences) as well, both positive and negative. For example, many program managers are now reporting concerns with their success in encouraging recycling. Although volumes of materials are being recycled that might otherwise have been put in landfills, managers believe the use of recyclable materials has significantly increased. Anecdotal comments such as these confirm their fears: "I don't worry about printing extra copies anymore because I'm using recycled paper and I'll put any copies not used in the recycling bin" and "I don't worry about buying small bottles of water to carry around because I can recycle them." As a result, environmentalists in some communities are now beginning to direct more of their efforts to the other two legs of their "three-legged stool": "Reduce use" and "Reuse."

CHAPTER SUMMARY

Key components of an evaluation and monitoring plan are determined by answers to the following questions:

- Why are you conducting this measurement, and who is the audience for the results?
- What will you measure?
- How will you conduct these measurements?
- When will these measurements be taken?
- How much will it cost?

Reasons *why* you are measuring will guide your research plan, as methodologies will vary according to your reason for measurement. Is it to fulfill a grant requirement? To do better the next time you conduct this same campaign? To (hopefully) get continued, even increased funding? To help you decide how to prioritize and allocate your resources going forward? Or to alert you to midcourse corrections you need to make in order to achieve goals?

What you will measure to achieve your evaluation purpose is likely to fall into one or more of five categories: inputs, outputs, outcomes, impacts, and return on investment. Input measures report on program resources expended. Output measures report on campaign activities, outcomes on target audience responses, and impacts on improvements in social conditions as a result of adoption of the targeted behavior. The final, ideal metric to report on is return on investment.

Optional techniques for *measurement* include surveys that are quantitative, qualitative, observational, or scientific/technical in nature, as well as ones that use control groups and rely on records and databases.

In this plan you will also determine *timing* for evaluations, considering opportunities to measure prior to campaign launch, during campaign implementation, and once the campaign has ended.

Finally, you will determine *costs* for your proposed efforts, which should be weighed in light of potential benefits.

RESEARCH HIGHLIGHT

Increasing Breast Cancer Screening Rates in Tokyo, Japan: Demonstrating the Benefits of Monitoring Efforts to Reach Goals (2009–2010)

Background

Breast cancer has been one of the most serious health issues in Japan, taking the lives of over 110,000 women[17] each year. One of the core reasons is low participation in breast cancer screening.

The Japanese government recommends that women over age 40 be screened for breast cancer (mammograms combined with clinical breast examinations) every two years and has promoted the message that early detection leads to a higher chance of cure. Still, compared to other developed countries, Japanese women's average breast cancer screening rates have stayed significantly low at 20% to 30%,[18] whereas rates in the U.S. and European countries are at approximately 70% to 80%.

To address this problem, the prefecture (jurisdiction) of Tokyo officially set a goal to increase its rates from 30.9%[19] (2008) to 50% (2012). On top of the awareness-building promotions, they decided to conduct a different type of intervention—a social marketing program—to create actual impact on changes in behaviors.[20]

Target Audience and Promotional Strategy

The intervention program was conducted in one city as a pilot area within the Tokyo prefecture. The target audience was women ages 50 to 59 (an age group whose breast cancer risk is highest but whose screening rates were low)[21] who resided in this city and were due to receive a screening test.

Based on the evidence-based recommendation by the U.S. Centers for Disease Control and Prevention (CDC), the promotional element of the program focused on a prompt designed to remind the target audience when they were due for screening. An additional reminder was to be sent to women who did not take action after the first one. Both prompts were directly mailed to homes from the City.

Monitoring Results and Need for Course Correction

Six months after the start of the client reminder program, interim results were monitored and showed that the initial reminder had successfully increased the city's breast cancer screening participation to over 40%. To ensure that their goal of 50% was met, however, the City decided to find opportunities to enhance effectiveness of the second reminder (prompt). A comprehensive research plan was developed and implemented to inform the team.

Methodology

As a first step, qualitative interviews were conducted to compare screening test participants with nonparticipants to understand the key factors that differentiated them. Through these interviews, the hypothesis was developed that there were different segments among the nonparticipants and that these segments had different barriers to screening, signaling a need for more targeted messages.

Final segmentation barriers grouped women based on (a) their readiness to take breast cancer screening and (b) their level of concern about breast cancer. Using this segmentation, an intervention program was placed. The research sample included 1,863 women in the city who did not have a breast cancer screening record for the past 24 months. They were first randomly split into two groups (Group 1 and Group 2) to ensure that both groups had a similar ratio of each of the developed segmentations (Subgroups A, B, and C; see Figure 15.4). As shown in Table 15.2, for Group 2, a tailored message was developed for each segment, printed, and sent via direct mail.

Figure 15.4 Participation flow.

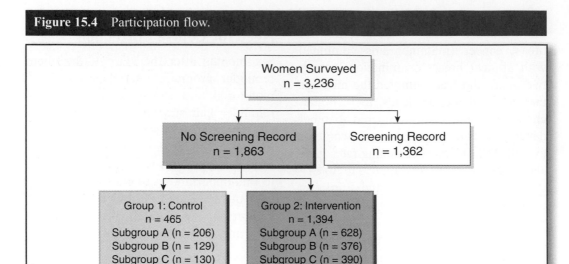

Table 15.2 Tailored Messages Sent

	Segment	Type of Message Sent	Tone of Design
Group 1	Control	Original recall reminder: "You are due for your cancer screening"	No specific design
Group 2— Subgroup A	High readiness for screening	Clear information List of where/when/how to take the screening	Checklist design ("The Breast Cancer Screening Handbook")
Group 2— Subgroup B	Low readiness for screening/bigger concern for cancer	Gain-framed message: "Detecting cancer early can lead to a higher chance of cure"	Friendly tone (Pink colors and illustrations)
Group 2— Subgroup C	Low readiness for screening/less concern for cancer	Loss-framed message: "Not detecting cancer early can increase level of fatality"	Alarming tone (Dark blue color)

To evaluate the effectiveness of this technique, women in Group 1 were sent the original recall reminder and served as a control.

Highlights of Findings

A significant increase in the screening rate was confirmed among all three intervention groups versus the control group, showing the effectiveness of prompts as well as tailored messages (see Table 15.3). The higher the readiness for screening (A > B & C), and the bigger the concern for cancer (B > C), the higher the screening rate.

With this program, the City was successfully able to increase their average

Table 15.3   Screening Rate Results[22]

	Control	Intervention
Subgroup A	7.3%	**25.5%**
Subgroup B	4.7%	**17.3%**
Subgroup C	4.6%	**13.3%**
Nonparticipants' Total Rate	5.8%	**19.9%**
City's Total Rate	45.4%	**53.0%** (+7.6 pts vs. control)

screening rates to achieve their planned goal of 50%.

The City's decision to take the time to monitor efforts "midstream," further understand the key differences between the "Doers (screening participants)" and "non-Doers (non-participants)," and then strategically take action based on their learning led to increased participation rates of 7.6 percentage points relative to the control group.

Implications

This intervention to increase breast cancer screening proved that a prompt with targeted messages based on audience barriers can significantly improve screening rates. While building awareness of the risk of cancer and the importance of early detection through PR is important, a follow-through prompt can be effective to actually inspire action. The findings from this program are now being reapplied to other cities in the Tokyo prefecture to meet the goal by 2012.

Furthermore, this case proved the importance of monitoring the social marketing effort before completion of the program in order to make meaningful midcourse corrections to ensure measureable outcomes for the activities.

CHAPTER 15 NOTES

1. Kotler, P. (1999). *Kotler on marketing: How to create, win and dominate markets* (p. 185). New York, NY: Free Press.

2. Retrieved October 26, 2010, from IPA Web site: Innovations for Poverty Action Web site: http://poverty-action.org/about/mission

3. Balane, L. (2009, March 5). Trying to quit smoking? Go to the bank. *Newsbreak.* Retrieved September 27, 2010, from http://www.abs-cbnnews.com/print/44458

4. Giné, X., Karlan, D., & Zinman, J. (2010, January). Put your money where your butt is: A commitment contract for smoking cessation. *American Economic Journal: Applied Economics, 2*(4), 213–235. Retrieved October 16, 2010, from http://www.aeaweb.org/articles.php?doi=10.1257/app.2.4.213

5. Balane, 2009, Trying to quit.

6. Giné et al., 2010, Put your money.

7. Stead, L., Perera, R., Bullen, C., Mant, D., & Lancaster, T. (2008). Nicotine replacement therapy for smoking cessation. *Cochrane Database of Systematic Reviews* (1).

8. Giné et al., 2010, Put your money.

9. Kotler, P., & Lee, N. (2006). *Marketing in the public sector: A roadmap for improved performance* (p. 266). Upper Saddle River, NJ: Wharton School.

10. Ibid., pp. 268–269.

11. The Ohio State University. (n.d.). National anti-drug campaign succeeds in lowering marijuana use, study suggests. *Research News.* Retrieved March 14, 2011, from http://research news.osu.edu/archive/aboveinfluence.htm

12. Ibid.

13. Adapted from an article that first appeared in the *Journal of Social Marketing*, Volume 1, Issue 1, Emerald Group Publishing Limited, February 2011. Nancy R. Lee, "Where's the Beef? Social Marketing in Tough Times," pp. 73–75.

14. American Lung Association. (2010, September 14). *New study finds positive return on investment for states that invest in quit smoking treatments* [Press release]. Retrieved March 15, 2011, from http://www.lungusa.org/press-room/press-releases/positive-roi-for-states.html.

15. Kotler & Lee, 2006, *Marketing in the public sector* (p. 266).

16. U.S. Department of Health and Human Services. (n.d.). *What is comparative effectiveness research.* Retrieved March 15, 2011, from http://www.effectivehealthcare.ahrq.gov/index.cfm/what-is-comparative-effectiveness-research1/

17. Center for Cancer Control and Information Services (National Cancer Center, Japan, 2009).

18. Comprehensive Survey of the Living Conditions of People on Health and Welfare (Ministry of Health, Labour and Welfare, 2008).

19. Ibid.

20. Information for this research highlight was provided by Akio Yonekura and Ishikawa Yoshiki, Cancer Scan Co., Ltd., Tokyo, Japan.

21. Tokyo Statistical Report of Breast Cancer Screening (Tokyo Metropolitan Government, 2009).

22. Cancer Scan Co., Ltd.,

Chapter 16

ESTABLISHING BUDGETS AND FINDING FUNDING

Harness all possible assets: Develop interventions and co-delivery through a coor-dinated coalition and effort on the part of the public, for profit, and NGO sectors.

—Dr. Jeff French
CEO Strategic Social Marketing

In this chapter, not only will you read about how to determine and justify budgets for your proposed plans, but you will also explore options for additional funding. You will read that we encourage you to seriously consider opportunities for corporate support for your initiatives, such as ones mentioned in the opening Marketing Highlight featuring the Heart Truth campaign. In the ethical considerations section of the chapter, we'll ask you to think back on your reaction to the following examples of corporate initiatives related to decreasing childhood obesity:

Sesame Street: A press release from the Sesame Workshop in September 2005 presented findings from a research study titled "The Effectiveness of Characters on Children's Food Choices" (the "Elmo/Broccoli Study"). It indicated that

> intake of a particular food increased if it carried a sticker of a *Sesame Street* character. For example, in the control group (no characters on either food) 78% of children participating in the study chose a chocolate bar over broccoli, whereas 22% chose the broccoli. However, when an Elmo sticker was placed on the broccoli and an unknown character was placed on the chocolate bar, 50% chose the chocolate bar and 50% chose the broccoli. Such outcomes suggest that the *Sesame Street* characters could play a strong role in increasing the appeal of healthy foods.[1]

Nickelodeon: In October 2005, Nickelodeon held its second annual Worldwide Day of Play, a part of its larger Let's Just Play initiative. The network went dark that Saturday for the first time in its 25-year history, from 12 P.M. to 3 P.M., replacing its usual program-ming with a broadcast message that encouraged kids to go outside and play. More than

60,000 kids registered online to get a number to wear to Day of Play events, and 40,000 kids attended events organized by Nickelodeon in selected American cities and abroad.[2] The annual campaign continued five years later. On Saturday, September 25, 2010, a special message was shown on the Nick channel screen: "Today is Nickelodeon's Worldwide Day of Play! We're outside playing and you should be too! So, turn off your TV, shut down your computer, put down that cell phone, and go ALL OUT! We'll be back at 3!"[3]

MARKETING HIGHLIGHT

The Heart Truth:
Mobilizing Partners to Help Spread the Word
(2002–2010)

Background

In 2000, only 34% of women in the U.S. knew that heart disease is the leading cause of death among women. Most thought that breast cancer was their greatest health threat.[4] Yet, at the time, one in three deaths in women was due to heart disease.[5] By 2009, a survey showed that awareness had increased to 54%.[6] This increase is due, perhaps in no small part, to the national social marketing campaign The Heart Truth—with the Red Dress brand playing a memorable, even "sticky" role. Although the campaign was conceived of and developed by the National Heart, Lung, and Blood Institute (NHLBI) and Ogilvy Public Relations Worldwide, partnerships formed

to support and fund nationwide exposure were key to success. This case highlights what partners were targeted, engaged, and formed—and what this provided in terms of campaign funding.[7]

Campaign Overview

The campaign *purpose* was to decrease heart disease among women, with a *focus* on increasing awareness among women that heart disease is their number one killer and influencing them to talk to their doctors, find out their risk, and take action to lower it. Using an audience segmentation tool similar to Alan Andreasen's nine factors presented in Chapter 6, the campaign team chose women ages 40 to 60 as their *target audience*, women at the time in life when their risk of heart disease begins to rise dramatically. Special emphasis was given to African-American and Hispanic women, as these groups are disproportionately affected by heart disease. The team conducted a comprehensive review of midlife women, including information on demographics; heart disease risk factors; lifestyle and psychographics; geographic and socioeconomic factors; cardiovascular health knowledge, attitudes, and behaviors; and media preferences. The resulting audience profile and subsequent formative research, including focus groups, drove the creation of campaign messages, materials, channels, and implementation strategies.

Planners were clear from their research efforts that the target audience was "asleep" relative to their personal risk and that the campaign needed to deliver a strong and urgent "wake-up call." Five specific message elements were crafted:

- Heart disease is the number one killer of women, but many women don't take their risk seriously or personally
- Heart disease can cause heart attack and death but can also lead to disability that can significantly decrease one's quality of life
- Having just one risk factor increases one's chance of getting heart disease, and the risk rises dramatically with each added risk factor
- Talk with your doctor, find out your risk, and take action today to lower it
- Americans can lower their risk by as much as 82% by leading a healthy lifestyle

Two creative elements were central to supporting the key messages. The first was an emphasis on the serious nature of the message through a strong campaign name: The Heart Truth, designed as a play on "the hard truth," provided a sense of urgency and reality about heart disease. The second element was the creation of the Red Dress as the national symbol for women and heart disease awareness, designed to emphasize that heart disease is not a "man's disease." It was paired with the tag line, "Heart Disease Doesn't Care What You Wear—It's the #1 Killer of Women." The Red Dress was introduced with print public service announcements at campaign launch in Washington, DC, in September 2002 (see Figure 16.1). The campaign's first year also included radio and television public service announcements, as well as a full suite of educational materials and a campaign Web site, www.hearttruth.gov. It was clear at this point that partners were key to the future of the campaign—critical to its growth, evolution, and sustainability.

Partnerships

As part of the campaign's planning, NHLBI held a Strategic Development Workshop involving more than 70 organizations committed to women's health. Input from the workshop was incorporated into campaign development, and many of these original groups became campaign partners. For example, three early partners were WomenHeart, the National Coalition for Women and Heart Disease (the nation's only advocacy group for women living with heart disease); NHLBI's sister government agency in the Department of Health and Human Services, the Office on Women's Health (OWH); and the American Heart Association. These organizations and others played an important role in providing supplemental funding, identifying spokespersons, and advancing the Red Dress and the overall women and heart disease movement. They also helped recruit professional organizations such as the American College of Cardiology and undertook key elements of the campaign. For example, the OWH took on the critical task of educating physicians and also engaged their regional offices in community training and public outreach.

Early on, the team developed a policy to guide the types of partners the team would seek and accept. This policy informed the campaign's initial (and continuing) efforts to identify, secure, and nurture campaign collaborators. It addressed issues such as types of companies a federally funded campaign would and would not be able to engage as partners, the defining features of desired partners, and expectations for partner usage of campaign logos, images, and messages. Three sectors were targeted: community partners, media partners, and corporate partners. Strategies to engage and recruit partners included the following:

Community Partners

Recognizing the power of national non-profit organizations with chapter and/or affiliate structures already working in the "women's health" space, the campaign team identified and sought collaborations with groups serving and representing women such as the General Federation of Women's Clubs. Other nonprofit partners included Haddassah, The Links, Inc., the National Latina Health Network, Miss Black USA Pageant and Scholarship, the Association of Black Cardiologists, Delta Phi Mu Sorority, and the Cardiology Associates Foundation. Initial efforts focused on equipping partners to incorporate campaign materials into their mission-based activities. As the campaign evolved, new programs were developed that enabled partners to embrace The Heart Truth and the Red Dress as their own, stimulating them to sponsor hundreds of local events such as health fairs, Red Dress fundraising galas, and local fashion shows coupled with educational activities. One example is the Cardiology Associates Foundation's Red Dress Style event. In 2010, the foundation hosted its fourth annual such event modeled after The Heart Truth's fashion show in New York. The event typically brings free heart health screenings and campaign educational materials to more than 500 people. In addition, the foundation brings The Heart Truth Red Dress Collection to a local shopping mall and holds cooking classes, heart health screenings, nutrition counseling, and workout demonstrations.

Media Partners

Partnerships with media corporations have contributed significantly to expanding the campaign's reach. *Woman's Day* and *Glamour*, two of the country's top-circulation women's magazines, were among the campaign's earliest and most active media partners. They helped introduce National Wear Red Day and have consistently published articles, cover stories, and columns. In 2004, the topic of women and heart disease and The Heart Truth campaign were featured in a *Time* magazine cover story, and *Prevention* did the first cover story using Red Dress imagery. Subsequent partnerships with Lifetime TV, CBSNews.com, Bravo, and others have played a significant role in generating editorial coverage and public service advertising. Beyond editorial coverage, these partners also have produced Web promotions and other types of integrated programming. In addition to engaging media corporations as partners, the campaign team implemented plans for aggressive earned media outreach for the campaign's major recurring events—National Wear Red Day and the annual Red Dress Collection fashion shows. These events have received extensive coverage, including *USA Weekend*, *Oprah*, *Today*, *People*, CNN, *Elle*, and the *Wall Street Journal*. To date, this strategy has resulted in earned media coverage totaling more than 4 billion audience impressions. National and local earned and social media outreach during other times of the year has focused on connecting the women's heart

disease issue with observances such as Mother's Day and coverage of relevant heart-related science findings and medical interventions (see Figure 16.1).

Corporate Partners

Based on the established partnership policy, the campaign team sought to engage corporate partners through aligning campaign assets, including the Red Dress brand, with sectors and companies that would find the relationship most appealing; that is, companies that counted women as major stakeholders and were involved in women's health issues.

One partnership, which some might consider a "strange bedfellow" for a government agency, involved the fashion industry. Given this industry's long-standing support of health issues as well as the shared demographic of women, the campaign team forged a partnership that was launched at Mercedes-Benz Fashion Week in New York in February 2003, with a display of designer red dresses under the tents at Bryant Park. The program has expanded to include an annual celebrity fashion show at Mercedes-Benz Fashion Week, a First Ladies Red Dress Collection (presented most recently at the George H. W. Bush Presidential Library and Museum), and dozens of local events that feature the campaign's collection of red dresses.

The expansion of the fashion industry partnership and its related promotional programming gave the campaign team a compelling selling point in engaging a growing number of corporate and media partners that recognized the potential impact of the Red Dress symbol and the significance of aligning with the issue.

Figure 16.1 Print public service announcement.[8]

Figure 16.2 Extending the brand with Swarovski Red Dress Pins.[9]

Figure 16.3 Cheerios helps spread the word.[10]

The team cultivated partnerships with major corporations, including Johnson & Johnson, Swarovski, Celestial Seasonings, and Diet Coke, which have sponsored the Red Dress Collection shows in various years, as well as a traveling road show offering free heart health screenings and educational materials (see Figure 16.2). These corporations and others—from General Mills to RadioShack to Albertsons—have helped the campaign reach millions of women where they live, work, and shop through placement of the Red Dress brand and messaging in corporate advertising and sales promotions, on in-store signage and product packages, and by sponsoring local events. For example, in 2007 and 2008, all brands of Cheerios cereal displayed the Red Dress image and information about women and heart disease (see Figure 16.3), and, in 2008, they included a cause-related marketing component to fund cholesterol screenings for low-income women.

Campaign Outcomes

In 1997, 30% of women were aware that heart disease is the leading cause of death among women. By 2003, after The Heart Truth had been operational for about a year, awareness had increased to 46% of women.[11] By 2009, it had climbed to 54% of women. Target audiences were awake.[12] In 2010, 58% of women recognized the Red Dress symbol and two thirds agreed that the Red Dress made them want to learn more about heart disease.[13] Furthermore, women started to take action to find out their risk and lower it. In 2009, 48% of women reported discussing heart disease with their doctors, up from 30% in 1997.[14] A study also showed that women who are aware of the threat of heart disease are 35% more likely to be physically active and 47% more likely to report weight loss than women who are less aware.

Partnerships played no small part in achieving these results. National and local partners in the government, media, and nonprofit sectors extended the campaign's reach, and many partners made monetary and/or "in-kind" contributions. By 2008, the campaign had about 65 national-level partners and many more at the local level. By March 2010, the campaign brand promotions on cereal, beverage, and other product packaging totaled more than 15 billion. In-kind promotional support from corporate partners was valued at more than $100 million, making it possible to execute the campaign's annual Red Dress Collection fashion shows and multiple traveling road show exhibits and health screenings. Corporate partners also contributed to the online impact, with offerings such as advertising, e-newsletters, Web banners, and blogs contributing millions of additional audience impressions.

Reflections/Lessons Learned

Almost from the beginning, The Heart Truth not only generated its own creative elements and programs, but also used its assets to help stimulate a host of other national and local educational initiatives, both large and small. The powerful appeal of the Red Dress played a substantial role in helping the campaign become a catalyst for change in women's heart disease. As the campaign grew and evolved, the team learned many lessons that served to refine future plans and directions. Best-practice social marketing relies on solid formative research, and The Heart Truth team reaped the benefits of investing in a full six months of research at the outset and further research as the campaign developed. The team learned that, once a solid strategy is formed, good judgment and discipline are needed to stay on track and resist the temptation to pursue off-course opportunities, even when they appear reasonable and attractive. The team also found that a little risk taking can sometimes be useful—the launch of the Red Dress through a partnership with the fashion industry proved to be a critical decision. Investing time and resources in developing a well-thought-out partnership strategy also was critical. However, the team learned that, over time, an ever-growing share of resources would be needed to maintain existing partners and seek new ones. Another important lesson was that engaging and retaining corporate partners meant understanding their business well and working to balance the corporate partners' needs with the needs of the campaign, a task that requires flexibility, agility, and patience.

STEP 9: ESTABLISH BUDGETS AND FIND FUNDING SOURCES

Step 9, the budgeting process, is "where the rubber hits the road." You are now ready to determine price tags for strategies and activities that you have identified in your plan, ones you believe are key to reaching behavior influence goals. Once this number is totaled, you will evaluate this potential cost by referring to anticipated benefits from targeted levels of behavior change, compare this with current funding levels, and, if needed, identify potential additional resources. This chapter will take you through each of these budgeting phases.

DETERMINING BUDGETS

In the commercial as well as nonprofit and public sectors, several approaches are often cited as possibilities to consider in determining marketing budgets.[15] The following three have the most relevance for social marketing:

The affordable method: Budgets are based on what the organization has available in the yearly budget or on what has been spent in prior years. For example, a county health department's budget for teen pregnancy prevention might be determined by state funds allocated every two years for the issue, and a local blood bank's budget for the annual blood drive might be established each year as a part of the organizational budgeting process.

The competitive-parity method: In this situation, budgets are set or considered on the basis of what others have spent for similar efforts. For example, a litter campaign budget might be established on the basis of a review of media expenses from other states that have been successful at reducing litter using mass media campaigns.

The objective-and-task method: Budgets are established by (a) reviewing specific objectives and quantifiable goals, (b) identifying the tasks that must be performed to achieve these objectives, and (c) estimating the costs associated with performing these tasks. The total is the preliminary budget.[16] For example, the budget for a utility's marketing effort for recycling might be based on estimated costs, including *staffing* of a new telephone service center for questions on what can be recycled; *plaques* for recognizing homeowner participation; and *promotional strategies*, including television ads, radio spots, statement stuffers, and flyers. These total costs are then considered in light of any projections of increased revenues or decreased costs for the utility.

The most logical of these approaches, and one consistent with our planning process, is the objective-and-task method. In this scenario, you will identify costs related to your marketing mix strategy (product, price, place, and promotion) as well as evaluation and monitoring efforts. This becomes a preliminary budget, one based on what you believe you need to do to achieve the goals established in Step 4 of your plan. (In subsequent sections of this chapter, we discuss options to consider when this preliminary budget exceeds currently available funds, including sources to explore for additional funding as well as the potential for revising strategies and/or reducing behavior change goals.)

More-detailed descriptions of typical costs associated with implementing the marketing plan follow. A brief example is included to further illustrate the nature of identifying strategies with budget implications. In this example, assume a hospital has developed a draft marketing plan to decrease the number of employees commuting to work in single-occupant vehicles (SOVs). The campaign *objective* is to influence employees to use public transportation, car pools, van pools, or walk or bike to work, with a *goal* to decrease the number of SOVs on campus by 10% (100 vehicles) over a 12-month period. The hospital is motivated by a desire to build a new wing, an effort that will require land use permits granted, in part, based on impacts on traffic congestion in the surrounding neighborhoods.

Product-related costs are most often associated with producing or purchasing any accompanying *tangible goods* and developing or enhancing associated *services* needed to support behavior change. Costs may include direct costs for providing these goods and services, or they may be indirect costs, such as staff time. Product-related cost considerations for the hospital will include the need to lease additional vans from the county's transit system, install new bike racks, and construct several additional showers for employee use if marketing goals are in fact met. Incremental service charges as a result of increased efforts might include costs for temporary personnel to provide ride share matching or to build and maintain a special online software program for ride sharing.

Price-related costs include those associated with incentives, recognition programs, and rewards. In some cases, they include net losses from sales of any goods and services associated with the marketing effort. Price-related costs for the hospital may include incentives, such as cash incentives for carpooling, reduced rates for parking spots close to the building, free bus passes, and occasional free taxi rides home promised to staff if they need to stay late. The draft plan also includes providing recognition pins for name tags, a strategy anticipated to make members of the program "feel good" as well as spread the word about the program to other employees during meetings, in the cafeteria, and the like. The hospital might also decide to reward those who have stuck with the program for a year with a free iPod in order to make their ride home on the bus or in the van more pleasant and encourage others to stick with the program.

Place-related costs involve providing new or enhanced access or delivery channels, such as telephone centers, online purchasing, extended hours, and new or improved locations. There may be costs related to distribution of any tangible goods associated with the program. In our example, there may be costs for creating additional parking spots for car pools close to the main entrance of the hospital or for staffing a booth outside the cafeteria for distributing incentives and actual ride share sign-up.

Promotion-related costs are the costs associated with developing, producing, and disseminating communications. Promotion-related costs for the hospital might include developing and producing fact sheets on benefits, posters, special brochures, and transportation fairs.

Evaluation-related costs include any planned measurement and tracking surveys. Evaluation-related costs for the hospital might include conducting a baseline and follow-up survey that measures employee awareness of financial incentives and ride share matching programs, as well as any changes in attitudes and intentions related to alternative transportation.

JUSTIFYING THE BUDGET

First, consider how those in the commercial marketing sector look at marketing budgets—it's all about the return on investment. We begin with a story from *Kotler on Marketing* that illustrates the marketing mindset, as well as a potential budget analysis:

> The story is told about a Hong Kong shoe manufacturer who wonders whether a
> market exists for his shoes on a remote South Pacific island. He sends an *order*

taker to the island who, upon cursory examination, wires back: "The people here don't wear shoes. There is no market." Not convinced, the Hong Kong shoe manufacturer sends a *salesman* to the island. This salesman wires back: "The people here don't wear shoes. There is a tremendous market."

Afraid that this salesman is being carried away by the sight of so many shoeless feet, the Hong Kong manufacturer sends a third person, this time a *marketer.* This marketing professional interviews the tribal chief and several of the natives, and finally wires back: "The people here don't wear shoes. However they have bad feet. I have shown the chief how shoes would help his people avoid foot problems. He is enthusiastic. He estimates that 70 percent of his people will buy the shoes at the price of $10 a pair. We probably can sell 5,000 pairs of shoes in the first year. Our cost of bringing the shoes to the island and setting up distribution would amount to $6 a pair. We will clear $20,000 in the first year, which, given our investment, will give us a rate of return on our investment (ROI) of 20 percent, which exceeds our normal ROI of 15 percent. This is not to mention the high value of our future earnings by entering this market. I recommend that we go ahead."[17]

As described in Chapter 15 in the section on ROI, consider the marketing budget as an investment, one that will be judged based on *outcomes* (levels of behavior change) relative to financial *inputs.* Theoretically, you want to calculate your costs for the targeted levels of behavior change and then compare them with the potential economic value of the behaviors influenced. The following examples are the types of simple, but not necessarily easy, questions you will want to answer for yourself and others:

- What is it worth in terms of medical and other societal costs for a health department to find 50 HIV-positive men in one city as a result of their testing efforts in gay bathhouses? How does that compare with the proposed marketing budget of $150,000 to support this effort? Is each "find" worth at least $3,000 ($150,000 ÷ 50)?
- What is the economic value of a 2% increase in seatbelt usage in a state? How many injuries and deaths would be avoided, and how do savings in public emergency and health care costs compare with a $250,000 budget for promotional activities proposed to achieve this increase?
- How does a budget of $100,000 for a state department of ecology to influence and support remodelers and small contractors to post their materials on an online exchange Web site compare with the value of 500 tons of materials being diverted from the landfill the first year—the goal in their marketing plan?
- If a county's campaign to increase spaying and neutering of pets is anticipated to persuade 500 more pet owners this year, compared to last year, how does a budget of $50,000 sound? Is it worth $100 for each "litter avoided"?

You may be surprised how grateful (even delighted) colleagues, funders, and management will be when you provide estimates on these returns on investment. This is only possible when you have established specific, measurable, attainable, relevant, and time sensitive (S.M.A.R.T.) goals for behavior changes, developed calculated strategies to support these goal levels, and then determined a budget based on each marketing-related expense.

FINDING SOURCES FOR ADDITIONAL FUNDING

What if the costs for the marketing activities you propose—ones you believe are needed to reach the agreed-upon goal—are more than is currently available in your agency's budget? Before reducing the goals, you have options for additional funding to explore. Each option will be illustrated with an example, and we use this as an opportunity to recall many of the cases highlighted in this text.

Government Grants and Appropriations

Federal, state, and local government agencies are the most common sources of funds and grants for social marketing efforts. Potential sources, especially for nonprofit organizations, include national, state, and local departments of health, human services, transportation, ecology, traffic safety, natural resources, fish and wildlife, parks and recreation, and public utilities.

Examples: In Chapter 6, we highlighted American Legacy's small innovative grants program, which recognizes that "One Size Never Fits All." One of the strengths of the program was its ability to scour the landscape for newer, nontraditional players and to bring a myriad of community-based organizations into the field of tobacco control. Beneficiaries of these grants ranged from prisoners in New York Sate and coal miners in West Virginia to Arab American waterpipe users in Pennsylvania and South Asian communities in California. Remember the effort to reduce deaths and injuries from small-farm tractor rollovers in the northeastern states, described in Chapter 7? Without the grants for roll-bars, it is unlikely sales would have increased 10 times in the six months after the intervention, and that the 58 farmers who reported having a close call after overturning their tractor would have "walked away" without an injury. And how much more scarce would water be for families in Jordan if USAID and Mercy Corps had not provided the revolving loan funds described in Chapter 11 that benefited more than 19,696 individuals, harvested 161,939 cubic meters of rainwater, and saved 39,945 cubic meters of treated municipal water?

Nonprofit/Foundations

There are more than 88,000 active independent corporate, community, and grant-making foundations operating in the United States alone (2010) with missions to contribute to many of the same social issues and causes addressed by social marketing efforts.[18] Kotler and Andreasen identify four major relevant groups: *family foundations*, in which funds are derived from members of a single family (e.g., Bill and Melinda Gates Foundation); *general foundations*, usually run by a professional staff awarding grants in many different fields of interest (e.g., Ford Foundation); *corporate foundations*, whose assets are derived primarily from the contributions of a for-profit business (e.g., Bank of America Foundation); and *community foundations*, set up to receive and manage contributions from a variety of sources in a local community, making grants for charitable purposes in a specific community or region.[19]

Examples: PATH's Safe Water Project, highlighted in Chapter 10, was launched with support from the Bill and Melinda Gates Foundation through its Global Development Program. In a description of their project, PATH acknowledges the importance of other partners as well:

> . . . commercial partners to refine product design, manufacturing, distribution, promotion and financing; research institutions to develop programmatic evaluation criteria, test products, and gain knowledge on safe water needs of low-income households; other nonprofit and nongovernmental organizations to find synergies in reaching target consumers, learn from their experience implementing and studying safe water initiatives, and share information derived from this project; and governments and policy-setting bodies to ensure that solutions are useful and sustainable in their constituent communities.[20]

And consider as well how the government in Maldives relied on The Promise Foundation to help fund an effort to provide counseling to support youth employment (see Chapter 4). You may recall that a program evaluation determined that the counseling interventions were key to reducing negative career beliefs and barriers to career development.

Advertising and Media Partners

Advertising agencies often provide pro bono services to support social causes, with contributions ranging from consulting on media buying and creative strategies to actually developing and producing advertising campaigns. Several factors motivate their choices, including opportunities to contribute to issues in the community, give their junior staff more experience, have more freedom to call the shots in developing creative strategies, and make new and important business contacts.[21]

The Ad Council, formed in 1942 as the War Ad Council to support efforts related to World War II, has played a significant role in producing, distributing, promoting, and evaluating public service communication programs. Familiar campaigns include Smokey Bear's "Only You Can Prevent Forest Fires," "Friends Don't Let Friends Drive Drunk," and McGruff the Crime Dog's "Take a Bite Out of Crime." Each year the council supports approximately 40 campaigns to enhance health, safety, and community involvement; strengthen families; and protect the environment, chosen from several hundred requests from nonprofit organizations and public sector agencies. Factors used for selection include criteria that the campaign must be noncommercial, nondenominational, and non-political in nature. It also needs to be perceived as an important issue and national in scope. When a proposal is selected, the council then organizes hundreds of professional volunteers from top advertising agencies, corporations, and the media to contribute to the campaign.[22] As you will read in Chapter 17, in 2010 the Ad Council supported First Lady Michelle Obama's Let's Move! initiative with several complementary campaigns to influence healthy eating and physical activity.

Television and radio stations are often approached to provide free or discounted ("two for one") airtime for campaigns with good causes. Even more valuable, they may be interested in having their sales force find corporate sponsors for campaigns, who then pay for media placement (e.g., for a campaign promoting bicycling, a media partnership between an outdoor equipment retailer, a health care organization, and a local television station). In this win-win-win situation, the social marketing campaign gets increased frequency and guaranteed placement of ads on programs that appeal to their target audience; the local corporations get to "do good" and "look good" in the community; and the television or radio stations get paid, which might not occur with public service advertising. The Heart Truth case example at the beginning of this chapter noted several media partners, including CBS News and *Women's Day* and *Glamour* magazines.

Coalitions and Other Partnerships

Many social marketing campaigns have been successful, at least in part, because of the resources and assistance gained from participating in coalitions and other similar partnerships. Coalition members may be able to pool resources to implement larger-scale campaigns. Networks of individual coalition members can provide invaluable distribution channels for campaign programs and materials (e.g., the local department of license office airs a traffic safety video in the lobby, where a captive audience waits for their number to be called).

Example: As evidenced by a tally of the cases highlighted in this text, support from coalitions and public/private/nonprofit partnerships appears to be the norm, illustrated by the following examples, to name a few:

- Chapter 4: The Green Network included a network of organizations (a social marketing nongovernmental organization [NGO], community clinics, pharmacists) to increase access to family planning services.
- Chapter 5: Persuading parents in Rajasthan, India, to administer the ORS-zinc solution for diarrhea when appropriate relied on efforts of NGOs, governmental agencies, retail outlets, and healthcare providers.

- Chapter 7: Influencing fisheries to change their practices involved consumers, non-profit organizations, restaurants, food suppliers, and retail stores that were organized and influenced by Monterey Bay Aquarium's Seafood Watch program.
- Chapter 9: Consider how much New York City relied on retailers such as nail salons and tattoo parlors to distribute their branded condoms.
- Chapter 11: Officials in Ireland recognized that their efforts to decrease use of plastic bags and increase use of reusable ones by imposing a 15-Eurocent tax would be fraught with difficulty without cooperation from the retail industry, revenue commissioners, and local authorities.
- Chapter 13: Persuading 30,000 of the 50,000 unbanked households in San Francisco to open a bank account relied on 75% of the banks and credit unions in the city to offer the branded Bank on San Francisco accounts.

Corporations

As Kotler and Lee describe in their book *Corporate Social Responsibility: Doing the Most Good for Your Company and Your Cause*, three trends in corporate giving are noteworthy, especially for social marketers: First, the good news is that giving is on an upward trend, with a report from Giving USA indicating that giving by for-profit corporations has risen from an estimated $9.6 billion in 1999 to $14.17 billion in 2009.[23] Second, there is an increased shift to strategic versus obligatory giving, with a desire, even expectation, for "doing well and doing good." More and more corporations are picking a few strategic areas of focus that fit their corporate values. They are selecting initiatives that support their business goals, choosing issues more closely related to their core products, and more interested in opportunities to meet marketing objectives, such as increased market share, better market penetration, or building a desired brand identity.[24] And this brings us to the third relevant trend. Many corporations are discovering (and deciding) that supporting social marketing initiatives and campaigns can be one of the most beneficial of all corporate social initiatives, especially for supporting their marketing efforts. In an article titled "Best of Breed" in the *Stanford Innovation Review* in the spring of 2004, Kotler and Lee described why corporations find this so attractive:

- It can support brand positioning (e.g., Subway partnering with the American Heart Association to influence healthy eating)
- It can create brand preference (e.g., Pampers' support of the SIDS Foundation to influence parents and caregivers to put infants to sleep on their back)
- It can build traffic in stores (e.g., Best Buy's recycling events at store locations)
- It can increase sales (e.g., Mustang Survival's partnership with Seattle Children's Hospital and Regional Medical Center to help the company capture a share of the toddler market)
- It can have a real impact on social change, and consumers make the connection (e.g., 7-Eleven's participation in the Don't Mess With Texas litter prevention campaign that has helped decrease litter by more than 50% in that state).[25]

Corporations have several ways to support your campaigns, as described in the following sections: cash grants and contributions, cause-related marketing campaigns, in-kind contributions, and use of their distribution channels.

Cash Grants and Contributions

Cash contributions from corporations (as opposed to their foundations) are awarded for a variety of purposes, including sponsorship mentions in communications, potential for building traffic at retail or Internet sites, and opportunities for visibility with key constituent groups.

Example: Child Care Resources is a nonprofit organization in Washington State providing information and referral assistance to families seeking child care, training and assistance for child care providers, and consulting and advocacy for quality child care. In the mid 1990s, Safeco, an insurance company based in Seattle, provided a generous grant to Child Care Resources to strengthen the ability of child care providers to promote and track immunizations

Figure 16.4   Door hanger used at child care centers to remind parents to check immunization status.[26]

of children in their care. Formative research with child care providers provided input for developing training and a kit of materials that included immunization tracking forms, posters, flyers, stickers, door hangers, and brochures for parents, with refrigerator magnets and immunization schedules (see Figure 16.4). In partnership with numerous local and state health agencies, Child Care Resources developed and disseminated more than 3,000 kits to child care providers in the first year of the grant. An evaluation survey among approximately 300 of the providers indicated that 94% felt the materials helped them encourage parents to keep their children's immunizations up-to-date. The grant was extended for a second year, and trainings and kit distribution were taken statewide under the direction of the Washington State Child Care Resource and Referral Network.

Cause-Related Marketing

Cause-related marketing (CRM) is an increasingly popular strategy with a win-win-win proposition. In the typical scenario, a percentage of sales of a company's product is devoted to a nonprofit organization (e.g., at one time a percentage of sales of Evian bottled water was contributed to the World Wildlife Fund). The strategy is based on the premise that buyers care about the civic virtue and caring nature of companies. When market offerings are similar, buyers have been shown to patronize the firms with better civic reputations. Carefully chosen and developed programs help a *company* achieve strategic marketing objectives (e.g., sell more product or penetrate new markets) and demonstrate social responsibility, with an aim of moving beyond rational and emotional branding to "spiritual" branding. At the same time, CRM raises funds and increases exposure for a *social issue or cause* and gives *consumers* an opportunity to be involved in improving the quality of life.[27] Well-known partnerships include programs such as American Express and Charge Against Hunger, Yoplait yogurt and breast cancer, and Lysol and Keep America Beautiful. National surveys indicate that the majority of consumers would be influenced to buy, or even switch and pay more for, brands when the product supports a cause, especially when product features and quality are equal. However, if the promotion rings hollow, customers may be cynical; if the charitable contribution doesn't amount to much or the promotion doesn't run long enough, customers may be skeptical; if the company chooses a cause of less interest to their customers, it will gain little; and if the company chooses a cause and other causes feel miffed, it may lose out.

In-Kind Contributions

For some corporations, in-kind donations are even more appealing than cash contributions. Not only do they represent opportunities to offload excess products or utilize "idle" equipment such as that used for printing, they also provide opportunities to connect consumers with the company's products and to connect the product with the organization's cause. The following example illustrates this opportunity well.

Example: Drowning is the second leading cause of unintentional-injury death for children in the United States. In Washington State alone, 90 children under the age of 15 drowned from 1999 to 2003. Sadly, in too many cases, drowning deaths could have been avoided if the child had been wearing a properly fitted life jacket. Although Washington State regulations require that children 12 years and younger wear a properly sized U.S. Coast Guard–approved life jacket on any boat under 19 feet long, not all children are wearing life jackets or ones that are properly fitted. In 1992, Mustang Survival, a life vest manufacturer, made a three-year commitment to a partnership that included Children's Hospital and Regional Medical Center and other members of a drowning prevention coalition. In addition to contributing free life jackets for special events, they also provided financial support, discount coupons, bulk buy programs, and in-kind printing (see Figure 16.5). Financial support was used to develop a parent's guide, children's activity booklet, and interactive display. Their support of the program continues more than 15 years later.

Use of Distribution Channels

Companies can provide tremendous visibility and support for your efforts by giving you space in their stores for such things as car seat safety checks (at car dealers), flu shots (at grocery stores), energy saving events like Rock the Bulb (at hardware stores, as highlighted in Chapter 13), and pet adoptions (at pet stores). In some cases, this can have a profound impact, as it did in the following example.

Figure 16.5 Coupon used to promote life vest use.[28]

Example: The EPA estimates that in 2007, citizens in the United States will generate 2 million tons of e-waste, or "tech trash"—old or obsolete cellular phones, rechargeable batteries, ink jet cartridges, televisions, computer components, monitors, appliances, and so on. The good news is that many of these materials can be conveniently recycled, even refurbished, at Best Buy stores, the largest U.S. retailer of consumer electronics. Just inside the door of every U.S. Best Buy store, you can find free recycling drop-off kiosks for cell phones, rechargeable batteries, and ink jet cartridges. As touted on their Web site, "No matter where you bought it, we'll recycle it . . . And we'll take just about anything electronic, including TVs, DVD players, computer monitors, audio and video cables, cell phones, and more." In partnership with the EPA, Best Buy also hosts and/or sponsors a series of weekend recycling events at its store parking lots across the United States. From 20 million pounds in 2006 to 120 million in 2009, Best Buy announced in 2010 that it is targeting 1 billion pounds in the next few years.[29]

APPEALING TO FUNDERS

The same principles we have outlined for influencing target audiences are applicable for influencing potential funders as well. They could be viewed simply as another type of target audience, and the same steps and customer orientation are called for:

- Begin by identifying and prioritizing segments (potential funders) who represent the greatest opportunities for funding your program. Several criteria may guide this prioritization, with a special focus on organizations where you have existing contacts and relationships, common areas of focus and concern, and similar target audiences, publics, or constituent groups.
- Formulate clear, specific potential requests.
- Spend time deepening your understanding of the funders' wants, needs, and perspectives. What are potential benefits of and concerns with your proposal? Who is the competition, and what advantages and disadvantages do you have?
- On the basis of this information, refine and finalize your specific request. Your preliminary inquiries, for example, may reveal that a large request (risking the

"door in your face") may in fact make it more likely that you will receive funding for a smaller one.

- Develop a strategy using all elements of the marketing mix, a proposal that (a) articulates clear value for the funder (what's in it for them) and benefits to the cause (target audiences), (b) addresses concerns and barriers, (c) ensures a smooth and responsible administrative process, and (d) provides assurance of measurable outcomes.

It is helpful to keep in mind that corporations evaluating an opportunity to support a social marketing effort are likely to consider the following questions:

- Is there a natural bond between the cause and the company?
- Is it an issue that our target audience cares about?
- Is there an opportunity for staff to be involved?
- Can we own or at least dominate the position of corporate partner?
- Can we stick with the program for at least two to three years?
- Is there synergy with our current distribution channels?
- Does it provide enhanced media opportunities?
- Can we develop an optimal donation model that provides sales incentives at an economically feasible per-unit contribution?
- Will we be able to absolutely measure our return on investment?

And, to underscore additional points made in the "Best of Breed" article in the *Stanford Innovation Review*, these partnerships must "pass the smell test." It is crucial that the social issue being addressed avoids any appearance of inauthenticity or hidden agendas. A tobacco company promoting parent-teen dialogue on the dangers of smoking, for an example, is likely to be viewed as inauthentic. Cynical consumers know the tobacco industry counts on early uptake among the youth population for a sustainable customer base. If there is the potential for even the appearance of a conflict of interest, companies should choose a different issue and social marketers should chose a different partner.

REVISING YOUR PLAN

What happens if funding levels are still inadequate to implement the desired plan? In this familiar scenario, you have several options to make ends meet:

Develop campaign phases: Spread costs out over a longer period of time, allowing for more time to raise funds or to use future budget allocations. Options for phasing could include targeting only one or a few target audiences the first year; launching the campaign in fewer geographic markets; focusing on only one or a few communication objectives (e.g., using the first year for awareness building); or implementing some strategies the first year and others in subsequent years (e.g., waiting until the second year to build the demonstration garden using recyclable materials).

Strategically reduce costs: Options might include *eliminating strategies and tactics* with questionable potential impact; *choosing less expensive options* for noncritical executional strategies (e.g., using black and white instead of four colors for brochures or lower-grade paper); and where feasible, *bringing some of the tasks in-house* (e.g., the development and dissemination of news releases and organization of special events).

Adjust goals: Perhaps the most important consideration is the potential need to return to Step 4 and adjust your goals. Clearly, in situations where you have chosen to spread campaign costs over a longer period of time, goals will need to be changed to reflect new time frames. In other situations where time frames cannot be adjusted and additional funding sources have been explored, and you have decided you need to eliminate one or more key strategies (e.g., television may not be an option, even though it was identified as key to reach and frequency objectives), you will then need to adjust the goal (e.g., reach 50% of the target audience instead of the 75% that television was anticipated to support). You are encouraged to then return to your managers, colleagues, and team members with frank discussions about the need to adjust preliminary goals so that "promises" are honest and realistic.

ETHICAL CONSIDERATIONS WHEN ESTABLISHING FUNDING

Ethical considerations regarding budgets and funding are probably familiar and include issues of responsible fiscal management, reporting, and soliciting of funds. Consider, though, the following additional dilemmas that could face a social marketer: What if a major tobacco company wanted to provide funding for television spots for youth tobacco prevention but didn't require the company's name to be placed in the ad? Is that okay with you? What if a major lumber and paper manufacturer wanted to provide funding for a campaign promoting recyclable materials and wanted the name of the company associated with the campaign? Any concerns? What if a fast-food chain wanted to be listed as a sponsor of magazine ads featuring the food guide pyramid? Is it okay to accept pro bono work from an advertising agency for a counter-alcohol campaign if the parent company has clients in the alcohol industry? In the opening of this chapter, you read about two corporate initiatives to help decrease childhood obesity (the Sesame Street and Nickelodeon projects). What did you think? Did you think they were well intended and a smart move on their part? Or were you put off in some way?

CHAPTER SUMMARY

Preliminary budgets are best determined by using the *objective-and-task method*, in which budgets are established by (a) reviewing specific objectives, (b) identifying the tasks that must be performed to achieve these objectives, and (c) estimating the costs associated with performing these tasks. These costs will include those related to developing and implementing elements of the marketing mix, as well as funds needed to support the evaluation and monitoring plan. And to justify them, you are encouraged to quantify the intended outcomes you are targeting for these outputs to produce.

When preliminary budgets exceed current funding, several major sources for additional funds are identified: government grants and appropriations, nonprofit organizations and foundations, advertising and media partners, coalitions and other partnerships, and corporations. You are also encouraged to consider more than cash grants and contributions from corporations, with cause-related marketing initiatives, in-kind contributions, and the use of their distribution channels being excellent opportunities as well.

If proposed budgets exceed funding sources even after exploring additional sources, you can consider creating campaign phases, strategically reducing costs, and/or adjusting the campaign goals you established in Step 7.

CHAPTER 16 NOTES

1. Sesame Workshop. (2005, September 20). *If Elmo eats broccoli, will kids eat it too? Atkins Foundation grant to fund further research* [Press release]. Retrieved July 26, 2011, from http://archive.sesameworkshop.org/aboutus/inside_press.php?contentId=15092302

2. Berry, L. L., Seiders, K., & Hergenroeder, A. (2006). Regaining the health of a nation: What business can do about obesity. *Organizational Dynamics, 35*(4), 341–356.

3. Wikipedia. (n.d.). *Worldwide Day of Play.* Retrieved March 16, 2011, from http://en.wikipedia.org/wiki/Worldwide_Day_of_Play

4. Christian, A. H., Rosamond, W., White, A., & Mosca, L. (2007). Nine-year trends and racial ethnic disparities in women's awareness of heart disease and stroke: An American Heart Association national study. *Journal of Women's Health, 16,* 68–81.

5. United States Department of Health and Human Services, National Institutes of Health, National Heart, Lung, and Blood Institute. (2007). *Key messages for The Heart Truth, February 2007.* Bethesda, MD: Unpublished report.

6. Mosca, L., Mochari-Greenberger, H., Dolor, R. J., Newby, L. K., & Robb, K. J. (2010, February 10). Twelve-year follow-up of American women's awareness of cardiovascular disease risk and barriers to heart health. *Circulation: Cardiovascular Quality and Outcomes, 3,* 120–127.

7. This case study was adapted, with updates, from a special section on The Heart Truth published in *Social Marketing Quarterly, XIV*(3), Fall 2008.

8. The Heart Truth.

9. Ibid.

10. Ibid.

11. Christian, et al., 2007, Nine-year trends.

12. Mosca, et al., 2010, Twelve-year follow-up.

13. Ibid.

14. Ibid.

15. Kotler, P., & Armstrong, G. (2001). *Principles of marketing* (pp. 528–529). Upper Saddle River, NJ: Prentice Hall.

16. Ibid., p. 529.

17. Kotler, P. (1999). *Kotler on marketing* (p. 31). New York, NY: Free Press.

18. Urban Institute, National Center for Charitable Statistics. (n.d.). *Number of private foundations in the United States, 2010.* Retrieved March 17, 2011, from http://nccsdataweb.urban.org/PubApps/profileDrillDown.php?state=US&rpt=PF

19. Kotler, P., & Andreasen, A. (1991). *Strategic marketing for nonprofit organizations* (p. 285). Englewood Cliffs, NJ: Prentice Hall.

20. PATH's Safe Water Project. (n.d.). *Partnerships for commercialization of household water treatment.* Retrieved March 16, 2011, from http://www.path.org/files/TS_safe_water_fs.pdf

21. Pringle, H., & Thompson, M. (1999). *Brand spirit: How cause-related marketing builds brands.* New York, NY: John Wiley; Earle, R. (2000). *The art of cause marketing.* Lincolnwood, IL: NTC Business Books.

22. Retrieved October 10, 2001, from Ad Council Web site: www.adcouncil.org & www.adcouncil.org/body_about.html

23. Retrieved March 17, 2011, from Giving USA Foundation Web site: http://www.givingusareports.org/

24. Kotler, P., & Lee, N. (2006). *Corporate social responsibility: Doing the most good for your company and your cause* (p. 9). New York, NY: John Wiley.

25. Ibid., pp. 119–129.

26. Materials developed by Child Care Resources and Safeco Insurance.

27. Pringle & Thompson, 1999, *Brand spirit*; Earle, 2000, *The art of cause marketing*.

28. Reprinted with permission of Children's Hospital and Regional Medical Center, Seattle, Washington.

29. Granger, T. (2010, April 27). *Best Buy targets 1 billion pounds of electronics recycling.* Retrieved July 26, 2011, from http://earth911.com/news/2010/04/27/best-buy-targets-1-billion-pounds-of-electronics-recycling/

Chapter 17

CREATING AN IMPLEMENTATION PLAN AND SUSTAINING BEHAVIOR

Numerous behaviors that support sustainability are susceptible to the most human of traits: forgetting. Fortunately, prompts can be very effective in reminding us to perform these activities.[1]

—Dr. Doug McKenzie-Mohr
McKenzie-Mohr & Associates Inc.

We envision a world where people are healthy and safe, financially secure, involved in protecting the environment, and contributing to their communities. We have written this book for the thousands of current and future practitioners on the front lines responsible for influencing public behaviors that will help create this reality.

After reading the prior 16 chapters, we hope you see social marketing as a process with a target audience focus and an intervention toolbox (4Ps) with more than messages, but tools you'll need to get the job done. You'll read in this final chapter about the importance of creating a detailed implementation plan to ensure accountability as well as sustainability. We hope you appreciate the rigor involved to achieve success and that you picked up on principles that will help ensure your desired outcomes—ones worth repeating and reviewing:

- Take advantage of prior and existing successful campaigns
- Start with target audiences most ready for action
- Promote single, simple, doable behaviors, ones that will have the most impact, greatest target audience willingness, and largest market opportunity
- Identify and remove barriers to behavior change
- Bring real benefits to the present
- Highlight costs of competing behaviors

- Search for and include tangible goods and services in your campaign, ones that will help your target audience perform the behavior
- Consider nonmonetary incentives in the form of recognition and appreciation
- Make access easy
- When appropriate, have a little fun with your messages
- Use media channels at the point of decision making
- Try for social and entertainment media channels
- Get commitments and pledges
- Use prompts for sustainability
- Create plans for social diffusion
- Track results and make adjustments

And we think this familiar quote from Margaret Mead introduces our final Marketing Highlight well: "Never doubt that a small group of thoughtful, committed citizens can change the world; indeed, it is the only thing that ever has."

MARKETING HIGHLIGHT

"Let's Move!"
First Lady Michelle Obama's Initiative to Reduce Childhood Obesity (2010)

The Problem

Childhood obesity in America is a national health crisis, with nearly one in every three children (31%) ages 2 to 19 overweight or obese.[2] Some even believe that the current generation is on track to have a shorter lifespan than their parents.[3] How did this happen? Many point to changes in lifestyle. Thirty years ago, kids were more likely to walk to school, participate regularly in gym classes, and play outside for hours after school before dinner. More meals were home cooked with reasonable portion sizes, and a vegetable on the plate was the norm. Eating fast food and snacking between meals was only an occasional treat, if not rare.[4] Children today lead a different lifestyle. Walking to school has been replaced by cars and buses. Physical education classes during school hours have been cut, and after-school play is now more defined by video games and the Internet. Working families are eating fewer home-cooked meals, snacking is the norm rather than the exception, and portion sizes have exploded.[5]

First Lady Michelle Obama wants to reverse these lifestyle trends and end this epidemic. In February 2010, she announced the launch of the Let's Move! initiative, one with a goal that children born today will reach adulthood at a healthy weight. She pointed to four areas of strategic focus:[6]

1. Empowering parents and caregivers to make healthy choices

2. Providing healthier foods at schools

3. Increasing access to healthy, affordable foods

4. Increasing physical activity

This case highlight presents major strategic elements of the initiative as it was launched in 2010, following our social marketing planning model.

Target Audiences and Desired Behaviors

Influencing these changes in lifestyle downstream will take "a village." On the Let's Move! Web site, six audiences in addition to children are identified, with five "simple steps" recommended for each audience segment (see Table 17.1). Each step, especially for the midstream and upstream audiences, is then elaborated upon in more depth with more specific action items (*behaviors*).

4Ps Strategies

A few of the major 4Ps strategies highlighted on the Let's Move! Web site in 2010, as well as in press releases, special reports, and news articles, include:

Product strategy examples include initiatives to promote *school kitchen gardens* and to get specially designed, child-sized *salad bars* into school cafeterias across the U.S.; a pledge from *major food and beverage manufacturers to reduce calories* in products by 1.5 trillion by the end of 2015 by lowering the calorie content of current products and reducing portion sizes of existing single-serving products; *free cookware kits* for chefs to use for cooking demonstrations at schools, donated by major cookware makers; and contests to create new healthier *recipes* developed by school nutrition professionals, chefs, and community members.

Price strategy examples included incentives of *prizes* worth $12,000 for winning recipes, and *grants* for projects to improve access to healthier foods.

Place strategy examples include influencing and equipping *grocery stores* and other *small businesses* and *retailers* to sell healthy food in communities that currently lack these choices at convenient locations.

Promotional strategy examples in addition to their *Web site* www.letsmove.gov include a Facebook page where success stories, videos, and photos can be shared; a "Walk to School Month" *event*, one in which schoolchildren in over 3,500 communities from all 50 states, the District of Columbia, and Puerto Rico participated; a variety of *public service announcements* developed by the Ad Council featuring Disney's well-known Beauty and the Beast characters encouraging kids to "discover the magic and beauty of healthy living"; Michelle Obama with Major League Baseball players encouraging parents to eat healthfully so "they can play an hour a day, every day";[7] *improved nutrition labels* on food packages, including larger font sizes; and a special *campaign logo and name* for each of the initiatives.

Table 17.1   Target Audiences and Desired Behaviors Downstream, Midstream, and Upstream

Target Audiences	Desired Behaviors
DOWNSTREAM	
• Kids	• Move every day. • Try a new fruit or veggie. • Drink lots of water. • Do jumping jacks to break up TV time. • Help make dinner.
MIDSTREAM	
• Parents	• Keep fresh fruit in a bowl within your child's reach to grab as a quick snack. • Take a walk with your family after dinner. • Plan a menu for the week. Get children involved in planning and cooking. • Turn off the TV during meals and share some family time. • Talk to the principal about organizing a school health team.
• Schools	• Create a school health advisory council. • Join the HealthierUS School Challenge. • Set a good example. Make your school a healthy workplace. • Incorporate nutrition education and physical education into the school day. • Plant a garden.
• Health Care Providers	• Join Let's Move! • Make BMI screening a standard part of your care. • Talk to your patients about breastfeeding and first foods. • Prescribe activity and healthy habits. • Be a leader in your community.
UPSTREAM	
• Mayors & Local Officials	• Become a Let's Move! city or town. • Help parents make healthy family choices. • Improve the health of schools. • Increase activity opportunities. • Make healthy food affordable and accessible.
• Community Leaders	• Help parents make healthy choices. • Advocate healthier schools. • Help children get physical activity. • Promote affordable, accessible food. • Start a community garden.
• Chefs	• Join Chefs Move to Schools. • Take on the HealthierUS School Challenge. • Learn about child nutrition programs. • Prep for the classroom. • Find recipes for success.

Partnerships and Measuring Outcomes

Several partnerships formed are critical for success, without which goals for the initiative are unlikely to be met, and there would be few, if any, systems for account-ability in place. Partnership for a Healthier America, an independent, nonpartisan organization, will focus on developing a strong network of members across the business, academic, and nonprofit sectors. The First Lady will serve as honorary chair of the partnership. In addition to convening and encouraging members' commitments, the organization will track and report performance of members to hold them accountable.[8] The Healthy Weight Commitment Foundation (HWCF) signed the agreement mentioned earlier, in which major food and beverage manufac-turers agreed to alter business practices. Under the terms of the agreement, the HWCF will report annually to the partner-ship on the progress being made toward this pledge. The Robert Wood Johnson Foundation will support a rigorous, inde-pendent evaluation of how the HWCF's efforts in the marketplace affect calories consumed by children and adolescents. Findings will be reported publicly.[9]

Year One Accomplishments

The following are among those accom-plished by February 2011, listed on the "Let's Move! Accomplishments Factsheet" at www.letsmove.gov:

- The Healthy, Hunger-Free Kids Act, a groundbreaking piece of legisla-tion, was signed into law so all kids have healthier food in school and even more have access to a healthy lunch.

- Three of the largest food service pro-viders have committed to improving the food they provide to schools to meet recommended levels of fat, sugar, and whole grains over the next five years, and to double the fruits and vegetables they serve over the next 10 years.

- A coalition of the Fruit and Vegetable Alliance; the Food, Family and Farming Foundation; and the United Fresh Produce Association has com-mitted over the next three years to put 6,000 salad bars in schools across the country, making fresh vegetables a more accessible choice for children.

- Nearly 2,000 chefs have volunteered to help schools in their community become healthier through the Chefs Move to Schools program, which pairs professional chefs with schools to help educate kids about making healthy food choices and engages the entire school community in helping to create healthier school menus.

- Nearly 500 communities across America have signed up for Let's Move Cities and Towns. Through this program, local leaders are bring-ing Let's Move! to their communi-ties and making commitments to significant changes in support of their communities' health.

- More and more families are seeing food and beverage packages with clear calorie information on grocery store shelves through a commitment from the American Beverage Association, the

Grocery Manufacturers Association, and the Food Marketing Institute to place clear calorie information on beverage and food packaging.

- The American Academy of Pediatrics and the American Academy of Family Physicians have pledged to have 100% of their doctors screen for BMI.

- Through Let's Move Faith and Communities, faith-based and community-based organizations have committed to walk 3 million miles, complete 500,000 Presidential Active Lifestyle Awards, and host 10,000 community gardens or farmers markets.

STEP 10: COMPLETE AN IMPLEMENTATION PLAN

For some, the implementation plan *is* the marketing plan, one that will reflect all prior decisions, and is considered your final major step in the planning process. It functions as a concise working document to share and track planned efforts. It provides a mechanism to ensure you and your team do what you said you wanted to do, on time, and within budget. It provides the map that charts your course, permitting timely feedback when you have wavered or need to take corrective actions. It is not the evaluation plan, although it incorporates evaluation activities. It is also not the same as a marketing plan for an entire program or organization, as the emphasis in this book has been on developing a marketing plan for a specific social marketing campaign.

Kotler and Armstrong describe *marketing implementation* as "the process that turns marketing strategies and plans into marketing actions in order to accomplish strategic marketing objectives."[10] They further emphasize that many managers think *doing things right* (implementation) is just as important as *doing the right things* (strategy). In this model, both are viewed as critical to success.

Key components to a comprehensive implementation plan include addressing the classic action planning elements of what will be done, by whom, when, and for how much.

- What will we do? Key activities necessary to execute strategies identified in the marketing mix and the evaluation plan are captured in this document. Many were reviewed and then confirmed in the budgeting process activity and will be incorporated in this section.
- Who will be responsible? For each of these major efforts, you will identify key individuals and/or organizations responsible for program implementation. In social marketing programs, typical key players include staff (e.g., program coordinators), partners (e.g., coalition members or other agencies), sponsors (e.g., a retail business or the media), suppliers (e.g., manufacturers), vendors (e.g., an advertising agency), consultants (e.g., for evaluation efforts), and other internal and external publics, such as volunteers, citizens, and lawmakers.

- When will it be done? Time frames are included for each major activity, typically noting expected start and finish dates.
- How much will it cost? Expenses identified in the budgeting process are then paired with associated activities.

Most commonly, these plans represent a minimum of one year of activities and, ideally, two or three years. In terms of format, options range from simple plans included in executive summaries of the marketing plan to complex ones developed using sophisticated software programs. Box 17.1 presents a summary of one section of a social marketing plan developed in 2006 for the Mental Health Transformation Grant Social Marketing Initiative in Washington State, a section focusing on influencing policy makers.

Box 17.1
A Social Marketing Plan for Eliminating the Mental Health Stigma: Special Section for Influencing Policymakers

1.0 Background, Purpose, and Focus

The purpose of this initiative is to reduce the stigma surrounding mental illness and the barriers it creates in the work setting, at home, within the health care system, and in the community. The focus is on increasing the understanding that people with mental illness can and do recover and live fulfilling and productive lives.

2.0 Situation Analysis

2.1 SWOT Analysis:

Strengths: Statewide transformation initiative with executive support, multiagency workgroup commitment, and marketing task group with strong consumer participation; recent legislative action on mental health issues, including: PACT teams, parity, and increased funding for children's mental health

Weaknesses: Limited budget, unrealistic expectations for a communications solution, and lack of consensus on the use of social marketing

Opportunities: Grant funding, governor endorsement, emerging coalitions, provider interest and support, and political curiosity

Threats: Competing projects/staff time limitations, constituent expectation that "campaign" can be all things to all people, and skepticism that marketing is a legitimate method for social change

2.2 This initiative will be built around the framework set forth by Patrick Corrigan, professor of psychiatry at Northwestern University, whose research suggests a target-specific stigma change model, identifying and influencing groups who have the power to change stigma and support adoption of the recovery model. Policymakers, the focus of this section of the plan, were identified as one of three priority audiences and will be addressed in Year 3 of the social marketing initiative. The full marketing plan includes sections targeting consumers and providers.

3.0 Target Audience Profile

- State legislators who are responsible for state-level policies and funding
- State agency officials who set reimbursement rules for the types of services that can be covered
- Local elected officials who are responsible for local policies and allocating funds to regional service providers

4.0 Marketing Objectives and Goals

4.1 We want this plan to influence policymakers to

- Pass legislation that enables "recovery" and "mental health transformation."
- Reallocate existing funds to put more resources into recovery, resulting in a decreased need for crisis intervention.
- Interpret regulations affecting people with mental illness using "recovery" lens.
- Ensure adequate funding to support recovery-oriented mental health services, including consumer participation.
- Support the provision of employment opportunities for consumers.
- Eliminate stigmatizing language and views and adopt a language and process that promotes recovery.

4.2 Goals

- Conduct a minimum of four speaking engagements with local elected officials.
- Conduct a minimum of six speaking engagements with state legislators.
- Conduct a minimum of five speaking engagements with state agency officials.

5.0 Target Audience Barriers, Benefits, and the Competition

5.1 Barriers

Perceived barriers to desired behaviors include (a) lack of knowledge about mental illness and funding/resource issues, (b) uncertainty that successful recovery is how the consumer defines it, and (c) uncertainty that recovery-oriented treatment systems can be devised where people with mental illness pose no greater violence risk to the community than people without mental illness.

(Continued)

(Continued)

5.2 Benefits/Motivators

Potential motivators include: consumer success stories and proof that the recovery model works and is an efficient way to spend tax dollars.

5.3 Competing Behaviors

Responding to public fear and belief in stereotypes, providing funding for crisis intervention before funding recovery-oriented self-help programs.

6.0 Positioning Statement

We plan to develop a speakers' bureau consisting of providers and consumers of mental health services that will educate policymakers about recovery and serve as living examples of success. We want them to view these speaking engagements as an opportunity to hear success stories from consumers and as a good source of information about mental health issues, including recovery and stigma. We will also develop white papers, in partnership with consumers and providers, and want policymakers to see these as a credible source of information about mental illness, recovery and resiliency, and stigma, and as a source of empirical evidence that the recovery model works, can be economical, and is a good investment.

7.0 Marketing Mix Strategies (4Ps)

7.1 Product

Core: Increased knowledge of mental illness and Washington's Mental Health Transformation Project

Actual: Strategic speaking engagements and presentations throughout the state, highlighting consumer success stories and the recovery model.

Augmented: White papers on the transformation effort in Washington State.

7.2 Price

Speaking engagements and white papers will be free. Media coverage will address public fear and instill hope for recovery. Advocacy awards will honor policy "heroes" who contribute to recovery and the breaking down of myths and stereotypes.

7.3 Place

Speaking engagements will be scheduled at locations and times throughout the state that are convenient for policymakers. White papers will be available on the Internet and downloadable for print. Hard copies will be mailed out individually and available at speaking engagements.

7.4 Promotion

Speaking engagements will be promoted in association newsletters, on listservs and at sessions at related conferences. White papers will be promoted via direct mail. A news bureau will be used to publicize awards, conduct editorial board meetings to discuss mental health transformation, and stimulate feature stories. Availability of speakers' bureau will be promoted through ongoing conversations with elected officials and their staff.

8.0 Evaluation Plan

Purpose and audience for evaluation: Speakers' bureau evaluation will measure change in policymaker knowledge of mental illness and recovery, change in belief that people with mental illness can live fulfilling lives in the community, disposition toward changing regulations and funding to support recovery-oriented services, and actual changes in policies, regulations, and funding. The marketing team will use evaluation findings to determine continuation, improvement, and expansion of speakers' bureau and policymaker strategies.

Output measures include number of speaking engagements conducted, number of white papers distributed, number of news articles and editorials printed, news stories aired, and editorial board meetings conducted.

Outcome measures include number of policymakers at speaking engagements, visits to Web site, increased knowledge about mental illnesses, increased knowledge about Washington's Mental Health Transformation Project, and decreased stigmatizing attitudes and beliefs by policymakers attending speaking engagements.

How and when to measure: Pre- and postworkshop questionnaires by speakers' bureau participants and audience members. Tracking of policy, regulation, and funding changes. Media monitoring for number of letters to the editor, retractions of stereotypical portrayals, feature stories on recovery, and media coverage of award recipients.

9.0 Budget

Budget estimate is for Year 3 for speakers' bureau and news bureau aimed at three target audiences—consumers, providers, and policymakers—and does not include all planned activities for Year 3. The project is funded by a Mental Health Transformation State Incentive Grant from the Substance Abuse and Mental Health Services Administration, U.S. Department of Health and Human Services.

(Continued)

(Continued)

Speakers' bureau	$70,000
Recovery and stigma materials (print and Web)	$20,000
News bureau	$15,000
Professional education	$10,000
Management & coordination	$20,000
Total for speakers' and news bureaus	$135,000

10.0 Implementation Plan

Key Activities	Responsibility/Lead	Timing	Budget
Project coordination and oversight	DOH	Ongoing	$30,000
Speakers' bureau coordination and scheduling	Washington Institute for Mental Illness Research and Training Finalize schedule for speaking engagements	1st quarter Quarterly	$70,000
Continuing availability of recovery and stigma materials in print and on the Web	DOH	Ongoing (started in Year 2)	$10,000
Policy white papers	Mental Health Transformation staff with DOH	1st quarter: Draft for review 2nd quarter: Finalize and print 2nd–4th quarters: Publicity and distribution	(Included in project coordination)

Source: Heidi Keller and Daisye Orr, Office of Health Promotion, Washington State Department of Health with Washington's Mental Health Transformation Project, Office of the Governor, 2006.

PHASING

As mentioned earlier in our discussion on budgeting in Chapter 16, when funding levels are inadequate to implement the desired plan, one tactic to consider is spreading costs over a longer period of time, allowing more time to raise funds or use future budget allocations. Natural options include creating phases that are organized (driven) by some element of the marketing plan: *target audience, geographic areas, campaign objectives, campaign goals, stages of change, products, pricing, distributional channels, promotional messages,* or *media channels.* The following provide examples of situations in which a particular framework might be most appropriate.

Phases Organized by Target Audience

In a differentiated strategy in which several market segments are targets for the campaign, each phase could concentrate on implementing strategies for a distinct segment. This would provide a strong focus for your efforts as well as increase resources behind them. For the Seafood Watch program highlighted in Chapter 7, deliberate phases included:

Phase 1: Influencing consumers to ask for and purchase "green fish"

Phase 2: Equipping restaurants and grocery stores to favor suppliers of "green fish"

Phase 3: Developing a recognition and certification program that recognizes "green fisheries"

Phases Organized by Geographic Area

Phasing by geographic area has several advantages. It may align with funding availability as well as offer the ability to pilot the campaign, measure outcomes, and then make important refinements prior to implementation. Most important, by using this option, you will also be implementing all of the strategic elements you chose for the marketing mix. You will just be concentrating them in one or a few geographic areas. In the tractor safety case in Chapter 7, phasing was accomplished by piloting and then expanding geographic areas for the rebate offer:

Phase 1: Program piloted in New York State

Phase 2: Program adopted by other northeastern states including Vermont, Pennsylvania, and New Hampshire, with each state determining its own sources of funding for rebates.

Phases Organized by Objective

In a situation in which a campaign has identified important objectives related to knowledge and beliefs as well as behavior, campaign phases can be organized and sequenced to support each objective. The litter prevention campaign in Washington State used this strategy, allowing more time to gain support of partners (e.g., law enforcement), secure sponsors (e.g., fast-food restaurants), and establish important infrastructures (e.g., identifying broad distribution channels for litterbags and incorporating questions on fines for litter in driver's education tests). In this example, phases reflect the process of moving target audiences from awareness to action—over time.

Phase 1: Creating awareness of laws and fines

Phase 2: Altering beliefs that "no one's watching" or cares by implementing a toll-free hotline for reporting littering

Phase 3: Changing littering behavior

Phases Organized by Goal

Campaigns may have established specific benchmarks for reaching interim goals, in which case, activities and resources would then be organized to support desired outcomes. The advantage of this framework is that funders and administrators "feel good" that the program will achieve targeted goals—eventually. Similar to phasing by geographic area, this approach does not require altering the marketing strategy you developed for the program. You read in Chapter 15 about targeted milestones to raise breast cancer screening rates in Japan from 30% in 2008:

Phase 1: To 40% by 2010

Phase 2: To 50% by 2012

Phases Organized by Stage of Change

In keeping with the objective of moving audiences through stages of change, it may make the most sense to phase a campaign effort by first targeting those "most ready for action" and then using this momentum to move on to other markets. In a campaign encouraging foodwaste composting, for example, efforts might be made to set up demonstration households in neighborhoods with eager volunteers who can then be influenced and equipped to spread the word to neighbors. In this case, phases might appear as follows:

Phase 1: Influence households with consistent participation in all curbside recycling (maintenance segment)

Phase 2: Influence households participating in paper and glass curbside recycling, but not yardwaste recycling (in action segment)

Phase 3: Influence households that have responded to and inquired about information in the past but are not regular curbside recyclers (contemplator segment)

Phases Organized by Introduction or Enhancement of Services or Tangible Goods

When new or improved services and tangible goods have been identified for a program plan, it may be necessary, even strategic, to introduce these over a period of time. A Women, Infants, and Children (WIC) program clinic, for example, might phase the introduction of service enhancements by starting with those perceived to have the most potential impact on increasing use of farmers' markets and then move on to those providing added value:

Phase 1: Counselor training and support materials

Phase 2: Market tours and transportation vouchers

Phase 3: Clinic classes on freezing and canning

Phases Organized by Pricing Strategies

A program may plan a pricing strategy in which significant price incentives are used early in the campaign as a way to create attention and stimulate action. In subsequent phases, efforts may rely on other elements of the marketing mix, such as improved distribution channels or targeted promotions. In the case of a utility promoting energy-efficient appliances, pricing strategies might change over time as follows:

Phase 1: Rebates for turning in old appliances

Phase 2: Discount coupons for energy-efficient appliances

Phase 3: Pricing similar to competing appliances and increased emphasis on contribution to the environment

Phases Organized by Distribution Channels

A campaign relying heavily on convenience of access might begin with implementing distribution channels that are the quickest, easiest, or least expensive to develop and then move on to more significant endeavors over time. Launching a prescription drug medications return program might progress over time as follows, allowing program managers to develop procedures that ensure secure as well as convenient return locations:

Phase 1: Pilot the program by accepting medications at county sheriff's office

Phase 2: Expand to major medical centers and hospitals

Phase 3: Expand to pharmacies

Phases Organized by Messages

When multiple campaign messages are needed to support a broad social marketing program (e.g., decreasing obesity), behavior change may be facilitated by introducing messages one at a time. This can help your target adopter spread costs for change over a period of time, as well as feel less overwhelmed (self-efficacy). The Ad Council's Small Steps campaign for the U.S. Department of Health and Human Services mentioned earlier could phase its 100 recommended actions in the following clustered way:

Phase 1: Steps at Work: Walk during your lunch hour. Get off a stop early and walk. Walk to a coworker's desk instead of e-mailing or calling them.

Phase 2: Steps When Shopping: Eat before grocery shopping. Make a grocery list before you shop. Carry a grocery basket instead of pushing a cart.

Phase 3: Steps When Eating: Eat off smaller plates. Stop eating when you are full. Snack on fruits and vegetables.

Phases Organized by Media Channels

At the onset of major threats such as the H1N1 flu, mad cow disease, and terrorist attacks, you may need to first reach broad audiences in a very short time. Once this phase is complete, efforts may shift to more targeted audiences through more targeted media channels. For H1N1 flu, for example, we saw media channels progress as follows:

Phase 1: Mass communication channels: news stories on TV, on radio, and in newspapers

Phase 2: Selective channels: posters, flyers, and signage (e.g., hand washing signs in restrooms)

Phase 3: Personal contact: health care workers making visits to schools to ensure policies were in place regarding attendance for sick children

Phases Organized by a Variety of Factors

In reality, it may be important, even necessary, to use a combination of phasing techniques. For example, campaign target audiences may vary by geographic area (e.g., farmers are more important target audiences for water conservation in rural areas than they are in urban communities). As a result, different communities may have different target audience phasing in their campaigns. As most practitioners will attest, campaigns will need to be meaningful to their specific communities or they will not receive the necessary support for implementation.

Phase 1: Rural communities target farmers and urban communities target large corporations for water conservation

Phase 2: Rural communities target businesses and urban communities target public sector agencies

Phase 3: Rural communities and urban communities target residential users

SUSTAINABILITY

At this point in the planning process, most strategies have been identified and scheduled to support desired behavior change objectives and goals. It is a worthwhile exercise, however, to give last minute consideration to any additional tactics to include in the plan that will keep your campaign visible and behavior change messages prominent after ads go off the air and news stories die down. Are there other mechanisms you could include in the campaign that will help your target audience sustain their behavior over the long term? In keeping with our stages of change theory and model, you should be specifically interested in ensuring that those in the action stage don't return to contemplation and that those in the maintenance stage don't return to irregular actions. In the following sections, ideas including the use of prompts, commitments, plans for social diffusion, and public infrastructures are presented.

Prompts

In their book *Fostering Sustainable Behavior*, McKenzie-Mohr and Smith offer insights, guidelines, tools, and checklists for the social marketer to consider for supporting continued behavior change. They describe prompts as

> visual or auditory aids which remind us to carry out an activity that we might otherwise forget. The purpose of a prompt is not to change attitudes or increase motivation, but simply to remind us to engage in an action that we are already predisposed to do.[11]

They have four recommendations for effective prompts:

1. Make the prompt noticeable, using eye-catching graphics

2. Make the prompt self-explanatory, including all information needed to take the appropriate action

3. Place the prompt as close as possible to where and when the action is to be taken

4. Use prompts to encourage positive behaviors rather than to avoid harmful ones

"Anchoring" is similar to prompting, where the desired behavior (e.g., flossing) is "anchored," or closely linked, to a current established behavior (e.g., brushing your teeth). Examples of both are illustrated in Table 17.2, and as a planning note, any new or additional prompts that you identify at this point should be noted in the appropriate 4Ps section of your marketing plan.

Commitments and Pledges

Gaining commitments, or pledges, from target adopters has also proven surprisingly effective. "Individuals who agreed to a small initial request were far more likely to agree to a subsequent larger request."[12] Examples include a backyard wildlife sanctuary program in which homeowners sign the application promising to follow the natural gardening guidelines, or WIC clinics in which clients who sign a receipt for farmers' market coupons state they are interested in using these in the next three months. Evidently, McKenzie-Mohr and Smith report, "when individuals agree to a small request, it often alters the way they perceive themselves." [13] Any commitments you decide to add to your plan at this point should be noted in the price strategy section. We consider it a form of a nonmonetary incentive, since making this commitment has been shown to act as an incentive to follow through with the behavior.

Table 17.2   Sustaining Behaviors and Campaign Efforts

Issue	Using Prompts to Sustain Behavior
Tobacco cessation	Electronic alerts during vulnerable times in the day that signal, "Come on, you can do it"
Binge drinking	Small posters in bar restroom stalls showing someone bending over "the porcelain god"
Physical activity	Wearing a pedometer to make sure you get 10,000 steps a day
Unintended pregnancies	Keeping a condom in a small case on a key chain
Fat intake	Detailed data on food labels indicating fat grams and percentage of calories
Fruits and vegetables	Placing fruits and vegetables in glass bowls at eye level in refrigerators
Water intake	Stickers at water coolers saying, "Have you had your 8 glasses today?"
Breastfeeding	Pediatricians encouraging a nursing mom to continue breastfeeding at the six-month checkup
Breast cancer	Shower nozzle hanger reminding about monthly breast self-exams
Folic acid	Keeping vitamin pills by the toothbrush as an established habit
Immunizations	Mailings recognizing and reminding when a child's immunization is due
Diabetes	Using a beeper as a reminder for blood glucose monitoring
Car seats	Keeping a car seat in all cars used frequently by a child
Drinking and driving	Making breathalyzers available in bars
Booster seats	Air fresheners for cars with reminders about booster seats
Drowning	Providing loaner life vests for toddlers at public beaches
Smoke alarms	Placing reminder stickers in planning calendars for checking batteries in smoke alarms
Waste reduction	Label on a bathroom towel dispenser suggesting, "Take only what you need. Towels are trees."
Foodwaste composting	Stickers on recycling containers recognizing a homeowner who also composts foodwaste
Reducing use	Messages at coffee stands suggesting that "the regulars" bring their own cups
Air pollution	Stickers inside car doors reminding car owners when it is time to get their tires inflated
Organ donation	Lawyers asking their clients who are organ donors if they have talked to their families about their wishes

In McKenzie-Mohr's 2011 edition of *Fostering Sustainable Behavior*, the following four guidelines for designing effective commitments are among those emphasized:[14]

1. Make commitments as public as possible (e.g., signs on lawns or signatures on a petition).

2. Seek commitments in groups (e.g., members of a church congregation pledge to conserve energy).

3. Engage the audience in performing the activity initially to increase their perception of commitment (e.g., having homeowners check the thermostat on their hot water heater will likely lead them to take the next step, setting it at 120 degrees).

4. Use existing, related contact points to solicit commitments (e.g., when purchasing paint, ask for a commitment to dispose of unused paint properly).

Plans for Social Diffusion

Before wrapping up the planning process, also take time to consider additional tactics to facilitate social diffusion—the spread of the adoption of a behavior from a few to many, a concept introduced in Chapter 6. McKenzie-Mohr suggests guidelines for this as well, including:[15]

1. Make support for behavior adoption visible (e.g., affix a decal to a recycling container indicating that "We compost").

2. Use durable versus temporary indicators (e.g., a Mutt Mitt station in a neighborhood versus yard signs encouraging picking up pet waste).

3. Engage well-known and well-respected people to make their support for a desired behavior visible (e.g., a city mayor speaking frequently about the advantages she sees from taking mass transit to city hall).

4. Make norms visible, especially when "most of us" are engaged in the behavior (e.g., a sign at the entrance to a grocery store stating 60% of shoppers bring their own bags at least once a month).

Utilizing Public Infrastructures to Increase and Maintain Visibility

If you are working in the public sector, you have numerous opportunities for sustained visibility, as you often have access to public places and signage at public agencies. Those working on traffic safety can negotiate for signage on roadways; those working on flu prevention have access to public restrooms for signage reminding people to wash their hands; those working on pedestrian safety can negotiate for tougher tests when getting a driver's license; and those working on decreasing secondhand tobacco smoke can work with school districts to send home "smoke-free home" pledge cards with the children. These are resources and opportunities that many in commercial marketing would envy and most would have a hard time paying for.

SHARING AND SELLING YOUR PLAN

Several techniques will help increase buy-in, approval, and support for your plan. First, include representatives from key internal and external groups on the planning team.

Consider those who have a role in approving the plan as well as those key to implementation. For a litter prevention campaign with an emphasis on enforcement, it would be critical that a member of the state patrol have input in the planning process; to increase WIC clients' use of farmers' markets, it would be important to have a representative from the farmers' market association present, especially to hear the results of research with clients on their experiences shopping at the market; and a city developing a pedestrian safety plan will benefit from having a police officer, an engineer, someone from the communications department, someone from a local business, and a citizen at the planning table.

Second, share a draft plan with decision makers and those key to implementation before finalizing your plan. Identify their concerns and address them. Be prepared to share the background data that led to your recommended strategies, and be prepared to compromise or modify a strategy based on their feedback. And surprise them with the targeted quantifiable goals you are proposing and how you plan to evaluate and report on campaign outcomes.

Finally, once the plan is finalized, consider developing and disseminating a concise summary of the plan. It could be as simple as a one-pager that presents the purpose, focus, target audience, objectives, key strategies, and evaluation plan. Where warranted, it could even be a more portable format such as a wallet-sized card or a more accessible one such as on your agency's Web site. Your intention is to position your campaign effort as one that is evidence based, strategically developed, and outcome driven.

ETHICAL CONSIDERATIONS WHEN IMPLEMENTING PLANS

In most of the chapters in this book, we have presented ethical considerations related specifically to each phase in the planning process. To highlight final considerations when developing an implementation plan and to summarize ethical considerations in general, we present the American Marketing Association members' code of ethics, published on their Web site (www.MarketingPower.com), in Box 17.2. Many of the principles apply to social marketing environments, with themes similar to those we have highlighted, including *Do no harm*, *Be fair*, *Provide full disclosure*, *Be good stewards*, *Own the problem*, *Be responsible*, and *Tell the truth*.

Box 17.2
Ethical Norms and Values for Marketers

Preamble

The American Marketing Association commits itself to promoting the highest standard of professional ethical norms and values for its members. Norms are established standards of conduct that are expected and maintained by society and/or professional organizations. Values represent the collective conception of what people find desirable, important and morally proper. Values serve as the criteria for evaluating the actions of others. Marketing practitioners must recognize that they not only serve their enterprises but also act as stewards of society in creating, facilitating and executing the efficient and effective transactions that are part of the greater economy. In this role, marketers should embrace the highest ethical norms of practicing professionals and the ethical values implied by their responsibility toward stakeholders (e.g., customers, employees, investors, channel members, regulators and the host community).

General Norms

1. Marketers must do no harm. This means doing work for which they are appropriately trained or experienced so that they can actively add value to their organizations and customers. It also means adhering to all applicable laws and regulations and embodying high ethical standards in the choices they make.

2. Marketers must foster trust in the marketing system. This means that products are appropriate for their intended and promoted uses. It requires that marketing communications about goods and services are not intentionally deceptive or misleading. It suggests building relationships that provide for the equitable adjustment and/or redress of customer grievances. It implies striving for good faith and fair dealing so as to contribute toward the efficacy of the exchange process.

3. Marketers must embrace, communicate and practice the fundamental ethical values that will improve consumer confidence in the integrity of the marketing exchange system. These basic values are intentionally aspirational and include honesty, responsibility, fairness, respect, openness and citizenship.

Ethical Values

Honesty—to be truthful and forthright in our dealings with customers and stakeholders. We will tell the truth in all situations and at all times.

- We will offer products of value that do what we claim in our communications.
- We will stand behind our products if they fail to deliver their claimed benefits.
- We will honor our explicit and implicit commitments and promises.

Responsibility—to accept the consequences of our marketing decisions and strategies.

- We will make strenuous efforts to serve the needs of our customers.
- We will avoid using coercion with all stakeholders.
- We will acknowledge the social obligations to stakeholders that come with increased marketing and economic power.

(Continued)

(Continued)

- We will recognize our special commitments to economically vulnerable segments of the market such as children, the elderly and others who may be substantially disadvantaged.

Fairness—to try to balance justly the needs of the buyer with the interests of the seller.

- We will represent our products in a clear way in selling, advertising and other forms of communication; this includes the avoidance of false, misleading and deceptive promotion.
- We will reject manipulations and sales tactics that harm customer trust.
- We will not engage in price fixing, predatory pricing, price gouging or "bait-and-switch" tactics.
- We will not knowingly participate in material conflicts of interest.

Respect—to acknowledge the basic human dignity of all stakeholders.

- We will value individual differences even as we avoid stereotyping customers or depicting demographic groups (e.g., gender, race, sexual orientation) in a negative or dehumanizing way in our promotions.
- We will listen to the needs of our customers and make all reasonable efforts to monitor and improve their satisfaction on an ongoing basis.
- We will make a special effort to understand suppliers, intermediaries and distributors from other cultures.
- We will appropriately acknowledge the contributions of others, such as consultants, employees and coworkers, to our marketing endeavors.

Openness—to create transparency in our marketing operations.

- We will strive to communicate clearly with all our constituencies.
- We will accept constructive criticism from our customers and other stakeholders.
- We will explain significant product or service risks, component substitutions or other foreseeable eventualities that could affect customers or their perception of the purchase decision.
- We will fully disclose list prices and terms of financing as well as available price deals and adjustments.

Citizenship—to fulfill the economic, legal, philanthropic and societal responsibilities that serve stakeholders in a strategic manner.

- We will strive to protect the natural environment in the execution of marketing campaigns.
- We will give back to the community through volunteerism and charitable donations.

- We will work to contribute to the overall betterment of marketing and its reputation.
- We will encourage supply chain members to ensure that trade is fair for all participants, including producers in developing countries.

Implementation

Finally, we recognize that every industry sector and marketing subdiscipline (e.g., marketing research, e-commerce, direct selling, direct marketing, advertising) has its own specific ethical issues that require policies and commentary. An array of such codes can be accessed through links on the AMA Web site. We encourage all such groups to develop and/or refine their industry and discipline-specific codes of ethics to supplement these general norms and values.

Source: American Marketing Association. (2004). Reprinted with permission. Retrieved from www.Marketing Power.com.

CHAPTER SUMMARY

Developing an implementation plan is Step 10, the final step in this marketing plan model. It turns strategies into actions and is critical to *doing things right*, even if you've planned *the right things*. An implementation plan functions as a concise working document that can be used to share and track planned efforts. It provides a mechanism to ensure that we do what we said we would do, on time, and within budgets. Key components of the plan include the following: What will you do? Who will be responsible? When will it be done? How much will it cost?

Formats for plans vary from simple plans incorporated in the executive summary of the marketing plan to complex plans using software programs. The ideal plan identifies activities over a period of two to three years.

Plans are often presented in phases, usually broken down into months or years. Several frameworks can be used to determine and organize phases, including *target audiences*, *geographic areas*, *campaign objectives*, *campaign goals*, *stages of change*, *products*, *pricing*, *distribution channels*, *promotional messages*, and *media channels*. Often it will be a combination of these factors.

Typical strategies to sustain visibility for your campaign, as well as target audience behaviors, include the use of prompts, commitments, social diffusion, and existing infrastructures. Prompt tactics and mechanisms include signage, stickers, mailings, electronic reminders, labels on packaging, and e-mail alerts. New or additional prompts you identify at this stage in the planning process are most often noted as promotional strategies, and commitments are nonmonetary incentives. Taking advantage of public places and agency partnerships may involve placing signage on government property or messaging in their existing materials (e.g., messages regarding texting and driving in driver's education tests).

Several techniques may be used to increase buy-in, approval, and support for your plan. First, include representatives from key internal and external groups on the planning team. Second, share a draft plan with decision makers and those key to implementation before finalizing your plan. Third, once the plan is finalized, consider developing and disseminating a concise summary of the plan. It could be as simple as a one-pager that presents the purpose, focus, target audience, objectives, key strategies, and evaluation plan.

RESEARCH HIGHLIGHT

Turn It Off: An Anti-idling Campaign (2007)

Doug McKenzie-Mohr, Ph.D.
Environmental Psychologist

Background

Each day millions of motorists unnecessarily idle their vehicle engines. For example, it is estimated that Canadians idle their vehicles an average of 5 to 10 minutes every day and that at any given time 56% of Canadian motorists are idling their engines when parked and sitting in their vehicles. Natural Resources Canada (NRCan) reports that if motorists reduced their idling by five minutes per day, Canadians would reduce their annual carbon monoxide emissions by over 1 million tons and over Can$1.7 million would be saved each and every day (assuming an average gasoline cost of $0.95 per liter).

With the support of Catherine Ray at NRCan and David Dilks of Lura Consulting, I developed a pilot project to reduce the extent to which Canadians idle their vehicles. This project utilized community-based social marketing.[16] Community-based social marketing is based on five steps: (1) carefully selecting the behavior to be targeted, (2) identifying the barriers and benefits to the action, (3) developing a strategy to overcome the barriers and enhance the perceived benefits, (4) piloting the strategy, and finally, (5) implementing on a broad scale. Following this process, we began by conducting barriers and benefits research, which involved conducting Canada-wide focus groups and survey research. This research identified several barriers to reducing idling as well as one significant perceived benefit. Regarding barriers, Canadians believed they should idle their vehicles for longer than three minutes before it was more fuel efficient to turn their engines off and then at a later time restart them (NRCan reports that the actual threshold is 10 seconds). Furthermore, they believed that it was necessary to warm their engines before driving (it is actually better for a vehicle to be driven to warm it up than to idle it) and that turning an engine off and on repeatedly would harm the starter. In addition, motorists reported forgetting to turn their engines off when parked and sitting in their vehicles. An effective anti-idling program would have to address each of these barriers as well as emphasize the reported benefit of enhancing air quality by turning off an engine when parked.

Objectives and Strategies

This pilot project sought to decrease both the frequency and duration of motorists' idling their vehicle engines. The project involved staff approaching motorists at Toronto schools and Toronto Transit Commission Kiss and Ride parking lots and speaking with them about the importance of turning off their vehicle engines when parked and sitting in their vehicles. Approached motorists were provided with an information card (see Figure 17.1), and signs reminding motorists to turn off their engines were posted at both the schools and the Kiss and Ride sites (see Figure 17.2). As part of the conversation, each motorist was asked to make a commitment to turn off the vehicle engine when parked. To assist motorists in remembering to turn off their engines, they were asked to place a sticker on their front windshields. The sticker served both as a prompt to turn off their engines and facilitated the development of community norms with respect to engine idling (the sticker, which was static-cling, could be pulled off, was transparent, and was placed on the front windshield of the

vehicle with the graphic and text viewable from both inside and outside the vehicle). Over 80% of the motorists who were asked to make a commitment to turn off their engines did so, and 26% placed the sticker on their front window (see Figure 17.3).

Figure 17.1   These information cards outline the benefits of reduced engine idling and are suitable for distribution at schools and other community locations.[17]

Figure 17.2 A sign used at schools and Kiss and Ride sites.[18]

Figure 17.3 Stickers given to motorists for their windows. [19]

Results

This project had three separate conditions. Two Kiss and Ride sites and two schools served as controls and received none of the above materials. In a second condition, two Kiss and Ride sites and two schools received only the signs. Finally, in the third condition, the personal conversations, which involved providing an information card and the sticker described above, were used in conjunction with signs. Note that the signs alone, which is what most municipalities would gravitate toward using, were completely ineffective. Motorists in the sign-only condition were no more likely to turn off their engines than those in the control group. However, the combination of signs, stickers, and information cards (third condition) dramatically affected idling. In this condition, there was a 32% reduction in idling and over a 70% reduction in the duration of idling. These results are based on over 8,000 observations of vehicles in the various parking lots. With the support of NRCan, this pilot project was subsequently implemented across two Canadian cities, Mississauga and Sudbury, with similar results. Most important, NRCan has made the materials from the project freely available to communities so that they can quickly and inexpensively implement their own anti-idling campaigns. As a consequence, municipalities across North America have implemented anti-idling programs based on this case study.

For further information, visit the Government of Canada's Idle Free Zone Web site (http://oee.nrcan.gc.ca/transportation/personal/idling.cfm). This site provides further details on delivering effective anti-idling programs as well as downloadable materials that can be used in a local program.

CHAPTER 17 NOTES

1. McKenzie-Mohr, D., Lee, N. R., Schultz, P. W., & Kotler, P. (2011). *Social marketing to protect the environment: What works* (p. 13). Thousand Oaks, CA: Sage.

2. Ogden, C. L., Carroll, M., Curtin, L., Lamb, M., & Flegal, K. (2010). Prevalence of high body mass index in US children and adolescents 2007–2008. *Journal of the American Medical Association, 303*(3), 242–249.

3. Olshansky, S. J., Passaro, D. J, Hershow, R. C., Layden, J., Carnes, B. A., Brody, J., . . . Ludwig, D. S. (2005, May 17). A potential decline in life expectancy in the United States in the 21st century. *The New England Journal of Medicine, 352*(11), 1138–1144.

4. Let's Move! (n.d.). *Learn the facts*. Retrieved November 26, 2010, from http://www.lets move.gov/learnthefacts.php

5. Ibid.

6. Let's Move! (n.d.). *America's move to raise A healthier generation of kids*. Retrieved November 26, 2010, from http://www.letsmove.gov/learnthefacts.php

7. Ad Council. (n.d.). *Nutrition education—Let's Move!* Retrieved November 26, 2010, from http:www.adcouncil.org/default.aspx?id=475

8. Retrieved November 26, 2010, from Partnership for a Healthy America Web site: http://www.ahealthieramerica.org/

9. Obama Foodorama. *Michelle Obama gets huge Let's Move! commitment from food corporations*. Retrieved May 17, 2010, from http://obamafoodorama.blogspot.com/

10. Kotler, P., & Armstrong, G. (2001). *Principles of marketing* (p. 71). Upper Saddle River, NJ: Prentice Hall.

11. McKenzie-Mohr, D., & Smith, W. (1999). *Fostering sustainable behavior: An introduction to community-based social marketing* (p. 101). Gabriola Island, British Columbia, Canada: New Society.

12. Ibid., p. 61.

13. Ibid., p. 48.

14. McKenzie-Mohr, D. (2011). *Fostering sustainable behavior: An introduction to community-based social marketing* (3rd ed., p. 56). Gabriola Island, British Columbia, Canada: New Society.

15. McKenzie-Mohr, 2011, *Fostering sustainable behavior* (p. 70).

16. McKenzie-Mohr & Smith, 1999, *Fostering sustainable behavior.*

17. Source: Natural Resources Canada.

18. McKenzie-Mohr & Smith, Fostering Sustainable Behavior, pp. 46-81.

19. Ibid.

EPILOGUE

We see a future world where people are healthy and safe, protecting the environment, contributing to their communities, and enhancing their own financial well-being. We believe that the discipline of social marketing, influencing public behaviors for societal good, is a key strategic model to help make this a reality.

For social marketing to be understood, regarded, and adapted around the world, we think there are four urgent needs:

1. Social marketing should be a required course for degrees in public health, public administration, political science, international studies, environmental studies, nursing, and medicine—all degrees whose graduates would benefit from the art and science of influencing patients', citizens', and policy makers' behaviors. Imagine the difference it would make to this field, as well as to the worlds' citizens, if thousands of graduates from these programs each year understood the term, its applications, and its strategic planning model. We think the best place for this to begin is with the Master's in Public Health degree.

2. Social marketing professionals need to be united. We need to embrace a common terminology and a strategic planning model, such as the one presented in this text. And all should be encouraged and supported to make it even better. Accountants have done this. So can we.

3. Social marketing professionals need the support of an international social marketing association, one that has chapters at the country, even local, levels. The newly formed International Social Marketing Association (2011) has a mission to provide a multitude of resources for individual members, as well as support for local chapters to be formed.

4. Social marketers need to consistently report on return on investment for programs. For every dollar spent, how many taxpayer dollars were saved? And given this, what is the rate of return on our investment? We have presented a detailed discussion on how to accomplish this in Chapter 15.

Thank you to all who are currently helping to complete these action steps, and to those who will be inspired to help in the future.

—Nancy Lee and Philip Kotler

APPENDIX A

SOCIAL MARKETING PLANNING WORKSHEETS

STEP 1: DESCRIBE THE BACKGROUND, PURPOSE, AND FOCUS OF YOUR PLAN

1.1 Summarize key *background* information leading to the development of this plan (e.g., increased rates of teen pregnancies, decreased salmon populations).

_____

_____

_____

_____

_____

1.2 What is the campaign *purpose*, the intended impact (benefit; e.g., reduced teen pregnancies, increased protection of salmon habitats)?

_____

_____

_____

_____

_____

1.3 What is the campaign *focus* (e.g., teen abstinence, residential gardening practices)?

_____

_____

_____

_____

_____

Refer to Chapter 5 for a detailed description of the process.

STEP 2: CONDUCT A SITUATION ANALYSIS

Organizational Factors

2.1   What organizational *strengths* will your plan maximize (e.g., resources, expertise, management support, internal publics, current alliances and partnerships, distribution channels)?

\
\

2.2   What organizational *weaknesses* will your plan minimize (e.g., resources, expertise, management support, internal publics, current alliances and partnerships, distribution channels)?

\
\

Environmental Forces

2.3   What environmental *opportunities* will your plan take advantage of (e.g., external publics and cultural, technological, demographic, natural, economic, and political/legal forces)?

\
\

2.4   What environmental *threats* will your plan prepare for (e.g., external publics and cultural, technological, demographic, natural, economic, and political/legal forces)?

\
\

Prior and Similar Efforts

2.5   What findings from *prior and similar efforts* are noteworthy, those of yours and others?

\
\

Refer to Chapter 5 for a detailed description of the process.

STEP 3: SELECT TARGET AUDIENCES

3.1 Describe the *primary target audiences* for your program/campaign in terms of size, problem incidence and severity, and relevant variables, including demographics, psychographics, geographics, behaviors, and/or stages of change:

_____

_____

_____

_____

_____

_____

3.2 If you have *additional important target audiences* that you will need to influence as well, describe them here:

_____

_____

_____

_____

_____

_____

_____

Refer to Chapter 6 for a detailed description of the process.

STEP 4: SET OBJECTIVES AND TARGET GOALS

Objectives

4.1 Behavior Objective:
What, very specifically, do you want to influence your target audience to *do* as a result of this campaign or project?

_____

_____

_____

4.2 Knowledge Objective:
Is there anything you need them to *know*, in order to act?

_____

_____

_____

4.3 Belief Objective:
Is there anything you need them to *believe*, in order to act?

_____

_____

_____

Goals

4.4 What quantifiable, measurable goals are you targeting? Ideally, these are stated in terms of *behavior change*. Other potential target goals are for campaign awareness, recall and/or response, and changes in knowledge, belief, or behavior intent levels.

_____

_____

_____

Refer to Chapter 7 for a detailed description of the process.

STEP 5: IDENTIFY TARGET AUDIENCE BARRIERS, BENEFITS, THE COMPETITION, AND INFLUENTIAL OTHERS

Barriers

5.1 Make a list of *barriers* your audience may have to adopting the desired behavior. These may be physical, psychological, skills, knowledge, awareness, attitudes, and so on.

1.

2.

3.

4.

5.

6.

7.

8.

9.

10.

Benefits

5.2 What are the key *benefits* your target audience will be motivated by?

Competition

5.3 What are the major competing *alternative behaviors*?

5.4 What *benefits* do your audiences associate with these behaviors?

5.5 What *costs* do your audiences associate with these behaviors?

Influential Others

5.6 Relative to the desired behavior, who does your target audience listen to, watch, and/or look up to?

5.7 What do you know about what these midstream audiences are currently saying and doing regarding the desired behavior?

Refer to Chapter 8 for a detailed description of the process.

STEP 6: DEVELOP A POSITIONING STATEMENT

Positioning Statement

6.1 Write a statement similar to the following, filling in the blanks:
"We want [TARGET AUDIENCE] to see [DESIRED BEHAVIOR] as [SET OF BENEFITS] and as more important and beneficial than [COMPETITION]."

Refer to Chapter 9 for a detailed description of the process.

STEP 7: DEVELOP MARKETING STRATEGIES

7.1 Product: Design the Product Platform

7.1.1 Core product: What is the major perceived benefit your target audience wants from performing the behavior that you will highlight? (Choose one or a few from those identified in 5.2.)

_____

_____

7.1.2 Actual product: What, if any, tangible goods and services will you be offering and/ or promoting (e.g., 100 native plants to choose from, fruits and vegetables, life vests, blood monitoring equipment, low-flow showerheads)?

_____

_____

7.1.3 Augmented product: Are there any additional tangible goods or services that would assist your target audience in performing the behavior (e.g., workshop on designing a native plant garden)?

Refer to Chapter 10 for a detailed description of the process.

7.2 Price: Fees and Monetary and Nonmonetary Incentives and Disincentives

7.2.1 If you will be including tangible goods and services in your campaign, what, if anything, will the target audience have to *pay* for them?

_____

_____

_____

7.2.2 Describe any *monetary incentives* for your target audience (e.g., coupons, rebates).

_____

_____

_____

7.2.3 Describe any *monetary disincentives* you will highlight (e.g., fines, increased taxes).

_____

_____

_____

7.2.4 Describe any *nonmonetary incentives* (e.g., recognition, reward).

_____

_____

_____

7.2.5 Describe any *nonmonetary disincentives* (e.g., negative visibility).

_____

_____

_____

Refer to Chapter 11 for a detailed description of the process.

7.3 Place: Develop the Place Strategy

As you determine each of the following, look for ways to make locations closer and more appealing, to extend hours, and to be there at the point of decision making.

7.3.1 *Where* will you encourage and support your target audience to *perform the desired behavior* and *when*?

_____

_____

_____

7.3.2 *Where* and *when* will the target audience acquire any related tangible objects?

_____

_____

_____

7.3.3 Are there any groups or individuals in the distribution channel that you will target to support efforts?

_____

_____

_____

Refer to Chapter 12 for a detailed description of the process.

7.4 Promotion: Decide on Messages, Messengers, Creative Strategies, and Communication Channels

7.4.1 Messages: What key messages do you want your campaign to communicate to target audiences?

_____

_____

_____

7.4.2 Messengers: Who will deliver the messages and/or be the perceived sponsor?

_____

_____

_____

7.4.3 Creative strategies: Summarize, describe, or highlight elements such as logos, taglines, copy, visuals, colors, script, actors, scenes, and sounds in broadcast media.

_____

_____

_____

7.4.4 Communication channels: What communication channels will you use?

_____

_____

_____

Refer to Chapters 13 and 14 for a detailed description of the process.

STEP 8: DEVELOP A PLAN FOR MONITORING AND EVALUATION

8.1   What is the *purpose* of this evaluation? Why are you doing it?

_____

_____

8.2   For *whom* is the evaluation being conducted? To whom will you present it?

_____

_____

8.3   *What goals* from Step 4 will be measured?

_____

_____

8.4   *What techniques and methodologies* will be used to conduct these measurements?

_____

_____

8.5   *When* will these measurements be taken?

_____

_____

8.6   *How* much will this cost?

_____

_____

Refer to Chapter 15 for a detailed description of the process.

STEP 9: ESTABLISH BUDGETS AND FIND FUNDING SOURCES

9.1 What costs will be associated with *product*-related strategies?

_____

_____

9.2 What costs will be associated with *price*-related strategies?

_____

_____

9.3 What costs will be associated with *place*-related strategies?

_____

_____

9.4 What costs will be associated with *promotion*-related strategies?

_____

_____

9.5 What costs will be associated with *evaluation*-related strategies?

_____

_____

9.6 If costs exceed currently available funds, what potential additional funding sources can be explored?

_____

_____

Refer to Chapter 16 for a detailed description of the process.

STEP 10: COMPLETE AN IMPLEMENTATION PLAN

10.1 Will there be phases to the campaign? How will they be organized (e.g., by audience, objectives, activities)?

_____

_____

_____

_____

_____

_____

_____

_____

10.2 For each phase, what will be done, who will be responsible, when will it be done, and for how much?

_____

_____

_____

_____

_____

_____

_____

_____

Refer to Chapter 17 for a detailed description of the process. For an electronic version of this plan, visit www.socialmarketingservice.com

APPENDIX B

SOCIAL MARKETING RESOURCES

Compiled by Mike Newton-Ward, Social Marketing Consultant, North Carolina Division of Public Health. He thanks participants on the Georgetown social marketing listserv for additional suggestions.

Blogs

Beyond Attitude: Community-Based Social Marketing Tips	www.beyondattitude.com/
Marketing in the Public Sector	http://jimmintz.wordpress.com/
Ogilvy PR, Social Marketing Exchange	http://smexchange.ogilvypr.com/
On Social Marketing and Social Change	http://socialmarketing.blogs.com/
Pulse+Signal	http://pulseandsignal.com/
Social Butterfly	www.fly4change.com/
Social Marketing Panorama	www.socialmarketingpanorama.com
Stephan Dahl's Blog	http://stephan.dahl.at/
The Social Marketing Place Blog	www.social-marketing.com/blog/

Books

Andreasen, A. (1995). *Marketing social change: Changing behavior to promote health, social development, and the environment.* San Francisco, CA: Jossey-Bass.

Andreasen, A. (Ed.). (2001). *Ethics in social marketing.* Washington, DC: Georgetown University Press.

Andreasen, A. (2001). *Marketing research that won't break the bank: A practical guide to getting the information you need* (2nd ed.). San Francisco, CA: Jossey-Bass.

Andreasen, A. (2006). *Social marketing in the 21st century.* Thousand Oaks, CA: Sage.

Andreasen, A., & Kotler, P. (2007). *Strategic marketing for non-profit organizations.* Upper Saddle River, NJ: Prentice Hall.

Basil, D. Z., & Wimer, W. W. (2007). *Social marketing: Advances in research & theory.* Binghamton, NY: Haworth Press.

Bearden, W. O., Netemeyer, R. G., & Haws, K.L. (1999). *Handbook of marketing scales: Multi-item measures for marketing and consumer behavior research* (2nd ed.). Thousand Oaks, CA: Sage.

Buros Institute. (2010). *The eighteenth mental measurements yearbook.* Lincoln, NE: Author.

Cheng, H., Kotler, P., & Lee, N. (2011). *Social marketing in public health: Global trends and success stories.* Sudbury, MA: Jones & Bartlett.

Donovan, R., & Henley, N. (2003). *Principles and practice of social marketing: An international perspective.* Victoria, Australia: Cambridge University Press.

French, J., Blair-Stevens, C., McVey, D., & Merritt, R. (2010). *Social marketing and public health: Theory and practice.* Oxford, England: Oxford University Press.

Galdwell, M. (2000). *The tipping point: How little things can make a big difference.* Boston, MA: Little, Brown.

Glanz, K., Rimer, B. K., & Lewis, M. L. (2008). *Health behavior and health education: Theory, research, and practice.* San Francisco, CA: Jossey-Bass.

Harvey, P. D. (1999). *Let every child be wanted: How social marketing is revolutionizing contraceptive use around the world.* Westport, CT: Auburn House.

Hastings, G. (2007). *Social marketing: Why should the devil have all the best tunes?* Oxford, England: Butterworth-Heinemann.

Hastings, G., Angus, K., & Bryant, C. (2011). *Sage handbook of social marketing.* Thousand Oaks, CA: Sage.

Heath, C., & Heath, D. (1995). *Made to stick: Why some ideas survive and others die.* New York, NY: Random House.

Heath, C., & Hcath, D. (1995). *Switch: How to change things when change is hard.* New York, NY: Broadway Books.

Kotler, P., & Lee, N. (2007). *Marketing in the public sector: A roadmap for improved performance.* Philadelphia, PA: Wharton School.

Kotler, P., & Lee, N. (2009). *Up and out of poverty: The social marketing solution.* Philadelphia, PA: Wharton School.

Kreuger, R. A., & Casey, M. A. (2000). *Focus groups: A practical guide for applied research* (3rd ed.). Thousand Oaks, CA: Sage.

Maibach, E., & Parrott, R. L. (Eds.). (1995). *Designing health messages.* Thousand Oaks, CA: Sage.

Mckenzie-Mohr, D. (2011). *Fostering sustainable behavior: An introduction to community-based social marketing.* Gabriola Island, BC, Canada: New Society.

Mckenzie-Mohr, D., Lee, N., Schultz, P. W., & Kotler, P. (2011). *Social marketing to protect the environment: What works.* Thousand Oaks, CA: Sage.

Prochaska, J. O., Norcross, J., & DiClemente, C. (1995). *Changing for good: A revolutionary six-stage program for overcoming bad habits, and moving your life positively forward.* New York, NY: Collins.

Siegel, M., & Lotenburg, L. D. (2007). *Marketing public health: Strategies to promote social change* (2nd ed.). Boston, MA: Jones & Bartlett.

Tobin, J., & Braziel, L. (2008). *Social media is like a cocktail party.* CreateSpace.

Weinreich, N. K. (2010). *Hands-on social marketing: A step-by-step guide.* Thousand Oaks, CA: Sage.

Conference Opportunities

1. *MARCOM Professional Development Annual Forum*, June, Ottawa, Canada

To view and download registration information, go to:
http://www.marcom.ca/

2. *Social Marketing in Public Health Annual Conference*, June, University of South Florida, Clearwater Beach, FL

Contact:
Continuing Professional Education
University of South Florida College of Public Health
813–974–9684
http://www.cme.hsc.usf.edu/smph/index.html

To view and download materials from previous conferences, go to:
http://www.cme.hsc.usf.edu/smph/presentations.html

3. *World Social Marketing Conference*, 2011, Dublin, Ireland

To view program information go to:
http://wsmconference.com/

(Next conference: April 21–22, 2013, Toronto, Canada)

E-Learning Tools and Online Courses

CDCynergy–Social Marketing Edition, online	www.orau.gov/cdcynergy/soc2webdefault.htm
Cullbridge Marketing and Communications, Tools of Change Webinars	www.webinars.cullbridge.com/
Social Marketing e-Learning Tool (Health Canada)	www.hc-sc.gc.ca/ahc-asc/activit/marketsoc/tools-outils/index_e.html
The National Training Collaborative for Social Marketing, USF Health, University of South Florida	http://hsc.usf.edu/medicine/ntcsm/TLM/present/index/index.htm
The Open University, United Kingdom, Social Marketing Course	http://openlearn.open.ac.uk/mod/oucontent/view.php?id=397437

Electronic Media

Centers for Disease Control and Prevention, Division of Nutrition, Physical Activity and Obesity, Social Marketing for Nutrition and Physical Activity Web course	www.cdc.gov/nccdphp/dnpa/socialmarketing/training/index.htm
Changing Transportation Behaviours: A Social Marketing Planning Guide	www.tc.gc.ca/media/documents/programs/ctb.pdf
Free-Range Thinking	www.agoodmanonline.com/newsletter/index.html
Social Marketing and Public Health: Lessons From the Field	http://socialmarketingcollaborative.org/smc/pdf/Lessons_from_field.pdf
Social Marketing Lite	www.aed.org/Publications/upload/Social-Marketing-Lite-1st-ed.pdf
Storytelling as Best Practice: How Stories Strengthen Your Organization, Engage Your Audience, and Advance Your Mission	www.agoodmanonline.com/publications/storytelling/index.html
The Basics of Social Marketing	http://socialmarketingcollaborative.org/smc/pdf/Social_Marketing_Basics.pdf
The Manager's Guide to Social Marketing	http://socialmarketingcollaborative.org/smc/pdf/Managers_guide.pdf
The Social Marketing Lady	www.socialmarketinglady.co.uk/
Theory-at-a-Glance	www.cancer.gov/PDF/481f5d53–63df-41bc-bfaf-5aa48ee1da4d/TAAG3.pdf
Why Bad Ads Happen to Good Causes: And How to Ensure That They Don't Happen to Yours	www.agoodmanonline.com/bad_ads_good_causes/index.html

Journals and Magazines

Advertising Age

Crain Communications, Inc.
http://adage.com/

American Journal of Health Behavior

American Academy of Health Behavior
http://131.230.221.136/ajhb/

Brand Week

VNU, Inc.
http://www.brandweek.com/bw/subscriptions.jsp

Cases in Public Health Communication & Marketing

Taylor & Francis
http://www.gwumc.edu/sphhs/departments/pch/phcm/resources/healthcomm.cfm

Health Marketing Quarterly

Haworth Press
http://www.haworthpress.com/store/product.asp?sku=J026

Journal of Consumer Research

University of Chicago Press
http://www.journals.uchicago.edu/JCR

Journal of Health Communication (online)

Taylor & Francis
http://www.tandf.co.uk/journals/titles/10810730.html

Journal of Marketing

American Marketing Association
http://www.marketingpower.com/AboutAMA/Pages/AMA%20Publications/AMA%
20Journals/Journal%200f%20Marketing/JournalofMarketing.aspx

Journal of Nonprofit & Voluntary Sector Marketing

John Wiley & Sons
http://www.wiley.com/WileyCDA/WileyTitle/productCd-NVSM.html

Journal of Public Policy and Marketing

American Marketing Association
http://www.marketingpower.com/AboutAMA/Pages/AMA%20Publications/AMA%
20Journals/Journal%200f%20Public%20Policy%20Marketing/JournalofPublicPolicy
Marketing.aspx

Journal of Social Marketing

Emerald Group Publishing Limited
http://www.emeraldinsight.com/journals.htm?issn=2042–6763

Social Marketing Quarterly

Taylor & Francis

http://www.tandf.co.uk/journals/titles/15245004.html
http://www.socialmarketingquarterly.com/

Listservs and e-Mail Digests

Dispatches: Insights on Brand Development from the Marketing Front (e-Mail Digest)

Brand Development Network International
To subscribe, send an e-mail to: loriv@bdn-intl.com,or call: 800–255–9831.

Fostering Sustainable Behavior Listserv

To subscribe, send an e-mail to: web@cbsm.com with "subscribe" in the subject.

Georgetown Social Marketing Listserv

1. Send an e-mail message (using plain text, not rich text nor html) to: listproc@georgetown.edu

2. In the *body* of the message, type "sub soc-mktg [your name]" (e.g., "sub soc-mktg Bob White").

Knowledge at Wharton (e-Mail Digest)

The Wharton School at the University of Pennsylvania

1. Go to: http://knowledge.wharton.upenn.edu/

2. Enter your e-mail address in the subscription box

Social Marketers Global Network of the International Social Marketing Association

http://www.socialmarketers.net/

Portable Media

CDCynergy-Social Marketing Edition Planning Tool (CD-ROM)

Purchase online at: http://www.tangibledata.com/CDCynergy-SOC

"Starter for 10" teaching and course materials (Memory Stick)

http://thensmc.com/content/starter-10

Special Emphasis: Selected Resources About Social Media

Centers for Disease Control and Prevention, e-Health Marketing

http://www.cdc.gov/healthmarketing/ehm/

HHS Center for New Media

http://www.newmedia.hhs.gov/

Mashable

http://mashable.com/

Pew Internet and American Life Project

www.pewinternet.com

Social Media at CDC

http://www.cdc.gov/socialmedia/

Television Series (Online)

PBS, Frontline, *The Persuaders*, http://www.pbs.org/wgbh/pages/frontline/shows/persuaders/

Twitter Feeds About Social Marketing and Communication

Alexandra Bornkessel, @SocialBttrfly

Andre Blackman, @mindofandre

Ann Aikin, @bujulicious

Carol Schecter, @Carol_Schechter

CDC e-Health, @CDC_eHealth

Centre of Excellence for Public Sector Marketing, @CEPSM

Craig Lefebvre, @chiefmaven

Erica Holt, @ericaholt

Erin Edgerton, @eedgerton

Holli Seitz, @hseitz

Jay Bernhardt, @jaybernhardt

Jeff French, @JeffFrenchSSM

Jim Mintz, @JimMintz

Kay White, @socialmktgNW

Lauren A. Becker, @LaurenBecker

Mike Newton-Ward, @sm1guru

Nedra Kline Weinreich, @nedra

Osocio Social Advertising, @osocio

Path of the Blueeye, @blueeyepath

Pew Internet & American Life Project, @Pew_Internet

R. Russell-Bennett, @DrBekMarketing

Salter Mitchell, @M4Change

Social Marketers Global Network, @socmarketersnet

Social Marketing at Australian National University, @mktg3024

Social Marketing East, @SMarketingeast

Stephan Dahl, @socMKT

Susannah Fox, @SusannahFox

The Social Change Hub, @SocialchangeHub

Upstream Social Marketing, @rebeccaupstream

Worldways Marketing, @worldways

Web Sites

A Goodman: Good Ideas for Good Causes	www.agoodmanonline.com/red.html
Academy for Educational Development, Center for Social Marketing and Behavior Change	http://csmbc.aed.org/index.htm
Academy for Educational Development, Social Marketing	www.aed.org/Approaches/ SocialMarketing/index.cfm
AdCouncil	www.adcouncil.org/
American Evaluation Association	www.eval.org/
American Marketing Association	www.marketingpower.com
Association of Consumer Research	www.acrwebsite.org
Australia and New Zealand Marketing Academy	www.anzmac.org
Center of Excellence for Public Sector Marketing	www.publicsectormarketing.ca/ home_e.html
Centers for Disease Control and Prevention, Division of Nutrition and Physical Activity, Index of Qualitative Research	www.cdc.gov/nccdphp/dnpa/ qualitative_research/index.htm
Centers for Disease Control and Prevention, Division of Nutrition, Physical Activity and Obesity, Social Marketing Resources	www.cdc.gov/nccdphp/dnpa/ socialmarketing/index.htm
Centers for Disease Control and Prevention, Gateway to Health Communication and Social Marketing Practice	www.cdc.gov/healthcommunication/ index.html
Centers for Disease Control and Prevention, National Center for Health Marketing	www.cdc.gov/healthmarketing/
Centre for Excellence in Public Sector Marketing	www.cepsm.ca/index.php/home

Florida Prevention Research Center at the University of South Florida, Obesity Prevention Coordinators' Social Marketing Guidebook	http://health.usf.edu/NR/ rdonlyres/1F6E6B64–967D-45D1– 8BC1–357EC9B3BC30/24125/ ObesityPreventionCoordinators SocialMarketingG.pdf
Fostering Sustainable Behavior, Community-Based Social Marketing	www.cbsm.com/
Frameworks Institute	www.frameworksinstitute.org/
George Washington University, School of Public Health and Health Services, Public Health Communication and Marketing, Health Communication Resources	www.gwumc.edu/sphhs/departments/ pch/phcm/resources/healthcomm.cfm
Harvard Business School *Working Knowledge* Newsletter	http://hbswk.hbs.edu/forms/newsletter .html
International Social Marketing Association	http://i-socialmarketing.org/
Marketing Sociale e Comunicazione per la Salute (Italy)	www.marketingsociale.net/
MRS Market Research	www.marketresearch.org.uk/index.htm
National Cancer Institute Health Behavior Constructs: Theory, Measurement and Research	http://cancercontrol.cancer.gov/brp/ constructs/index.html
National Centre for Health Marketing	www.nsmcentre.org.uk/
Nielsen Online	www.nielsen-online.com/intlpage.html
Osocio Social Advertising and Non-profit Campaigns	http://osocio.org/
Path of the Blueeye Project	www.pathoftheblueeye.com/
Population Services International (PSI)	www.psi.org
Social Marketing Downunder (New Zealand, Australia, and South Pacific)	socialmarketing.co.nz
Social Marketing Institute	www.social-marketing.org/
Social Marketing National Excellence Collaborative (Turning Point)	http://socialmarketingcollaborative.org/ smc/

Stanford Social Innovation Review	ssireview.org
Stanford University Persuasive Technology Lab	captology.stanford.edu/
Tangible Data.com (URL at which to order copies of CDCynergy-Social Marketing Edition CD ROM planning tool)	www.tangibledata.com/CDCynergy -SOC
The Institute for Social Marketing, University of Stirling, Scotland	www.ism.stir.ac.uk/
The Queensland, Australia, Government's Social Marketing Final Report	www.premiers.qld.gov.au/publications/ categories/reports/social-marketing .aspx
The Social Marketing Network, Health Canada	www.healthcanada.gc.ca/ socialmarketing
The Social Marketing Place	social-marketing.com/
The Social Marketing Toolbox	http://socialmarketing-toolbox.com/ content/getting-started-1
Tools of Change	www.toolsofchange.com/
University of Lethbridge (Canada), Faculty of Management	www.uleth.ca/man/research/centres/ csrm/related.shtml
University of South Florida, Graduate Certificate in Social Marketing and Public Health	http://gradcerts.usf.edu/certinfo .asp?ccode=XSP

Name Index

Abdulla, A., 101, 105
Abu-Bader, A., 158
Academy for Educational Development (AED),
    3, 63, 182
Adams, M., 384
Ad Council, 335, 349, 377, 386, 422–423, 431,
    434, 445, 457
Adler, R., 352–354, 384
AEA Technology PLC, 284
Agha, S., 104
Ajzen, I., 198–199, 210
Allen, E., 352
Allen, R. H., 104
Allinson, L., 350
American Academy of Pediatrics, 65, 72
American Cancer Society, 299, 300
American Diabetes Association, 29
American Heart Association, 17, 29, 413
American Humane, 31
American Lung Association, 158, 299, 402–403, 410
American Marketing Association, 9–10, 28,
    450–453
American Red Cross, 31
America's Blood Centers (ABC), 189–190, 210
Andreasen, A. R., xi, 7, 9, 12, 13, 14, 25, 28, 41,
    51, 52–53, 54, 81, 88, 96, 99, 104, 105, 148,
    152, 159, 194–195, 210, 274, 284, 370, 385,
    412, 422, 431, 472
Angus, K., 473
Apps for Healthy Kids, 252–253, 261
Arab American Institute, 158
Armstrong, G., 104, 139, 158, 159, 226, 260, 261,
    262, 283, 349, 374, 379, 386, 431, 437, 457
Arulmani, G., 101, 105
Association of SIDS and Infant Mortality
    Programs, 72

Bachman, J. G., 105
Bagozzi, R. P., 28, 188, 209
Baker, S., 284
Balakrishnan, J., 107
Balane, L., 409, 410
Bandura, A., 199

Barnes, D. K. A., 238
Basil, D. Z., 472
Bastani, R., 158
Bayes, B., 184
Bayside Climate Change Action Group, 350
BBC News, 284
Bearden, W. O., 473
Begier, E., 237
Berkowitz, A., 195–196, 211
Bernhardt, J., 7
Bernstein, K., 237
Berry, L. L., 430
Bikes Belong Foundation, 306–308, 310
Bill Moyers reports, 30
Birmingham Health and Wellbeing
    Partnership, 209
Black, R. E., 125
Blair-Stevens, C., 14, 473
Bloom, P., 13
Bornstein, D., 77
Boschi-Pinto, C., 125
Bott, J., 309
Brennan, L., 76, 77
Broder, M., 210
Brody, J., 457
Browne, R. C., 348
Brown, K. M., 197
Brown, K. R. M., 210
Brown, T., 251, 261
Bryant, C., 41, 81, 473
Bryce, J., 125
Bueckert, D., 283
Buehler, R., 308, 310
Bullen, C., 410
Bureau of Justice Statistics, 31
Burke, R., 237
Burn, S. M., 333, 349
Buros Institute, 473
Byers, R. H., 29

California Center for Public Advocacy, 366
Carducci, V., 349
Carlin-Menter, S., 283

SUBJECT INDEX

ABOUT THE AUTHORS

Nancy R. Lee, MBA, is president of Social Marketing Services, Inc., in Seattle, Washington, and an adjunct faculty member at the University of Washington as well as at the University of South Florida, where she teaches social marketing and marketing in the public sector. With more than 25 years of practical marketing experience in the public and private sectors, Ms. Lee has held numerous corporate marketing positions, including vice president and director of marketing for Washington State's second-largest bank and director of marketing for the region's Children's Hospital and Medical Center.

Ms. Lee has consulted with more than 100 nonprofit organizations and has participated in the development of more than 200 social marketing campaign strategies for public sector agencies. Clients in the public sector include the Centers for Disease Control and Prevention (CDC), Environmental Protection Agency (EPA), Washington State Department of Health, Office of Crime Victims Advocacy, county Health and Transportation Departments, Department of Ecology, Department of Fisheries and Wildlife, Washington Traffic Safety Commission, City of Seattle, and Office of Superintendent of Public Instruction. Campaigns developed for these clients targeted issues listed below:

- Health: teen pregnancy prevention, HIV/AIDS prevention, nutrition education, sexual assault, diabetes prevention, adult physical activity, tobacco control, arthritis diagnosis and treatment, immunizations, dental hygiene, senior wellness, and eating disorder awareness
- Safety: drowning prevention, senior fall prevention, underage drinking and driving, youth suicide prevention, binge drinking, pedestrian safety, and safe gun storage
- Environment: natural gardening, preservation of fish and wildlife habitats, recycling, trip reduction, water quality, and water and power conservation

She has conducted social marketing workshops around the world (Jordan, South Africa, Ghana, Ireland, Australia, Singapore, Canada) for more than 2,000 public sector employees involved in developing public behavior change campaigns in the areas of health, safety, the environment, and financial well-being. She has been a keynote speaker on social marketing at conferences for improved water quality, energy conservation, family planning, nutrition, recycling, teen pregnancy prevention, influencing financial behaviors, and tobacco control.

Ms. Lee has coauthored seven other books with Philip Kotler: *Social Marketing: Improving the Quality of Life* (2002); *Corporate Social Responsibility: Doing the Most Good for Your Company and Your Cause* (2005); *Marketing in the Public Sector: A Roadmap for Improved Performance* (2006); *Social Marketing: Influencing Behaviors for Good* (2008); *Up and Out of Poverty: The Social Marketing Solution* (2009); *Social Marketing in Public Health* (2010); and *Social Marketing to Protect the Environment* (2011). She has also contributed articles to the *Stanford Social Innovation Review, Social*

Marketing Quarterly, Journal of Social Marketing and *The Public Manager.* (See more on Nancy Lee at www.socialmarketingservice.com)

Philip Kotler is the S. C. Johnson & Son Distinguished Professor of International Marketing at the J. L. Kellogg Graduate School of Management, Northwestern University, Evanston, Illinois. Kellogg was voted Best Business School for six years in *Business Week*'s survey of U.S. business schools. It is also rated Best Business School for the Teaching of Marketing. Professor Kotler has significantly contributed to Kellogg's success through his many years of research and teaching there.

He received his master's degree at the University of Chicago and his Ph.D. degree at MIT, both in economics. He did postdoctoral work in mathematics at Harvard University and in behavioral science at the University of Chicago.

Professor Kotler is the author of *Marketing Management: Analysis, Planning, Implementation and Control,* the most widely used marketing book in graduate business schools worldwide; *Principles of Marketing; Marketing Models; Strategic Marketing for Non-Profit Organizations; The New Competition; High Visibility; Social Marketing; Marketing Places; Marketing for Congregations; Marketing for Hospitality and Tourism; The Marketing of Nations;* and *Kotler on Marketing.* He has published over 100 articles in leading journals, several of which have received best-article awards.

Professor Kotler was the first recipient of the Distinguished Marketing Educator Award (1985) given by the American Marketing Association (AMA). The European Association of Marketing Consultants and Sales Trainers awarded him their prize for Marketing Excellence. He was chosen as the Leader in Marketing Thought by the Academic Members of the AMA in a 1975 survey. He also received the 1978 Paul Converse Award of the AMA, honoring his original contribution to marketing. In 1995, Sales and Marketing Executives International (SMEI) named him Marketer of the Year.

Professor Kotler has consulted for such companies as IBM, General Electric, AT&T, Honeywell, Bank of America, Merck, and others in the areas of marketing strategy and planning, marketing organization, and international marketing.

He has been chairman of the College of Marketing of the Institute of Management Sciences, director of the American Marketing Association, trustee of the Marketing Science Institute, director of the MAC Group, former member of the Yankelovich Advisory Board, and a member of the Copernicus Advisory Board. He is a member of the Board of Governors of the School of the Art Institute of Chicago and a member of the advisory board of the Drucker Foundation. He has received honorary doctoral degrees from Stockholm University, University of Zurich, Athens University of Economics and Business, DePaul University, the Cracow School of Business and Economics, Groupe H.E.C. in Paris, the University of Economics and Business Administration in Vienna, the Catholic University of Santo Domingo, and the Budapest School of Economic Science and Public Administration.

He has traveled extensively throughout Europe, Asia, and South America, advising and lecturing to many companies and organizations. This experience expands the scope and depth of his programs, enhancing them with an accurate global perspective.

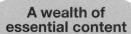
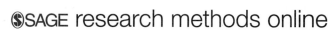